*As this appalling ocean surrounds the verdant land,
so in the soul of man there lies one insular Tahiti,
full of peace and joy, but encompassed by all
the horrors of the half-known life.*

*God help thee! Push not off from that isle,
thou canst never return.*

—HERMAN MELVILLE

TAHITI
HANDBOOK

TAHITI
HANDBOOK

INCLUDING EASTER ISLAND AND THE COOKS
FOURTH EDITION

DAVID STANLEY

MOON
TRAVEL
HANDBOOKS

TAHITI HANDBOOK
FOURTH EDITION

Published by
Avalon Travel Publishing
5855 Beaudry St.
Emeryville, CA 94608, USA

Printed by
Colorcraft Ltd.

ISBN: 1-56691-140-0
ISSN: 1082-4855

Please send all comments, corrections, additions, amendments, and critiques to:

**MOON TRAVEL HANDBOOKS:
TAHITI, FOURTH EDITION
AVALON TRAVEL PUBLISHING
5855 BEAUDRY ST.
EMERYVILLE, CA 94608
e-mail:
atpfeedback@avalonpub.com
www.travelmatters.com**

Printing History
1st edition—1989
4th edition—June 1999
5 4 3

Editor: Asha Johnson
Production & Design: Carey Wilson
Cartography: Chris Folks, Allen Leech, and Mike Morgenfeld
Index: Asha Johnson

Front cover photo: Bora Bora. Courtesy of The Photo Network

All photos by David Stanley unless otherwise noted.

Distributed in the United States and Canada by Publishers Group West

Printed in China

Although the author and publisher have made every effort to ensure that the information was correct at the time of going to press, the author and publisher do not assume and hereby disclaim any liability to any party for any loss or damage caused by errors, omissions, or any potential travel disruption due to labor or financial difficulty, whether such errors or omissions result from negligence, accident, or any other cause.

CONTENTS

Cross-references in **bold type** within the text of the book refer to citations in the general index.

INTRODUCTION

TAHITI-POLYNESIA

EASTER ISLAND

COOK ISLANDS

MAPS

MAP SYMBOLS

═══ Primary Road	○ City	▲ Mountain
═══ Secondary Road	○ Town	🖋 Waterfall
======== Unpaved Road	• Accommodation	Reef
-------- Trail	▪ Sight	Water
✗ Airfield/Airstrip	⌞ Golf Course	

CHARTS

ABBREVIATIONS

a/c—air-conditioned
ATM—automated teller
   machine
B.P.—*boîte postale*
C—Centigrade
CDW—collision damage waiver
CFP—French Pacific Franc
cm—centimeters
EEZ—Exclusive Economic
   Zone
E.U.—European Union
4WD—four-wheel drive
I.—island

Is.—islands
kg—kilogram
km—kilometer
kph—kilometers per hour
LDS—Latter-day Saints
   (Mormons)
LMS—London Missionary
   Society
mm—millimeters
MV—motor vessel
No.—number
N.Z.—New Zealand
NZ$—New Zealand dollars

PK—*pointe kilométrique*
pp—per person
P.W.D.—Public Works
   Department
SDA—Seventh-Day Adventist
SPF—South Pacific Forum
STD—sexually transmitted
   disease
tel.—telephone
U.S.—United States
US$—U.S. dollars
WW II—World War Two

ACKNOWLEDGMENTS

The nationalities of those listed below are identified by the following signs which follow their names: au (Australia), ch (Switzerland), ck (Cook Islands), de (Germany), dk (Denmark), es (Spain), fr (France), gb (Great Britain), hk (Hong Kong), nc (New Caledonia), nl (Netherlands), no (Norway), nz (New Zealand), pf (Tahiti-Polynesia), pt (Portugal), and us (United States).

Some of the antique engravings by M.G.L. Domeny de Rienzi are from the classic three-volume work *Oceanie ou Cinquième Partie du Monde* (Paris: Firmin Didot Frères, 1836).

Special thanks to Armand Kuris (us) for correcting the section on coral reefs, to Robert Rousseau (fr) for climate charts, to Antonio Trindade (pt) for surfing tips, to David Fanshawe (gb) and Ad Linkels (nl) for information on Pacific music, to Madame Jacques Brel for kind permission to reproduce *Les Marquises* and to Lynne Lipkind for providing the translation, to Tatiana Blanc (nc) of the Pacific Community and Chantale and Philippe (pf) of the Institut National de la Statistique for statistical support, to Charlie Appleton (au) for photos and documentation of his return to Mount Aorai, to Leslie McDonald (us) for a frank report on Moorea, to Dr. Georgia Lee (us) for help in updating Easter Island, to Ben Ponia (ck) for an update on the Cook Islands cultured pearl industry, to Warwick Latham (ck) for feedback from Penrhyn, to Ylva Carosone (au) for Tahiti website reviews, to Danee Hazama (pf) for supplying last-minute price information, and to my wife Ria de Vos for her continuing assistance, suggestions, and support.

Thanks too to the following readers who took the trouble to write us letters about their trips:

Kilali Alailima (us), Kim Birkedahl (dk), Larry Bleidner (us), John Blyth (gb), Tracy Brassfield (us), Claire Brenn (ch), Carl P. Budrecki (us), Rowland Burley (hk), Thom Burns (us), Bob Duchan (us), Fredrik S. Heffermehl (no), Caroline Green (gb), Gisela Comas Garcia (es), William F. Hachmeister (us), Morina Harder (us), Ed Hartz (nz), Roger Hill (gb), Kirk W. Huffman (es), Martin J. Kahn (us), Fr. John Knoernschild (us), Christoph Kopke (gb), Sheena Leatham (us), John Maidment (gb), Allegra Marshall (au), Merritt Maxim (us), Jim McLauchlin (us), John Metzger (us), Erica Noorlander (nl), Simone Neull (gb), Lorraine Oak (us), B. Orenstein (us), Yolanda Ortiz de Arri (es), Rick Range (us), Steven A. Rasmussen (us), Jonathan Reap (us), Shawn Rohan (us), Francesc Rubio i Barceló (es), Paul A. Runyon (us), Bev Schmidt (us), Nan Schmitz (us), Carol Stetser (us), Tae Sung (us), Robert Takashi Imagire (ck), Antonio Trindade (pt), C. Webb (us), Hugh Williams (us), J.R. Williams (us), Sidsel Wold (no), Anselm Zänkert (de), and Arthur & Jane Zeeuw (nl).

All their comments have been incorporated into the volume you're now holding. To have your own name included here next edition, write: David Stanley, c/o Moon Travel Handbooks, P.O. Box 3040, Chico, CA 95927-3040, U.S.A. (e-mail: travel@moon.com)

Attention Hotel Keepers, Tour Operators, Divemasters

The best way to keep your listing in *Tahiti Handbook* up to date is to send us current information about your business. If you don't agree with what we've written, please tell us why—there's never any charge or obligation for a listing. Thanks to the following island tourism workers and government officials who *did* write in:

Scott Arlander (ck), Hugh Baker (ck), Bill Bates (ck), Rebecca Blackburn (ck), Jason Brown (ck), Ingrid Caffery (pf), Marie-Isabelle Chan (pf), Anne Condesse (pf), Nancy Daniels (us), Kathy Davis (us), Neil Dearlove (ck), Andrea and Juergen Eimke (ck), Brenda Farnsworth (ck), Didier Forget (pf), Gary Johns (au), Jan Kristensson (ck), Georges Moulon (pf), Nan Noovao (ck), Vaiata Noel (pf), Coral Perry (us), Gilles Pétré (pf), François Profit (pf), Trina Pureau (ck), Marie-Claude Rajaud (pf), Dorice Reid (ck), Elliot Smith (ck), and Madeilene Sword (ck).

From the Author

While out researching my books I find it cheaper to pay my own way, and you can rest assured that nothing in this book is designed to repay freebies from hotels, restaurants, tour operators, or airlines. I prefer to arrive unexpected and uninvited, and to experience things as they really are. On the road I seldom identify myself to anyone. Unlike many other travel writers I don't allow myself to be chaperoned by local tourist offices or leave out justified criticism that might impact book sales. The essential difference between this handbook and the myriad travel brochures free for the taking in airports and tourist offices all across the region is that this book represents you, the traveler, while the brochures represent the travel industry. The companies and organizations included herein are there for information purposes only, and a mention in no way implies an endorsement.

YOU WILL HAVE THE LAST WORD

Travel writing is among the least passive forms of journalism, and every time you use this book you become a participant. I've done my best to provide the sort of information I think will help make your trip a success, and now I'm asking for your help. If I led you astray or inconvenienced you, I want to know, and if you feel I've been unfair somewhere, don't hesitate to say. If you thought I sounded naive, starry eyed, co-opted, servile, or unable to separate the good from the bad, tell me that too. Some things are bound to have changed by the time you get there, and if you write and tell me I'll correct the new edition, which is probably already in preparation even as you read this book.

Unlike many travel writers, this author doesn't accept "freebies" from tourism businesses or obtain VIP treatment by announcing who he is to one and all. At times that makes it difficult to audit the expensive or isolated resorts, therefore comments from readers who stayed at the upmarket places are especially welcome, particularly if the facilities didn't match the rates. If you feel you've been badly treated by a hotel, restaurant, car rental agency, airline, tour company, dive shop, or whoever, please let me know, and if it concurs with other information on hand, your complaint certainly will have an impact. Of course, we also want to hear about the things you thought were great. Reader's letters are examined during the concluding stages of editing the book, so you really will have the final say.

When writing, please be as precise and accurate as you can. Notes made on the scene are far better than later recollections. Write comments in your copy of *Tahiti Handbook* as you go along, then send me a summary when you get home. If this book helped you, please help me make it even better. Address your feedback to:

David Stanley
c/o Moon Publications Inc.
P.O. Box 3040
Chico, CA 95927-3040, U.S.A.
fax 1-530/345-6751
e-mail: travel@moon.com

ACCOMMODATIONS PRICE RANGES

Throughout this handbook, accommodations are generally grouped in the price categories which follow. Of course, currency fluctuations and inflation can lead to slight variations.

Shoestring	under US$15 double
Budget	US$15-35 double
Inexpensive	US$35-60 double
Moderate	US$60-85 double
Expensive	US$85-110 double
Premium	US$110-150 double
Luxury	over US$150 double

INTRODUCTION
Tahiti-Polynesia, Easter Island, Cook Islands

King Pomare II

METRO GOLDWIN MAYER

Tarita co-starred with Marlon Brando in the 1962 MGM film Mutiny on the Bounty.

M.G.L. DOMENY DE RIENZI

INTRODUCTION

The Polynesian triangle between Hawaii, New Zealand, and Easter Island stretches 8,000 km across the central Pacific Ocean—a fifth of the earth's surface. Since the late 18th century, when Captain Cook first revealed Polynesia to European eyes, artists and writers have sung the praises of the graceful golden-skinned peoples of the "many islands."

This vast region is divided into two cultural areas, Western Polynesia (Tonga, Niue, and Samoa) and Eastern Polynesia (Tahiti-Polynesia, Easter Island, Cook Islands, Hawaii, and New Zealand). While the three Eastern Polynesian territories covered in this book display some homogeneity, there are also striking contrasts resulting from a history of French, Chilean, and New Zealand colonial rule.

Polynesia consists of boundless ocean and little land. Together Tahiti-Polynesia, Easter Island, and Cook Islands control 7,215,000 square kilometers of the South Pacific Ocean, an area only slightly smaller than the 48 contiguous states of the continental United States. From Rarotonga to Easter Island is about as far as from Denver to Boston. Yet in land area, the three together total just a bit more than Rhode Island. Fewer than a quarter of a million people are fortunate enough to live on these sunny tropical isles.

The striking scenic beauty of Tahiti-Polynesia combines well with the archaeological mysteries of Easter Island and the easygoing island life in the Cooks. These three territories are closely linked by air with good connections to both Americas, Europe, and Australasia. It's a fascinating area to explore, abounding in man-made attractions, exotic legends, and stunning scenes. You'll find that travel is easy with good facilities along the way. Through this book we've tried to show you the best of the region without ignoring the worst. Paradise it may not be, but it's still a remarkable part of our world.

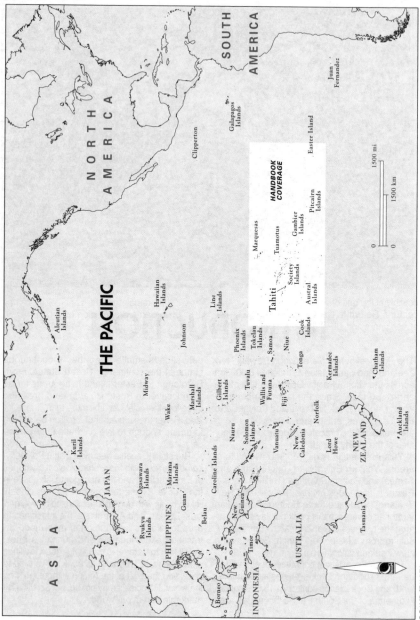

THE PACIFIC

HANDBOOK COVERAGE

© DAVID STANLEY

THE LAND

Darwin's Theory of Atoll Formation

The famous formulator of the theory of natural selection surmised that atolls form as high volcanic islands subside into lagoons. The original island's fringing reef grows into a barrier reef as the volcanic portion sinks. When the last volcanic material finally disappears below sea level, the coral rim of the reef/atoll remains to indicate how big the island once was.

Of course, all this takes place over millions of years, but deep down below every atoll is the old volcanic core. Darwin's theory is well-illustrated at Bora Bora, where a high volcanic island remains inside the rim of Bora Bora's barrier reef; this island's volcanic core is still sinking imperceptibly at the rate of one centimeter a century. Return to Bora Bora in 25 million years and all you'll find will be a coral atoll like Rangiroa or Manihi.

Charles Darwin

Hot Spots

High or low, all of the islands have a volcanic origin best explained by the "Conveyor Belt Theory." A crack opens in the earth's mantle and volcanic magma escapes upward. A submarine volcano builds up slowly until the lava finally breaks the surface, becoming a volcanic island. The Pacific Plate moves northwest approximately 10 centimeters a year; thus, over geologic eons the volcano disconnects from the hot spot or crack from which it emerged. As the old volcanoes disconnect from the crack, new ones appear to the southeast, and the older islands are carried away from the cleft in earth's crust from which they were born.

The island then begins to sink under its own weight and erosion also cuts into the now-extinct volcano. In the warm, clear waters a living coral reef begins to grow along the shore. As the island subsides, the reef continues to grow upward. In this way a lagoon forms between the reef and the shoreline of the slowly sinking island.

This barrier reef marks the old margin of the original island.

As the hot spot shifts southeast in an opposite direction from the sliding Pacific Plate (and shifting magnetic pole of the earth), the process is repeated, time and again, until whole chains of islands ride the blue Pacific. Weathering is most advanced on the composite islands and atolls at the northwest ends of the Society, Austral, Tuamotu, Marquesas, and Cooks chains. Maupiti and Bora Bora, with their exposed volcanic cores, are the oldest of the larger Society Islands. The Tuamotus have eroded almost to sea level; the Gambier Islands originated out of the same hot spot and their volcanic peaks remain inside a giant atoll reef. The same progression of youth, maturity, and old age can be followed in Rarotonga, Aitutaki, and Manihiki. In every case, the islands at the southeast end of the chains are the youngest.

By drilling into the Tuamotu atolls, scientists have proven their point conclusively: the coral formations are about 350 meters thick at the southeast end of the chain, 600 meters thick at Hao near the center, and 1,000 meters thick at Rangiroa near the northwest end of the Tuamotu Group. Clearly, Rangiroa, where the volcanic rock is now a kilometer below the surface, is many millions of years older than the Gambiers, where a volcanic peak still stands 482 meters above sea level. Geologists estimate that Tahiti is two to three million years old, Bora Bora seven million years old, and the Tuamotus 10 to 40 million years old.

Equally fascinating is the way ancient atolls have been uplifted by adjacent volcanoes. The upper crust of earth is an elastic envelope enclosing an incompressible fluid. When this envelope is stretched taut, the tremendous weight of a volcano is spread over a great area, deforming the seabed. In the Cook Islands, for example, Atiu, Mauke, Mitiaro, and Mangaia were uplifted by the weight of Aitutaki and Rarotonga.

Island-building continues at an active undersea volcano called MacDonald, 50 meters below sea level at the southeast end of the Australs. The crack spews forth about a cubic mile of lava every century and someday MacDonald too will poke its smoky head above the waves. The theories of plate tectonics, or the sliding crust of the earth, seem proven in the Pacific.

Life of an Atoll

A circular or horseshoe-shaped coral reef bearing a necklace of sandy, slender islets *(motu)* of debris thrown up by storms, surf, and wind is known as an atoll. Atolls can be up to 100 km across, but the width of dry land is usually only 200-400 meters from inner to outer beach. The central lagoon can measure anywhere from one km to 50 km in diameter; huge Rangiroa Atoll is 77 km long. Entirely landlocked lagoons are rare; passages through the barrier reef are usually found on the leeward side. Most atolls are no higher than four to six meters.

A raised or elevated atoll is one that has been pushed up by some trauma of nature to become a platform of coral rock rising up to 20 meters above sea level. Raised atolls are often known for their huge sea caves and steep oceanside cliffs. The only raised atoll in Tahiti-Polynesia is crescent-shaped Makatea in the northwestern corner of the Tuamotu group. It is 100 meters high, seven km long, and 4.5 km wide. In Cook Islands, Atiu, Mitiaro, Mauke, and Mangaia are raised atolls.

Where the volcanic island remains there's often a deep passage between the barrier reef and shore; the reef forms a natural breakwater, which shelters good anchorages. Australia's Great Barrier Reef is 1,600 km long and 25 to 44 km offshore. Soil derived from coral is extremely poor in nutrients, while volcanic soil is known for its fertility. Dark-colored beaches are formed from volcanic material; the white beaches of travel brochures are entirely coral-based. The black beaches are cooler and easier on the eyes, plantlife grows closer and provids patches of shade; the white beaches are generally safer for swimming, as visibility is better.

CORAL REEFS

To understand how a basalt volcano becomes a limestone atoll, it's necessary to know a little about the growth of coral. Coral reefs cover some 200,000 square km worldwide, between 35 degrees north and 32 degrees south latitude. A reef is created by the accumulation of millions of calcareous skeletons left by myriad generations

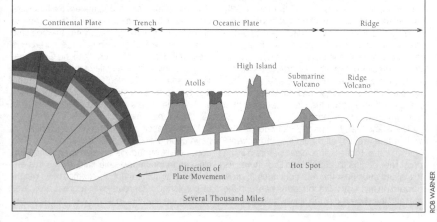

CROSS SECTION OF AN OCEANIC PLATE

Continental Plate | Trench | Oceanic Plate | Ridge

High Island

Submarine Volcano

Ridge Volcano

Atolls

Direction of Plate Movement

Hot Spot

Several Thousand Miles

ROB WARNER

CORALS OF THE PACIFIC

acropora

staghorn fire coral (Millepora accicornis)

table coral

mushroom coral (Fungia fungites)

elkhorn fire coral (Millepora platyphylla)

brain coral (Meandrina)

honeycomb coral (Favia matthaii)

DIANA LASICH HARPER

of tiny coral polyps, some no bigger than a pinhead. Though the skeleton is usually white, the living polyps are of many different colors. The individual polyps on the surface often live a long time, continuously secreting layers to the skeletal mass beneath the tiny layer of flesh.

Coral polyps thrive in clear salty water where the temperature never drops below 18° C. They must also have a base not more than 50 meters below the water's surface on which to form. The coral colony grows slowly upward on the consolidated skeletons of its ancestors until it reaches the low-tide mark, after which development extends outward on the edges of the reef. Sunlight is critical for coral growth. Colonies grow quickly on the ocean side due to clearer water and a greater abundance of food. A strong, healthy reef can grow four to five centimeters a year. Fresh or cloudy water inhibits coral growth, which is why villages and ports all across the Pacific are located at the reef-free mouths of rivers. Hurricanes can kill coral by covering the reef with sand, preventing light and nutrients from getting through. Erosion caused by logging or urban development can have the same effect.

Polyps extract calcium carbonate from the water and deposit it in their skeletons. All limy reef-building corals also contain microscopic algae within their cells. The algae, like all green plants, obtain energy from the sun and contribute this energy to the growth of the reef's skeleton. As a result, corals behave (and look) more like plants than animals, competing for sunlight just as terrestrial plants do. Many polyps are also carnivorous; with minute stinging tentacles they supplement their energy by capturing tiny planktonic animals and organic particles at night. A small piece of coral is a colony composed of large numbers of polyps.

Coral Types

Corals belong to a broad group of stinging creatures, which includes polyps, soft corals, stony corals, sea anemones, sea fans, and jellyfish. Only those types with hard skeletons and a single hollow cavity within the body are considered true corals. Stony corals such as brain, table, staghorn, and mushroom corals have external skeletons and are important reef builders. Soft corals, black corals, and sea fans have internal skeletons. The fire corals are recognized by their

BOB HALSTEAD

smooth, velvety surface and yellowish brown color. The stinging toxins of this last group can easily penetrate human skin and cause swelling and painful burning that can last up to an hour. The many varieties of soft, colorful anemones gently waving in the current might seem inviting to touch, but beware: many are also poisonous.

The corals, like most other forms of life in the Pacific, colonized the ocean from the fertile seas of Southeast Asia. Thus the number of species declines as you move east. Over 600 species of coral make their home in the Pacific, compared to only 48 in the Caribbean. The diversity of coral colors and forms is endlessly amazing. This is our most unspoiled environment, a world of almost indescribable beauty.

Exploring a Reef

Until you've explored a good coral reef, you haven't experienced one of the greatest joys of nature. While one cannot walk through pristine forests due to the lack of paths, it's quite possible to swim over untouched reefs. Coral reefs are the most densely populated living space on earth—the rainforests of the sea! It's wise to bring along a high quality mask you've checked thoroughly beforehand as there's nothing more disheartening than a leaky, ill-fitting mask. Otherwise dive shops throughout the region rent or sell snorkeling gear, so do get into the clear, warm waters around you.

Conservation

Coral reefs are one of the most fragile and complex ecosystems on earth, providing food and shelter for countless species of fish, crustaceans (shrimps, crabs, and lobsters), mollusks (shells), and other animals. The coral reefs of the South Pacific protect shorelines during storms, supply sand to maintain the islands, furnish food for the local population, form a living laboratory for science, and are major tourist attractions. Without coral, the South Pacific would be immeasurably poorer.

Hard corals grow only about 10 to 25 millimeters a year and it can take 7,000-10,000 years for a coral reef to form. Though corals look solid they're easily broken; by standing on them, breaking off pieces, or carelessly dropping anchor you can destroy in a few minutes what took so long to form. Once a piece of coral breaks off it dies, and it may be years before the coral reestablishes itself and even longer before the broken piece is replaced. The "wound"

THE GREENHOUSE EFFECT

The gravest danger facing the atolls of Oceania is the greenhouse effect, a gradual warming of Earth's environment due to fossil fuel combustion and the widespread clearing of forests. By the year 2030 the concentration of carbon dioxide in the atmosphere will have doubled from preindustrial levels. As infrared radiation from the sun is absorbed by the gas, the trapped heat melts mountain glaciers and the polar ice caps. In addition, seawater expands as it warms up, so water levels could rise almost a meter by the year 2100, destroying shorelines created 5,000 years ago.

A 1982 study demonstrated that sea levels had already risen 12 centimeters in the previous century; in 1995 2,500 scientists from 70 countries involved in an Intergovernmental Panel on Climate Change commissioned by the United Nations completed a two-year study with the warning that over the next century air temperatures may rise as much as 5° Celsius and sea levels could go up 95 centimeters. Not only will this reduce the growing area for food crops, but rising sea levels will mean salt water intrusion into groundwater supplies—a horrifying prospect if accompanied by the droughts that have been predicted. Coastal erosion will force governments to spend vast sums on road repairs and coastline stabilization.

Increasing temperatures may already be contributing to the dramatic jump in the number of hurricanes in the South Pacific. In 1997 and 1998 the El Niño phenomenon brought with it a round of devastating hurricanes, many hitting Cook Islands and Tahiti-Polynesia, which are usually missed by such storms.

Coral bleaching occurs when an organism's symbiotic algae are expelled in response to environmental stresses, such as changes in water temperature, and widespread instances of bleaching and reefs being killed by rising sea temperatures have been confirmed in Tahiti-Polynesia and Cook Islands. To make matters worse, the coral-crunching crown-of-thorns starfish (*taramea* in Tahitian) is again on the rise throughout the South Pacific (probably due to sewage and fertilizer runoff that nurture the starfish larvae). Reef destruction will reduce coastal fish stocks and impact tourism.

As storm waves wash across the low-lying atolls, eating away the precious land, the entire populations of archipelagos such as the Tuamotus and Northern Cooks may be forced to evacuate long before they're actually flooded. The construction of seawalls to keep out the rising seas would be prohibitively expensive and may even do more harm than good by interfering with natural water flows.

Unfortunately, those most responsible for the problem, the industrialized countries led by the United States (and including Australia) have strongly resisted taking any action to significantly cut greenhouse gas emissions, and new industrial polluters like India and China are sure to make matters much worse. And as if that weren't bad enough, the hydrofluorocarbons (HFCs) presently being developed by corporate giants like Du Pont to replace the ozone-destructive chlorofluorocarbons (CFCs) used in cooling systems are far more potent greenhouse gases than carbon dioxide. This is only one of many similar consumption-related problems, and it seems as if one section of humanity is hurtling down a suicidal slope, unable to resist the momentum, as the rest of our race watches the catastrophe approach in helpless horror. It will cost a lot to rewrite our collective ticket but there may not be any choice.

may become infected by algae, which can multiply and kill the entire coral colony. When this happens over a wide area, the diversity of marinelife declines dramatically.

Swim beside or well above the coral. Avoid bumping the coral with your fins, gauges, or other equipment and don't dive during rough sea conditions. Proper buoyancy control is preferable to excessive weight belts. Snorkelers should check into taking along a float-coat, which will allow equipment adjustments without standing on coral.

We recommend that you not remove seashells, coral, plantlife, or marine animals from the sea. Doing so upsets the delicate balance of nature, and coral is much more beautiful underwater anyway! This is a particular problem along shorelines frequented by large numbers of tourists, who can completely strip a reef in very little time. If you'd like a souvenir, content yourself with what you find on the beach (although even a seemingly empty shell may be inhabited by a hermit crab). Also think twice about purchasing jewelry or souvenirs made from coral or seashells. Genuine traditional handicrafts that incorporate shells are one thing, but by purchasing unmounted seashells or mass-produced coral curios you are contributing to the destruction of the marine environment. The triton shell, for example, keeps in check the reef-destroying crown-of-thorns starfish.

The anchors and anchor chains of private yachts can do serious damage to coral reefs. Pronged anchors are more environmentally friendly than larger, heavier anchors, and plastic tubing over the end of the anchor chain helps minimize the damage. If at all possible, anchor in sand. A longer anchor chain makes this easier, and a good windlass is essential for larger boats. A recording depth sounder will help locate sandy areas when none are available in shallow water. If you don't have a depth sounder and can't see the bottom, lower the anchor until it just touches the bottom and feel the anchor line as the boat drifts. If it "grumbles" lift it up, drift a little, and try again. Later, if you notice your chain grumbling, motor over the anchor, lift it out of the coral and move. Not only do sand and mud hold better, but your anchor will be less likely to become fouled. Try to arrive before 1500 to be able to see clearly where you're anchoring—Polaroid sunglasses make it easier to distinguish corals. If you scuba dive with an operator who anchors incorrectly, let your concerns be known.

There's an urgent need for stricter government regulation of the marine environment, and in some places coral reefs are already protected. Appeals such as the one above have only limited impact—legislators must write stricter laws and impose fines. If you witness dumping or any other marine-related activity you think might be illegal, don't become directly involved but take a few notes and calmly report the incident to the local authorities or police at the first opportunity. You'll learn something about their approach to these matters and make them aware of your concerns.

Resort developers can minimize damage to their valuable reefs by providing public mooring buoys so yachts don't have to drop anchor and pontoons so snorkelers aren't tempted to stand on coral. Licensing authorities can make such amenities mandatory whenever appropriate, and in extreme cases, endangered coral gardens should be declared off limits to private boats. As consumerism spreads, once-remote areas become subject to the problems of pollution and overexploitation: the garbage is visibly piling up on many shores. As a visitor, don't hesitate to practice your conservationist attitudes, and leave a clean wake.

CLIMATE

The Pacific Ocean has a greater impact on the world's climate than any other geographical feature on earth. By taking heat away from the equator and toward the poles, it stretches the bounds of the area in which life can exist. Broad circular ocean currents flow from east to west across the tropical Pacific, clockwise in the North Pacific, counterclockwise in the South Pacific. North and south of the "horse latitudes" just outside the tropics the currents cool and swing east. The prevailing winds move the same way: the southeast trade winds south of the equator, the northeast trade winds north of the equator, and the low-pressure "doldrums" in between. Westerlies blow east above the cool currents north and south of the tropics. This natural air-conditioning system brings warm water to Australia and Japan, cooler water to Peru and California.

PAPEETE'S CLIMATE

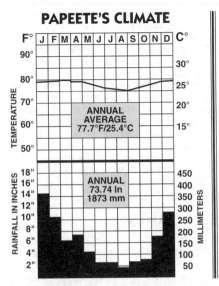

ANNUAL
AVERAGE
77.7°F/25.4°C

ANNUAL
73.74 In
1873 mm

RAROTONGA'S CLIMATE

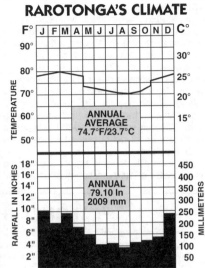

ANNUAL
AVERAGE
74.7°F/23.7°C

ANNUAL
79.10 In
2009 mm

The climate of the high islands is closely related to these winds. As air is heated near the equator it rises and flows at high altitudes toward the poles. By the time it reaches about 30 degrees south latitude it will have cooled enough to cause it to fall and flow back toward the equator near sea level. In the southern hemisphere the rotation of the earth deflects the winds to the left to become the southeast trades. When these cool moist trade winds hit a high island, they are warmed by the sun and forced up. Above 500 meters elevation they begin to cool again and their moisture condenses into clouds. At night the winds do not capture much warmth and are more likely to discharge their moisture as rain. The windward slopes of the high islands catch the trades head-on and are usually wet, while those on the leeward side may be dry.

Rain falls abundantly and frequently in the islands during the southern summer months (Nov.-April). This is also the hurricane season south of the equator, a dangerous time for cruising yachts. However, New Zealand and southern Australia, outside the tropics, get their finest weather at this time; many boats head south to sit it out. The southeast trade winds or *alizés*

sweep the South Pacific May-Oct., the cruising season. Cooler and drier, these are the ideal months for travel in insular Oceania, though the rainy season is only a slight inconvenience and the season shouldn't be a pivotal factor in deciding when to go.

Over the past few years climatic changes have turned weather patterns upside down, so don't be surprised if you get prolonged periods of rain and wind during the official "dry season" and drought when there should be rain. A recent analysis of data shows that in 1977 the belt of storms and winds shifted abruptly eastwards, making Tonga and Melanesia drier and Tahiti-Polynesia wetter. Hurricanes are also striking farther east and El Niño is expected to recur more frequently.

Temperatures range from warm to hot year-round; however, the ever-present sea moderates the humidity by bringing continual cooling breezes. Areas nearer the equator (the Marquesas and Northern Cooks) are hotter than those farther south (the Australs and Southern Cooks). There's almost no twilight in the tropics, which makes Pacific sunsets brief. When the sun begins to go down, you have less than half an hour before darkness.

When to Go

Compared to parts of North America and Europe, the seasonal climatic variations in Polynesia are not extreme. There is a hotter, more humid season Nov.-April and a cooler, drier time May-October. These contrasts are more pronounced in areas closer to the equator such as the Marquesas and less noticeable in Cook Islands. Hurricanes can also come during the "rainy" season but they only last a few days a year. The sun sets around 1800 year-round and there aren't periods when the days are shorter or longer.

Seasonal differences in airfares are covered in the **Getting There** section that follows and these should be more influential in deciding when to go. On Air New Zealand flights from North America to Cook Islands the low season is mid-April to August, the prime time to go there. To Tahiti, on the other hand, June to August is the high tourist season for airfares, festivals, and tourism in general. French tourists are notorious for scheduling their trips in August, and New Zealanders crowd into Rarotonga in July and August to escape the winter weather back home. Christmas is also busy with islanders returning home.

In short, there isn't really any one season that is the "best" time to come. Go whenever you can, but book your airline seat well in advance as many flights from the U.S. run 90% full.

TROPICAL HURRICANES

The official hurricane (or cyclone) season south of the equator is Nov.-April, although hurricanes have also occurred in May and October. Since the ocean provides the energy, these low pressure systems can only form over water with a surface temperature above 27° C; during years when water temperatures are high (such as during the recent El Niño) their frequency increases. The rotation of the earth must give the storm its initial spin, and this occurs mostly between latitudes five and 20 on either side of the equator.

As rainfall increases and the seas rise, the winds are drawn into a spiral that reaches its maximum speed in a ring around the center. In the South Pacific a cyclone develops as these circular winds, rotating clockwise around a center, increase in velocity: force eight to nine winds blowing at 34 to 47 knots are called a gale, force 10 to 11 at 48 to 63 knots is a storm, force 12 winds revolving at 64 knots or more is a hurricane. Wind speeds can go as high as 100 knots with gusts to 140 on the left side of the storm's path in the direction it's moving.

The eye of the hurricane can be 10 to 30 kilometers wide and surprising clear and calm, although at sea, contradictory wave patterns continue to wreak havoc. In the South Pacific most hurricanes move south at speeds of five to 20 knots. As water is sucked into the low-pressure eye of the hurricane and waves reach 14 meters in height, coastlines can receive a surge of up to four meters of water, especially if the storm enters a narrowing bay or occurs at high tide.

M.G.L. DOMENY DE RIENZI

a waterspout during a tropical cyclone or hurricane

FLORA AND FAUNA

FLORA

The variety of floral species encountered in the Pacific islands declines as you move away from the Asian mainland. Although some species may have spread across the islands by means of floating seeds or fruit, wind and birds were probably more effective. The microscopic spores of ferns, for example, can be carried vast distances by the wind. In the coastal areas of Tahiti most of the plants now seen have been introduced by humans.

Distance, drought, and poor soil have made atoll vegetation among the most unvaried on earth. Though a tropical atoll might seem "lush," no more than 15 native species may be present! On the atolls, taro, a root vegetable with broad heart-shaped leaves, must be cultivated in deep organic pits. The vegetation of a raised atoll is apt to be far denser, with many more species, yet it's likely that fewer than half are native.

The high islands of Polynesia support a great variety of plantlife, while the low islands are restricted to a few hardy, drought-resistant species such as coconuts and pandanus. Rainforests fill the valleys and damp windward slopes of the high islands, while brush and thickets grow in more exposed locations. *Mape* (Tahitian chestnut) grows along the streams. Other trees you'll encounter include almond, candlenut, casuarina (ironwood), flamboyant, barringtonia, *purau* (wild hibiscus), pistachio, and rosewood. Mountain bananas *(fei)* grow wild in the high country. Along the coast, fruits such as avocado, banana, custard apple, guava, grapefruit, lime, lychee, mango, orange, papaya, pineapple, watermelon, and a hundred more are cultivated. Hillsides in the drier areas are covered with coarse grasses. The absence of leaf-eating animals allowed the vegetation to develop largely without the protective spines and thorns found elsewhere.

Here in Polynesia the air is sweet with the bouquet of tropical blossoms such as bursting bougainvillea, camellia, frangipani, ginger, orchids, poinsettia, and pitate jasmine. The fragrant flowers of the Polynesian hibiscus *(purau)* are yellow, not red or pink as on the Chinese hibiscus. A useful tree, the hibiscus has a soft wood used for house and canoe construction, and bast fiber used to make cordage and mats. The national flower, the delicate, heavily scented *tiare Tahiti (Gardenia tahitiensis),* can have anywhere from six to nine white petals. It blooms year-round, but especially from September to April. In his *Plants and Flowers of Tahiti* Jean-Claude Belhay writes: "The tiare is to Polynesia what the lotus is to India: a veritable symbol." Follow local custom by wearing this blossom or a hibiscus behind your left ear if you're happily taken, behind your right ear if you're still available.

Mangroves can occasionally be found along some high island coastal lagoons. The cable roots of the saltwater-tolerant red mangrove anchor in the shallow upper layer of oxygenated mud, avoiding the layers of hydrogen sulfide below. The tree provides shade for tiny organisms dwelling in the tidal mudflats—a place for birds to nest and for fish or shellfish to feed and spawn. The mangroves also perform the same task as land-building coral colonies along the reefs. As sediments are trapped between the roots, the trees extend farther into the lagoon, creating a unique natural environment. The past decade has seen widespread destruction of the mangroves.

FAUNA

Land Animals

Few land animals reached the eastern Pacific without the help of man. Ancient Polynesian navigators introduced pigs, dogs, and chickens; they also brought along rats. Captain Cook contributed cattle, horses, and goats; Captain Wallis left behind cats. Whalers dropped more goats off in the Marquesas. Giant African snails *(Achatina fulica)* were brought to Tahiti from Hawaii in the 1960s by a local policeman fond of fancy French food. He tried to set up a snail farm with the result that some escaped, multiplied, and now crawl wild, destroying the vegetation. Dogs and roosters add to the sounds of the night.

BENGT DANIELSSON

Colonies of black noodies nest in palm trees throughout the islands.

Birds

Of the 90 species of birds in Tahiti-Polynesia, 59 are found in the Society Islands, of which 33 are native. Among the seabirds are the white-tailed tropic birds, brown and black noddies, white and crested terns, petrels, and boobies. The *itatae* (white tern), often seen flying about with its mate far from land, lays a single egg in the fork of a tree without any nest. The baby terns can fly soon after hatching. Its call is a sharp ke-ke-yek-yek. The *oio* (black noddy) nests in colonies, preferably in palm trees, building a flat nest of dead leaves, sticks, and stems. It calls a deep cra-cra-cra. The hopping Indian mynah bird *(Acridotheres tristis)* with its yellow beak and feet was introduced from Indonesia at the turn of the century to help control insects. Today these noisy, aggressive birds are a ubiquitous pest—feeding on fruit trees and forcing the native finches and blue-tinged doves out of their habitat.

Birdwatching is a highly recommended pursuit for the serious Pacific traveler; you'll find it opens unexpected doors. Good field guides are few (ask at local bookstores, museums, and cultural centers), but a determined interest will bring you into contact with fascinating people and lead to great adventures. The best time to observe forest birds is in the very early morning—they move around a lot less in the heat of the day.

Fish

The South Pacific's richest store of life is found in the silent underwater world of the pelagic and lagoon fishes. It's estimated that half the fish remaining on our globe are swimming in this great ocean. Coral pinnacles on the lagoon floor provide a safe haven for angelfish, butterfly fish, damselfish, groupers, soldierfish, surgeonfish, triggerfish, trumpet fish, and countless more. These fish seldom venture more than a few meters away from the protective coral, but larger fish such as barracuda, jackfish, parrot fish, pike, stingrays, and small sharks range across lagoon waters that are seldom deeper than 30 meters. The external side of the reef is also home to many of the above, but the open ocean is reserved for bonito, mahimahi, swordfish, tuna, wrasses, and the larger sharks. Passes between ocean and lagoon can be crowded with fish in transit, offering a favorite hunting ground for predators.

In the open sea the food chain begins with phytoplankton, which flourish wherever ocean upswellings bring nutrients such as nitrates and phosphates to the surface. In the western Pacific this occurs near the equator, where massive currents draw water away toward Japan and Australia. Large schools of fast-moving tuna ply these waters feeding on smaller fish, which consume tiny phytoplankton drifting near the sunlit surface. The phytoplankton also exist in tropical lagoons where mangrove leaves, sea grasses, and other plant material are consumed by far more varied populations of reef fish, mollusks, and crustaceans.

It's believed that most Pacific marine organisms evolved in the triangular area bounded by New Guinea, the Philippines, and the Malay Peninsula. This "Cradle of Indo-Pacific Marinelife" includes a wide variety of habitats and has remained stable through several geological ages. From this cradle the rest of the Pacific was colonized.

Marine Mammals

While most people use the terms dolphin and porpoise interchangeably, a porpoise lacks the dolphin's beak (although many dolphins are also beakless). There are 62 species of dolphins, and only six species of porpoises. Dolphins leap from the water and many legends tell of their

saving humans, especially children, from drowning (the most famous concerns Telemachus, son of Odysseus). Dolphins often try to race in front of ferries and large ships. The commercialization of dolphins in aquariums or enclosures for the amusement of humans is a questionable activity.

Whales generally visit the tropical South Pacific between July and October. Humpbacks arrive about this time to give birth in the warm waters. As the weather grows warmer they return to the summer feeding areas around Antarctica. (Sadly, Japanese whalers continue to hunt the animals in Antarctica for "scientific purposes," and endangered fin and humpback whales are usually hidden among the 400 minke whale kills reported each year. Whale meat is openly available at Tokyo restaurants.)

Sharks

The danger from sharks (*mao* in Tahitian, *requin* in French) has been greatly exaggerated. Of some 300 different species, only 28 are known to have attacked humans. Most dangerous are the white, tiger, and blue sharks. Fortunately, all of these inhabit deep water far from the coasts. An average of only 50 shark attacks a year occur worldwide, so considering the number of people who swim in the sea, your chances of being involved are about one in ten million. In the South Pacific, shark attacks on snorkelers or scuba divers are extremely rare and the tiny mosquito is a far more dangerous predator.

Sharks are not aggressive where food is abundant, but they can be very nasty far offshore. You're always safer if you keep your head underwater (with a mask and snorkel), and don't panic if you see a shark—you might attract it. Even if you do, they're usually only curious, so keep your eye on the shark and slowly back off. The swimming techniques of humans must seem very clumsy to fish, so it's not surprising if they want a closer look.

Sharks are attracted by shiny objects (a knife or jewelry), bright colors (especially yellow and red), urine, blood, spearfishing, and splashing (divers should ease themselves into the water). Sharks normally stay outside the reef, but get local advice. White beaches are safer than dark, and clear water safer than murky. Avoid swimming in places where sewage or edible wastes enter the water, or where fish have just been cleaned. You should also exercise care in places where local residents have been fishing with spears or even hook and line that day.

Never swim alone if you suspect the presence of sharks. If you see one, even a supposedly harmless nurse shark lying on the bottom, get out of the water calmly and quickly, and go elsewhere. Studies indicate that sharks, like most other creatures, have a "personal space" around them that they will defend. Thus an attack could be a shark's way of warning someone to keep his distance, and it's a fact that over half the victims of these incidents are not eaten but merely bitten. Sharks are much less of a problem in the South Pacific than in colder waters because small marine mammals (commonly hunted by sharks) are rare here, so you won't be mistaken for a seal or an otter.

Let common sense be your guide, not irrational fear or carelessness. Many scuba divers come actually *looking* for sharks, and local divemasters seem able to swim among them with impunity. If you're in the market for some shark action, dive shops at Bora Bora and Rangiroa can provide it. Just be aware that getting into the water with feeding sharks always entails some danger, and the divemaster who admits this and lays down some basic safety guidelines (such as keeping your hands clasped or arms folded) is probably a safer bet than the macho man who just says he's been doing it for years without incident.

However, supplying food to any kind of wild creature destroys their natural feeding habits and handling marine life can have unpredictable consequences. Never snorkel on your own (without the services of an experienced guide) near a spot where shark feeding is practiced as you never know how the sharks will react to a surface swimmer without any food for them. More study is required to determine whether shark feeding by tourism operators tends to attract sharks to lagoons and beaches used for public recreation. Like all other wild animals, sharks deserve to be approached with respect.

Sea Urchins

Sea urchins (living pincushions) are common in tropical waters. The black variety is the most dangerous: their long, sharp quills can go right

through a snorkeler's fins. Even the small ones, which you can easily pick up in your hand, can pinch you if you're careless. They're found on rocky shores and reefs, never on clear, sandy beaches where the surf rolls in.

Most sea urchins are not poisonous, though quill punctures are painful and can become infected if not treated. The pain is caused by an injected protein, which you can eliminate by holding the injured area in a pail of very hot water for about 15 minutes. This will coagulate the protein, eliminating the pain for good. If you can't heat water, soak the area in vinegar or urine for a quarter hour. Remove the quills if possible, but being made of calcium, they'll decompose in a couple of weeks anyway—not much of a consolation as you limp along in the meantime. In some places sea urchins are considered a delicacy: the orange or yellow urchin gonads are delicious with lemon and salt.

Other Hazardous Creatures

Although jellyfish, stonefish, crown-of-thorns starfish, cone shells, eels, and poisonous sea snakes are dangerous, injuries resulting from any of these are rare. Gently apply methylated spirit, alcohol, or urine (but not water, kerosene, or gasoline) to areas stung by jellyfish. Inoffensive sea cucumbers (bêche-de-mer) punctuate the lagoon shallows, but stonefish also rest on the bottom and are hard to see due to camouflaging; if you happen to step on one, its dorsal fins inject a painful poison, which burns like fire in the blood. Fortunately, stonefish are not common.

It's worth knowing that the venom produced by most marine animals is destroyed by heat, so your first move should be to soak the injured part in very hot water for 30 minutes. (Also hold an opposite foot or hand in the same water to prevent scalding due to numbness.) Other authorities claim the best first aid is to squeeze blood from a sea cucumber scraped raw on coral directly onto the wound. If a hospital or clinic is nearby, go there immediately.

Never pick up a live cone shell; some varieties have a deadly stinger dart coming out from the pointed end. The tiny blue-ring octopus is only five centimeters long but packs a poison that can kill a human. Eels hide in reef crevices by day; most are harmful only if you inadvertently poke your hand or foot in at them. Of course, never tempt fate by approaching them (fun-loving divemasters sometimes feed the big ones by hand and stroke their backs).

Reptiles and Insects

Land snakes don't exist in eastern Polynesia and the sea snakes are shy and inoffensive. This, and the relative absence of leeches, poisonous plants, thorns, and dangerous wild animals, makes the South Pacific a paradise for hikers. One creature to watch out for is the centipede, which often hides under stones or anything else lying around. It's a long, flat, fast-moving insect not to be confused with the round, slow, and harmless millipede. The centipede's bite, though painful, is not lethal to a normal adult.

Geckos and skinks are small lizards often seen on the islands. The skink hunts insects by day; its tail breaks off if you catch it, but a new one quickly grows. The gecko is nocturnal and has no eyelids. Adhesive toe pads enable it to pass along vertical surfaces, and it changes color to avoid detection. Unlike the skink, which avoids humans, geckos often live in people's homes, where they eat insects attracted by electric lights. Its loud clicking call may be a territorial warning to other geckos. Two species of geckos are asexual: in these, males do not exist and the unfertilized eggs hatch into females identical to the mother. Geckos are the highest members of the animal world where this phenomenon takes place. During the 1970s a sexual species of house gecko was introduced to Samoa and Vanuatu, and in 1988 it arrived on Tahiti. These larger, more aggressive geckos have drastically reduced the population of the endemic asexual species.

Five of the seven species of sea turtles are present in Polynesia (the green, hawksbill, leatherback, loggerhead, and olive ridley turtles). These magnificent creatures are some-

LOUISE FOOTE

times erroneously referred to as "tortoises," which are land turtles. All species of sea turtles now face extinction due to ruthless hunting, egg harvesting, and beach destruction. Sea turtles come ashore Nov.-Feb. to lay their eggs on the beach from which they themselves originally hatched, but female turtles don't commence this activity until they are twenty years old. Thus a drop in numbers today has irreversible consequences a generation later, and it's estimated that breeding females already number in the hundreds or low thousands. Turtles are often choked by floating plastic bags they mistake for food, or they drown in fishing nets.

HISTORY

THE ERA OF DISCOVERY AND SETTLEMENT

Prehistory

Oceania is the site of many "lasts." It was the last area on earth to be settled by humans, the last to be discovered by Europeans, and the last to be both colonized and decolonized. Sometime after about 1600 B.C., broad-nosed, light-skinned Austronesian peoples entered the Pacific from Indonesia or the Philippines. The Austronesians had pottery and advanced outrigger canoes. Their distinctive *lapita* pottery, decorated in horizontal

LOUIS LE BRETON

a tattooed Marquesan woman from Dumont d'Urville's Voyage au Sud Pole *(1846)*

geometric bands and dated from 1500 to 500 B.C., has been found at sites ranging from New Britain to New Caledonia, Tonga, and Samoa. *Lapita* pottery has allowed archaeologists to trace the migrations of an Austronesian-speaking race, the Polynesians, with some precision, and recent comparisons of DNA samples have confirmed that they traveled from Taiwan to the Philippines, Indonesia, New Guinea, Fiji, and Samoa.

The colorful theory that Oceania was colonized from the Americas is no longer seriously entertained. The Austronesian languages are today spoken from Madagascar through Indonesia all the way to Easter Island and Hawaii, half the circumference of the world! All of the introduced plants of old Polynesia, except the sweet potato, originated in Southeast Asia. The endemic diseases of Oceania, leprosy and the filaria parasite (which causes elephantiasis), were unknown in the Americas. The amazing continuity of Polynesian culture is illustrated by motifs in contemporary tattooing and tapa, which are very similar to those on ancient *lapita* pottery.

The Colonization of Polynesia

Three thousand five hundred years ago the early Polynesians set out from Southeast Asia on a migratory trek that would lead them to make the "many islands" of Polynesia their home. Great voyagers, they sailed their huge double-hulled canoes far and wide, steering with huge paddles and pandanus sails. To navigate they read the sun, stars, currents, swells, winds, clouds, and birds. Sailing purposefully, against the prevailing winds and currents, the *Lapita* peoples reached the Bismarck Archipelago by 1500 B.C., Tonga (via Fiji) by 1300 B.C., and Samoa by 1000 B.C. Around the time of Christ they pushed out from this primeval area, remembered as Havaiki, into the eastern half of the Pacific.

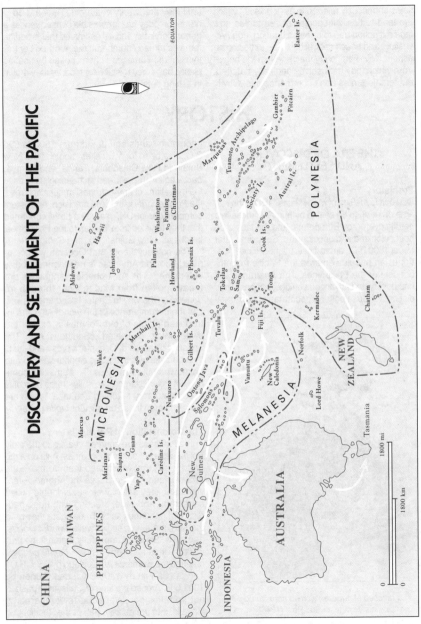

DISCOVERY AND SETTLEMENT OF THE PACIFIC

EQUATOR

CHINA

TAIWAN

PHILIPPINES

INDONESIA

AUSTRALIA

Tasmania

New Guinea

MICRONESIA

Marcus

Wake

Marianas

Saipan

Guam

Yap

Caroline Is.

Marshall Is.

Nukuoro

Ontong Java

Solomons

MELANESIA

Vanuatu

New Caledonia

Lord Howe

Norfolk

Gilbert Is.

Tuvalu

Fiji Is.

Kermadec

NEW ZEALAND

Chatham

Midway

Hawaii

Johnston

Palmyra

Washington

Fanning

Christmas

Howland

Phoenix Is.

Tokelau

Samoa

Tonga

Cook Is.

Society Is.

Marquesas

Tuamoto Archipelago

Austral Is.

Gambier

Pitcairn

Easter Is.

POLYNESIA

1800 mi

1800 km

0

0

© DAVID STANLEY

Perhaps due to rising overpopulation in Samoa, some Polynesians pressed on to the Society Islands and the Marquesas by A.D. 300. Easter Island (A.D. 400), Hawaii (A.D. 500), and Mangareva (A.D. 900) were all reached by Polynesians from the Marquesas. Migrants to the Tuamotus (A.D. 900), the Cook Islands (A.D. 900), and New Zealand (A.D. 1100) were from the Society Islands. The stone food pounders, carved figures, and tanged adzes of Eastern Polynesia are not found in Samoa and Tonga (Western Polynesia), indicating that they were later, local developments of Polynesian culture.

These were not chance landfalls but planned voyages of colonization: the Polynesians could (and often did) return the way they came. That one could deliberately sail such distances against the tradewinds and currents without the help of modern navigational equipment was proved in 1976 when the *Hokule'a*, a reconstructed ocean-going canoe, sailed 5,000 km south from Hawaii to Tahiti. The expedition's Micronesian navigator, Mau Piailug, succeeded in setting a course by the ocean swells and relative positions of the stars alone, which guided them very precisely along their way. Other signs used to locate an island were clouds (which hang over peaks and remain stationary), seabirds (boobies fly up to 50 km offshore, frigate birds up to 80 km), and mysterious *te lapa* (underwater streaks of light radiating 120-150 km from an island, disappearing closer in).

Since 1976 the *Hokule'a* has made several additional return trips to Tahiti; during 1985-87 Hawaiian navigator Nainoa Thompson used traditional methods to guide the *Hokule'a* on a 27-month "Voyage of Rediscovery" that included a return west-east journey between Samoa and Tahiti. To date the vessel has logged over 100,000 km using traditional methods, introducing Polynesian voyaging to countless thousands. In 1992 the canoe *Te Aurere* sailed from New Zealand to Rarotonga for the Festival of Pacific Arts—the first such voyage in a thousand years—where it joined the *Hokule'a* and a fleet of other canoes in a dramatic demonstration of the current revival of traditional Polynesian navigation. In 1995 the *Hokule'a* led a three-canoe flotilla from Hawaii to Tahiti, returning in May with another three double-hulled canoes, which joined them in the Marquesas. A voyage from Hawaii to Easter Island is planned for the millennium. (For more information on the *Hokule'a*, click on http://leahi.kcc.hawaii.edu/org/pvs.)

The Polynesians were the real discoverers of the Pacific, completing all their major voyages long before Europeans even dreamed this ocean existed. In double canoes lashed together to form rafts, carrying their plants and animals with them, they penetrated as close to Antarctica as the South Island of New Zealand, as far north as Hawaii, and as far east as Easter Island—a full 13,000 km from where it's presumed they first entered the Pacific!

the double-hulled
sailing canoe, Hokule'a

EASTERN POLYNESIAN CHRONOLOGY

A.D. 300: Polynesians reach the Marquesas

A.D. 800: Polynesians reach the Society Islands

1521: Magellan sights Pukapuka in the Tuamotus

1595: Mendaña contacts the Marquesas

1606: Quirós passes through the Tuamotus

1722: Roggeveen sights Easter Island and Bora Bora

1767: Englishman Samuel Wallis contacts Tahiti

1768: Frenchman Bougainville visits Tahiti

1769: Captain Cook observes transit of Venus at Tahiti

1774: Spanish priests spend one year on Tahiti

1777: last of Capt. Cook's four visits to Tahiti

1788: Bligh's HMS *Bounty* at Tahiti

1789: Captain Bligh sights Aitutaki

1797: arrival on Tahiti of first Protestant missionaries

1803: Pomare II flees to Moorea

1812: Pomare's subjects convert to Protestantism

1815: Pomare II reconquers Tahiti

1818: foundation of Papeete by Rev. Crook

1823: missionary John Williams arrives at Rarotonga

1827: 50-year reign of Queen Pomare IV begins

1834: French Catholic missionaries arrive at Mangareva

1836: French Catholic priests are expelled from Tahiti

1838: French gunboat demands compensation

1842: French protectorate is declared over Tahiti and the Marquesas
Herman Melville visits Tahiti-Polynesia

1844: Mormon missionaries arrive on Tubuai, Austral Islands

1844-1847: Tahitian War of Independence

1847: Queen Pomare accepts French protectorate

1862: Easter Islanders kidnaped by Peruvian slavers

1865-1866: 1,010 Chinese laborers arrive on Tahiti

1877: death of Queen Pomare IV

1880: French protectorate changes into a colony

1884: a fire destroys much of Papeete

1887: France annexes the Leeward Islands

1888: British protectorate declared in Southern Cooks

1888: Chile annexes Easter Island

1889: British protectorate declared in Northern Cooks

1889: French protectorate declared over Australs

1890: British missionaries depart Leeward Islands

1891: Paul Gauguin arrives at Tahiti

1900: Austral Islands annexed by France

1901: Cook Islands transferred to New Zealand

1903: Paul Gauguin dies on Hiva Oa

1908: phosphate mining begins at Makatea

1914: German cruisers shell Papeete

1917: W. Somerset Maugham arrives to research a book about Gauguin

1918: influenza epidemic kills 20% of population of Tahiti

1942: American military base is established on Bora Bora

1945: Tahitians become French citizens

1946: Tahiti-Polynesia becomes an overseas territory

1946: territorial assembly created

1953: Chilean Navy takes over Easter Island

1958 : Pouvanaa a Oopa is arrested

1961: opening of Faa'a Airport on Tahiti

1962: French halt nuclear testing in Algeria

1963: French nuclear testing moves to Polynesia

1965: Cook Islands becomes self-governing phosphate mine closes on Makatea

1966: first atmospheric nuclear explosion in the Tuamotus

1974: French nuclear testing moves underground

1977: Tahiti-Polynesia is granted partial internal autonomy

1984: internal autonomy increases slightly

1987: Université française du Pacifique is established

1992: President Mitterrand suspends nuclear testing

1994: income tax introduced in Tahiti-Polynesia

1995: President Chirac restarts nuclear testing

1996: nuclear testing ends and site is dismantled

1998: Value Added Tax inflicted on Tahiti-Polynesia

Neolithic Society

The Polynesians kept gardens and a few domestic animals. Taro was cultivated in organic pits; breadfruit was preserved by fermentation through burial (still a rare delicacy). Stone fishponds and fish traps were built in the lagoons. Pandanus and coconut fronds were woven into handicrafts. On the larger islands these practices produced a surplus, which allowed the emergence of a powerful ruling class. The common people lived in fear of their gods and chiefs.

The Polynesians were cannibals, although the intensity of the practice varied from group to group: cannibalism was rife in the Marquesas but relatively rare on Tahiti. Early European explorers were occasionally met by natives who would kneel beside them on the shore, squeezing their legs and pinching their posteriors to ascertain how tasty and substantial these white people would be to eat. It was believed that the mana or spiritual power of an enemy would be transferred to the consumer; to eat the body of one who was greatly despised was the ultimate revenge. Some Melanesians perceived the pale-skinned newcomers with "odd heads and removable skin" (hats and clothes) as evil spirits, perhaps ancestors intent on punishing the tribe for some violation of custom.

Jean-Jacques Rousseau and the 18th-century French rationalists created the romantic image of the "noble savage." Their vision of an ideal state of existence in harmony with nature disregarded the inequalities, cannibalism, and warfare that were a central part of island life, just as much of today's travel literature ignores the poverty and political/economic exploitation many Pacific peoples now face. Still, the legend of the South Pacific maintains its magic hold.

EUROPEAN CONTACT

European Exploration

The first Europeans on the scene were the Spaniards. In 1595, on his second trip from Peru to the Solomon Islands, Álvaro de Mendaña discovered the southern Marquesas Islands. He stayed only a few days and Europeans didn't return for over a century. The systematic European exploration of the Pacific in the 18th century

was actually a search for *terra australis incognita,* a great southern continent believed to balance the continents of the north. Dutchman Jacob Roggeveen's 1722 voyage failed to discover the unknown continent, but he did find Easter Island and narrowed the area of conjecture considerably.

In 1745, the British Parliament passed an act promising £20,000 to the first British subject who could, in a British ship, discover and sail through a strait between Hudson's Bay and the South Seas. Thus many explorers were spurred to investigate the region. This route would have proven infinitely shorter than the one around Cape Horn, where the weather was often foul and the ships in perpetual danger; on Samuel Wallis's voyage of 1766-67, his two ships took four months to round the chaotic Straits of Mag-

WILLIAM HODGES

Omai, a native of Huahine, sailed to England with Cook's colleague, Captain Furneaux, aboard the Adventure, *and immediately became the talk of London. For many Europeans he epitomized the "noble savage," but to those who came to know him, he was a sophisticated man with a culture of his own.*

Captain Cook and his officers sharing a meal with Tahitians

ellan. In June 1767 Wallis "discovered" Tahiti (which was already well populated at the time).

Captain Cook

The extraordinary achievements of James Cook (1728-1779) on his three voyages in the ships *Endeavor, Resolution, Adventure,* and *Discovery* left his successors with little to do but marvel over them. A product of the Age of Enlightenment, Cook was a mathematician, astronomer, practical physician, and master navigator. Son of a Yorkshire laborer, he learned seamanship on small coastal traders plying England's east coast. He joined the British Navy in 1755 and soon made a name for himself in Canada where he surveyed the St. Lawrence River, greatly contributing to the capture of Quebec City in 1759. Later he charted the coast of Newfoundland. Chosen to command the *Endeavor* in 1768 though only a warrant officer, Cook was the first captain to eliminate scurvy from his crew (with sauerkraut).

The scientists of his time needed accurate observations of the transit of Venus, for if the passage of Venus across the face of the sun were measured from points on opposite sides of the earth, then the size of the solar system could be determined for the first time. In turn, this would make possible accurate predictions of the movements of the planets, vital for navigation at sea. Thus Cook was dispatched to Tahiti, and Father Hell (a Viennese astronomer of Hungarian origin) to Vardo, Norway.

So as not to alarm the French and Spanish, the British admiralty claimed Cook's first voyage (1768-71) was primarily to take these measurements. His real purpose, however, was to further explore the region, in particular to find *terra australis incognita.* After three months on Tahiti, he sailed west and spent six months exploring and mapping New Zealand and the whole east coast of Australia, nearly tearing the bottom off his ship, the *Endeavor,* on the Great Barrier Reef in the process. Nine months after returning to England, Cook embarked on his second expedition (1772-75), resolving to settle the matter of *terra australis incognita* conclusively. In the *Resolution* and *Adventure,* he sailed entirely around the bottom of the world, becoming the first to cross the Antarctic Circle and return to tell about it.

In 1773 John Harrison won the greater part of a £20,000 reward offered by Queen Anne in 1714 "for such Person or Persons as shall discover the Longitude at Sea." Harrison won it with the first marine chronometer (1759), which accompanied Cook on his second and third voyages. Also on these voyages was Omai, a native of Tahiti who sailed to England with Cook in 1774. Omai immediately became the talk of London, the epitome of the "noble savage," but to those who knew him he was simply a sophisticated man with a culture of his own.

In 1776 Cook set forth from England for a third voyage, supposedly to repatriate Omai but really to find a Northwest Passage from the Pacific to

MUTINY ON THE *BOUNTY*

In 1788 the HMS *Bounty* sailed from England for the Pacific to collect breadfruit plants to supplement the diet of slaves in the West Indies. Because the *Bounty* arrived at Tahiti at the wrong time of year, it was necessary to spend a long five months there collecting samples, and during this time, part of the crew became overly attached to that isle of pleasure. On 28 April 1789, in Tongan waters, they mutinied against Lt. William Bligh under 24-year-old Master's Mate Fletcher Christian. Bligh was set adrift in an open boat with the 18 men who chose to go with him. He then performed the amazing feat of sailing 6,500 km in 41 days, reaching Dutch Timor to give the story to the world.

After the mutiny, the *Bounty* sailed back to Tahiti. An attempt to colonize Tubuai in the Austral Islands failed, and Fletcher Christian set out with eight mutineers, 18 Polynesian men and women, and one small girl, to find a new home where they would be safe from capture. In 1791 the crew members who elected to remain on Tahiti were picked up by the HMS *Pandora* and returned to England for trial. Three were executed. The *Bounty* sailed through the Cook Islands, Tonga, and Fiji, until Christian remembered the discovery of tiny Pitcairn Island by Captain Carteret of the *Swallow* in 1767. They changed course for Pitcairn and arrived on

15 January 1790. After removing everything of value, the mutineers burned the *Bounty* to avoid detection. For 18 years after the mutiny, the world knew nothing of the fate of the *Bounty,* until the American sealer *Topaz* called at Pitcairn for water in 1808 and solved the mystery.

Actor Erroll Flynn's first screen role was as Fletcher Christian in a 1933 Australian movie titled *In the Wake of the Bounty.* The famous mutiny captured the popular imagination after an account by American writers Charles Nordhoff and James Norman Hall was published in 1934, and a year later Frank Lloyd's film *Mutiny on the Bounty* with Charles Laughton as a cruel Captain Bligh and Clark Gable as a gallant Fletcher Christian won the Oscar for Best Picture. Lloyd presented the affair as a simplistic struggle between good and evil, and two subsequent remakes were more historically accurate. The extravagant 1962 version starring Trevor Howard as Captain Bligh and Marlon Brando as Fletcher Christian is well remembered in Tahiti due to Brando's continuing involvement in the area, but the 1984 film with Sir Anthony Hopkins as a purposeful Bligh and Mel Gibson portraying an ambiguous Christian comes closer to reality and the views of Moorea are stunning. All these are well worth viewing on video.

Robert Dodd's famous 1790 painting of Fletcher Christian aboard HMS Bounty bidding farewell to Captain Bligh and the loyal members of his crew.

ROBERT DODD

the Atlantic. He rounded Cape Horn and headed due north, discovering Kauai in the Hawaiian Islands on 18 January 1778. After two weeks in Hawaii, Cook continued north via the west coast of North America but was forced back by ice in the Bering Strait. With winter coming, he returned to Hawaiian waters and located the two biggest islands of the group, Maui and Hawaii. On 14 February 1779, in a short, unexpected, petty skirmish with the Hawaiians, Cook was killed. Today he remains the giant of Pacific exploration.

The Fatal Impact

Most early contacts with Europeans had a hugely disintegrating effect on native cultures. When introduced into the South Pacific, European sicknesses—mere discomforts to them—devastated whole populations. Measles, influenza, tuberculosis, dysentery, smallpox, typhus, typhoid, and whooping cough were deadly because the islanders had never developed resistance to them. The European's alcohol, weapons, and venereal disease further accelerated the process.

CONVERSION, COLONIALISM, AND NUCLEAR TESTS

Conversion

The systematic explorations of the 18th century were stimulated by the need for raw materials and markets as the Industrial Revolution took hold in Europe. After the American Revolution, much of Britain's colonizing energy was deflected toward Africa, India, and the Pacific. This gave them an early lead, but France wasn't far behind. As trade developed in the late 18th and early 19th centuries, ruffian whalers, sealers, and individual beachcombers flooded in. Most were unsavory characters who acted as mercenaries or advisors to local chiefs, but one, Herman Melville, left a valuable account of early Polynesia.

After the easily exploited resources were depleted, white traders and planters arrived to establish posts and to create copra and cotton plantations on the finest land. Missionaries came to "civilize" the natives by teaching that all their customs—cannibalism, warring with their neighbors, having more than one wife, wearing leaves instead of clothes, dancing, drinking kava, chewing betel nut, etc.—were wrong. They taught hard work, shame, thrift, abstention, and obedience. Tribes now had to wear sweaty, rainsoaked, germ-carrying garments of European design. Men dressed in singlets and trousers, and the women in Mother Hubbards, one-piece smocks trailing along the ground. To clothe themselves and build churches required money, obtained only by working as laborers on European plantations or producing a surplus of goods to sell to European traders. In many instances this austere, harsh Christianity was grafted onto the numerous taboo systems of the Pacific.

Members of the London Missionary Society arrived at Tahiti in 1797, though it was not until 1815 that they succeeded in converting the Tahitians. One famous LMS missionary, the Rev. John Williams, spread Protestantism to the Cook Islands (1823) and Samoa (1830). The children of some of the European missionaries who "came to do good, stayed to do well" as merchants. Later, many islanders themselves became missionaries: some 1,200 of them left their homes to carry the word of God to other islands. The first Catholic priests arrived in Polynesia in 1834. They competed with the Protestants for influence and divided islands on religious grounds.

After the 1840s, islanders were kidnapped by "blackbirders," who sold them as slaves. Worst were the Peruvians, who took 3,634 islanders to Peru in 1862 and 1863, of whom only 148 were returned. The populations of Easter Island and some of the northern Cooks were devastated.

Colonialism

The first European colonies in Oceania were Australia (1788) and New Zealand (1840). Soon after, the French seized Tahiti-Polynesia (1842) and New Caledonia (1853). A canal across Central America had already been proposed and Tahiti was seen as a potential port of call on the sea routes to Australia and New Zealand. The French annexed several other island groups near Tahiti in the 1880s. Missionary pressure led Britain to declare a protectorate over Cook Islands in 1888, the same year Chile annexed Easter Island, forestalling further French advances in those directions. In 1901 Britain transferred responsibility for Cook Islands to New Zealand.

By the late 19th century, the colonies' tropical produce (copra, sugar, vanilla, cacao, and fruits)

WHAT'S IN A NAME?

Over the years that portion of Eastern Polynesia controlled by France has been called many things. After 1880 it was the Etablissements français de l'Oceánie, becoming Polynésie française or French Polynesia in 1957, the designation still officially recognized by the colonial (and postal) authorities. French-occupied Polynesia better reflects the political reality, but variations like (french) Polynesia and "French" Polynesia are also seen. Recently the pro-French faction in the Territorial Assembly has adopted Tahiti Nui or "Greater Tahiti" to give the impression that they enjoy a lot more autonomy than is the case, whereas the pro-independence camp calls their country Te Ao Maohi, which translates to Land of the Moahi. Maohinui is also heard. Tourism officials on Tahiti often use Tahiti and Its Islands, whereas we prefer Tahiti-Polynesia. When in doubt, "Tahiti" will get you by, although there's a lot more to this colorful region than just its largest and best-known island.

had become more valuable and accessible; minerals, such as phosphates and guano, were also exploited. Total control of the assets gained by exploiting these resources passed to large European trading companies, which owned the plantations, ships, and retail stores. This colonial economy led to a drop in the indigenous populations in general by a third, not to mention the destruction of their cultures.

There were fundamental differences in approach between the British and French colonial administrations in the South Pacific. While the French system installed "direct rule" by French officials appointed by the French government, the British practiced "indirect rule" with the *ariki* (chiefs) retaining most of their traditional powers. Not only was this form of government cheaper, but it fostered stability. British colonial officials had more decision-making authority than their French counterparts who had to adhere to instructions received from Paris. And while the French sought to undermine local traditions in the name of assimilation, the British (and later New Zealanders) defended the native land tenure on which traditional life was based.

During World War II, large American staging and supply bases were created on Bora Bora, Aitutaki, and Penrhyn to support the southern supply routes to Australia and New Zealand. The airfields built on those islands during the war are still in use today.

In 1960 the United Nations issued a Declaration of Granting of Independence to Colonial Countries and Peoples, which encouraged the trend toward self-government, and in 1965 Cook Islands achieved de facto independence in association with New Zealand. As a French colony, Tahiti-Polynesia has a degree of internal autonomy, although great power continues to be wielded by appointed French officials who are not responsible to the local assembly. Decolonization is a hot issue on Tahiti, where one of the South Pacific's only active independence movements is found. Easter Island also remains an old-fashioned colony of Chile.

French Power

New Caledonia, Tahiti-Polynesia, and Wallis and Futuna are part of a worldwide chain of French colonies also including Kerguelen, Guiana, Martinique, Guadeloupe, Mayotte, Reunion, and St. Pierre and Miquelon, under the DOM-TOM (Ministry of Overseas Departments and Territories). It costs France billions of francs a year to maintain this system, a clear indicator that it's something totally different from colonial empires of the past, which were based on economic exploitation, not subsidies. A closer analogy is the American network of military bases around the world, which serves a similar purpose—enforcing hegemony. For over thirty years France has been willing to spend vast sums to perpetuate its status as a medium-sized world power.

These conditions contradict what has happened elsewhere in the South Pacific. During the 1960s and 1970s, as Britain, Australia, and New Zealand voluntarily withdrew from their Pacific colonies, French pretensions to global status grew stronger. This digging in created the anachronism of a few highly visible bastions of white colonialism in the midst of a sea of English-speaking self-governing nations. When French officials summarily rejected all protests against their nuclear testing and suppression of independence movements, most Pacific islanders were outraged.

The final round of nuclear testing in the Tuamotu Islands in 1995 was a watershed as French national prestige had seldom sunk as low, both in the Pacific and around the world. Since that debacle, France has tried to mend fences by supplying economic aid to the independent states and granting enhanced autonomy to its colonies. In recent years France has come to realize that its interests in the Pacific are as well served by emphasizing social, cultural, and economic matters as by outright political and military domination. French universities have been established on Tahiti and New Caledonia. As France becomes fully integrated into the new Europe, it's quite likely the ability and desire to maintain remote colonies will decline, and the decolonization process will finally be concluded.

Nuclear Testing

No other area on earth was more directly affected by the nuclear arms race than the Pacific. From 6 August 1945 until 27 January 1996, scarcely a year passed without one nuclear power or another testing their weapons here. The U.S., Britain, and France exploded over 250 nuclear bombs at Bikini, Enewetak, Christmas Island, Moruroa, and Fangataufa, an average of over six a year for over 40 years, more than half of them by France. The U.S. and British testing was only halted by the 1963 Partial Nuclear Test Ban Treaty with the Soviets, while the French tests continued until unprecedented worldwide protests made it clear that the Cold War really was over (as usual, France was a slow learner).

The British and American test sites in Micronesia are now part of independent countries, but the Marshallese still suffer radiation sickness from U.S. testing in the 1940s and 1950s (some of it deliberately inflicted by the use of islanders as human guinea pigs), and the French are still covering up the consequences of their tests. The end result of nuclear testing in Micronesia and Polynesia is ticking away in the genes of thousands of servicemen and residents present in those areas during the tests, and at the fragile underground Tuamotu test site used by the French.

The fact that the nuclear age began in their backyard at Hiroshima and Nagasaki has not been lost on the islanders. They have always seen few benefits coming from nuclear power, only deadly dangers. On 6 August 1985 eight member states of the South Pacific Forum signed the South Pacific Nuclear-Free Zone Treaty, also known as the Treaty of Rarotonga, which bans nuclear testing, land-based nuclear weapon storage, and nuclear waste dumping on their territories. Each country may decide for itself if nuclear-armed warships and aircraft are to be allowed entry. Of the five nuclear powers, China and the USSR promptly signed the treaty, while the U.S., France, and Britain only signed in March 1996 when it became obvious they could no longer use the region as a nuclear playground.

frangipani

DIANA LASICH HARPER

ECONOMY

The greatest source of income for all three territories included herein is budgetary aid from the mother country. France, Chile, and New Zealand each spend millions of dollars a year subsidizing the public services of their dependencies. Tourism comes a distant second, and in recent years cultured pearls have become the leading export of Tahiti-Polynesia and Cook Islands.

One of the few potential sources of real wealth are the undersea mineral nodules within the huge exclusive economic zones (EEZ) of Tahiti-Polynesia and Cook Islands. Three known nodule deposits sit in over 6,000 meters of water in the Pacific: one stretches from Mexico to a point southeast of Hawaii; another is between Hawaii and the Marshall Islands; a third is in Tahiti-Polynesia and Cook Islands. The potato-sized nodules contain manganese, cobalt, nickel, and copper; total deposits are valued at US$3 trillion, enough to supply the world for thousands of years. Over the past decade Japan has spent US$100 million on seabed surveys in preparation for eventual mining, although that's still decades away.

In 1976 the French government passed legislation that gave it control of this zone, not only along France's coastal waters but also around all her overseas territories and departments. The National Marine Research Center and private firms have already drawn up plans to recover nickel, cobalt, manganese, and copper nodules from depths of over 4,000 meters. The French government has adamantly refused to give the Territorial Assembly any jurisdiction over this tremendous resource, an important indicator as to why they are determined to hold onto their colony at any price.

TOURISM

Tourism is the world's largest and fastest-growing industry, increasing 260% between 1970 and 1990. Some 593 million people traveled abroad in 1996 compared to only 25 million in 1950, and each year over 25 million first-world tourists visit third-world countries, transferring an estimated US$25 billion from North to South. Tourism is the only industry that allows a net flow of wealth from richer to poorer countries, and in the islands it's one of the few avenues open for economic development, providing much-needed foreign exchange required to pay for imports. Unlike every other export, purchasers of tourism products pay their own transportation costs to the market.

New Zealand is the main source of visitors to Cook Islands, while most of Easter Island's arrivals are from Europe and Chile. Americans and French are the largest single groups of travelers to Tahiti-Polynesia. On a per-capita basis, Cook Islands gets more tourists than any other South Pacific country, and it's the number one industry throughout this part of the world. Yet the "tyranny of distance" has thus far prevented the islands from being spoiled.

Arrival levels from New Zealand are expected to remain stable in coming years, and Japan, Europe, and North America are seen as the main growth markets for South Pacific tourism. Japanese interest in the region increased dramatically in the late 1980s, and Japanese companies now own several top hotels in Tahiti-Polynesia. Increasing numbers of European and North American visitors can be expected if airfares remain low and the region's many advantages over competing Mediterranean and Caribbean destinations can be effectively marketed.

Only about 40% of the net earnings from tourism actually stays in the host country. The rest is "leaked" in repatriated profits, salaries for expatriates, commissions, imported goods, food, fuel, etc. Top management positions usually go to foreigners, with local residents offered low-paying service jobs. To encourage hotel construction, local governments must commit themselves to crippling tax concessions and large infrastructure investments for the benefit of hotel companies. The cost of airports, roads, communications networks, power lines, sewers, and waste disposal can exceed the profits from tourism.

Tourism-related construction can cause unsightly beach erosion due to the clearing of vegetation and the extraction of sand. Resort sewage causes lagoon pollution, while the reefs are blasted to provide passes for tourist craft and stripped of corals or shells by visitors. Locally scarce water supplies are diverted to hotels, and foods such as fruit and fish can be priced beyond the reach of local residents. Access to the ocean can be blocked by wall-to-wall hotels.

Although tourism is often seen as a way of experiencing other cultures, it can undermine those same cultures. Traditional dances and ceremonies are shortened or changed to fit into tourist schedules, and mock celebrations are held out of season and context, and their significance is lost. Cheap mass-produced handicrafts are made to satisfy the expectations of visitors; thus the Balinese carvings sold on Bora Bora. Authenticity is sacrificed for immediate profits. While travel cannot help but improve international understanding, the aura of glamour and prosperity surrounding tourist resorts can present a totally false image of a country's social and economic realities.

To date, most attention has focused on luxury resorts and all-inclusive tours—the exotic rather than the authentic. Packaged holidays create the illusion of adventure while avoiding all risks and individualized variables, and on many tours the only islanders seen are maids and bartenders. This elitist tourism perpetuates the colonial master-servant relationship as condescending foreigners instill a feeling of inferiority in local residents and workers. Fortunately, in all three territories included in this book, an excellent alternative exists in the form of local guesthouse tourism.

THE PEOPLE

The aquatic continent of Oceania is divided into three great cultural areas: Polynesia and Melanesia lie mostly below the equator while Micronesia is above it. The name Polynesia comes from the Greek words *poly* (many) and *nesos* (islands). The Polynesian Triangle has Hawaii at its north apex, New Zealand 8,000 km to the southwest, and Easter Island an equal distance to the southeast. Melanesia gets its name from the Greek word *melas* (black), probably for the dark appearance of its inhabitants as seen by the early European navigators. Micronesia comes from the Greek word *mikros* (small), thus, the "small islands."

The term Polynesia was coined by Charles de Brosses in 1756 and applied to all the Pacific islands. The present restricted use was proposed by Dumont d'Urville during a famous lecture at the Geographical Society in Paris in 1831. At the same time he also proposed the terms Melanesia and Micronesia for the regions that still bear those names. The terms are not particularly good, considering that all three regions have "many islands" and "small islands"; in Melanesia it is not the islands, but the people, that are black.

Cook Islands and Tahiti-Polynesia are highly urbanized, and the rapid growth of Papeete has led to high levels of unemployment and social problems such as alcoholism, petty crime, and domestic violence. Cook Islanders migrate to New Zealand, people from the Australs, Tuamotus, and Marquesas to Tahiti, and Tahitians to New Caledonia, creating the problem of idled land and abandoned homes. In Cook Islands more islanders now live off their home islands than on them. Yet the region's charming, gentle, graceful peoples remain high among its attractions.

THE POLYNESIANS

The Polynesians, whom Robert Louis Stevenson called "God's best, at least God's sweetest work," are a tall, golden-skinned people with straight or wavy, but rarely fuzzy, hair. They have fine features, almost intimidating physiques, and a soft, flowing language. One theory holds that the Polynesians evolved their great bodily stature through a selective process on their long ocean voyages, as the larger individuals with more body fat were better able to resist the chill of evaporating sea spray on their bodies (polar animals are generally larger than equatorial animals of the same species for the same reason). Other authorities ascribe their huge body size to a high-carbohydrate vegetable diet.

The ancient Polynesians developed a rigid social system with hereditary chiefs; descent was

ARCHIVES NATIONALES, SECTION OUTRE-MER, FRANCE

Polynesian girl, Tahiti

usually through the father. In most of Polynesia there were only two classes, chiefs and commoners, but in Hawaii, Tahiti, and Tonga an intermediate class existed. Slaves were outside the class system entirely, but slavery was practiced only in New Zealand, the Cook Islands, and Mangareva. People lived in scattered dwellings rather than villages, although there were groupings around the major temples and chiefs' residences. Their economy centered on fishing and agriculture. Land was collectively owned by families and tribes. Though the land was worked collectively by commoners, the chiefly families controlled and distributed its produce by well-defined customs. Large numbers of people could be mobilized for public works or war.

Two related forces governed Polynesian life: mana and *tapu*. Our word "taboo" originated from the Polynesian *tapu*. Numerous taboos regulated Polynesian life, such as prohibitions against taking certain plants or fish that were intended for chiefly use. Mana was a spiritual power—gods and high chiefs had the most and commoners had the least. Early missionaries would often publicly violate the taboos and smash the images of the gods to show that their mana had vanished.

Gods

The Polynesians worshipped a pantheon of gods, who had more mana than any human. The most important were Tangaroa (the creator and god of the oceans), and Oro, or Tu (the god of war), who demanded human sacrifices. The most fascinating figure in Polynesian mythology was Maui, a Krishna- or Prometheus-like figure who caught the sun with a cord to give its fire to the world. He lifted the firmament to prevent it from crushing mankind, fished the islands out of the ocean with a hook, and was killed trying to gain the prize of immortality for humanity. Also worth noting is Hina, the heroine who fled to the moon to avoid incest with her brother and so that the sound of her tapa beater wouldn't bother anyone. Tane (the god of light) and Rongo (the god of agriculture and peace) were other important gods. This polytheism, which may have disseminated from Raiatea in the Society Islands, was most important in Eastern Polynesia. The *Arioi* confraternity, centered in Raiatea and thought to be possessed by the gods, traveled about putting on dramatic representations of the myths.

The Eastern Polynesians were enthusiastic temple builders, evidenced today by widespread ruins. Known by the Polynesian name *marae,* these platform and courtyard structures of coral and basalt blocks often had low surrounding walls and internal arrangements of upright wooden slabs. Once temples for religious cults, they were used for seating the gods and for presenting fruits and other foods to them at ritual feasts. Sometimes, but rarely, human sacrifices took place on the *marae*. Religion in Western Polynesia was very low-key, with few priests or cult images. No temples have been found in Tonga and very few in Samoa. The gods of Eastern Polynesia were represented in human form. The ancestors were more important as a source of descent for social ranking, and genealogies were carefully preserved. Surviving elements of the old religion are the still-widespread belief in spirits *(aitu),* the continuing use of traditional medicine, and the influence of myth. More than 150 years after conversion by early missionaries, most Polynesians maintain their early Christian piety and fervid devotion.

TAHITI IN LITERATURE

Over the years European writers have traveled to Polynesia in search of Bougainville's Nouvelle Cythère or Rousseau's noble savage. Brought to the stage and silver screen, their stories entered the popular imagination alongside Gauguin's rich images, creating the romantic myth of the South Seas paradise presently cultivated by the travel industry. An enjoyable way to get a feel for the region is to read a couple of the books mentioned below before you come.

Herman Melville, author of the whaling classic *Moby Dick* (1851), deserted his New Bedford whaler at Nuku Hiva in 1842 and *Typee* (1846) describes his experiences there. An Australian whaling ship carried Melville on to Tahiti, but he joined a mutiny on board, which landed him in the Papeete *calabooza* (prison). His second Polynesian book, *Omoo* (1847), was a result. In both, Melville decries the ruin of Polynesian culture by Western influence.

Robert Louis Stevenson

Pierre Loti's *The Marriage of Loti* (1880) is a sentimental tale of the love of a young French midshipman for a Polynesian girl named Rarahu. Loti's naïveté is rather absurd, but his friendship with Queen Pomare IV and his fine imagery make the book worth reading. Loti's writings influenced Paul Gauguin to come to Tahiti.

In 1888-90 Robert Louis Stevenson, famous author of *Treasure Island* and *Kidnapped,* cruised the Pacific in his schooner, the *Casco.* His book *In the South Seas* describes his visits to the Marquesas and Tuamotus. Stevenson settled at Tautira on Tahiti-iti for a time, but eventually retired at Apia in Samoa, which offered the author better mail service. In 1890 Stevenson and his family bought a large tract of land just outside Apia and built a large, framed house called Vailima. In 1894 he was buried on Mt. Vaea, just above his home.

Jack London and his wife Charmian cruised the Pacific aboard their yacht, the *Snark,* in 1907-09. A longtime admirer of Melville, London found only a wretched swamp at Taipivai in the Marquesas. His *South Sea Tales* (1911) was the first of the 10 books that he wrote on the Pacific. London's story "The House of Mapuhi," about a Jewish pearl buyer, earned him a costly lawsuit. London was a prod-uct of his time, and the modern reader is often shocked by his insensitive portrayal of the islanders.

In 1913-14 the youthful poet Rupert Brooke visited Tahiti, where he fell in love with Mamua, a girl from Mataiea whom he immortalized in his poem "Tiare Tahiti." Later Brooke fought in WW I and wrote five famous war sonnets. He died of blood poisoning on a French hospital ship in the Mediterranean in 1915.

W. Somerset Maugham toured Polynesia in 1916-17 to research his novel, *The Moon and Sixpence* (1919), a fictional life of Paul Gauguin. Maugham's *A Writer's Notebook,* published in 1984, 19 years after his death, describes his travels in the Pacific. On Tahiti Maugham discovered not only material for his books but by chance located a glass door pane with a female figure painted by Gauguin himself, which he bought for 200 francs. In 1962 it sold at Sotheby's in London for $37,400.

American writers Charles Nordhoff and James Norman Hall came to Tahiti after WW I, married Tahitian women, and collaborated on 11 books. Their most famous was the *Bounty Trilogy* (1934), which tells of Fletcher Christian's *Mutiny on the Bounty,* the escape to Dutch Timor of Captain Bligh and his crew in *Men Against the Sea,* and the mutineer's fate in *Pitcairn's Island.* Three generations of filmmakers have selected this saga as their way of presenting paradise.

Hall remained on Tahiti until his death in 1951 and he was buried on the hill behind his home at Arue. His last book, *The Forgotten One,* is a collection of true stories about expatriate intellectuals and writers lost in the South Seas. Hall's account of the 28-year correspondence with his American friend Robert Dean Frisbie, who settled on Pukapuka in the Cook Islands during the 1920s, is touching.

James A. Michener joined the U.S. Navy in 1942 and ended up visiting around 50 South Sea islands, among them Bora Bora. His *Tales of the South Pacific* (1947) tells of the impact of WW II on the South Pacific and the Pacific's impact on those who served. It was later made into the long-running Broadway musical, *South Pacific.* Michener's *Return to Paradise* (1951) is a readable collection of essays and short stories.

Art

The Polynesians used no masks and few colors, usually leaving their works unpainted. Art forms were very traditional, and there was a defined class of artists producing works of remarkable delicacy and deftness. Three of the five great archaeological sites of Oceania are in Polynesia: Easter Island, Huahine, and Tongatapu (the other two are Pohnpei and Kosrae in Micronesia).

RELIGION

Religion plays an important role in the lives of the Pacific islanders, holding communities together and defending moral values. No other non-European region of the world is as solidly Christian as the South Pacific, and the South Pacific is one of the few areas of the world with a large surplus of ministers of religion. The first missionaries to arrive were Protestants, and the Catholic fathers who landed almost 40 years later had to rely on French military backing to establish missions in Tahiti and the Marquesas. Thus the established Protestant denominations are progeny of the London Missionary Society, the Evangelicals of Tahiti-Polynesia and the Cook Islands Christian Church. On Easter Island, Catholicism predominates.

Since the 1960s, the old rivalry between Protestant and Catholic has been largely replaced by an avalanche of well-financed American fundamentalist missionary groups that divide families and spread confusion in an area already strongly Christian. While the indigenous churches have long been localized, the new evangelical sects are dominated by foreign personnel, ideas, and money. The ultraconservative outlook of the new religious imperialists continues the tradition of allying Christianity with colonialism or neocolonialism.

Of course, the optimum way to experience religion in the South Pacific is to go to church on Sunday. Just be aware that the services can last one and a half hours and will usually be in the Polynesian tongue, French, or Spanish. If you decide to go, don't get up and walk out in the middle—see it through. You'll be rewarded by the joyous singing and fellowship, and you'll encounter the islanders on a different level. After church, people gather for a family meal or picnic and spend the rest of the day relaxing and socializing. If you're a guest in an island home you'll be invited to accompany them to church.

The Mormons

Mormon missionaries arrived on Tubuai in the Austral Islands as early as 1844, and today "Mormonia" covers much of the South Pacific. According to the Book of Mormon, American Indians are descendants of the 10 lost tribes of Israel and to hasten the second coming of Christ, they must be reconverted. Like Thor Heyerdahl, Mormons believe American Indians settled Polynesia, so the present church is willing to spend a lot of time and money spreading the word. The pairs of clean-cut young Mormon "elders" seen on the outliers, each in shirt and tie, riding a bicycle or driving a minibus, are sent down from the States for two-year stays.

You don't have to travel far in the South Pacific to find the assembly-line Mormon chapels, schools, and sporting facilities, paid for by church members who are expected to contribute 10% of their incomes. The Mormon church spends over US$500 million a year on foreign missions and sends out almost 50,000 missionaries, more than any other American church by far. Mormon fascination with genealogy parallels the importance of descent in Polynesian society where it often determines land rights. There's a strong link to Hawaii's Brigham Young University (www.byuh.edu), and many island students help pay for their schooling by representing their home country at the Mormon-owned Polynesian Cultural Center on Oahu. In Melanesia, Mormon missionary activity is a recent phenomenon, as prior to a "revelation" in 1978, blacks were barred from the Mormon priesthood.

Other Religious Groups

More numerous than the Mormons are adherents of the **Seventh-Day Adventist Church,** a politically ultra-conservative group that grew out of the 19th-century American Baptist movement. This is the largest nonhistorical religious group in the South Pacific, with a large following in Tahiti-Polynesia. The SDA Church teaches the imminent return of Christ, and Saturday (rather than Sunday) is observed as the Sabbath. SDAs regard the human body as the temple of the

Holy Spirit, thus much attention is paid to health matters. Members are forbidden to partake of certain foods, alcohol, drugs, and tobacco, and the church expends considerable energy on the provision of medical and dental services. They're also active in education and local economic development. Like many of the fundamentalist sects, the SDAs tend to completely obliterate traditional cultures.

The **Assemblies of God** (AOG) is a Pentecostal sect founded in Arkansas in 1914 and presently headquartered in Springfield, Missouri. Although the AOG carries out some relief work, it opposes social reform in the belief that only God can solve humanity's problems. Disgraced American tele-evangelists Jimmy Swaggart and Jim Bakker were both former AOG ministers.

The **Jehovah's Witnesses** originated in 19th century America and since 1909 their headquarters has been in Brooklyn, from whence their worldwide operations are financed. Jehovah's Witnesses' teachings against military service and blood transfusions have often brought them into conflict with governments, and they in turn regard other churches, especially the Catholic Church, as instruments of the Devil. Members must spread the word by canvassing their neighborhood door-to-door, or by standing on streetcorners offering copies of *The Watchtower*. This group focuses mostly on Christ's return, and since "the end of time" is fast approaching, it has little interest in relief work. They're numerous in Tahiti-Polynesia.

LANGUAGE

Some 1,200 languages, a third of the world's total, are spoken in the Pacific islands, though most have very few speakers. The Austronesian language family includes over 900 distinct languages spoken in an area stretching from Madagascar to Easter Island. The Polynesians speak about 21 closely related languages with local variations and consonantal changes. They're mutually unintelligible to those who haven't learned them, although they have many words in common. For instance, the word for land varies between *whenua, fenua, fanua, fonua, honua, vanua,* and *henua*. In the Polynesian languages the words are softened by the removal of certain consonants. Thus the Tagalog word for coconut, *niog,* became *niu, ni,* or *nu*. They're musical languages whose accent lies mostly on the vowels. Polynesian is rhetorical and poetical but not scientific, and to adapt to modern life many words have been borrowed from European languages; these too are infused with vowels to make them more melodious to the Polynesian ear. Thus in Tahitian governor becomes *tavana* and frying pan *faraipani*. Special vocabularies used to refer to or address royalty or the aristocracy also exist.

CONDUCT AND CUSTOMS

Foreign travel is an exceptional experience enjoyed by a privileged few. Too often, tourists try to transfer their lifestyles to tropical islands, thereby missing out on what is unique to the region. Travel can be a learning experience if approached openly and with a positive attitude, so read up on the local culture before you arrive and become aware of the social and environmental problems of the area. A wise traveler soon graduates from hearing and seeing to listening and observing. Speaking is good for the ego and listening is good for the soul.

The path is primed with packaged pleasures, but pierce the bubble of tourism and you'll encounter something far from the schedules and organized efficiency: a time to learn how other people live. Walk gently, for human qualities are as fragile and responsive to abuse as the brilliant reefs. The islanders are by nature soft-spoken and reserved. Often they won't show open disapproval if their social codes are broken, but don't underestimate them: they understand far more than you think. Consider that you're only one of thousands of visitors to their islands, so don't expect to be treated better than anyone else. Respect is one of the most important things in life and humility is also greatly appreciated.

Don't try for a bargain if it means someone will be exploited. What enriches you may violate others. Be sensitive to the feelings of those you wish to "shoot" with your camera and ask their permission first. Don't promise things you can't or won't deliver. Keep your time values to yourself; the islanders lead an unstressful lifestyle and assume you are there to share it.

If you're alone you're lucky, for the single traveler is everyone's friend. Get away from other tourists and meet the people. There aren't many places on earth where you can still do this meaningfully, but the South Pacific is one. If you do meet people with similar interests, keep in touch by writing. This is no tourist's paradise, though, and local residents are not exhibits or paid performers. They have just as many problems as you, and if you see them as real people you're less likely to be viewed as a stereotypical tourist. You may have come to escape civilization, but keep in mind that you're just a guest.

Most important of all, try to see things their way. Take an interest in local customs, values, languages, challenges, and successes. If things work differently than they do back home, give thanks—that's why you've come. Reflect on what you've experienced and you'll return home with a better understanding of how much we all have in common, outwardly different as we may seem. Do that and your trip won't have been wasted.

Women

In many traditional island cultures a woman seen wandering aimlessly along a remote beach was thought to be in search of male companionship, and "no" meant "yes." Single women hiking, camping, sunbathing, and simply traveling alone may be seen in the same light, an impression strongly reinforced by the type of videos available in the islands. In some cultures local women rarely travel without men, and some day-hikes, excursions, and interisland ship journeys mentioned in this book may be uncomfortable or even dangerous for women who are unprepared.

Two women together will have less to worry about in most cases, especially if they're well covered and look purposeful.

Women traveling alone should avoid staying in isolated tourist bungalows by themselves—it's wise to team up with other travelers before heading to the outer islands. In many Polynesian cultures there's a custom known as "sleep crawling" in which a boy silently enters a girl's home at night and lies beside her to prove his bravery. Visiting women sometimes become objects of this type of unwanted attention even in well-known resorts like Bora Bora and Moorea.

Children

Karen Addison of Sussex, England, sent us the following:

Traveling with children can have its ups and downs, but in the Pacific it's definitely an up. Pacific islanders are warm, friendly people, but with children you see them at their best. Your children are automatically accepted, and you, as an extension of them, are as well. As the majority of the islands are free of any deadly bugs or diseases, acclimatizing to the water, food, and climate would be your paramount concern. Self-contained units, where you can do your own cooking, are easy to find and cheap; having set meals every day gives children a sense of security. Not having television as a distraction, I've attempted to teach my son the rudiments of reading and writing. As a single mother with a little boy, traveling with him opened my eyes to things I'd normally overlook and has been an education to us both.

M.G.L. DOMENY DE RIENZI

canoes at Nuku Hiva, Marquesas Islands

ON THE ROAD

SPORTS AND RECREATION

Scuba Diving

Scuba diving is offered in resort areas throughout Polynesia. Commercial scuba operators know their waters and will be able to show you the most amazing things in perfect safety. Dive centers on Aitutaki, Bora Bora, Easter Island, Fakarava, Huahine, Manihi, Moorea, Nuku Hiva, Raiatea, Rangiroa, Rarotonga, Tahiti, and Tikehau operate year-round, with marinelife most profuse July to November. Before strapping on a tank and fins you'll have to show your scuba certification card, and occasionally divers are also asked to show a medical report from their doctor indicating that they are in good physical condition. Most dive shops tack on an extra US$10 or more for "equipment rental" (regulator, buoyancy compensator, and gauges) and frequent divers will save a lot by bringing their own. The waters are warm, varying less than one degree centigrade between the surface and 100 meters, so a wetsuit is not essential (although it will protect you from coral cuts). Many of the scuba operators listed in this book offer introductory "resort courses" for those who only want a taste of scuba diving, and full CMAS, NAUI, or PADI open-water certification courses for those wishing to dive more than once or twice. Scuba training will enhance your understanding and enjoyment of the sea. Lagoon diving is recommended for beginners; those with some experience will find the most beautiful coral along reef dropoffs and the most fish around passes into the lagoon. Precise information on scuba diving is provided throughout this handbook, immediately after the sightseeing sections.

Snorkeling

Scuba diving can become expensive if you get addicted, but snorkeling is practically free—all you need to do is a acquire a mask and pipe. Many scuba operators will take snorkelers out

10 SAFETY RULES OF DIVING

1. The most important rule in scuba diving is to BREATHE CONTINUOUSLY. If you establish this rule, you won't forget and hold your breath, and overexpansion will never occur.

2. COME UP AT A RATE OF 18 METERS PER MINUTE OR LESS. This allows the gas dissolved in you body under pressure to come out of solution safely and also prevents vertigo from fast ascents. Always make a precautionary decompression stop at a depth of five meters.

3. NEVER ESCAPE TO THE SURFACE. Panic is the diver's worst enemy.

4. STOP, THINK, THEN ACT. Always maintain control.

5. PACE YOURSELF. KNOW YOUR LIMITATIONS. A DIVER SHOULD ALWAYS BE ABLE TO REST AND RELAX IN THE WATER. Proper use of the buoyancy vest will allow you to rest on the surface and maintain control under water. A diver who becomes fatigued in the water is a danger to himself and his buddy.

6. NEVER DIVE WITH A COLD. Avoid alcoholic beverages but drink plenty of water. Get a good night's sleep and refrain from strenuous physical activities on the day you dive. Dive conservatively if you are overweight or more than 45 years of age. Make fewer dives the last two days before flying and no dives at all during the final 24 hours.

7. PLAN YOUR DIVE. Know your starting point, your diving area, and your exit areas. DIVE YOUR PLAN.

8. NEVER EXCEED THE SAFE SPORT DIVING LIMIT OF 30 METERS. Make your first dive the deepest of the day.

9. All equipment must be equipped with QUICK RELEASES.

10. WEAR ADEQUATE PROTECTIVE CLOTHING AGAINST SUN AND CORAL.

on their regular trips for a third to a quarter the cost of scuba diving. This is an easy way to reach some good snorkeling spots, just don't expect to be chaperoned for that price.

Be careful, however, and know the dangers. Practice snorkeling on a shallow sandy bottom and don't head into deep water or swim over coral until you're sure you've got the hang of it. Breathe easily; don't hyperventilate. When snorkeling on a fringing reef, beware of deadly currents and undertows in channels that drain tidal flows. Observe the direction the water is flowing before you swim into it. If you feel yourself being dragged out to sea through a reef passage, try swimming across the current rather than against it. If you can't resist the pull at all, it may be better to let yourself be carried out. Wait till the current diminishes, then swim along the outer reef face until you find somewhere to come back in. Or use your energy to attract the attention of someone onshore.

Snorkeling on the outer edge or drop-off of a reef is thrilling for the variety of fish and corals, but attempt it only on a very calm day. Even then it's wise to have someone stand onshore or paddle behind you in a canoe to watch for occasional big waves, which can take you by surprise and smash you into the rocks. Also, beware of unperceived currents outside the reef—you may not get a second chance.

A far better idea is to limit your snorkeling to the protected inner reef and leave the open waters to the scuba diver. You'll encounter the brightest colors in shallow waters anyway as beneath six meters the colors blue out as short wavelengths are lost. By diving with a tank you trade off the chance to observe shallow water species in order to gain access to the often larger deep water species. The best solution is to do a bit of both. In any case, avoid touching the reef or any of its creatures as the contact can be very harmful to both you and the reef. Take only pictures and leave only bubbles.

Ocean Kayaking

This is a viable sport best practiced in sheltered lagoons, such as those of Raiatea/Taha'a, Bora Bora, and Aitutaki. You can rent kayaks in some places, but it's better to bring your own folding kayak. See **Getting Around,** later in this chapter, for more information on kayaking.

TAHITIAN DANCE MOVEMENTS

anuanua
rainbow

ao
day

here
to love

maeva
welcome

mana'o
to think

marama
moon

ori
to walk

LOUISE FOOTE

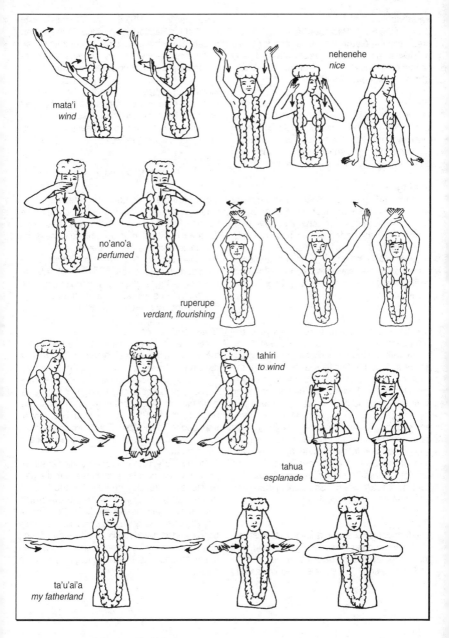

mata'i
wind

nehenehe
nice

no'ano'a
perfumed

ruperupe
verdant, flourishing

tahiri
to wind

tahua
esplanade

ta'u'ai'a
my fatherland

Yachting

Cruising the South Pacific by yacht is also covered below in **Getting Around,** and for those with less time there are several established yacht charter operations based at Raiatea. See **Yacht Charters** for more information.

Hiking

This is an excellent, inexpensive way to see the islands. A few of the outstanding treks covered in this handbook are Mt. Aorai on Tahiti, Vaiare to Paopao on Moorea, and the Cross-island Track on Rarotonga. There are many others.

Surfing

Famous surfing spots include Tahiti's Papara Beach, Huahine's Fare Reef, and Easter Island. The top surfing season is generally July to September when the tradewinds push the Antarctic swells north. During the hurricane season from January to March tropical storms can generate some spectacular waves. Prime locales for windsurfing include Rarotonga's Muri Lagoon and many others.

Fishing

Sportfishing is a questionable activity—especially spearfishing, which is sort of like shooting a cow with a handgun. An islander who spearfishes to feed his family is one thing, but the tourist who does it for fun is perhaps worthy of the attention of sharks. Deep-sea game fishing from gas-guzzling powerboats isn't much better, and it's painful to see noble fish slaughtered and strung up just to inflate someone's ego. That said, one has to admit that taking fish from the sea one by one for sport is never going to endanger the stocks the way net fishing by huge trawlers does. On most big-game boats, the captain keeps the catch. Sportfishing is covered throughout this handbook.

Golf

The former New Zealand administrators left behind several golf courses in Cook Island, and major international competitions are held at Tahiti's Olivier Breaud Golf Course. Greens fees vary considerably, from US$45 at the Olivier Breaud to US$7 at the Rarotonga Golf Club. Club and cart rentals are usually available for a bit less than the greens fees and all of the courses have clubhouses with pleasant colonial-style bars.

More Information

Package tours incorporating the activities just mentioned are described under **Getting There** in this introduction. Turn to that section for information on bicycling as well.

ENTERTAINMENT

Many big hotels run "island nights," or feasts where you get to taste the local food and see traditional dancing. If you don't wish to splurge on the meal it's sometimes possible to witness the spectacle from the bar for the price of a drink or a cover charge. These events are held weekly on certain days, so ask. On most islands Friday night is the time to let it all hang out; on Saturday many people are preparing for a family get-together or church on Sunday.

Music and Dance

Traditional music and dance is alive and well in the South Pacific, especially the exciting *tamure* dancing of Tahiti-Polynesia and Cook Islands. The slit-log gong beaten with a wooden stick is now a common instrument throughout Polynesia, even though the Eastern Polynesians originally had skin drums. The *to'ere* slit drum was only introduced to Tahiti from Western Polynesia after 1915, and it's marvelous the way the Tahitians have made it their own.

In the early 19th century, missionaries replaced the old chants of Polynesia with the harmonious gospel singing heard in the islands today, yet even the hymns were transformed into an original Oceanic medium. Contemporary Pacific music includes bamboo bands, brass bands, and localized Anglo-American pop. String bands have made European instruments such as the guitar and ukulele an integral part of Pacific music.

HOLIDAYS AND FESTIVALS

The special events of Tahiti-Polynesia, Easter Island, and Cook Islands are described in the respective chapters. Their dates often vary from year to year, so it's a good idea to contact the local tourist information office soon after your arrival to learn just what will be happening during your stay.

The most important annual festivals are the Tapati Rapa Nui festival on Easter Island (late January or early February), the Heiva i Tahiti at Papeete and Bora Bora (first two weeks of July), and the Constitution Celebrations on Rarotonga (early August). Since 1987 a Marquesas Islands Festival has been held about every four years (the next will be in December 1999). Catch as many as of these you can and try to participate in what's happening, rather than merely watching like a tourist.

ARTS AND CRAFTS

The traditional handicrafts that have survived best are the practical arts done by women (weaving, basketmaking, tapa). In cases where the items still perform their original function, they remain as vital as ever. Among the European-derived items are the patchwork quilts *(tifaifai)* of Tahiti and the Cooks. Whenever possible buy handicrafts from local women's committee shops, church groups, local markets, or from the craftspeople themselves, but avoid objects made from turtle shell/leather, clam shell, or marine mammal ivory, which are prohibited entry into many countries under endangered species acts. Failure to declare such items to customs officers can lead to heavy fines. Also resist the temptation to purchase jewelry or other items made from seashells and coral, the collection of which damages the reefs. Souvenirs made from straw or seeds may be held for fumigation or confiscated upon arrival.

Weaving

Woven articles are the most widespread handicrafts. Pandanus fiber is the most common, but coconut leaf and husk, vine tendril, banana stem, tree and shrub bark, the stems and leaves of water weeds, and the skin of the sago palm leaf are all used. On some islands the fibers are passed through a fire, boiled, then bleached in the sun. Vegetable dyes of very lovely mellow tones are sometimes used, but gaudier store dyes are much more prevalent. Shells are occasionally utilized to cut, curl, or make the fibers pliable. Polynesian woven arts are characterized by colorful, skillful patterns.

a contemporary tapa design from Fatu Hiva, Marquesas Islands

ACCOMMODATIONS

Hotels

With *Tahiti Handbook* in hand you're guaranteed a good, inexpensive place to stay on every island. Each and every hotel in the three territories is included herein, not just a selection. We consistently do this to give you a solid second reference in case your travel agent or someone else recommends a certain place. To allow you the widest possible choice, all price categories are included, and throughout we've tried to indicate which properties offer value for money. If you think we're wrong or you were badly treated, be sure to send a us written complaint. Equally important, let us know when you agree with what's here or if you think a place deserves a better rave. Your letter will have an impact!

We don't solicit freebies from the hotel chains; our only income derives from the price you paid for this book. So we don't mind telling you that, as usual, most of the luxury hotels are just not worth the exorbitant prices they charge. Many simply recreate Hawaii at twice the cost, offering far more luxury than you need. Even worse, they tend to isolate you in a French/American/Kiwi environment, away from the South Pacific you came to experience. Most are worth visiting as sightseeing attractions, watering holes, or sources of entertainment, but unless you're a millionaire sleep elsewhere. There are always middle-level hotels that charge half what the top-end places ask, while providing adequate comfort. And if you really *can* afford US$500 a night and up, you might do better chartering a skippered or bareboat yacht!

Dormitory, "bunkroom," or backpacker accommodations are available on all of the main is-

ECOTOURISM

Recently "ecotourism" has become the thing, and with increasing concern in Western countries over the damaging impact of solar radiation, more and more people are looking for land-based activities as an alternative to lying on the beach. This trend is also fueled by the "baby boomers" who hitchhiked around Europe in the 1970s. Today they're looking for more exotic locales in which to practice "soft adventure tourism" and they've got a lot more disposable income this time around. In the South Pacific the most widespread manifestation of the ecotourism/adventure phenomenon is the current scuba diving boom, and tours by chartered yacht, ocean kayak, surfboard, bicycle, or on foot are proliferating.

This presents both a danger and an opportunity. Income from visitors wishing to experience nature gives local residents and governments an incentive for preserving the environment, although tourism can quickly degrade that environment through littering, the collection of coral and shells, and the development of roads, docks, and resorts in natural areas. Means of access created for ecotourists often end up being used by local residents whose priority is not conservation. Perhaps the strongest argument in favor of the creation of national parks and reserves in the South Pacific is the ability of such parks to attract visitors from industrialized countries while at the same time creating a framework for the preservation of nature. For in the final analysis, it is governments that must enact regulations to protect the environment—market forces usually do the opposite.

Too often what is called ecotourism is actually packaged consumer tourism with a green coating, or just an excuse for high prices. Some four-wheel-drive jeep safaris, jet boat excursions, and helicopter trips have more to do with ecoterrorism than ecotourism. A genuine ecotourism resort will be built of local materials using natural ventilation. This means no air conditioning and only limited use of fans. The buildings will fit into the natural landscape and not restrict access to customary lands or the sea. Local fish and vegetables will have preference over imported meats on tourist tables, and wastes will be minimized. The use of aggressive motorized transport will be kept to an absolute minimum. Cultural sensitivity will be enhanced by profit sharing with the landowning clans and local participation in ownership. It's worth considering all of this, as a flood of phony ecotourism facilities are popping up.

"Club Bed" at Fare, Huahine, is popular among budget travelers.

lands, with communal cooking facilities usually provided. If you're traveling alone these are excellent since they're just the place to meet other travelers. Couples can usually get a double room for a price only slightly above two dorm beds. For the most part, the dormitories are safe and congenial for those who don't mind sacrificing their privacy to save money.

In Tahiti-Polynesia there's a bed and breakfast *(logement chez l'habitant)* program where you pay a set fee to stay with a local family in their own home. Meals may not be included in the price, but they're often available, tending toward your host family's fare of seafood and native vegetables.

ACCOMMODATIONS PRICE RANGES

Throughout this handbook, accommodations are generally grouped in the price categories which follow. Of course, currency fluctuations and inflation can lead to slight variations.

Shoestring	under US$15 double
Budget	US$15-35 double
Inexpensive	US$35-60 double
Moderate	US$60-85 double
Expensive	US$85-110 double
Premium	US$110-150 double
Luxury	over US$150 double

Needless to say, always ask the price of your accommodations before accepting them. In cases where there's a local and a tourist price, you'll always pay the higher tariff if you don't check beforehand. Hotel prices are usually fixed and bargaining isn't the normal way to go.

Be aware that some of the low-budget places included in this book are a lot more basic than what is sometimes referred to as "budget" accommodations in the States. The standards of cleanliness in the common bathrooms may be lower than you expected, the furnishings "early attic," the beds uncomfortable, linens and towels skimpy, housekeeping nonexistent, and window screens lacking, but ask yourself, where in the U.S. are you going to find a room for a similar price? Luckily, good medium-priced accommodations are usually available for those of us unwilling to put up with spartan conditions, and we include all of them in this book too.

When picking a hotel, keep in mind that although a thatched bungalow is cooler and infinitely more attractive than a concrete box, it's also more likely to have insect problems. If in doubt check the window screens and carry mosquito coils and/or repellent. Hopefully there'll be a resident lizard or two to eat the bugs. Always turn on a light before getting out of bed to use the facilities at night, as even the finest hotels in the tropics have cockroaches.

A room with cooking facilities can save you a lot on restaurant meals, and some moderately priced establishments have weekly rates. If you have to choose a meal plan, take only breakfast and dinner (Modified American Plan or *demi-pension*) and have fruit for lunch. As you check into your room, note the nearest fire exits. And don't automatically take the first room offered; if you're paying good money look at several, then choose. Single women intending to stay in isolated tourist bungalows should try to find someone with whom to share.

Reserving Ahead

Booking accommodations in advance usually works to your disadvantage as full-service travel agents will begin by trying to sell you their most expensive properties (which pay them the highest commissions) and work down from there. The quite adequate middle and budget places included in this handbook often aren't on their screens or are sold at highly inflated prices. Herein we provide the rates for direct local bookings, and if you book through a travel agent abroad you could end up paying considerably more as multiple commissions are tacked on. Thus we suggest you avoid making any hotel reservations at all before arriving in the South Pacific (unless you're coming for a major event).

We don't know of any island where it's to your advantage to book ahead in the medium to lower price range, but you can sometimes obtain substantial discounts at the luxury hotels by including them as part of a package tour. Even then, you'll almost always find medium-priced accommodations for less than the package price and your freedom of choice won't be impaired. If, however, you intend to spend most of your time at a specific first-class hotel, you'll benefit from bulk rates by taking a package tour instead of paying the higher "rack rate" the hotels charge to individuals who just walk in off the street. Call Air New Zealand's toll-free number and ask them to mail you their *Go As You Please* brochure, which lists deluxe hotel rooms in Cook Islands and Tahiti that can be booked on an individual basis at slightly reduced rates. Also call Discover Wholesale Travel and some of the other agents listed herein in **Getting There.**

Camping

Your number-one home away from home is a tent. There are organized campgrounds in Tahiti-Polynesia and on Easter Island, but camping is forbidden in Cook Islands. Make sure your tent is water- and mosquito-proof, and try to find a spot swept by the trades. Never camp under a coconut tree, as falling coconuts hurt (actually, coconuts have two eyes so they only strike the wicked). If you hear a hurricane warning, pack up your tent and take immediate cover with the locals.

FOOD

The traditional diet of the Pacific islanders consists of root crops and fruit, plus lagoon fish and the occasional pig. The vegetables include taro, yams, cassava (manioc), breadfruit, and sweet potatoes. The sweet potato is something of an anomaly—it's the only Pacific food plant with a South American origin. How it got to the islands is not known.

Taro is an elephant-eared plant cultivated in freshwater swamps. Papaya (pawpaw) is nourishing: a third of a cup contains as much vitamin C as 18 apples. To ripen a green papaya overnight, puncture it a few times with a knife. Don't overeat papaya—unless you *need* an effective laxative.

Raw fish (*poisson cru* or *sashimi*) is an appetizing dish enjoyed in many Pacific countries. To prepare it, clean and skin the fish, then dice the fillet. Squeeze lemon or lime juice over it, and store in a cool place about 10 hours. When it's ready to serve, add chopped onions, garlic, green peppers, tomatoes, and coconut cream to taste. Local fishmongers know which species make the best raw fish, but know what you're doing before you join them—island stomachs are probably stronger than yours. Health experts recommend eating only well-cooked foods and peeling your own fruit, but the islanders swear by raw fish.

Lobsters have become almost an endangered species on some islands due to the high prices they fetch on restaurant tables. Countless more are airfreighted to Hawaii. Before asking for one of these creatures to be sacrificed for your dinner, consider that the world will be poorer for it. Coconut crabs are even more threatened and it's al-

THE COCONUT PALM

Human life would not be possible on most of the Pacific's far-flung atolls without this all-purpose tree. It reaches maturity in eight years, then produces about 50 nuts a year for 60 years. Aside from the tree's esthetic value and usefulness in providing shade, the water of the green coconut provides a refreshing drink, and the white meat of the young nut is a delicious food. The harder meat of more mature nuts is grated and squeezed, which creates a coconut cream that is eaten alone or used in cooking. The oldest nuts are cracked open and the hard meat removed then dried to be sold as copra. It takes about 6,000 coconuts to make a ton of copra. Copra is pressed to extract the oil, which in turn is made into candles, cosmetics, and soap. Scented with flowers, the oil nurtures the skin.

The juice or sap from the cut flower spathes of the palm provides toddy, a popular drink; the toddy is distilled into a spirit called arrack, the whiskey of the Pacific. Otherwise the sap can be boiled to make candy. Millionaire's salad is made by shredding the growth cut from the heart of the tree. For each salad, a fully mature tree must be sacrificed.

The nut's hard inner shell can be used as a cup and makes excellent firewood. Rope, cordage, brushes, and heavy matting are produced from the coir fiber of the husk. The smoke from burning husks is a most effective mosquito repellent. The leaves of the coconut tree are used to thatch the roofs of the islanders' cottages or are woven into baskets, mats, and fans. The trunk provides timber for building and furniture. Actually, these are only the common uses: there are many others as well.

DIANA LASICH HARPER

Every part of the coconut tree (Cocus nucifera) *can be used.*

most scandalous that local governments should allow them to be fed to tourists. Sea turtles are other delicacy to avoid, although it's seldom offered to tourists.

Cooking

The ancient Polynesians stopped making pottery over a millennium ago and instead developed an ingenious way of cooking in an underground earth oven known as an *ahimaa*. First a stack of dry coconut husks is burned in a pit. Once the fire is going well, coral stones are heaped on top, and when most of the husks have burnt away the food is wrapped in banana leaves and placed on the hot stones—fish and meat below, vegetables above. A whole pig may be cleaned, then stuffed with banana leaves and hot stones. This cooks the beast from inside out as well as outside in, and the leaves create steam. The food is then covered with more leaves and stones, and after about two and a half hours everything is cooked.

SERVICES AND INFORMATION

VISAS AND OFFICIALDOM

If you're from an English-speaking country or Western Europe you won't need a visa to visit these territories. The only exception is Easter Island, where New Zealanders need one, in which case the visa is best obtained before leaving home. If you're from New Zealand check the latest requirements with your airline well ahead, as consulates are few and far between.

Everyone must have a passport, sufficient funds, and a ticket to leave. Your passport should be valid six months beyond your departure date. Some officials object to tourists who intend to camp or stay with friends, so write the name of a likely hotel on your arrival card (don't leave that space blank).

Customs

Agricultural regulations in the islands prohibit the import of fresh fruit, flowers, meat (including sausage), live animals and plants, as well as any old artifacts that might harbor pests. If in doubt, ask about having your souvenirs fumigated by the local agricultural authorities and a certificate issued prior to departure. Canned food, biscuits, confectionery, dried flowers, mounted insects, mats, baskets, and tapa cloth are usually okay. If you've been on a farm, wash your clothes and shoes before going to the airport, and if you've been camping, make sure your tent is clean.

Yacht owners should think twice before taking their pet dog along, as regulations in the rabies-free South Pacific are strict. Most countries require the animal to be held in quarantine on board for four to nine months. A bond of US$250 may be required, and it will be a hassle to get the money back come time to leave. You may be denied permission to dock or will get a shorter visa if you have a dog. Pets found ashore illegally can be confiscated and destroyed. Cats and birds may be happy spending a year aboard, but it's no life for a dog.

MONEY

All prices quoted herein are in Pacific francs (CFP), U.S. dollars, or New Zealand dollars unless otherwise stated. Each Monday the *Wall Street Journal* runs a "World Value of the Dollar" column that lists the current exchange rates of all foreign currencies. If you have access to the internet you'll find the rates at www.oanda.com.

Both Tahiti and Rarotonga airports have banks that change money at normal rates (check the Airport listings at the end of those chapter introductions). French francs in cash are the best currency to carry to Tahiti-Polynesia as they're exchanged at a fixed rate without any commission. However, if you don't already have them, just go with whatever currency you have.

The bulk of your travel funds should be in traveler's checks, preferably American Express as they have travel service offices in Papeete and Rarotonga. To claim a refund for lost or stolen American Express traveler's checks call the local office (listed in the respective chapters) or their Sydney office collect (tel. 61-2/9886-0689). They'll also cancel lost credit cards, as long as you know the numbers. The banks best represented in this part of the world are the ANZ Bank, the Bank of Hawaii, and the Westpac Bank, so if you need to have money sent, you'll want to work through one of them.

If you want to use a credit card, always ask beforehand, even if a business has a sign or brochure that says it's possible. Visa and MasterCard can be used to obtain cash advances at banks in most countries, but remember that cash advances accrue interest from the moment you receive the money—ask your bank if they have a debit card that allows charges to be deducted from your checking account automatically.

When you rent a car the agency will probably ask you to sign a blank credit card charge slip as security on the vehicle. As you do so, be sure to count the number of pages in the slip, and if you later pay cash and the blank slip is returned to you, make you sure you get all the pages back. Otherwise a dishonest operator could have removed the page to be sent to the credit card company with the intention of processing the charge a second time. Another way to protect yourself is to retain the blank slip as proof that it was returned when you paid cash, but be sure to write Void across it in case it's stolen or lost. Also keep your signed cash receipt, and don't let your credit card out of sight, even for a moment. Credit card fraud is not common in the South Pacific, but cases have occurred.

Many banks now have automated teller machines (ATMs) outside their offices and these provide local currency against checking account Visa and MasterCard at good rates without commission. Occasionally the machines don't work due to problems with the software, in which case you'll almost always be able to get a cash advance at the counter inside. To avoid emergencies, it's better not to be 100% dependent on ATMs. Ask your bank what fee they'll charge if you use an ATM abroad and find out if you need a special personal identification number (PIN).

Upon departure avoid getting stuck with leftover local banknotes, as currencies such as the Pacific franc and Chilean peso are difficult to change and heavily discounted even in neighboring countries. Change whatever you have left over into the currency of the next country on your itinerary, but don't wait to do it at the airport.

Cost-wise, you'll find Cook Islands and Easter Island a lot less expensive than Tahiti-Polynesia. Thus it's smart to spend those extra days of relaxation on Rarotonga rather than on Moorea or Bora Bora. Bargaining is not common: the first price you're quoted is usually it. Tipping is *not* customary in the South Pacific and can generate more embarrassment than gratitude.

POST AND TELECOMMUNICATIONS

Postal Services

Always use airmail when posting letters from the islands. Airmail takes two weeks to reach North America and Europe, surface mail takes up to six months. Postage rates to the U.S. are medium-priced from Cook Islands and very expensive from Tahiti-Polynesia. Plan your postcard writing accordingly.

When writing to South Pacific individuals or businesses, include the post office box number (or *Boîte Postale* in Tahiti-Polynesia), as mail delivery is rare. If it's a remote island or small village you're writing to, the person's name will be sufficient. Sending a picture postcard to an islander is a very nice way of saying thank you.

When collecting mail at poste restante (general delivery), be sure to check under the initials of your first and second names, plus any initial that is similar. Have your correspondents print and underline your last name.

Telephone Services

Cook Islands and Tahiti-Polynesia have card telephones and these are very handy. If you'll be staying in the islands more than a few days and intend to make your own arrangements, it's wise to purchase a local telephone card at a post office right away. In this handbook we provide all the numbers you'll need to make hotel reservations, check restaurant hours, find out about cultural shows, and compare car rental rates, saving you a lot of time and inconvenience.

By using a telephone card to call long distance you limit the amount the call can possibly cost and won't end up overspending should you forget to keep track of the time. On short calls you avoid three-minute minimum charges. International telephone calls placed from hotel rooms are always much more expensive than the same calls made from public phones using telephone cards. What you sacrifice is your privacy as anyone can stand around and listen to your call, as often happens. Card phones are usually found outside post offices or telephone centers. Check that the phone actually works before bothering to arrange your numbers and notes, as they're often out of service.

A local telephone call will be under US$0.20 in Cook Islands but in Tahiti-Polynesia they cost over US$0.50. A three-minute station-to-station call to the U.S. will cost under US$7 from Tahiti-Polynesia but US$12 from Cook Islands. Calling from the U.S. to the the islands is cheaper than going in the other direction, so if you want to talk to someone periodically, leave a list of your travel dates and hotel telephone numbers (provided in this book) where friends and relatives can try to get hold of you. All the main islands have direct dialing via satellite. One reader on a wide-ranging trip said he found it very effective to leave an extra copy of this book with his family. Not only were they able to follow his travels around the Pacific, but they had all the telephone and fax numbers needed to contact him.

To place a call to a Pacific island from outside the region, first dial the international access code (check your phone book), then the country code, then the number. The country codes are 56-32 Easter Island, 682 Cook Islands, and 689 Tahiti-Polynesia. There are no local area codes, but local telephone numbers have five digits in Cook Islands, six digits in Tahiti-Polynesia and Easter Island.

If a fax you are trying to send to the South Pacific doesn't go through smoothly on the first or second try, wait and try again at another time of day. If it doesn't work then, stop trying as the fax machine at the other end may not be able to read your signal, and your telephone company will levy a minimum charge for each attempt. Call the international operator to ask what is going wrong.

Electronic Mail

An increasing number of tourism-related businesses in the islands have e-mail addresses, which makes communicating with them from abroad a lot cheaper and easier. To allow ourselves the flexibility of updating our listings more frequently, we have committed most e-mail and website addresses to this book's backmatter (some overseas addresses meant to be used prior to arrival are embedded in the introductions). If you use the web, have a look at that part of the appendix now, if you haven't already done so.

When sending e-mail to the islands never include a large attached file with your message unless it has been specifically requested as the recipient may have to pay US$1 a minute in long-distance telephone charges to download it. This serious breach of etiquette is not the best way to win friends or influence people.

TIME

The international date line generally follows 180 degrees longitude and creates a difference of 24 hours in time between the two sides. Everything in the Eastern Hemisphere west of the date line (including Fiji and New Zealand) is a day later, everything in the Western Hemisphere east of the line (including the areas covered in this book and North America) is a day earlier (or behind). Air travelers lose a day when they fly west across the date line and gain it back when they return. Keep track of things by repeating to yourself, "If it's Sunday in Seattle, it's Monday in Manila."

You're better calling from North America to the South Pacific in the evening as it will be mid-afternoon in the islands (plus you'll probably benefit from off-peak telephone rates). From Europe, call very late at night. In the other direction, if you're calling from the islands to North America or Europe, do so in the early morning as it will already be afternoon in North America and evening in Europe.

In this book all clock times are rendered according to the 24-hour airline timetable system, i.e. 0100 is 1:00 a.m., 1300 is 1:00 p.m., 2330 is 11:30 p.m. The islanders operate on "coconut time"—the nut will fall when it is ripe. In the languid air of the South Seas punctuality takes on a new meaning. Appointments are approximate and service relaxed. Even the seasons are fuzzy: sometimes wetter, sometimes drier, but almost always hot. Slow down to the island pace and get in step with where you are. You may not get as much done, but you'll enjoy life a lot more. Daylight hours in the tropics run 0600-1800 with few seasonal variations.

WEIGHTS AND MEASURES

The metric system is used throughout the region. Study the conversion table in the back of this handbook if you're not used to thinking metric. Most distances herein are quoted in kilometers—they become easy to comprehend when you know than one km is the distance a normal person walks in 10 minutes. A meter is slightly more than a yard and a liter is just over a quart.

Unless otherwise indicated, north is at the top of all maps in this handbook. When using official topographical maps you can determine the scale by taking the representative fraction (RF) and dividing by 100. This will give the number of meters represented by one centimeter. For example, a map with an RF of 1:10,000 would represent 100 meters for every centimeter on the map.

Electric Currents

If you're taking along a plug-in razor, radio, computer, electric immersion coil, or other electrical appliance, be aware that 220 volts AC is commonly used in the islands. Take care, however, as some luxury hotel rooms have 110-volt outlets as a convenience to North American visitors. A 220-volt appliance will only run too slowly in a 110-volt outlet, but a 110-volt appliance will quickly burn out and be destroyed in a 220-volt outlet.

Most appliances require a converter to change from one voltage to another. You'll also need an adapter to cope with different socket types, which vary between round two-pronged plugs in the French territories and three-pronged plugs with the two on top at angles in the Cooks. Pick up both items before you leave home, as they're hard to find in the islands. Some sockets have a switch that must be turned on. Remember voltages if you buy duty-free appliances: dual voltage (110/220 V) items are best.

Videos

Commercial travel video tapes make nice souvenirs, but always keep in mind that there are three incompatible video formats loose in the world: NTSC (used in North America), PAL (used in Britain, Germany, Japan, Australia, New Zealand, and Cook Islands), and SECAM (used in France, Tahiti-Polynesia, and Russia). Don't buy prerecorded tapes abroad unless they're of the system used in your country.

MEDIA AND INFORMATION

Daily newspapers are published in Tahiti-Polynesia (*La Dépêche de Tahiti* and *Les Nouvelles de Tahiti*) and Cook Islands *(Cook Islands News)*. Weekly papers of note include the *Tahiti Beach Press* and the *Cook Islands Press*. Turn to Resources at the end of this book for more Pacific-oriented publications.

Radio

A great way to keep in touch with world and local affairs is to take along a small AM/FM shortwave portable radio. Your only expense will be the radio itself and batteries. In this handbook we've provided the names and frequencies of a few local stations, so set your tuning buttons to these as soon as you arrive.

You can also try picking up the BBC World Service on your shortwave receiver at 5.98, 7.15, 9.66, 9.74, 11.77, 11.96, 12.08, or 15.36 MHz (15.36 MHz generally works best). For Radio Australia try 6.08, 7.24, 9.66, 11.88, 12.08, 15.51, and 17.71 MHz. Look for Radio New Zealand International at 6.10, 6.14, 9.87, 11.69, 11.73, and 17.67 MHz. These frequencies vary according to the time of day and work best at night. (Unfortunately both RNZI and Radio Australia have recently faced cutbacks that could impact their services.)

Information Offices

All the territories have official tourist information offices. Their main branches open during normal business hours but the information desks at the airports open only for the arrival of international flights, if then. Always visit the local tourist office to pick up brochures and ask questions. Their overseas offices, listed in this handbook's appendix, often mail out useful information on their country and most have internet websites.

HEALTH

For a tropical area, the South Pacific's a healthy place. The sea and air are clear and usually pollution-free. The humidity nourishes the skin and the local fruit is brimming with vitamins. If you take a few precautions, you'll never have a sick day. Malaria and cholera don't exist here. The information provided below is intended to make you knowledgeable, not fearful. If you have access to the internet, check www.cdc.gov/travel/index.htm for up-to-the-minute information.

The government-run medical facilities mentioned in this book typically provide free medical treatment to local residents but have special rates for foreigners. It's usually no more expensive to visit a private doctor or clinic, and often it's actually cheaper. Private doctors can afford to provide faster service since everyone is paying, and we've tried to list local doctors and dentists throughout the handbook. In emergencies and outside clinic hours, you can always turn to the government-run facilities. Unfortunately, very few facilities are provided for travelers with disabilities.

American-made medications may by unobtainable in the islands, so along bring a supply of whatever you think you'll need. If you need to replace anything, quote the generic name at the pharmacy rather than the brand name. Otherwise go to any Chinese general store (in Tahiti-Polynesia) and ask the owner to recommend a good Chinese patent medicine for what ails you. The cost will be a third of what European medicines or herbs cost, and the Chinese medicine is often as effective or more so. Antibiotics should only be used to treat serious wounds, and only after medical advice.

Travel Insurance

The sale of travel insurance is big business but the value of the policies themselves is often questionable. If your regular group health insurance also covers you while you're traveling abroad it's probably enough (although medical costs in Tahiti-Polynesia are high). Most policies only pay the amount above and beyond what your national or group health insurance will pay and are invalid if you don't have any health insurance at all. You may also be covered by your credit card company if you paid for your plane ticket with the card. Buying extra travel insurance is about the same as buying a lottery ticket: there's always the chance it will pay off, but it's usually money down the drain.

If you do opt for the security of travel insurance, make sure emergency medical evacuations are covered. Some policies are invalid if you engage in any "dangerous activities," such as scuba diving, parasailing, surfing, or even riding a motor scooter, so be sure to read the fine print. Scuba divers should know that there's a recompression chamber at Papeete but an emergency medical evacuation will still be costly and there isn't any point buying a policy that doesn't cover it. Medical insurance especially designed for scuba divers is available from **Divers Alert Network** (6 West Colony Place, Durham, NC 27705, U.S.A.; tel. 1-800/446-2671 or 1-919/684-2948, fax 1-919/490-6630, www.dan.ycg.org). In Australia, New Zealand, or the South Pacific, write Box 134, Carnegie, Victoria 3163, Australia (tel. 61-3/9563-1151, fax 61-3/9563-1139).

Some companies will pay your bills directly while others require you to pay and collect receipts that may be reimbursed later. Ask if travel delays, lost baggage, and theft are included. In practice, your airline probably already covers the first two adequately and claiming something extra from your insurance company could be more trouble than it's worth. Theft insurance never covers items left on the beach while you're in swimming. All this said, you should weigh the advantages and decide for yourself if you want a policy. Just don't be influenced by what your travel agent says as they'll only want to sell you coverage in order to earn another commission.

Acclimatizing

Don't go from winter weather into the steaming tropics without a rest before and after. Minimize jet lag by setting your watch to local time at your destination as soon as you board the flight. Westbound flights into the South Pacific from North America or Europe are less jolting since you follow the sun and your body gets a few hours extra sleep. On the way home you're moving against the sun and the hours of sleep your body loses cause jet lag. Airplane cabins have low humidity, so drink lots of juice or water instead of carbonated drinks, and don't overeat in-flight. It's also wise to forgo coffee, as it will only keep you awake, and alcohol, which will dehydrate you.

Scuba diving on departure day can give you a severe case of the bends. Before flying there should be a minimum of 12 hours surface interval after a non-decompression dive and a minimum of 24 hours after a decompression dive. Factors contributing to decompression sickness include a lack of sleep and/or the excessive consumption of alcohol before diving.

If you start feeling seasick onboard a ship, stare at the horizon, which is always steady, and stop thinking about it. Anti-motion-sickness pills are useful to have along; otherwise, ginger helps alleviate seasickness. Travel stores sell acubands that find a pressure point on the wrist and create a stable flow of blood to the head, thus miraculously preventing seasickness!

The tap water is safe to drink in the main towns, but ask first elsewhere. If in doubt, boil it or use purification pills. Tap water that is uncomfortably hot to touch is usually safe. Allow it to cool in a clean container. Don't forget that if the tap water is contaminated, the local ice will be too. Avoid brushing your teeth with water unfit to drink, and wash or peel fruit and vegetables if you can. Cooked food is less subject to contamination than raw.

Frequently the feeling of thirst is false and only due to mucous membrane dryness. Gargling or taking two or three gulps of warm water should be enough. Keep moisture in your body by having a hot drink like tea or black coffee, or any kind of slightly salted or sour drink in small quantities. Salt in fresh lime juice is remarkably refreshing.

Sunburn

Though you might like to think that getting a tan will make you look healthier and more attractive, it's actually very damaging to the skin, which becomes dry, rigid, and prematurely old and wrinkled, especially on the face. Begin with short exposures to the sun, perhaps half an hour at a time, followed by an equal time in the shade. Avoid the sun 1000-1500, the most dangerous time. Clouds and beach umbrellas will not protect you fully. Wear a T-shirt while snorkeling to protect your back. Drink plenty of liquids to keep your pores open. Sunbathing is also the main cause of cataracts to the eyes, so wear sunglasses and a wide-brimmed hat, and beware of reflected sunlight.

Use a sunscreen lotion containing PABA rather than oil, and don't forget to apply it to your nose, lips, forehead, neck, hands, and feet. Sunscreens protect you from ultraviolet rays (a leading cause of cancer), while oils magnify the sun's effect. A 15-factor sunscreen provides 93% protection (a more expensive 30-factor sunscreen is only slightly better at 97% protection). Apply the lotion *before* going to the beach to avoid being burned on the way, and reapply every couple of hours to replace sunscreen washed away by perspiration. Swimming also washes away your protection. After sunbathing take a tepid shower rather than a hot one, which would wash away your natural skin oils. Stay moist and use a vitamin E evening cream to preserve the youth of your skin. Calamine ointment soothes skin already burned, as does coconut oil. Pharmacists recommend Solarcaine to soothe burned skin. Rinsing off with a vinegar solution reduces peeling, and aspirin relieves some of the pain and irritation. Vitamin A and calcium counteract overdoses of vitamin D received from the sun. The fairer your skin, the more essential it is to take care.

As earth's ozone layer is depleted due to the commercial use of chlorofluorocarbons (CFCs) and other factors, the need to protect oneself from ultraviolet radiation is becoming more urgent. In 1990 the U.S. Centers for Disease Control and Prevention in Atlanta reported that deaths from skin cancer increased 26% between 1973 and 1985. Previously the cancers didn't develop until age 50 or 60, but now much younger people are affected.

Ailments

Cuts and scratches infect easily in the tropics and take a long time to heal. Prevent infection from coral cuts by immediately washing wounds with soap and fresh water, then rubbing in vinegar or alcohol (whiskey will do)—painful but effective. Use an antiseptic like hydrogen peroxide and an antibacterial ointment such as neosporin, if you have them. Islanders usually dab coral cuts with lime juice. All cuts turn septic quickly in the tropics, so try to keep them clean and covered.

For bites, burns, and cuts, an antiseptic such as Solarcaine speeds healing and helps prevent infection. Pure aloe vera is good for sunburn, scratches, and even coral cuts. Bites by *no no* sandflies itch for days and can become infected. Not everyone is affected by insect bites in the same way. Some people are practically immune to insects, while traveling companions experiencing exactly the same conditions are soon covered with bites. You'll soon know which type you are.

Prickly heat, an intensely irritating rash, is caused by wearing heavy clothing that is inappropriate for the climate. When sweat glands are blocked and the sweat is unable to evaporate, the skin becomes soggy and small red blisters appear. Synthetic fabrics like nylon are especially bad in this regard. Take a cold shower, apply calamine lotion, dust with talcum powder, and take off those clothes! Until things improve, avoid alcohol, tea, coffee, and any physical activity that makes you sweat. If you're sweating profusely, increase your intake of salt slightly to avoid fatigue, but not without concurrently drinking more water.

Use antidiarrheal medications such as Lomotil or Imodium sparingly. Rather than take drugs to plug yourself up, drink plenty of unsweetened liquids like green coconut or fresh fruit juice to help flush yourself out. Egg yolk mixed with nutmeg helps diarrhea, or have a rice and tea day. Avoid dairy products. Most cases of diarrhea are self-limiting and require only simple replacement of the fluids and salts lost in diarrheal stools. If the diarrhea is persistent or you experience high fever, drowsiness, or blood in the stool, stop traveling, rest, and consider seeing a doctor. For constipation eat pineapple or any peeled fruit.

AIDS

In 1981 scientists in the United States and France first recognized the Acquired Immune Deficiency Syndrome (AIDS), which was later discovered to be caused by a virus called the Human Immuno-deficiency Virus (HIV). HIV breaks down the body's immunity to infections leading to AIDS. The virus can lie hidden in the body for up to 10 years without producing any obvious symptoms or before developing into the AIDS disease and in the meantime the person can unknowingly infect others.

HIV lives in white blood cells and is present in the sexual fluids of humans. It's difficult to catch and is spread mostly through sexual intercourse, by needle or syringe sharing among intravenous drug users, in blood transfusions, and during pregnancy and birth (if the mother is infected). Using another person's razor blade or having your body pierced or tattooed are also risky, but the HIV virus cannot be transmitted by shaking hands, kissing, cuddling, fondling, sneezing, cooking food, or sharing eating or drinking utensils. One cannot be infected by saliva, sweat, tears, urine, or feces; toilet seats, telephones,

swimming pools, or mosquito bites do not cause AIDS. Ostracizing a known AIDS victim is not only immoral but also absurd.

Most blood banks now screen their products for HIV, and you can protect yourself against dirty needles by only allowing an injection if you see the syringe taken out of a fresh unopened pack. The simplest safeguard during sex is the proper use of a latex condom. Unroll the condom onto the erect penis; while withdrawing after ejaculation, hold onto the condom as you come out. Never try to recycle a condom, and pack a supply with you as it's a nuisance trying to buy them locally.

HIV is spread more often through anal than vaginal sex because the lining of the rectum is much weaker than that of the vagina, and ordinary condoms sometimes tear when used in anal sex. If you have anal sex, only use extra-strong condoms and special water-based lubricants since oil, Vaseline, and cream weaken the rubber. During oral sex you must make sure you don't get any semen or menstrual blood in your mouth. A woman runs 10 times the risk of contracting AIDS from a man than the other way around, and the threat is always greater when another sexually transmitted disease (STD) is present.

The very existence of AIDS calls for a basic change in human behavior. No vaccine or drug exists that can prevent or cure AIDS, and because the virus mutates frequently, no remedy may ever be totally effective. Other STDs such as syphilis, gonorrhea, chlamydia, hepatitis B, and herpes are far more common than AIDS and can lead to serious complications such as infertility, but at least they can usually be cured.

The euphoria of travel can make it easier to fall in love or have sex with a stranger, so travelers must be informed of these dangers. As a tourist you should always practice safe sex to prevent AIDS and other STDs. You never know who is infected or even if you yourself have become infected. It's important to bring the subject up *before* you start to make love. Make a joke out of it by pulling out a condom and asking your new partner, "Say, do you know what this is?" Or perhaps, "Your condom or mine?" Far from being unromantic or embarrassing, you'll both feel more relaxed with the subject off your minds and it's much better than worrying afterwards if you might have been infected. The golden rule is safe sex or no sex.

By 1999 an estimated 33 million people worldwide were HIV carriers, and millions had already died of AIDS. In the South Pacific, the number of cases is still extremely small compared to the 650,000 confirmed HIV infections in the United States. However it's worth noting that other STDs are rampant on some islands, demonstrating that the type of behavior leading to the rapid spread of AIDS is present.

An HIV infection can be detected through a blood test because the antibodies created by the body to fight off the virus can be seen under a microscope. It takes at least three weeks for the antibodies to be produced and in some cases as long as six months before they can be picked up during a screening test. If you think you may have run a risk, you should discuss the appropriateness of a test with your doctor. It's always better to know if you are infected so as to be able to avoid infecting others, to obtain early treatment of symptoms, and to make realistic plans. If you know someone with AIDS you should give them all the support you can (there's no danger in such contact unless blood is present).

Toxic Fish

Over 400 species of tropical reef fish, including wrasses, snappers, groupers, jacks, moray eels, surgeonfish, shellfish, and especially barracudas are known to cause seafood poisoning (ciguatera). There's no way to tell if a fish will cause ciguatera: a species can be poisonous on one side of the island, but not on the other.

In 1976 French and Japanese scientists working in the Gambier Islands determined that a one-celled dinoflagellate or plankton called *Gambierdiscus toxicus* was the cause. Normally these microalgae are found only in the ocean depths, but when a reef ecosystem is disturbed by natural or human causes they can multiply dramatically in a lagoon. The dinoflagellates are consumed by tiny herbivorous fish and the toxin passes up through the food chain to larger fish where it becomes concentrated in the head and guts. The toxins have no effect on the fish that feed on them.

Tahiti-Polynesia's 700-800 cases of ciguatera a year are more than in the rest of the South Pacific combined, leading to suspicions that the former French nuclear testing program is responsible. Ciguatera didn't exist on Hao atoll in the Tuamotus until military dredging for a 3,500-

meter runway began in 1965. By mid-1968 43% of the population had been affected. Between 1971 and 1980 over 30% of the population of Mangareva near the Moruroa nuclear test site suffered from seafood poisoning. The symptoms (numbness and tingling around the mouth and extremities, reversal of hot/cold sensations, prickling, itching, nausea, vomiting, erratic heartbeat, joint and muscle pains) usually subside in a few days. Induce vomiting, take castor oil as a laxative, and avoid alcohol if you're unlucky. Symptoms can recur for up to a year, and victims may become allergic to all seafoods. In the Marshall Islands, an injected drug called Mannitel has been effective in treating ciguatera, but as yet little is known about it.

Avoid biointoxication by cleaning fish as soon as they're caught, discarding the head and organs, and taking special care with oversized fish caught in shallow water. Small fish are generally safer. Whether the fish is consumed cooked or raw has no bearing on this problem. Local residents often know from experience which species may be eaten.

Other Diseases

Infectious hepatitis A (jaundice) is a liver ailment transmitted person to person or through unboiled water, uncooked vegetables, or other foods contaminated during handling. The risk of infection is highest among those who eat village food, so if you'll be spending much time in rural areas, consider getting an immune globulin shot, which provides six months protection. Better is a vaccine called Havrix, which provides up to 10 years protection (given in two doses two weeks apart, then a third dose six months later). If you've ever had hepatitis A in your life you are already immune. Otherwise, you'll know you've got the hep when your eyeballs and urine turn yellow. Time and rest are the only cure. Viral hepatitis B is spread through sexual or blood contact.

Typhoid fever is caused by contaminated food or water, while tetanus (lockjaw) occurs when cuts or bites become infected. Horrible disfigur-

ing diseases such as leprosy and elephantiasis are hard to catch, so it's unlikely you'll be visited by one of these nightmares of the flesh.

More of a problem is dengue fever, a mosquito-transmitted disease endemic in the South Pacific. Signs are headaches, sore throat, pain in the joints, fever, chills, nausea, and rash. This painful illness also known as "breakbone fever" can last anywhere from five to 15 days. Although you can relieve the symptoms somewhat, the only real cure is to stay in bed, drink lots of water, and wait it out. Avoid aspirin as this can lead to complications. No vaccine exists, so just try to avoid getting bitten (the *Aedes aegypti* mosquito bites only during the day). Dengue fever can kill infants so extra care must be taken to protect them if an outbreak is in progress.

Vaccinations

Most visitors are not required to get any vaccinations at all before coming to the South Pacific. Tetanus, diphtheria, and typhoid fever shots are not required, but they're worth considering if you're going off the beaten track. Tetanus and diphtheria shots are given together, and a booster is required every 10 years. The typhoid fever shot is every three years. Polio is believed to have been eradicated from the region.

A yellow-fever vaccination is required if you've been in an infected area within the six days prior to arrival. Yellow fever is a mosquito-borne disease that only occurs in Central Africa and northern South America (excluding Chile), places you're not likely to have been just before arriving in the South Pacific. Since the vaccination is valid 10 years, get one if you're an inveterate globe-trotter.

Immune globulin (IG) and the Havrix vaccine aren't 100% effective against hepatitis A, but they do increase your general resistance to infections. IG prophylaxis must be repeated every five months. Hepatitis B vaccination involves three doses over a six-month period (duration of protection unknown) and is recommended mostly for people planning extended stays in the region.

WHAT TO TAKE

Packing

Assemble everything you simply must take and cannot live without—then cut the pile in half. If you're still left with more than will fit into a medium-size suitcase or backpack, continue eliminating. You have to be tough on yourself and just limit what you take. Now put it all into your bag. If the total (bag and contents) weighs over 16 kg, you'll sacrifice much of your mobility. If you can keep it down to 10 kg, you're traveling *light*. Categorize, separate, and pack all your things into clear plastic bags or stuff sacks for convenience and protection from moisture. Items that might leak should be in resealable bags. In addition to your principal bag, you'll want a day pack or flight bag. When checking in for flights, carry anything that cannot be replaced in your hand luggage.

Your Luggage

A soft medium-size backpack with a lightweight internal frame is best. Big external-frame packs are fine for mountain climbing but get caught in airport conveyor belts and are very inconvenient on public transport. The best packs have a zippered compartment in back where you can tuck in the hip belt and straps before turning your pack over to an airline or bus. This type of pack has the flexibility of allowing you to simply walk when motorized transport is unavailable or unacceptable; and with the straps zipped in it looks like a regular suitcase, should you wish to go upmarket for a while.

Make sure your pack allows you to carry the weight on your hips, has a cushion for spine support, and doesn't pull backwards. The pack should strap snugly to your body but also allow ventilation to your back. It should be made of a water-resistant material such as nylon and have a Fastex buckle.

Look for a pack with double, two-way zipper compartments and pockets you can lock with miniature padlocks. They might not *stop* a thief, but they will deter the casual pilferer. A 60-cm length of lightweight chain and another padlock will allow you to fasten your pack to something. Keep valuables locked in your bag, out of sight, as even upmarket hotel rooms aren't 100% safe.

Clothing and Camping Equipment

Take loose-fitting cotton washable clothes, light in color and weight. Synthetic fabrics are hot and sticky, and most of the things you wear at home are too heavy for the tropics—be prepared for the humidity. Dress is casual, with slacks and a sports shirt okay for men even at dinner parties. Local women often wear long colorful dresses in the evening, but respectable shorts are okay in daytime. The pareu (pronounced "par-RAY-o") is a bright two-meter piece of cloth both men and women wrap about themselves as an all-purpose garment. Any islander can show you how to wear it. If in doubt, bring the minimum with you and buy tropical garb upon arrival. Stick to clothes you can rinse in your room sink. In midwinter (July and August) it can be cool at night in the Cooks and even Moorea, so a light sweater or windbreaker may come in handy.

Take comfortable shoes that have been broken in. Running shoes and rubber thongs (flip-flops) are handy for day use but will bar you from nightspots with strict dress codes. Scuba divers' wetsuit booties are lightweight and perfect for both crossing rivers and lagoon walking, though an old pair of sneakers may be just as good (never use the booties to walk on breakable coral).

DIANA LASICH HARPER

Go native in a Tahitian pareu. Throw one corner over your right shoulder, then pass the other under your left arm and pull tight. Tie the ends and you're dressed.

A small nylon tent guarantees backpackers a place to sleep every night (except in Cook Islands), but it *must* be mosquito- and waterproof. Get one with a tent fly, then waterproof both tent and fly with a can of waterproofing spray. You'll seldom need a sleeping bag in the tropics, so that's one item you can easily cut. A youth hostel sleeping sheet is ideal—all HI handbooks give instructions on how to make your own or buy one at your local hostel. You don't really need to carry a bulky foam pad, as the ground is seldom cold.

Below we've provided a few checklists to help you assemble your gear. The listed items combined weigh well over 16 kg, so eliminate what doesn't suit you:

> pack with internal frame
> day pack or airline bag
> sun hat or visor
> essential clothing only
> bathing suit
> sturdy walking shoes
> rubber thongs
> rubber booties
> nylon tent and fly
> tent-patching tape
> mosquito net
> sleeping sheet

> portable shortwave radio
> camera and 10 rolls of film
> compass
> pocket flashlight
> extra batteries
> candle
> pocket alarm calculator
> extra pair of eyeglasses
> sunglasses
> mask and snorkel
> padlock and lightweight chain
> collapsible umbrella
> string for a clothesline
> powdered laundry soap (inside several plastic bags)
> universal sink plug
> mini-towel
> silicon glue
> sewing kit
> mini-scissors
> nail clippers
> fishing line for sewing gear
> plastic cup and plate
> can and bottle opener
> corkscrew
> penknife
> spoon
> water bottle
> matches
> tea bags

Accessories

Bring some reading material, as good books can be hard to find in the islands and any books at all in English are rare in Tahiti-Polynesia. A mask and snorkel are essential equipment—you'll be missing half of the Pacific's beauty without them. Scuba divers will bring their own regulator, buoyancy compensator, and gauges to avoid rental fees and to eliminate the possibility of catching a transmissible disease from rental equipment. A lightweight three-mm Lycra wetsuit will provide protection against marine stings and coral.

Neutral gray eyeglasses protect your eyes from the sun and give the least color distortion. Take an extra pair (if you wear them).

Also take along postcards of your hometown and snapshots of your house, family, workplace, etc; islanders love to see these. Always keep a promise to mail islanders the photos you take of them.

Toiletries and Medical Kit

Since everyone has his/her own medical requirements and brand names vary from country to country, there's no point going into detail here. Note, however, that even the basics (such as aspirin) are unavailable on some outer islands, so be prepared. Bring medicated powder for prickly heat rash. Charcoal tablets are useful for diarrhea and poisoning (they absorb the irritants). Bring an adequate supply of any personal medications, plus your prescriptions (in generic terminology).

High humidity causes curly hair to swell and bush, straight hair to droop. If it's curly have it cut short or keep it long in a ponytail or bun. A good cut is essential with straight hair. Water-based makeup is preferable, as the heat and humidity cause oil glands to work overtime. High-quality locally made shampoo, body oils, and insect repellent are sold on all the islands, and the bottles are conveniently smaller than those sold in Western countries. See **Health** for more ideas.

> wax earplugs
> soap in plastic container
> soft toothbrush
> toothpaste
> roll-on deodorant
> shampoo
> comb and brush
> skin creams
> makeup
> tampons or napkins
> white toilet paper
> vitamin/mineral supplement
> insect repellent
> PABA sunscreen
> lip balm
> a motion-sickness remedy
> contraceptives
> iodine
> water-purification pills
> delousing powder
> a diarrhea remedy
> Tiger Balm
> a cold remedy
> Alka-Seltzer
> aspirin
> antihistamine
> antifungal
> Calmitol ointment
> antibacterial ointment
> antiseptic cream
> disinfectant
> simple dressings
> adhesive bandages (like Band-Aids)
> painkiller
> prescription medicines

Money and Documents

All post offices have passport applications. If you lose your passport you should report the matter to the local police at once, obtain a certificate or receipt, then proceed to your consulate (if any!) for a replacement. If you have your birth certificate with you it expedites things considerably. Don't bother getting an international driver's license as your regular license is all you need to drive here (except in Cook Islands where you'll be required to buy a local license).

Traveler's checks in U.S. dollars are recommended, and in the South Pacific, American Express is the most efficient company when it comes to providing refunds for lost checks. Bring along a small supply of US$1 and US$5 bills to use if you don't manage to change money immediately upon arrival or if you run out of local currency and can't get to a bank. In the French territories French francs in cash are best currency to have as they're exchanged at a fixed rate without commission.

Carry your valuables in a money belt worn around your waist or neck under your clothing; most camping stores have these. Make several photocopies of the information page of your passport, personal identification, driver's license, scuba certification card, credit cards, airline tickets, receipts for purchase of traveler's checks, etc.—you should be able to get them all on one page. On the side, write the phone numbers you'd need to call to report lost documents. A brief medical history with your blood type, allergies, chronic or special health problems, eyeglass and medical prescriptions, etc., might also come in handy. Put these inside plastic bags to protect them from moisture, then carry the lists in different places, and leave one at home.

How much money you'll need depends on your lifestyle, but time is also a factor. The longer you stay, the cheaper it gets. Suppose you have to lay out US$1,000 on airfare and have (for example) US$50 a day left over for expenses. If you stay 15 days, you'll average US$117 a day ($50 times 15 plus $1,000, divided by 15). If you stay 30 days, you'll average US$83 a day. If you stay 90 days, the per-day cost drops to US$61. If you stay a year it'll cost only US$53 a day.

> passport
> airline tickets
> scuba certification card
> driver's license
> traveler's checks
> some U.S. cash
> credit card
> photocopies of documents
> money belt
> address book
> notebook
> envelopes
> extra ballpoint pens

FILM AND PHOTOGRAPHY

Scan the ads in photographic magazines for deals on mail-order cameras and film, or buy at a discount shop in any large city. Run a roll of film through your camera to be sure it's in good working order; clean the lens with lens-cleaning tissue and check the batteries. Remove the batteries from your camera when storing it at home for long periods. Register valuable cameras or electronic equipment with customs before you leave home so there won't be any argument over where you bought the items when you return, or at least carry a copy of the original bill of sale.

The type of camera you choose could depend on the way you travel. If you'll be staying mostly in one place, a heavy single-lens reflex (SLR) camera with spare lenses and other equipment won't trouble you. If you'll be moving around a lot for a considerable length of time, a 35-mm automatic compact camera will be better. The compacts are mostly useful for close-up shots; landscapes will seem spread out and far away. A wide-angle lens gives excellent depth of field, but hold the camera upright to avoid converging verticals. A polarizing filter prevents reflections from glass windows and water, and makes the sky bluer.

Take double the amount of film and mailers you think you'll need: film is expensive in the islands, and even then you never know if it's been spoiled by an airport X-ray on the way there. On a long trip mailers are essential as exposed film shouldn't be held for long periods. Choose 36-exposure film over 24-exposure to save on the number of rolls you have to carry. In Tahiti-Polynesia camera film costs over double what you'd pay in the U.S., but you can import 10 rolls duty free. When purchasing film in the islands take care to check the expiration date.

Films are rated by their speed and sensitivity to light, using ISO numbers from 25 to 1600. The higher the number, the greater the film's sensitivity to light. Slower films with lower ISOs (like 100-200) produce sharp images in bright sunlight. Faster films with higher ISOs (like 400) stop action and work well in low-light situations, such as in dark rainforests or at sunset. If you have a manual SLR you can avoid overexposure at midday by reducing the exposure half a stop, but *do* overexpose when photographing dark-skinned islanders. From 1000 to 1600 the light is often too bright to take good photos, and panoramas usually come out best early or late in the day.

Keep your photos simple with one main subject and an uncomplicated background. Get as close to your subjects as you can and lower or raise the camera to their level. Include people in the foreground of scenic shots to add interest and perspective. Outdoors a flash can fill in unflattering facial shadows caused by high sun or backlit conditions. Most of all, be creative. Look for interesting details and compose the photo before you push the trigger. Instead of taking a head-on photo of a group of people, step to one side and ask them to face you. The angle improves the photo. Photograph subjects coming toward you rather than passing by. Ask permission before photographing people. If you're asked for money (rare) you can always walk away—give your subjects the same choice.

When packing, protect your camera against vibration. Checked baggage is scanned by powerful airport X-ray monitors, so carry both camera and film aboard the plane in a clear plastic bag and ask security for a visual inspection. Some airports will refuse to do this, however. A good alternative is to use a lead-laminated pouch. The old high-dose X-ray units are seldom seen these days but even low-dose inspection units can ruin fast film (400 ASA and above). Beware of the cumulative effect of X-ray machines.

Keep your camera in a plastic bag during rain and while traveling in motorized canoes, etc. In the tropics the humidity can cause film to stick to itself; silica-gel crystals in the bag will protect film from humidity and mold growth. Protect camera and film from direct sunlight and load the film in the shade. When loading, check that the takeup spool revolves. Never leave camera or film in a hot place like a car floor, glove compartment, or trunk.

GETTING THERE

Preparations

First decide where and when you're going and how long you wish to stay. Some routes are more available or practical than others. Most North Americans and Europeans will pass through Los Angeles International Airport (code-named LAX) on their way to Tahiti, although it's also possible to arrive via Honolulu. Many people think of Tahiti as somewhere far away on the other side of the globe, but it's only 7.5 hours from Los Angeles; since it takes about five hours to fly from Los Angeles to Hawaii, the flight to Tahiti is only 2.5 hours longer.

Your plane ticket will be your biggest single expense, so spend some time considering the possibilities. Before going any further, read this entire chapter right through and check the Transportation sections in the Tahiti-Polynesia, Easter Island, and Cook Islands introductions, which provide more detailed information. If you're online peruse the internet sites of the airlines that interest you, then call them directly over their toll-free 800 numbers to get current information on fares. The following airlines have flights from the United States:

Air France: tel. 1-800/237-2747, www.airfrance.com, flies to Tahiti

Air New Zealand: tel. 1-800/262-1234, www.airnz.co.nz, flies to Rarotonga and Tahiti

AOM French Airlines: tel. 1-800/892-9136, www.flyaom.com, flies to Tahiti

Air Tahiti Nui: tel. 1-877/824-4846, fly@airtahitinui.pf, flies to Tahiti

Canada 3000: tel. 1-416/674-0257, www.canada3000.com, flies to Rarotonga from Vancouver and Honolulu

Corsair: tel. 1-800/677-0720, www.corsair-int.com, flies to Tahiti

Hawaiian Airlines: tel. 1-800/367-5320, www.hawaiianair.com, flies to Tahiti

LanChile Airlines: tel. 1-800/735-5526, www.lanchile.com, flies to Easter Island and Tahiti

Sometimes Canada and parts of the U.S. have different toll-free numbers, so if the number given above doesn't work, dial 800 information at 1-800/555-1212 (all 800 and 888 numbers are free). In Canada, Air New Zealand's toll-free number is tel. 1-800/663-5494.

Call all of these carriers and say you want the *lowest possible fare*. Cheapest are the excursion fares but these often have limitations and restrictions, so be sure to ask. Some have an advance-purchase deadline, which means it's wise to begin shopping early. Also check the fare seasons.

If you're not happy with the answers you get, call the number back later and try again. Many different agents take calls on these lines, and some are more knowledgeable than others. The numbers are often busy during peak business hours, so call first thing in the morning, after dinner, or on the weekend. *Be persistent.*

Other Airlines

The international airlines listed below don't fly directly between North America and the South Pacific, but they do service Tahiti:

Aircalin: tel. 1-800/677-4277, www.aircalin.nc, flies from Nouméa to Tahiti

Qantas Airways: tel. 1-800/227-4500, www.qantas.com.au, flies from Australia to Tahiti

Cheaper Fares

Over the past few years South Pacific airfares have been deregulated and companies like Air New Zealand no longer publish set fare price lists. Their internet websites are also evasive, usually with tariff information kept secret (they might have prices for their all-inclusive package tours on the web but not air prices alone). Finding your way through this minefield can be the least enjoyable part of your pre-trip planning, but you'll definitely pay a premium if you take the easy route and accept the first or second fare you're offered.

With fares in flux, the airline employees you'll get at the numbers listed above probably won't quote you the lowest fare on the market but at least you'll have their official price to use as a benchmark. After you're heard what they have to say, turn to a "discounter," specialist travel agencies that deal in bulk and sell seats and rooms at wholesale prices. Many airlines have more seats than they can market through normal channels, so they sell their unused long-haul capacity to "consolidators" or "bucket shops" at discounts of 40-50% off the official tariffs. The discounters buy tickets on this gray market and pass the savings along to you. Many such companies run ads in the Sunday travel sections of newspapers like the *San Francisco Examiner, New York Times,* or *Toronto Star,* or in major entertainment weeklies.

Despite their occasionally shady appearance, most discounters and consolidators are perfectly

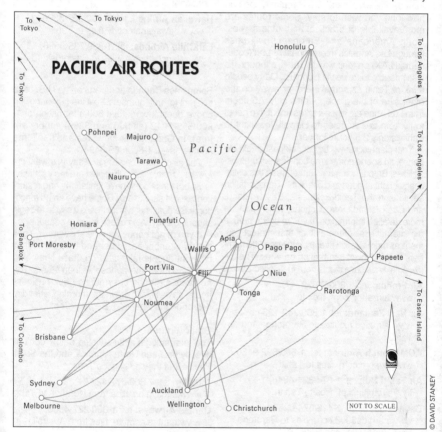

PACIFIC AIR ROUTES

NOT TO SCALE

© DAVID STANLEY

legitimate, and your ticket will probably be issued by the airline itself. Most discounted tickets look and are exactly the same as regular full-fare tickets but they're usually nonrefundable. There may also be other restrictions not associated with the more expensive tickets and penalties if you wish to change your routing or reservations. Rates are competitive, so allow yourself time to shop around. A few hours spent on the phone, doing time on hold and asking questions, could save you hundreds of dollars.

Travel Agents

Be aware that any travel agent worth his/her commission will probably want to sell you a package tour, and it's a fact that some vacation packages actually cost less than regular roundtrip airfare! If they'll let you extend your return date to give you some time to yourself this could be a good deal, especially with the hotel thrown in for "free." But check the restrictions.

Pick your agent carefully as many don't want to hear about discounts, cheap flights, or complicated routes, and will give wrong or misleading information in an offhand manner. They may try to sell you hotel rooms you could get locally for a fraction of the cost. Agencies belonging to the American Society of Travel Agents (ASTA), the Alliance of Canadian Travel Associations (ACTA), or the Association of British Travel Agents must conform to a strict code of ethics. Some protection is also obtained by paying by credit card.

Once you've done a deal with an agent and have your ticket in hand, call the airline again over their toll-free reservations number to check that your flight bookings and seat reservations are okay. If you got a really cheap fare, make sure the agent booked you in the same class of service as is printed on your ticket. For example, if you've got a K-coded ticket but your agent was only able to get a higher B-code booking, you could be denied boarding at the airport (in fact, few agents would risk doing something like this). A crooked agent might also tell you that you're free to change your return reservations when in fact you're not.

One of the most knowledgeable Canadian travel agents for South Pacific tickets is the **Adventure Centre** (25 Bellair St., Toronto, Ontario M5R 3L3; tel. 1-800/267-3347 or 1-416/922-7584, fax 1-416/922-8136, www.trek.ca, e-mail: info@tor.

trek.ca) with offices in Calgary (tel. 1-403/283-6115), Edmonton (tel. 1-403/439-0024), and Vancouver (tel. 1-604/734-1066). Ask for their informative brochure *South Pacific Airfare Specials*.

Similar tickets are available in the U.S. from the **Adventure Center** (1311 63rd St., Ste. 200, Emeryville, CA 94608, U.S.A.; tel. 1-800/227-8747 or 1-510/654-1879, fax 1-510/654-4200, e-mail: tripinfo@adventure-center.com).

Discover Wholesale Travel (2192 Dupont Dr., Ste. 116, Irvine, CA 92612, U.S.A.; tel. 1-800/576-7770, 1-800/759-7330, or 1-949/833-1136, fax 1-949/833-1176, www.discovertravel.net, e-mail: disc_tvl@ix.netcom.com) sells discounted air tickets and offers rock-bottom rates on rooms at the top hotels of Tahiti-Polynesia. They sometimes have significantly lower fares for passengers booking within two weeks of departure ("distressed seats"). President Mary Anne Cook claims everyone on her staff has 10 years experience selling the South Pacific and "most importantly, we all love the area!"

Some of the cheapest return tickets to Tahiti and Rarotonga are sold by **Fiji Travel** (8885 Venice Blvd., Ste. 202, Los Angeles, CA 90034, U.S.A.: tel. 1-800/500-3454 or 1-310/202-4220, fax 1-310/202-8233, www.fijitravel.com). They make their money through high volume, and to attract customers they keep their profit margins as low as possible. Thus you should absorb the airline's time with all your questions about fare seasons, schedules, etc., and only call companies like Fiji Travel and Discover Wholesale Travel after you know exactly what you want and how much everybody else is charging.

One U.S. agent willing to help you work out a personalized itinerary is Rob Jenneve of **Island Adventures** (574 Mills Way, Goleta, CA 93117, U.S.A.; tel. 1-800/289-4957 or 1-805/685-9230, fax 1-805/685-0960, e-mail: motuman@aol.com). Rob can put together flight and accommodation packages that are only slightly more expensive than the cheapest return airfare, and it's often possible to extend your return date to up to 30 days on the lowest fares or up to 90 days for a bit more. This option combines the benefits of packaged and independent travel, and you could end up spending a week at a medium-priced hotel with transfers for only US$50-100 more than you'd have to spend anyway just to get to the islands! Rob also books complex circle-Pacific routes and can steer you to deluxe resorts that offer value for money.

Student Fares

If you're a student, recent graduate, or teacher, you can sometimes benefit from lower student fares by booking through a student travel office. There are two rival organizations of this kind: Council Travel Services, with offices in college towns across the U.S. and a sister organization in Canada known as Travel Cuts; and STA Travel (Student Travel Australia) with a wholesale division known as the Student Travel Network. Both organizations require you to pay a nominal fee for an official student card, and to get the cheapest fares you have to prove you're really a student. Slightly higher fares on the same routes are available to nonstudents, so they're always worth checking.

STA Travel (www.sta-travel. com) offers special airfares for students and young people under 26 years with minimal restrictions. Their prices on roundtrip fares to single destinations are competitive but they don't sell more complicated tickets (standard routings like Los Angeles-Tahiti-Auckland-Sydney-Bangkok-London-Los Angeles are their style). Call their toll-free number (tel. 1-800/777-0112) for the latest information.

Different student fares are available from **Council Travel Services,** a division of the nonprofit Council on International Educational Exchange (CIEE). Both they and **Travel Cuts** (tel. 1-800/667-2887) in Canada are stricter about making sure you're a "real" student: you must first obtain the widely recognized International Student Identity Card (US$20) to get a ticket at the student rate. Some fares are limited to students and youths under 26 years of age, but part-time students and teachers also qualify. There are special connecting flights to Los Angeles from other U.S. points.

STUDENT TRAVEL OFFICES

STA Travel, 297 Newbury St., Boston, MA 02115, U.S.A (tel. 617/266-6014)

STA Travel, 429 S. Dearborn St., Chicago, IL 60605, U.S.A. (tel. 312/786-9050)

STA Travel, 920 Westwood Blvd., Los Angeles, CA 90024, U.S.A. (tel. 310/824-1574)

STA Travel, 10 Downing St. (6th Ave. and Bleecker), New York, NY 10014, U.S.A. (tel. 212/627-3111)

STA Travel, 3730 Walnut St., Philadelphia, PA 19104, U.S.A. (tel. 215/382-2928)

STA Travel, 51 Grant Ave., San Francisco, CA 94108, U.S.A. (tel. 415/391-8407)

STA Travel, 4341 University Way NE, Seattle, WA 98105, U.S.A. (tel. 206/633-5000)

STA Travel, 2401 Pennsylvania Ave. #G, Washington, DC 20037, U.S.A. (tel. 202/887-0912)

STA Travel, 222 Faraday St., Carlton, Melbourne 3053, Australia (tel. 61-3/9349-2411)

STA Travel, 855 George St., Sydney, NSW 2007, Australia (tel. 61-2/9212-1255)

STA Travel, 10 High St., Auckland, New Zealand (tel. 64-9/309-0458)

STA Travel, #02-17 Orchard Parade Hotel, 1 Tanglin Rd., Singapore 1024 (tel. 65/737-7188)

STA Travel, Suite 1406, 33 Surawong Rd., Bangkok 10500, Thailand (tel. 66-2/236-0262)

STA Travel, Bockenheimer Landstrasse 133, D-60325 Frankfurt, Germany (tel. 49-69/703-035)

STA Travel, 117 Euston Rd., London NW1 2SX, United Kingdom (tel. 44-171/465-0484)

Seasons

The month of outbound travel from the U.S. determines which seasonal fare you'll pay; inquiring far in advance may help you to schedule your vacation to take advantage of lower fares.

Air New Zealand has their low (or "basic") season on flights to Cook Islands from mid-April to August, shoulder season Sept.-Nov. and in March, and high (or "peak") season Dec.-February. They've made April-Nov.—the top months in the South Pacific—their off-season because that's winter in Australia and New Zealand. If you're only going to the islands and can make it at that time, it certainly works to your advantage.

However, if you're flying to Tahiti on one of the three French carriers, the high seasons are timed to correspond to holiday time in Europe: June to mid-September and December. This also applies on Air New Zealand if you're not going beyond Tahiti (if you're continuing to Rarotonga normal Air New Zealand seasons apply to the whole ticket).

Circular Tickets

If you plan a wide-ranging trip with stops on several continents, the **Global Explorer** may be the ticket for you. This fare allows six free stops selected from over 400 destinations on 28,500 miles of routes. You can use the services of any of these airlines: Air Liberté, Air Pacific, American Airlines, British Airways, Canadian Airlines, Deutsche Airlines, and Qantas. This costs US$3,089 in the U.S. or CDN$3,969 in Canada, and additional stops after the first six are US$100 each. You must purchase the pass a week in advance and it's valid one year. Date changes and the first rerouting are free (additional reroutings US$100). Ask Qantas about this ticket.

A similar fare available only in the South Pacific and Europe is the **World Navigator,** which encompasses the networks of Aircalin, Air New Zealand, Air UK, Ansett Australia, Emirates, KLM Royal Dutch Airlines, Northwest Airlines, Kenyan Airlines, and South African Airways. From London, the World Navigator costs £1,099/1,199/1,299 in the low/shoulder/peak seasons (the low season is April to June only). From Australia, it's A$2,569/2,779/2,979/3,189 according to season with the lowest season running from mid-January to February and October to mid-November.

In North America, Air New Zealand sells a **World Escapade** valid for a round-the-world journey on Air New Zealand, Ansett Australia, and Singapore Airlines. You're allowed 29,000 miles with unlimited stops at US$2,799. One transatlantic and one transpacific journey must be included, but the ticket is valid one year and backtracking is allowed.

Air New Zealand's **Pacific Escapade** allows a circle-Pacific trip on the same three airlines. With this one you get 22,000 miles at US$2,600 with all the stops you want (maximum of three each in Australia and New Zealand). You'll have to transit Singapore at least once and travel must begin in either Los Angeles or Vancouver

---

COUNCIL TRAVEL OFFICES

Council Travel, 2486 Channing Way, Berkeley, CA 94704, U.S.A. (tel. 510/848-8604)

Council Travel, 273 Newbury St., Boston, MA 02115, U.S.A. (tel. 617/266-1926)

Council Travel, 1153 N. Dearborn St., 2nd Floor, Chicago, IL 60610, U.S.A. (tel. 312/951-0585)

Council Travel, 10904 Lindbrook Dr., Los Angeles, CA 90024, U.S.A. (tel. 310/208-3551)

Council Travel, One Datran Center, Suite 220, 9100 S. Dadeland Blvd., Miami, FL 33156, U.S.A. (tel. 305/670-9261)

Council Travel, 205 East 42nd St., New York, NY 10017-5706, U.S.A. (tel. 212/822-2700)

Council Travel, 1430 SW Park Ave., Portland, OR 97201, U.S.A. (tel. 503/228-1900)

Council Travel, 953 Garnet Ave., San Diego, CA 92109, U.S.A. (tel. 619/270-6401)

Council Travel, 530 Bush St., San Francisco, CA 94108, U.S.A. (tel. 415/421-3473)

Council Travel, 1314 N.E. 43rd St., Suite 210, Seattle, WA 98105, U.S.A. (tel. 206/632-2448)

Travel Cuts, 187 College St., Toronto, ON M5T 1P7, Canada (tel. 416/979-2406)

Travel Cuts, 567 Seymour St., Vancouver, BC V6B 3H6, Canada (tel. 604/681-9136)

SYFS, 102/12-13 Koasan Rd., Banglumpoo, Bangkok 10200, Thailand (tel. 66-2/282-0507)

HKST, 921a Star House, Tsimshatsui, Kowloon, Hong Kong (tel. 852/2730-3269)

CIEE, Cosmos Aoyama, B1, 5-53-67 Jingumae, Shibuya-ku, Tokyo, Japan (tel. 81-3/5467-5501)

Council Travel, 18 Graf Adolph Strasse, D-40212 Düsseldorf 1, Germany (tel. 49-211/363-030)

Council Travel, 22 rue des Pyramides, 75001 Paris, France (tel. 33-1/4455-5544)

Council Travel, 28A Poland St., near Oxford Circus, London W1V 3DB, United Kingdom (tel. 44-171/437-7767)

(no add-ons). On both Escapades, should you go over the allowable mileage, 4,500 extra miles are US$300. Reservation changes are free the first time but extra after that.

Northwest Airlines in conjunction with Air New Zealand offers a **Circle-Pacific fare** of US$2,650 from Los Angeles with add-on airfares available from other North American cities. This ticket allows four free stopovers in Asia and the South Pacific, additional stops US$50 each. To reissue the ticket also costs US$50. It's valid six months and date changes are free. You must travel in a continuous circle without any backtracking. Air Pacific also has a Circle-Pacific fare, so compare.

Onward Tickets

All of the South Pacific countries require an onward ticket as a condition for entry. Although the immigration officials don't always check it, the airlines usually do. If you're planning a long trip including locally arranged sea travel between countries, this can be a nuisance. One way to satisfy the ticket-to-leave requirement is to purchase a full-fare one-way economy ticket out of the area from Air New Zealand (valid one year). As you're about to depart for the next country on your route have the airline reissue the ticket, so it's a ticket to leave from there. Otherwise buy a full-fare ticket across the Pacific with stops in all the countries you'll visit, then use it *only* to satisfy check-in staff and immigration. When you finally complete your trip return the ticket to the issuing office for a full refund. Remember that airline tickets are often refundable only in the place of purchase and that the sort of deals and discount airfares available elsewhere are not available in the South Pacific. Have your *real* means of departure planned.

AIR SERVICES

From North America

Air France, Air New Zealand, Air Tahiti Nui, AOM French Airlines, and Corsair are the major carriers serving Tahiti and Rarotonga out of Los Angeles, although Air France, Air Tahiti Nui, AOM French Airlines, and Corsair only go as far as Tahiti. Corsair also flies Oakland-Tahiti.

The only U.S. airline serving Tahiti is **Hawaiian Airlines,** which offers flights to Papeete via its base in Honolulu with connections to/from

Las Vegas, Los Angeles, San Francisco, Portland, and Seattle. From the West Coast to Tahiti a 14-day advance-purchase roundtrip is US$690/890 low/high season plus tax. Fare seasons to Tahiti are complicated, so call well ahead. Date changes after ticketing are US$75. A free stop in Honolulu is available on this fare.

From November to April only, **Canada 3000** has direct weekly flights from Toronto and Vancouver to Rarotonga via Honolulu (tickets on charter carriers such as Canada 3000 embody numerous burdensome restrictions and should only be considered if the savings is very large). Air New Zealand passengers originating in Canada must change planes in Honolulu or Los Angeles.

Air New Zealand

In the 1950s Air New Zealand pioneered its "Coral Route" using Solent flying boats, and today the carrier has achieved a death grip over long-haul air routes into the region by allowing stopovers in Tahiti-Polynesia, Cook Islands, Fiji, Samoa, and Tonga as part of through services between North America and New Zealand.

Air New Zealand's first priority is to fly people to Auckland, and it's sometimes cheaper to buy a return ticket to Auckland with a couple of free stops in the islands than a roundtrip ticket from Los Angeles only as far as Tahiti-Rarotonga-Fiji. If you don't wish to visit New Zealand, you can transit Auckland the same day. Despite Air New Zealand's frequent services, travelers in Europe and North America often have difficulty booking stops in the islands on their way down under and it's advisable to reserve seats well ahead. Air New Zealand's near monopoly does have the advantage of allowing you to include a number of countries in a single ticket if you do some advance planning.

The cheapest tickets involve a number of restrictions. On Air New Zealand if you're only flying to Tahiti the high season runs from July to mid-August and in mid-December; the rest of the year is low season. The cheapest fare is the "Economy APEX" at US$1,008/1,187 low/high return between Los Angeles and Tahiti. You must purchase this at least seven days in advance, there's a 35% cancellation penalty, and the maximum stay is two months. The full unrestricted fare is US$1,349/1,892.

From Los Angeles to Rarotonga, a return "No Stop Apex" ticket is US$888/1,048/1,298 low/shoulder/high at the beginning of the week (US$200 cheaper from Honolulu). To set out on Thursday, Friday, Saturday or Sunday is US$60 more. The maximum stay is one month and you must pay at least 21 days before departure (50% cancellation penalty). If you book on shorter notice the fare is almost 50% higher.

It's not that much more expensive to add a couple of islands. Air New Zealand's "Coral Experience" allows one stop plus your destination with additional stops available at US$145 each. Thus you can fly Los Angeles-Tahiti-Rarotonga-Fiji-Los Angeles for US$1,143/1,343/1,593 low/shoulder/high season if you leave at the beginning of the week for a trip of three months maximum. Add US$150 if wish to extend your period of stay to six months, plus another US$60 if you'd like to set out on Thursday, Friday, Saturday, or Sunday. Drop either Tahiti, Rarotonga, or Fiji from your itinerary and you'll save US$145. Trips originating in Honolulu are US$200 cheaper in all cases. Remember that the "Coral Experience" must be purchased 14 days in advance and there's a US$75 penalty to change your flight dates. A 35% cancellation fee also applies after the 14-day ticket deadline.

For a more wide-ranging trip with fewer restrictions, ask for Air New Zealand's "Coral Explorer Airpass," which costs US$1,758/2,008/2,258 low/shoulder/high season. This worthwhile ticket allows you to fly Los Angeles-Tahiti-Rarotonga-Fiji-Auckland-Tongatapu-Apia-Honolulu-Los Angeles or vice versa. Extend the ticket to Australia for US$100 more; eliminate Auckland-Tongatapu-Apia and it's about US$100 less. Begin in Honolulu and it's US$200 less again. You can stay up to one year but rerouting costs US$75 (date changes are free). There's no advance purchase requirement and you can go any day. To follow the same routing minus two stops on a six-month "Coral Experience" with all its restrictions costs US$1,633/1,883/2,133.

In Canada, Air New Zealand calls the same thing by different names: the "No Stop Apex" is the "Shotover Fare" while the "Coral Experience"

is the "Bungy Fare" (the "Explorer" is still the "Explorer"). There's also a cheaper "Backpacker Downunder" fare which must be purchased 14 days in advance and does not cover hotel expenses due to flight misconnections.

On most tickets special "add-on" fares to Los Angeles or Vancouver are available from cities right across the U.S. and Canada. One problem with Air New Zealand is its unfriendly schedules, which are built around Auckland and Los Angeles. Air New Zealand's Tahiti schedules are especially inconvenient as Papeete is only a stopover and flight times are planned so the aircraft arrive in Auckland in the morning. Air New Zealand flights back to Los Angeles depart Papeete well after midnight, costing you another night's sleep.

Air New Zealand's cabin service is professional, and you'll like the champagne breakfasts and outstanding food with complimentary beer and wine. Another plus are the relaxing seats with adjustable head rests and lots of leg room. The *Blue Pacific* videos about their destinations are entertaining the first time you see them, but after a while you get bored. The only reading material provided is the *Pacific Wave* inflight magazine, the *Skyshop* duty free catalog, and the *Primetime* entertainment magazine. These are unlikely to hold your attention for long, so bring along a book or magazine of your own (the daily newspaper is provided only to passengers in first class).

French Charter Flights

The French tour company **Nouvelles Frontières** or "New Frontiers" handles weekly charter flights from Paris and Los Angeles/Oakland to Tahiti on their own airline, **Corsair.** A round-the-world routing Los Angeles/Oakland-Tahiti-Nouméa-Bangkok-Paris-Los Angeles/Oakland is also possible on Corsair.

Seasons are based on the exact date of each flight with the low or "green" season Jan.-June and Sept.-November. Many restrictions and penalties apply. On the cheapest tickets you must

pay 50% of the price upon booking and the balance 21 days before departure. There are no refunds if you decide to cancel. To change the date of your return flight is US$100, provided you do so 15 days in advance. Corsair reserves the right to alter flight times up to 48 hours without compensation, but if you miss your flight you lose your money. Still, if you're sure when you'll be traveling, the Corsair fare of around US$600/700 low/high roundtrip plus tax is a couple of hundred dollars lower than anything offered by the scheduled airlines.

Nouvelles Frontières (www.nouvelles-frontieres.fr) has 200 offices in France and 40 others around the world, including these: 12 East 33rd St., 10th Floor, New York, NY 10016, U.S.A. (tel. 1-212/779-0600, fax 1-212/779-1007); Air Promotions Systems, 5757 West Century Blvd., Ste. 660, Los Angeles, CA 90045-6407, U.S.A. (tel. 1-800/677-0720 or 1-310/670-7318, fax 1-310/338-0708, www.corsair-int.com, e-mail: webmaster @corsair-int.com); and 2/3 Woodstock St., London W1R 1HE, England (tel. 44-171/355-3952, fax 44-171/491-0684).

From Australia

Qantas flies to Tahiti from Auckland and Sydney, and since the Australian government sold Qantas and deregulated airfares, the cost of flying out of Australia has dropped dramatically. Now you can often find deals much better than the published Apex fares, especially during off months.

Air New Zealand is competing fiercely in the Australian market, and they offer competitive fares to Rarotonga and Tahiti via Auckland. You can usually buy such tickets for a lower price than you'd pay at the airline office itself by working through an agent specializing in bargain airfares. Check the travel sections in the weekend papers and call Flight Centres International. For information on slightly reduced fares available from STA Travel, see **Student Fares,** above. Hideaway Holidays mentioned under **Organized Tours,** below, offers a variety of standard package tours to Tahiti that combine accommodations with cheap group airfares.

The Circle-Pacific and round-the-world fares described above are also available here. Apex (advance purchase excursion) tickets must be bought 14 days in advance and heavy cancellation penalties apply. The low season for flights

from Australia to Tahiti is Feb.-May. July-Sept. and mid-December to mid-January is the high season, and the other months are shoulder. To Rarotonga the low season is mid-January to June, mid-July to mid-September, and mid-October to November, but this does vary.

From New Zealand

Unrestricted low airfares to the South Pacific are surprisingly hard to come by in New Zealand. Some tickets have advance purchase requirements, so start shopping well ahead. Ask around at a number of different travel agencies for special unadvertised or under-the-counter fares. Agents to call include STA Travel and Flight Centres International. Fares to Tahiti often allow a stop in the Cook Islands, but it's hard to get a seat on these fully booked planes.

From Auckland, a 45-day roundtrip excursion fare to Tahiti on Air New Zealand costs NZ$1,211 in February, March, October, and November, NZ$1,293 in May, June, and mid-July to mid-September, and NZ$1,417 other months. It is possible to change flight dates. One-year, seven-day advance purchase fares to Rarotonga are NZ$1,056/1,296 low/high. It's often cheaper to buy a package tour to the islands with airfare, accommodations, and transfers included, but these are usually limited to seven nights on one island and you're stuck in a boring touristic environment. Ask if you'll be allowed to extend your return date and still get the low inclusive tour price.

From South America

LanChile Airlines flies from Santiago to Tahiti via Easter Island three times a week, with additional flights during the high southern summer season. The regular one-way fare Santiago-Easter-Tahiti is US$1,133 economy class. Santiago-Easter Island is US$448 each way.

LanChile's 30-day roundtrip excursion fare between Tahiti and Santiago, with a stopover on Easter Island, costs US$1,200. If you only want to visit Easter Island, 30-day excursion tickets Tahiti-Easter Island-Tahiti are available in Papeete, but it's cheaper to buy a tour package from one of the agencies mentioned in this book's Papeete section (from Tahiti, low season fares are available March-November).

LanChile offers a variety of "Pacific Circuit

Fares" including Miami/Los Angeles-Santiago-Easter Island-Tahiti-Honolulu-Los Angeles (US$1,645), New York-Santiago-Easter Island-Tahiti-Honolulu-Los Angeles (US$1,775), and Los Angeles-Santiago-Easter Island-Tahiti-Los Angeles (US$1,828), all valid one year. From Australia or New Zealand you can get Sydney/Melbourne/Brisbane-Auckland-Tahiti-Easter Island-Santiago-Los Angeles-Australia (US$2,091).

LanChile must rate as one of the most unreliable carriers flying to the South Pacific, and service irregularities are routine. The Santiago-Easter Island portion of their Tahiti service is often heavily booked, so try to reserve far in advance, although this can be hard to do.

From Europe

Since few European carriers reach the South Pacific, you may have to use a gateway city such as Singapore, Sydney, Honolulu, or Los Angeles. Air New Zealand offers nonstop flights London-Los Angeles five times a week and Frankfurt-Los Angeles three times a week, with connections in L.A. to their Coral Route. Air France, AOM French Airlines, and Corsair fly to Tahiti from Paris via Los Angeles or Oakland.

Air New Zealand reservations numbers around Europe are tel. 03/202-1355 (Belgium), tel. 0800/907-712 (France), tel. 01/3081-7778 (Germany), tel. 1678-76126 (Italy), tel. 08-002527 (Luxembourg), tel. 06/022-1016 (Netherlands), tel. 900/993241 (Spain), tel. 020/792-939 (Sweden), tel. 0800/557-778 (Switzerland), and tel. 44-181/741-2299 (United Kingdom). Call them up and ask about their Coral Route fares. Be aware that Air New Zealand flights from Europe are heavily booked and reservations should be made far in advance.

The British specialist in South Pacific itineraries is **Trailfinders** (44-50 Earls Court Rd., Kensington, London W8 6FT; tel. 44-171/938-3366, fax 44-171/937-9294), in business since 1970. They offer a variety of discounted round-the-world tickets through the South Pacific which are often much cheaper than the published fares. For example, a routing via Easter Island and Tahiti is £1,150. Call or write for a free copy of their magazine, *Trailfinder,* which appears in April, July, and December. **Bridge the World** (47 Chalk Farm Rd., Camden Town, London NW1 8AN; tel. 44-171/911-0900, fax 44-171/813-

3350, e-mail: sales@bridge-the-world.co.uk) has a ticket that includes Fiji, Rarotonga, Tahiti, and a variety of stops in Asia for £935. Check the ads in the London entertainment magazines for other such companies.

In Holland **Pacific Island Travel** (Herengracht 495, 1017 BT Amsterdam, the Netherlands; tel. 31-20/626-1325, fax 31-20/623-0008, e-mail: pitnet@xs4all.nl) sells most of the air passes and long-distance tickets mentioned in this section, plus package tours. **Barron & De Keijzer Travel** (Herengracht 340, 1016 CG Amsterdam, the Netherlands; tel. 31-20/625-8600, fax 31-20/622-7559) sells Air New Zealand's Coral Route with travel via London. Also in Amsterdam, **Reisbureau Amber** (Da Costastraat 77, 1053 ZG Amsterdam, the Netherlands; tel. 31-20/685-1155, fax 31-20/689-0406) is one of the best places in Europe to pick up books on the South Pacific.

In Switzerland try **Globetrotter Travel Service** (Rennweg 35, CH-8023 Zürich, Switzerland; tel. 41-1/213-8080, fax 41-1/213-8088), with offices in Baden, Basel, Bern, Luzern, St. Gallen, Thun, Winterthur, Zug, and Zürich. Their quarterly newsletter, *Ticket-Info,* lists hundreds of cheap flights, including many through the South Pacific.

Bucket shops in Germany sell a "Pacific Airpass" on Air New Zealand from Frankfurt to the South Pacific that allows all the usual Coral Route stops and is valid six months. All flights must be booked prior to leaving Europe, and there's a charge to change the dates once the ticket has been issued. One agency selling such tickets is **Walther-Weltreisen** (Hirschberger Strasse 30, D-53119 Bonn; tel. 49-228/661-239, fax 49-228/661-181). The **Pacific Travel House** (Bayerstrasse 95, D-80335 München; tel. 49-89/530-9293) offers a variety of package tours.

Elsewhere in Europe, inclusive tours to Tahiti-Polynesia are most easily booked through Nouvelles Frontières offices.

Important Note

Airfares, rules, and regulations tend to fluctuate a lot, so some of the information above may have changed. This is only a guide; we've included a few fares to give you a rough idea how much things might cost. Your travel agent will know what's available at the time you're ready to travel, but if you're not satisfied with his/her advice, keep shopping around. The biggest step is deciding to go—once you're over that, the rest is easy!

PROBLEMS

When planning your trip allow a minimum two-hour stopover between connecting flights at U.S. airports, although with airport delays on the increase even this may not be enough. In the islands allow at least a day between flights. In some airports flights are not called over the public address system, so keep your eyes open. Whenever traveling, always have a paperback or two, some toiletries, and a change of underwear in your hand luggage.

If your flight is canceled due to a mechanical problem with the aircraft, the airline will cover your hotel bill and meals. If they reschedule the flight on short notice for reasons of their own or you're bumped off an overbooked flight, they should also pay. They may not feel obligated to pay, however, if the delay is due to weather conditions, a strike by another company, national emergencies, etc., although the best airlines still pick up the tab in these cases. Just don't expect much from local, "third-level" airlines on remote islands where such difficulties are routine.

It's an established practice among airlines to provide light refreshments to passengers delayed two hours after the scheduled departure time and a meal after four hours. Don't expect to get this on an outer island, but politely request it if you're at a gateway airport. If you are unexpectedly forced to spend the night somewhere, an airline employee may hand you a form on which they offer to telephone a friend or relative to inform them of the delay. Don't trust them to do this, however. Call your party yourself if you want to be sure they get the message.

Overbooking

To compensate for no-shows, most airlines overbook their flights. To avoid being bumped, ask for your seat assignment when booking, check in early, and go to the departure area well before flight time. Of course, if you *are* bumped by a reputable international airline at a major airport you'll be regaled with free meals and lodging and sometimes even free flight vouchers (don't expect anything like this from a domestic carrier on a remote Pacific island).

Whenever you break your journey for more than 72 hours, always reconfirm your onward reservations and check your seat assignment at the same time. Get the name of the person who takes your reconfirmation so they cannot later deny it. Failure to reconfirm could result in the cancellation of your complete remaining itinerary. This could also happen if you miss a flight for any reason. If you want special vegetarian or kosher food in-flight, request it when buying your ticket, booking, and reconfirming.

When you try to reconfirm your Air New Zealand flight the agent will tell you that this formality is no longer required. Theoretically this is true, but unless you request your seat assignment in advance, either at an Air New Zealand office or over the phone, you could be "bumped" from a full flight, reservation or no reservation. Air New Zealand's ticket cover bears this surprising message:

. . . no guarantee of a seat is indicated by the terms "reservation," "booking," "O.K." status, or the times associated therewith.

They do admit in the same notice that confirmed passengers denied seats may be eligible for compensation, so if you're not in a hurry, a night or two at an upmarket hotel with all meals courtesy of Air New Zealand may not be a hardship. Your best bet if you don't want to get "bumped" is to request seat assignments for your entire itinerary before you leave home, or at least at the first Air New Zealand office you pass during your travels. Any good travel agent selling tickets on Air New Zealand should know enough to automatically request your seat assignments as they make your bookings. In the islands Air New Zealand offices will still accept a local contact telephone number from you. Check Air New Zealand's reconfirmation policy at one of their offices as it could change.

Baggage

International airlines allow economy-class passengers either 20 kilos of baggage or two pieces not over 32 kilos each (ask which applies to you). Under the piece system, neither bag must have a combined length, width, and height of over 158 centimeters (62 inches) and the two pieces together must not exceed 272 centimeters (107 inches). On most long-haul tickets to/from North America or Europe, the piece system applies to all sectors, but check this with the airline. The frequent flier programs of some major airlines allow participants to carry up to 10 kilos of excess baggage free of charge. Commuter carriers sometimes restrict you to as little as 10 kilos total, so it's better to pack according to the lowest common denominator.

Bicycles, folding kayaks, and surfboards can usually be checked as baggage (sometimes for an additional US$50-100 charge), but sailboards may have to be shipped airfreight. If you do travel with a sailboard, be sure to call it a surfboard at check-in.

Tag your bag with name, address, and phone number inside and out. Stow anything that could conceivably be considered a weapon (scissors, penknife, toy gun, mace, etc.) in your checked luggage. One reason for lost baggage is that some people fail to remove used baggage tags after they claim their luggage. Get into the habit of tearing off old baggage tags, unless you want your luggage to travel in the opposite direction! As you're checking in, look to see if the three-letter city codes on your baggage tag receipt and boarding pass are the same.

If your baggage is damaged or doesn't arrive at your destination, inform the airline officials *immediately* and have them fill out a written report; otherwise future claims for compensation will be compromised. Airlines usually reimburse out-of-pocket expenses if your baggage is lost or delayed over 24 hours. The amount varies from US$25 to US$50. Your chances of getting it are better if you're polite but firm. Keep receipts for any money you're forced to spend to replace missing articles.

Claims for lost luggage can take weeks to process. Keep in touch with the airline to show your concern and hang on to your baggage tag until the matter is resolved. If you feel you did not receive the attention you deserved, write the airline an objective letter outlining the case. Get the names of the employees you're dealing with so you can mention them in the letter. Of course, don't expect any pocket money or compensation on a remote outer island. Report the loss, then wait till you get back to their main office. What-

ever happens, try to avoid getting angry. The people you're dealing with don't want the problem any more than you do. (Most of the foregoing information applies only to international flights and not domestic services within Tahiti-Polynesia and Cook Islands.)

BY BOAT

Even as much Pacific shipping was being sunk during WW II, airstrips were springing up on all the main islands. This hastened the inevitable replacement of the old steamships with modern aircraft, and it's now extremely rare to arrive in the South Pacific by boat (private yachts excepted). Most islands export similar products and there's little interregional trade; large container ships headed for Australia, New Zealand, and Japan don't usually accept passengers.

Those bitten by nostalgia for the slower prewar ways may like to know that a couple of passenger-carrying freighters do still call at the islands, though their fares are much higher than those charged by the airlines. A specialized agency booking such passages is **TravLtips** (Box 188, Flushing, NY 11358, U.S.A.; tel. 1-800/872-8584 or 1-718/939-2400, fax 1-718/939-2047, www. TravLtips.com, e-mail: info@travltips.com). Also try **Freighter World Cruises** (180 South Lake Ave., Ste. 335, Pasadena, CA 91101, U.S.A.; tel. 1-818/449-9200, fax 1-818/449-9573, www. gus.net/travel/fwc/fwc.html).

These companies can place you aboard a British-registered **Bank Line** container ship on its way around the world from Europe via the Panama Canal, Papeete, Nouméa, Suva, Lautoka, Port Vila, Santo, Honiara, and Papua New Guinea. A round-the-world ticket for the four-month journey is US$12,125, but segments are sold if space is available 30 days before sailing. These ships can accommodate only about a dozen passengers, so inquire well in advance.

Nature Expeditions International (6400 E. El Dorado Circle, Ste. 210, Tucson, AZ 85715, U.S.A.; tel. 1-800/869-0639 or 1-520/721-6712, fax 1-520/721-6719, www.naturexp.com, e-mail: NaturExp@aol.com) books cruises to the farthest corners of Polynesia on the expedition ship *World Discoverer.* Passengers land on remote islands from Zodiacs and there are on-board lectures by world authorities. Twice a year there's an 18-day cruise from Easter Island to Tahiti via Pitcairn, Mangareva, and the Marquesas (from US$6,930 pp double occupancy, airfare extra). One-week trips from Tahiti to Rarotonga and island-hoping cruises from Tahiti to Apia or Fiji to Rorotonga are also offered. Nature Expeditions operates very good two-week archaeology tours to Easter Island.

Quest Nature Tours (36 Finch Ave. West, Toronto, Ontario M2N 2G9, Canada; tel. 1-800/387-1483 or 1-416/221-3000, fax 1-416/221-5730, e-mail: travel@worldwidequest.com) books an annual 27-night cruise in April from Chile to Tahiti that visits such remote islands as Easter, Pitcairn, Mangareva, Rapa, Raivavae, and more. Cabins on the Russian mini-cruise ship begin at US$5,995 pp double occupancy, plus gratuities and US$595 port taxes, but including return airfare from Los Angeles.

Adventure cruises to the Marquesas Islands aboard the freighter *Aranui* are described in the Tahiti-Polynesia introduction. **Radisson Seven Seas Cruises** offers tourist trips around Tahiti-Polynesia on the huge cruise ship *Paul Gauguin* and cruises are also operated by **Renaissance Cruises.** Outstanding one-week catamaran cruises around the Leeward, Tuamotu, and Marquesas islands are offered by **Archipels Croisieres** (details in the introduction to Tahiti-Polynesia).

ORGANIZED TOURS

Packaged Holidays
While packaged travel certainly isn't for everyone, reduced group airfares and hotel rates make some tours worth considering. For two people with limited time and a desire to stay at a first-class hotel, this may be the cheapest way to go. The "wholesalers" who put these packages together get their rooms at rates far lower than individuals pay. Special-interest tours are very popular among sportspeople who want to be sure they'll get to participate in the various activities they enjoy. The main drawback to the tours is that you're on a fixed itinerary in a touristic environment, out of touch with local life. Singles pay a healthy supplement. Some of the companies mentioned below do not accept consumer inquiries and require you to work through a travel agent.

Specialists in tours (and all travel arrangements) to Tahiti-Polynesia include the following companies:

Discover Wholesale Travel (2192 Dupont Dr., Ste. 116, Irvine, CA 92612, U.S.A.; tel. 1-800/576-7770, 1-800/759-7330, or 1-949/833-1136, fax 1-949/833-1176)

Islands in the Sun (2381 Rosecrans Ave. #325, El Segundo, CA 90245-4913, U.S.A.; tel. 1-800/828-6877, fax 1-310/536-6266)

Jetset Tours (5120 West Goldleaf Circle, Los Angeles, CA 90056, U.S.A.; tel. 1-604/664-0595, fax 1-604/683-2522, www.jetsettours.com)

Manuia Tours (74 New Montgomery St., San Francisco, CA 94105, U.S.A.; tel. 1-415/495-4500, fax 1-415/495-2000)

Pleasant Holidays (Box 5020, Westlake Village, CA 91359-5020, U.S.A.; tel. 1-800/644-3515, fax 1-619/283-3131, www.pleasantholidays.com)

Runaway Tours (120 Montgomery St., Ste. 800, San Francisco, CA 94104, U.S.A.; tel. 1-800/622-0723, fax 1-800/882-2999)

Tahiti Legends (Box 733, Corona del Mar, CA 92625, U.S.A.; tel. 1-800/200-1213 or 1-714/673-0816, fax 1-714/673-5397, www.tahitilegends.com, e-mail: info@tahitilegends.com)

Tahiti Nui's Island Dreams (Box 9170, Seattle, WA 98109, U.S.A.; tel. 1-800/359-4359 or 1-206/216-2900, fax 1-206/216-2906)

Tahiti Vacations (9841 Airport Blvd., Ste. 1124, Los Angeles, CA 90045, U.S.A.; tel. 1-800/553-3477 or 1-310/337-1040, fax 1-310/337-1126, www.tahitivacation.com)

Check them all for specials before booking a tour or cruise to Tahiti. (Some, such as Runaway Tours, will only accept bookings through travel agents.)

Sunspots International (1918 N.E. 181st, Portland, OR 97230, U.S.A.; tel. 1-800/334-5623 or 1-503/666-3893, fax 1-503/661-7771, www.sunspotsintl.com) has an informative color brochure on Cook Islands, plus a good website. **Sunmakers** (100 West Harrison, South Tower, Ste. 350, Seattle, WA 98119-4123, U.S.A.; tel. 1-800/359-4359 or 1-206/216-2900, fax 1-206/216-2906) books customized itineraries in Cook Islands and Tahiti-Polynesia. **Travel Arrangements Ltd.** (1268 Broadway, Sonoma, CA 95476, U.S.A.; tel. 1-800/392-8213 or 1-707/938-1118, fax 1-707/938-1268) has a color brochure depicting upmarket accommodations in Cook Islands and another on yacht charters at Tahiti. **Tahiti Vacations** (address above) offers three-night Easter Island extensions to their Tahiti packages at US$799 including airfare from Tahiti, accommodations, and an island tour.

Club Méditerranée (40 W. 57th St., New York, NY 10019, U.S.A.; tel. 1-800/147-1522 in the U.S. or 1-800/465-6633 in Canada, fax 1-212/750-1696) offers one-week packages to their resort villages on Bora Bora and Moorea. Package prices include room (double occupancy), food, land and water sports, evening entertainment, and transfers, but airfare and bicycle rentals are extra. Due to all the activities, Club Med's a good choice for singles and couples; families with small children should look elsewhere. Book a couple of months in advance, especially if you want to travel in July, August, or December. For more information on *le Club,* see the **Moorea** and **Bora Bora** chapters in this handbook.

From Australia and New Zealand
Hideaway Holidays (Val Gavriloff, 994 Victoria Rd., West Ryde, NSW 2114, Australia; tel. 61-2/9807-4222, fax 61-2/9808-2260, www.hideawayholidays.com.au, e-mail: sales@hideawayholidays.com.au) specializes in off-the-beaten-track packages to every part of the South Pacific and can organize complicated itineraries.

Qantas Jetabout Holidays (Level 6, 141 Walker St., North Sydney, NSW 2060, Australia; tel. 1-300/360-347 or 61-2/9957-0538, fax 61-2/9957-0393, www.qantas.com.au) offers a variety of standard package tours to Tahiti. In Europe these trips can be booked through Jetabout Holidays, Sovereign House, 361 King St., Hammersmith, London W6 9NJ, England (tel. 44-181/748-8676, fax 44-181/748-7236).

From New Zealand **ASPAC Vacations Ltd.**

(Box 4330, Auckland; tel. 64-9/623-0259, fax 64-9/623-0257, e-mail: southpacific@aspac-vacations.co.nz) has packaged tours and cruises to most of the areas covered in this book. **Travel Arrangements Ltd.** (Box 297, Auckland; tel. 64-9/379-5944, fax 64-9/373-2369) offers sailing holidays and package tours through the region.

Scuba Tours
The South Pacific is one of the world's prime scuba locales, and most of the islands have excellent facilities for divers. Although it's not that difficult to make your own arrangements as you go, you should consider joining an organized scuba tour if you want to cram in as much diving as possible. To stay in business, the dive travel specialists mentioned below are forced to charge prices similar to what you'd pay on the beach, and the convenience of having everything prearranged is often worth it. Before booking, find out exactly where you'll be staying and ask if daily transfers and meals are provided. Of course, diver certification is mandatory.

Live-aboard catamarans in the Tuamotus and Marquesas offer scuba tours. They're a bit more expensive than hotel-based diving, but you're offered up to five dives a day and a total experience. Some repeat divers won't go any other way.

One of the top American scuba wholesalers selling the South Pacific is **Poseidon Ventures Tours** (359 San Miguel Dr., Newport Beach, CA 92660, U.S.A.; tel. 1-800/854-9334 or 1-949/644-5344, fax 1-949/644-5392, www.poseidontours.com, e-mail: poseidon@fea.net; or 3724 FM 1960 West, Ste. 114, Houston, TX 77068, U.S.A.; tel. 1-281/586-7800, fax 1-281/586-7870).

In 1998 the noted underwater photographer and author, Carl Roessler, closed down See & Sea Travel Service which he'd founded in 1966 and became an independent consultant providing advice on scuba facilities and sites worldwide. He makes his money out of "finder fees" paid by selected island suppliers, and his 35 years of experience leading dive tours around the Pacific costs nothing extra to you. Check out his website at www.divxprt.com/see&sea and if you like what you see, get in touch with him at **Sea Images** (Box 471899, San Francisco, CA 94147, U.S.A.; tel. 1-415/922-5807, fax 1-415/922-5662, e-mail: divxprt@ix.netcom.com).

Alternatively, you can make your own arrangements directly with island dive shops. Information about these operators is included under the heading Sports and Recreation in the respective destination chapters of this book.

Tours for Seniors

Since 1989 the **Pacific Islands Institute** (Box 1926, Kailua, HI 96734, U.S.A.; tel. 1-808/262-8942, fax 1-808/263-0178, www.pac-island.com, e-mail: info@pac-island.com) has operated educational tours to most of the South Pacific countries in cooperation with Hawaii Pacific University. Their **Elderhostel** people-to-people study programs designed for those aged 55 or over (younger spouses welcome) are offered between four and six times a year. A 14-day tour to Rarotonga is US$3,056 from Honolulu, otherwise it's US$5,056 for 21 days to Rarotonga, Tahiti, Moorea, Huahine, and Aitutaki. These culturally responsible trips are highly recommended.

Surfing Tours

The largest operator of surfing tours to the South Pacific is **The Surf Travel Company** (Box 446, Cronulla, NSW 2230, Australia; tel. 61-2/9527-4722, fax 61-2/9527-4522, www.surftravel.com.au, e-mail: surftrav@ozemail.com.au) with packages to Moorea and Easter Island. In New Zealand book through Mark Thompson (7 Danbury Dr., Torbay, Auckland; tel./fax 64-9/473-8388). **Waterways Travel** (15145 Califa St., Ste. 1, Van Nuys, CA 91411, U.S.A.; tel. 1-800/928-3757 or 1-818/376-0341, fax 1-818/376-0353, www.waterwaystravel.com) books surfing tours to Tahiti.

Bicycle Tours

About the only North American company offering tours especially designed for cyclists is **Cyclevents** (Box 7491, Jackson, WY 83002-7491, U.S.A.; tel. 1-888/733-9615 or 1-307/733-9615, fax 1-307/734-8581, www.cyclevents.com, e-mail: biking@cyclevents.com). Five times a year there are 12-day cycle tours of Tahiti-Polynesia (US$1,750, double occupancy). Interisland travel between Tahiti, Moorea, Huahine, and Raiatea is included, as are accommodations, most food, and guides, but airfare is extra and you have to bring your own bicycle on the flight.

Yacht Tours and Charters

If you were planning to spend a substantial amount to stay at a luxury resort, consider chartering a yacht instead! Divided among the members of your party the per-person charter price will be about the same, but you'll experience much more of the Pacific's beauty on a boat than you would staying in a hotel room. All charterers visit remote islands accessible only by small boat and thus receive special insights into island life unspoiled by normal tourist trappings. Of course, activities such as sailing, snorkeling, and general exploring by sea and land are included in the price.

Yacht charters are available either "bareboat" (for those with the skill to sail on their own) or "crewed" (in which case charterers pay a daily fee for a skipper plus his/her provisions). On a "flotilla" charter a group of bareboats follows an experienced lead yacht.

The Moorings (4th Floor, 19345 U.S. 19 North, Clearwater, FL 34624, U.S.A.; tel. 1-800/535-7289, fax 1-813/530-9747, www.moorings.com, e-mail: yacht@moorings.com) offers bareboat and crewed yacht charters from their base at Raiatea. Prices range US$430-1,030 a day with the low season Nov.-March. Prices are for the entire boat, but extras are airfare, food (US$32 pp daily), skipper (US$140 daily plus food, if required), and cook (US$120 plus food, if desired). They check you out to make sure you're really capable of handling their vessels. Other obligatory extras are security insurance (US$25 a day), cancellation insurance (US$75 pp), and 3% local tax. Always ask about "specials," such as nine days for the price of seven (reservations clerks often don't volunteer this information). Their New Zealand office is **The Moorings Yacht Charters** (Box 90413, Auckland, New Zealand; tel. 64-9/377-4840, fax 64-9/377-4820, e-mail: info@clubseafarer.co.nz).

The Moorings' Raiatea competitors, Tahiti Yacht Charters and Stardust Marine, are represented by **Tahiti Nui Travel** (B.P. 718, 98713 Papeete; tel. 54-02-00, fax 42-74-35, www.tahiti-nui.com, e-mail: info@tahitinuitravel.pf). It's always wise to compare prices and service before booking.

A few private brokers arranging bareboat or crewed yacht charters at Raiatea are **Sun Yacht Charters** (Box 737, Camden, ME 04843, U.S.A.;

tel. 1-800/772-3500, fax 1-207/236-3972, www. sunyachts.com), **Charter World Pty. Ltd.** (23 Passchendaele St., Hampton, Melbourne 3188, Australia; tel. 61-3/9521-0033, fax 61-3/9521-0081), **Sail Connections Ltd.** (Box 3234, Auckland 1015, New Zealand; tel. 64-9/358-0556, fax 64-9/358-4341, e-mail: jeni@sailconnections.co.nz), **Yachting Partners International** (28-29 Richmond Pl., Brighton, Sussex, BN2 2NA, United Kingdom; tel. 44-1273/571-722, fax 44-1273/571-720, e-mail: ypi@ypi.co.uk), and **Crestar Yachts Ltd.** (125 Sloane St., London SW1X 9AU, United Kingdom; tel. 44-171/730-9962, fax 44-171/824-8691). As they don't own their own boats (as The Moorings does), they'll be more inclined to fit you to the particular boat that suits your individual needs.

One of the most experienced brokers arranging such charters is **Ocean Voyages Inc.** (1709 Bridgeway, Sausalito, CA 94965, U.S.A.; tel. 1-800/299-4444 or 1-415/332-4681, fax 1-415/332-7460, www.crowleys.com/ocean.htm, e-mail: voyages@ix.netcom.com). Unlike their competitors, Ocean Voyages organizes "shareboat" charters in which singles and couples book a cabin on yachts sailing to the remotest corners of Polynesia. Ask about shareboat yacht cruises on fixed itineraries of anywhere from one week to two months. Individuals are welcome and there are about 50 departures a year on a range of vessels. They offer one-week catamaran cruises especially designed for individual scuba divers to the remote islands of the Marquesas (US$2,450 pp)—the *crème de la crème* of Polynesian dive experiences. Other catamarans cruise the Leeward and Tuamotu islands costing US$1,975 pp for six nights in the Leewards and US$1,080 pp for three nights in the Tuamotus. This is perfect if you're alone or in a party of two and don't wish to charter an entire bareboat yacht.

For groups four or six Ocean Voyages books charter vessels such as the catamaran *Fai Manu* at US$7,950/8,950 for four/six persons a week. The smaller *Coup de Coeur* is designed for couples who pay US$3,500 a week to share the 12-meter yacht with Thierry and Luisa Jubin on a dream cruise. Prices include everything other than bar and land excursions. Ocean Voyages also organizes an annual yacht trip from Mangareva to Pitcairn, about the only practicable way of actually spending a few days there. See **Transportation** in the Tahiti-Polynesia introduction for more information on yacht charters.

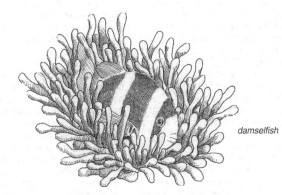

damselfish

DIANA LASICH HARPER

GETTING AROUND

Both Tahiti-Polynesia and Cook Islands have their own local airline servicing the outer islands. These flights, described in the respective chapters of this guide, can be booked upon arrival. Air Tahiti and Air Rarotonga fly small aircraft, so only 10-16 kilograms free baggage may be allowed. A typical interisland flight will cost around US$75 in Cook Islands and US$90 in Tahiti-Polynesia.

Ninety-nine percent of international travel around the South Pacific is by air. With few exceptions travel by boat is a thing of the past. Local boats to the outer islands within a single country are available everywhere, however. Among the local trips you can easily do by regularly scheduled boat are Tahiti-Moorea and Tahiti-Bora Bora. Details of these and other shipping possibilities are explored in the Tahiti-Polynesia and Cook Islands introductions.

BY SAILING YACHT

Getting Aboard

Hitch rides into the Pacific on yachts from California, Panama, New Zealand, and Australia, or around the yachting triangle Papeete-Suva-Honolulu. At home, scrutinize the classified listings of yachts seeking crews, yachts to be delivered, etc., in magazines like *Yachting, Cruising World, Sail,* and *Latitude 38.* You can even advertise yourself for about US$25 (plan to have the ad appear three months before the beginning of the season). Check the bulletin boards at yacht clubs. The **Seven Seas Cruising Association** (1525 South Andrews Ave., Ste. 217, Fort Lauderdale, FL 33316, U.S.A.; tel. 1-954/463-2431, fax 1-954/463-7183, www.ssca.org, e-mail: SSCA1@ibm.net) is in touch with yachties all around the Pacific, and the classified section "Crew Exchange" in their monthly *Commodores' Bulletin* contains ads from captains in search of crew.

Cruising yachts are recognizable by their foreign flags, wind-vane steering gear, sturdy appearance, and laundry hung out to dry. Put up notices on yacht club and marine bulletin boards, and meet people in bars. When a boat is hauled

out, you can find work scraping and repainting the bottom, varnishing, and doing minor repairs. It's much easier, however, to crew on yachts already in the islands. In Tahiti, for example, after a month on the open sea, some of the original crew may have flown home or onward, opening a place for you. Pago Pago, Vava'u, Suva, Musket Cove, and Port Vila are other places to look for a boat.

If you've never crewed before, it's better to try for a short passage the first time. Once at sea on the way to Tahiti, they won't turn around to take a seasick crew member back to Hawaii. Good captains evaluate crew on personality, attitude, and a willingness to learn more than experience, so don't lie. Be honest and open when interviewing with a skipper—a deception will soon become apparent.

It's also good to know what a captain's *really* like before you commit yourself to an isolated month with her/him. To determine what might happen should the electronic gadgetry break down, find out if there's a sextant aboard and whether he/she knows how to use it. A rundown-looking boat may often be mechanically unsound too. Also be concerned about a skipper who doesn't do a careful safety briefing early on, or who seems to have a hard time hanging onto crew. If the previous crew have left the boat at an unlikely place such as the Marquesas, there must have been a reason. Once you're on a boat and part of the yachtie community, things are easy. (P.S. from veteran yachtie Peter Moree: "We do need more ladies out here—adventurous types naturally.")

Time of Year

The weather and seasons play a deciding role in any South Pacific trip by sailboat and you'll have to pull out of many beautiful places, or be unable to stop there, because of bad weather. The favorite season for rides in the South Pacific is May-Oct.; sometimes you'll even have to turn one down. Around August or September start looking for a ride from the South Pacific to Hawaii or New Zealand.

Be aware of the hurricane season: Nov.-March in the South Pacific, July-Dec. in the northwest

Pacific (near Guam), and June-Oct. in the area between Mexico and Hawaii. Few yachts will be cruising those areas at these times. A few yachts spend the winter at Pago Pago and Vava'u (the main "hurricane holes"), but most South Pacific cruisers will have left for hurricane-free New Zealand by October.

Also, know which way the winds are blowing; the prevailing trade winds in the tropics are from the northeast north of the equator, from the southeast south of the equator. North of the tropic of Cancer and south of the tropic of Capricorn the winds are out of the west. Due to the action of prevailing southeast tradewinds, boat trips are smoother from east to west than west to east throughout the South Pacific, so that's the way to go.

Yachting Routes

The South Pacific is good for sailing; there's not too much traffic and no piracy like you'd find in the Mediterranean or in Indonesian waters. The common yachting route or "Coconut Milk Run" across the South Pacific utilizes the northeast and southeast trades: from California to Tahiti via the Marquesas or Hawaii, then Rarotonga, Niue, Vava'u, Suva, and New Zealand. Some yachts continue west from Fiji to Port Vila. In the other direction, you'll sail on the westerlies from New Zealand to a point south of the Australs, then north on the trades to Tahiti.

Some 300 yachts leave the U.S. West Coast for Tahiti every year, almost always crewed by couples or men only. Most stay in the South Seas about a year before returning to North America, while a few continue around the world. About 60-80 cross the Indian Ocean every year (look for rides from Sydney in May, Cairns or Darwin June-Aug., Bali Aug-Oct., Singapore Oct-Dec.); around 700 yachts sail from Europe to the Caribbean (from Gibraltar and Gran Canaria Oct.- December).

Cruising yachts average about 150 km a day, so it takes about a month to get from the U.S. west coast to Hawaii, then another month from Hawaii to Tahiti. To enjoy the finest weather conditions many yachts clear the Panama Canal or depart California in February to arrive in the Marquesas in March. From Hawaii, yachts often leave for Tahiti in April or May. Many stay on for the *Heiva i Tahiti* festival, which ends on 14

July, at which time they sail west to Vava'u or Suva, where you'll find them in July and August. In mid-September the yachting season culminates with a race by about 40 boats from Musket Cove on Fiji's Malololailai Island to Port Vila (it's very easy to hitch a ride at this time). By late October the bulk of the yachting community is sailing south via New Caledonia to New Zealand or Australia to spend the southern summer there. In April or May on alternate years (1999, 2001, etc.) there's a yacht race from Auckland and Sydney to Suva, timed to coincide with the cruisers' return after the hurricane season.

Blue Water Rallies (Peter Seymour, Windsor Cottage, Chedworth, Cheltenham, Gloucestershire GL54 4AA, United Kingdom; tel./fax 01285/720-904) organizes annual round-the-world yachting rallies, departing Europe each October. Inquiries from both owners and potential crew members are welcome for these 20-month circumnavigations that visit Galapagos, the Marquesas, Tahiti, Tonga, and Fiji. Blue Water's professional support services will help make that "voyage of a lifetime" a reality! Similar events are organized by Jimmy Cornell's **World Cruising** (Box 165, London WC1B 3XA, United Kingdom; tel. 44-171/405-9905, fax 44-171/831-0161), departing Fort Lauderdale, Florida, in February.

Be aware that a law enacted in New Zealand in 1995 requires foreign yachts departing New Zealand to obtain a "Certificate of Inspection" from the New Zealand Yachting Federation prior to customs clearance. This regulation has led to a 30% decline in the number of yachts visiting New Zealand, and it's wise to consider alternative summer anchorages before sailing into a situation where some clerk may force you to spend of thousands of dollars upgrading safety standards on your boat before you'll be permitted to leave.

Life Aboard

To crew on a yacht you must be willing to wash and iron clothes, cook, steer, keep watch at night, and help with engine work. Other jobs might include changing and resetting sails, cleaning the boat, scraping the bottom, pulling up the anchor, and climbing the main mast to watch for reefs. Do more than is expected of you. A safety harness must be worn in rough weather. As a guest in someone else's home you'll want to wash your dishes promptly after use and put them, and all other gear, back where you found them. Tampons must not be thrown in the toilet bowl. Smoking is usually prohibited as a safety hazard.

You'll be a lot more useful if you know how to tie knots like the clove hitch, rolling hitch, sheet bend, double sheet bend, reef knot, square knot, figure eight, and bowline. Check your local library for books on sailing or write away for the comprehensive free catalog of nautical books available from International Marine Publishing, Box 548, Black Lick, OH 43004, U.S.A. (tel. 1-800/262-4729, fax 1-614/759-3641, www.pbg.mcgraw-hill.com/im).

Anybody who wants to get on well under sail must be flexible and tolerant, both physically and emotionally. Expense-sharing crew members pay US$50 a week or more per person. After 30 days you'll be happy to hit land for a freshwater shower. Give adequate notice when you're ready to leave the boat, but *do* disembark when your journey's up. Boat people have few enough opportunities for privacy as it is. If you've had a good trip, ask the captain to write you a letter of recommendation; it'll help you hitch another ride.

Food for Thought

When you consider the big investment, depreciation, cost of maintenance, operating expenses, and considerable risk (most cruising yachts are not insured), travel by sailing yacht is quite a luxury. The huge cost can be surmised from charter fees (US$500 a day and up for a 10-meter yacht). International law makes a clear distinction between passengers and crew. Crew members paying only for their own food, cooking gas, and part of the diesel are very different from charterers who do nothing and pay full costs. The crew is there to help operate the boat, adding safety, but like passengers, they're very much under the control of the captain. Crew has no say in where the yacht will go.

The skipper is personally responsible for crew coming into foreign ports: he's entitled to hold their passports and to see that they have onward tickets and sufficient funds for further traveling. Otherwise the skipper might have to pay their hotel bills and even return airfares to the crew's country of origin. Crew may be asked to pay a share of third-party liability insurance. Possession of dope can result in seizure of the yacht. Because of such considerations, skippers often hesitate to accept crew. Crew members should remember that at no cost to themselves they can learn a bit of sailing and visit places nearly inaccessible by other means. Although not for everyone, it's *the* way to see the real South Pacific, and folks who arrive by *vaa* or *vaka* (sailing canoe) are treated differently than other tourists.

OTHER TRAVEL OPTIONS

By Car

A rental car with unlimited mileage will generally cost around US$40 a day in Cook Islands and US$70 in Tahiti-Polynesia. The price of a liter of gasoline also varies considerably: Cook Islands US$0.79 and Tahiti-Polynesia US$1.12. To determine the price of an American gallon, multiply either of these by 3.7854.

Due to the alternative means of travel available, you only really need to consider renting a car in Tahiti-Polynesia. In Cook Islands one must pay a stiff fee for a local driver's license (international driver's license is not recognized) and it's better to tour that territory by rented bicycle anyway. Bicycle is also the way to see Bora Bora.

The car rental business is very competitive and it's possible to shop around for a good deal upon arrival. Although the locally operated companies may offer cheaper rates than the international franchises, it's also true that the agents of Avis, Budget, Europcar, and Hertz are required to maintain recognized standards of service and they have regional offices where you can complain if anything goes seriously wrong. Always find out if insurance, mileage, and tax are included, and check for restrictions on where you'll be allowed to take the car. If in doubt, ask to see a copy of their standard rental contract before making reservations.

Driving is on the right (as in continental Europe and North America) in Tahiti-Polynesia and Easter Island, and on the left (as in Britain, New Zealand, and Japan) in Cook Islands. If you do rent a car, remember those sudden tropical downpours and don't leave the windows open. Also avoid parking under coconut trees (a falling nut might break the window), and never go off and leave the keys in the ignition.

By Bicycle

Bicycling in the South Pacific? Sure, why not? It's cheap, convenient, healthy, quick, environmentally sound, safe, and above all, *fun.* You'll be able to go where and when you please, stop easily and often to meet people and take photos, save money on taxi fares—really *see* the countries. Cycling every day can be fatiguing, however, so it's smart to have bicycle-touring experience beforehand. Most roads are flat along the coast, but be careful on coral roads, especially inclines: if you slip and fall you could hurt yourself badly. On the high islands interior roads tend to be very steep. Never ride your bike through mud.

A sturdy, single-speed mountain bike with wide wheels, safety chain, and good brakes might be ideal. Thick tires and a plastic liner between tube and tire will reduce punctures. Know how to fix your own bike. Take along a good repair kit (pump, puncture kit, freewheel tool, spare spokes, cables, chain links, assorted nuts and bolts, etc.) and a repair manual; bicycle shops are poor to nonexistent in the islands. Don't try riding with a backpack: sturdy, waterproof panniers (bike bags) are required; you'll also want a good lock. Refuse to lend your bike to *anyone.*

Most international airlines will carry a bicycle as checked luggage, usually free but sometimes at the standard overweight charge or for a flat US$50 fee. The charter carriers are the more likely to charge extra, but verify the airline's policy when booking. Take off the pedals and panniers, turn the handlebars sideways and tie them down, deflate the tires, and clean off the dirt before checking in (or use a special bike-carrying bag) and arrive at the airport early. The commuter airlines usually won't accept bikes on their small planes. Interisland boats sometimes charge a token amount to carry a bike; other times it's free. If you'd just like to rent a bicycle locally, you'll have many opportunities to do so at very reasonable prices in Cook Islands.

By Ocean Kayak

Ocean kayaking is experiencing a boom in Hawaii, but the South Pacific is still largely virgin territory. Virtually every island has a sheltered lagoon ready-made for the excitement of kayak touring, but this effortless transportation mode hasn't yet arrived, so you can be a real independent 20th-century explorer! Many international airlines accept folding kayaks as checked baggage at no charge.

For a better introduction to ocean kayaking than is possible here, check at your local public library for sea kayaking manuals. Noted author Paul Theroux toured the entire South Pacific by kayak, and his experiences are recounted in *The Happy Isles of Oceania: Paddling the Pacific* (London: Hamish Hamilton, 1992).

By Canoe

If you get off the beaten track, it's more than likely that a local friend will offer to take you out in his outrigger canoe. Never attempt to take a dugout canoe through even light surf: you'll be swamped. Don't try to pull or lift a canoe by its outrigger—it will break. Drag the canoe by holding the solid main body. A bailer is *essential* equipment.

DIANA LASICH HARPER

TAHITI-POLYNESIA
Te Ao Maohi

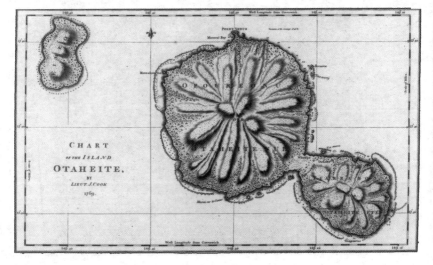

Captain Cook's 1769 map of Tahiti and Moorea

Parau na te Varua ino (Words of the Devil); *Paul Gauguin; National Gallery of Art, Washington; gift of the W. Averell Harriman Foundation in memory of Marie N. Harriman*

M.G.L. DOMENY DE RIENZI

the Tahitian fleet preparing to attack Moorea, 1774 (after William Hodges)

INTRODUCTION

Legendary Tahiti, isle of love, has long been the vision of "la Nouvelle Cythère," the earthly paradise. Explorers Wallis, Bougainville, and Cook all told of a land of spellbinding beauty and enchantment, where the climate was delightful, hazardous insects and diseases unknown, and the islanders, especially the women, among the handsomest ever seen. Rousseau's "noble savage" had been found! A few years later, Fletcher Christian and Captain Bligh acted out their drama of sin and retribution here.

A list of the famous authors who came and wrote about these islands reads like the curriculum of a high-school literature course: Herman Melville, Robert Louis Stevenson, Pierre Loti, Rupert Brooke, Jack London, W. Somerset Maugham, Charles Nordhoff and James Norman Hall (the Americans who wrote *Mutiny on the Bounty*), among others. Exotic images of uninhibited dancers, fragrant flowers, and pagan gods fill the pages. Here, at least, life was meant to be enjoyed.

The most unlikely PR man of them all was a once-obscure French painter named Paul Gauguin, who transformed the primitive color of Tahiti and the Marquesas into powerful visual images seen around the world. When WW II shook the Pacific from Pearl Harbor to Guadalcanal, rather than bloodcurdling banzais and saturation bombings, Polynesia got a U.S. serviceman named James A. Michener, who added Bora Bora to the legend. Marlon Brando arrived in 1961 on one of the first jets to land in Polynesia and, along with thousands of tourists and adventurers, has been coming back ever since.

The friendly, easygoing manner of the people of Tahiti-Polynesia isn't only a cliché! Tahiti gets just 165,000 tourists a year (compared to the seven million that visit Hawaii) and many are French nationals visiting friends, so you won't be facing a tourist glut! Despite over a century and a half of French colonialism, the Tahitians retain many of their old ways, be it in personal dress, Polynesian dancing, or outrigger canoe racing.

POLYNESIA AT A GLANCE

	POPULATION (1996)	AREA (HECTARES)
WINDWARD ISLANDS	**162,686**	**118,580**
Tahiti	150,721	104,510
Moorea	11,682	12,520
LEEWARD ISLANDS	**26,838**	**38,750**
Huahine	5,411	7,480
Raiatea	10,063	17,140
Taha'a	4,470	9,020
Bora Bora	5,767	2,930
Maupiti	1,127	1,140
AUSTRAL ISLANDS	**6,563**	**14,784**
Rurutu	2,015	3,235
Tubuai	2,049	4,500
TUAMOTU ISLANDS	**14,283**	**72,646**
Rangiroa	1,913	7,900
Manihi	769	1,300
GAMBIER ISLANDS	**1,087**	**4,597**
MARQUESAS ISLANDS	**8,064**	**104,930**
Nuku Hiva	2,375	33,950
Hiva Oa	1,837	31,550
TAHITI-POLYNESIA	**219,521**	**354,287**

Relax, smile, and say *bonjour* to strangers—you'll almost always get a warm response. Welcome to paradise!

THE LAND

Tahiti-Polynesia (or Te Ao Maohi as it is known to the Polynesians themselves) consists of five great archipelagos, the Society, Austral, Tuamotu, Gambier, and Marquesas islands, arrayed in chains running from northwest to southeast. The Society Islands are subdivided into the Windwards, or *Îles du Vent* (Tahiti, Moorea, Maiao, Tetiaroa, and Mehetia), and the Leewards, or *Îles Sous-le-Vent* (Huahine, Raiatea, Taha'a, Bora Bora, Maupiti, Tupai, Maupihaa/Mopelia, Manuae/Scilly, and Motu One/Bellingshausen).

Together the 35 islands and 83 atolls of Tahiti-Polynesia total only 3,543 square km in land area, yet they're scattered over a vast area of the southeastern Pacific Ocean, between 7° and 28° south latitude and 131° and 156° west longitude. Papeete (149° west longitude) is actually eight degrees *east* of Honolulu (157° west longitude). Though Tahiti-Polynesia is only half the size of Corsica in land area, if Papeete were Paris then the Gambiers would be in Romania and the Marquesas near Stockholm. At 5,030,000 square km the territory's 200-nautical-mile exclusive economic zone is by far the largest in the Pacific islands.

There's a wonderful geological diversity to these islands midway between Australia and South America—from the dramatic, jagged volcanic outlines of the Society and Marquesas islands, to the 400-meter-high hills of the Australs and Gambiers, to the low coral atolls of the Tuamotus. All of the Marquesas are volcanic islands, while the Tuamotus are all coral islands or atolls. The Societies and Gambiers include both volcanic and coral types.

Tahiti, around 4,000 km from both Auckland and Honolulu or 6,000 km from Los Angeles and Sydney, is not only the best known and most populous of the islands, but also the largest (1,045 square km) and highest (2,241 meters). Bora Bora and Maupiti are noted for their combination of high volcanic peaks within low coral rings. Rangiroa is one of the world's largest coral atolls while Makatea is an uplifted atoll. In the Marquesas, precipitous and sharply crenelated mountains rise hundreds of meters, with craggy peaks, razorback ridges, plummeting waterfalls, deep, fertile valleys, and dark broken coastlines

pounded by surf. Compare them to the pencil-thin strips of yellow reefs, green vegetation, and white beaches enclosing the transparent Tuamotu lagoons. In all, Tahiti-Polynesia offers some of the most varied and spectacular scenery in the entire South Pacific.

Climate

The hot and humid summer season runs Nov.-April. The rest of the year the climate is somewhat cooler and drier. The refreshing southeast trade winds blow consistently May-Aug., varying to easterlies Sept.-December. The northeast trades

TAHITI-POLYNESIA

SOUTH

PACIFIC

OCEAN

Hatutu · Coral Is.
Eiao
Motu Iti ·
Nuku Hiva · ·Ua Huku
Ua Pou° ·Fatu Huku
Marquesas Tahuata° ·Motane
Islands Fatu Hiva°

Tepoto
Manihi Takaroa ·Napuka
Ahe· ·Tikei
Mataiva· Rangiroa Takapoto Tuamotu
Motu-Iti· Arutua Puka Puka··
Bellingshausen Tikehau ·Aratika Islands
·Scilly Bora-Bora Makatea Apataki ·Raraka Takume
Maupiti· Kaukura° Toau ·· ·Katiu Taenga ·Fangatau
Tahaa Niau° ·Makemo Raroia Fakahina
Mopelia Raiatea° ·Huahine Fakarava Faaite ·· ·Hiti Nihiru
Society Islands Moorea Tetiaroa Tahanea·· Motutunga ·Rekareka Tatakoto
Maiao Anaa·· North Marutea ·Hikueru
Tahiti Mehetia Hararaiki ·Tauere
Reitoru· Pukaroa
Marokau· Amanu· ·Hao Aki-Aki ·Reao
Ravahere ·Manuhangi ·Vahitahi
Hereheretue Nengonengo· ·Paraoa Nukutavake
Manuhangi· Vairaatea Pinaki
Nukutipipi Ahunui
Vanavana· Tureia
·Maria Tematangi· Moruroa Maturei·· Tenararo Marutea
Vavao
Fangataufa· ·Maria

Austral

Islands

Maria
·Rurutu
Rimatara°
·Tubuai
·Raivavae

Morane· ·Temoe
Mangareva
Gambier
Islands

Rapa Iti·

0   250 mi

0   250 km

© DAVID STANLEY

Jan.-April coincide with the hurricane season. The trade winds cool the islands and offer clear sailing for mariners, making May-Oct. the most favorable season to visit. (In fact, there can be long periods of fine, sunny weather anytime of year and these seasonal variations should not be a pivotal factor in deciding when to come.)

The trade winds are caused by hot air rising near the equator, which then flows toward the poles at high altitude. Cooler air drawn toward the vacuum is deflected to the west by the rotation of the earth. Tahiti-Polynesia's proximity to the intertropical convergence zone (5° north and south of the equator), or "doldrum zone"—where the most heated air is rising—explains the seasonal shift in the winds from northeast to southeast.

Hurricanes are relatively rare, although they do hit the Tuamotus and occasionally Tahiti (but almost never the Marquesas). From November 1980 to May 1983 an unusual wave of eight hurricanes and two tropical storms battered the islands due to the El Niño phenomenon. The next hurricane occurred in December 1991. In November 1997 two hurricanes struck Maupiti and neighboring isles, one passed over the Tuamotus in February 1998, and another hit Huahine in April 1998, again the fault of El Niño. A hurricane would merely inconvenience a visitor staying at a hotel, though campers and yachties might get blown into oblivion. The days immediately following a hurricane are clear and dry.

Rainfall is greatest in the mountains and along the windward shores of the high islands. The Societies are far damper than the Marquesas. In fact, the climate of the Marquesas is erratic: some years the group experiences drought, other years it could rain the whole time you're there. The low-lying Tuamotus get the least rainfall of all. Tahiti-Polynesia encompasses such a vast area that latitude is an important factor: at 27° south latitude Rapa is far cooler than Nuku Hiva (9° south).

Winds from the southeast (maraamu) are generally drier than those from the northeast or north. The northeast winds often bring rain: Papenoo on the northeast side of Tahiti is twice as wet as rain-shadowed Punaauia. The annual rainfall is extremely variable, but the humidity is generally high, reaching 98%. In the evening the heat of the Tahiti afternoons is replaced by soft, fragrant mountain breezes called hupe, which drift down to the sea. Tahiti-Polynesia enjoys some of the cleanest air on earth—air that hasn't blown over a continent for weeks.

Tahiti and Moorea have a solar (rather than a lunar) tide which means that the low tides are at sunrise and sunset, high tides at noon and midnight. Because of this, snorkeling in or near a reef passage will be safest in the morning as the water flows in. Shallow waters are best traversed by yachts around noon when the water is high and slack, and visibility is at its peak.

HISTORY

Polynesian Culture

The eastern Polynesian islands, including those of Tahiti-Polynesia, were colonized at uncertain

a chief mourner before a cadaver, 1773 (after William Hodges)

M.G.L. DOMENY DE RIENZI

ARCHAEOLOGY

The first archaeological survey of Tahiti-Polynesia was undertaken in 1925 by Professor Kenneth P. Emory of Honolulu's Bernice P. Bishop Museum. Emory's successor, Professor Yosihiko Sinoto of the same museum, has carried out extensive excavations and restorations in the area since 1960. In 1962, at a 9th-century graveyard on Maupiti's Motu Paeao, Emory and Sinoto uncovered artifacts perfectly matching those of the first New Zealand Maoris. A few years later, at Ua Huka in the Marquesas, Sinoto discovered a coastal village site dating from A.D. 300, the oldest yet found in Eastern Polynesia. Sinoto was responsible for the restoration of the Maeva *marae* on Huahine and many historical *marae* on Tahiti, Moorea, Raiatea, and Bora Bora. During construction of the Bali Hai Hôtel on Huahine in 1973-77 Sinoto's student diggers located 10 flat hand clubs of the *patu* model, previously thought to exist only in New Zealand, plus some planks of a 1,000-year-old sewn double canoe.

dates during the 1st millennium A.D. It's thought that about A.D. 300 the Polynesians reached the Marquesas from Samoa, and sometime around A.D. 500 they sailed on from the Marquesas to Hawaii and Easter Island. They were on the Society Islands by 800 and sailed from there to the Cooks and New Zealand around 1000, completing the occupation of the Polynesian triangle. On these planned voyages of colonization they carried all the plants and animals needed to continue their way of life.

The Polynesians lived from fishing and agriculture, using tools made from stone, bone, shell, and wood. The men were responsible for planting, harvesting, fishing, cooking, and house and canoe building; the women tended the fields and animals, gathered food and fuel, prepared food, and made tapa clothes and household items. Both men and women worked together in family or community groups, not as individuals.

The Polynesians lost the art of pottery making during their long stay in Havaiki (possibly Samoa) and had to cook their food in underground ovens *(umu)*. It was sometimes *tapu* for men and women to eat together. Breadfruit, taro, yams,

sweet potatoes, bananas, and coconuts were cultivated (the Polynesians had no cereals). Pigs, chickens, and dogs were also kept for food, but the surrounding sea yielded the most important source of protein.

Canoes were made of planks stitched together with sennit and caulked with gum from breadfruit trees. Clothing consisted of tapa (bark cloth). Both men and women wore belts of pandanus leaves or tapa when at work, and during leisure, a skirt that reached to their knees. Ornaments were of feathers, whale or dolphin teeth, and flowers. Both sexes were artfully tattooed using candlenut oil and soot.

For weapons there were clubs, spears, and slings. Archery was practiced only as a game to determine who could shoot farthest. Spear throwing, wrestling, boxing, kite flying, surfing, and canoe racing were popular sports. Polynesian music was made with nasal flutes and cylindrical sharkskin or hollow slit drums. Their dancing is still appreciated today.

The museums of the world possess many fine stone and wood tikis in human form from the Marquesas Islands, where the decorative sense was highly developed. Sculpture in the Australs was more naturalistic, and only here were female tikis common. The Tahitians showed less interest in the plastic arts but excelled in the social arts of poetry, oratory, theater, music, song, and dance. Life on the Tuamotus was a struggle for existence, and objects had utilitarian functions. Countless Polynesian cult objects were destroyed in the early 19th century by overzealous missionaries.

Prior to European contact three hereditary classes structured the Society Islands: high chiefs *(ari'i),* lesser chiefs *(raatira),* and commoners *(manahune).* A small slave class *(titi)* also existed. The various *ari'i* tribes controlled wedge-shaped valleys, and their authority was balanced. None managed to gain permanent supremacy over the rest. In this rigid hierarchical system, where high chiefs had the more *mana* than commoners, marriage or even physical contact between persons of unequal mana was forbidden. Children resulting from sexual relations between the classes were killed.

Religion centered around an open-air temple, called a *marae,* with a stone altar. Here priests prayed to the ancestors or gods and conducted all the significant ceremonies of Polynesian life. An individual's social position was determined by his or her family connections, and the recitation of one's genealogy confirmed it. Human sacrifices took place on important occasions on a high chief's *marae*. Cannibalism was rife in the Marquesas and was also practiced in the Tuamotus.

Members of the Raiatea-based Arioi Society traveled through the islands performing ritual copulation and religious rites. The fertility god Oro had descended on a rainbow to Bora Bora's Mount Pahia, where he found a beautiful *vahine*. Their child was the first Arioi. In their pursuit of absolute *free* love, the Arioi shared spouses and killed their own children.

But the Arioi were not the only practitioners of infanticide in Tahiti-Polynesia. The whole social structure could be threatened by a surplus of children among the chiefly class. Such children might demand arable land from commoners who supplied the chiefs with food. And a struggle between too many potential heirs could create strife. Thus the *ari'i* often did away with unwanted infants after birth (rather than before birth as is the accepted practice today). The Arioi Society itself may have been a partial solution as unwanted *ari'i* children were assigned a benign role as Arioi with the assurance that they themselves would never produce any offspring.

European Exploration

While the Polynesian history of the islands goes back at least 1,700 years, the European period only began in the 16th century when the Magellan expedition sailed past the Tuamotus and Mendaña visited the Marquesas. The Spaniard Quirós saw the Tuamotus in 1606, as did the Dutchmen Le Maire and Schouten in 1616, the Dutchman Roggeveen in 1722, and the Englishman Byron in 1765. But it was not until 18 June 1767 that Capt. Samuel Wallis on the HMS *Dolphin* happened upon Tahiti. He and most of his contemporary explorers were in search of *terra australis incognita,* a mythical southern landmass thought to balance the Northern Hemisphere.

At first the Tahitians attacked the ship, but after experiencing European gunfire they decided to be friendly. Eager to trade, they loaded the Englishmen down with pigs, fowl, and fruit. Iron was in the highest demand, and Tahitian women lured the sailors to exchange nails for love. Consequently, to prevent the ship's timbers from being torn asunder for the nails, no man was allowed onshore except in parties strictly for food and water. Wallis sent ashore a landing party, which named Tahiti "King George III Island," turned some sod, and hoisted the Union Jack. A year later the French explorer Louis-Antoine de Bougainville arrived on the east coast, unaware of Wallis's discovery, and claimed Tahiti for the king of France.

Wallis and Bougainville only visited briefly, leaving it to Capt. James Cook to really describe Polynesia to Europeans. Cook visited "Otaheite" four times, in 1769, 1773, 1774, and 1777. His first three-month visit was to observe the transit of

the ceding of Matavai, Tahiti, to English missionaries in 1797

M.G.L. DOMENY DE RIENZE

the planet Venus across the face of the sun. The second and third were in search of the southern continent, while the fourth was to locate a northwest passage between the Pacific and Atlantic oceans. Some of the finest artists and scientists of the day accompanied Captain Cook. Their explorations added the Leeward Islands, two Austral islands, and a dozen Tuamotu islands to European knowledge. On Tahiti Cook met a high priest from Raiatea named Tupaia, who had an astonishing knowledge of the Pacific and could name dozens of islands. He drew Cook a map that included the Cook Islands, the Marquesas, and perhaps also some Samoan islands!

In 1788 Tahiti was visited for five months by HMS *Bounty* commanded by Lt. William Bligh with orders to collect young breadfruit plants for transportation to the West Indies. However, the famous mutiny did not take place at Tahiti but in Tongan waters, and from there Bligh and loyal members of his crew managed to escape by navigating an open boat 6,500 km to Dutch Timor. In 1791, the HMS *Pandora* came to Tahiti in search of the *Bounty* mutineers, intending to take them to England for trial. They captured 14 survivors of the 16 who had elected to stay on Tahiti when Fletcher Christian and eight others left for Pitcairn. Although glamorized by Hollywood, the mutineers helped destroy traditional Tahitian society by acting as mercenaries for rival chiefs. In 1792 Bligh returned to Tahiti in another ship and completed his original mission.

By the early 19th century, ruffian British and American whalers were fanning out over the Pacific. Other ships traded with the islanders for sandalwood, bêche-de-mer, and mother-of-pearl, as well as the usual supplies. They brought with them smallpox, measles, influenza, tuberculosis, scarlet fever, and venereal diseases, which devastated the unprepared Polynesians. Slave raids, alcohol, and European firearms did the rest.

Kings and Missionaries

In March 1797 the ship *Duff* dropped off on Tahiti 18 Protestant missionaries and their wives after a 207-day journey from England. By this time Pomare, chief of the area adjoining Matavai Bay, had become powerful through the use of European tools, firearms, and mercenaries. He welcomed the missionaries but would not be converted; infanticide, sexual freedom, and

human sacrifices continued. By 1800 all but five of the original 18 had left Tahiti disappointed.

In 1803 Pomare I died and his despotic son, Pomare II, attempted to conquer the entire island. After initial success he was forced to flee to Moorea in 1808. Missionary Henry Nott went with him, and in 1812 Pomare II turned to him for help in regaining his lost power. Though the missionaries refused to baptize Pomare II himself because of his heathen and drunken habits, his subjects on Moorea became nominal Christians. In 1815 this "Christian king" managed to regain Tahiti and overthrow paganism. Instead of being punished, the defeated clans were forgiven and allowed to become Christians. The persistent missionaries then enforced the Ten Commandments and dressed the Tahitian women in "Mother Hubbard" costumes—dresses that covered their bodies from head to toe. Henceforth singing anything but hymns was banned, dancing proscribed, and all customs that offended puritanical sensibilities wiped away. Morality police terrorized the confused Tahitians in an eternal crusade against sin. Even the wearing of flowers in the hair was prohibited.

In *Omoo* (1847) Herman Melville comments:

Doubtless, in thus denationalizing the Tahitians, as it were, the missionaries were prompted by a sincere desire for good; but the effect has been lamentable. Supplied with no amusements, in place of those forbidden, the Tahitians, who require more recreation than other people, have sunk into a listlessness, or indulge in sensualities, a hundred times more pernicious than all the games ever celebrated in the Temple of Tanee.

The Rape of Polynesia

Upon Pomare II's death from drink at age 40 in 1821, the crown passed to his infant son, Pomare III, but he passed away in 1827. At this juncture the most remarkable Tahitian of the 19th century, Aimata, half-sister of Pomare II, became Queen Pomare Vahine IV. She was to rule Tahiti, Moorea, and part of the Austral and Tuamotu groups for half a century until her death in 1877, a barefoot Tahitian Queen Victoria. She allied herself closely with the London Missionary

Society (LMS), and when two French-Catholic priests, Honoré Laval and François Caret, arrived on Tahiti in 1836 from their stronghold at Mangareva (Gambier Islands), she expelled them promptly.

This affront brought a French frigate to Papeete in 1838, demanding $2,000 compensation and a salute to the French flag. Although the conditions were met, the queen and her chiefs wrote to England appealing for help, but none came. A Belgian named Moerenhout who had formerly served at the U.S. consul was appointed French consul to Queen Pomare in 1838, and soon after a second French gunboat returned in 1839 and threatened to bombard Tahiti unless 2,000 Spanish dollars were paid and Catholic missionaries given free entry. Back in Mangareva, Laval pushed forward a grandiose building program, which wiped out 80% of the population of the Gambiers from overwork.

In September 1842, while the queen and George Pritchard, the English consul, were away, he tricked four local chiefs into signing a petition asking to be brought under French "protection." This demand was immediately accepted by French Admiral Abel Dupetit-Thouars, who was in league with Moerenhout, and on 9 September 1842 they forced Queen Pomare to accept a French protectorate. When the queen tried to maintain her power and keep her red-and-white royal flag, Dupetit-Thouars deposed the queen on 8 November 1843 and occupied her kingdom, an arbitrary act that was rejected by the French king, who reestablished the protectorate in 1844. Queen Pomare fled to Raiatea and Pritchard was deported to England in March 1844, bringing

AUCKLAND INSTITUTE AND MUSEUM

DAVID STANLEY

Pomare V's mother died in 1877 after reigning for 50 troubled years during which she was exhorted to accept a French protectorate over her Polynesian kingdom. A less heroic figure than his mother, King Pomare V (above left) the fifth and last of his name to hold the throne, took over a luckless dynasty and also took to drink. He was particularly fond of Benedictine and although the distinctive symbol enshrined forever atop his pylon-shaped mausoleum at Arue (above right) appears to be a massive Benedictine bottle, it is actually a Grecian vase. He died in 1891, an unhappy man.

Britain and France to the brink of war. The Tahitians resisted for three years: old French forts and war memorials recall the struggle.

A French Protectorate

At the beginning of 1847, when Queen Pomare realized that no British assistance was forthcoming, she and her people reluctantly accepted the French protectorate. As a compromise, the British elicited a promise from the French not to annex the Leeward Islands, so Huahine, Raiatea, and Bora Bora remained independent until 1887. The French had taken possession of the Marquesas in 1842, even before imposing a protectorate on Tahiti. The Austral Islands were added in 1900 and only prior British action prevented the annexation of the Cook Islands. French missionaries attempted to convert the Tahitians to Catholicism, but only in the Marquesas were they fully successful.

Queen Pomare tried to defend the interests of her people as best she could, but much of her nation was dying: between the 18th century and 1926 the population of the Marquesas fell from 80,000 to only 2,000. In April 1774 Captain Cook had tried to estimate the population of Tahiti by counting the number of men he saw in a fleet of war canoes and ascribing three members to each one's family. Cook's figure was 204,000, but according to anthropologist Bengt Danielsson, the correct number at the time of discovery was about 150,000. By 1829 it had dropped to 8,568, and a low of 7,169 was reached in 1865. The name "Pomare" means "night cough," from *po,* night, plus *mare,* cough, because Pomare I's infant daughter died of tuberculosis in 1792.

Pomare V, the final, degenerate member of the line, was more interested in earthly pleasures than the traditions upheld by his mother. In 1880, with French interests at work on the Panama Canal, a smart colonial administrator convinced him to sign away his kingdom for a 5,000-franc-a-month pension. Thus, on 29 June 1880 the protectorate became the full French colony it is today, the "Etablissements français de l'Océanie." In 1957 the name was changed to "Polynésie française." Right up until the 1970s the colony was run by governors appointed in Paris who implemented the policies of the French government. There was no system of indirect rule through local chiefs as was the case in the

British colonies: here French officials decided everything and their authority could not be questioned. Even the 18-member Conseil Générale created in 1885 to oversee certain financial matters had its powers reduced in 1899 and was replaced in 1903 by an impotent advisory council composed of French civil servants. The only elected official with any authority (and a budget) was the mayor of Papeete.

The most earthshaking event between 1880 and 1960 was a visit by two German cruisers, the *Scharnhorst* and *Gneisenau,* which shelled Papeete, destroying the marketplace on 22 September 1914. (Two months later both were sunk by the British at the Battle of the Falkland Islands.) A thousand Tahitian volunteers subsequently served in Europe, 300 of them becoming casualties. On 2 September 1940 the colony declared its support for the Free French, and soon after Pearl Harbor the Americans arrived to establish a base on Bora Bora. Polynesia remained cut off from occupied metropolitan France until the end of the war, although several hundred Tahitians served with the Pacific battalion in North Africa and Italy. In 1946 the colony was made an overseas territory or *territoire d'outre-mer* (TOM) endowed with an elected territorial assembly. Representation in the French parliament was also granted.

The economy of the early colonial period had been based on cotton growing (1865-1900), vanilla cultivation (1870-1960), pearl shell collecting (1870-1960), copra making, and phosphate mining (1908-1966). These were to be replaced by nuclear testing (1963-1996), tourism (1961-present), and cultured pearls (1968-present).

The Nuclear Era

The early 1960s were momentous times for Polynesia. Within a few years, MGM filmed *Mutiny on the Bounty,* an international airport opened on Tahiti, and the French began testing their atomic bombs. After Algeria became independent in July 1962 the French decided to move their Sahara nuclear testing facilities to Moruroa Atoll in the Tuamotu Islands, 1,200 km southeast of Tahiti. In 1963, when all local political parties protested the invasion of Polynesia by thousands of French troops and technicians sent to establish a nuclear testing center, President Charles de Gaulle simply outlawed political parties. The French set off their first atmospheric nuclear explosion at Moruroa on 2 July 1966, spreading contamination as far as Peru and New Zealand. In 1974 international protests forced the French to switch to the underground tests that continued until 1996. During those three decades of infamy 181 nuclear explosions, 41 of them in the atmosphere, rocked the Tuamotus.

In the 1960s-70s, as independence blossomed across the South Pacific, France tightened its strategic grip on Tahiti-Polynesia. The spirit of the time is best summed up in the life of one man, Pouvanaa a Oopa, an outspoken WW I hero from Huahine. In 1949 he became the first Polynesian to occupy a seat in the French Chamber of Deputies. His party gained control of the territorial assembly in 1953 and in 1957 he was elected vice-president of the newly formed Government Council. In 1958 Pouvanaa campaigned for independence in a referendum vote, but when this failed due to a controversy over the imposition of an income tax, the French government reestablished central control and had Pouvanaa arrested on trumped-up charges of arson. He was eventually sentenced to an eight-year prison term, and exiled to France for 15 years. De Gaulle wanted Pouvanaa out of the way until French nuclear testing facilities could be established in Polynesia, and he was not freed until 1968. In 1971 he won the "French" Polynesian seat in the French Senate, a post he held until his death in early 1977. Tahitians refer to the man as *metua* (father), and his statue stands in front of Papeete's Territorial Assembly.

Pouvanaa's successors, John Teariki and Francis Sanford, were also defenders of Polynesian autonomy and opponents of nuclear testing. Their combined efforts convinced the French government to grant Polynesia a new statute with a slightly increased autonomy in 1977. In 1982 the neo-Gaullist Tahoeraa Huiraatira (Popular Union) won the territorial elections, and the pronuclear, anti-independence mayor of Pirae, Gaston Flosse, became head of the local government. Flosse's reputation for fixing government contracts while in office earned him the title "Mr. Ten Percent" from the Paris newspaper *Libération.* To stem growing support for independence, Flosse negotiated enhanced autonomy for the territory in 1984 and 1996.

The leading antinuclear, pro-independence party is the Tavini Huiraatira, the Polynesian Liberation Front, formed in 1978 by Faa'a mayor Oscar Temaru. For the 1996 territorial election Temaru's party merged with Jacqui Drollet's la Mana Te Nunaa and together they increased their assembly representation from four to 10. Yet Flosse and Tahoeraa Huiraatira (which got 22 seats in 1996) remain in office today, largely thanks to massive French subsidies and a gerrymandered electoral system. The *indépendentistes* are strongest in Papeete, weakest in the Tuamotus and Marquesas—areas heavily dependent on French aid—and one vote in the Australs, Tuamotus, and Marquesas is worth almost three on Tahiti. French civil servants and military personnel can vote in local elections after six months residence in the territory, and they vote for Flosse's party as a block. (Just prior to the 1996 election the territorial government handed out free housing in marginal ridings, but delayed transfer of the ownership papers until after the election, and Tahoeraa Huiraatira candidates won several of those seats by a handful of votes. This is only one example of the type of chicanery that keeps Flosse's party in power.)

The independence cause was given impetus by a heavy-handed last fling at nuclear testing by the French government. In April 1992, President Mitterrand halted the testing program at Moruroa, but in June 1995, newly elected President Jacques Chirac ordered a resumption of underground nuclear testing in the Tuamotus, and despite worldwide protests the first test was carried out on 5 September 1995. Early the next morning nonviolent demonstrators blocked the runway of Faa'a Airport because they believed Gaston Flosse was attempting to escape on a flight to France. When the police charged the protesters to clear the runway, the demonstration turned into an ugly riot in which the airport and Papeete were ransacked.

Already in 1987 and 1991 there had been rioting by youths from squatter settlements near the airport where unemployment runs at 80%, and this time they were joined by union members who had been meeting in a stadium between Papeete and the airport. The incensed unionists said they could not stand by and watch as defenseless protesters (including a group of children) were beaten. After radio appeals for calm from Oscar Temaru the trouble subsided, but on 9 September French riot police raided the offices of A Tia I Mua, the trade union blamed for the rioting. The *gendarmes* bludgeoned and handcuffed everyone present, then dragged them from the building in a brutal manner. For 34 hours the accused were humiliated and held in intolerable conditions at the *gendarmerie* on avenue Bruat in central Papeete before being delivered to the sanctuary of a local prison. The union's leader, Hiro Tefaarere, was held for two months, but he now sits in the territorial assembly as an elected member from Oscar Temaru's party.

Meanwhile at the Moruroa test site, two large Greenpeace protest vessels had been boarded by tear gas-firing French commandos and impounded (the ships were not released until six months later). With the local opposition crushed, the rest of the Chirac tests went ahead without incident. However, worldwide condemnation of the series reached unprecedented levels, and in January 1996 the French announced that the testing had been completed. The facilities on Moruroa have since been decommissioned and it's almost inconceivable that the testing could ever resume, yet deadly radiation may already be leaking into the sea through cracks in the atoll's porous coral cap. A mantle of secrecy continues to hang over the France's former nuclear playground in the South Pacific and the credibility of official French sources on this subject is almost nil. (For more information, turn to **The Nuclear Test Zone** in the Tuamotu Islands section.)

GOVERNMENT

In 1885 an organic decree created the colonial system of government, which remained in effect until the proclamation of a new statute in 1958. In 1977 the French granted the territory partial internal self-government, and Francis Sanford was elected premier of "autonomous" Polynesia. A new local-government statute, passed by the French parliament and promulgated on 6 September 1984, gave slightly more powers to the Polynesians, and in 1996 additional powers were transferred to the territory to slow the momentum toward full independence. Yet the constitution of the Republic of France remains the supreme law of the land. Territorial laws can be overridden by the French Parliament or the Constitutional Commission, and administrative decisions by territorial officials can be overturned by French judges.

A Territorial Assembly elects the president of the government, who chooses 15 cabinet ministers. The 41 assembly members are elected every five years from separate districts, with 22 seats from Tahiti/Moorea, eight from the Leeward Islands, five from the Tuamotus and Gambiers, three from the Australs, and three from the Marquesas. The territory is represented in Paris by two elected deputies, a senator, and a social and economic counselor. The French government, through its high commissioner (called governor until 1977), retains control over foreign relations, immigration, defense, justice, the police, the municipalities, higher education, TV and radio, property rights, and the currency.

Tahiti-Polynesia is divided into 48 communes, each with an elected Municipal Council, which chooses a mayor from its ranks. Every main town on an island will have its *mairie* (town hall). These elected municipal bodies, however, are controlled by appointed French civil servants, who run the five administrative subdivisions. The administrators of the Windward, Tuamotu-Gambier, and Austral subdivisions are based at Papeete, while the headquarters of the Leeward Islands administration is at Uturoa (Raiatea), and that of the Marquesas Islands is at Taiohae (Nuku Hiva).

The territorial flag consists of horizontal red, white, and red bands with a double-hulled Polynesian sailing canoe superimposed on the white band. On the canoe are five figures representing the five archipelagos.

ECONOMY

Government Spending
Tahiti-Polynesia has the highest per capita gross domestic product (GDP) in the South Pacific, about US$15,500 pp or seven times as much as Fiji. Paris contributes little to the territorial budget, but it finances the many departments and services under the direct control of the high commissioner, spending an average of US$1 billion a year in the territory or almost a third of the

GDP. Most of it goes to the military and to the 2,200 expatriate French civil servants who earn salaries 84% higher than those doing the same work in France. Of the total workforce of 45,000, about 16,500 work for some level of government while the other 28,500 are privately employed.

The inflow of people and money since the early 1960s has substituted consumerism for subsistence, and except for tourism and cultured pearls, the economy of Tahiti-Polynesia is now totally dominated by French government spending. The nuclear testing program provoked an influx of 30,000 French settlers, plus a massive infusion of capital, which distorted the formerly self-supporting economy into one totally dependent on France. In the early 1960s, many Polynesians left their homes for construction jobs with the *Centre d'Expérimentations du Pacifique* (CEP), the government, and the hotel chains. Now that the volume of this work is decreasing, most of them subsist in precarious circumstances on Tahiti, dependent on government spending.

In 1994 the territorial government introduced an income tax of two percent on earnings over CFP 150,000 a month where none had previously existed, plus new taxes on gasoline, wine, telecommunications, and unearned income. The conclusion of nuclear testing in 1996 meant that 1,000 local workers had to be laid off and tax revenues on military imports suddenly dropped. To compensate for this and to shore up the political fortunes of their local allies, the French government agreed to a "Pacte de Progrès," which will provide the territory with an additional subsidy of US$200 million a year until 2005.

Trade

Prior to the start of nuclear testing, trade was balanced. Only 30 years later, 1996 imports stood at CFP 89,388 million while exports amounted to just CFP 15,452 million, one of the highest disparities in the world. Much of the imbalance is consumed by the French administration itself, and 17% of imports are related to military activities. Foreign currency spent by tourists on imported goods and services also helps steady the situation. A plan exists to lift income from exports and tourism to 50% of the value of imports by the year 2003.

Nearly half the imports come from France, which has imposed a series of self-favoring restrictions. Imports include food, fuel, building material, consumer goods, and automobiles. The main agricultural export from the outer islands is copra; copra production has been heavily subsidized by the government since 1967 to discourage migration to Tahiti. The copra is crushed into coconut oil and animal feed at the Papeete mill, while cultured pearls from farms in the Tuamotus are the biggest export by far. Perfume, vanilla, and monoï oil are also exported.

Indirect taxes, such as licensing fees and customs duties of 20-200%, have long accounted for over half of territorial government revenue, and the price of many imported goods is more than doubled by taxation. There's also a flat 35% levy on businesses, which is simply passed along to consumers. In late 1998 it was announced that customs duties were to be phased out and replaced by a *taxe sur la valeur ajoutée* (TVA) or value added tax (VAT). Since 1 January 1998 a 3% TVA has been added to the price of most goods and services, and this is to be increased to 15% over five years.

Agriculture

Labor recruiting for the nuclear testing program caused local agriculture to collapse in the mid-'60s. Between 1962 and 1988 the percentage of the workforce employed in agriculture dropped from 46% to 10% and it has declined even further since then; today agriculture and fishing account for under four percent of salaried employment. Exports of coffee and vanilla had ceased completely by 1965 and coconut products dropped 40% despite massive subsidies. Vanilla, copra, and coconut oil combined now compose only four percent of exports. South Korean companies pay US$1.5 million a year in licensing fees to fish the territory's exclusive economic zone.

About 80% of all food consumed locally is imported. Tahiti-Polynesia does manage, however, to cover three-quarters of its own fruit requirements, and most of the local pineapple and grapefruit crop goes to the fruit-juice factory on Moorea. In the 1880s-90s four million oranges a year were exported to Australia, New Zealand, and California. The industry was wiped out by a blight at the turn of the century, and now only a few trees grow wild.

Local vegetables supply half of local needs, while Tahitian coffee covers 20% of consumption. Considerable livestock is kept in the Marquesas. Large areas have been planted in Caribbean pine to provide for future timber needs. Aquaculture, with tanks for freshwater shrimp, prawns, live bait, and green mussels, is being developed. Most industry is related to food processing (fruit-juice factory, brewery, soft drinks, etc.) or coconut products. It's rumored that marijuana *(pakalolo)* is now the leading cash crop, though you won't be aware of it.

Cultured Pearls

Tahiti-Polynesia's cultured-pearl industry, now second only to tourism as a money earner, originated in 1963 when an experimental farm was established on Hikueru atoll in the Tuamotus. The first commercial farm opened on Manihi in 1968, but the real boom only began in the late 1980s and today hundreds of cooperative and private pearl farms operate on 26 atolls, employing thousands of people. Fourteen large companies account for half of production with the rest coming from 50 smaller companies and 450 family operations. The industry is drawing many Tahitians back to ancestral islands they abandoned after devastating hurricanes in 1983. Pearl farming is ecologically benign, relieving pressure on natural stocks and creating a need to protect marine environments. Pollution from fertilizer runoff or sewage can make a lagoon unsuitable for pearl farming, which is why the farms are concentrated on lightly populated atolls where other forms of agriculture are scarcely practiced.

Unlike the Japanese cultured white pearl, the Polynesian black pearl is created only by the giant blacklipped oyster *(Pinctada margaritifera),* which thrives in the Tuamotu lagoons. Beginning in the 19th century the oysters were collected by Polynesian divers who could dive up to 40 meters. The shell was made into mother-of-pearl buttons; finding a pearl this way was pure chance. By the middle of this century overharvesting had depleted the slow-growing oyster beds and today live oysters are collected only to supply cultured-pearl farms. The shell is now a mere by-product, made into decorative items or exported. The strings of oysters must be monitored constantly and lowered or raised if there are variations in water temperature.

It takes around three years for a pearl to form in a seeded oyster. A spherical pearl is formed when a Mississippi River mussel graft is introduced inside the coat; the oyster only creates a hemispherical half pearl if the graft goes between the coat and the shell. Half pearls are much cheaper than real pearls and make outstanding rings and pendants. Some of the grafts used are surprisingly large and the layer of nacre around such pearls may be relatively thin, but only an X-ray can tell. Thin coating on a pearl greatly reduces its value.

The cooperatives sell their production at Papeete auctions in April and October. The pearls are usually offered to bidders in unmixed batches. Local jewelers vie with Japanese buyers at these events, with some 65,000 black pearls changing hands for about US$5 million. Private producers sell their pearls through independent dealers or plush retail outlets in Papeete. Every year about a million black pearls worth US$150 million are exported to Japan, Hong Kong, Singapore, and the U.S., making the territory the world's second-largest source of loose pearls (after Australia which produces the smaller yellow pearls). By comparison, the combined export value of coconut oil, copra, mother of pearl shells, vanilla, fruit, and vegetables is paltry at around US$8 million.

Tourism

In general, two kinds of people visit Tahiti-Polynesia: packaged tourists on two-week trips from the States, Japan, or France, who book all their accommodations in advance, stay at the top hotels, and travel interisland by air; and independent budget travelers (often young Europeans), who have more time, find a place to stay upon arrival, and travel by boat as much as possible. Tahiti, Moorea, Huahine, Raiatea, and Bora Bora are popular among both groups for their combination of beaches, mountain scenery, easy access, and good facilities. The Society group is closely linked by sea and air, an island-hopper's playground.

Tourism only got underway with the opening of Faa'a Airport in 1961 and today Tahiti-Polynesia is second only to Fiji as a South Pacific tourist center, with 180,440 visitors in 1997, a quarter of them from France and another quarter from the United States. Japan, New Zealand, Germany, Italy, Britain, Canada, and New Caledonia also account for significant numbers. Even though flying from Los Angeles to Tahiti takes only three hours longer than flying to Honolulu, tourism is far less developed here than it is in Hawaii. A single Waikiki hotel could have more rooms than the entire island of Tahiti; Hawaii gets more visitors in 10 days than Tahiti-Polynesia gets in a year.

Miscalculations of distance and reports of high prices have kept Tahiti out of the American mass market, and high local labor costs have hampered development (the minimum wage is CFP 505 an hour). Now tourism by high-budget Japanese (especially honeymooners) is being vigorously promoted and the number of European visitors is growing quickly. The US$360 million a year generated by tourism covers 28% of Tahiti-Polynesia's import bill and provides thousands of jobs, but 80% of the things tourists buy are also imported.

Transnational corporations, either hotel chains, tour companies, or airlines, dominate the tourist industry. Top management of the big hotels is invariably French or foreign, as ownership rests with Japanese (Beachcomber Parkroyal, Bora Bora Lagoon, Kia Ora Village), French (Sofitel/Accor, Club Med, Méridien), and American (Bali Hai and Outrigger) corporations. Air New Zealand promotes Tahiti only as a stopover on the way to Auckland, limiting many tourists to a few nights in Papeete.

Many Polynesians are rather nervous about this transnational tourism development, and in June 1991 Moorea voters decided against a US$93.4 million Sheraton hotel and Arnold Palmer championship golf course that Japanese investors had wanted to build on their island. In May 1990 the traditional owners of Tupai, just north of Bora Bora, blocked the atoll's sale to a Japanese corporation that had intended to build a major resort there. On Tahiti, protest occupations by hundreds of Tahitians from April 1992 to January 1996 tried unsuccessfully to halt construction of Hôtel Le Méridien near the Museum of Tahiti in Punaauia. Tourism from Japan almost dried up during the 1995 nuclear testing but visitor levels are growing again.

In some cases quick resort development seems to have been at the expense of the environment. We've recently received complaints from readers about improper waste disposal on Tahiti, Huahine, and Bora Bora. An American reader sent us this:

We did some fantastic snorkeling until we discovered that we had swum right through the resort's raw sewage as it was piped out between the rocks in front of their beach. We figured this out after we both got sick— dizzy, weak, nauseous, and faint. Raw sewage was a recurring impediment to our enjoyment of Tahiti's gorgeous lagoons and it was disgusting to see how the big resorts (and probably local folks too) are undermining the islands' greatest treasure.

BUYING A BLACK PEARL

The relative newness of this gemstone is reflected in varying prices. A radiant, perfectly round, smooth, and flawless pearl with a good depth of metallic green/blue can sell for many times more than a similar pearl with only one or two defects. The luster is more important than the color. Size can vary from eight millimeters to 20 millimeters with the larger pearls that much more expensive. Black pearls are now in fashion in Paris, so don't expect any bargains. A first-class necklace can cost as much as US$50,000 and individual pearls of high quality cost US$1,000 and up, but slightly flawed pearls are much cheaper (beginning at US$100). The "baroque" pearls still make exquisite jewelry when mounted in gold and platinum.

Consider purchasing a loose pearl and having it mounted back home. If you think you might do this, check with your local jeweler before leaving for Tahiti. Half the fun is in the shopping, so be in no hurry to decide and don't let yourself be influenced by a driver or guide who may only be after a commission. If no guide is involved the shop may even pay the commission to you in the form of a discount (ask). It's preferable to buy pearls at a specialized shop rather than somewhere that also sells pareus and souvenirs (and never buy a pearl from a person on the street). A reputable dealer will always give you an invoice or certificate verifying the authenticity of your pearl. If you've made an expensive choice ask the dealer to make a fresh X-ray right in front of you in order to be sure of the quality.

the cover of an official brochure promoting tourism as a source of income for Tahiti-Polynesia

THE PEOPLE

The 1996 population of 219,521 is around 68% Polynesian, 11% European, 12% Polynesian/European, five percent Chinese, and three percent Polynesian/Chinese. All are French citizens. About 69% of the total population lives on Tahiti (compared to only 25% before the nuclear-testing boom began in the 1960s), but a total of 65 far-flung islands are inhabited.

The indigenous people of Tahiti-Polynesia are the Maohi or Eastern Polynesians (as opposed to the Western Polynesians in Samoa and Tonga), and some local nationalists refer to their country as Te Ao Maohi. The word *colon* formerly applied to Frenchmen who arrived long before the bomb and made a living as planters or traders, and practically all of them married Polynesian women. Most of these *colons* have already passed away and their descendants are termed *demis,* or *afa.* The present Europeans

are mostly recently arrived metropolitan French *(faranis).* Most *faranis* live in urban areas or are involved in the administration or military. Their numbers increased dramatically in the 1960s and 1970s. In contrast, very few Polynesians have migrated to France although 7,000 reside in New Caledonia.

Local Chinese *(tinito)* dominate the retail trade throughout the territory. In Papeete and Uturoa entire streets are lined with Chinese stores, and individual Chinese merchants are found on almost every island. During the American Civil War, when the supply of cotton to Europe was disrupted, Scotsman William Stewart decided to set up a cotton plantation on the south side of Tahiti. Unable to convince Tahitians to accept the heavy work, Stewart brought in a contingent of 1,010 Chinese laborers from Canton in 1865-66. When the war ended the enterprise went bankrupt, but many of the Chinese managed to stay on as market gardeners, hawkers, and opium dealers. Things began changing in 1964 when France recognized mainland China and granted French citizenship to the territory's Chinese (most other Tahitians had become French citizens right after WW II). The French government tried to assimilate the Chinese by requiring that they adopt French-sounding names and by closing all Chinese schools. Despite this, the Chinese community has remained distinct.

From 1976 to 1983 some 18,000 people migrated to the territory, 77% of them from France and another 13% from New Caledonia. Nearly 1,000 new settlers a year continue to arrive. Some 40,000 Europeans are now present in the territory, plus 8,000 soldiers, policemen, and transient officials. Most Tahitians would like to see this immigration restricted, as it is in virtually every other Pacific state. Yet with the integration of the European Union, all 370 million E.U. citizens may soon gain the right to live in Polynesia. French citizens even have a tax incentive to come since they become legal residents after six months and one day in the territory and are thus exempt from French income tax (in Tahiti-Polynesia the tax rate is only 2%).

There's an undercurrent of anti-French sentiment; English speakers are better liked by the Tahitians. Yet inevitably the newcomers get caught up in the Polynesian openness and friendliness—even the surliest Parisian. In fact, the Gallic charm you'll experience even in government offices is a delight. Tahiti-Polynesia really is a friendly place.

The New Class Structure

The creation of the Centre d'Expérimentations du Pacifique (CEP) in the early 1960s upset the economic and social equilibrium, drove up the cost of living, created artificial needs, and led to a migration toward Papeete. In 1962 46% of the labor force was engaged in fishing and agriculture. Since then there's been a massive shift to public and private services and about 80% of the working population of 58,000 are now employees. Of these, 40% work for the government, 40% in services, 11% in industry, and only eight percent in fishing and agriculture.

Civil servants in Tahiti-Polynesia get 84% higher salaries than their counterparts in France and pay only three percent income tax. There are generous expatriation benefits, and six months' paid leave is earned after three years. The minimum monthly wage in the territory is US$1,500 in the public sector, but only US$850 in the private sector. Living standards in Tahiti-Polynesia may be far higher than in the surrounding insular countries due to the subsidies, yet this expansion of wealth has created inequalities; also, the number of unemployed or underemployed is increasing. The gap between an affluent foreign clique and the impoverished Tahitian masses has created an explosive situation.

In October 1987 the French high commissioner used riot police flown in from Paris to suppress a dockworkers' strike, leading to serious rioting in Papeete and US$50 million in damage. The mayor of Papeete accused French officials of deliberately provoking the violence as a way of breaking the union, which handled cargo bound for the nuclear testing facilities. Most of those eventually convicted of looting were not strikers at all but unemployed Tahitian youths who took advantage of the disturbance to grab consumer goods. Fresh rioting in July 1991 forced the territorial government to cancel tax increases on gasoline, alcohol, and tobacco meant to cover a US$73.4 million budget deficit. The strikers said these levies placed an intolerable burden on Tahitian families and called for the imposition of income tax on salaries over US$3,000 a month instead. In the end France agreed to pick up part of the deficit bill to restore calm. Further rioting occurred in September 1995.

An estimated 20,000 poor, unemployed, and marginalized Tahitians live in *bidonvilles* or slums on the outskirts of Papeete. In the valley shanty-towns behind Papeete and Faa'a 10-15 Polynesians are crammed into each neat flower-decked plywood house. Many are children, as a government subsidy of US$50 per month per child encourages big families. Opportunities for young Tahitians with a taste for the consumer society are not adequate. Every year 3,000 young people turn 18 and begin competing for scarce jobs. The present social structure places *farani* officials at the top, followed by *demis* in the lower echelons of business and government, while *maohis* (indigenous people) work for wages or subsist at the bottom of the shredded social fabric.

Tahitian Life

For the French, lunch is the main meal of the day, followed by a siesta. Dinner may consist of leftovers from lunch. Tahitians traditionally eat their main meal of fish and native vegetables in the evening, when the day's work is over. People at home often take a shower before or after a meal and put flowers in their hair. Traditionally a flower behind the left ear means a person has a partner while a blossom behind the right ear means one is still looking. If folks are in a good mood a guitar or ukulele might appear.

Tahitians often observe with amusement or disdain the efforts of individuals to rise above the group. In a society where sharing and reciprocal generosity have traditionally been important qualities, the deliberate accumulation of personal wealth was always viewed as a vice. Now with the influx of government and tourist money, Tahitian life is changing, quickly in Papeete, more slowly in the outer islands. To prevent the Polynesians from being made paupers in their own country, foreigners other than French are not usually permitted to purchase land here and 85% of the land is still owned by the Polynesians. A new impoverished class is forming among those who have sold their ancestral lands to recent French immigrants.

The educational curriculum is entirely French. Children enter school at age three and for 12 years study the French language, literature, culture, history, and geography, but not much about

Polynesia. Although 80% of the population speaks Tahitian at home there is little formal training in it (teaching in Tahitian has only been allowed since 1984). The failure rate ranges 40-60%, and most of the rest of the children are behind schedule. The brightest students are given scholarships to continue studying, while many of the dropouts become delinquents. About a quarter of the schools are privately run by the churches, but these must teach exactly the same curriculum or lose their subsidies. The whole aim is to transform the Polynesians into Pacific French. In 1987 the Université française du Pacifique (B.P. 4635, 98713 Papeete; tel. 42-16-80, fax 41-01-31) opened on Tahiti, specializing in law, humanities, social sciences, languages, and science.

Most Tahitians live along the coast because the interior is too rugged and possibly inhabited by *tupapau* (ghosts). Some people leave a light on all night in their home for the latter reason. A traditional Tahitian residence consists of several separate buildings: the *fare tutu* (kitchen), the *fare tamaa* (dining area), the *fare taoto* (bedrooms), plus bathing and sanitary outhouses. Often several generations live together, and young children are sent to live with their grandparents. Adoption is commonplace and family relationships complex. Young Tahitians generally go out as groups, rather than on individual "dates."

The lifestyle may be summed up in the words *aita e peapea* (no problem) and *fiu* (fed up, bored). About the only time the normally languid Tahitians go really wild is when they're dancing or behind the wheel of a car.

Sex

Since the days of Wallis and Bougainville, Tahitian women have had a reputation for promiscuity. Well, for better or worse, this is largely a thing of the past, if it ever existed at all. As a short-term visitor your liaisons with Tahitians are likely to remain polite. Westerners' obsession with the sexuality of Polynesians usually reflects their own frustrations, and the view that Tahitian morality is loose is rather ironic considering that Polynesians have always shared whatever they have, cared for their old and young, and refrained from ostracizing unwed mothers or attaching stigma to their offspring. The good Christian Tahitians of today are highly moral and compassionate.

a Polynesian vahine

ARCHIVES NATIONALES, SECTION OUTRE-MER, FRANCE

Polynesia's *mahus* or "third sex" bear little of the stigma attached to female impersonators in the West. A young boy may adopt the female role by his own choice or that of his parents, performing female tasks at home and eventually finding a job usually performed by women, such as serving in a restaurant or hotel. Generally only one *mahu* exists in each village or community, proof that this type of individual serves a certain sociological function. George Mortimer of the British ship *Mercury* recorded an encounter with a *mahu* in 1789. Though Tahitians may poke fun at a *mahu,* they're fully accepted in society, seen teaching Sunday school, etc. Many, but not all, *mahus* are also homosexuals. Today, with money all-important, some transvestites have involved themselves in male prostitution and the term *raerae* has been coined for this category. Now there are even Miss Tane (Miss Male) beauty contests! All this may be seen as the degradation of a phenomenon that has always been a part of Polynesian life.

Religion

Though the old Polynesian religion died out in the early 19th century, the Tahitians are still a strongly religious people. Protestant missionaries arrived on Tahiti 39 years before the Catholics and 47 years before the Mormons, so almost half of the Polynesians now belong to the Evangelical Church, which is strongest in the Austral and Leeward Islands. Until the middle of the 20th century this church was one of the only democratic institutions in the colony and it continues to exert strong influence on social matters (for example, it has resolutely opposed nuclear testing).

Of the 35% of the total population who are Catholic, half are Polynesians from the Tuamotus and Marquesas, and the other half are French. Another eight percent are Seventh-Day Adventists and seven percent are Mormons. A Mormon group called Sanitos, which rejects Brigham Young as a second prophet, has had a strong following in the Tuamotus since the 19th century. Several other Christian sects are also represented, and some Chinese are Buddhists. It's not unusual to see two or three different churches in a village of 100 people. All the main denominations operate their own schools. Local ministers and priests are powerful figures in the outer-island communities. One vestige of the pre-Christian religion is a widespread belief in ghosts *(tupapau)*.

Protestant church services are conducted mostly in Tahitian, Catholic services are in French. Sitting through one (one to two hours) is often worthwhile just to hear the singing and to observe the women's hats. Never wear a pareu to church—you'll be asked to leave. Young missionaries from the Church of Latter-day Saints (Mormons) continue to flock to Polynesia from the U.S. for two-year stays. They wear short-sleeved white shirts with ties and travel in pairs—you may spot a couple.

The most sinister religious development in recent years occurred on Faaite atoll in the Tuamotus in early September 1987. A pair of self-proclaimed fundamentalist crusaders from the "charismatic renewal movement" managed to instill such intense revivalist fervor in the villagers that six people were actually burned to death, some by their own children, to exorcise "devils" that threatened the island with disaster. A radio alert brought the mayor and a Catholic priest to the scene just in time to prevent another four "impure souls" from being sacrificed to the "healing" fire. In 1990 24 Faaite villagers were found guilty of the act, and ringleader François Mauati was sentenced to 14 years of imprisonment.

Language

French is spoken throughout the territory, and visitors will sometimes have difficulty making themselves understood in English, although most of those involved in the tourist industry speak some English. Large Chinese stores often have someone who speaks English, though members of the Chinese community use Hakka among themselves. Young Polynesians often become curious and friendly when they hear you speaking English. Still, unless you're on a package tour everything will be a lot easier if you know at least a little French. Check out some French language recordings from your local public library to brush up your high school French before you arrive. The "Capsule French Vocabulary" at the end of this book may also help you get by. (It's often the recently arrived French immigrants who are the most arrogant, a reflection of the way monolingual English-speakers are treated in France itself.)

Tahitian has been recognized as an official language alongside French only since 1980. Contemporary Tahitian is the chiefly or royal dialect used in the translation of the Bible by early Protestant missionaries, and today, as communications improve, the outer-island dialects are becoming mingled with the predominant Tahitian. Tahitian or Maohi is one of a family of Austronesian languages spoken from Madagascar through Indonesia, all the way to Easter Island and Hawaii. The related languages of Eastern Polynesia (Hawaiian, Tahitian, Tuamotuan, Mangarevan, Marquesan, Rarotongan, Maori) are quite different from those of Western Polynesia (Samoan, Tongan). Among the Polynesian languages the consonants did the changing rather than the vowels. The k and l in Hawaiian are generally rendered as a t and r in Tahitian.

Instead of attempting to speak French to the Tahitians—a foreign language for you both—turn to the Tahitian vocabulary at the end of this book and give it a try. Remember to pronounce each vowel separately, a as the *ah* in "far," e as the *ai* in "day," i as the *ee* in "see," o as the *oh* in "go," and u as the *oo* in "lulu"—the same as in Latin or Spanish. Written Tahitian has only eight consonants: *f, h, m, n, p, r, t, v.* Two consonants never follow one another, and all words end in a vowel. No silent letters exist in Tahitian, but there is a glottal stop, often marked with an apostrophe. A slight variation in pronunciation or vowel length can change the meaning of a word completely, so don't be surprised if your efforts produce some unexpected results!

Some of the many English words that have entered Tahitian through contact with early seamen include: *faraipani* (frying pan), *manua* (man of war), *matete* (market), *mati* (match), *moni* (money), *oniani* (onion), *painapo* (pineapple), *pani* (pan), *pata* (butter), *pipi* (peas), *poti* (boat), *taiete* (society), *tapitana* (captain), *tauera* (towel), and *tavana* (governor).

Writer Pierre Loti was impressed by the mystical vocabulary of Tahitian:

The sad, weird, mysterious utterances of nature: the scarcely articulate stirrings of fancy. . . . Faa-fano: *the departure of the soul at death.* Aa: *happiness, earth, sky, paradise.* Mahoi: *essence or soul of God.* Tapetape: *the line where the sea grows deep.* Tutai: *red clouds on the horizon.* Ari: *depth, emptiness, a wave of the sea.* Po: *night, unknown dark world, Hell.*

CONDUCT AND CUSTOMS

The dress code in Tahiti-Polynesia is very casual—you can even go around barefoot. Cleanliness *is* important, however. Formal wear or jacket and tie are unnecessary (unless you're to be received by the high commissioner!). One exception is downtown Papeete, where scanty dress would be out of place. For clothing tips, see **What to Take** in the main introduction.

People usually shake hands when meeting; visitors are expected to shake hands with everyone present. If a Polynesian man's hand is dirty he'll extend his wrist or elbow. Women kiss each other on the cheeks. When entering a private residence it's polite to remove your shoes. It's okay to show interest in the possessions of a host, but don't lavish too much praise on any single object or he/she may feel obligated to give it to you. It's rude to refuse food offered by a Tahitian, but don't eat everything on your plate just to be polite, as this will be a signal to your host that you want another helping. Often guests in a private home are expected to eat while the family watches.

All the beaches of Tahiti-Polynesia are public to one meter above the high-tide mark, although some watchdogs don't recognize this. Topless sunbathing is completely legal in Tahiti-Polynesia and commonly practiced at resorts by European tourists, though total nudity is only practiced on offshore *motu* and floating pontoons.

Despite the apparent laissez-faire attitude promoted in the travel brochures and this book, female travelers should take care: there have been sexual assaults by Polynesian men on foreign women. Peeping toms can be a nuisance both in budget accommodations and on beaches away from the main resorts, and women should avoid staying alone in isolated tourist bungalows or camping outside organized campgrounds. A California reader who was there in September 1998 sent us this:

My friend and I must have been unusual looking travelers. Though we dressed in pants and baggy clothes when we had to go to town, our age (we're both 26) and not unattractive appearance drew some very undesirable attention. Video rental stores are a common sight here and the local men seem to have developed ideas about what white women are after from watching blue movies. So we found ourselves being threatened time and again by aggressive local men. On Bora Bora we took an all-day outrigger trip and found ourselves left alone with the guides in the afternoon. We didn't know how to cancel at that point, so we were taken to a motu *for lunch. The two male guides extended our time on the* motu *so long that we were both sunburnt despite 45 block and entirely missed the afternoon activities we had paid for. At 1530 we had to insist they bring us back to shore. We didn't panic on the* motu *and escaped unhurt, but I think it is essential that you include a caution for all single women traveling in Tahiti to make sure there are other guests, including couples* or men, on these daytrips before putting themselves in the hands of strangers. We had to forego any future island trips, including safaris, for fear of the guides themselves. Based on our experience I would say that for women, even in pairs, things like hiking, hitchhiking, or walking along the road should not be taken lightly. The harassment continued even in very rural parts of the islands and we had to learn to be very unfriendly, even rude, to keep men from aggressively entering our space/lives. Our joke came to be, "women wandering alone?—must be looking for sex," as this was definitely the local male mindset and it was evidenced by the fact that young Tahitian women were never seen walking around away from their parent's homes, but young men were everywhere. Even at the main resorts we had problems with the entertainment staff hitting on us every time we went to a show. On Moorea we'd booked a charming beach fare and spent a positively terrible first night there. The locks on our unit were unreliable and we were soon discovered by the local men, several of whom began to slink around quietly behind our bungalow or watch us from the shadows at the corner of the beach. As it got dark, we kept hearing people standing directly outside our bungalow or darting past our windows. It was terrifying and we slept in shifts, barricading the door and arming ourselves as best we could. It wasn't until 0400 that the bastards finally left the area. There was no other reason they should have been there— a wall was directly behind the place and only other guests slept nearby. I'm sure we were targeted for more than theft. The next morning we insisted on having our deposit back and moved to the Sofitel Ia Ora where we felt safe, although the motu guides there still did their best to get us into their boats (we began to call that the motu scam). I think women visitors are best not even saying hello to men who approach them here— rudeness seems to be the only reaction that does not signal the wrong thing. Don't think we didn't see the humor in some of this and make the most of our stay—but it would have been helpful if we'd known about it beforehand from your book.

In addition to the situation outlined above, we've heard of cases of laundry being stolen from the line, hotel and car break-ins, park muggings, and even mass holdups at knifepoint, but luckily such things are still the exception here and it's highly unlikely you'll become a victim of armed robbery. Do keep an eye on your valuables, however.

ON THE ROAD

Highlights

Tahiti-Polynesia abounds in things to see and do, including many in the "not to be missed" category. Papeete's colorful morning market and captivating waterfront welcome you to Polynesia. Travelers should not pass up the opportunity to take the ferry ride to Moorea and see the island's stunning Opunohu Valley, replete with splendid scenery, lush vegetation, and fascinating archaeological sites. Farther afield, an even greater concentration of old Polynesian *marae* (temples) awaits visitors to Maeva on the enchanting island of Huahine. The natural wonders of Bora Bora have been applauded many times, but neighboring Maupiti offers more of the same, though its pleasures are less well known. Polynesia's most spectacular atoll may be Rangiroa, where the Avatoru and Tiputa passes offer exciting snorkel rides on the tide flows. The shark feeding and manta ray viewing on Rangiroa, Bora Bora, and other islands, and dolphin encounters on Moorea, are memorable experiences.

Sports and Recreation

As elsewhere in the South Pacific, **scuba diving** is the most popular sport among visitors, and well-established dive shops exist on Tahiti, Moorea, Huahine, Raiatea, Bora Bora, Rangiroa, Manihi, Tikehau, Fakarava, and Nuku Hiva. The best coral and marinelife viewing by far is available in the Tuamotus and serious divers won't go wrong by choosing Rangiroa, the shark-viewing capital of Polynesia. In the warm waters of Polynesia wetsuits are not required. If you take a scuba certification course make sure it's PADI accredited as the French CMAS certification may not be recognized elsewhere.

There's good **surfing** around Tahiti, Moorea, Huahine, and Raiatea, usually hurricane swells on the north shores Oct.-March (summer) and Antarctic swells on the south shores from April-Sept. (winter). The summer swells are the same ones that hit Hawaii three or four days earlier and the reef breaks off the north shore of Moorea work better than Tahiti's beach breaks. The most powerful, hollow waves are in winter. The reef breaks in the passes are a lot longer paddle than those off the beach (where you can expect lots of company).

Excellent, easily accessible **hiking** areas exist on Tahiti, Moorea, and Nuku Hiva. **Horseback riding** is readily available on Moorea, Huahine, Raiatea, and in the Marquesas with the Huahine and Raiatea operations especially recommended. **Golfers** will certainly want to complete all 18 holes at the International Golf Course Olivier Breaud on Tahiti, the territory's only major course. The Society Islands are a sailor's paradise with numerous protected anchorages and excellent **sailing** weather, which is why most of Tahiti-Polynesia's charter yacht operations are concentrated on Raiatea.

Entertainment

The big hotels on Tahiti, Moorea, Huahine, and Bora Bora offer exciting dance shows several nights a week. They're usually accompanied by a barbecue or traditional feast, but if the price asked for the meal is too steep, settle for a drink at the bar and enjoy the show (no cover charge). Many of the regular performances are listed in this book, but be sure to call the hotel to confirm the time and date as these do change to accommodate tour groups.

On Friday and Saturday nights discos crank up in most towns and these are good places to meet the locals. The nonhotel bar scene is limited mostly to Papeete and Uturoa. The drinking age in Tahiti-Polynesia is officially 18, but it's not strictly enforced.

Music and Dance

Though the missionaries banned dancing completely in the 1820s and the 19th-century French colonial administration only allowed performances that didn't disturb Victorian decorum, traditional Tahitian dancing experienced a revival in the 1950s with the formation of Madeleine Moua's Pupu Heiva dance troupe, followed in the 1960s by Coco Hotahota's Temaeva and Gilles Hollande's Ora Tahiti. These groups rediscovered the near-forgotten myths of old Polynesia and popularized them with exciting music, dance, song, and costumes. During major festivals several dozen troupes consisting of 20-50 dancers and 6-10 musicians participate in thrilling competitions.

The Tahitian *tamure* or *'ori Tahiti* is a fast, provocative, erotic dance done by rapidly shifting the weight from one foot to the other. The rubber-legged men are almost acrobatic, though their movements tend to follow those of the women closely. The tossing, shell-decorated fiber skirts *(mores)*, the hand-held pandanus wands, and the tall headdresses add to the drama.

Dances such as the *aparima, 'ote'a,* and *hivinau* reenact Polynesian legends, and each movement tells part of a story. The *aparima* is a dance resembling the Hawaiian hula or Samoan siva executed mainly with the hands in a standing or sitting position. The hand movements repeat the story told in the accompanying song. The *'ote'a* is a theme dance executed to the accompaniment of drums with great precision and admirable timing by a group of men and/or women arrayed in two lines. The *ute* is a restrained dance based on ancient refrains.

Listen to the staccato beat of the *to'ere,* a slit rosewood drum, each slightly different in size and pitch, hit with a stick. A split-bamboo drum *(ofe)* hit against the ground often provides a contrasting sound. The *pahu* is a more conventional bass drum made from a hollowed coconut tree trunk with a sharkskin cover. Its sound resembles the human heartbeat. The smallest *pahu* is the *fa'atete,* which is hit with sticks. Another traditional Polynesian musical instrument is the bamboo nose flute *(vivo),* which sounds rather like the call of a bird, though today guitars and ukuleles are more often seen. The ukulele was originally the *braguinha,* brought to Hawaii by Portuguese immigrants a century ago. Homemade ukuleles with the half-shells of coconuts as sound boxes emit pleasant tones, while those sporting empty tins give a more metallic sound. The hollow, piercing note produced by the conch shell or *pu* once accompanied pagan ceremonies on the *marae.*

Traditional Tahitian vocal music was limited to polyphonic chants conveying oral history and customs, and the contrapuntal *himene* or "hymn" sung by large choirs today is based on those ancient chants. The spiritual quality of the *himene* can be electrifying, so for the musical experience of a lifetime, attend church any Sunday.

Stone Fishing

This traditional method of fishing is now practiced only on very special occasions in the Leeward Islands. Coconut fronds are tied end to end until a line a half-km long is ready. Several dozen outrigger canoes form a semicircle. Advancing slowly together, men in the canoes beat the water with stones tied to ropes. The frightened fish are thus driven toward a beach. When the water is shallow enough, the men leap from their canoes, push the leaf line before them, yell, and beat the water with their hands. In this way the fish are literally forced ashore into an open bamboo fence, where they are caught. See **Taha'a** for more information.

Public Holidays and Festivals

Public holidays in Tahiti-Polynesia include New Year's Day (1 January), Gospel Day (5 March), Good Friday and Easter Monday (March/April), Labor Day (1 May), Victory Day (8 May), Ascension Day (May), Pentecost or Whitmonday (May/June), Internal Autonomy Day (29 June), Bastille Day (14 July), Assumption Day (15 August), All Saints' Day (1 November), Armistice Day (11 November), and Christmas Day (25 December). Ironically, Internal Autonomy Day really commemorates 29 June 1880 when King Pomare V was deposed and Tahiti-Polynesia became a full French colony, not 6 September 1984 when the territory achieved a degree of internal autonomy. *Everything* will be closed on these holidays (and maybe also the days before and after—ask).

The big event of the year is the two-week-long **Heiva i Tahiti,** which runs from the end of June to Bastille Day (14 July). Formerly known as La Fête du Juillet or the Tiurai Festival (the Tahitian word *tiurai* comes from the English July), the Heiva originated way back in 1882. Today it brings contestants and participants to Tahiti from all over the territory to take part in elaborate processions, competitive dancing and singing, feasting, and partying. There are bicycle, car, horse, and outrigger-canoe races, petanque, archery, and javelin-throwing contests, fire walking, sidewalk bazaars, arts and crafts exhibitions, tattooing, games, and joyous carnivals. **Bastille Day** itself, which marks the fall of the Bastille in Paris on 14 July 1789 at the height of the French Revolution, features a military parade in the capital. Ask at the Papeete tourist office about when to see the historical reenactments at Marae Arahurahu, the canoe race along Papeete waterfront, horse racing at the Pirae track, and the traditional dance competitions at the Moorea ferry landing. Tickets to most Heiva events are sold at the Cultural Center in Papeete or at the door. As happens during carnival in Rio de Janeiro, you must pay to sit in the stands and watch the best performances, but acceptable seats begin at just CFP 500 and you get four hours or more of unforgettable nonstop entertainment.

The July celebrations on Bora Bora are as good as those on Tahiti, and festivals are also held on Raiatea and Taha'a at that time. Note that all ships, planes, and hotels are fully booked around 14 July, so be in the right place beforehand or get firm reservations, especially if you want to be on Bora Bora that day. At this time of year, races, games, and dance competitions take place on many different islands, and the older women prove themselves graceful dancers and excellent singers.

Chinese New Year in January or February is celebrated with dances and fireworks. **World Environment Day** (5 June) is marked by guided excursions to Tahiti's interior and on the following weekend special activities are arranged at tourist sites around the island. The **Agricultural Fair** on Tahiti in mid-August involves the construction of a Tahitian village. The **Carnival** parade through Papeete is held at the end of October. On **All Saints' Day** (1 November) when the locals illuminate the cemeteries at Papeete, Arue, Punaauia, and elsewhere with candles. On **New Year's Eve** the Papeete waterfront is beautifully illuminated and there's a seven-km foot race. For advance information on special events and sporting competitions contact **Tahiti Manava** (B.P. 1710, 98713 Papeete; tel. 50-57-12, fax 45-16-78).

Major Sporting Events

The **Moorea Blue Marathon** has been held every February since 1988 (in 1997 Patrick Muturi of Kenya set the record time of two hours and 21.5 minutes). A traditional Maohi sports festival in late April features javelin throwing, rock lifting, coconut tree climbing, coconut husking, races while carrying loads of fruit, etc. Triathlons involving swimming, bicycling, and running are held on Moorea in April and May. The **Tahiti Open** at the Atimaono golf course on Tahiti is in July. The **Te Aito** individual outrigger canoe race is held on Tahiti around the end of July. The **Hawaiki Nui Va'a** outrigger canoe race in early November is a stirring three-day event with canoe teams crossing from Huahine to Raiatea the first day, Raiatea to Taha'a the second, and Taha'a to Bora Bora the third.

Shopping

Most local souvenir shops sell Marquesas-style wooden "tikis" carved from wood or stone. The original Tiki was a god of fertility, and really old tikis are still shrouded in superstition. Today they're viewed mainly as good luck charms and often come decorated with mother-of-pearl. Other items carved from wood include mallets (to beat tapa cloth), *umete* bowls, and slit *to'ere* drums. Carefully woven pandanus hats and mats come from the Australs. Other curios to buy include hand-carved mother-of-pearl shell, sharks'-tooth pendants, hematite (black stone) carvings, and bamboo fishhooks.

Black-pearl jewelry is widely available throughout Tahiti-Polynesia. The color, shape, weight, and size of the pearl are important. The darkest pearls are the most valuable. Prices vary considerably, so shop around before purchasing pearls.

As this is a French colony, it's not surprising that many of the best buys are related to fashion. A tropical shirt, sundress, or T-shirt is a purchase of immediate usefulness. The pareu is a typically Tahitian leisure garment consisting of a brightly colored hand-blocked or painted local fabric about two meters long and a meter wide. There are dozens of ways both men and women can wear a pareu and it's the most common apparel for local women throughout the territory, including Papeete, so pick one up! Local cosmetics like Monoï Tiare Tahiti, a fragrant coconut-oil skin moisturizer, and coconut-oil soap will put you in form. Jasmine shampoo, cologne, and perfume are also made locally from the tiare Tahiti flower. Vanilla is used to flavor coffee.

Early missionaries introduced the Tahitians to quilting, and two-layer patchwork *tifaifai* have now taken the place of tapa (bark cloth). Used as bed covers and pillows by tourists, *tifaifai* is still used by Tahitians to cloak newlyweds and to cover coffins. To be wrapped in a *tifaifai* is the highest honor. Each woman has individual quilt patterns that are her trademarks and bold floral designs are popular, with contrasting colors drawn from nature. A good *tifaifai* can take up to six months to complete and cost US$1,000. The French artist Henri Matisse, who in 1930 spent several weeks at the now-demolished Hôtel Stuart on Papeete's boulevard Pomare, was so impressed by the Tahitian *tifaifai* that he applied the same technique and adopted many designs for his *"gouaches découpees."*

Those who have been thrilled by hypnotic Tahitian music and dance will want to take some Polynesian music home with them on cassette (CFP 2,000) or compact disc (CFP 3,000), available at hotels and souvenir shops throughout the islands. The largest local company producing these CDs is Editions Manuiti or Tamure Records (B.P. 755, 98713 Papeete; tel. 42-82-39, fax 43-27-24). Among the well-known local singers and musicians appearing on Manuiti are Bimbo, Charley Mauu, Guy Roche, Yves Roche, Emma Terangi, Andy Tupaia, and Henriette Winkler. Small Tahitian groups like the Moorea Lagon Kaina Boys, the Barefoot Boys, and Tamarii Punaruu, and large folkloric ensembles such as Maeva Tahiti, Tiare Tahiti, and Coco's Temaeva (often recorded at major festivals) are also well represented. The Tahitian recordings of the Hawaiian artist Bobby Holcomb are highly recommended. Turn to **Resources** at the end of this book for specific CD listings.

Hustling and bargaining are not practiced in Tahiti-Polynesia: it's expensive for everyone. Haggling may even be considered insulting, so just pay the price asked or keep looking. Many local food prices are subsidized by the government. You can sometimes avoid whopping markups and taxes by purchasing food and handicrafts from the producers themselves at markets or roadside stalls.

ACCOMMODATIONS AND FOOD

Accommodations
A wise government regulation prohibiting buildings higher than a coconut tree outside Papeete means that most of the hotels are low-rise or consist of small Tahitian *fare*. As the lagoon waters off the northwest corner of Tahiti become increasingly polluted with raw sewage, hotels like the Beachcomber and Maeva Beach fall back on their swimming pools. On most of the outer islands open to foreign tourists, the water is so clear it makes pools superfluous.

Hotel prices range from CFP 800 for a dormitory bed all the way up to CFP 70,000 single or double without meals, plus tax. Price wars often erupt between rival hotels, and at times you're charged less than the prices quoted herein! When things are really slow even the luxury hotels sometimes discount their rooms. If your hotel can't provide running water, electricity, air-conditioning, or something similar because of a hurricane or otherwise, ask for a price reduction. You'll often get 10% off. The budget places often provide cooking facilities; this allows you to save a lot on food.

A eight percent room tax used to finance tourism promotion is added to the room rates at the hotels (never included in the quoted price), but it doesn't apply to pensions and family-operated accommodations. Some islands such as Moorea and Bora Bora add a room tax of CFP 150 pp per day to accommodation bills to cover municipal services. Many small hotels add a surcharge to your bill if you stay only one night and some charge a supplement during the high seasons (July, August, and around Christmas). Discounts may be offered during the low months of February, March, September, and October.

A tent saves the budget traveler a lot of money and proves very convenient to fall back on. The Polynesians don't usually mind if you camp, and quite a few French locals also have tents. Regular campgrounds exist on Moorea, Huahine, Raiatea, and Bora Bora, catering to the growing number of camper-tourists. On Rangiroa it's possible to camp at certain small hotels (listed herein). On the outer islands camping should be no problem, but ask permission of the landowner, or pitch your tent well out of sight of the road. Please ensure this same hospitality for the next traveler by not leaving a mess. Make sure your tent is water- and mosquito-proof, and never pitch a tent directly below coconuts hanging from a tree or a precariously leaning trunk.

Paying Guests
A unique accommodations option worth looking into is the well-organized homestay program, in

which you get a private room or bungalow with a local family. *Logement chez l'habitant* is available on all the outer islands, and even in Papeete itself; the tourist office supplies printed lists. Many travel agents abroad won't book the cheaper hotels or lodgings with the inhabitants because no commissions are paid, but you can make reservations directly with the owners themselves either by mail or phone. Letters are usually not answered, so calling ahead from Papeete is best; things change fast and the printed listings are often out of date. One Papeete travel agency specializing in such bookings is **Tekura Tahiti Travel** (B.P. 2971, 98713 Papeete; tel. 43-12-00, fax 42-84-60, e-mail: go@tahiti-tekuratravel.com) in Papeete's Vaima Center, although they tend to work with the more upmarket places. Most pensions don't accept credit cards, and English may not be spoken.

These private guesthouses can be hard to locate. There's usually no sign outside, and some don't cater to walk-in clients who show up unexpectedly. Also, the limited number of beds in each may all be taken. Sometimes you'll get air-port transfers at no additional charge if you book ahead. Don't expect hot water in the shower or a lot of privacy. Blankets and especially towels may not be provided. Often meals are included (typically seafood), which can make these places quite expensive. If you're on a budget, ask for a place with cooking facilities and prepare your own food. The family may loan you a bicycle and can be generally helpful in arranging tours, etc. It's a great way to meet the people while finding a place to stay.

In really remote areas residents are often very hospitable and may offer to put you up. Try to find some tangible way to show your apprecia-tion, such as paying for the groceries or giving a gift. It wouldn't hurt to offer cash payment if a stranger helps you when you're in a jam. Once you get home, don't forget to mail prints of any photos you've taken. If you do make friends on one island, ask them to write you a letter of in-troduction to their relatives on another.

Food and Drink

The restaurants are often exorbitant, but you can bring the price way down by ordering only a single main dish. Fresh bread and cold water come with the meal. Avoid appetizers, alcohol, and desserts. No service charges are tacked on, and tipping is unnecessary. So it's really not as expensive as it looks! US$15 will usually see you through an excellent no-frills lunch of fried fish at a small French restaurant. The same thing in a deluxe hotel dining room will be about 50% more. Even the finest places are afford-able if you order this way.

Most restaurants post their menu in the win-dow. If not, have a look at it before sitting down. Check the main plates, as that's all you'll need to take. If the price is right, the ambience congenial, and local French are at the tables, sit right down. Sure, food at a snack bar would be half as much, but your Coke will be extra, and in the end it's smart to pay a little more to enjoy excellent cui-sine once in a while. Steer clear of restaurants where you see a big plastic bottle of mineral water on every table, as this will add a couple of hundred francs to your bill. Also beware of set meals designed for tourists, as these usually cost double the average entree. If you can't order à la carte walk back out the door.

Local restaurants offer French, Chinese, Viet-namese, Italian, and, of course, Tahitian dishes. The *nouvelle cuisine Tahitienne* is a combination of European and Asian recipes, with local seafoods and vegetables, plus the classic *maa Tahiti* (Tahitian food). The French are famous for their sauces, so try something exotic. Lunch is the main meal of the day in Tahiti-Polynesia, and many restaurants offer a *plat du jour* de-signed for regular customers. This is often dis-played on a blackboard near the entrance and is usually good value. Most restaurants stop serv-ing lunch at 1400, dinner at 2200. Don't expect snappy service: what's the rush, anyway?

If it's all too expensive, groceries are a good al-ternative. There are lots of nice places to pic-nic, and at CFP 40 a loaf, that crisp French white bread is incredibly cheap and good. French *baguettes* are subsidized by the government, unlike that awful sliced white bread in a plastic package, which is CFP 250 a loaf! Cheap red wines like Selection Faragui are imported from France in bulk and bottled locally in plastic bot-tles. Add a nice piece of French cheese to the above and you're ready for a budget traveler's banquet. *Casse-croûtes* are big healthy sand-wiches made with those long French baguettes at about CFP 250—a bargain.

HINANO BEER

The Brasserie de Tahiti was launched in 1914 and for the next 39 years the denizens of Polynesia were able to quench their thirst with a brew known as Aorai. The operation underwent a major modernization in 1955, and the hearty Hinano of today was born to the delight of beer drinkers. Since 1976 the Tahiti brewery has received technical support from the Dutch brewer Heineken whose beer is bottled in Papeete under license. A non-alcoholic beer called Vaitia was first produced in 1982, and in 1992 the Hei-Lager light beer was added to the line. Hei-Lager Gold followed in 1994. The computer-controlled cannery that opened on Tahiti in 1989 has made it possible to export canned Hinano to beer connoisseurs around the world. At present the company produces over 30 million liters of Hinano a year, and can fill 32,000 bottles and 22,000 cans an hour. It's one of the world's great beers.

There's also Martinique rum and Hinano beer (CFP 140 in grocery stores), brewed locally by the Brasserie de Tahiti. Founded in 1914, this company's first beer was called Aorai and today they produce Heineken as well as Hinano. Remember the deposit on Hinano beer bottles (CFP 30/60 on small/large bottles), which makes beer cheap to buy cold and carry out. Supermarkets aren't allowed to sell alcohol after 1700 daily or on Sunday or holidays (stock your fridge in the morning).

Moorea's famous Rotui fruit drinks are sold in tall liter containers in a variety of types. The tastiest is perhaps *pamplemousse* (grapefruit), produced from local Moorea fruit, but the pineapple juice is also outstanding. At about CFP 250 a carton, they're excellent value. At CFP 100, bottled Eau Royale mineral water is also quite cheap.

If you're going to the outer islands, take as many edibles with you as possible; it's always more expensive there. Keep in mind that virtually every food plant you see growing on the islands is cultivated by someone. Even fishing floats or seashells washed up on a beach, or fish in the lagoon near someone's home, may be considered private property.

Tahitian Food

If you can spare the cash, attend a Tahitian *tamaaraa* (feast) at a big hotel and try some Polynesian dishes roasted in an *ahimaa* (underground oven). Basalt stones are preheated with a wood fire in a meter-deep pit, then covered with leaves. Each type of food is wrapped separately in banana leaves to retain its own flavor and lowered in. The oven is covered with more banana leaves, wet sacking, and sand, and left one to three hours to bake: suckling pig, mahimahi, taro, *umara* (sweet potato), *uru* (breadfruit), and *fafa,* a spinachlike cooked vegetable made from taro tops.

Also sample the gamy flavor of *fei,* the red cooking banana that flourishes in Tahiti's uninhabited interior. The Tahitian chestnut tree *(mape)* grows near streams and the delicious cooked nuts can often be purchased at markets. *Miti hue* is a coconut-milk sauce fermented with the juice of river shrimp. Traditionally *ma'a Tahiti* is eaten with the fingers.

Poisson cru (ia ota), small pieces of raw bonito (skipjack) or yellowfin marinated with lime juice and soaked in coconut milk, is enjoyable, as is *fafaru* ("smelly fish"), prepared by marinating pieces of fish in seawater in an airtight coconut-shell container. As with the durian, although the smell is repugnant, the first bite can be addicting. Other typical Tahitian plates are chicken and pork casserole with *fafa,* pork and cabbage casserole *(pua'a chou),* and goat cooked in ginger.

Po'e is a sticky sweet pudding made of starchy banana, papaya, taro, or pumpkin flour, flavored with vanilla, and topped with coconut-milk sauce. Many varieties of this treat are made throughout Polynesia. *Faraoa ipo* is Tuamotu coconut bread. The local coffee is flavored with vanilla bean and served with sugar and coconut cream.

SERVICES AND INFORMATION

Visas and Officialdom

Everyone other than French citizens needs a passport. French are admitted freely for an un-limited stay, and citizens of the European Union (E.U.) countries, Australia, Norway, and Switzerland, get three months without a visa. Citizens of the United States, Canada, New Zealand, Japan, and 13 other countries can obtain a one-month stay free upon arrival at Papeete. If you require a visa, make sure the words *valable pour la Polynésie Française* are endorsed on the visa as visas for France are not accepted.

Extensions of stay are possible after you arrive, but they cost CFP 3,000 and you'll have to go to the post office to buy a stamp. You'll also

BREADFRUIT

The breadfruit *(uru)* is the plant most often associated with the South Pacific. The theme of a man turning himself into such a tree to save his family during famine often recurs in Polynesian legends. Ancient voyagers brought breadfruit shoots or seeds from Southeast Asia. When baked in an underground oven or roasted over flames, the fruit of the now-seedless Polynesian variety resembles bread. Joseph Banks, botanist on Captain Cook's first voyage, wrote:

If a man should in the course of his lifetime plant 10 trees, which if well done might take the labor of an hour or thereabouts, he would completely fulfill his duty to his own as well as future generations.

The French naturalist Sonnerat transplanted breadfruit to Reunion in the Indian Ocean as early as 1772, but it's Captain William Bligh who shall always be remembered when the plant is mentioned. In 1787 Bligh set out to collect young shoots in Tahiti for transfer to the West Indies, where they were to be planted to feed slaves. On the way back, his crew mutinied in Tongan waters and cast off both breadfruit and Bligh. The indomitable captain managed to reach Dutch Timor in a rowboat and in 1792 returned to Tahiti with another ship to complete his task.

The breadfruit *(Artocarpus altilis)*, a tall tree with broad green leaves, provides shade as well as food. A well-watered tree can produce as many as 1,000 pale green breadfruits a year. Robert Lee Eskridge described a breadfruit thus:

Its outer rind or skin, very hard, is covered with a golf-ball-like surface of small irregular pits or tiny hollows. An inner rind about a half-inch thick surrounds the fruit itself, which when baked tastes not unlike a doughy potato. Perhaps fresh bread, rolled up until it becomes a semifirm mass, best describes the breadfruit when cooked.

The starchy, easily digested fruit is rich in vitamin B. When consumed with a protein such as fish or meat it serves as an energy food. The Polynesians learned to preserve breadfruit by pounding it into a paste, which was kept in leaf-lined pits to ferment into *mahi*. Like the coconut, the breadfruit tree itself had many uses, including the provision of wood for outrigger canoes.

breadfruit (Artcarpus altilis)

DIANA LASICH HARPER

FRENCH CONSULATES GENERAL

Australia: St. Martin's Tower, 31 Market St., Sydney, NSW 2000 (tel. 61-2/9261-5779); 492 St. Kilda Rd., Melbourne, Victoria 3004 (tel. 61-3/9820-0921); 6 Perth Ave., Yarralumla, Canberra, ACT 2600 (tel. 61-2/6216-0100, fax 61-2/6216-0127, www.france.net.au/official)

Canada: French consulates general are found in Moncton, Montreal, Ottawa, Quebec, Toronto, and Vancouver.

Chile: Ave. Condell 65, Providencia, Santiago de Chile (tel. 56-2/225-1030, fax 56-2/274-1353)

Fiji: Dominion House, Thomson St., Private Mail Bag, Suva (tel. 679/300-991, fax 679/301-894)

Hawaii: 1099 Alakea St., 18th Floor, Honolulu, HI 96813 (tel. 1-808/547-5625, fax 1-808/547-5880)

Japan: 11-44, 4 Chome, Minami Azabu, Minato-Ku, Tokyo 106 (tel. 81-3/5420-8800, fax 81-3/5420-8847); Ohbayashi Bldg., 24th Floor, 4-33, Kitahama-Higashi, Chuo-Ku, Osaka 540 (tel. 81-6/946-6181)

Hong Kong: Admiralty Center Tower 2, 26th Floor, 18 Harcourt Rd., Hong Kong (tel. 852/2529-4351, fax 852/2861-0019)

New Zealand: 1 Willeston St., Box 1695, Wellington (tel. 64-4/472-0200, fax 64-4/472-5887)

Singapore: 5 Gallop Rd., Singapore 1025 (tel. 65/466-4866, fax 65/469-0907)

U.S.A.: French consulates general exist in Atlanta, Boston, Chicago, Houston, Los Angeles, Miami, New Orleans, New York, San Francisco, and Washington. Get the address of the one nearest you by dialing the toll-free number of Air France.

---

holiday, you can easily get around this requirement by purchasing a refundable Air New Zealand ticket back to the U.S. or wherever before leaving home. If you catch a boat headed to Fiji, for example, simply have the airline reissue the ticket so it's a ticket to leave from your next destination—and on you go.

Yacht Entry

The main port of entry for cruising yachts is Papeete. Upon application to the local *gendarmerie,* entry may also be allowed at Moorea, Huahine, Raiatea, Bora Bora, Rurutu, Tubuai, Raivavae, Rangiroa, Mangareva, Nuku Hiva, Hiva Oa, and Ua Pou. Have an accurate inventory list for your vessel ready. Even after clearance, you must continue to report your arrival at each respective office every time you visit any of those islands (locations and phone numbers are provided throughout this book). The *gendarmes* are usually friendly and courteous, if you are. Boats arriving from Tonga, Fiji, and the Samoas must be fumigated (also those which have called at ports in Central or South America during the previous 21 days).

Anyone arriving by yacht without an onward ticket must post a

need to show "sufficient funds" and your ticket to leave Tahiti-Polynesia and provide one photo. North Americans are limited to three months total; if you know you'll be staying over a month, it's better to get a three-month visa at a French consulate prior to arrival, making this formality unnecessary.

Tahiti-Polynesia requires a ticket to leave of everyone (including nonresident French citizens). If you arrive without one, you'll be refused entry or required to post a cash bond equivalent to the value of a full-fare ticket back to your home country. If you're on an open-ended

bond or *caution* at a local bank equivalent to the airfare back to their country of origin. In Taiohae the bond is US$1,200 pp, but in Papeete it's only US$600 (for Americans). This is refundable upon departure at any branch of the same bank, less a three percent administrative fee. Make sure the receipt shows the currency in which the original deposit was made and get an assurance that it will be refunded in kind. If arriving at Papeete use the Westpac Bank, which will hold your bond in dollars; in the Marquesas there's only Banque Socredo. To reclaim the bond you'll also need a letter from Immigration verifying that you've been officially checked out. If any individual on the yacht doesn't have the bond money, the captain is responsible.

Once the bond is posted, a "temporary" three-month visa (CFP 3,000) is issued, which means you have three months to get to Papeete where an additional three months (another CFP 3,000) may be granted. After that you have to leave although boats can be left at Raiatea Carenage another six months. Yachts staying longer than one year are charged full customs duty on the vessel. Actually, the rules are not hard-and-fast, and everyone has a different experience. Crew changes should be made at Papeete. Visiting yachts cannot be chartered to third parties without permission.

After clearing customs in Papeete, outbound yachts may spend the duration of their period of stay cruising the outer islands. Make sure every island where you *might* stop is listed on your clearance. Duty-free fuel may be purchased immediately after clearance. The officials want all transient boats out of the country by 31 October, the onset of the hurricane season.

Money

The French Pacific franc or *Cour de Franc Pacifique* (CFP) is legal tender in Tahiti-Polynesia, Wallis and Futuna, and New Caledonia (there is no difference between the banknotes circulating in those territories). There are beautifully colored big banknotes of CFP 500, 1,000, 5,000, and 10,000, and coins of CFP 1, 2, 5, 10, 20, 50, and 100.

The CFP is fixed at one French franc (FF) to 18.18 Pacific francs (or one Euro to CFP 119.25), so you can determine how many CFP you'll get for your dollar or pound by finding out how many FF you get, then multiplying by 18.18. Or to put it another way, 5.5 FF equals CFP 100, so divide the number of FF you get by 5.5 and multiply by 100. At last report US$1 = CFP 106, but a rough way to convert CFP into U.S. dollars would be simply to divide by 100, so CFP 1,000 is US$10, etc.

All banks levy a stiff commission on foreign currency transactions. The Banque Socredo and the Banque de Polynésie deduct CFP 400 commission, the Westpac Bank CFP 450, and the Banque de Tahiti CFP 500. Traveler's checks attract a rate of exchange about 1.5% higher than cash, but a passport is required for identification (photocopies are sometimes accepted). The easiest way to avoid the high commissions and long bank lines is to change enough to cover your entire stay at the first opportunity to do so, then guard all that cash with your life (keep it in a moneybelt firmly strapped around your body while you're awake and shoved under the middle of the mattress at night while you're sleeping). If you are changing a very large amount of money it might be worth your while to compare the rates of all four banks as their rates do vary slightly.

The best currency to have with you is

EXCHANGE RATES
(approximate figures for orientation only)

One French Franc = 18.18 Pacific Francs
One U.S. Dollar = 106 Pacific Francs
One Canadian Dollar = 71 Pacific Francs
One Australian Dollar = 69 Pacific Francs
One New Zealand Dollar = 58 Pacific Francs
One Pound Sterling = 171 Pacific Francs
One Swiss Franc = 74 Pacific Francs
One German Mark = 61 Pacific Francs
One Dutch Guilder = 54 Pacific Francs
100 Japanese Yen = 94 Pacific Francs

French francs *in cash* as these are converted back and forth at the fixed rate of CFP 18.18 to one FF without any commission charge (traveler's checks in FF *are* subject to commission). However, it certainly isn't worth buying FF with dollars before leaving home for this purpose alone. If prior to departure you find you've changed too much and want your FF back, don't wait to do it at the airport as that branch may refuse and even the Papeete branches may be reluctant to carry out an operation on which they won't earn their blessed commission. How the introduction of the Euro in France will affect all of this was still unclear at press time. If you're from the States, you might also bring a few U.S. dollars in small bills to cover emergency expenses.

Credit cards are accepted in many places on the main islands, but Pacific francs in cash are easier to use at restaurants, shops, etc. If you wish to use a credit card at a restaurant, ask first. Visa and MasterCard credit cards are universally accepted in the Society Islands, but American Express is not. The American Express representative on Tahiti is Tahiti Tours (B.P. 627, 98713 Papeete, tel. 54-02-50) at 15 rue Jeanne d'Arc near the Vaima Center in Papeete. Most banks will give cash advances on credit cards, but it's still wise to bring enough traveler's checks to cover all your out-of-pocket expenses, and then some.

An alternative are the ATM machines outside Banque Socredo offices throughout the territory (including at Faa'a airport). These give a rate slightly better than traveler's checks without commission, however checking account ATM cards may not work despite advertised links to international services like Cirrus. Credit card withdrawals work better, but keep in mind that a high rate of interest is charged from the moment you receive the money (avoid this by leaving a balance with your credit card company). Some readers have reported problems with ATMs that gave "amount too high" messages instead of banknotes. This situation should improve as the banks upgrade their computer systems.

On most outer islands credit cards, traveler's checks, and foreign banknotes won't be accepted, so it's essential to change enough money before leaving Papeete. Apart from Tahiti, there are banks on Bora Bora, Huahine, Hiva Oa, Moorea, Nuku Hiva, Raiatea, Rangiroa, Rurutu, Taha'a, Tubuai, and Ua Pou. All of these islands have Banque Socredo branches, and the Banque de Tahiti (86% of which is owned by the Bank of Hawaii) is represented on six of them. Bora Bora, Moorea, and Raiatea each have four different banks. If you're headed for any island other than these, take along enough CFP in cash to see you through.

Costs

Although Tahiti is easily the most expensive corner of the South Pacific, it also has the lowest inflation rate in the region (only 1.5% in 1996, compared to 10% and up in many neighboring countries). Fortunately, facilities for budget travelers are now highly developed throughout the Society Islands, often with cooking facilities that allow you to save a lot on meals. Bread (and indirectly the ubiquitous baguette sandwiches) are heavily subsidized and a real bargain. Beer, fruit juice, and mineral water from grocery stores are reasonable. Cheap transportation is available by interisland boat, and on Tahiti there's *le truck*. Bicycles can be hired in many places.

On 1 January 1998 a value added tax (VAT) or *taxe sur la valeur ajoutée* (TVA) came into effect at the rate of 1% on accommodations and prepaid meals, 2% on store purchases, and 3% on restaurants, bars, car rentals, and excursions. This tax is usually included in the basic price and it's expected to rise in future years.

Time is what you need the most of to see Tahiti-Polynesia on the cheap, and the wisdom to avoid trying to see and do too much. There are countless organized tours and activities designed to separate you and your money, but none are really essential and the beautiful scenery, spectacular beaches, challenging hikes, and exotic atmosphere are free. Bargaining is not common in Tahiti-Polynesia, and no one will try to cheat you (with the exception of the odd taxi driver). There's *no tipping*.

Post

The 34 regular post offices and 58 authorized agencies throughout Tahiti-Polynesia are open weekdays 0700-1500. Main branches sell ready-made padded envelopes and boxes. Parcels with an aggregate length, width, and height of over 90 cm or weighing more than 20 kg cannot be mailed. Rolls (posters, calendars, etc.) longer than 90 cm are also not accepted. Letters cannot weigh over two kg and when mailing parcels it's much cheaper to keep the weight under two kilograms. Registration *(recommandation)* is CFP 500 extra and insurance *(envois avec valeur déclarée)* is also possible. Always use airmail *(poste aérienne)* when posting a letter; surface mail takes months to arrive. Postcards can still take up to two weeks to reach the United States. Though twice as expensive as in Cook Islands or Fiji, the service is quite reliable.

To pick up poste restante (general delivery) mail, you must show your passport and pay CFP 55 per piece. If you're going to an outer island and are worried about your letters being returned to sender after 30 days (at Nuku Hiva after 15 days), pay CFP 2,000 per month for a *garde de courrier,* which obliges the post office to hold all letters for at least two months. If one of your letters has "please hold" marked on it, the local postmaster may decide to hold all your mail for two months, but you'll have to pay the CFP 2,000 to collect it. Packages may be returned after one month in any case. For a flat fee of CFP 2,000 you can have your mail forwarded for one year. Ask for an *"Ordre de Réexpédition Temporaire."*

There's no residential mail delivery in Tahiti-Polynesia and what appear to be mail boxes along rural roads are actually bread delivery boxes! Almost everybody has a post office box, rendered B.P. *(Boîte Postale)* in this book. Since there are usually no street addresses, always include the B.P. and postal code when writing to a local address, plus the name of the commune or village and the island. The postal authorities recognize "French Polynesia" as the official name of this country, and it's better to add "South Pacific" to that for good measure. Tahiti-Polynesia issues its own colorful postage stamps—available at local post offices. They make excellent souvenirs.

Telecommunications

Local telephone calls are CFP 50, and the pay phones usually work! A flashing light means you're about to be cut off, so have another coin ready. However, most public telephones now accept local telephone cards only (no coins). All calls within a single island are considered local calls, except on Tahiti, which is divided into two zones. Long-distance calls are best placed at

post offices, which also handle fax *(télécopier)* services. Calls made from hotel rooms are charged double or triple—you could be presented with a truly astronomical bill. Collect calls overseas are possible to Australia, Canada, France, Mexico, New Zealand, and the U.S. (but not to the U.K.): dial 19 and say you want a *conversation payable a l'arrivée.* For information (in French), dial 12; to get the operator, dial 19.

Anyone planning on using the phone should pick up a local telephone card *(télécarte),* sold at all post offices. They're valid for both local and overseas calls, and are available in denominations of 30 units (CFP 1,000), 60 units (CFP 2,000), and 150 units (CFP 5,000). It's cheaper than paying cash for long distance and you don't get hit with stiff three-minute minimum charges for operator-assisted calls (CFP 1,056 to the U.S.). North American AT&T, HTC, and Teleglobe Canada telephone cards can be used in Tahiti-Polynesia.

To dial overseas direct from Tahiti, listen for the dial tone, then push 00 (Tahiti's international access code). When you hear another dial tone, press the country code of your party (Canada and the U.S. are both 1), the city or area code, and the number. The procedure is clearly explained in notices in English in the phone booths. If calling from abroad, Tahiti-Polynesia's telephone code is 689.

The cost of placing international calls was sharply reduced in 1997, and with a card the cost per minute is now CFP 180 to Australia, New Zealand, and Hawaii, CFP 200 to the U.S. and Canada, and CFP 300 to Britain and Germany. Calls to any of these countries (except Germany and the UK) are half price from midnight to 0600. To call Tahiti-Polynesia direct from the U.S. or Canada, one must dial 011-689 and the six-digit telephone number. International access codes do vary, so always check in the front of your local telephone book. If you need to consult the Tahiti-Polynesia phone book, ask to see the *annuaire* at any post office.

Throughout this book we've tried to supply the local telephone numbers you'll need. Most tourist-oriented businesses will have someone handy who speaks English, so don't hesitate to call ahead. You'll get current information, be able to check prices and perhaps make a reservation, and often save yourself a lot of time and worry.

Electronic mail is still in its infancy here but those e-mail addresses that do exist should be listed at www.tahiti.com/directories/zframes/yel-low-pages.htm. A selection of Tahiti-related websites and e-mail addresses are included in this book's appendix.

Business Hours and Time

Businesses open early in Tahiti-Polynesia and often close for a two-hour siesta at midday. Normal office hours are weekdays 0730-1130/1330-1630. Many shops keep the same schedule but remain open until 1730 and Saturday 0730-1200. A few shops remain open at lunchtime and small convenience stores are often open Saturday afternoon until 1800 and Sunday 0600-0800. Banking hours are variable, either 0800-1530 or 0800-1100/1400-1700 weekdays. A few banks in Papeete open Saturday morning (check the sign on the door).

Tahiti-Polynesia operates on the same time as Hawaii, 10 hours behind Greenwich mean time or two hours behind California (except May-Oct., when it's three hours). The Marquesas are 30 minutes ahead of the rest of Tahiti-Polynesia. Tahiti-Polynesia is east of the international date line, so the day is the same as that of the Cook Islands, Hawaii, and the U.S., but a day behind Fiji, New Zealand, and Australia.

Media

Two French-owned morning papers appear daily except Sunday. *Les Nouvelles de Tahiti* (B.P. 1757, 98713 Papeete; tel. 43-44-45, fax 42-18-00) was founded in 1961 and currently has a circulation of 6,700 copies. In 1964 *La Dépêche de Tahiti* (B.P. 50, 98713 Papeete; tel. 46-43-43, fax 46-43-50) merged with an existing paper and 14,000 copies a day are presently sold. In 1989 the previously locally owned *LesNouvelles* was purchased by the Hersant publishing empire, which also owns *La Dépêche. La Dépêche* provides more international news, but both papers run a constant barrage of stories emphasizing the economic dangers of independence.

The free weekly *Tahiti Beach Press* (B.P. 887, 98713 Papeete; tel. 42-68-50, fax 42-33-56), edited by Jan Prince, includes tourist information and is well worth perusing to find out which local companies are interested in your business. The same folks put out the monthly newspaper *Tahi-ti Today* with more in-depth articles (to subscribe mail a check for US$34 to the address above). If you read French, the monthly magazine *Tahiti-Pacifique* (www.tahitiweb.com/f/info) is a lively observer of political and economic affairs (single copies CFP 500, airmail subscription US$100).

Television was introduced to Tahiti in 1965 and state-owned Radio-Télévision Française d'Outre-Mer (RFO) broadcasts on two channels in French and (occasionally) Tahitian. (After the 1996 election a Court of Appeal found that RFO's coverage was biased in favor of the ruling party, and for this and other reasons, fresh elections were ordered in 11 ridings.) A private commercial television station, Canal Polynésie, and two cable companies (Téléfenua and Canal +) also operate. There are nine private radio stations and it's fun to listen to the Tahitian-language stations, which play more local music than the French stations. The Tahitian call-in shows with messages to families on outer islands are a delightful slice of real life.

Among the FM radio stations you can receive around Papeete is **Radio Tahiti** (RFO), a government-run station picked up at 89.0 or 91.8 MHz. Their main news of the day (in French) is at 0630 but it's mostly official propaganda. **Radio 1** (98.7, 100.0, and 103.8 MHz) gives a more independent news report at 0630, but it's better known as Tahiti's rock music station. More rock and rap can be heard on **NRJ** (88.6 and 103.0 MHz). **Radio Bleue** (88.2, 88.5, 93.3, 96.0, 97.0, and 100.3 MHz) presents a mix of Tahitian, French, and Anglo-American music. For more local music, tune in **Radio Tiare** (104.2 and 105.9 MHz), Radio 1's sister station. **Radio Te Reo o Tefana** (92.8 and 94.4 MHz) is a pro-independence station based at Faa'a, which features Tahitian talk shows and local music. Outside Tahiti the frequencies used by these stations varies (Radio Tahiti is on 89.0 MHz at Taravao and 738 kHz AM elsewhere. Radio 1 uses 90.9 MHz at Taravao and 100.9 MHz at Raiatea, while Radio Tiare is at 98.3 MHz at Taravao.) None of the local AM/FM stations broadcast in English.

Information

Tahiti-Polynesia has one of the best-equipped tourist offices in the South Pacific, Tahiti Tourisme (B.P. 65, 98713 Papeete; tel. 50-57-00, fax 43-66-19, www.tahiti-tourisme.com, e-mail:

tahiti-tourisme@mail.pf). For a list of their overseas offices, turn to the Information Offices appendix at the back of this book. Within Tahiti-Polynesia the same organization calls itself the Tahiti Manava Visitors Bureau and operates tourist information offices on Tahiti, Moorea, Huahine, Raiatea, Bora Bora, and Hiva Oa. These offices can provide free brochures and answer questions, but they're not travel agencies, so you must make your own hotel and transportation bookings. Ask for their current information sheets on the islands you intend to visit.

Health

Public hospitals are found in Papeete (Tahiti), Taravao (Tahiti), Afareaitu (Moorea), Uturoa (Raiatea), Mataura (Tubuai), Taiohae (Nuku Hiva), and Atuona (Hiva Oa). Most other islands have only infirmaries or dispensaries. Medical treatment is not free and in non-life-threatening situations it's better to see a private doctor or dentist whose attention will cost you no more but whose services are generally more convenient. Private clinics are found throughout the Society Islands but there are none on the eastern outer islands (there, ask for the *infirmerie*). Papeete's Mamao Hospital (tel. 46-62-62) has one of only two recompression chambers in the South Pacific.

TRANSPORTATION

Getting There

Aircalin, Air France, Air New Zealand, Air Tahiti Nui, AOM French Airlines, Corsair, Hawaiian Airlines, Lan Chile Airlines, and Qantas Airways all have flights to Papeete. For more information on these, turn to the Introduction.

In 1990 France's state-owned national airline, **Air France** (tel. 800/237-2747), bought out privately owned UTA French Airlines to become *the* international carrier to the French colonies in the South Pacific. Both Air France and **AOM**

French Airlines (9841 Airport Blvd., Ste. 1120, Los Angeles, CA 90045, U.S.A.; tel. 800/892-9136) fly four times a week from Paris to Papeete via Los Angeles. Air France also flies nonstop between Tokyo and Papeete once a week. AOM (Air Outre-Mer), owned by the French bank Crédit Lyonnais, has a policy of consistently setting their fares slightly below those of Air France while offering comparable service.

The charter airline **Corsair,** owned by the French tour operator Nouvelles Frontières (APS, Inc., 5757 West Century Blvd., Ste. 660, Los Angeles, CA 90045-6407, U.S.A.; tel. 800/677-0720 or 310/670-7318, fax 310/338-0708, www.nouvelles-frontieres.fr, e-mail: webmaster@corsair-int.com), also has scheduled Paris-Los Angeles-Papeete flights twice a week, plus Paris-Oakland-Papeete weekly. Corsair prices their tickets differently than the other carriers: you pay according to the season in which each leg is actually flown, whereas all of the other airlines base their fares on the season when the journey begins and heavy cancellation penalties apply. Thus while Corsair may be cheaper, it's also more complicated, and requires more careful planning. The seating on Corsair and AOM planes is reported to be rather cramped. (On the French carriers the high season months from Los Angeles to Tahiti are July to mid-September and part of December. June is also high season on Air France. Air New Zealand's seasons are quite different with the shoulder season in March and from September to November, and the high season from December to February. Always compare airfares before booking.)

Air New Zealand (tel. 800/262-1234 or 800/663-5494) has eight-hour flights from Los Angeles to Papeete twice a week, with connections to/from many points in North America and Western Europe. These flights continue southwest to Auckland with one calling at Rarotonga and Fiji. **Qantas** (tel. 800/227-4500) flies from Melbourne to Papeete via Auckland with connections for six other Australian cities. **Hawaiian Airlines** (tel. 800/367-5320) offers weekly nonstop service to Papeete from Honolulu with connections from Los Angeles, Las Vegas, San Francisco, Portland, and Seattle.

Aircalin (tel. 1-310/670-7302) has flights from Nouméa to Papeete via Wallis Island or Nadi.

These services also have connections to/from Australia.

Lan Chile Airlines (tel. 800/735-5526) runs their Boeing 767 service from Santiago to Tahiti via Easter Island three times a week.

A new, locally owned airline, **Air Tahiti Nui** (B.P. 1673, 98713 Papeete; tel. 46-02-02, fax 46-02-90, e-mail: fly@airtahitinui.pf), began service from Papeete in November 1998. Their 286-seat Airbus flies to Los Angeles three times a week, and to Tokyo twice a week.

By Boat

The only scheduled international passenger-carrying freighter service to Tahiti is the monthly Bank Line service from Le Havre (France) to Auckland via the Panama Canal. The local agent is **Agence Maritime de Fare Ute** (B.P. 9003, 98715 Papeete; tel. 42-55-61, fax 42-86-08).

Getting Around by Air

The domestic carrier, **Air Tahiti** (B.P. 314, 98713 Papeete; tel. 86-42-42, fax 86-40-69, e-mail: rtahitim@mail.pf), flies to 37 airstrips in every corner of Tahiti-Polynesia, with important hubs at Papeete (Windward Islands), Bora Bora (Leeward Islands), Rangiroa (western Tuamotus), Hao (eastern Tuamotus), and Nuku Hiva (Marquesas). Their fleet consists of three 66-seat ATR 72s, three 48-seat ATR 42s, and two 19-seat Dornier 228s. The Italian-made ATRs are economical in fuel consumption and maintenance requirements, and perform well under island conditions. The high-winged design makes them perfect for aerial sightseeing along the way.

Air Tahiti doesn't allow stopovers on their tickets, so if you're flying roundtrip from Tahiti to Bora Bora and want to stop at Raiatea on the way out and Huahine on the way back, you'll have to purchase four separate tickets (total CFP 30,500). Ask about their "Pass Bleu," which allows you to visit these islands plus Moorea for CFP 20,000 (certain restrictions apply). An "Excursion Bleue" allows a 30% reduction on a roundtrip to any island in the Society or North Tuamotu groups provided you fly on off-peak "blue" flights.

No student discounts are available, but persons under 25 and over 60 can get discounts of up to 50% on certain flights by paying CFP 1,000 for a discount card *(carte de réduction)*. Family re-

duction cards (CFP 2,000) provide a potential 50% reduction for the parents and 75% off for children 16 and under. Identification and one photo are required, and application must be made at least three working days before you wish to travel.

Better than point-to-point fares are the six Air Tahiti **Air Passes.** These are valid 28 days, but only one stopover can be made on each island included in the package. For example, you can go Papeete-Moorea-Huahine-Raiatea-Maupiti-Bora Bora-Papeete for CFP 30,500. Otherwise pay CFP 45,500 for Papeete-Moorea-Huahine-Raiatea-Bora Bora-Rangiroa-Manihi-Papeete. This compares with an individual ticket price of CFP 41,400 to do the first circuit, CFP 69,800 for the second, which makes the air passes good value. Air Passes that include the Austral Islands are CFP 50,500 (compared to CFP 81,400 on an individual basis); with the Tuamotu and Marquesas islands they're CFP 87,000 (compared to CFP 116,000). All flights must be booked in advance but date changes are possible. Air Tahiti's agent in North America (tel. 800/553-3477) will have current information. The passes are nonrefundable once travel has begun.

Air Tahiti's "Decouverte Marquises" fare allows you to fly from Papeete to Nuku Hiva for CFP 49,900 return; to Atuona, Ua Pou, or Ua Huka it's CFP 54,900 return. This is for a stay of between seven and 15 days with only one reservation change allowed. There's a 25% cancellation penalty and you can only fly on low-load "blue" flights (not valid around Christmas or Easter or in July and August). This ticket is only available in Papeete.

Air Tahiti also offers packages to almost all their destinations including airfare, transfers, hotel rooms (double occupancy), and the occasional breakfast or excursion. Of course, they only use the more upmarket hotels, but if you were planning to stay in one of them anyway, Air Tahiti's packages are cheaper than what you'd pay directly. Cruise packages are also offered. All the possibilities are clearly outlined (in French) with exact prices given in Air Tahiti's well-designed timetable.

Air Tahiti tickets are refundable at the place of purchase, but you must cancel your reservations at least two hours before flight time to avoid a CFP 1,000 penalty. Do this in person and have your flight coupon amended as no-shows are

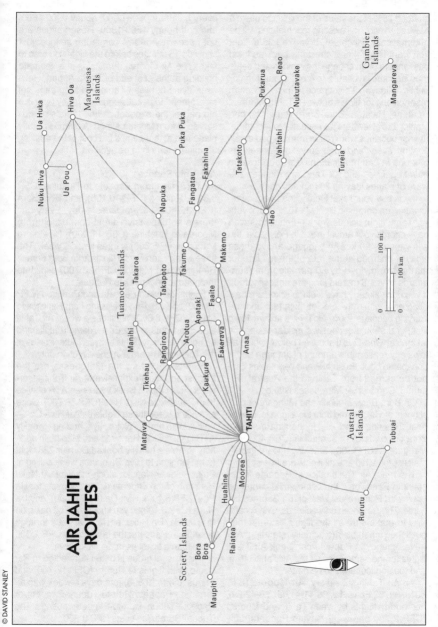

© DAVID STANLEY

AIR TAHITI
ROUTES

charged 25% of the value of the ticket to make a new reservation (all existing reservations will be automatically canceled). If you're told a flight you want is full, keep checking back as local passengers often change their minds and seats may become available (except around major public holidays). It's not necessary to reconfirm reservations for flights between Tahiti, Moorea, Huahine, Raiatea, Bora Bora, Rangiroa, and Manihi, but elsewhere it's essential to reconfirm. (If your bookings were made from abroad do reconfirm *everything* upon arrival in Papeete as mix-ups in communications between foreign travel agencies and Air Tahiti are routine.) Beware of planes leaving 20 minutes early.

If you buy your ticket locally, the baggage allowance on domestic flights is 10 kg, but if your Air Tahiti flight tickets were purchased seven days prior to your arrival in Tahiti-Polynesia, the allowance is 20 kg. All baggage above those limits is charged at the rate of the full fare for that sector divided by 80 per kilogram (surfboards over 1.8 meters long are not accepted). If you don't already have a plane ticket, are traveling only within the Society Islands, and are carrying baggage above Air Tahiti's absurd 10-kg limit, you should seriously consider taking the jet cruiser *Ono-Ono* discussed below, which allows any reasonable amount of luggage and is cheaper to boot. Fresh fruit and vegetables cannot be carried from Tahiti to the Austral, Tuamotu, Gambier, or Marquesas islands.

On Bora Bora, Maupiti, and Mangareva passengers are transferred from the airport to town by boat. This ride is included in the airfare at Bora Bora but costs extra at Maupiti (CFP 400) and Mangareva (CFP 500). Smoking aboard the aircraft is prohibited and all flights are free seating.

The main Air Tahiti office in Papeete is upstairs in Fare Tony, the commercial center off boulevard Pomare just west of rue Georges Lagarde. They're closed on weekends. Check carefully to make sure all the flights listed in their published timetable are actually operating! Any travel agency in Papeete can book Air Tahiti flights for the same price as the Air Tahiti office, and the service tends to be better.

An Air Tahiti subsidiary, **Air Moorea** (B.P. 6019, 98702 Faa'a; tel. 86-41-41, fax 86-42-69), has hourly flights between Tahiti and Moorea (CFP 2,700 one-way) leaving Papeete daily every half hour 0600-0900, hourly 0900-1600, and half hourly 1600-1800. Reservations are not necessary on this commuter service: just show up 15 minutes before the flight you wish to take. The Air Moorea terminal is in a separate building at the east end of Faa'a Airport. However, flying between Tahiti and Moorea is not recommended because going over by ferry is a big part of the experience and there's no bus service to/from Moorea Airport. A cramped, stuffy plane ride at three times the cost of the relaxing 30-minute ferry is to be avoided.

Air Tahiti Services
Air Tahiti flies from Papeete to Huahine (CFP 8,800), Raiatea (CFP 10,100), and Bora Bora (CFP 12,400) several times a day. Every day there's an expensive direct connection from Moorea to Huahine (CFP 11,000); Raiatea to Maupiti (CFP 5,600) is three times a week. The three weekly transversal flights from Bora Bora to Rangiroa and Manihi (CFP 20,700) eliminate the need to backtrack to Papeete.

Flights between Papeete and Rangiroa (CFP 13,600) operate daily, continuing from Rangiroa to Manihi (CFP 8,800) five times a week. Air Tahiti also has flights to the East Tuamotu atolls and Mangareva. Many flights between outer islands of the Tuamotus operate in one direction only.

Flights bound for the Marquesas are the longest and most expensive of Air Tahiti's services. Five times a week there's an ATR service from Papeete to Nuku Hiva (CFP 28,700). Once or twice a week these flights call at Hiva Oa on their way to or from Nuku Hiva, and one weekly ATR flight calls at Rangiroa and Manihi. In addition, there's a heavily booked Dornier 228 flight from Rangiroa to Hiva Oa once a week calling at Puka Puka or Napuka along the way. At Nuku Hiva one of the Papeete flights connects for Ua Pou (CFP 5,100), Hiva Oa (CFP 8,800), and Ua Huka (CFP 5,100). If you know you'll be going on to Hiva Oa, Ua Huka, or Ua Pou, get a through ticket from Papeete; the fare is only CFP 1,300 more than a ticket as far as Nuku Hiva.

The Austral group is better connected to Papeete, with flights to Rurutu (CFP 17,700) and Tubuai (CFP 19,800) four days a week with alternating Papeete-Rurutu-Tubuai-Papeete or Papeete-Tubuai-Rurutu-Papeete routings. The Tubuai-Rurutu leg costs CFP 8,300.

During July and August, the peak holiday season, extra flights are scheduled. Air Tahiti is fairly reliable; still, you should never schedule a flight back to Papeete on the same day that your international flight leaves Tahiti. It's always wise to allow a couple of days' leeway in case there's a problem with the air service. Save your trip around Tahiti until the end.

Getting Around by Sea

To save money, most budget travelers tour Tahiti-Polynesia by boat. There's a certain romance and adventure to taking an interisland freighter and you can go anywhere by copra boat, including islands without airstrips and resorts. Ships leave Papeete regularly for the different island groups. You'll meet local people and fellow travelers and receive a gentle introduction to the island of your choice. Problems about overweight baggage, tight reservations, and airport transport are eliminated, and thanks to government subsidies travel by ferry or passenger-carrying freighter is four times cheaper than the plane. Seasickness, cockroaches, diesel fumes, and the heavy scent of copra are all part of the experience.

Below you'll find specific information on the main interisland boats; the tourist office in Papeete also has lists. Prices and schedules have been fairly stable over the past few years, and new services are being added all the time. Lots of visitors travel this way to Moorea and Bora Bora, so don't feel intimidated if you've never done it before.

For the cheapest ride and the most local color, travel deck class. There's usually an awning in case of rain, and you'll be surrounded by Tahitians, but don't count on getting a lot of sleep if you go this way—probably no problem for one night, right? Lay your mat pointed to one side

of the boat because if you lie parallel to the length of the boat you'll roll from side to side. Don't step over other peoples' mats, but if you must, first remove your shoes and excuse yourself. Otherwise take a cabin, which you'll share with three or four other passengers, still cheaper than an airplane seat. Food is only included on really long trips (ask), but snacks may be sold on board. On a long trip you're better off taking all your own food than buying a meal plan.

For any boat trip farther than Moorea check the schedule and pick up tickets the day before at the company office listed below. If you're headed for a remote island outside the Societies or want cabin class, visit the office as far in advance as possible. Take along your passport as they may insist on checking the expiration date of your visa before selling you a ticket to a point outside the Society Islands. Except on the tourist-class *Aranui,* it's not possible (nor recommended) to book your passage before arriving on Tahiti. If you really want to go, there'll be something leaving around the date you want. On an outer island, be wary when someone, even a member of the crew, tells you the departure time of a ship: they're as apt to leave early as late.

Boat trips are always smoother northwest-bound than southeast-bound because you go with the prevailing winds. Take this into consideration if you plan to fly one way, in which case it would be better to come back by air. *Bon voyage.*

Ferry to Moorea

Two types of ferries travel to Moorea: two fast 320-passenger catamarans carrying walk-on commuters only (30 minutes), and two large car ferries with a capacity for 400 foot-passengers and 80 vehicles (one hour). Departure times are posted at the ferry landing on the Papeete waterfront (punctual) and reservations are not required: you buy your ticket just before you board. Stroll around the open upper deck and enjoy the scenic one-hour crossing.

The high-speed catamarans *Aremiti III* (B.P. 9254, 98715 Papeete; tel. 42-88-88, fax 42-83-83) and *Tamahine Moorea* (B.P. 3917, 98713 Papeete; tel. 43-76-50, fax 42-10-49) make five or six trips a day between Tahiti and Moorea at CFP 900 pp. The ultimate in speed is the *Tamarii Moorea VIII,* a very fast Corsaire 6000 ferry brought into service in June 1996. On the Moorea cats you're allowed to sit or stand outside on the roof and get an all-round view, which makes them fun and well worth taking at least once.

The car ferries *Tamarii Moorea* and *Aremiti Ferry* shuttle four or five times a day between Papeete and Vaiare Wharf on Moorea (CFP 800 one-way, students and children under 13 CFP 400, car CFP 2,000, scooter CFP 500, bicycle free).

A bus meets all ferries on the Moorea side and will take you anywhere on that island for CFP 200. Just don't be too slow boarding the bus or it could be full. The Moorea ferries carry over a million passengers a year making Papeete the third-largest port under the French flag (after Calais and Cherbourg) as far as passenger movements go.

Ono-Ono

Jet Cruiser to the Leeward Islands

In 1994 the high-speed monohull *Ono-Ono* (Sociéte Polynesienne d'Investissement Maritime, B.P. 16, 98713 Papeete; tel. 45-35-35, fax 43-83-45, e-mail: onoono@mail.pf) began whisking passengers from Papeete to Huahine, Raiatea, Taha'a, and Bora Bora. This Australian-built 48-meter jet boat carries 450 passengers at speeds of up to 35 knots, cutting traveling times from Papeete to Huahine to just three and a half hours (CFP 4,944), to Raiatea four and a half hours (CFP 5,499), to Taha'a five and a half hours (CFP 6,055), and to Bora Bora eight hours (CFP 6,610). Children under 12 years of age pay half price on tickets to/from Papeete. Bicycles are CFP 1,200, surfboards CFP 650.

The *Ono-Ono* departs Papeete's Moorea ferry wharf Monday and Wednesday at 0900, Friday at 1630, departing Bora Bora for the return trip on Tuesday and Thursday at 0700, Sunday at 1200. On Saturday there's a shorter interisland run within the Leeward Islands only (about CFP

1,778 a hop). *Ono-Ono* is seldom full and tickets can be purchased an hour before departure (for insurance purposes, the booking agent will need to know the name and age of each passenger). To refund a ticket is CFP 1,000. The *Ono-Ono* ticket cover instructs you to check in at the harbor 45 minutes before the scheduled departure time and you should do so as they often leave half an hour early! Canceled services with little notice are also quite routine.

Place your luggage in a special baggage container near the gangway (there are none of the worries about overweight luggage you might have on Air Tahiti). Another big advantage that this ferry has over the plane is that on Tahiti, Huahine, Raiatea, and Taha'a you'll arrive right in the center of town, eliminating the need for airport transfers. Seating is 10 or 12 abreast in rows of airplane-style seats on two enclosed decks, plus on a covered deck at back where you can sit outside. Though over twice as expensive as the cargo boats or ferry, it's half the price of going by air and certainly makes getting around these enchanting islands a lot easier.

Ferry to the Leeward Islands

The **Compagnie Maritime Raromatai Nui** (B.P. 50712, 98716 Pirae; tel. 43-19-88, fax 43-19-99), with an office in a red-and-white kiosk at the Moorea ferry wharf in Papeete, handles the car-carrying, 400-passenger *Raromatai Ferry,* which departs Papeete to Huahine, Raiatea, Taha'a, and Bora Bora on Tuesday and Friday afternoons. This ship uses a landing behind the tourist office in downtown Papeete, not the wharf at Motu Uta where *Taporo VI* and the *Vaeanu* dock. Tickets for walk-on passengers are usually available just prior to departure. Prices from Papeete to Bora Bora are CFP 3,200 for a seat in the salon, CFP 5,000 pp in a four-berth cabin, CFP 10,000 for a car, CFP 500 for a bicycle. A double "cruise cabin" is CFP 20,000 for two people. There are discounts for students and those 18 and under.

The *Raromatai Ferry* salon is a spacious sitting room with aircraft-style Pullman seats, but French TV shows blast at you nonstop and the powerful air-conditioning means you freeze at night unless you've got a sleeping bag. The *Raromatai Ferry* rolls a lot in rough weather. Between the Leeward Islands the *Raromatai Ferry* is a good deal (CFP 1,000 salon interisland) for these daylight crossings (southbound), with an excellent open promenade deck on top. Unfortunately this ship is often out of service for one reason or another.

Cargo Ships to the Leeward Islands

The cargo ship MV *Taporo VI* departs Papeete's Motu Uta wharf every Monday, Wednesday, and Friday afternoon around 1600. *Taporo VI* calls at Huahine at 0200, Raiatea at 0530, and Taha'a at 0700, reaching Bora Bora at 1000 Tuesday, Thursday, and Saturday. It departs Bora Bora for Papeete once again Tuesday, Thursday, and Saturday at 1130, calling at Raiatea at 1400 and Huahine at 1700, reaching Papeete early Wednesday, Friday, and Sunday morning (you can stay on board till dawn).

Northbound the MV *Vaeanu* leaves Papeete Monday, Wednesday, and Friday at 1700; south-

bound it leaves Bora Bora Tuesday at 1030, Thursday at noon, and Sunday at 0900.

The timings are more civilized if you stay on the boat right through to Bora Bora northbound: you get to see the sunset over Moorea, go to bed, and when you awake you'll be treated to a scenic cruise past Taha'a and into the Bora Bora lagoon. Getting off at Huahine at 0200 is no fun (although there is a good shelter on the wharf where you can spend the rest of the night for free). Southbound between Bora Bora, Raiatea, and Huahine you travel during daylight hours which makes it easy to island hop back (you'll save a day by taking the *Ono-Ono* between Bora Bora and Taha'a/Raiatea). The only fly in the ointment is that southbound you must board at Huahine just before dark and all of the sheltered places in which to stretch your mat may be taken. However, there's usually ample sleeping space left on the *Vaeanu* and there will be no distur-

---

LEEWARD ISLANDS FERRY SCHEDULES

MV *Ono-Ono* (450 passengers)
MV *Vaeanu* (121 passengers)

	NORTHBOUND					PORTS OF CALL			SOUTHBOUND				
A	C	E	G	J				B	D	F	H	I	K
0900	1630	—	1700	1700	dep.	Papeete	arr.	1415	1915	—	0300	0400	0200
1230	1945	—	0200	0200	arr.	Huahine	dep.	1045	1545	—	1800	1900	1700
1245	2000	1500	0300	0300	dep.	Huahine	arr.	1030	1530	1130	1700	1800	1600
1330	2100	1600	0500	0500	arr.	Raiatea	dep.	0930	1430	1030	1500	1600	1400
1345	2115	1615	0630	0630	dep.	Raiatea	arr.	0915	1415	1015	1400	1500	1300
1430	—	1700	—	0730	arr.	Taha'a	dep.	0815	1345	0915	1300	—	1200
1440		1710	—	0800	dep.	Taha'a	arr.	0800	1300	0900	1230	—	1100
1615	2300	1815	0930	1000	arr.	Bora Bora	dep.	0700	1200	0800	1030	1200	0900

A—*Ono Ono* departs Papeete Monday and Wednesday
B—*Ono Ono* departs Bora Bora Tuesday and Thursday
C—*Ono Ono* departs Papeete Friday
D—*Ono Ono* departs Bora Bora Sunday
E—*Ono Ono* departs Huahine Saturday
F—*Ono Ono* departs Bora Bora Saturday
G—*Vaeanu* departs Papeete Monday and Wednesday
H—*Vaeanu* departs Bora Bora Tuesday
I—*Vaeanu* departs Bora Bora Thursday
J—*Vaeanu* departs Papeete Friday
K—*Vaeanu* departs Bora Bora Sunday

Schedules may be modified during holidays or otherwise.

bances before Tahiti. If the risk of being forced to sleep on deck under the stars (and possibly the rain) intimidates you, there's always the option of finally splurging on the high-speed ferry *Ono-Ono* straight back to Papeete.

Although the ships do make an effort to stick to their timetables, the times are approximate—ask at the company offices. They're more likely to be running late on the return trip from Bora Bora to Tahiti (unlike the *Ono-Ono,* which tends to run a little early). Expect variations if there's a public holiday that week. Also beware of voyages marked "carburant" on the schedules because when fuel *(combustible)* is being carried, only cabin passengers are allowed aboard (this often happens on the Wednesday departures from Papeete). Northbound you won't get much sleep due to noise and commotion during the early-morning stops. No mattresses or bedding are provided for deck passengers. In Papeete, board the ship two hours prior to departure to be sure of a reasonable place on deck to sleep (mark your place with a beach mat). Luckily these ships aren't promoted in the Australian guidebooks, so they aren't overwhelmed by tourists. If you've got some time to kill before your ship leaves Papeete, have a look around the coconut-oil mill next to the wharf.

On *Taporo VI* the deck fare from Papeete to any of the Leeward Islands is CFP 1,709. However, they accept only a limited number of deck passengers (who sleep on pallets in three large open containers on the upper rear deck), so it's important to book ahead at the **Compagnie Française Maritime de Tahiti** (B.P. 368, 98713 Papeete; tel. 42-63-93, fax 42-06-17; open weekdays 0730-1100/1330-1700, Saturday 0730-1100) in Fare Ute. The two four-bed cabins are CFP 20,000 each (seldom full). If you're only traveling between the islands of Huahine, Raiatea, Taha'a, and Bora Bora, the interisland deck fares are under CFP 1,000 each trip. If you jump off for a quick look around while the ship is in port, you may be asked to buy another ticket when you reboard. A bicycle is about CFP 600 extra. No meals are included, so take food and water with you.

The *Vaeanu* carries a much larger number of deck and cabin passengers, and you can usually buy a ticket at their office (B.P. 9062, 98715 Papeete; tel. 41-25-35, fax 41-24-34) facing the wharf at Motu Uta a few hours prior to departure (except on holidays). Do buy your ticket before boarding, however, as there can be problems for anyone trying to pay once the ship is underway. In the Leeward Islands buy a ticket from the agent on the wharf as soon as the boat arrives. The *Vaeanu* offers mats in the spacious hold down below or floor space on the enclosed upper rear deck (with the lights on all night). Most travelers prefer the *Vaeanu* as there's a lot more elbowroom and shade than on *Taporo VI.* The passengers and crew on both boats are mostly Tahitian as tourists and French usually take the *Ono-Ono,* but *Vaeanu* and *Taporo VI* are excellent options for the adventurous traveler.

The Compagnie Française Maritime de Tahiti also runs a supply ship from Papeete to Maiao occasionally, so ask. (The CFMT itself has a place in local history, having been founded around 1890 by Sir James Donald, who had the contract to supply limes to the British Pacific fleet. At the turn of the century Donald's schooner, the *Tiare Taporo,* was the fastest in Polynesia, and the CFMT is still the Lloyd's of London agent.)

Barge to Maupiti

The government supply barges *Meherio* or *Maupiti Tou Ai's* leave Papeete for Maupiti Wednesday at 1900 (20 hours) calling at Raiatea on the way. Tickets to Maupiti are available from the **Direction de l'Equipment** (weekdays 0730-1500; B.P. 85, 98713 Papeete; tel. 42-44-92, fax 43-32-69) at Motu Uta, costing CFP 2,221 from Papeete or CFP 1,058 from Raiatea.

Ships to the Austral Islands

The **Service de Navigation des Australes** (B.P. 1890, 98713 Papeete; tel. 42-93-67, fax 42-06-09), at the Motu Uta interisland wharf on the west side of the copra sheds in Papeete, runs the *Tuhaa Pae II* to the Austral Islands two or three times a month: CFP 12,500 a day including meals cabin class for the 10-day roundtrip. One-way deck/cabin fares from Papeete are CFP 3,799/6,649 to Rurutu, Rimatara, or Tubuai, CFP 5,475/9,582 to Raivavae, CFP 7,486/13,101 to Rapa. Between Rurutu and Tubuai it's CFP 1,780 deck. No meals are included, but food can be ordered at CFP 2,300 pp a day extra (take your own). Some of the cabins are below the waterline and very hot. The rear deck has a diesely romantic feel, for a day or two. For sanitary reasons the seats have been removed from the ship's toilets (squat). The *Tuhaa Pae II* calls at Rimatara, Rurutu, Tubuai, Raivavae, and about once a month Rapa Iti. Maria Atoll is visited annually. Their schedule changes at a moment's notice, so actually going with them requires persistence. Consider going out by boat and returning on the plane.

Ships to the Tuamotus and Gambiers

The motor vessel *Dory* (B.P. 9274, 98715 Papeete; tel. 42-30-55, fax 42-06-15) leaves from Motu Uta every Monday at 1300 for Tikehau (Tuesday 0600), Rangiroa (Tuesday 1200), Arutua (Wednesday 0600), and Kaukura (Wednesday 1400), arriving back in Papeete Thursday at 0800. This routing means it takes only 23 hours to go from Papeete to Rangiroa but 44 hours to return. There are five double and two triple cabins, and cabin/deck fares are CFP 3,535/5,050 each way. Meals are not included. This small 26-meter vessel tosses a lot in rough weather as it visits the islands to pick up fish and deliver frozen bread, chicken, and ice cream. Their Papeete office is across the hall from the *Aranui* office at Motu Uta. Foreign visitors use this boat regularly, so it's a good bet. The same company runs the *Cobia II* to the Tuamotus, departing Monday at 1200 for Kaukura (Tuesday 0800), Arutua (Tuesday 1300), Apataki (Tuesday 1630), Aratika (Wednesday 0700), and Toau (Wednesday 1330), returning to Papeete Friday at 1000 (also CFP 2,500 one-way). No cabins are available and you must take all your own food.

The *Vai-Aito* (tel. 43-99-96, fax 43-53-04) departs Motu Uta every other Saturday morning for Rangiroa (CFP 4,000 deck from Papeete), Kaukura (CFP 4,500), Apataki (CFP 5,000), Ahe (CFP 5,400), Manihi (CFP 5,800), Aratika (CFP 6,300), Kauehi (CFP 6,600), Raraka (CFP 7,100), and Fakarava (CFP 7,600). A complete roundtrip costs CFP 15,000.

The 48-meter cargo boat *Manava II* (B.P. 1816, 98713 Papeete; tel. 43-83-84, fax 42-25-57) runs to the northern Tuamotus (Rangiroa, Tikehau, Mataiva, Ahe, Manihi, Takaroa, Takapoto, Aratika, Kauehi, Fakarava, Toau, Apataki, Arutua, and Kaukura) once or twice a month. There are no cabins: the deck passage to Rangiroa is CFP 4,000 (meals CFP 1,800 a day extra).

Many smaller copra boats, such as the *Au' Ura Nui III, Hotu Maru, Kauaroa Nui, Kura Ora II, Mareva Nui, Nuku Hau, Rairoa Nui, Ruahatu, Saint Xavier Maris Stella,* and *Vai Aito* also service the Tuamotus. For the Gambiers, it's the monthly *Manava IV* (B.P. 1291, 98713 Papeete; tel. 43-32-65, fax 41-31-65) which does an 18-day roundtrip to Rikitea and the southern Tuamotus. Ask about ships of this kind at the large workshops west of Papeete's Motu Uta interisland wharf.

Ships to the Marquesas

Every two weeks the 75-meter cargo ship *Taporo IV* departs Papeete Thursday at 1700 for Takapoto, Tahuata, Hiva Oa, Nuku Hiva, and Ua Pou, charging passengers CFP 20,200 deck or CFP 30,300 cabin one-way from Papeete to any port in the Marquesas. It takes three and a half days on the open sea to reach the first Marquesan island, so you should certainly try for a cabin. Otherwise you can do the whole eight-day roundtrip for CFP 40,400 deck or CFP 60,600 cabin, but only three to eight hours are spent at each port so you should plan on getting off somewhere and flying back.

The *Taporo IV* has two four-berth cabins and 12 seats on deck. Food is included but it's marginal, so take extras and bring your own bowl. Meals are served at 0600, 1030, and 1730. No pillows or towels are supplied in the cabins and the shower is only open three hours a day. The agent is **Compagnie Française Maritime de Tahiti** (B.P. 368, 98713 Papeete; tel. 42-63-93, fax 42-06-17) at Fare Ute. At island stops *Taporo IV* lowers a container that it uses as an office onto the wharfs.

The *Tamarii Tuamotu II* also departs for the Marquesas monthly with only deck passage available (no cabins). Passage is cheaper at CFP 7,500 each way, plus CFP 2,000 a day for meals, but this ship visits various Tuamotu atolls in each direction, so it takes a lot longer to get to the Marquesas and is only for the very hardy. It calls at every inhabited bay in the Marquesas (this alone takes 12 days). Check at their city office, the Bureau Tamarii Tuamotu (Jacques Wong, B.P. 2606, 98713 Papeete; tel./fax 42-95-07), 43 avenue du Prince Hinoï, corner of rue des Remparts (next to the Europcar office on the east side of the street). It may be out of service.

The *Aranui*

The *Aranui*, a passenger-carrying freighter revamped for tourism, cruises 15 times a year between Papeete and the Marquesas. The ship calls at most of the inhabited Marquesas Islands, plus a couple of the Tuamotus. The routing might be Papeete-Takapoto-Ua Pou-Nuku Hiva-Hiva Oa-Fatu Hiva-Hiva Oa-Ua Huka-Nuku Hiva-Ua Pou-Rangiroa-Papeete. A vigorous daily program with fairly strenuous but optional hikes is included in the tour price. The only docks in the Marquesas are at Taiohae, Vaipaee, Hakahau, and Atuona; elsewhere everyone goes ashore in whale boats, a potential problem for passengers with mobility limitations. Still, the *Aranui* is fine for the adventuresome visitor who wants to see a lot in a short time.

This modern 105-meter freighter had its inaugural sailing in 1990, replacing a smaller German-built boat that had served the Marquesas since 1981. It's clean and pleasant compared to the other ships, but far more expensive. A hundred passengers are accommodated in 40 a/c double cabins or given mattresses on the bridge deck. The cheapest cabin with shared bath for a 15-day, eight-island cruise to the Tuamotus and Marquesas is CFP 304,868 pp roundtrip (double occupancy), all meals included. Cabins with private bath start at CFP 350,632 pp. Single occupancy costs 50% more. There's also an a/c dormitory with upper and lower berths that works out a third cheaper and, of course, doesn't involve a single supplement. A US$75 port tax is extra. Less expensive one-way deck fares are supposed to be for local residents only but it's sometimes possible for tourists to go one way on deck. You can also travel interisland within the Marquesas on deck (about CFP 2,000 a hop), but it's highly unlikely you'd be permitted to do a roundtrip that way. In any case, deck passage can be hot, noisy, and tiring on such a long trip. If traveling one way, pick Nuku Hiva as your destination as you'll save on the exorbitant airport transfers of that island.

Despite the fares charged, don't expect cruise-ship comforts on the *Aranui*. Accommodations are spartan (but adequate), and meals are served in two shifts due to lack of space in the dining area. Aside from three classes of cabins (the cheaper ones are cramped), there's a large covered area where the deck passengers sleep. The roster of American/French/German passengers is congenial.

The *Aranui*'s Papeete office (**Compagnie Polynésienne de Transport Maritime,** B.P. 220, 98713 Papeete; tel. 42-62-40, fax 43-48-89) is at the interisland wharf at Motu Uta. The CPTM's U.S. office is at 2028 El Camino Real South, Ste. B, San Mateo, CA 94403, U.S.A. (tel. 800/972-7268 or 1-650/574-2575, fax 1-650/574-6881, e-mail: cptm@aranui.com). In the U.S. advance bookings can be made through Tahiti Vacations (tel. 800/553-3477, www.tahitivacation.com) or any of the agents listed at www.aranui.com. One Australian reader wrote: "The trip is fantastic and I hope to do it again soon." (The *Aranui* recently costarred with Warren Beatty and Annette Bening in the Warner Brothers film *Love Affair*.)

Tourist Cruises

In 1998 the tall-masted cruise ships *Wind Song* and *Club Med 2* were withdrawn from Tahiti and replaced by the conventional, 320-passenger *Paul Gauguin,* built at St. Nazaire, France, in 1997 and presently operated by Radisson Seven Seas Cruises (600 Corporate Dr., Ste. 410, Fort Lauderdale, FL 33334, U.S.A.; tel. 1-800/477-7500 or 1-800/333-3333, www.rssc.com). This ship does seven-night cruises from Papeete to Rangiroa, Bora Bora, Raiatea, and Moorea year-round, beginning at US$3,195 pp a week double-occupancy for one of the 14 cabins on the bottom deck including airfare from Los Angeles

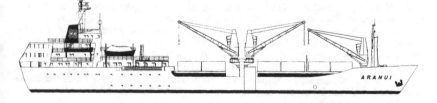

(US$189 port charges are extra). Upper deck cabins with balconies start at US$4,295 pp. There's a spa and fitness center, watersports platform, and lecture program.

Beginning in late 1999 Renaissance Cruises (www.renaissancecruises.com) will operate 10-night cruises from Papeete to the Leeward Islands on the 690-passenger Liberian cruise ship *R3*. The 15 inside cabins on the lowest deck begin at US$2,699 pp double occupancy, plus US$99 port fees, roundtrip airfare from Los Angeles included. Cabins with balconies start at US$3,499 pp (these sale prices could rise). The main market for both of these vessels is the U.S. west coast, which is almost as close to Tahiti as it is to the better-known cruising grounds in the Caribbean.

Since early 1998 the 34-meter mini-cruiseship *Haumana* has done luxury cruises around Raiatea, Taha'a, and Bora Bora. The 21 cabins are US$1,215/1,630 pp double occupancy (plus US$45 port fees) for a three/four-day cruise including excursions. It's run by **Bora Bora Pearl Cruises** (B.P. 9274, 98715 Papeete; tel. 43-43-03, fax 43-17-86, e-mail: haumana@spm.pf). Tour operators such as Tahiti Vacations can book yacht tours in the same area for less money, such as six days on the *Danae III* at US$985 pp. They also offer yacht cruises of the Marquesas Islands.

Also consider **Archipels Croisieres** (B.P. 1160, 98729 Papetoai, Moorea; tel. 56-36-39, fax 56-35-87, www.archipels.com, e-mail: archi-moo@mail.pf), which operates all-inclusive cruises on 17-meter, eight-passenger catamarans. There are three possibilities: a six-night tour of the Leeward Islands is US$1,880 pp, two/three nights cruising the Rangiroa lagoon is US$790/1,030 pp, and seven nights touring five islands in the Marquesas Islands is US$2,050 pp (all double occupancy). Shore excursions and almost everything other than interisland airfare and alcohol is included. A 5% discount is allowed if you book two of the three options back to back. If you don't require the glamour (and large crowds) of large cruise ship, these trips bring you a lot closer to the islands and departures are guaranteed even if only two people reserve. For couples it's much cheaper than chartering a yacht and your experienced crew does all the work. In North America, Tahiti Vacations (tel. 1-

800/553-3477, www.tahitivacation.com) can handle reservations.

Yacht Charters

Yachts are for rent from **Tahiti Yacht Charter** (B.P. 608, 98713 Papeete; tel. 45-04-00, fax 42-76-00, e-mail: tyc@mail.pf) with a base on the Papeete waterfront almost opposite Air France. Their Leeward Island base (tel. 66-28-86, fax 66-28-85) at the Marina Apooiti, one km west of Raiatea Airport, has 10 charter yachts available. Prices begin at CFP 245,000 a week for a six-person Oceanis 350 and increase to CFP 574,000 for a 10-person Kennex 445 catamaran with a supplement in July and August. Charters longer than a week are discounted. A skipper will be CFP 12,000 a day, a cook CFP 10,000.

The South Pacific's largest bareboat yacht charter operation is **The Moorings Ltd.** (B.P. 165, 98735 Uturoa; tel. 66-35-93, fax 66-20-94, e-mail: moorings@mail.pf), a Florida company with 30 yachts based at Raiatea's Marina Apooiti. Bareboat prices begin at US$3,000 a week for a yacht accommodating six and go up to US$6,000 for an eight-person catamaran. Prices are higher during the April-Oct. high season. Provisioning is US$32 pp a day (plus US$120 a day for a cook, if required). If you're new to sailing, a skipper must be hired at US$140 a day and the charterer is responsible for the skipper/cook's provisions. Local tax is three percent, security insurance, US$25 a day, and the starter kit, US$97 and up. This may seem like a lot, but split among a nautical-minded group it's comparable to a deluxe hotel room. Charterers are given a complete briefing on channels and anchorages, and provided with a detailed set of charts. All boats are radio-equipped, and a voice from the Moorings is available to talk nervous skippers in and out. Travel by night is forbidden, but by day it's easy sailing. All charters are from noon to noon. Book through The Moorings Ltd., 19345 US 19 North, Ste. 402, Clearwater, FL 34624-3147, U.S.A. (tel. 1-800/535-7289, fax 1-813/530-9747, www.moorings.com, e-mail: yacht@moorings.com). Ask about "specials" when calling.

A third yacht charter operation, the French-operated **Stardust Marine** (B.P. 331, 98735 Uturoa; tel. 66-23-18, fax 66-23-19), is based at Raiatea's Faaroa Bay. A four-person bareboat yacht is US$337/442/503 in the low/intermediate/high season with substantial reductions for periods over eight or 15 days. Their top-of-the-line eight-passenger deluxe catamaran is US$669/882/951 and there are eight other categories in between. The high season is July and August, intermediate April-June and Sept.-November. If you can schedule a 15-day trip between January and March you can have a bareboat yacht for as little as US$242 a day! Those without the required sailing skills will have to hire a skipper at US$140 a day.

Bookings for all three companies above can be made through **Tahiti Nui Travel** (B.P. 718, 98713 Papeete; tel. 54-02-00, fax 42-74-35, e-mail: info@tahitinuitravel.pf) in Papeete's Vaima Center. Check their internet website at www.tahiti-nui.com for the current prices of all boats.

The territory's top charter vessel may be the luxury catamaran *Tara Vana* built in 1993. When Captain Richard Postma arrived on Bora Bora from Hawaii in 1972 the waitress at Club Med refused to serve him his first cold beer in four weeks. Later she married him and he's been sailing there ever since. Cruises within the Leeward Islands are US$1,650/1,980 a night for two/four people including food and wine, and sportfishing is a specialty. Book through **Solace Destinations** (Box 15245, Newport Beach, CA 92659, U.S.A.; tel. 1-800/548-5331, fax 1-714/650-7175, www.innovision1.com/solace, e-mail: solace@innovision1.com).

Le Truck

Polynesia's folkloric *le truck* provides an entertaining unscheduled passenger service on Tahiti, Huahine, and Raiatea. Passengers sit on long wooden benches in back and there's no problem with luggage. Fares are fairly low and often posted on the side of the vehicle. You pay through the window on the right side of the cab. Drivers are generally friendly and will stop to pick you up anywhere if you wave—they're all self-employed, so there's no way they'd miss a fare! On Tahiti the larger *trucks* leave Papeete for the outlying districts periodically throughout the day until 1700; they continue running to Faa'a Airport and the Maeva Beach Hôtel until around 2200. On Huahine and Raiatea service is usually limited to a trip into the main town in the morning and a return to the villages in the afternoon. On Moorea and Bora Bora buses or *trucks* meet the boats

from Papeete. No public transportation is available on the roads of the Austral, Tuamotu, Gambier, or Marquesas islands.

Car Rentals

Car rentals are available at most of the airports served by Air Tahiti and they're more expensive on the Leeward Islands than on Tahiti or Moorea due to a lack of competition. On Tahiti there's sometimes a mileage charge, whereas on Moorea, Huahine, Raiatea, and Bora Bora all rentals come with unlimited mileage. Public liability insurance is included by law, but collision damage waiver (CDW) insurance is extra. The insurance policies don't cover flat tire repair, stolen radios or accessories, broken keys, or towing charges if the renter is found to be responsible. If you can get a small group together, consider renting a minibus for a do-it-yourself island tour. Unless you have a major credit card you'll have to put a cash deposit down on the car. Your home driver's license will be accepted, although you must have had your driver's license for at least a year. Some companies rent to persons aged 18-24, but those under 25 must show a major credit card and the deductible amount not covered by the CDW insurance will be much higher.

Except on Tahiti, rental scooters are usually available and a strictly enforced local regulation requires you to wear a helmet *(casque)* at all times (CFP 5,000 fine for failure to comply). On some outer islands you can rent an open two-seater "fun car" slightly bigger than a golf cart and no helmet or driver's license is required for these. These and bicycles carry no insurance.

One major hassle with renting cars on the outer islands is that they usually give you a car with the fuel tank only a quarter full, so immediately after renting you must go to a gas station and tank up. Try to avoid putting in more gas than you can use by calculating how many km you might drive, then dividing that by 10 for the number of liters of gasoline you might use. Don't put in over CFP 2,000 (about 20 liters) in any case or you'll be giving a nice gift to the rental agency (which, of course, is their hope in giving you a car that's not full). Gas stations are usually only in the main towns and open only weekdays during business hour, plus perhaps a couple of hours on weekend mornings. Expect to pay around CFP 112 a liter for gas, which works out to just over US$4 per American gallon—the South Pacific's highest priced gasoline to drive the most region's expensive rental cars.

Two traffic signs to know: a white line across a red background indicates a one-way street, while a slanting blue line on a white background means no parking. At unmarked intersections in Papeete, the driver on the right has priority. As in continental Europe and North America, driving is on the right-hand side of the road. The seldom-observed speed limit is 40 kph in Papeete, 60 kph around the island, and 90 kph on the RDO expressway. Drive with extreme care in congested areas—traffic accidents are frequent.

A good alternative to renting a car are the 4WD jeep safaris offered on Tahiti, Moorea, Huahine, Raiatea, and Bora Bora. These take you along rough interior roads inaccessible to most rental vehicles and the guides know all the superlative spots. Prices vary CFP 3,500-7,000 pp depending on how far you go.

Others

Taxis are a rip-off throughout Tahiti-Polynesia and are best avoided. If you must take one, always verify the fare before getting in. The hitching is still fairly good in Polynesia, although local residents along the north side of Moorea are fed up with it and don't stop. Hitching around Tahiti is only a matter of time.

Bicycling on the island of Tahiti is risky due to wild devil-may-care motorists, but most of the outer islands (Moorea included) have excellent, uncrowded roads. It's wiser to use *le truck* on Tahiti, though a bike would come in handy on the other islands where *le truck* is rare. The distances are just made for cycling!

International Airport

Faa'a Airport (PPT), 5.5 km southwest of Papeete, handles around 32,000 domestic, 2,300 international, and 1,000 military flights a year. The runway was created in 1959-61, using material dredged from the lagoon or trucked in from the Punaruu Valley. A taxi into town is CFP 1,500, or CFP 2,500 after 2000. *Le truck* up on the main highway will take you to the same place for only CFP 120 (CFP 200 at night) and starts running around 0530.

Many flights to Tahiti arrive in the middle of the night, but you can stretch out on the plastic benches inside the terminal (open 24 hours a day). Be aware that the persons who seem to be staffing the tourist information counter at the airport during the night may in fact be taxi drivers who will say anything to get a fare. We've received complaints from readers who were driven all over town from one closed hostel to another, only to be presented with a tremendous bill (you have been warned). Unless you're willing to spend a lot of money for the possibility of a few hours sleep it's better to wait in the terminal until dawn.

The Westpac Bank (tel. 82-44-24), to the left as you come out of customs, opens weekdays 0730-1200/1245-1600, and one hour before and after the arrival and departure of all international flights. They charge commission CFP 450 on all traveler's checks (but no commission on French francs in cash). For other currencies, their rate is 1% better for traveler's checks than it is for cash. There's also a Banque Socredo branch (tel. 83-86-95) next to the Air Tahiti ticket office facing the parking lot at the far right (west) end of the airport. This office is not easily visible from inside the terminal, so search. It's open weekdays 0800-1200/1400-1700 (no exchanges after 1630) and an adjacent ATM machine is accessible 24 hours.

The airport luggage-storage counter is open weekdays 0700-1800, weekends 0700-1200/1400-1830, and two hours before and after international departures. They charge CFP 180 per day for a handbag, CFP 360 for a suitcase, backpack, or golf bags, CFP 600 for a bicycle, and CFP 1,000 for surfboards. If they're closed when you arrive, ask at the nearby snack bar. The left-luggage counter is poorly marked; it's to the right as you come out of customs and just outside the main terminal in an adjacent building.

Air Tahiti has a ticket office in the terminal open daily 0530-1730. These car rental companies have counters at the airport: Avis, Daniel, Europcar, Hertz, and Pierrot et Jacqueline. The airport post office is open weekdays 0600-1000/1300-1600, weekends 0600-1000. Several coin and card phones available at airport. The snack bar at the airport is open 24 hours (CFP 200 for cafe au lait). Public toilets are located near the snack bar and upstairs from the bank. The airport information number is tel. 86-60-61.

You can spend your leftover Pacific francs at the duty-free shops in the departure lounge, but don't expect any bargains. The Fare Hei, just outside the terminal, sells shell and flower leis for presentation to arriving or departing passengers.

All passengers arriving from Samoa or Fiji must have their baggage fumigated upon arrival, a process that takes about two hours (don't laugh if you're told this is to prevent the introduction of the "rhinoceros" into Polynesia—they mean the rhinoceros *beetle*). Fresh fruits, vegetables, and flowers are prohibited entry. Free luggage carts are supplied. There's no airport tax.

dolphin fish

LOUISE FOOTE

M.G.L. DOMENY DE RIENZI

TAHITI

Tahiti, largest of the Societies, is an island of legend and song lying in the eye of Polynesia. Though only one of 118, this lush island of around 150,000 inhabitants is paradise itself to most people. Here you'll find an exciting city, big hotels, restaurants, nightclubs, things to see and do, valleys, mountains, reefs, trails, and history, plus transportation to everywhere. Since the days of Wallis, Bougainville, Cook, and Bligh, Tahiti has been the eastern gateway to the South Pacific.

In 1891 Paul Gauguin arrived at Papeete after a 63-day sea voyage from France. He immediately felt that Papeete "was Europe—the Europe which I had thought to shake off . . . it was the Tahiti of former times which I loved. That of the present filled me with horror." So Gauguin left the town and rented a native-style bamboo hut in Mataiea on the south coast, where he found happiness in the company of a 14-year-old Tahitian *vahine* whose "face flood-ed the interior of our hut and the landscape round about with joy and light." Somerset Maugham's *The Moon and Sixpence* is a fictional tale of Gauguin's life on the island.

Legends created by the early explorers, amplified in Jean-Jacques Rousseau's "noble savage" and taken up by the travel industry, make it difficult to write objectively about Tahiti. Though the Lafayette Nightclub is gone from Arue and Quinn's Tahitian Hut no longer graces Papeete's waterfront, Tahiti remains a delightful, enchanting place. In the late afternoon, as Tahitian crews practice canoe racing in the lagoon and Moorea gains a pink hue, the romance resurfaces. If you steer clear of the traffic jams and congestion in commercial Papeete and avoid the tourist ghettos west of the city, you can get a taste of the magic Gauguin encountered. But whether you love or hate the capital, it's only on the outer islands of Polynesia, away from the motorists and the military complexes, that the full flavor lingers.

The Land

The island of Tahiti (1,045 square km) accounts for almost a third of the land area of Tahiti-Polynesia. Like Hawaii's Maui, Tahiti was formed over a million years ago by two or three shield volcanoes joined at the isthmus of Taravao. These peaks once stood 3,000 meters above the sea, or 12,700 meters high counting from the seabed. Today the rounded, verdant summits of Orohena (2,241 meters) and Aorai (2,066 meters) rise in the center of Tahiti-nui and deep valleys radiate in all directions from these central peaks. Steep slopes drop abruptly from the high plateaus to coastal plains. The northeast coast is rugged and rocky, without a barrier reef, and thus exposed to intense, pounding surf; villages lie on a narrow strip between mountains and ocean. The south coast is broad and gentle with large gardens and coconut groves; a barrier reef shields it from the sea's fury.

Tahiti-iti (also called the Taiarapu Peninsula) is a peninsula with no road around it. It's a few hundred thousand years younger than Tahiti-nui and Mount Rooniu (1,323 meters) forms its heart. The populations of big (nui) and small (iti) Tahiti are concentrated in Papeete and along the coast; the interior of both Tahitis is almost uninhabited. Contrary to the popular stereotype, mostly brown/black beaches of volcanic sand fringe this turtle-shaped island. To find the white/golden sands of the travel brochures, you must cross over to Moorea.

Environmental Concerns

Nonstop development over the past 35 years has had a heavy impact on the crowded 40-km coastal strip around Papeete. Aside from high-profile traffic congestion, the lagoon off northwestern Tahiti has been seriously affected by the quarrying of coral building materials from the seabed (halted in 1987), soil erosion resulting from construction work on adjacent hillsides, and inadequate treatment of sewage and solid wastes.

Half of the coastline between Punaauia and Arue is now artificial or reclaimed, and mud carried into the lagoon from unprotected terraces at building sites has increased turbidity, suffocating coral growth and causing flooding. A 1993 case study released by the South Pacific Regional Environment Program reports heavy metal concentrations on the lagoon floor up to 12 times higher than normal with especially high contamination in the port area. The SPREP study warns that "faecal pollution rules out swimming from most of the beaches within Papeete urban

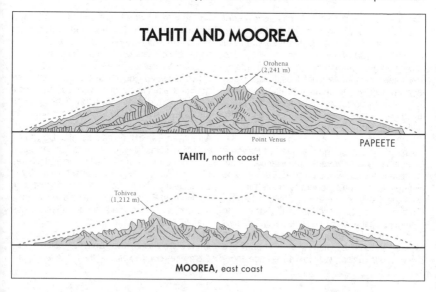

TAHITI AND MOOREA

Orohena
(2,241 m)

Point Venus   PAPEETE

TAHITI, north coast

Tohivea
(1,212 m)

MOOREA, east coast

area, because of the lack of a coherent, integrated waste water collection and treatment system, and because effluent is still often disposed of straight into the lagoon."

The city's six official solid waste dumps are not only ugly, but they create a stench due to the lack of sorting and frequent fires. Recently a large amount was spent on a methane-producing incinerator in the heavily populated Tipaerui Valley above the Hôtel Matavai, but this sparked heated protests from local residents who felt endangered by emissions and in early 1994 part of the plant was closed. According to the SPREP study, Papeete's "water is piped from many open, above-ground catchments that have uneven degrees of protection and control, and is often untreated and not potable." Even in par-

adise, progress has a price which we as consumers must pay in the end.

Orientation

Almost everyone arrives at Faa'a International Airport five km west of Papeete, the capital and main tourist center of Tahiti-Polynesia. East of Papeete are Pirae, Arue, and Mahina, with a smattering of hotels and things to see, while south of Faa'a lie the commuter communities Punaauia, Paea, and Papara. On the narrow neck of Tahiti is Taravao, a refueling stop on your 117-km way around Tahiti-nui. Tahiti-iti is a backwater, with dead-end roads on both sides. Boulevard Pomare curves around Papeete's harbor to the tourist office near the market—that's where to begin. Moorea is clearly visible to the northwest.

PAPEETE

Papeete (pa-pay-EH-tay) means "Water Basket." The most likely explanation for this name is that islanders originally used calabashes enclosed in baskets to fetch water at a spring behind the present Territorial Assembly. Founded as a mission station by the Rev. William Crook in 1818, whalers began frequenting Papeete's port in the 1820s as it offered better shelter than Matavai Bay. It became the seat of government when young Queen Pomare IV settled here in 1827. The French governors who "protected" the island from 1842 also used Papeete as their headquarters.

Today Papeete is the political, cultural, economic, and communications hub of Tahiti-Polynesia. Over 100,000 people live in this cosmopolitan city, crowded between the mountains and the sea, and its satellite towns, Faa'a, Pirae, and Arue—over half the people on the island. "Greater Papeete" extends for 32 km from Paea to Mahina. In addition, thousands of French soldiers are stationed here, mostly hardened foreign legionnaires and paramilitary police. The French Naval facilities in the harbor area were constructed in the 1960s to support nuclear testing in the Tuamotus.

Since the opening of Faa'a International Airport in 1961 Papeete has blossomed with new hotels, expensive restaurants, bars with wild dancing, radio towers, skyscrapers, and elec-

tric rock bands pulsing their jet-age beat. Where a nail or red feather may once have satisfied a Tahitian, VCRs and Renaults are now in demand. Over 35,000 registered vehicles jam Tahiti's 200 km of roads. Noisy automobiles, motorcycles, and mopeds clog Papeete's downtown and roar along boulevards Pomare and Prince Hinoï buffeting pedestrians with pollution and noise. Crossing the street you can literally take your life in your hands.

Yet along the waterfront the yachts of many countries rock luxuriously in their Mediterranean moorings (anchor out and stern lines ashore). Many of the boats are permanent homes for expatriate French working in the city. "Bonitiers" moored opposite the Vaima Center fish for *auhopu* (bonito) for the local market. You should not really "tour" Papeete, just wander about without any set goal. Visit the highly specialized French boutiques, Chinese stores trying to sell everything, and Tahitians clustered in the market. Avoid the capital on weekends when life washes out into the countryside; on Sunday afternoons it's a ghost town. Explore Papeete, but make it your starting point—not a final destination.

Orientation

Thanks to airline schedules you'll probably arrive at the crack of dawn. Change money at the airport bank or use a couple of US$1 bills to take *le truck* to Papeete market. The helpful tourist office on the waterfront opens early, as do the banks nearby. You'll probably want a hotel in town for the first couple of nights to attend to "business": reconfirm your flights, check out the boats or planes, then take off for the outer islands.

A trip around the island will fill a day if you're waiting for connections, and Papeete itself can be fun. Fare Ute, north of French naval headquarters, was reclaimed with material dredged from the harbor in 1963. West across a bridge, past more military muscle, is Motu Uta, where you can jump aboard a passenger-carrying freighter. The high-speed boats and all of the Moorea ferries leave from the landing behind the tourist office downtown. For a day at the beach take *le truck* to Point Venus.

SIGHTS

Papeete
Begin your visit at teeming **Papeete market** (rebuilt 1987) where you'll see Tahitians selling fish, fruit, root crops, and breadfruit; Chinese gardeners with their tomatoes, lettuce, and other vegetables; and French or Chinese offering meat and bakery products. The colorful throng is especially picturesque 1600-1700 when the fishmongers spring to life. Fish and vegetables are sold downstairs on the main floor, handicrafts,

pareus, and snacks upstairs on the balcony. The flower displays outside make great photos and the vendors are quite friendly. The biggest market of the week begins around 0500 Sunday morning and is over by 0730.

The streets to the north of the market are lined with two-story Chinese stores built after the great fire of 1884. The US$14.5-million **Town Hall** on rue Paul Gauguin was inaugurated in 1990 on the site of a smaller colonial building demolished to make way. The architect designed the three-story building to resemble the palace of Queen Pomare that once stood on Place Tarahoi near the present post office. The Town Hall gardens are a nice place to sit.

Notre Dame Catholic Cathedral (1875) is on rue du Général de Gaulle, a block and a half southeast of the market. Notice the Polynesian faces and the melange of Tahitian and Roman dress on the striking series of paintings of the crucifixion inside. Diagonally across the street is the **Vaima Center,** Papeete's finest window shopping venue, erected in 1977.

Farther down on rue de Gaulle is Place Tarahoi. The **Territorial Assembly** on the left occupies the site of the former royal palace, demolished in 1966. The adjacent residence of the French high commissioner is private, but the assembly building and its lovely gardens are worth a brief visit. In front of the entrance gate is a monument erected in 1982 to **Pouvanaa a Oopa**

Papeete as it looked around the turn of the century

HUNGARIAN ETHNOGRAPHICAL MUSEUM, BUDAPEST

THE STREETS OF PAPEETE

Papeete's streets bear the names of an odd assortment of French politicians, officials, military leaders, missionaries, and explorers, many of them unfamiliar to English speakers. The city's principal coastal boulevard is named for the Pomare dynasty, which ruled during the implantation of French colonialism. Similarly, Prince Hinoï (1869-1916), who succeeded the puppet king Pomare V, lent his name to the main avenue leading east from the harbor. Papeete's most prominent park bears the name of French explorer Louis-Antoine de Bougainville (1729-1811), whereas Captain Samuel Wallis who arrived a year earlier is not remembered and Captain Cook merits only a small sidestreet west of the center. In contrast, an important bypass behind downtown celebrates Dumont d'Urville (1790-1842), a French explorer who visited Tahiti 55 years after Wallis.

Admiral Abel Dupetit-Thouars, who declared a French protectorate over Tahiti in 1842, and Admiral Armand Bruat, the first French governor, are acclaimed by streets near the residence of the present French High Commissioner. A busy east-west thoroughfare passing here bears the names of four prominent Frenchmen: Commandant Destremeau, who defended Papeete against German cruisers in 1914, General De Gaulle (1890-1970), who initiated nuclear testing in Polynesia in 1966, Maréchal Foch (1851-1929), the Allied military commander during the closing months of WW I, and Georges Clémenceau (1841-1929), the French premier during and after WW I.

Less known are the church leaders whose names have been attached to streets around Papeete's Catholic cathedral. Rue Monseigneur Tepano Jaussen, the road leading to the bishop's palace, recalls Florentin Étienne Jaussen (1815-1891) who was appointed vicar apostolic in 1851. This road crosses a street which commemorates Venerable Anne-Marie Javouhey (1779-1851), who founded the Sisters of St. Joseph of Cluny, which did Catholic missionary work in the French colonies. A road between Papeete's city hall and the market honors Gilles Colette, the free-thinking parish priest of Papeete in the late 19th century.

Protestants have been awarded a nearby back-street named for Huguenot missionary Charles Viénot, who promoted Protestant education on Tahiti around the turn of the century. The street between rues Viénot and Jaussen recalls Edouard Ahnne, the director of Catholic boys schools on Tahiti in the early 20th century and leader of the campaign to recognize the Free French forces at the beginning of WW II.

The street in front of the Catholic cathedral recognizes Jeanne d'Arc (1412-31), the national hero of France who was burned at the stake for heresy after helping to save France from the wicked English. Rue des Poilus Tahitiens, in front of the war memorial on avenue Bruat, memorializes the Tahitian volunteers who fought for France in WW I. Rue de la Canonnière Zélée nearby salutes the French warship sunk at Papeete by German cruisers in 1914. And last but not least, rue Paul Gauguin passes in front of Papeete city hall, a bastion of minor officialdom, the very class so despised by the painter during his lifetime.

(1895-1977), a Tahitian WW I hero who struggled all his life for the independence of his country. The plaque on the monument says nothing about Pouvanaa's fight for independence and against the bomb! In July 1995 nearly a third of the adult population of Tahiti gathered here to protest French nuclear testing in the Tuamotus.

Beside the post office across the busy avenue from Place Tarahoi is **Parc Bougainville** with its garden café. A monument to Bougainville himself, who sailed around the world in 1766-69, is flanked by two old naval guns. One, stamped "Fried Krupp 1899," is from Count Felix von Luckner's famous raider *Seeadler,* which ended up on the Maupihaa reef in 1917; the other is

off the French gunboat *Zélée,* sunk in Papeete harbor by German cruisers in 1914.

Much of the bureaucracy works along avenue Bruat just west, a gracious tree-lined French provincial avenue. The protectorate's first governor, Admiral Armand Bruat, set up a military camp here in 1843. You may observe French justice in action at the **Palais de Justice** (weekdays 0800-1100). The public gallery is up the stairway and straight ahead. Opposite the police station farther up avenue Bruat is the War Memorial.

Back on the waterfront just before the Protestant church is the **Tahiti Perles Center** (B.P. 850, 98713 Papeete; tel. 50-53-10). A black pearl museum (weekdays 0800-1200 and 1400-

POUVANAA A OOPA

Pouvanaa a Oopa was born at Maeva on Huahine in 1895 and during WW I he served in France. In 1942 he denounced war profiteers and was placed under arrest on Huahine. A year later he managed to escape with another man by canoe to Bora Bora in the hope of obtaining American help, but was arrested and returned to Huahine three days later. After the war Pouvanaa continued to oppose the colonial administration and to advocate a freer political alliance with France. He was elected a deputy to the French parliament in 1949, 1952, and 1956 on an autonomy program. In 1957 he became vice-president of the local administration and campaigned for independence in the 1958 referendum, but the No side got only 35% of the vote throughout the territory. Later that year he was falsely accused of trying to set Papeete aflame and was sentenced to 15 years imprisonment. Finally pardoned in 1968, Pouvanaa was elected a senator in the French parliament two years later, a post he held until his death in 1977. Known to the Tahitians as *metua* (spiritual father), Pouvanaa a Oopa remains a symbol of the Polynesian struggle for independence.

1730, Saturday 0900-1200; admission free) and aquarium are the main attractions, but look around the showroom where the famous black pearls are sold. A 20-minute video presentation shown on request explains how cultured black pearls are "farmed" in the Gambier Islands. The

center is owned by a pioneer of the black pearl industry, Robert Wan, whose nine farms in the Gambier and Tuamotu groups are linked to Tahiti by his own charter airline Wanair.

Next to the pearl museum is the headquarters of the **Evangelical Church** in Tahiti-Polynesia, with a church dating from 1875 but rebuilt in 1981, a girls' hostel, public cafeteria, and health clinic. It was here that the London Missionary Society established Paofai Mission in 1818. The British consulate occupied the hostel site from 1837 to 1958 and George Pritchard, an early British consul, had his office here.

Continue west along the bay past the outrigger racing canoes to the "neo-Polynesian" **Cultural Center** (1973) or Te Fare Tahiti Nui, which houses a public library, notice boards, and auditoriums set among pleasant grounds. This complex is run by the Office Territorial d'Action Culturelle (OTAC), which organizes the annual Heiva Festival and many other events. The municipal swimming pool is beyond (go upstairs to the restaurant for a view). Return to the center of town along the waterfront.

Another walk takes you east from downtown to the Catholic **Archbishop's Palace** (1869), a lonely remnant of the Papeete that Gauguin saw. To get there, take the road behind the Catholic cathedral, keep straight, and ask for the *archevêché catholique*. Without doubt, this is the finest extant piece of colonial architecture in a territory of fast-disappearing historic buildings. The park grounds planted in citrus and the modern open-air church nearby (to the right) also merit a look. The huge mango trees in front of the church were planted in 1855 by Tahiti's first bishop, Monseigneur Tepano Jaussen.

Fautaua Valley
If you'd like to make a short trip out of the city, go to the Hôtel de Ville and take a Mamao-Titioro *truck* to the **Bain Loti,** three km up the Fautaua Valley from the Mormon Temple. A bust of writer Pierre Loti marks the spot where he had the love affair described in *The Marriage of Loti.* Today the local kids swim in a pool in the river here.

A dirt road continues three km farther up the Fautaua Valley but because it's part of a water catchment, private cars are prohibited, so you must walk. From the end of the road, a trail straight ahead leads directly to **Fautaua Falls** (30 minutes) with several river crossings. Back a bit on the left, just before the end of the road, is a wooden footbridge across the river. Here begins a steep one-hour trail up to a 19th-century French fort at the top of the falls. The fort controlled the main trail into Tahiti's interior, and it's still an excellent hiking area. There's a CFP 600 pp charge to go up the valley, and it's only open on weekdays. Go early and make a day of it.

Back on avenue Georges Clemenceau near the Mormon Temple is the impressive **Kanti Chinese Temple,** built in 1987, which is usually open mornings until noon.

East of Papeete

Arue (a-roo-AY) and Point Venus can be done easily as a half-day side trip from Papeete by *le truck* (12 km each way). Begin by taking a Mahina *truck* from near the tourist office to the **tomb of King Pomare V** at PK 4.7 Arue, five km outside the city. The mausoleum surmounted by a Grecian urn was built in 1879 for Queen Pomare IV, but her remains were subsequently removed to make room for her son, Pomare V, who died of drink in 1891 at the age of 52 (Paul Gauguin witnessed the funeral). Irreverent tour guides often remark that the urn resembles a bottle of Benedictine, Pomare V's favorite liqueur. A century earlier, on 13 February 1791, his grandfather, Pomare II, then nine, was made first king of Tahiti on the great *marae* that once stood on this spot. Pomare II became the first Christian convert and built a 215-meter-long version of King Solomon's Temple here, but nothing remains of either temple.

At PK 5.4, Arue, next to the École Maternelle Ahutoru, stand the tombs of Pomare I, II, III, and IV in the **Cimetière Pomare.** This less-known site is not signposted, but a building across the street is marked Artisanat. A board next to the cemetery clearly identifies the many Pomare graves here. The colonial-style **Mairie de Arue** (1892) is at PK 5.6.

The **Royal Matavai Bay Resort Hôtel** (PK 8.1) on One Tree Hill, a couple of km east of the Pomare graves, was built in 1968 on a spectacular series of terraces down the hillside to conform to a local regulation that no building should be more than two-thirds the height of a coconut tree. There's a superb view of Point Venus, Tahiti, and Moorea from the Governor's Bench on the knoll beyond the swimming pool above the hotel entrance. In Matavai Bay below the resort, Capt. Samuel Wallis anchored in 1767, after having "discovered" Tahiti. There's good swimming off the black beach below the hotel.

Catch another *truck* or walk on to **Point Venus** (PK 10). Captain Cook camped on this point between the river and the lagoon during his visit to observe the transit of the planet Venus across the sun on 3 June 1769. Captain Bligh also occupied Point Venus for two months in 1788 while collecting breadfruit shoots for transportation to the West Indies. On 5 March 1797, the first members of the London Missionary Society landed here, as a monument recalls. From Tahiti, Protes-

M.G.L. DOMENY DE RIENZI

Matavai Bay, Tahiti, as it appeared in the early 19th century

tantism spread throughout Polynesia and as far as Vanuatu.

Today there's a park on the point, with a 25-meter-high lighthouse (1867) among the palms and ironwood trees. The view of Tahiti across Matavai Bay is superb, and twin-humped Orohena, highest peak on the island, is in view (you can't see it from Papeete itself). Topless sunbathing is common on the wide dark sands along the bay and you can see pareus being made in the handicraft center in the park. Weekdays, Point Venus is a peaceful place, the perfect choice if you'd like to get away from the rat race in Papeete and spend some time at the beach (weekends it gets crowded).

SPORTS AND RECREATION

Information on the **International Golf Course Olivier Breaud** on the south coast at Atimaono, can be found later in this chapter.

Tahiti Plongée (B.P. 2192, 98713 Papeete; tel./fax 41-00-62), also known as "Club Corail Sub," offers scuba diving several times daily from its base at the Hôtel Te Puna Bel Air, Punaauia. The charge is CFP 4,000 per dive all-inclusive, or CFP 19,000 for a five-dive card, CFP 30,000 for 10 dives. You can ocean dive Tues.-Sun. at 0800 and on Wednesday and Saturday at 1400; lagoon diving is daily at 1000 and weekdays at 1400 (no diving on Monday). Divemaster Henri Pouliquen was one of the first to teach scuba diving to children. The youngest person Henri has taken down was aged two years, six months—the oldest was a woman of 72 on her first dive. Since 1979 Tahiti Plongée has arranged over 10,000 dives with children, certainly a unique achievement. Another specialty is diving for people with disabilities.

Diving is also offered by a new scuba operation at the **Sofitel Maeva Beach** (B.P. 6008, 98702 Faa'a; tel. 42-80-42, fax 43-84-70) and by **Eleuthera Plongée** (tel. 42-49-29) at the Marina Taina in Punaauia.

On the other side of Papeete, you can dive with Pascal Le Cointre of the **Yacht Club of Tahiti** (B.P. 51167, 98716 Pirae; tel. 42-23-55, fax 43-64-36) at PK 4, Arue. Outings are offered at 0900 and 1400 daily except Sunday afternoon and Monday. It's CFP 5,000 for one dive or

CFP 22,500 for five dives. A certification course costs the same as five dives, plus CFP 2,200/2,500 for CMAS/PADI registration (log book CFP 1,600 extra)—good value.

International Tahiti Immersions (Joël Roussel, tel./fax 57-77-93), at the Marina Puunui on the southeast side of the island, does scuba diving at CFP 5,000 a dive.

If you want to set out on your own, **Nauti-Sport** (B.P. 62, 98713 Papeete; tel. 50-59-59, fax 42-17-75; weekdays 0800-1145/1315-1700, Saturday 0730-1130) in Fare Ute sells every type of scuba gear and also rents tanks (CFP 2,500). The **Centre de Plongée Dolphin Sub** (B.P. 5213, 98716 Pirae; tel. 45-21-98, fax 43-39-49) behind Nauti-Sport offers scuba trips at 0845 and 1400 daily at competitive prices and has information on diving all around Polynesia.

Most diving is on the Punaauia reef. Other favorite scuba locales include a scuttled Pan Am Catalina PBY seaplane near the airport, its upper wing 12 meters down; and a schooner wreck, 10 meters down, about 45 meters from the breakwater at the entrance to the harbor.

The **Ski Nautique Club de Tahiti** (tel. 77-22-62; Tues.-Fri. 1200-1800, weekends 0900-1800) on the waterfront at the Hôtel Te Puna Bel Air, Punaauia, offers water-skiing at CFP 2,300 or CFP 20,000 for 10 sessions.

The **Tura'i Mata'are Surfing School** (B.P. 4232, 98713 Papeete; tel./fax 41-91-37), at Kelly Surf Boutique in the Fare Tony Commercial Center on boulevard Pomare, Papeete, teaches surfing and body surfing to persons from the age of eight and up. Their half-day introduction to surfing is CFP 4,000, and courses with five three-hour lessons (CFP 18,000) or 10 lessons (CFP 25,000) are offered. Boards and transportation are supplied and a certificate is issued.

Papeete's **municipal swimming pool** (tel. 42-89-24) is open to the public Tues.-Fri. 1145-1600, Saturday and Sunday 0730-1700 (CFP 350). Most evenings after 1800 **soccer** is practiced in the sports field opposite the municipal swimming pool.

MOUNTAIN CLIMBING

Tahiti's finest climb is to the summit of **Aorai** (2,066 meters), second-ranking peak on the island. (Some guides claim 2,110-meter Piti Hiti is the second-highest peak on Tahiti but it's actually a shoulder of Orohena.) A beaten 10-km track all the way to the top of Aorai makes a guide unnecessary, but food, water, flashlight, and long pants *are* required, plus a sleeping bag and warm sweater if you plan to spend the night up there. At last report the refuges at Fare Mato (1,400 meters) and Fare Ata (1,800 meters) were in good shape with drinking water available and splendid sunset views. Each refuge sleeps about 10 persons on the floor at no charge.

The trailhead is at Fare Rau Ape (600 meters) near **Le Belvédère** (tel. 42-73-44), a fancy French restaurant seven km up a rough, potholed road from Pirae. Taxis want CFP 5,000 for the trip from Papeete and few people live up there, so hitching would be a case of finding tourists headed for the restaurant, and weekends are best for this. You could rent a small car at the kilometer rate but parking near the restaurant is limited.

The restaurant does provide their clients with free *truck* transportation from most Papeete hotels and this the easiest way to get there. You can reserve the Belvédère *truck* at the Hôtel Royal Papeete reception or at Tahiti Nui Travel in the Vaima Center. Of course, in order to use it you'll be required to take a complete meal including salad, dessert, coffee, and wine at CFP 4,500. The specialty is fondue bourguignone, a meat fondue, but you can substitute mahi mahi,

steak, or shish kebab. The *truck* departs most Papeete hotels at 1130 and 1630, leaving the restaurant for the return trip to Papeete at 1430 and 1930.

To make a day of it, catch the 1130 *truck* up to the restaurant on the understanding that you'll be eating dinner and returning to town on the 1930 *truck* (make sure all of this is clearly understood before you pay—Tina Brichet at Le Belvédère speaks good English). This would give you all afternoon to cover part of the trail, although it's unlikely you'd have time to reach the top (even if you only get as far as Fare Mato it's still well worth the effort). Take a sandwich along for lunch. You should be able to leave some clean clothes at the restaurant to change into for dinner, and be sure to bring your bathing suit and a towel in case you have time to use their swimming pool. If you can get in all of this, the CFP 4,500 pp price becomes quite reasonable.

A large signboard outside the restaurant maps out the hike. Just above the restaurant is the French Army's Centre d'Instruction de Montagne, where you can sign a register. From Fare Rau Ape to the summit takes seven hours: an hour and a half to Hamuta, another two to Fare Mato (good view of Le Diadème, not visible from Papeete), then two and a half hours to Fare Ata, where most hikers spend the first night in order to cover the last 40 minutes to the summit the following morning. The hut at Fare Ata is in a low depression 100 meters beyond an open shelter.

You'll get this unobstructed view of Le Diadème from the Mt. Aorai Trail.

DAVID STANLEY

The view from Aorai is magnificent, with Papeete and many of the empty interior valleys in full view. To the north is Tetiaroa atoll, while Moorea's jagged outline fills the west. Even on a cloudy day the massive green hulk of neighboring Orohena (2,241 meters) often towers above the clouds like Mt. Olympus. A bonus is the chance to see some of the original native vegetation of Tahiti, which survives better at high altitudes and in isolated gullies. In good weather Aorai is exhausting but superb; in the rain it's a disaster.

When the author of this book climbed Aorai some years ago, the trip could be done by anyone in reasonable physical shape. Later we heard that the trail had deteriorated, with sheer slopes and slippery, crumbling ridges to be negotiated. In the past we've asked readers to write in with current information on Aorai, and we're grateful to Charlie Appleton of Paddington, Australia, for sending us this report:

The trail has been restored and is now well maintained. The chalets at Fare Mato and Fare Ata were in excellent order, the former sitting on a recently reconstructed platform. They'll sleep 12-15 without difficulty, and both have drinking water and solar electricity! Just above Fare Mato cables have been fixed along the section of trail with the steepest drops on both sides, allowing some fairly inexperienced hikers I met to traverse it with confidence. Very few people do the climb, and if you go in the middle of the week you can expect to have the mountain to yourself. It might be worth mentioning that the compelling reason for spending the night on top (apart from sunset and sunrise) is that those who make the roundtrip in a day are likely to find that by the time they near the summit the mountain will have put on its midday hat of clouds, limiting their views.

Orohena

Aorai's neighbor **Orohena** (2,241 meters) is seldom climbed, since the way involves considerable risks. The route up Orohena begins at the office of the Sheriff de Mahina, opposite the military laboratories (PK 11). Follow the road five km straight up through Mahinarama subdivision. At about 600 meters elevation, where Allée Tuauru on the right climbs to Residence Les Hauts de Mahinarama, you see a red fire hydrant and a dirt road with a chain across it straight ahead. Park here and hike up this road past two large water tanks (these directions could change due to ongoing residential development in this area).

A jeep track built into the slope in 1975 follows the contour six km up the Tuauru River valley to the **Thousand Springs** at 900 meters elevation. Anyone at Mahinarama will be able to direct you to the "Route des Mille Sources." The actual Orohena trail begins at the Thousand Springs and climbs steeply to Pito Iti where hikers spend the night before ascending Orohena the following morning. A guide is most certainly required to climb Orohena, but anyone can do the Thousand Springs hike on their own, enjoying good views of the rounded peaks of Orohena to the left and Aorai's long ridge to the right. There's nothing special to see at the Thousand Springs, so turn back whenever you like.

Mt. Marau

The road inland from directly opposite Faa'a Airport goes under the RDO bypass road and up the side of the island to an excellent viewpoint over northwestern Tahiti. It's a rough 10 km drive which should only be attempted in dry weather. From the TV tower at the end of the track it's only 30 minutes on foot to the summit of Mt. Marau (1,493 meters). From here you'll get another incredible view down into the Plateau of Oranges to the south, up the Fautaua Valley to the north, and along the ridge to Le Diadème and Aorai to the east.

Guides

These and other hikes on Tahiti are led on weekends and holidays by **Pierre Florentin** (B.P. 5323, 98716 Pirae; tel./fax 43-72-01), a professional mountain guide with 20 years of experience. Pierre charges a fixed rate of CFP 16,000 a day for groups of up to eight persons maximum—well worth considering if there are a few of you. The trips offered include climbs up Orohena (three days) and Aorai (two days), the hike across Tahiti-iti (two days), and day-trips to Fautaua Falls, Papenoo Falls, Mt. Marau, a lava tube, etc. Pierre also organizes hang gliding from Mt. Marau. Transport to the trailheads is included, but backpacks and tents are extra (if required), and participants must bring their own food. Pierre's services are highly recommended for small groups of serious hikers/climbers concerned about both safety and success.

Another professional guide, **Angélien Zéna** (B.P. 7426, 98719 Taravao; tel. 57-22-67), specializes in hikes around the Pari Coast at the east end of Tahiti-iti, the "Circuit Vert." Angélien's three-day trip costs CFP 110,000 for up to 10 persons, meals and transport from/to Taravao included. Time off is allowed for swimming and fishing. A boat from Vairao to Vaipoiri Grotto is used on the two-day hikes, and day-trips can also be arranged. Even if there are only a few of you, it's worth calling both Pierre and Angélien to learn if they have any trips scheduled that you might join.

Vincent Dubousquet (tel. 43-25-95 or 77-24-37) takes visitors on an easy walk up the Fautaua Valley near Papeete at CFP 7,000 pp for two or CFP 5,500 for three or more. A bit more challenging are his climbs of Mont Marau or Aorai, both CFP 8,000/6,000. The two-day trek along the Pari Coast is CFP 15,000/12,000 including food. Experienced hikers can join him in scaling Mt. Mouaputa on Moorea (CFP 10,000/8,000). These are only Vincent's most popular hikes and he knows many more.

PRACTICALITIES

ACCOMMODATIONS

Most of the places to stay are in the congested Punaauia-to-Mahina strip engulfing Faa'a International Airport and Papeete and they tend to offer much poorer value for many than comparable accommodations on Moorea, which is only a short ferry ride away. The hotel listings that follow are arranged clockwise around the island in each category. With the closure of the Hiti Mahana Beach Club near Point Venus in 1995 there are no longer any regular campgrounds on Tahiti. Recently several new medium-priced places to stay have sprung up on the Tahiti-iti peninsula and south side of Tahiti, offering the chance to break your trip around the island. These (and the selections in Punaauia within commuting distance of Papeete) are covered later in this chapter.

Budget
Many backpackers head straight for **Hostel Teamo** (B.P. 2407, 98713 Papeete; tel. 42-47-26, fax 43-56-95), 8 rue du Pont Neuf, Quartier Mission, a century-old house in an attractive neighborhood near the Archbishop's Palace, just a short walk east of downtown. To get there from the market head inland on rue François Cardella. It's a little hard to find the first time, but convenient once you know it. Shared dormitory-style accommodations with variable cooking facilities are CFP 1,200 pp in a nine-bed dorm or CFP 1,500 pp in a better six-bed dorm. Private rooms are CFP 3,500 double with shared bath, CFP 4,000 double with private bath (bring your own towel). There's a nice veranda with French TV, but the managers can be temperamental and theft is not unknown (even food left in the fridge may not be considered sacred). Checkout time is 1000, but you can stay until 1900 for an additional CFP 800 pp fee (otherwise, you must leave). The receptionist will hold your luggage at CFP 150 a day and will provide free transportation to the airport if you're catching a late flight. Their minibus also meets international flights at the airport and provides free transfers to the hostel. It's all rather basic (and we've received letters from several readers who thought it was *awful*) but Teamo remains the choice of those looking for the cheapest possible place.

Nearby on busy rue du Frère Alain is the **Tahiti Budget Lodge** (B.P. 237, 98713 Papeete; tel. 42-66-82, fax 43-06-79), a quiet white wooden house with green trim, straight back on rue Édouard Ahnne from the market. The 11 four-bed rooms are CFP 1,900 pp, CFP 3,900 double with shared bath, CFP 4,800 double with private bath. Some rooms don't have locks on the doors. Communal cooking facilities are provided (but screens on the windows are not). They charge CFP 500 pp to leave your luggage until

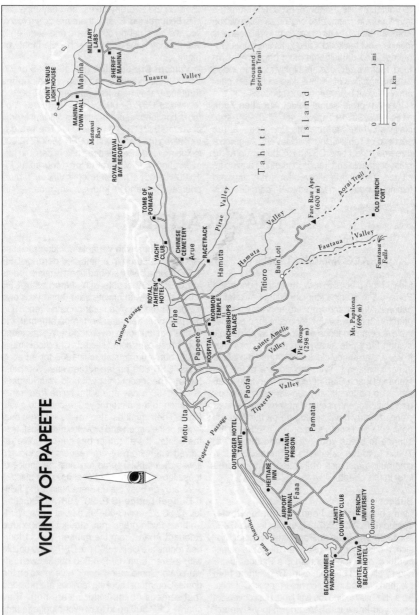

VICINITY OF PAPEETE

MILITARY LABS

POINT VENUS LIGHTHOUSE

SHERIFF DE MAHINA

Mahina

Tuauru Valley

Thousand Springs Trail

MAHINA TOWN HALL

Matavai Bay

ROYAL MATAVAI BAY RESORT

Tahiti   Island

1 mi

1 km

TOMB OF POMARE V

Pirae Valley

Fare Rau Ape (600 m)

Aorai Trail

OLD FRENCH FORT

CHINESE CEMETERY

RACETRACK

Arue

Hamuta

Valley

YACHT CLUB

Hamuta

Fautaua   Valley

Bain Loti

Fautaua Falls

Titioro

ROYAL TAHITIEN HOTEL

Taunoa Passage

MORMON TEMPLE

Pirae

ARCHBISHOPS PALACE

Papeete

HOSPITAL

Sainte Amelie Valley

Mt. Papaiona (696 m)

Pic Rouge (298 m)

Paofai

Tipaerui   Valley

Motu Uta

Pamatai

Papeete Passage

OUTRIGGER HOTEL TAHITI

NUUTANIA PRISON

HEITIARE INN

Faaa

AIRPORT TERMINAL

TAHITI COUNTRY CLUB

FRENCH UNIVERSITY

Outumaoro

Faaa Channel

BEACHCOMBER PARKROYAL

SOFITEL MAEVA BEACH HOTEL

© DAVID STANLEY

2000, or CFP 1,000 per piece to leave items for one week. Although not without problems (or mosquitos), it's better kept and less crowded than Teamo for only a little more money. Just don't show up in the middle of the night expecting to get a room as you'll be most unwelcome. Instead wait in the airport until *le truck* begins running at daybreak.

Women can stay at the five-story **Foyer de Jeunes Filles de Paofai** (B.P. 1719, 98713 Papeete; tel. 46-06-80) near the Protestant church on boulevard Pomare. This Evangelical Church-operated women's residence provides 125 beds in rooms of two, three, four, or six beds at CFP 2,000 a day, CFP 30,000 a month, breakfast included. There's a 2200 curfew daily, except Wednesday, Friday, and Saturday when it's midnight. This hotel is officially open to travelers in July and August only (although you can always try other months—they may have beds available). The majority of the guests are outer-island Polynesian women aged 16-23, so it's a good opportunity for female travelers to meet local women.

Inexpensive

On the mountain side of the highway at PK 8.3, Punaauia, not far from the Centre Commercial Moana Nui, is a five-bed dormitory run by **Moana Surf Tours** (Moana David, B.P. 6734, 98702 Faa'a; tel./fax 43-70-70). A place here is CFP 10,300 a day including breakfast, dinner, and unlimited surf transfers to breaks off Tahiti and Moorea. Reductions are possible for long stays.

In a pinch, **Pension Dahl Fifi** (Joséphine Dahl, tel. 82-63-30), directly across the street from the airport terminal (the second house on the left up the hill beside Blanchisserie Pressing Mea Ma), has three rooms with bath at CFP 3,500/6,000 single/double, breakfast included. Communal cooking facilities are available, but the location is noisy due to the nearby industrial laundry and airport.

The **Heitiare Inn** (Raymond Tarahu, B.P. 6830, 98702 Faa'a; tel. 83-33-52 or 82-77-53) at PK 4.3, Faa'a, a km east of the airport, has six rooms at CFP 4,000/5,000 single/double with shared bath, CFP 5,000/6,000 with a/c, and CFP 7,000/7,500 with a/c and private bath. Breakfast is included and communal cooking facilities are provided. The location isn't great and troops

from a nearby military base often kick up a storm at the Inn's snack bar in the middle of the night.

Chez Myrna (Myrna Dahmeyer, B.P. 790, 98713 Papeete; tel. 42-64-11), Chemin vicinal de Tipaerui 106, half a km up the road from the Hôtel Matavai, offers two shared-bath rooms at CFP 3,500/4,500 single/double with breakfast (minimum stay two nights). Dinner is CFP 1,500 (if desired). Myrna's husband, Walter, is a German expat who has been on Tahiti for 30 years. There's no sign outside, so call ahead.

The **Hôtel Shogun** (Bruno Gatto, B.P. 2880, 98713 Papeete; tel. 43-13-93, fax 43-27-28), 10 rue du Commandant Destremeau, Papeete, has seven a/c rooms with bath facing the noisy road at CFP 6,000 single or double, or CFP 6,500 single or double on the back side. A monthly rate of CFP 90,000 double is available.

The **Hôtel Mahina Tea** (B.P. 17, 98713 Papeete; tel. 42-00-97), up rue Sainte-Amélie from avenue Bruat, is about the only regular economy-priced hotel in the city. The 16 rooms are CFP 4,000 single or double, reduced to CFP 3,400/3,700 single/double if you stay three or more nights. A room with twin beds instead of a double bed is CFP 500 more. Six small studios with cooking facilities cost CFP 90,000 a month double. All rooms have private bath with hot water. No cooking facilities are provided in the daily rental rooms but you may use the shared fridge downstairs. The Mahina Tea does occasionally get some village-style noise from the surrounding houses. This family-operated place has been around for many years but it's not overrun by the backpack brigade. An easy walk from town, the Mahina Tea is excellent value for Papeete.

Expensive

The high-rise **Hôtel Prince Hinoï** (B.P. 4545, 98713 Papeete; tel. 42-32-77, fax 42-33-66), avenue du Prince Hinoï at boulevard Pomare, has 72 small a/c rooms at CFP 10,260 single or double plus tax but including breakfast. The New Diamond Casino is on the 2nd floor of this six-story hotel.

The venerable **Hôtel Royal Papeete** (B.P. 919, 98713 Papeete; tel. 42-01-29, fax 43-79-09), downtown on boulevard Pomare opposite the Moorea ferry landing, has 78 large a/c rooms beginning at CFP 9,000/10,500/12,000 single/double/triple plus tax. The Royal Papeete

the black volcanic sands of Tahiti

TINI COLOMBEL, TAHITI TOURISME

should be your choice if you want to stay right in the belly of Papeete's nightlife quarter. The hotel's two lively nightclubs downstairs offer free admission to guests and the Royal Casino is open nightly. Just make sure you don't get a room directly above the clubs unless you like being rocked to sleep by a disco beat. There's a Hertz desk at the Royal Papeete.

Hôtel Kon Tiki Pacific (B.P. 111, 98713 Papeete; tel. 43-72-82, fax 42-11-66), nearby at 271 boulevard Pomare, has long been popular among French military personnel in transit and its high-rise building opposite the Moorea ferry wharf offers excellent views into the nearby French naval base. The 44 spacious a/c rooms begin at CFP 8,500/9,900/11,900 single/double/triple plus tax. Don't accept one of the noisy rooms near the elevator, which are always offered first. Instead, get one with a balcony on the front side of the building and immerse yourself in the intrigue.

Premium

The **Tahiti Country Club** (B.P. 13019, 98717 Punaauia; tel. 42-60-40, fax 41-09-28) is up on the hillside at PK 7.2, Punaauia, just under two km southwest of the airport. The 40 a/c rooms with TV in a neat two-story building are CFP 14,000 single, double, or triple plus tax (children under 12 free), plus 8% tax and CFP 4,500 pp

extra for breakfast and dinner (if desired). Thirty-six additional rooms were to be added in 1999. If you come during business hours and ask at the office behind the tennis courts they may give you a discount on the room rates. A swimming pool is on the premises. The hike up to this hotel from the main road is quite a workout! There's a Europcar desk here. The nearby Hôtel Te Puna Bel Air is presently closed.

The 138-room **Hôtel Matavai** (B.P. 32, 98713 Papeete; tel. 42-67-67, fax 42-36-90) is CFP 12,000/16,000/20,000 single/double/triple plus tax with bath, TV, and two double beds. You can almost tell this four-floor edifice was once a Holiday Inn. During the 1995 nuclear testing series the Matavai was used to billet French riot police flown in to guard Papeete. Tennis and squash courts, mini-golf, a swimming pool, and other sporting facilities are on the premises. Airport transfers are free.

The six-story **Hôtel Tiare Tahiti** (B.P. 2359, 98713 Papeete; tel. 43-68-48, fax 43-68-47), at 417 boulevard Pomare on the waterfront next to the post office, has 38 a/c rooms beginning at CFP 12,000/14,000 double/triple plus tax (the first child under 12 free). Ask for an upstairs room with a balcony facing the harbor. Opened in December 1996, the Tiare Tahiti is not worth 50% more than the three places listed under "Expensive" above.

The **Hôtel Le Mandarin** (B.P. 302, 98713 Papeete; tel. 42-16-33, fax 42-16-32), 51 rue Colette, is a modern hotel whose 37 a/c rooms are overpriced at CFP 12,400/14,000/16,000 single/double/triple (children under 12 free). One reader reported that her room was dirty and in poor repair, the charges for laundry and drinks were excessive, and the service was lacking.

The **Royal Tahitien Hôtel** (B.P. 5001, 98716 Pirae; tel. 42-81-13, fax 41-05-35), at PK 3.5, directly behind the Mairie de Pirae, is a peaceful two-story building facing beautifully kept grounds on a litter-strewn black-sand beach. You're unlikely to see anyone swimming here as the water is murky with no coral, but the windsurfing is good. The 40 a/c rooms are CFP 16,000 single or double, CFP 19,000 triple, plus tax. Breakfast and dinner served on the attractive terrace overlooking the lagoon are CFP 4,400 pp extra (in general, the food prices here are exorbitant). You'll get better value for this kind of money on Moorea.

Luxury

The French-owned **Sofitel Maeva Beach** (B.P. 6008, 98702 Faa'a; tel. 42-80-42, fax 43-84-70) at PK 7.5, Punaauia, was built by UTA French Airlines in the late 1960s. The 224 a/c rooms in this pyramidal high-rise cost CFP 20,000 single or double garden view, CFP 23,000 lagoon view, CFP 25,000 panoramic view plus tax (children under 12 free). The seven-story Maeva Beach faces a man-made white beach but with pollution on the increase in the adjacent Punaauia Lagoon, most swimmers stick to the hotel pool. Tennis courts are available and scuba diving is offered. For CFP 700 pp roundtrip the hotel's recreation people will shuttle you out to their offshore sunbathing pontoon anchored above a snorkeling locale (no lifeguard or shade). Up to five persons can go deep sea fishing at CFP 48,000/75,000 a half/full day for the boat. Numerous cruising yachts anchor offshore and use the resort's wharf to tie up their dinghies. Europcar has a desk here.

The Japanese-owned **Tahiti Beachcomber Parkroyal** (B.P. 6014, 98702 Faa'a; tel. 86-51-10, fax 86-51-30), at PK 7, Faa'a, is a former Travelodge built in 1974. It's the first place west of the airport, and a smart international hotel. The 180 a/c rooms in the main building begin at CFP 29,300 single or double; for one of the 32

overwater bungalows add 50% again. Children under 14 sharing the room with their parents stay for free. A breakfast and dinner meal plan is CFP 6,500 pp extra. Tahitian dancing and crafts demonstrations are regular features. The hotel pool is reserved for guests and the beach is artificial, but the attendants in the water sports kiosk on the beach will gladly ferry you out to the nudist pontoons anchored in mid-lagoon for CFP 800 roundtrip. Other paid activities include waterskiing, kayaking, winsurfing, and scuba diving. The Automatic Currency Exchange machine in the lobby of this hotel changes the banknotes of nine countries for CFP 400 commission. Europcar and Hertz have desks here.

The **Outrigger Hôtel Tahiti** (B.P. 416, 98713 Papeete; tel. 53-23-77, fax 53-28-77), at PK 2.6 between Papeete and the airport, reopened in 1999 after being completely redeveloped by Outrigger Hotels of Hawaii. This site was once the residence of Princess Pomare, daughter of the last king of Tahiti, and from 1961 to 1996 a historic colonial-style hotel stood there. The 163 a/c rooms with fridge are divided between a large three-story building and garden and lagoon front bungalows. Rates begin at CFP 27,500 and increase to CFP 50,000 for the best suite. There's a swimming pool, 300-seat conference room, and an overwater restaurant with splendid sunset views of Moorea. It's the closest luxury hotel to central Papeete.

The **Royal Matavai Bay Resort Hôtel** (B.P. 14700, 98701 Arue; tel. 46-12-34, fax 48-25-44) at PK 8, Mahina, was built by Pan American Airways in 1968. Formerly known as the Tahara'a Hôtel, and a Hyatt Regency from 1988 to 1997, it's owned by Réginald Flosse, son of the territory's president, Gaston Flosse. Fully renovated in 1998, the 190 spacious a/c rooms begin at CFP 27,000 single or double, CFP 32,000 triple (children under 18 free). For breakfast and dinner, add CFP 5,500 pp. Happy hour at the hotel bar is 1730-1830. Built on a hillside overlooking Matavai Bay, this is one of the few hotels in the world where you take an elevator *down* to your room. The views from the balconies are superb and a black-sand beach is at the foot of the hill. The Royal Matavai Bay provides a shuttle service to and from Papeete for guests. Europcar has a desk here.

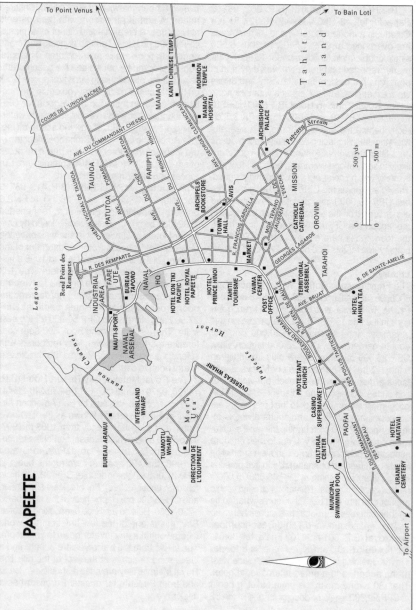

PAPEETE

© DAVID STANLEY

FOOD

Food Trailers

In the early evening take a stroll along the Papeete waterfront near the Moorea ferry landing, past the dozens of gaily lit vans known as *les roulottes* which form a colorful night market. Here you'll find everything from couscous, pizza, waffles, crêpes, and *brouchettes* (shish kebab) to steak with real *pommes frites*. There's no better place to try *poisson cru*. As the city lights wink gently across the harbor, sailors promenade with their *vahines*, adding a touch of romance and glamour. The food and atmosphere are excellent, and even if you're not dining, it's a scene not to miss. The most crowded *roulottes* generally have the best food but you may have to wait as lots of people bring large bowls to be filled and taken home. No alcohol is available.

Self-Service

Poly-Self Restaurant (tel. 43-75-32), 8 rue Gauguin behind the Banque de Polynésie, dispenses filling Chinese-style lunches at about CFP 800. It's unpretentious but a little overpriced.

The **Foyer de Jeunes Filles de Paofai** (tel. 46-06-80) opposite the Protestant church has a good modern self-service cafeteria open weekdays for lunch 1130-1300. Alcohol is not available here.

Snack Bars

To sample the cuisine of the people, check out the Chinese/Tahitian eateries on rue Cardella right beside the market. Try *ma'a tinito*, a mélange of red beans, pork, macaroni, and vegetables on rice (CFP 750). A large Hinano beer at these places is around CFP 350.

Acajou (tel. 43-19-22), 7 rue Cardella by the market, half a block from the tourist office, serves a large coffee with fresh buttered bread which makes an excellent CFP 250 breakfast or mid-morning snack.

Some of the cheapest and freshest baguette sandwiches in town are sold over the counter at **Boulangerie L'Epi d'Or** (tel. 43-07-13), 26 rue du Maréchal Foch near the market.

Inexpensive grilled meat and fish dishes are the specialty at **Snack Paofai** (tel. 42-95-76; Monday to Saturday 0500-1400) near Clinique Paofai. A complete meal chosen from among the specials listed on the blackboard and consumed on their airy terrace will run CFP 750, but arrive before 1300 or you'll find little left. On Thursday they prepare a special couscous dish. It's among the best values in town, as you'll gather from all the Tahitians eating there.

If you're catching the interisland boats *Vaeanu* or *Taporo VI* from Motu Uta, check out the **Restaurant Motu Uta** behind the *Vaeanu* office near the wharf. They offer takeaway lunches and big bottles of cold beer. Also check the food trailers at the south end of the parking lot near the tall blue port administration building, 75 meters from Motu Uta wharf.

Asian

The most popular Chinese restaurant in Papeete may be the **Waikiki Restaurant** (tel. 42-95-27; open daily 1100-1300 and 1800-2100, closed Sunday lunch and Monday dinner), rue Leboucher 20, near the market.

The inexpensive **Cathay Restaurant** (tel. 42-99-67), 28 rue du Maréchal Foch, also near the market, serves large portions of dishes *maa tinito* and steak frites, accompanied by large Hinano beers.

Papeete's finest Cantonese restaurant is **Restaurant Le Plazza** (tel. 42-16-33) at the Hôtel Mandarin, 26 rue des Écoles. Their specialty is Chinese fondue at CFP 3,300 pp for four to seven persons, CFP 3,100 pp for eight or more. You must reserve 24 hours in advance.

Restaurant La Saigonnaise (tel. 42-05-35; closed Sunday) on avenue du Prince Hinoï has moderately expensive Vietnamese food. Saigonese soup makes a good lunch.

Italian

For a taste of the Mediterranean, **La Pizzeria** (tel. 42-98-30; open Mon.-Sat. 1130-2200), on boulevard Pomare near the Tahiti Pearl Center, prepares real pizza in a brick oven. The prices are reasonable for the waterfront location—they're all spelled out in a big blackboard menu.

Pizzeria Lou Pescadou (tel. 43-74-26; open Mon.-Sat. 1100-1430 and 1630-2300), on rue Anne-Marie Javouhey a long block back from the Vaima Center, is friendly, unpretentious, breezy, inexpensive, and fun. Their pizza pesca-

The food trucks along the Papeete waterfront are about the best places in the city to eat.

DAVID STANLEY

tore (CFP 650) makes a good lunch, and a big pitcher of ice water is included in the price. Owner Mario Vitulli may be from Marseilles, but you won't complain about his spaghetti—a huge meal for about CFP 700. And where else will you get unpitted olives on a pizza? Non-alcoholic drinks are on the house while you stand and wait for a table. The service is lively, and Lou Pescadou is very popular among local French, a high recommendation.

More good pizza in the CFP 700-1,000 range is baked at **Don Camillo** (tel. 42-80-96), 14 rue des Écoles, next to the Piano Bar.

Other Restaurants

The *plat du jour* at **Big Burger** (tel. 43-01-98; closed Sunday), opposite MacDonald's, is often big value (CFP 1,400), and it's not fast food as the name implies. All of their one-person pizzas are CFP 800.

Restaurant La Madona (tel. 45-16-52; open Mon.-Sat. 1130-1400, Friday and Saturday 1900-2200), below Hôtel Shogun, specializes in seafood such as *poisson cru* (CFP 1,100), sashimi (CFP 1,200), mahimahi (CFP 1,600), and shrimps (CFP 1,700-2,300). **Salvani's Snack Express** (tel. 45-16-52) next door has inexpensive sandwiches and *plats du jour* at lunchtime.

For a change of pace have a lunch at the **Restaurant Tiare** at the Lycée Hôtelier Taaone (tel. 45-23-71), a bit east of Pirae Municipal Market. The food is prepared and served by

students, and it's open Oct.-June Tues.-Fri. noon-1400, except during the Christmas holidays, when it's closed.

Cafes

Le Retro (tel. 42-86-83) on the boulevard Pomare side of the Vaima Center is *the* place to sit and sip a drink while watching the passing parade. The fruit-flavored ice cream is intense and for yachties a banana split after a long sailing trip can be heavenly. The atmosphere here is thoroughly Côte d'Azur.

L'Oasis du Vaima (tel. 45-45-01), on the back side of the Vaima Center in front of the Air New Zealand office, is another scene in which to be seen, especially by the trendy youths who drop by in the late afternoon.

The Papeete equivalent of a Hard Rock Cafe is **Morrison's Café** (tel. 42-78-61; weekdays 1100-0100, Saturday 1600-0100), upstairs in the Vaima Center, which offers a full pub menu (not cheap), and a swimming pool. Here MTV-deprived local youths get a chance to mix with island-hopping yachties on an airy terrace with a view of Tahiti.

On boulevard Pomare across the park from the Moorea ferry landing is a row of sidewalk cafes frequented by French servicemen, happy hookers, gays, and assorted groupies. Some establishments even have a happy hour. This is a good place to sit and take in the local color of every shade and hue.

When the heat gets to you, **Pâtisserie La Marquisienne** (tel. 42-83-52), 29 rue Colette, offers coffee and pastries in a/c comfort. It's popular among French expats.

Groceries

Downtown there's **Casino** ((tel. 43-70-40; open Mon.-Sat. 0630-1900, Sunday 0630-1200), a large supermarket on rue du Commandant Destremeau. Get whole barbecued chickens and chow mein in the deli section.

At PK 8.3 Punaauia, just south of the junction of the auto route to Papeete, is the **Centre Commercial Moana Nui**, Tahiti's first enclosed shopping mall, which opened in 1986. Some of the cheapest groceries on the island are available at the large adjoining supermarket, **Continent** (tel. 43-25-32; Mon.-Sat. 0800-2000, Sunday 0800-1200). The deli section has a good selection of takeaway items including barbecued chickens, and there's also a snack bar on the mall. Continent doesn't only sell groceries but also clothing and souvenirs at the best prices you'll find around here.

Other big supermarkets around the island include a second **Continent** (tel. 45-42-22) at PK 4.5, Arue, **Supermarche Venustar** (tel. 48-10-13; Mon.-Sat. 0600-1930, Sunday 0600-1200) at the turnoff to Point Venus on the circle island highway (PK 10), and **Casino** in Taravao. All of these are good places to pick up picnic supplies.

ENTERTAINMENT AND EVENTS

Five Papeete cinemas show B-grade films dubbed into French (admission CFP 800). The Concorde is in the Vaima Center; Hollywood I and II are on rue Lagarde beside the Vaima Center; Liberty Cinema is on rue du Maréchal Foch near the market; and the Mamao Palace is near Mamao Hospital.

All three entertainment district hotels—the Prince Hinoï, Royal Papeete, and Kon Tiki—have gambling casinos where local residents unload excess cash.

Ask for the monthly program of activities at the Departement Fêtes et Manifestations in the **Cultural Center** (B.P. 1709, 98713 Papeete; tel. 54-45-44, fax 42-85-69) at Te Fare Tahiti Nui on the waterfront.

Nightlife

After dark when the tourists have returned to their swank beach hotels, local carousers and French sailors take over the little bars crowding the streets around rue des Écoles. The places with live music or a show generally impose a CFP 1,000-1,500 cover charge, which includes one drink. Nothing much gets going before 2200, and by 0100 everything is very informal for the last hour before closing. For the glitzy capital of a leading French resort, the nightlife is surprisingly downmarket.

The **Piano Bar** (tel. 42-88-24), beside Hôtel Prince Hinoï on rue des Écoles, is the most notorious of Papeete's *mahu* (transvestite) discos. It's open daily 1500-0300 with a special show at 0130. **Le Club 5** nearby features female stripping. The CFP 1,500 cover charge on Friday and Saturday includes one drink; during the week there's no cover but it's obligatory to have a drink and a dress code is in effect. Young French servicemen are in their element in these places.

a Tahitian dancer at a Papeete hotel

TAHITI TOURISME

Café des Sports on the corner across the street from the Piano Bar has beer on tap and usually no cover. More locals than tourists patronize this colorful establishment, where a good Tahitian band plays on weekends. Just don't believe the low drink prices advertised outside.

French soldiers and sailors out of uniform patronize the bars along boulevard Pomare opposite the Moorea ferry landing, such as **La Cave** (tel. 42-01-29) inside the Hôtel Royal Papeete (entry through the lobby), which has live Tahitian music for dancing on Friday and Saturday 2200-0300 (CFP 1,000 cover charge, free for Royal Papeete guests). Male visitors should ensure they've got their steps right before inviting any local ladies onto the floor—or face immediate rejection. **Le Tamure Hut** (tel. 42-01-29), also at the Royal Papeete, is one of the few downtown Papeete clubs that caters to visitors. Through the music and decor they've attempted to recapture the nightlife milieu of a decade or more ago, before Quinn's Tahitian Hut closed in 1973. It's open Friday and Saturday 2100-0300, cover charge CFP 1,000 (includes one drink).

Paradise Night Club (tel. 42-73-05; open nightly 1900-0100, weekends until 0200), next to Hôtel Kon Tiki opposite the Moorea ferries, has an island night every Thursday at 1900 with Polynesian karaoke. Other nights it's West African and reggae music. Monday to Thursday admission is CFP 1,500 pp including one drink, or CFP 2,000 on weekends. Popular French singers perform here on Friday and Saturday nights, and a dress code applies. Their restaurant serves dinners with meat dishes or seafood in the CFP 1,400-2,800 range. **Chaplin's Cafe** next door is a popular hangout for French sailors.

The **Tiki d'Or Bar Américain,** 26 rue Georges Lagarde near the Vaima Center, gets lively around happy hour. You'll locate it by the ukuleles and impromptu singing.

Le Rolls Club Discotheque (tel. 43-41-42) in the Vaima Center (opposite Big Burger) is Papeete's top youth disco and sharp dress is in order (open Thurs.-Sat. nights, admission CFP 1,500).

Cultural Shows for Visitors

A Tahitian dance show takes place in the Bougainville Restaurant, downstairs at the **Hôtel Maeva Beach** (tel. 42-80-42), Friday and Saturday at 2000. If you're not interested in having dinner, a drink at the Bar Moorea by the pool will put you in position to see the action (no cover charge). Sunday this hotel presents a full Tahitian feast at 1200, complete with earth oven *(ahimaa)* and dancing at 1300.

The **Beachcomber Parkroyal Hôtel** (tel. 86-51-10) stages one of the top Tahitian dance shows on the island; attend for the price of a drink at the bar near the pool (no cover charge). Tahiti's top dance troupe, Coco's Temaeva, often performs here (check). The dancers' starting time tends to vary (officially, Wednesday, Friday, and Sunday at 2000), so arrive early and be prepared to wait. For something special try the Tahitian feast on Sunday—CFP 4,850. The seafood dinner show on Friday is CFP 6,250.

At the **Royal Matavai Bay Resort Hôtel** (tel. 46-12-34) the Tahitian dancing is Friday and Saturday at 2000 and Sunday at 1300.

There's often Tahitian dancing in the **Captain Bligh Restaurant** (tel. 43-62-90) at the Punaauia Lagoonarium (PK 11.4) on Friday and Saturday nights at 2100 (call ahead to check). The buffet here is CFP 3,500.

SHOPPING

Normal shopping hours in Papeete are weekdays 0730-1130 and 1330-1730, Saturday 0730-1200. Papeete's largest shopping complex is the **Vaima Center,** where numerous shops sell black pearls, designer clothes, souvenirs, and books. It's certainly worth a look; then branch out into the surrounding streets. **Galerie Winkler** (tel. 42-81-77), 17 rue Jeanne d'Arc beside American Express, sells contemporary paintings of Polynesia.

Galerie d'Art Reva Reva (tel. 43-32-67, fax 58-46-78), 36 rue Lagarde, displays the works of Moorea artist François Ravello and other local painters. They also may have copies of an illustrated book on Bobby Holcomb called *Bobby: Polynesian Visions* with reproductions of many of his paintings.

O.P.E.C. (tel. 45-36-26), 20 rue Gauguin (upstairs), and **Tahiti Pearl Dream** (tel. 43-43-68), rue Leboucher 10 (upstairs), are black pearl sales rooms a block from the market. They'll show you a free video about the pearls if they

Don't overlook the local fashions. **Marie Ah You** (tel. 42-05-56) on the waterfront between the Vaima Center and the tourist office sells very chic island clothing—at prices to match. Several shops along rue Paul Gauguin flog slightly cheaper tropical garb.

The **Music Shop** (tel. 42-85-63), 13 rue du General de Gaulle, opposite Concorde Cinema behind the Vaima Center, has a large selection of compact discs of Tahitian music. You can use headphones to listen to the music.

If you're a surfer, check **Shop Tahiti** (tel. 42-66-51), 10 rue Édouard Ahnne near the market, for boards, plus all attendant gear. **Caroline** (tel. 42-98-86), 41 rue Colette, and **Waikiki Beach** (tel. 42-34-97), 9 rue Jeanne d'Arc, also sell surfing gear.

Nauti-Sport (tel. 50-59-59) in Fare Ute carries a good selection of quality snorkeling/dive masks at reasonable prices.

The **Philatelic Bureau** (tel. 41-43-35, fax 45-25-86) at the main post office sells the stamps and first-day covers of all the French Pacific territories. Some are quite beautiful and inexpensive. (To get on their mailing list write: Centre philatélique, 8 rue de la Reine Pomare IV, 98714 Papeete.)

Photo Lux (tel. 42-84-31), 30 rue du Maréchal Foch near the market, has some of the cheapest color print film you'll find, and they repair Minolta cameras.

SERVICES

Money

A good place to change is the Banque de Polynesie (tel. 46-66-74; Mon.-Thur. 0745-1530, Friday 0745-1430, Saturday 0800-1130), boulevard Pomare 355, directly across from the tourist office. They take CFP 400 commission. The Banque de Tahiti (tel. 41-70-14; weekdays 0800-1145/1330-1630, Saturday 0800-1130) in the Vaima Center charges CFP 500 commission. The Westpac Bank (tel. 46-79-79) near the Catholic cathedral takes CFP 450.

Several banks around town have automatic tellers where you can get cash advances on credit cards. For example, Banque Socredo (tel. 45-31-83), boulevard Pomare 411, on the waterfront just east of the post office, has an outside

a Marquesan woodcarving

think you're a potential buyer. Several dozen other jewelers around Papeete, including **Vaima Perles** (tel. 42-55-57) and **Maison Sibani** (tel. 54-24-24) in the Vaima Center, also sell pearls and it's wise to visit several before making such an important purchase.

For reproductions of authentic Marquesan woodcarvings, have a look in **Manuia Curios** (tel. 42-04-94) on the east side of the cathedral. Upstairs in the market is another good place to buy handicrafts, or just a pareu. Surprisingly, handicrafts are often cheaper in Papeete than on their island of origin.

ATM accessible 24 hours a day. Adjacent is a nifty Automatic Currency Exchange machine, which changes the banknotes of nine countries for CFP 400 commission (an identical machine is at the Beachcomber Parkroyal Hôtel).

Post and Telecommunications
The main post office (weekdays 0700-1800, Saturday 0800-1100) is on boulevard Pomare across from the yacht anchorage. Pick up poste restante (general delivery) mail downstairs (CFP 55 per piece). The public fax number at Papeete's main post office is fax 689/43-68-68, and you'll pay CFP 250 a page to pick up faxes sent to this number. The post office is also a place to make a long-distance telephone call, but there's a stiff three-minute minimum for operator-assisted calls and it's cheaper to use a telephone card for such calls.

Around Tahiti, small branch post offices with public telephones are found in Arue, Faa'a Airport, Mahina, Mataiea, Paea, Papara, Papeari, Pirae, Punaauia, and Taravao.

If you have an American Express card you can have your mail sent c/o Tahiti Tours, B.P. 627, 98713 Papeete. Their office (tel. 54-02-50) is at 15 rue Jeanne d'Arc next to the Vaima Center.

Courier Services
TTI-Tahiti (B.P. 6480, 98702 Faa'a; tel. 83-00-24, fax 83-76-27; daily 0700-1700) at Faa'a Airport is the DHL Worldwide Express agent. Cowan et Fils (tel. 42-44-25) at the airport is the United Parcel Service agent with next day air letter service. Federal Express (B.P. 9689, 98715 Papeete; tel. 45-36-45, fax 45-36-46) is at Global Air Cargo on rue des Remparts.

Immigration Office
If you arrived by air, visa extensions are handled by the Direction du Contrôle de l'Immigration (DCILEC, B.P. 6362, 98702 Faa'a; tel. 82-10-10, fax 86-60-20; open weekdays 0800-1200/1400-1700) at the airport (up the stairs beside the snack bar). Yachties are handled by the immigration office (tel. 42-40-74; Mon.-Thurs. 0730-1100/1330-1530, Friday 0730-1100/1330-1500) next to a small Banque Socredo branch on the waterfront behind Tahiti Tourisme in the center of town. Be patient and courteous with the officials if you want good service.

For those uninitiated into the French administrative system, the police station (in emergencies tel. 17) opposite the War Memorial on avenue Bruat deals with Papeete matters, while the *gendarmerie* (tel. 46-73-73) at the head of avenue Bruat is concerned with the rest of the island. The locally recruited Papeete police wear blue uniforms, while the paramilitary French-import *gendarmes* are dressed in khaki.

Consulates
The honorary consul of Australia (tel. 43-88-38), at the Qantas office in the Vaima Center, can issue Australian visas. In case of need, Canadians should turn to the Australian consul for emergency assistance. The honorary consul of New Zealand (tel. 54-07-40; weekdays 0900-1500) is upstairs in the Air New Zealand office, also in the Vaima Center. The honorary British consul is Transpolynésie (tel. 85-58-75) opposite the Outrigger Hôtel Tahiti in Faa'a. The honorary consul of Germany is Claude-Eliane Weinmann (tel. 42-99-94), on rue Tihoni Te Faatau, the road off avenue du Prince Hinoï next to the Lycée Hôtelier Paaone in Afareru on the far east side of the city. Other countries with honorary consuls at Papeete are Austria (tel. 43-91-14), Belgium (tel. 82-54-44), Chile (tel. 43-89-19), Denmark (tel. 54-04-54), Finland (tel. 43-60-67), Holland (tel. 42-49-37), Italy (tel. 43-45-01), Norway (tel. 43-79-72), South Korea (tel. 43-64-75), and Sweden (tel. 42-73-93). There's no U.S. diplomatic post in Tahiti-Polynesia. All visa applications and requests for replacement of lost passports must be sent to the U.S. Embassy (tel. 679/314-466) in Suva, Fiji. Japan is also *not* represented.

Laundromats
Central Pressing (tel. 42-08-74), 72 rue Albert Leboucher, offers a special service to visitors: for CFP 580 they'll wash, dry, and fold one kg of laundry. It's on the street behind the Hôtel Royal Papeete.

Laverie Gauguin Pressing Lavomatic (tel. 43-71-59; Mon.-Sat. 0630-1200/1330-1730), rue Gauguin 64, charges CFP 700 to wash six kg, another CFP 700 to dry, and CFP 100 for soap.

Laverie Automatique "Lavex ça m'plein" (tel. 41-26-65; Mon.-Sat. 0600-2000, Sunday 0800-1200), 301 boulevard Pomare opposite the

Moorea ferry wharf, is CFP 700 to wash up to seven kilograms, plus CFP 800 to dry same.

Public Toilets

Public toilets are found next to the immigration office near the small Banque Socredo behind Tahiti Tourisme, at the bus stop opposite Hôtel Le Mandarin beside the Hôtel de Ville, and on the waterfront opposite Air France. The ones near immigration are the most likely to be open regularly, so locate them early in your stay.

Yachting Facilities

Yachts must report their arrival to the port authorities over VHF channel 12 before entering the pass. The yacht master, customs, and immigration are all in the building next to Banque Socredo behind Tahiti Tourisme. A one-time entry fee and optional daily electricity and water hookup are charged. Yachts pay a daily fee based on the length of the vessel to moor Mediterranean-style (stern-to, bow anchor out) along the quay on boulevard Pomare. For half price you can anchor farther west along the boulevard at Hokulea Beach. It's also possible to anchor at the Hôtel Maeva Beach or to dock at the Marina Taina (tel. 41-02-25) in Punaauia, both accessible via the Faa'a Channel without exiting the lagoon. Visiting boats can use one of the anchor buoys at the **Yacht Club of Tahiti** (B.P. 1456, 98713 Papeete; tel. 42-78-03) at PK 4, Arue, for a monthly charge. Tahiti's sunny west and south coasts are excellent cruising grounds, while there are few good anchorages on the windward, rainy, and often dangerous east and north coasts.

INFORMATION

Tahiti Tourisme (B.P. 65, 98713 Papeete; tel. 50-57-00, fax 43-66-19) at Fare Manihini, a neo-Polynesian building on the waterfront not far from the market, can answer questions and supply a free map of Papeete. Ask for their lists of "small hotel" accommodations on virtually all of the islands, and inquire about special events and boats to the outer islands. The office is open weekdays 0730-1700, Saturday 0800-1200. The CFP 100 cold drink machine outside their office is also notable.

The Institut Territorial de la Statistique (B.P. 395, 98713 Papeete; tel. 54-32-32, fax 42-72-52; Mon.-Thurs. 0730-1500, Friday 0730-1200), 2nd floor, Bloc Donald (behind Voyagence Tahiti, opposite the Vaima Center), puts out a monthly publication called *Te Avei'a, Bulletin d'Information Statistique* (CFP 700). Their annual abstract *La Polynésie en Bref* is also useful.

Bookstores

You'll find Papeete's biggest selection of books in English at Librairie Archipels (B.P. 20676, 98713 Papeete; tel. 42-47-30, fax 45-10-27), 68 rue des Remparts.

The Librairie du Vaima/Hachette (B.P. 2399, 98713 Papeete; tel. 45-57-44, fax 45-53-45), in the Vaima Center, and Polygraph (B.P. 707, 98713 Papeete; tel. 42-80-47, fax 43-97-89), 12 avenue Bruat, are Papeete's largest French bookstores (and most of their titles are in French). Librairie Le Petit Prince (B.P. 13080, 98717 Punaauia; tel. 43-26-24) in the Centre Commercial Moana Nui, Punaauia, has a few international newspapers and magazines in English.

There's a newsstand (tel. 41-02-89) with magazines in English in front of the Vaima Center by the taxi stand on boulevard Pomare.

Maps

Topographical maps (CFP 1,500 a sheet) of some islands are available from the Section Topographie of the Service de l'Urbanisme (B.P. 866, 98713 Papeete; tel. 46-81-67, fax 43-49-83), 4th floor, Administrative Building, 11 rue du Commandant Destremeau.

La Boutique Klima (B.P. 31, 98713 Papeete; tel. 42-00-63, fax 43-28-24), 13 rue Jaussen behind the cathedral, sells nautical charts (CFP 2,600) and many interesting French books on Polynesia.

Nauti-Sport (tel. 50-59-59) in Fare Ute also retails French nautical charts of Polynesia at CFP 3,000 a sheet, and Marine Corail (tel. 42-82-22) nearby has more of the same (compare).

Libraries

A public library (tel. 54-45-44; open Mon.-Thurs. 0800-1700, Friday 0800-1600) is located in the Cultural Center. To take three books out for 15 days you must buy an annual card for CFP

4,000. The padded chairs in their air-conditioned reading room are great for relaxing.

The Université Française du Pacifique Bibliothèque (B.P. 4532, 98713 Papeete; tel. 45-01-65, fax 41-34-25; Mon.-Fri. 0800-1800, Saturday 0830-1200), is on the top floor at 21 rue Cook, between Commandant Destremeau and boulevard Pomare, Paofai (entry from the back of the building).

Travel Agencies
One of Papeete's most reliable regular travel agencies is Tahiti Tours (B.P. 627, 98713 Papeete; tel. 54-02-50), 15 rue Jeanne d'Arc next to the Vaima Center.

Tahiti Nui Travel (B.P. 718, 98713 Papeete; tel. 54-02-00, fax 42-74-35) in the Vaima Center often has cheap package tours to Easter Island (check the vouchers carefully). Vahini Tahiti Travel (tel. 42-44-38) next to Tahiti Nui Travel also has three-night packages to Easter Island costing about US$660 all inclusive. Before booking one of these, check the price of a return air ticket alone at the LanChile office in the same center (low off-season fares available March-Nov.). It's sometimes cheaper to make a side trip to Easter Island from Tahiti than to go to the Marquesas! New Zealanders require a Chilean visa to visit Easter Island but most other nationalities need only a passport.

Airline Offices
Reconfirm your international flight at your airline's Papeete office. Most of the airline offices are in the Vaima Center: Air New Zealand (tel. 54-07-47), Hawaiian Airlines (tel. 42-15-00), LanChile (tel. 42-64-55), and Qantas (tel. 43-06-65). AOM French Airlines (tel. 54-25-25) is at 90 rue des Remparts. Corsair (tel. 42-28-28) is at boulevard Pomare 297 next to the Hôtel Royal Papeete. Air France (tel. 42-22-22), which also represents Aircalin, is on boulevard Pomare near avenue Bruat.

HEALTH

Mamao Territorial Hospital (tel. 46-62-62) is always crowded with locals awaiting free treatment, so unless you've been taken to the recompression chamber there, you're better off attending a private clinic. The Clinique Paofai (B.P. 545, 98713 Papeete; tel. 43-02-02) on boulevard Pomare accepts outpatients weekdays 0630-1700, Saturday 0730-1130, emergencies anytime. The facilities and attention are excellent, but be prepared for fees of around CFP 3,000.

Dr. Bernard Bensaid and Dr. Bruno Voron operate a Cabinet Médical (tel. 43-10-43; open weekdays 0700-1330/1500-1800, Saturday 0700-1200, Sunday 0730-1000) in the building above the pharmacy opposite the Catholic cathedral.

In case of emergencies around Papeete call S.O.S. Médecins at tel. 42-34-56. To call an ambulance dial 15.

Two dentists, Dr. Michel Ligerot and Dr. Valérie Galano-Serra (tel. 43-32-24), are on the 2nd floor of the building next to the Hôtel Tiare Tahiti at boulevard Pomare 415.

The Pharmacie de la Cathedrale (tel. 42-02-24) across the street from the Catholic cathedral opens weekdays 0730-1800, Saturday 0730-1200. There are many other pharmacies around Papeete.

TRANSPORTATION

For information on air and sea services from Tahiti to other Polynesian islands, see the **Transportation** section in the introduction to Tahiti-Polynesia.

Le Truck
You can go almost anywhere on Tahiti by *les trucks,* converted cargo vehicles with long benches in back. *Trucks* marked Outumaoro run from Papeete to Faa'a International Airport and the Maeva Beach Hôtel every few minutes during the day, with sporadic service after dark until 2000 daily, then again in the morning from 0500 on. On Sunday long-distance *trucks* run only in the very early morning and evening; weekdays the last trip to Mahina, Paea, and points beyond is around 1700.

Trucks to Arue, Mahina, Papenoo, Taravao, and Tautira leave from boulevard Pomare across the street from Tahiti Tourisme. Those to the airport, Outumaoro, Punaauia, Paea, and Papara are found on rue du Maréchal Foch near the market. Local services to Motu Uta, Mission,

DAVID STANLEY

flower sellers, Papeete market

Mamao, Titioro, and Tipaeriu depart from rue Colette near the Hôtel de Ville.

Destinations and fares are posted on the side of the vehicle: CFP 120 to the airport, CFP 140 to Punaauia, CFP 160 to Mahina, CFP 170 to Paea, CFP 190 to Papara, CFP 200 to Mataiea, CFP 240 to Papeari, CFP 300 to Taravao, CFP 330 to Pueu, and CFP 350 to Teahupoo or Tautira. After dark all *truck* fares increase. Outside Papeete you don't have to be at a stop: *trucks* stop anywhere if you wave. Luggage rides for free.

Taxis

Taxis in Papeete are expensive, and it's important not to get in unless there's a meter that works or you've agreed to a flat fare beforehand. The minimum fare is CFP 800 during the day or CFP 1,200 at night (2000-0600 daily). Add to this the per kilometer charge of CFP 120 by day or CFP 240 at night. The flat rate per hour is CFP 4,000 during the day or CFP 6,000 at night. Waiting time is CFP 2,000 an hour by day, CFP 3,000 at night. Baggage is CFP 100 per piece at night

only. Expect to pay at least CFP 800 for a short trip within Papeete, CFP 1,500 to the airport, or CFP 1,800 to the Royal Matavai Bay Resort Hôtel or Maeva Beach. Taxi stands are found at the Vaima Center (tel. 42-33-60) and the airport (tel. 83-30-07). If you feel cheated by a taxi driver, take down the license number and complain to the tourist office, although what you consider a ripoff may be the correct amount. We have received many complaints about Papeete taxi drivers and they're best avoided if at all possible.

Car Rentals

Check the car as carefully as they check you; be sure to comment on dents, scratches, flat tires, etc. All the car rental agencies include third-party public liability insurance in the basic price, but collision damage waiver (CDW) varies from CFP 700 to CFP 2,000 extra per day with CFP 20,000 and up deductible (called the *franchise* in French). Most agencies charge the client for damage to the tires and stolen accessories, insurance or no insurance, and Tahiti insurance isn't valid if you take the car across to Moorea. You'll also pay for towing if you are judged responsible. On Tahiti the car comes full of gas, and you'll see Mobil and Total gas stations all around the island. As yet it's still free to park on the street anywhere in Papeete, which helps explain the heavy traffic. European-style parking fee machines are sure to make their debut on streetcorners before long!

If you want to whiz the island and pack in as many side trips as you can in one day, an unlimited-mileage rental is for you, and with a few people sharing it's not a bad deal. You should only consider renting on a per-kilometer basis if you plan to keep the car for at least three days and intend to use it only for short hops. Most agencies impose a 50-km daily minimum on their per-km rentals to prevent you from traveling *too* slowly; most rentals are for a minimum of 24 hours. Many car rental companies have kiosks inside Faa'a Airport, and most offer clients a free pickup and drop-off service to the hotels and airport.

Avis/Pacificar (B.P. 4466, 98713 Papeete; tel. 41-93-93, fax 42-19-11), 56 rue des Remparts at pont de l'Est, at the east end of rue Paul Gauguin, is open 24 hours a day. If the main office is closed, the guard in the parking lot can give you a car. They also have a kiosk facing the Moorea ferry wharf, a desk at the airport, and an office next to the military barracks in Taravao. Avis/Pacificar has unlimited km cars from CFP 8,000/13,000/18,800 for one/two/three days, plus CFP 1,200 a day insurance.

Also open 24 hours is **Europcar** (tel. 45-24-24, fax 41-93-41, www.europcar.com), at the corner of avenue du Prince Hinoï and rue des Remparts, two blocks back from Moorea ferry wharf, at the Moorea ferry wharf, the airport, and several hotels. Their Fiat Pandas are CFP 1,700, plus CFP 36 a km. With unlimited kms and insurance it's CFP 7,600/13,000/18,000 for one/two/three days. Europcar also has a depot at Taravao (tel. 57-01-11). Their minimum age is only 18 but the insurance coverage is limited for those under 25.

Hertz (tel. 42-04-71, fax 42-48-62), at Paradise Tours, on Vicinal de Tipaerui opposite Hôtel Matavai, has cars from CFP 2,350 a day, plus CFP 36 a km, plus CPF 1,250 insurance. Otherwise it's CFP 7,750/18,800/36,800 for one/three/seven days with unlimited mileage and insurance.

A good place to try for a per-km rental is **Robert Rent-a-Car** (B.P. 1047, 98713 Papeete; tel. 42-97-20) on rue du Commandant Destremeau (from CFP 1,200 daily, plus CFP 35 a km, plus CFP 700 insurance). Robert's unlimited km rentals begin at CFP 5,600 including insurance. They may offer you an upgrade at no charge.

More expensive is **Garage Daniel** (B.P. 1445, 98713 Papeete; tel. 82-30-04, fax 85-62-64), at PK 5.5 across the highway from the airport terminal. Their cheapest Citroën begins at CFP 1,600 a day, plus CFP 31 a km, plus CFP 1,000 insurance, or CFP 10,000/15,000/30,000 for two/three/seven days with unlimited mileage (insurance included).

The least expensive Citroën available from **Location de Voitures Pierrot et Jacqueline** (B.P. 1855, 98713 Papeete; tel. 42-74-49 or 81-94-00, fax 81-07-77) is CFP 1,700 a day, plus CFP 30 a km and CFP 1,000 insurance. With unlimited kms it's CFP 10,000/15,000/30,000 for two/three/seven days, insurance included. They'll allow you to take their car to Moorea if you ask before, but the insurance won't be valid over there. The minimum age to rent is 18. This friendly, efficient

company has an office near the Total oil tanks and Mobil service station at Fare Ute (open weekdays 0730-1100/1400-1730, Saturday 0730-1100), and another at the airport.

Bicycle Rentals

Unfortunately the dangerously fast and furious traffic on Tahiti's main highways makes cycling hazardous and unpleasant, and motor scooter rentals have been discontinued after fatal accidents. Nevertheless, **Rando Cycles** (tel./fax 41-22-08; weekdays 0800-1200/1400-1700, Saturday 0800-1200), at PK 20.2, Paea, rents bicycles at CFP 1,500/9,000 a day/week, or CFP 2,500 a weekend (Saturday morning to Monday before 0900).

Garage Bambou (B.P. 5592, 98716 Pirae; tel. 42-80-09), on avenue Georges Clemenceau near the Chinese temple, sells new Peugot bicycles from CFP 35,000 and does repairs.

Local Tours

William Leeteg of **Adventure Eagle Tours** (B.P. 6719, 98702 Faa'a; tel. 41-37-63 or 77-20-03) takes visitors on a full-day tour around the island at CFP 3,800 (admissions and lunch not included). William speaks good English and will do special guided tours for groups of up to seven.

Patrice Bordes of **Tahiti Safari Expédition** (B.P. 14445, 98701 Arue; tel. 42-14-15, fax 42-10-07) and several other companies offer 4WD jeep tours to Mt. Marau, the Papenoo Valley, and Lake Vaihiria.

Marama Tours (B.P. 6266, 98702 Faa'a; tel. 83-96-50, fax 82-16-75), at the airport and several deluxe hotels, does six-hour circle-island tours at CFP 4,000 and a 4WD island crossing via Lake Vaihiria at CFP 7,000. They also have a circle-Moorea tour from Tahiti at CFP 9,000 including the ferry. Also offered are day tours by air to Tetiaroa (CFP 24,500) and Bora Bora (CFP 26,900). **Tahiti Nui Travel** (tel. 54-02-00) at the Vaima Center and various hotels offers much the same.

Day Cruises

Many of the yachts and catamarans tied up along the waterfront opposite the Vaima Center offer excursions to Tetiaroa, deep-sea fishing, scuba diving, yacht charters, etc. Departures are often announced on notice boards and a stroll along there will yield current information. **Archipels Croisières** (tel. 56-36-39) operates a day cruise around Moorea on a 34-meter classic schooner departing from the Punaauia resorts. It's about CFP 11,000 pp including a buffet lunch).

Getting Away

The **Air Tahiti** booking office (tel. 43-39-39, weekdays 0730-1200/1300-1630) is upstairs in Fare Tony off boulevard Pomare between the post office and Vaima Center. **Air Moorea** (tel. 86-41-41) is at Faa'a International Airport. Interisland services by air and sea are covered in the introduction to Tahiti-Polynesia.

The ferries to Moorea depart from the landing just behind the tourist office downtown. The *Raromatai Ferry* and *Ono-Ono* to the Leeward Islands also leave from there, as do cruise ships and a few other small boats. All other interisland ships, including the cargo vessels *Taporo VI* and *Vaeanu*, leave from the Tuamotu wharf or Quai des Caboteurs in Motu Uta, across the harbor from downtown Papeete. You can catch *le truck* directly to Motu Uta from the Hôtel de Ville. The ticket offices of some of the vessels are in Fare Ute just north of downtown, while others are at Motu Uta (addresses given in the introduction to Tahiti-Polynesia).

AROUND TAHITI

A 117-km Route de Ceinture (Belt Road) runs right around Tahiti-nui, the larger part of this hourglass-shaped island. Construction began in the 1820s as a form of punishment. For orientation you'll see red-and-white kilometer stones, called PK *(pointe kilométrique),* along the inland side of the road. These are numbered in each direction from the Catholic cathedral in Papeete, meeting at Taravao.

Go clockwise to get over the most difficult stretch first; also, you'll be riding on the inside lane of traffic and less likely to go off a cliff in case of an accident (an average of 55 people a year are killed and 700 injured in accidents on this island). Southern Tahiti is much quieter than the northwest, whereas from Paea to Mahina it's even hard to slow down as tailgating motorists roar behind you.

If you're a bit adventurous it's possible to do a circle-island tour on *le truck,* provided you get an early start and go clockwise with no stop until Taravao. *Trucks* don't run right around the island, although some go as far as Tautira and Teahupoo on Tahiti-iti. *Trucks* and buses to Tautira leave from boulevard Pomare opposite the tourist office about six times a day with the first around 0830. Some *trucks* to Tautira go via the south coast, so if you want to be sure you'll be able to do a full circle trip, ask for one going via Papenoo. If you're told none are available or it looks like they won't be going for quite a while, switch to asking for a *truck* to Papenoo itself, then hitch from the end of its line or wait there for an onward *truck.*

Once at Taravao, walk across the peninsula (15 minutes) and look for another *truck* coming from Teahupoo or elsewhere to take you back to Papeete along the south coast. They stop running in the early afternoon, but if you get stuck, it's comforting to know that hitchhiking *(l'autostop)* is fairly easy and relatively safe on Tahiti. The local people are quite receptive to foreign visitors, so you'll improve your chances if it's obvious you're not French. For instance, try using a destination sign (never used by locals). There's lots of traffic along the straight south coast highway all day and it's almost certain you'll get a ride eventually. However you travel around Tahiti, it's customary to smile and wave to the Tahitians you see (outside Papeete).

The Northeast Coast

The coast is very rugged all along the northeast side of the island with no barrier reef from Port Venus to Mahaena. The **leper colony** at Orofara (PK 13.2) was founded in 1914. Previously the colony was on Reao atoll in the Tuamotus, but this proved too remote to service. Although leprosy is a thing of the past, about 50 of the former patients' children who grew up there and have nowhere else to go remain at Orofara today. They make money by selling cheap woodcarvings.

From November to March surfers ride the waves at Chinaman's Bay, Papenoo (PK 16), one of the best rivermouth beach breaks on the north side of the island. The bridge over the

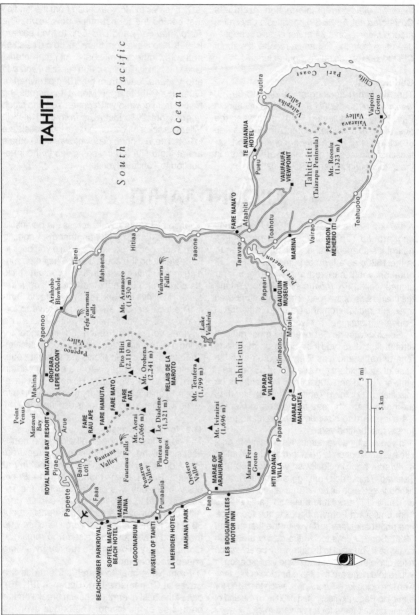

TAHITI

South Pacific Ocean

Point Venus
Matavai Bay
ROYAL MATAVAI BAY RESORT
Arahoho Blowhole
Papenoo
Tiarei
Mahaena
Hitiaa
Te Anuanua Hotel
Tautira
Vaiterapa Valley
Vaiufaufa Viewpoint
Pari Coast
Cliffs
Pueu
Vaitepiha Valley
Afaahiti
Fare Nana'o
Toahotu
Vairao
Teahupoo
Mt. Rooniu (1,323 m)
Tahiti-iti (Taiarapa Peninsula)
Vaipoiri Grotto
Vairaava Valley
Marina
Pension Meherio Iti
Taravao
Port Phaeton
Faaone
Vaiharuru Falls
Mt. Aramaoro (1,530 m)
Tefaaurumai Falls
Orofara Leper Colony
Mahina
Papenoo Valley
Pito Hiti (2,110 m)
Mt. Orohena (2,241 m)
Relais de la Maroto
Lake Vaihiria
Papeari
Gauguin Museum
Mataiea
Tahiti-nui
Atimaono
Papara Village
Marae of Mahaiatea
Papara
Hiti Moana Villa
Marae Fern Grotto
Mt. Tetufera (1,799 m)
Mt. Iviraiai (1,696 m)
Mt. Tetufera
Fare Rau Ape
Fare Hamuta
Fare Mato
Fare Ata
Mt. Aorai (2,066 m)
Le Diademe (1,321 m)
Plateau of Oranges
Ordeto Valley
Marae of Arahurahu
Punaruu Valley
Fautaua Falls
Fautaua Valley
Bain Loti
Pirae
Papeete
Faaa
Marina Taina
Beachcomber Parkroyal
Sofitel Maeva Beach Hotel
Lagoonarium
Museum of Tahiti
La Meridien Hotel
Mahana Park
Les Bougainvillees Motor Inn
Punaauia
Paea
Arue

0   5 km
0   5 mi

© DAVID STANLEY

broad **Papenoo River** (PK 17.9) allows a view up the largest valley on Tahiti. A paved road leads a km up the valley to the rough track across the island via the Relais de la Maroto (18 km) and Lake Vaihiria (25 km). You wouldn't get far in an ordinary car and even a 4WD jeep could get stuck. (See **Lake Vaihiria.**)

At the **Arahoho Blowhole** (PK 22), jets of water shoot up through holes in the lava rock beside the highway at high tide. It's dangerous to get too close to the blowhole as a sudden surge could toss you out to sea! Carefully lock your car here. Just a little beyond the blowhole, a road to the right leads 1.3 km up to the three **Tefa'aurumai Waterfalls** (admission free), also known as the Faarumai Falls. Vaimahuta Falls is accessible on foot in five minutes along the easy path to the right across the bridge. The 30-minute trail to the left leads to two more waterfalls, Haamaremare Iti and Haamaremare Rahi. The farthest falls has a pool deep enough for swimming. Bring insect repellent and beware of theft if you park a rental car at these falls.

At **Mahaena** (PK 32.5) is the battleground where 441 well-armed French troops defeated a dug-in Tahitian force twice their size on 17 April 1844 in the last fixed confrontation of the French-Tahitian War. The Tahitians carried on a guerrilla campaign another two years until the French captured their main mountain stronghold. No monument commemorates the 100 Tahitians who died combating the foreign invaders here.

The French ships *La Boudeuse* and *L'Étoile,* carrying explorer Louis-Antoine de Bougainville, anchored by the southernmost of two islets off **Hitiaa** (PK 37.6) on 6 April 1768. Unaware that an Englishman had visited Tahiti a year before, Bougainville christened the island "New Cythera," after the Greek isle where love goddess Aphrodite rose from the sea. A plaque near the bridge recalls the event. The clever Tahitians recognized a member of Bougainville's crew as a woman disguised as a man, and an embarrassed Jeanne Baret entered history as the first woman to sail around the world. (Bougainville lost six large anchors during his nine days at this dangerous windward anchorage.)

From the bridge over the Faatautia River at PK 41.8 **Vaiharuru Falls** are visible in the distance. The American filmmaker John Huston intended to make a movie of Herman Melville's *Typee*

Captain Louis-Antoine de Bougainville

here in 1957, but when Huston's other Melville film, *Moby Dick,* became a box-office flop, the idea was dropped.

Tahiti-iti

At Taravao (PK 53), on the strategic isthmus joining the two Tahitis where the PKs meet, is an **old fort** built by the French in 1844 to cut off the Tahitians who had retreated to Tahiti-iti after the battle mentioned above. Germans were interned here during WW II, and the fort is still occupied today by the 1st Company of the Régiment d'Infanterie de Marine du Pacifique.

The small assortment of grocery stores, banks, post office, gasoline stations, and restaurants at Taravao make it a good place to break your trip around the island. Lunch is served at **Restaurant Chez Guilloux** (closed Monday; tel. 57-12-91), opposite Casino supermarket, a hundred meters down the road to Tautira from the Westpac Bank in Taravao. They have large bottles of Hinano (CFP 400) and sandwiches (CFP 350), plus more formal dishes such as steak (CFP 1,450), mahimahi (CFP 1,500), and Chinese food (CFP 1,000). It's popular among French locals. Another excellent choice is **Restaurant Chez Jeannine** (tel. 57-29-82; closed Wednesday), on the main highway next to

Europcar, which specializes in seafoods and Vietnamese dishes.

If you have your own transportation, three roads are explorable on rugged Tahiti-iti. If you're hitching or traveling by *le truck,* choose the excellent 18-km highway that runs east from Taravao to quaint little **Tautira.** Two Spanish priests from Peru attempted to establish a Catholic mission at Tautira in 1774 but it lasted for only one year. Scottish author Robert Louis Stevenson stayed at Tautira for two months in 1888 and called it "the most beautiful spot, and its people the most amiable, I have ever found." The road peters out a few km beyond Tautira but you can continue walking 12 km southeast to the Vaiote River where there are petroglyphs, sacred rocks, and *marae.* These are difficult to find without a guide, and a few km beyond are the high cliffs that make it impractical to try hiking around the Pari Coast to Teahupoo. Intrepid sea kayakers have been known to paddle the 30 km around, although there's a wild four-km stretch not protected by reefs and most visitors go by speedboat.

The unoccupied beach at the mouth of the **Vaitepiha River** near Tautira is a potential campsite. A dirt road runs two km up the right bank of the river, where you could find more secluded places to camp. If you're keen, hike beyond the end of the road for a look at this majestic, unoccupied valley and a swim in the river. In the dry season rugged backpackers could hike south across the peninsula to the Vaiarava Valley and Teahupoo in two days, but a guide is definitely necessary. The ruins of at least three old *marae* are at the junction of the Vaitia and Vaitepiha rivers a couple of hours inland, and it's reported that tikis are hidden in there.

Another paved nine-km road climbs straight up the Taravao Plateau from just before the hospital in Taravao, 600 meters down the Tautira road from Casino supermarket. If you have a car or scooter and only time to take in one of Tahiti-iti's three roads, this one should be your choice. At the 600-meter level on top is the **Vaiufaufa Viewpoint,** with a breathtaking view of both Tahitis. No one lives up here: in good weather it would be possible to pitch a tent on the grassy hill above the reservoir at the end of the road (or sleep in your car if it's cold and raining). You'll witness spectacular sunsets from here and the herds of cows grazing peacefully among the grassy meadows give this upland an almost Swiss air. A rough side road near the viewpoint cuts down to rejoin the Tautira road.

The third road on Tahiti-iti runs 18 km along the south coast to Teahupoo. Seven km east of Taravao is a **marina** with an artificial beach (PK 7). American pulp Western writer Zane Grey had his fishing camp near here in the 1930s. Just east of the marina is **Toouo Beach,** a long stretch of natural white sand beside the road where you'll see fishermen spearing by torchlight on the opposite reef in the evening. In the afternoon it's a great picnic spot. The two huge moorings near the shore were used by ocean liners before Papeete harbor was developed in the 1960s as this is the finest natural deep-water harbor on Tahiti. Some of Tahiti's finest reef break surfing is possible out there in the Tapuaeraha Pass, but you'll need a boat.

Worth seeking out is **Marae Nu'utere,** 500 meters up a side road on the west side of the École Maternelle Tefaao at Vairao, PK 9.5 east of Taravao on the Teahupoo road. This large stone platform with a huge *ora* (banyan tree) growing in the center belonged to the female chief of the district. It was restored in 1994 and an explanatory board has been posted. Yachts can tie up to a pier near the *mairie* in Vairoa. An oceanographic research station studying shrimp breeding is nearby.

The **Teahupoo** road ends abruptly at a river crossed by a narrow footbridge. There's an excellent mountain view from this bridge, but walk east along the beach to get a glimpse of Polynesian village life. After a couple of km the going becomes difficult due to yelping dogs, seawalls built into the lagoon, fences, fallen trees, and *tapu* signs. Beyond is the onetime domain of the "nature men" who tried to escape civilization by living alone with nature over half a century ago.

Three hours on foot from the end of the road is **Vaipoiri Grotto,** a large water-filled cave best reached by boat. Try hiring a motorized canoe or hitch a ride with someone at the end of the road. Beyond this the 350-meter-high cliffs of the Pari Coast terminate all foot traffic along the shore; the only way to pass is by boat. All the land east of Teahupoo is well fenced off, so finding a campsite would involve getting someone's permission. It's probably easier to look elsewhere.

One option is **Le Bon Jouir** (Annick Paofai, B.P. 9171, 98715 Papeete; tel. 57-02-15, fax 43-69-70) beyond the end of the road on Pari Coast. The three bungalows start at CFP 4,000 double, otherwise a mattress in a large dorm is CFRP 2,000. You can cook for yourself or order breakfast and dinner at CFP 3,500 pp a day. Return boat transfers are CFP 2,000 pp and it costs CFP 500 a day for parking in Teahupoo. It's in a verdant location backed by hills.

Gauguin Museum

Port Phaeton on the southwest side of the Taravao Isthmus is a natural "hurricane hole" with excellent holding for yachts in the muddy bottom and easy access to Taravao from the head of the bay. (The entire south coast of Tahiti is a paradise for yachties with many fine protected anchorages.) Timeless oral traditions tell that the first Polynesians to reach Tahiti settled at Papeari (PK 56—measured now from the west). In precontact times the chiefly family of this district was among the most prestigious on the island.

The Gauguin Museum (B.P. 7029, 98719 Taravao; tel. 57-10-58; open daily 0900-1700, CFP 500 admission) is at PK 51.7 in Papeari District. Opened in 1965 thanks to grant from the Singer Foundation of sewing machine fame, the museum tells the painter's tormented life story and shows the present locations of his works throughout the world. Strangely, Gauguin's Tahitian mistresses get little attention in the museum. Twenty-five of his minor works are exhibited. Most of the photos of his paintings are numbered and you may be able to borrow a catalog (from the gift shop, go around clockwise). The two-meterish, two-ton stone tiki on the museum grounds is said to be imbued with a sacred *tapu* spell.

THE PAINTER PAUL GAUGUIN

One-time Paris stockbroker Paul Gauguin arrived at Papeete in June 1891 at age 43 in search of the roots of "primitive" art. He lived at Mataiea with his 14-year-old mistress Teha'amana for a year and a half, joyfully painting. In August 1893 he returned to France with 66 paintings and about a dozen woodcarvings, which were to establish his reputation. Unfortunately, his exhibition flopped and in August 1895 Gauguin returned to Tahiti a second time, infected with VD and poor, settling at Punaauia. After an unsuccessful suicide attempt he recovered somewhat, and in 1901 a Paris art dealer named Vollard signed a contract with Gauguin, assuring him a monthly payment of 350 francs and a purchase price of 250 francs per picture. His financial problems alleviated, the painter left for Hiva Oa, Marquesas Islands, to find an environment uncontaminated by Western influences. During the last two years of his life at Atuona, Gauguin's eccentricities put him on the wrong side of the ecclesiastical and official hierarchies. He died in May 1903 at age 53, a near outcast among his countrymen in the islands, yet today a Papeete street and school are named after him!

Teha'amana, who lived with Gauguin at Mataiea from 1892 to 1893, was the painter's great love and is mentioned often in Noa Noa.

Tahitians believe this tiki, carved on the island of Raivavae hundreds of years ago, still lives. The three Tahitians who moved the statue here from Papeete in 1965 all died mysterious deaths within a few weeks. A curse is still said to befall all who touch the tiki.

A **botanical garden** rich in exotic species is part of the Gauguin Museum complex (CFP 400 additional admission). This 137-hectare garden was created in 1919-21 by the American botanist Harrison Smith (1872-1947), who introduced over 200 new species to the island, among them the sweet grapefruit (pomelo), mangosteen, rambutan, and durian. A large Galapagos tortoise traipses through the east side of the gardens, the last of several such animals given to the children of writer Charles Nordhoff way back in the 1930s. Yachts can enter the lagoon through Temarau Pass and anchor just west of the point here.

The attractive **Gauguin Museum Restaurant** (tel. 57-13-80), a km west of the museum, hosts circle-island tour groups for lunch. Even without the food it's worth a stop to see the fish swimming in the enclosure around the wharf and to take in the view.

At PK 49 is the **Jardin Public Vaipahi** with a lovely waterfall minutes from the road (admission free). It's a good substitute if you missed the botanical garden. A few hundred meters west of Vaipahi is the **Bain du Vaima**, a strong freshwater spring with several deep swimming pools. This is one of the favorite free picnic spots on the island and on weekends it's crowded with locals. Yachts can anchor offshore.

Lake Vaihiria

The unmarked road to Lake Vaihiria begins at PK 47.6 between a housing settlement and a Mormon church (Église de Jesus-Christ des Saints des Derniers Jours), just before the bridge over the Vairaharaha River, as you travel west. The rough track leads 12 km up to Lake Vaihiria, Tahiti's only lake, following the Vaihiria River, which has been harnessed for hydroelectricity. Two km up the road you'll encounter a white hydro substation and the first of a series of Piste Privée signs advising motorists that the road is closed to rental cars (vehicles de location), though open to pedestrians. For those who don't mind taking risks, in dry weather a rental car

could continue another five km to a dam and the lower power station, provided the chain across the road isn't locked.

A km beyond is an archaeological site with restored marae. Three km beyond this (11 km from the main road) is a second dam and an upper (larger) power station. Beyond this point only a 4WD vehicle could proceed, passing prominent Danger signs, another km up a concrete track with a 37-degree incline to Lake Vaihiria itself.

Sheer cliffs and spectacular waterfalls squeeze in around the spring-fed lake, and the shore would make a fine campsite (though overrun by mosquitoes). Native floppy-eared eels known as puhi taria, up to 1.8 meters long, live in these cold waters, as do prawns and trout. With its luxuriant vegetation this rain-drenched 473-meter-high spot is one of the most evocative on the island.

The track proceeds up to the 780-meter level and through the 110-meter Urufau Tunnel (opened in 1989) and over to the Papenoo Valley, the caldera of Tahiti-nui's great extinct volcano. The ancient Tahitians considered this the realm of the gods and the **Marae Farehape** is near the Relais de la Maroto. Another large dam, the Barage Tahinu, is a couple of km west of the Relais. Developed since 1980, these facilities now supply over a third of Tahiti's electric requirements. On the slopes of Orohena, eight km north of the Relais and 10 km short of Papenoo, is the access to the **Parc naturel Te Faaiti,** Tahiti's first (and as yet undeveloped) territorial park. On the east side of the Papenoo Valley stands Mt. Aramaoro (1,530 meters).

From coast to coast it's a four-hour, 40-km trip by 4WD jeep, or two days on foot. You must wade through the rivers about 20 times. The easiest way to do this trip is seated in a chauffeur-driven 4WD jeep booked through any of the tour companies that leave their brochures at Tahiti Tourisme. Expect to pay CFP 9,500 pp including lunch and drinks or CFP 7,000 without lunch (four-person minimum participation). These trips don't usually operate during the rainy season (Nov.-March).

The 12-room **Relais de la Maroto** (B.P. 20687, 98713 Papeete; tel. 57-90-29, fax 57-90-30) is at the junction of the Vaituoru and Vainavenave rivers in the upper Papenoo Valley, about five km north of the tunnel. The only access is by 4WD, helicopter, or foot (the Papenoo River must be forded 10 times between here and the north coast highway). This cluster of solid concrete buildings was built to house workers during construction of the hydroelectric installations here, and rooms with bath start at CFP 8,800 single or double. Add CFP 5,000 pp for breakfast and dinner, plus CFP 14,500 pp for return transfers from Papeete. Local French often come here for the weekend and the flashy restaurant, wine cellar, and disco are designed to cater to them. Despite this, the Relais does provide a good base for exploring the many waterfalls and archaeological remains in this area if your budget is generous enough.

The South Coast

Tahiti-Polynesia's only golf course, the **International Golf Course Olivier Breaud** (B.P. 12017, 98712 Papara; tel. 57-43-41; open daily 0800-1700) at PK 41, Atimaono, stretches up to the mountainside on the site of Terre Eugenie, a cotton and sugar plantation established by Scotsman William Stewart at the time of the U.S. Civil War (1863). Many of today's Tahitian Chinese are descended from Chinese laborers imported to do the work, and a novel by A. T'Serstevens, *The Great Plantation,* was set here. The present 5,405-meter, 18-hole course was laid out by Californian Bob Baldock in 1970 with a par 72 for men, par 73 for women. If you'd like to do a round, the greens fees are CFP 4,500, and clubs

and cart rent for another CFP 3,000. Since 1981 the Tahiti Open in July has attracted golf professionals from around the Pacific. The course restaurant is said to be good.

Behind the golf course is the **Parc d'Atimaono,** a favorite hiking area. A road closed to cars, which begins next to the golf course parking lot, leads several km up into this area, though you may be charged CFP 500 as a "day visitor" to the golf course.

The **Marae of Mahaiatea** (PK 39.2) at Papara was once the most hallowed temple on Tahiti, dedicated to the sea god Ruahatu. After a visit in 1769 Captain Cook's botanist Joseph Banks wrote, "It is almost beyond belief that Indians could raise so large a structure without the assistance of iron tools." Less than a century later planter William Stewart raided the *marae* for building materials, and storms did the rest. All that's left of the 11-story pyramid today is a rough heap of stones, but still worth visiting for its aura and setting. You could swim and snorkel off the beach next to the *marae,* but watch the currents. The unmarked turnoff to the *marae* is a hundred meters west of Beach Burger, then straight down to the beach. From April to October surfers often take the waves at black-colored **Papara Beach** on nearby Popoti Bay (PK 38.5), one of the top beach break sites on southern Tahiti.

By the church at **Papara** (PK 36) is the grave of Dorence Atwater (1845-1910), U.S. consul to Tahiti from 1871-88. Atwater's claim to fame

Tahiti's Mahaiatea Marae as illustrated in James Wilson's A Missionary Voyage *(London, 1779). This 11-step pyramid was once the largest pagan temple on the island.*

dates back to the American Civil War, when he recorded the names of 13,000 dead Union prisoners at Andersonville Prison, Georgia, from lists the Confederates had been withholding. Himself a Union prisoner, Atwater escaped with his list in March 1865. Atwater's tombstone provides details. Across the street from the church is a Centre Artisanal selling handicrafts, and a Sea Shell Museum. A commercial bird park and greenhouse called **Mataoa Gardens** is at PK 34.5.

Maraa Fern Grotto (PK 28.5) is by the road just across the Paea border. An optical illusion, the grotto at first appears small but is quite deep and some Tahitians believe *varua ino* (evil spirits) lurk in the shadowy depths. Others say that if you follow an underground river back from the grotto you'll emerge at a wonderful valley in the spirit world. Paul Gauguin wrote of a swim he took across the small lake in the cave; you're also welcome to jump in the blue-gray water. You can fill your water bottle with fresh mineral water from eight spouts next to the parking lot. Maraa Pass is almost opposite the grotto and yachts can anchor in the bay.

On the mountain side of the road at PK 26.5 is the small **Ava Tea Distillery** (B.P. 10398, 98711 Paea; tel. 53-32-43), which can be visited daily 0900-1200/1400-1700. Ring the bell as you enter.

The Southwest Coast
The **Marae Arahurahu** at PK 22.5, Paea, is up the road inland from Magasin Laut—take care, the sign faces Papeete, so it's not visible if you're traveling clockwise. This temple, lying in a tranquil, verdant spot under high cliffs, is perhaps Tahiti's only remaining pagan mystery. The ancient open altars built from thousands of cut stones were completely restored in 1954 (open daily, admission free). Historical pageants (CFP 1,500 admission) recreating pagan rites are performed here on Saturdays from July to September.

For some hiking, Paea's **Orofero Valley** is recommended and camping might be possible up beyond the end of the road (six km). From the main highway take the first paved road inland south of the large Catholic church by the Vaiatu River at PK 21.5. You can drive a car three km up. When you get to the *tapu* sign, park, cross the river, and continue up the other side on foot. A jeep track runs another three km up the valley (half-hour walk), through half a dozen river crossings (wear rubber booties or zories). At the end of the road a tall waterfall is to the left and the trail continues ahead. Orofero is one of the few Tahitian valleys free of trash!

You get a good view of Moorea from **Mahana Park** (admission free) at PK 18.3, Papehue. This is a public beach park with a restaurant (tel. 48-19-99) and cafe. Pedal boats and kayaks are for rent.

The West Coast
Paea and Punaauia are Tahiti's sheltered "Gold Coast," with old colonial homes hidden behind trees along the lagoonside and *nouveau riche* villas dotting the hillside above. **Hôtel Le Méridien** at PK 15, Punaauia, opened in 1998 amid considerable local controversy as Tahitian protesters had been occupying the site for nearly four years to protect an ancient Moahi burial ground and to defend one of the last remaining customary accesses to the sea. In January 1996 French *gendarmes* were called in to evict the demonstrators and construction went ahead under tight security.

At Fishermen's Point, Punaauia, is the **Museum of Tahiti and the Islands** (B.P. 6272, 98702 Faa'a; tel. 58-34-76; open Tues.-Sun. 0930-1730; admission CFP 500), which opened in 1977. Located in a large, modern complex on Punaauia Bay, about a km down a narrow road from PK 14.8, this worthwhile museum has four halls devoted to the natural environment, the origins of the Polynesians, Polynesian culture, and the history of Polynesia. Outside is a huge double-hulled canoe and Captain Cook's anchor from Tautira. Most of the captions are in French, Tahitian, and English (photography allowed).

When the waves are right, you can sit on the seawall behind the museum and watch the Tahitian surfers bob and ride, with the outline of Moorea beyond. It's a nice picnic spot. On your way back to the main highway from the museum, look up to the top of the hill at an **old fort** used by the French to subjugate the Tahitians in the 1840s. The crown-shaped pinnacles of **Le Diadème** (1,321 meters) are also visible from this road.

If you want to see pollution on a massive scale, follow the route up the once-beautiful **Punaruu Valley** behind the Punaauia industrial zone (PK 14.8). You can drive a normal car five km up a

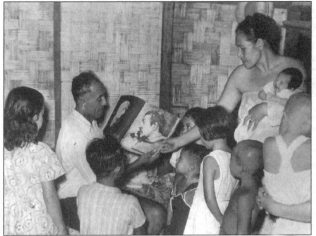

BENGT DANIELSSON

This photo, taken by Bengt Danielsson in the 1950s and published in his book Gauguin in the South Seas, *shows Emile Marae a Tai, son of Gauguin and his vahine, Pau'ura a Tai. The resemblance is striking.*

valley incredibly trashed out with garbage dumps all the way. At the end of the valley is a water catchment and, although the way leads on to the fantastic Plateau of Oranges, entry is forbidden. Tahitian enterprises dump their refuse in valleys all around the island, but this has got to be the ugliest! Here paradise ends.

From 1896 to 1901 Gauguin had his studio at PK 12.6 Punaauia, but nothing remains of it; his *Two Tahitian Women* was painted here. The **Lagoonarium** (B.P. 2381, 98713 Papeete; tel. 43-62-90; closed Monday), below the lagoon behind Captain Bligh Restaurant at PK 11.4, Punaauia, provides a vision of the underwater marinelife of Polynesia safely behind glass. The big tank full of black-tip sharks is a feature. Entry is CFP 500 pp, open daily, free for restaurant customers, and CFP 300 for children under 12. The shark feeding takes place around noon. Straight out from the Lagoonarium is the Passe de Taapuna, southern entrance to the Punaauia Lagoon and another popular surfing venue.

At PK 8, Outumaoro, is the turnoff for the RDO bypass to Papeete, Tahiti's only superhighway! Follow the Université signs from here up to the ultramodern campus of the **French University of the Pacific** (tel. 80-38-03) with its fantastic hilltop view of Moorea.

On the old airport road just north are Tahiti's biggest hotels: the **Sofitel Maeva Beach** (PK 7.5) and **Beachcomber Parkroyal** (PK 7), each

worth a stop—though their beaches are polluted. From the point where the Beachcomber Parkroyal is today, the souls of deceased Tahitians once leapt on their journey to the spirit world. A sunset from either of these hotels, behind Moorea's jagged peaks across the Sea of the Moon, would be a spectacular finale to a circle-island tour. The **Mairie de Faa'a** (PK 5) was erected in the traditional Maohi style in 1989 (Faa'a mayor Oscar Temaru is the territory's leading independence advocate). As you reenter Papeete, **Uranie Cemetery** (PK 1.5) is on your right.

The west coast of Tahiti can also be visited as a day-trip from Papeete; start by taking *le truck* to the Fern Grotto at Paea, then work your way back. *Trucks* back to Papeete from the vicinity of the Maeva Beach Hôtel run late into the night, but the last one from the Museum of Tahiti is around 1630.

ACCOMMODATIONS AROUND TAHITI

Accommodations near Taravao
Fare Nana'o (B.P. 7193, 98719 Taravao; tel. 57-18-14, fax 57-76-10), operated by sculptor Jean-Claude Michel and his wife Monique Meriaux, is an unusual place to stay. It's beside the lagoon in a colorful compound overflowing with vegetation and fragments of sculpture, very near the PK 52

marker a km north of the old French fort at Tar-avao. The six thatched *fare* vary in price, from CFP 5,000 double for the treehouse (you climb up a tree), CFP 5,500 double for an overwater *fare* on stilts (you must wade through the lagoon), CFP 6,500 double for one of the two units with cooking facilities, to CFP 8,500 double for the only room with private bath and hot water. A third person is CFP 1,000 extra in all these, and the weekly discount is 10% (no credit cards). Although unique and wonderful, Fare Nana'o is not for everyone: the walls are constructed of tree trunks and branches left partially open, there's no hot water, flashlights are required to reach the shared toilet and shower at night, and you may be visited in the night by crabs, spiders, lizards, and a marauding cat. This Robinson Crusoe-style place has had TV exposure in Los Angeles, so advance reservations are necessary, especially on weekends. Inexpensive.

A good sightseeing base is **Chez Jeannine** (Jeannine Letivier, B.P. 7310, 98719 Taravao; tel./fax 57-07-49), also known as "L'Eurasienne," on the Route de Plateau five km above Taravao. You'll need a rented car to stay here as it's way up on the road to the Vaiufaufa Viewpoint and *le truck* doesn't pass anywhere nearby. The four two-story bungalows with cooking facilities and wicker furniture are CFP 6,000/30,000/80,000 double a day/week/month, while the five rooms above the restaurant are CFP 4,000/20,000/50,000. Chez Jeannine opened in 1997 and the cool breezes and good views are complemented by a swimming pool. Information is available at Restaurant Chez Jeannine (closed Wednesday) next to Europcar in Taravao. Inexpensive.

The **Te Anuanua Hôtel** (Hilda Lehartel, B.P. 1553, 98713 Papeete; tel./fax 57-12-54), just east of the church in Pueu at PK 10, Tahiti-iti, has four duplex bungalows. Garden bungalows here are CFP 5,500/6,500 single/double plus tax but including breakfast; the lagoonfront bungalows are CFP 1,000 more. Check the rooms before checking in, as some lack window screens, fans, or functioning plumbing. On weekends the disco pulses from 2200 to 0300. A nice seafood restaurant faces the lagoon, making the Te Anuanua worth a stop as you travel around the island. This hotel doesn't have a beach, but there's a pool and the crystal clear water off their wharf invites one to jump in. Moderate.

The backpackers best bet is probably **Chez Mado** (tel. 57-32-77 or 57-00-57), the snack bar on the east beach at the end of the road in Tautira. The friendly folks running the restaurant accommodate visitors in their own home at CFP 3,000 pp including all meals. The snack bar is usually closed on Monday and Tuesday, so it would be best to call ahead those days (a good idea anytime). Tautira makes a good base for hikers and it would be fun to spend a couple of nights in this attractive village. Budget.

On the opposite side of the Tahiti-iti peninsula is **Pension Meherio Iti** (Maria Maitere, B.P. 3695, 98713 Papeete; tel. 57-74-31 or 77-22-73), at PK 11.9 in Vairao district on the road to Teahupoo. Four rooms are available in a house next to the main road at CFP 3,500/4,000/4,500 single or double depending on whether the room has cooking facilities or private bath. There are also three newer bungalows with cooking facilities down near the lagoon, 400 meters off the road. These cost CFP 6,000 double in the garden or CFP 7,000 on the beach (extra person CFP 700). This place is usually fully booked by local French families on weekends but a possibility during the week. Inexpensive.

Southwest Side of Tahiti

Lovely sea and mountain views await you at **Papara Village** (Thomas Chave, B.P. 12379, 98712 Papara; tel. 57-41-41, fax 57-79-00), at PK 38.5, Papara, up on a hill a km off the south coast highway. The two solid bungalows with private bath, fridge, and TV (but no cooking) are CFP 5,000/7,500 single/double. There's also a large family bungalow with kitchen at CFP 15,000 for up to four persons. A swimming pool is on the premises and this is the closest place to stay to the golf course. It's sort of like a luxury hotel at half the price, but unless you take the family bungalow, food will be a problem. Moderate.

Hiti Moana Villa (Steve Brotherson, B.P. 10865, 98711 Paea; tel. 57-93-93, fax 57-94-44), at PK 32, is an attractive small resort right on the lagoon between Papara and Paea. The eight deluxe apartments each have a kitchen, living room, TV, terrace, and private bath at CFP 8,000 single or double, or CFP 12,500 for four persons (minimum stay three nights). There's a swimming pool and pontoon, and the manager will loan a boat and motor free (you pay the gas). This place is usually full—especially on weekends—and advance bookings are recommended. Moderate.

Les Bougainvillées Motor Inn (B.P. 63, 98713 Papeete; tel. 53-28-02, fax 43-77-11) is at PK 22, Paea (lagoon side). The eight apartments with kitchen, living room, TV, terrace, and private bath in a four-story building facing the swimming pool are CFP 8,000 for two people, or CFP 12,000 for up to four people. The minimum stay is three nights and reduced rates are offered for long stays. It's a cozy arrangement with access to the beach via the owners' driveway, but call ahead for reservations as it's often full. Moderate.

Pension Te Miti (Frédéric Cella, B.P. 130088, 98717 Punaauia; tel./fax 58-48-61) at PK 18.5, Paea, is in Papehue village, 450 meters up off the main road. Five rooms in two adjacent houses cost CFP 4,500 double in a small room, or CFP 6,000 double in a large room. Backpackers and surfers often stay in the four-mattress dormitory at CFP 1,500 pp. There's a communal fridge but no cooking facilities. Breakfast is CFP 250, dinner CFP 1,200. Use of the washing machine is CFP 500. It's run by a young French couple named Frédéric and Crystal and their future plans include a campground across the road. Airport transfers are CFP 2,000 pp but it's easy to get here on *le truck.* Inexpensive.

Chez Armelle (Armelle Faille, B.P. 388640, 98718 Punaauia; tel. 58-42-43, fax 58-42-81), at PK 15.5 in Punaauia (almost opposite a large Mobil service station), has eight rooms at CFP 4,500/6,000 single/double. A bed in a six-bed dorm is CFP 2,000. Some of the rooms have private bath, and communal cooking facilities are provided. Dinner is available at CFP 1,000 pp and breakfast is included in all rates. It's right on the beach (though the rooms are not), but this pension caters more to French migrants planning long stays: you get seven nights for the price of six, and one month is CFP 120,000 double. There's a two-night minimum stay and the managers can be rather abrupt with English speakers. Snorkeling gear, surfboards, canoes, and bicycles are loaned free. Airport transfers are CFP 1,000 pp return. Inexpensive.

In June 1998 the **Hôtel Le Méridien** (B.P. 380595, 98718 Punaauia; tel. 47-07-07, fax 47-07-08) opened at PK 15, Punaauia, about nine km southwest of the airport. The 138 a/c rooms in the four-story main building begin at CFP 34,650 single or double, CFP 41,650 triple, while the 12 overwater bungalows are CFP 48,300 single or double, CFP 55,300 triple, plus tax. A huge sand-bottomed swimming pool linked to the beach and a 500-seat conference center are on the premises. The waters off their sandy beach are pollution-free, the Museum of Tahiti and the Islands is just a 15-minute walk away, and the sunsets over Moorea are superb. Luxury.

strand morning glory (Ipomoea pes-caprae)

OTHER WINDWARD ISLANDS

Maiao

Maiao, or Tapuaemanu, 70 km southwest of Moorea, is a low coral island with an elongated, 180-meter-high hill at the center. On each side of this hill is a large greenish blue lake. Around Maiao is a barrier reef with a pass on the south side accessible only to small boats. Some 250 people live in a small village on the southeast side of 8.3-square-km Maiao, all of them Polynesians. Problems with an Englishman, Eric Trower, who attempted to gain control of Maiao for phosphate mining in the 1930s, have resulted in a ban on Europeans and Chinese residing on the island. Most of the thatch used in touristic constructions on Moorea and Tahiti originates on Maiao.

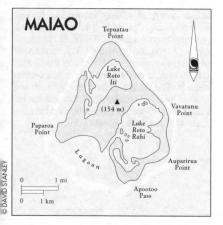

There are no tourist accommodations on Maiao and an invitation from a resident is required to stay. There's no airstrip. For information on the monthly supply ship from Papeete, contact the **Compagnie Française Maritime de Tahiti** (B.P. 368, 98713 Papeete; tel. 42-63-93) at Fare Ute. A roundtrip voyage on this ship would at least give you a glimpse of Maiao.

Mehetia

Mehetia is an uninhabited volcanic island about 100 km east of Tahiti. The island is less than two km across, but its Mount Fareura reaches 435 meters. There's no lagoon and anchorage is untenable. A difficult landing is possible on a black beach on the northwest side of the island. Anglers from the south coast of Tahiti visit occasionally.

TETIAROA

Tetiaroa, 42 km north of Tahiti, is a low coral atoll with a turquoise lagoon and 13 deep-green coconut-covered islets totaling 490 hectares. Only small boats can enter the lagoon. Tahuna Iti has been designated a seabird refuge (fenced off), the lagoon a marine reserve. Three-km-long Rimatuu islet served as a retreat for Tahitian royalty and the remains of Polynesian *marae* and giant *tuu* trees may be seen.

In 1904 the Pomare family gave Tetiaroa, once a Tahitian royal retreat, to a Canadian dentist named Walter J. Williams to pay their bills. Dr. Williams, who served as British consul from 1916 until his death in 1937, had a daughter who sold Tetiaroa to actor Marlon Brando in 1966. Brando came to Tahiti in 1960 to play Fletcher Christian in the MGM film *Mutiny on the Bounty* and ended up marrying his leading lady, Tarita Teriipaia (who played Mameetee, the chief's daughter). She and her family still run the small tourist resort on Motu Onetahi. Tarita and Marlon had two children, son Teihotu, born in 1965, and daughter Cheyenne, born in 1970.

The gunshot death of Dag Drollet, Cheyenne's ex-boyfriend and father of her son Tuki, at the Brando residence in Los Angeles in 1990, resulted in a 10-year prison sentence for Cheyenne's half-brother, Christian Brando, on a plea bargain. On Easter Sunday 1995 Cheyenne committed suicide and was buried next to Dag in the Drollet family crypt on Tahiti. These tragedies continue to haunt the Brando family, and the resort on Tetiaroa has been seriously neglected as a result. Brando is seldom present on Tetiaroa these days, and when he's on the atoll it's closed to tourists.

Getting There

A reservation office (B.P. 2418, 98713 Papeete; tel. 82-63-03, fax 85-00-51) in the Air Moorea ter-

TETIAROA

Auroa
Oroatera
Tauini Hira
Anae
Tiaraunu
Motu Aie
Honuea   L a g o o n
AIRSTRIP   HOTEL
Onetahi
Rimatuu
Tahuna Iti
Tahuna
Rahi
0   2 mi
Reiono
0   2 km

© DAVID STANLEY

minal at Faa'a International Airport arranges flights to Tetiaroa. A seven-hour day-trip including airfare, bird island tour, and lunch is CFP 23,800 pp. If you arrange this trip through your hotel, their commission will inflate the price. To stay in a rustic bungalow at the **Tetiaroa Village Hôtel** costs CFP 31,000/56,000/72,000 single/double/triple for a one-night package, or CFP 41,900/77,800/107,700 for a two-night package, air ticket, bungalow, meals, and excursion included. If you arrive in the morning you must also leave in the morning. To be frank, ᴵ. need of major renovations and you'll ɮ to see the traces of past glory being slowₗ away by termites. So—though the price may ᵤ gest it—don't come expecting anything resem. bling a luxury resort, and be prepared to rough it.

Aremiti Pacific Cruises (tel. 42-88-88) at the Moorea ferry wharf has tours to Tetiaroa on Wednesday and Sunday at CFP 14,000 pp including lunch and a guided tour of bird island. Other yachts and catamarans tied up opposite the Vaima Center offer day-trips to Tetiaroa and their departure times and rates are posted. Prices vary according to whether lunch is included and the quality of the boat, and you can sometimes go for as little as CFP 7,000 (meals not included). On all of the boat trips to Tetiaroa, be aware that up to three hours will be spent traveling each way and on a day-trip you'll only have about four hours on the atoll. The boat trip tends to be rough and many people throw up their fancy lunch on the way back to Papeete. (In mid-1995 Marlon Brando won a lawsuit to prohibit "floating hotels" in the Tetiaroa lagoon, so overnight trips many now only be possible for those staying at the Tetiaroa Village Hôtel.)

Cruising yachts with careless captains sometimes make an unscheduled stop at low-lying Tetiaroa is it's directly on the approach to Papeete from Hawaii. Several good boats have ended their days here.

M.G.L. DOMENY DE RIENZI

MOOREA
INTRODUCTION

Moorea, Tahiti's heart-shaped sister island, is clearly visible across the Sea of the Moon, just 16 km northwest of Papeete. This enticing island offers the white-sand beaches rare on Tahiti, plus long, deep bays, lush volcanic peaks, and a broad blue-green lagoon. Much more than Tahiti, Moorea is the laid-back South Sea isle of the travel brochures. Bora Bora may have a reputation as Polynesia's most beautiful island, but easily accessible Moorea seems to merit the distinction more (it's also a lot less expensive). And when Papeete starts to get to you, Moorea is only a hop away.

With a population of just 12,000, Moorea lives a quiet, relaxed lifestyle; coconut, pineapple, and vanilla plantations alternate with pleasant resorts and the vegetation-draped dwellings of the inhabitants. Tourism is concentrated along the north coast around Paopao and Club Med; many of the locals live in the more spacious south. Yet like Bora Bora, Moorea is in danger of becoming overdeveloped and heavy traffic already roars along the north coastal road all day. The choicest sections of shoreline have been barricaded by luxury resorts. On the plus side, most of the hotels are clusters of thatched bungalows, and you won't find many of the monstrous steel, glass, and cement edifices that scream at you in Hawaii. Still, the accommodations are plentiful and good, and weekly and monthly apartment rentals make even extended stays possible. Don't try to see Moorea as a day-trip from Tahiti: this is a place to relax!

The Land

This triangular, 125-square-km island is the surviving southern rim of a shield volcano once 3,000 meters high. Moorea is twice as old as its Windward partner, Tahiti, and weathering is noticeably advanced. The two spectacular bays cutting into the north coast flank Mt. Rotui (899 meters), once Moorea's core. The crescent of jagged peaks facing these long northern bays is scenically superb.

Shark-tooth-shaped Mouaroa (880 meters) is a visual triumph, but Mt. Tohivea (1,207 meters) is higher. Polynesian chiefs were once buried in caves along the cliffs. Moorea's peaks protect the north and northwest coasts from the rain-bearing southeast trades; the drier climate and scenic beauty explain the profusion of hotels along this side of the island. Moorea is surrounded by a coral ring with several passes into the lagoon. Three *motu* enhance the lagoon, one off Afareaitu and two off Club Med.

Moorea's interior valley slopes are unusually rich, with large fruit and vegetable plantations and human habitation. At one time or another, coconuts, sugarcane, cotton, vanilla, coffee, rice, and pineapples have all been grown in the rich soil of Moorea's plantations. Stock farming and fishing are other occupations. Vegetables like taro, cucumbers, pumpkins, and lettuce, and fruit such as bananas, oranges, grapefruit, papaya, star apples, rambutans, avocados, tomatoes, mangoes, limes, tangerines, and breadfruit make Moorea a veritable Garden of Eden.

History

Legend claims that Aimeho (or "Eimeo," as Captain Cook spelled it) was formed from the second dorsal fin of the fish that became Tahiti. The present name, Moorea, means "offshoot." It has also been called Fe'e or "octopus" for the eight

---

MONOÏ OIL

The Maohi women produce monoï by squeezing coconut pulp to liberate the oil which is then allowed to cure for several weeks. Blossoms of the tiare Tahiti, a white-petaled flower often used as a symbol of Tahiti, are added to the oil to give it a special fragrance. Monoï is judged by its fluidity and purity, and it's primarily a skin conditioner used as a moisturizer after showers or in traditional Polynesian massage. On Tahiti, newborn babies are bathed in monoï rather than water during their first month of life. Monoï is also a sure remedy for dry hair. It doesn't prevent sunburn and can even magnify the sun's rays, but it does provide instant relief for sunburned skin.

---

ridges that divide the island into eight segments. A hole right through the summit of Mt. Mouaputa (830 meters) is said to have been made by the spear of the demigod Pai, who tossed it across from Tahiti to prevent Mt. Rotui from being carried off to Raiatea by Hiro, the god of thieves.

Captain Samuel Wallis was the European discoverer of the Windward Islands in 1767. After leaving Tahiti, he passed along the north coast of Moorea without landing. He named it Duke of York's Island. The first European visitors were botanist Joseph Banks, Lieutenant Gore, the surgeon William Monkhouse, Herman Sporie. Captain Cook anchored in Opunohu Bay for one week in 1777, but he never visited the bay that today bears his name! His visit was uncharacteristically brutal, as he smashed the islanders' canoes and burned their homes when they refused to return a stolen goat.

In 1792 Pomare I conquered Moorea using arms obtained from the *Bounty* mutineers. Moorea had long been a traditional place of refuge for defeated Tahitian warriors, thus in 1808 Pomare II fled into exile here after his bid to bring all Tahiti under his control failed. A party of English missionaries established themselves at Papetoai in 1811, and Moorea soon earned a special place in the history of Christianity: here in 1812 the missionaries finally managed to convert Pomare II after 15 years of trying. On 14 February 1815, Patii, high priest of Oro, publicly accepted Protestantism and burned the old heathen idols at Papetoai, where the octagonal church is today. Shortly afterward the whole population followed Patii's example. The *marae* of Moorea were then abandoned and the Opunohu Valley depopulated. The first Tahitian translation of part of the Bible was printed on Moorea in 1817. From this island Protestantism spread throughout the South Pacific.

After Pomare II finally managed to reconquer Tahiti in 1815 with missionary help (the main reason for his "conversion"), Moorea again became a backwater. American novelist Herman Melville visited Moorea in 1842 and worked with other beachcombers on a sweet-potato farm in Maatea. His book *Omoo* contains a marvelous description of his tour of the island. Cotton and coconut plantations were created on Moorea in the 19th century, followed by vanilla and coffee

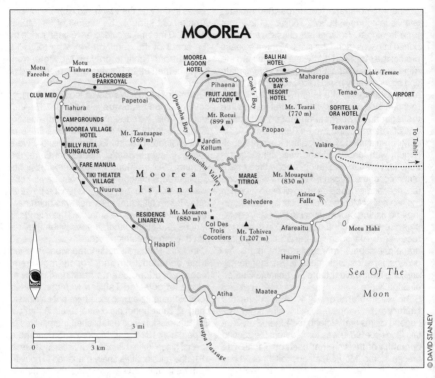

MOOREA

Moorea Island

Sea Of The Moon

© DAVID STANLEY

in the 20th, but only with the advent of the travel industry has Moorea become more than a beautiful backdrop for Tahiti.

Orientation

If you arrive by ferry you'll get off at Vaiare, four km south of Temae Airport. Your hotel may be at Maharepa (Hôtel Bali Hai), Paopao (Bali Hai Club, Motel Albert), Pihaena (Moorea Lagoon Hôtel), or Tiahura (Club Med, the campgrounds, Moorea Village Hôtel), all on the north coast. The Paopao hotels enjoy better scenery, but the beach is far superior at Tiahura. Add a CFP 150

pp per day municipal services tax to the accommodations prices quoted below.

The PKs (kilometer stones) on Moorea are measured in both directions from PK 0 at the access road to Temae Airport. They're numbered up to PK 35 along the north coast via Club Med and up to PK 24 along the south coast via Afareaitu, meeting at Haapiti halfway around the island.

Our circle-island tour and the accommodations and restaurant listings below begin at Vaiare Wharf and go counterclockwise around the island in each category.

SIGHTS

Northeast Moorea

You'll probably arrive on Moorea at **Vaiare Wharf,** which is officially PK 4 on the 59-km road around the island. To the north is the **Sofitel la Ora** (PK 1.3), built in the mid-1970s. If you have your own transport, stop here for a look around the resort and a swim. It's also enjoyable to walk north along the beach from this hotel or even to go snorkeling. At PK 1 on the main road, high above the la Ora, is a fine **lookout** over the deep passage, romantically named the Sea of the Moon, between Tahiti and Moorea.

One of the only public beach parks on Moorea is at **Temae,** about a km down a gravel road to the right a bit before you reach the airport access road. Watch out for black spiny sea urchins here. The Temae area is a former *motu* now linked to the main island and surfers will find an excellent long right wave around the point next to the airstrip. There's good snorkeling near Lilishop Boutique at **Maharepa** (PK 4). Look for the gaudy pareus hanging outside—the beach access is a few hundred meters to the east.

Around Cook's Bay

On the grounds of the American-owned **Hôtel Bali Hai** at PK 5.3 are replicas of historic an-chors lost by captains Bougainville and Cook in the 18th century. Just past the Bali Hai on the mountain side of the road is the "White House," the stately mansion of a former vanilla plantation, now used as a pareu salesroom.

At the entrance to Cook's Bay (PK 7) is the **Galerie Aad Van der Heyde** (tel. 56-14-22), as much a museum as a gallery. Aad's paintings hang outside in the flower-filled courtyard; in-side are his black-pearl jewelry, a large collection of Marquesan sculpture, and more paintings.

Teva Yrondi's **Aquarium de Moorea** (B.P. 483, 98728 Maharepa; tel. 56-24-00, fax 56-30-00; Tues.-Sun. 0930-1200/1430-1730), just south of the Cooks Bay Resort, displays turtles, crabs, coral, seashells, pearls, and jewelry in tanks that had once held tropical fish. Out back is a garden with a large travelers tree in the middle. Dozens of birds are attracted by feeders near the beach and you can see fish in an enclosure by their dock. Although the intention is to sell you a black pearl, the aquarium is worth treating as a mu-seum and admission is free.

Also as good as a museum is the **Galerie Baie de Cook** (B.P. 103, 98728 Maharepa; tel. 56-25-67; open daily 0900-1700; admission free), op-posite Club Bali Hai. Here you can inspect paint-

an old photo of
Mouaroa across
Cook's Bay, Moorea

ings by local artists, several huge Polynesian canoes, and a good collection of old artifacts. **Paopao Market** is almost defunct but it's still worth stopping to admire the large wall painting of a market scene by Temae artist François Ravello.

A rough four-km dirt road up to the paved Belvédère viewpoint road begins just west of the bridge at Paopao (PK 9), and it's nice to hike up it past the pineapple plantations. This is a good shortcut to the Opunohu Valley.

On the west side of Cook's Bay, a km farther along the north-coast highway, is a new **Catholic church** (PK 10). In the older St. Joseph's Church next door is an interesting altar painting with Polynesian angels done by the Swedish artist Peter Heyman in 1948. Unfortunately this building is not being maintained and is presently closed (although you may still be able to peek at the painting through the windows).

It's possible to visit the sales room (but not the production facilities) of the Distillerie de Moorea **fruit-juice factory** (B.P. 23, 98728 Temae; tel. 56-11-33, fax 56-21-52, daily 0800-1600), up off the main road at PK 12. Aside from the excellent papaya, grapefruit, and pineapple juices made from local fruits, the factory produces apple, orange, and passion fruit juices from imported concentrate, with no preservatives added. They also make 40-proof brandies (carambola or "star fruit," ginger, grapefruit, mango, orange, and pineapple flavors) and 25-proof liqueurs (coconut, ginger, and pineapple varieties). These are for sale and if they think you might buy a bottle they'll invite you to sample the brews (no free samples for obvious backpackers).

Opunohu Bay to Le Belvédère

The Moorea Lagoon Hôtel at PK 14 is the only large hotel between Paopao and Tiahura. A trail up **Mt. Rotui** (899 meters) begins opposite the "Faimano Village" accommodations nearby. Go up the driveway directly opposite Faimano Village and turn right before the house on the hill. A red arrow painted on a coconut tree points the way, but you may have to contend with the local dogs as you start up the hill. Once up behind the house the trail swings right and onto the ridge, which you follow to the summit. The land at the trailhead belongs to the Faimano Village's owner and he doesn't mind climbers, but you should ask permission to proceed of anyone you happen to meet near the house. From on top you'll have a sweeping

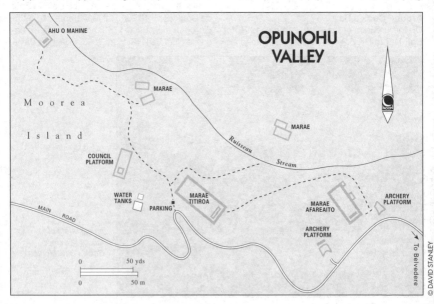

DAVID STANLEY

Moorea's Rotui rises above a country road.

view of the entire north coast. It's better not to go alone as there are vertical drops from the ridge and steep rocks in places, and after rains the trail could be dangerous. This is not a climb to be undertaken lightly.

Reader Greg Sawyer of Lafayette, Indiana, sent us this:

The trail up Mt. Rotui is quite strenuous but you're rewarded with billion-dollar views. It should only be attempted in fair weather, as it follows a razorback ridge quite narrow in places. In the rain it would be dangerous. Start very early and allow most of a day to really enjoy the trail and views (though fit people could push it through in four to five hours return). Mt. Rotui is Moorea's second-highest peak, and lies alone between the two bays on the north shore. There's little shade and no water but there are a couple of fixed ropes near the top at a couple of short steep pitches. Take care. The trail is not maintained but it's easy to follow once found. Just get to and stay on the ridgeline.

At PK 17.5 is the **Jardin Kellum Stop** (tel. 56-18-52) a tropical garden along Opunohu Bay with a colonial-style house built in 1920. Marie Kellum is an amateur archaeologist whose personal collection is full of interest and she can tell you anything you need to know about Tahitian medicinal plants. Until 1962 the Kellum family owned most of the Opunohu Valley. The garden is open Wednesday to Saturday mornings until noon. Ring the cow bell on the gate—it's CFP 300 pp admission. A famous yacht anchorage called Robinson's Cove is just offshore. From the unspoiled surroundings it's easy to understand why the 1984 remake of *The Bounty* was filmed here.

Shrimp are bred in large basins at the head of Opunohu Bay (PK 18). From here a paved five-km side road runs up the largely uninhabited **Opunohu Valley** to the Belvédère viewpoint. After two km you reach the junction with the dirt connecting road from Cook's Bay previously mentioned, then another km up and on the right is the **Lycée Professionnel Agricole,** Moorea's agricultural high school. This worthy institution, with students from all the islands of Tahiti-Polynesia, has hundreds of hectares planted in pineapples, vanilla, coffee, fruit trees, decorative flowers, and native vegetables on land seized from a German company in 1914. (In 1991 Moorea voters rejected a proposal to build a Sheraton resort and golf course in this area.)

Another km above this is **Marae Titiroa,** largest of a group of Polynesian temples restored in 1969 by Prof. Y.H. Sinoto of Honolulu. The small platform or *ahu* at the end of this *marae* was a sacred area reserved for the gods, and stone backrests for chiefs and priests are also seen. Here the people offered gifts of tubers, fish, dogs, and pigs, and prayed to their gods, many of whom were deified ancestors. Near the water tanks just 50 meters northwest of Marae Titiroa is a long council platform, and 50 meters farther are two smaller *marae* surrounded by towering Tahitian chestnut trees *(mape).* The most evocative of the group is four-tiered **Marae Ahu o Mahine,** about 250 meters down the trail.

Some 500 ancient structures have been identified in this area, and if you're very keen, you should be able to find a few in the forest across the stream, evidence of a large population with a highly developed social system. Following the acceptance of Christianity in the early 19th century, the Opunohu Valley's importance declined sharply. Today lots of side trails lead nowhere in particular but you'll discover many crumbling marae walls. Naturalists will enjoy the natural vegetation.

Continue up the main road from Marae Titiroa about 200 meters and watch for some stone **archery platforms** on the left. Here kneeling nobles once competed to see who could shoot an arrow the farthest. The bows and arrows employed in these contests were never used in warfare. Just up on the left is access to another archery platform and **Marae Afareaito.** The stone slabs you see sticking up in the middle of the *marae* were backrests for participants of honor.

From the archaeological area the winding road climbs steeply another km to the **Belvédère,** or Roto Nui, a viewpoint high up near the geographical center of the island. Much of northern Moorea is visible from here and it's easy to visualize the great volcano that once existed. Mt. Rotui (899 meters) in front of you was once the central core of an island more than three times as high as the present. The north part is now missing, but the semicircular arch of the southern half is plain to see. (An ice cream from the *roulotte* in the parking lot may be a welcome treat.)

Although most easily toured by rental car, this intriguing area can also be explored on foot. If you're staying anywhere around Cook's Bay, begin by hiking up the dirt road from the bridge in Paopao. If staying at Tiahura, take the boat bus to Cook's Bay. After "doing" the *marae* and Belvédère (and perhaps the Col des Trois Cocotiers hike below), walk down the Opunohu Valley road if you're returning to Tiahura or back down the dirt road to Cook's Bay. Take water and a picnic lunch and make a day of it.

Col des Trois Cocotiers

An adventurous three-hour hike off the paved Belvédère highway begins at the first turnoff to the right above junction with the Cook's Bay road. Three coconut trees once stood high up on a 400-meter-high ridge between Mt. Mouaroa and Mt. Tohivea called the Col des Trois Cocotiers though only one of the trees remains today.

Follow the green signs southwest 800 meters down a dirt road to a noisy generator and pig farm where a chain blocks the way. Park and continue down the road to a stream. About 50 meters up the hill from the stream is a barbed wire gate. Here you take the footpath to the right and continue straight ahead to a corner where you get your first clear view of the remaining coconut tree far up on the ridge. About 100 meters beyond the viewpoint is a side trail to the right that drops sharply toward another stream. This way is marked by bright green paint marks and older red marks (the trail straight ahead continues another five minutes up the fern-covered slope to Colline Maraamu where it too drops to the river, but the first descent is the more common way to go). You cross the stream and follow it up toward the ridge keeping a sharp eye out for paint marks (don't continue straight up the hill from the stream). After crossing the stream half a dozen times you go up the hill, taking care not to lose the trail. Turn right along the ridge at the top and continue to the coconut tree where you'll have a 360-degree view. On the way back down also beware of getting lost.

At times the way is not easy to follow, and if you're at all uncertain about your ability as a mountaineer it might be better to inquire about organized hiking tours up this way (see the listing for Ron's Adventure Tours under **Transportation,** below).

Papetoai to Club Med

Return to the main highway and continue west. The octagonal **Protestant church,** behind the post office at Papetoai (PK 22), was built on the site of the temple of the god Oro in 1822. Despite having been rebuilt several times, the church is known as "the oldest European building still in use in the South Pacific."

As the road begins to curve around the northwest corner of Moorea, you pass a number of large resort hotels, including the **Beachcomber Parkroyal** (PK 24.5), **Club Med** (PK 26.5), and the **Moorea Village Hôtel** (PK 27); only Club Med forbids you to walk through their grounds to the beach (there are no public beaches anywhere along here). It's possible to snorkel out to Tarahu and Tiahuru *motu* from this beach; recreation people at the Beachcomber Parkroyal and Moorea Beach Hôtel could also ferry you over. Try feeding bread to the fish. There's excellent reef break surfing in Taotai Pass off the Parkroyal.

Patrice Bredel's **Galerie Api** (tel. 56-13-57, fax 56-28-27; Mon.-Sat. 0930-1200/1430-1730), on the beach northeast of Club Med, displays the works of local artist François Ravello who paints in a Gauguin-like style. Bredel's personal collection of old Pacific artifacts is fascinating. In **Le Petit Village** shopping mall, across the street from Club Med, are a tourist information kiosk, bank, grocery store, snack bar, gas station, and many tourist shops.

Southern Moorea

The south coast of Moorea is much quieter than the north. You'll drive for kilometers through the open coconut plantations past unspoiled villages and scenic vistas. At PK 31 is **Tiki Theater Village,** described below under "Entertainment," the only one of its kind in the territory. Just past the Fire Department at PK 31.5 Haapiti is **Marae Nuurua,** on the beach across the soccer field. This three-tiered *marae* restored in 1991 bears a petroglyph of a turtle, and beyond is the much higher rubble heap of an unrestored *marae.*

At PK 33 you can have your photo taken in front of a huge fiberglass Tahitian warrior! It's also fun to stop for an upmarket lunch or a drink at **Résidence Linareva** (PK 34). Linareva's up-scale floating seafood restaurant, the *Tamarii Moorea I,* is an old ferryboat that once plied between Moorea and Tahiti. Colorful reef fish swim around the dock, which also affords an excellent mountain view. Drop into **Pai Moana Pearls** (tel. 56-25-25) next to the hotel driveway and ask for a free copy of owner Rick Steger's excellent brochure on pricing pearls.

At PK 35/24, Haapiti, the kilometer numbering begins its descent to Temae Airport. The twin-towered **Église de la Sainte Famille** (1891) at Haapiti was once the head church of the Catholic mission on the island. There's good anchorage here for yachts entering Matauvau Pass and a tall left hander for surfers out there (Tubb's Pub offers surf shuttles).

Tiny Motu Hahi lies just off **Afareaitu** (PK 9), the administrative center of Moorea. After Papetoai, this was the second center of missionary activity on Moorea, and on 30 June 1817, at the printing works at Afareaitu, King Pomare II ceremonially printed the first page of the first book ever published on a South Pacific island, a Tahitian translation of the Gospel of St. Luke. Before the press

was moved to Huahine a year later, over 9,000 books totaling more than half a million pages had been printed at Afareaitu! After 1821 the London Missionary Society established its Academy of the South Seas here to instruct the children of the missionaries and the Tahitian chiefs.

From opposite the old Protestant church (1912) in Afareaitu, the road between Magasin Ah Sing and a school leads up the **Afareaitu Valley** to a high waterfall, which cascades down a sheer cliff into a pool, a one-hour walk. You can drive a car two-thirds of the way up the valley. Park at the point where a normal car would have problems and hike on up the road to the right. When this road begins to climb steeply, look for a well-beaten footpath on the right, which will take you directly to the falls. You'll need a bit of intuition to find the unmarked way on your own.

You get a good view of Mt. Mouaputa, the peak pierced by Pai's spear, from the hospital just north of Afareaitu.

The access road to a different waterfall, **Atiraa Falls,** is a little beyond the hospital at Afareaitu. Admission to this one is CFP 200 pp, but at least the way is clearly marked. It's a 30-minute hike from the parking area.

Across the Island

An excellent day hike involves taking a morning bus to Vaiare Wharf, then hiking over the mountains to Paopao. From there you can catch another bus back to your accommodations, or try hitching. The shaded three-hour trail, partly marked by red, white, and green paint dabbed on tree and rock, does demand attention and perseverance, however. There are a few steep ascents and descents, and after rains it can be muddy and slippery.

Take the road inland beside Magasin Chez Meno, about 50 meters south of the first bridge south of the Vaiare ferry wharf. As you follow the dirt road up the valley, you'll take two forks to the right. Don't cross the stream after the second fork but go left and walk past some houses, just beyond which is an old Polynesian *marae* on the left. Further along you cross the stream and continue past a number of local gardens. The trail to Paopao leads off to the left near the last garden, and once you're on it it's fairly easy to follow if you keep your eyes open. When you see an old stone stairway on the left five minutes after leaving the gardens you'll know you're on the correct trail. All of the locals know about this trail and if you say "Paopao?" to them in a questioning way, they'll point you in the right direction. (It's hard to understand why Tahiti Tourisme, which has millions to spend on lavish overseas promotions can't find a few francs to erect proper trail markers here.)

When you reach the divide, go a short distance south along the ridge to a super viewpoint. On a clear day the rounded double peak of Orohena, Tahiti's highest, will be visible, plus the whole interior of Moorea. On the way down the other side avoid taking the wrong turn at a bamboo grove. You'll come out among the pineapple plantations of central Moorea behind Paopao. It's not possible to do this hike eastbound from Paopao to Vaiare without a guide, but westbound an experienced hiker should have no difficulty and it's worth going simply to see a good cross section of the vegetation. Don't miss it, but do take water and wear sturdy shoes.

SPORTS AND RECREATION

M.U.S.T. Plongée Scuba Diving, or Moorea Underwater Scuba-diving Tahiti (B.P. 336, 98728 Paopao; tel. 56-17-32, fax 56-15-83), has their base on the dock behind the Cook's Bay Resort Hôtel. They offer diving daily except Monday at 0900 and 1400 for CFP 5,000 for one dive, CFP 22,500 for five dives. If you pay by credit card there's a 3% surcharge. Divemaster Philippe Molle, author of a well-known French book on scuba diving, knows 20 different spots in and outside the reef.

Moorea's only female divemaster, Ms. Pascale Souquieres, runs **Moorea Fun Dive** (B.P. 737, 98728 Maharepa; tel. 56-40-38, fax 56-40-74) at the Moorea Lagoon Hôtel. It's CFP 4,500 a dive or CFP 4,500 a dive for five dives or more including all gear (except a wetsuit, which is CFP 300 extra). Hotel pickups are offered twice a day for almost anywhere on northern Moorea. This is a professional yet laid-back operation we can recommend.

Bernard and Collette Begliomini's **Bathy's Club** (B.P. 1247, 98729 Papetoai; tel. 56-31-

44, fax 56-38-10), at the Beachcomber Parkroyal, offers scuba diving for CFP 5,000, diving with dolphins CFP 13,000. This is the only PADI five-star facility in the territory. Bathy's and M.U.S.T. do underwater fish, eel, and shark feeding. Sometimes the swarm of fish becomes so thick the guide is lost from sight, yet as the resident shark scatters the mass of fish to steal the bait, the divemaster is seen again patting *le requin* as it passes. (It's still unknown if this activity will eventually attract sharks into the Moorea lagoon but to date no incidents have been reported.)

Marc Quattrini's **Scubapiti** (B.P. 58H, 98729 Haapiti, Moorea; tel. 56-12-67, fax 56-20-38), at Résidence Les Tipaniers, offers scuba diving daily at 0900 and 1430 (CFP 5,500). Instead of putting on a show, Marc keeps things natural on his cave, canyon, and drift dives. He also offers PADI or CMAS scuba certification courses and free hotel transfers from anywhere in northwestern Moorea.

The "Activities Nautiques" kiosk on the wharf at the **Beachcomber Parkroyal** (tel. 55-19-19) rents jet-skis at CFP 6,500 for half an hour, CFP 10,000 for one hour, or try your hand at parasailing (CFP 5,000).

Surfing is possible in most of the passes around the island or off the beach next to the airstrip, but it's not quite as good as on Tahiti or Huahine. A boat or a long paddle is required to reach the reef breaks.

Deep-sea fishing is offered by **Tea Nui Charters** (Chris Lilley, B.P. 194, 98728 Maharepa; tel. 56-15-08, fax 41-32-97) at CFP 12,000/17,000 pp for a half/full day (four-person minimum).

For horseback riding try **Rupe-Rupe Ranch** (tel. 56-26-52), or the "Crazy Horse Coral," at PK 2 between Vaiare Wharf and the Sofitel Ia Ora. To take one of their 12 horses along the beach for an hour is CFP 3,000. Group rides commence at 0830, 1400, and 1600, but it's best to call ahead.

Tiahura Ranch (tel. 56-28-55) across the highway from the Moorea Village Hôtel offers horseback riding at 0900 and 1615 daily except Monday (CFP 3,000 for 1.5 hours). You must reserve at least an hour in advance.

PRACTICALITIES

ACCOMMODATIONS

Camping

One of the South Pacific's nicest campgrounds is **Camping Chez Nelson** (Nelson and Josiane Flohr, tel. 56-15-18), beside the Hôtel Hibiscus, just south of Club Med (PK 27, Tiahura). It's beautifully set in a coconut grove right on the same beach tourists at the fancy resorts are paying hundreds of dollars a day to enjoy. The camping charge is CFP 700 pp, with toilets, showers, refrigerator, and good communal cooking facilities provided. No tents are for rent, but the 10 two-bed "dormitory" rooms go for CFP 1,000 pp (CFP 1,500 for one night). The five beach cabins with shared bath are CFP 2,200 single or double (CFP 2,500 for one night); four larger *fare* near the office are CFP 2,500 single or double (CFP 3,000 for one night). They also have three larger bungalows with kitchen and private bath at CFP 6,000 double. For CFP 300 pp (minimum of seven) they'll ferry you across to a *motu* for snorkeling. The campground office is open only during normal business hours. Josiane is a little eccentric and can be rather reserved at first, but she has a heart of gold. The place is clean, quiet, breezy, spacious, and well equipped, but unfortunately, however, there have been reports of theft here, so don't leave valuables unattended or within reach of an open window at night.

A second, smaller campground is just a little south of Chez Nelson, near the Moorea Village Hôtel. Friendly **Moorea Camping** (tel. 56-14-47, fax 56-30-22), also known as "Chez Viri et Claude," faces the same white-sand beach and has nine four-bed dorms at CFP 800 pp (CFP 1,000 for one night), plus another nine double rooms in a long building at CFP 2,000 single or double (CFP 3,000 for one night). The five beachfront bungalows with fridge are CFP 4,000 single or double (CFP 5,000 for one night). Camping is CFP 700 pp (CFP 800 for one night). The reception is open 0800-1200/1330-1700 only (closed Sunday afternoon). Communal kitchen and washing facilities are provided, and

they'll loan you snorkeling gear and perhaps even a canoe. Bus trips around the island are CFP 1,000 pp if at least six people sign up and they can also take you to a *motu*. The activities manager, Coco (one of the nicest Tahitians you'll ever meet), will be able fill you in on all the cheapest deals around Moorea. He'll also help

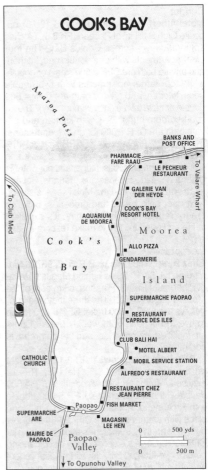

COOK'S BAY

Avaroa Pass

BANKS AND POST OFFICE

PHARMACIE FARE RAAU

LE PECHEUR RESTAURANT

To Vaiare Wharf

GALERIE VAN DER HEYDE

COOK'S BAY RESORT HOTEL

AQUARIUM DE MOOREA

To Club Med

M o o r e a

C o o k ' s

ALLO PIZZA

GENDARMERIE

B a y

I s l a n d

SUPERMARCHE PAOPAO

RESTAURANT CAPRICE DES ILES

CLUB BALI HAI

MOTEL ALBERT

MOBIL SERVICE STATION

CATHOLIC CHURCH

ALFREDO'S RESTAURANT

RESTAURANT CHEZ JEAN PIERRE

Paopao

FISH MARKET

SUPERMARCHE ARE

MAGASIN LEE HEN

MAIRIE DE PAOPAO

Paopao Valley

0   500 yds

0   500 m

To Opunohu Valley

© DAVID STANLEY

you book trips even if you're not staying here. But as at Chez Nelson, we've heard of things going missing from the dorms, so chain your pack to something solid and keep the top locked. Break-ins often occur when everybody is at a party on the veranda and the campground is empty. Despite the insecurity, both campgrounds are great for young low-budget travelers and other adventurers—you'll meet some wonderful people. Two grocery stores (with cold beer) are between the two camping grounds.

Budget

Motel Albert (Iris Haring, tel./fax 56-12-76), opposite Club Bali Hai at Paopao (PK 8.5), catches splendid views across Cook's Bay. The four older apartments with one double bed, kitchen, and private bath are CFP 3,500 single or double, while four larger apartments with two double beds, kitchen, and private bath are CFP 4,500 double or triple (two-night minimum stay). The 10 two-bedroom bungalows with kitchen and private bath are CFP 7,000 for up to four persons. The cheaper apartments are often taken by monthly rentals at CFP 80,000 or 90,000. Each unit has cooking facilities, fridge, and hot water in a garden setting on spacious grounds. Several stores are nearby and the Mobil service station next door sells bread and groceries. Bicycles are for rent at CFP 1,200 a day. It's excellent value and often full (try to make reservations).

Inexpensive

Chez Dina (Dina Dhieux, B.P. 512, 98728 Maharepa; tel. 56-10-39) is behind Magasin Vairagi Pihaena at PK 13, Pihaena, a km east of the Moorea Lagoon Hôtel. The three thatched bungalows are CFP 4,500 triple, CFP 5,000 for up to five (reductions on a weekly basis). Cooking facilities are provided, and the bathroom is communal.

Billy Ruta Bungalows (tel. 56-12-54) is right on the beach at PK 28.3, Tiahura. The 12 thatched A-frame bungalows begin at CFP 4,000 double without kitchenette, CFP 5,000 double with kitchenette. Another eight rooms in a long block with shared bath are CFP 3,000 single or double, and they sometimes allow camping at CFP 500 pp. There's occasionally disco dancing here on weekends. Billy drives the local school and church *truck* and is a very friendly guy.

Chez Pauline (Jean-Pierre Bouvier, tel. 56-11-26) at PK 9, Afareaitu, is between the two stores near the church. It's a lovely old colonial house with three rooms with double beds and shared bath at CFP 4,000/5,000 single/double including breakfast. One larger room sleeping five is CFP 10,000. A picturesque restaurant with tikis on display rounds out this establishment, which has great atmosphere. Dinner here is around CFP 3,000 (fish and Tahitian vegetables) and it must be ordered in advance.

Moderate

The **Cook's Bay Resort Hôtel** (Béatrice and François Michel, B.P. 30, 98728 Temae; tel. 56-10-50, fax 56-29-18) is beside the highway at the entrance to Cook's Bay (PK 7.2). You can't miss this mock-colonial edifice constructed in 1985, with its false-front Waikiki feel. The 76 rooms cost CFP 6,500 single or double with fan, CFP 8,500 with a/c, plus tax. The accommodations are rather small and spartan with old furniture, but at least they're clean and each room has a fridge. Don't bother taking the a/c as it probably won't work anyway. The resort also has 24 wooden bungalows opposite the wharf at CFP 8,500 single or double in the garden or CFP 9,500 facing the water. Discounts are sometimes offered. The breakfast and dinner plan here is CFP 3,800 pp, but plenty of better restaurants are nearby. You can swim or snorkel off the pier, and there's also a swimming pool. Moorea's top dive shop is on the premises, and all the usual resort activities and entertainment are available. The Cook's Bay caters mostly to people on cheap Hawaii-style packages, and this captured clientele helps explain the variable service. Many readers liked this resort, but a few did not. The views of the bay are stunning. (A late report indicates that this resort has closed due to financial difficulties and that guests are now accommodated at the adjacent Hôtel Kaveka, which also may soon go under.)

Several small places near the Moorea Lagoon Hôtel (PK 14) rent bungalows. **Chez Nani** (Maeva Bougues, B.P. 117, 98713 Papeete; tel. 56-19-99) on the west side of the hotel has three thatched bungalows with kitchenettes at CFP 7,000 single or double. The signposted **Faimano Village** (Hinano Feidel, B.P. 588, 98728 Maharepa; tel. 56-10-20, fax 56-36-47) next to Chez Nani has seven lovely thatched *fare* with cooking facilities at CFP 11,500 for up to six persons with private bath, CFP 8,000/8,500 double/triple with shared bath (two-night minimum stay). Faimano Village has a nice garden setting facing the beach and easygoing individual atmosphere but single women should avoid it as there have been reports of prowlers. Doors and windows cannot be locked. **Chez Francine** (Francine Lumen, B.P. 659, 98728 Maharepa; tel. 56-13-24), 400 meters farther west, doesn't have a sign but look for three buildings with red tile roofs between the highway and the shore. A two-room house is CFP 8,000 double with kitchenette or CFP 6,500 double without kitchenette.

Fare Vai Moana (B.P. 1181, 98729 Papetoai; tel./fax 56-17-14) is at Pizzeria Jeannot, a large restaurant overlooking the beach adjacent to Camping Chez Nelson at PK 27, Tiahura. The 12 attractive thatched bungalows near the beach are CFP 8,000 double in the garden or CFP 12,000 facing the beach, plus tax. Half board at their seafood restaurant is CFP 2,900 pp.

Moorea Fare Auti'ura (Viri Pere, tel. 56-14-47, fax 56-30-22), opposite Moorea Camping at PK 27.5, Tiahura, has six thatched bungalows on elevated concrete platforms at CFP 6,000 single or double (minimum stay two nights). Cooking facilities are provided. It's run by Moorea Camping, so check there if nobody seems to be around.

Fare Mato Tea (Iris Cabral, B.P. 1111, 98729 Papetoai; tel. 56-14-36), on the beach just south of Billy Ruta (PK 29, Tiahura), is okay if you're a family or group: CFP 8,500 for four, CFP 10,500 for six (minimum stay two nights). All eight large thatched *fare* on the spacious grounds have full cooking facilities and private bath. It's a do-your-own-thing type of place.

Near the south end of the west coast strip (PK 30) is **Fare Manuia** (Jeanne Salmon, tel. 56-26-17) with six *fare* with cooking facilities at CFP 8,000 for up to four people, CFP 10,000 for up to six people, or CFP 12,000 on the beach.

Polynesian Bungalows (B.P. 1234, 98729 Papetoai; tel. 56-30-77, fax 56-32-15) is squeezed in front of Tiki Theater Village at PK 31. The 12 large thatched bungalows with kitchenettes are CFP 8,000 single or double plus tax with reduced weekly and monthly rates. You have to walk through Tiki Village to get to the beach, so it's not as good a choice as the two places listed above.

Résidence Linareva (B.P. 1, 98729 Haapiti) tel. 56-15-35, fax 56-25-25) sits amid splendid mountain scenery at PK 34 on the wild side of the island. Prices begin at CFP 7,200/8,200/9,900 single/double/triple, with 20% weekly discounts. Each of the seven units is unique, with TV, fan, and full cooking facilities. Bicycles and an outrigger canoe are loaned free.

Expensive

Résidence Les Tipaniers (B.P. 1002, 9827 Papetoai; tel. 56-12-67, fax 56-29-25) at PK 25.9, Tiahura, is cramped around the reception, but better as you approach the beach. The 22 bungalows start at CFP 8,500/10,200 single/double (those with kitchen are a few thousand francs extra). The hotel also has five self-catering lagoonside bungalows at PK 21 on Opunohu Bay costing CFP 7,500 plus tax for up to four persons with weekly rates available. Les Tipaniers' well known restaurant offers Italian dishes. They'll shuttle you over to a nearby *motu* for snorkeling or loan you a bicycle or outrigger canoe at no charge. This hotel has a good reputation and a resident divemaster.

The **Hôtel Hibiscus** (B.P. 1009, 98729 Papetoai; tel. 56-12-20, fax 56-20-69), on beach right next to Club Med (PK 27), offers 29 thatched bungalows beneath the coconut palms at CFP 11,000 triple in the garden or CFP 13,000 on the beach, plus tax. A fourth person is CFP 1,000 extra. There's a 20% discount on a weekly basis. The breakfast and dinner plan is CFP 3,900 pp, but all units have kitchenettes so this is a good choice for families. You don't get a lot of mosquitos here because Club Med fumigates their adjacent property daily (you do get occasional disco noise from the same source).

The **Moorea Village Hôtel** (B.P. 1008, 98729 Papetoai; tel. 56-10-02, fax 56-22-11), also called "Fare Gendron," at PK 27.9, Tiahura, offers 70 fan-cooled thatched bungalows beginning at CFP 8,000/9,000 single/double plus tax, or CFP 11,500 for up to four people. To be on the beach is another CFP 2,500. The 10 new units with kitchen are double price; all units have fridges. The breakfast and dinner plan costs CFP 3,900 pp. Saturday at 1900 there's a barbecue; the Tahitian feast with Polynesian dancing is Sunday at noon. There are lots of free activities, such as the canoe trip to the *motu*, outrigger canoes, tennis, snorkeling, and swimming pool. Though on the package tour circuit, this place is also somewhat of a hangout for local Tahitians, and the management leaves a lot to be desired.

Premium

The 63-room **Hôtel Bali Hai** (B.P. 26, 98728 Temae; tel. 56-13-52, fax 56-19-22) at PK 5.3, Maharepa, caters mainly to American tour groups staying three, four, or seven nights. If you go for stuff like that you'll love the Bali Hai. Standard rooms are CFP 11,500 single or double, bungalows from CFP 14,000 (children under 12 free). The cheaper rooms are rather gloomy and it's better to go for a bungalow if you stay here. For breakfast and dinner add CFP 4,500 pp extra. Rides on the Bali Hai's thatched catamaran *Liki Tiki* are CFP 2,000 and up. Happy hour here is daily 1700-1900 with live music and pocorn, and Wednesday there's a dance show. The Bali Hai was founded by the so-called Bali Hai Boys, ex-Californians Hugh, Jay, and Muk, who arrived on Moorea in 1959 to take over a vanilla plantation but ended up inventing the overwater bungalow right here in 1961.

Club Bali Hai (B.P. 8, 98728 Maharepa; tel. 56-13-68, fax 56-13-27) at PK 8.5, Paopao, has 20 rooms in the main two-story building starting at CFP 12,000 single or double, and 19 beachfront or overwater bungalows at CFP 18,000 or 24,000. Slightly reduced room rates are available to walk in guests. Only the bungalows include cooking facilities, but most rooms have a spectacular view of Cook's Bay. There's a swimming pool by the bay. Many units have been sold to affluent Americans on a time-share basis, with each owner getting two weeks a year at the Club. Enjoy reduced-price drinks, free popcorn, and Tahitian trio music during happy hour at the lagoonside bar Tuesday and Friday 1800-1900—a Moorea institution. The snack bar serves a wicked hot dog at lunchtime. We've heard Club Bali Hai welcomes visiting yachties warmly.

The **Moorea Lagoon Hôtel** (B.P. 11, 98728 Temae; tel. 56-14-68, fax 56-26-25) at PK 14, Pihaena, is CFP 11,000/12,000 single/double garden view, CFP 14,000/15,000 lagoon view, CFP 16,000/17,000 beachfront for the 45 tightly packed thatched bungalows, plus tax. Breakfast and dinner are another CFP 3,600 pp. It's

more isolated than most of the other resorts, but the beach is fine, there's a pool, and scuba diving is offered. The property is to be redeveloped with 55 outwater bungalows by Outrigger Hotels of Hawaii and until the work is complete, the hotel may be closed.

The **Moorea Beach Club** (B.P. 1017, 98729 Papetoai; tel. 56-15-48, fax 56-25-70), formerly the Climate de France, is the easternmost hotel on the white sandy shores of the Tiahura tourist strip (PK 25.8). The 40 a/c rooms with fridge begin at CFP 12,000 single, double, or triple, plus 8% tax and CFP 4,800 pp extra for breakfast and dinner (if desired). These standard units are on two floors, so you will have someone above or below. **Fare Condominium** (B.P. 1052, 98729 Papetoai; tel. 56-26-69, fax 56-26-22) at the Moorea Beach Club is managed separately from the rest of the resort and it's a good choice for families or small groups. An a/c garden bungalow with cooking facilities and TV will cost CFP 15,500 double or triple, CFP 18,000 for up to six persons. The same thing on the beach is CFP 18,400 for up to three or CFP 20,400 for up to six. Outrigger canoes, tennis, snorkeling, and fishing gear are free.

Luxury

The **Sofitel la Ora** (B.P. 28, 98728 Temae; tel. 56-12-90, fax 56-12-91), at PK 1.3 between Vaiare and the airport, sits on one of the finest beaches on the island with a splendid view of Tahiti. The 110 thatched bungalows begin at CFP 23,200 single or double plus tax (children under 12 free). Upgrade to a/c if possible. Breakfast and dinner are CFP 5,600 pp extra together. The meals here are often not up to scratch (the Molokai Restaurant has better food and service than La Pérouse) and because the Sofitel is rather isolated some of the Paopao restaurants won't pick up diners here (Le Pêcheur might). Unfortunately, the service deteriorates fast when large groups are present and some of the local staff are rude and unhelpful (several complaints have been received). We've heard of local children with improper toilet training being allowed in the hotel pool, so use the beach. There's a Europcar desk in the lobby.

The 147-room **Moorea Beachcomber Parkroyal** (B.P. 1019, 98729 Papetoai; tel. 55-19-19, fax 55-19-55) at PK 24.5, was erected on an artificial beach in 1987 and purchased in 1989 by Japanese interests. It's Moorea's top hotel. The 49 standard a/c rooms in the main building start are CFP 28,800 single or double plus tax, but it's better value to pay CFP 30,900 for a garden bungalow. Beach bungalows are CFP 35,000. For one of the 50 overwater bungalows, have your CFP 39,100 ready (50% less than you'd pay for the same thing on Bora Bora). Third persons are CFP 6,000, but children under 16 are free. The breakfast and dinner plan is CFP 6,500 pp (alternative eateries are quite a walk away). There's a pool and the full spectrum of paid sporting activities is available (only daytime tennis, snorkeling gear, and canoeing are free for guests). The hotel's dolphins are a big attraction and you'll see them standing on their heads and roughhousing at all hours day and night. Europcar has a desk here.

Club Méditerranée (B.P. 1010, 98729 Papetoai; tel. 55-00-00, fax 55-00-10) at PK 26.5, Tiahura, has 350 simple fan-cooled bungalows. You can reserve one by paying CFP 14,000 pp a day (double occupancy) at the Club Med office in the Vaima Center, Papeete (B.P. 575, 98713 Papeete; tel. 42-96-99, fax 42-16-83). Children under 12 are CFP 7,000, under four CFP 1,400. The price includes buffet breakfast, lunch, and dinner, and a wide range of regimented activities (including one scuba dive a day), but no airport transfers. Unlimited beer and wine come with lunch and dinner, but other drinks are expensive and laundry charges will knock your socks off! The PADI scuba diving center here is for guests only. Sunbathing in the raw is permitted on the small *motu* just offshore (the tiniest of bottoms is required in front of the resort). Club Med's for you if nonstop activity is a high priority, otherwise all the canned entertainment can be to the detriment of peace at night, and occasional helicopter landings beside the restaurant often interrupt afternoon naps. Clocks inside the village are set ahead to give guests an extra hour in the sun. Club Med's G.O.s *(gentils organisateurs)* tend to resist the unusual or nonroutine (such as requesting a specific room or not sitting where you're told in the restaurant), so try to "go with the flow" (i.e., conform). It's not a "swinging singles club" anymore, but rather a haven for couples where singles can also be found. Nonguests can

purchase a CFP 5,500 day pass valid for lunch and some sporting activities. Don't attempt to trespass as these guys are security freaks. The Moorea Club Med has been around for quite a while and it can't compare to the newer, smaller, and smarter Club Med on Bora Bora.

FOOD

Aside from the hotel restaurants, table hoppers are catered to by a mixed bag of eateries along the east side of Cook's Bay. **Restaurant Le Mahogany** (tel. 56-39-73; closed Wednesday), at PK 4, Maharepa, is a new place offering French and Chinese dishes. A bit west is **Le Cocotier Restaurant** (tel. 56-12-10; Mon.-Sat. 1100-1430/1730-2100) meat dishes priced CFP 1,400-1,650 and fish at CFP 1,350-2,400. There's a menu at the entrance and it's quite popular.

Snack Le Sylésie (tel. 56-15-88), next to the post office at PK 5.5, Maharepa, has a nice terrace and fast service—perfect for breakfast. It's also good for pastries, sandwiches, and crepes, and try the coconut ice cream. Of course, the coffee here is *magnifique!*

Le Pêcheur Restaurant (tel. 56-36-12; closed Sunday), also at Maharepa (PK 6), near the pharmacy at the east entrance to Cook's Bay, has an excellent reputation for its seafood dishes, which begin around CFP 1,500. The service is also good and on Saturday night there's local entertainment. If you lack transport, they'll come pick you up.

The overwater **Fishermen's Wharf Restaurant** (tel. 56-15-56; Tues.-Sat. 1130-1400/1700-2100) near the Cook's Bay Resort Hôtel also serves seafood in the CFP 1,500-1,900 range. Readers report that while the view from their terrace is superb, the food is variable.

Cook's Pizza (tel. 56-10-50), across the street from the Cook's Bay Resort Hôtel (PK 7.2), has small/large thick or thin crust pizzas beginning at CFP 900/1,300—not bad for Moorea. **Allo Pizza** (tel. 56-18-22; daily except Tuesday 1100-2100), opposite the *gendarmerie* in Paopao (PK 7.8), dispenses large takeaway pizzas costing CFP 900-1,300, which you must consume picnic-style somewhere.

Restaurant Caprice des Îles (tel. 56-44-24; closed Tuesday), occupies a thatched pavilion next to Supermarché Paopao on the mountain

a charming Polynesian woman

side of the road, 150 meters north of Club Bali Hai. They offer Italian pastas (CFP 800-1,400), Chinese dishes (CFP 900-1,900), Tahitian dishes (CFP 1,000-1,900), and French dishes (CFP 1,300-2,400)—more expensive than other places along this way. We've heard rave reviews of their seafood but the pastas can be rather heavy in such a warm climate.

Restaurant Chez Jean Pierre (tel. 56-18-51; closed Wednesday), close to the market, is reasonable and has roast suckling pig in coconut milk on Saturday night. Cheaper still is the outdoor snack bar at Paopao Market, which is only open in the evening (a huge swordfish steak for CFP 900).

Alfredo's Restaurante Italiano (tel. 56-17-71; open daily), on the inland side of the road a few hundred meters south of Club Bali Hai, has some of the island's top pizza and pasta, plus a few reasonably priced fish and meat dishes. The piña coladas aren't bad either. It's owned by an American named Syd Pollock who has been running hotels and restaurants around Polynesia for years. He's an interesting guy to chat with and he does hotel pickups on request. Recommended.

Also check **Chez Michèle** (tel. 56-34-80), by the river at the head of Cooks Bay, which lists their menu on a blackboard facing their terrace.

Restaurants near Club Med

Le Garden (tel. 56-47-00), in Le Petit Village shopping mall opposite Club Med, has ice-cream sundaes at CFP 650, and it's also a good place for breakfast (omelettes CFP 300-500, served 0900-1430). The continental breakfast is served 0800-1100 only.

Nearby is **Restaurant L'Aventure** (tel. 56-23-36; Tuesday 1830-2100, Wed.-Sun. 1200-1400/1830-2100) with salads (CFP 400-900), pastas (CFP 800-1,600), and meat and fish dishes (CFP 1,000-1,800). Specials are advertised on a blackboard menu.

Good pizza and ocean views are available at beachfront **Le Sunset Pizzeria** (tel. 56-26-00) at the Hôtel Hibiscus (but avoid the salads). **Pâtisserie Le Sylésie II** (tel. 56-20-45) is nearby.

Groceries

If you've got access to cooking facilities, shop at one of the many grocery stores spread around Moorea. The largest and cheapest is **Toa Moorea** (tel. 56-18-89; Mon.-Thurs. 0800-1900, Friday and Saturday 0800-2000, Sunday 0600-1200), a km south of the Vaiare ferry wharf.

Libre Service Maharepa (tel. 56-35-90), at PK 5.5, is almost opposite the Banque de Tahiti. **Supermarché Pao Pao** (tel. 56-17-34), 150 meters north of Club Bali Hai, opens Mon.-Sat. 0530-1200/1400-1800, Sunday 0500-1000. At the head of Cook's Bay you have a choice of **Magasin Lee Hen** (tel. 56-15-02; daily 0600-1200/1400-1830) or **Supermarché Are** (tel. 56-10-28) just west of the bridge nearby.

The nearest grocery store to the three small hotels near Faimano Village is **Magasin Vairagi Pihaena,** a km east of the Moorea Lagoon Hôtel. The supermarket in Le Petit Village opposite Club Med opens Monday, Friday, and Saturday 0830-1800, Tues.-Thurs. 0830-1230/1430-1830, and Sunday 0800-1200.

All you're likely to find at the **municipal market** at Paopao is a limited selection of fish. Fresh produce is much harder to obtain on Moorea than it is on Tahiti, so buy things when you see them and plan your grocery shopping carefully. Ask the stores what time the bread arrives, then be there promptly. The hybrid lime-grapefruit grown on Moorea has a thick green skin and a unique flavor.

ENTERTAINMENT

Disco
The disco at **Billy Ruta Bungalows** (tel. 56-12-54), at PK 28.3, Tiahura, is a nice, very Polynesian scene with a good music mix of Tahitian, French, American, reggae, etc. It's a fun place that gets very busy with some very talented dancers (Friday and Saturday from 2230). Otherwise there's a show and disco at **Club Med** (tel. 55-00-00) Friday and Saturday nights at 2130 (CFP 2,500 cover charge includes CFP 1,800 in drinks).

Cultural Shows for Visitors
See Tahitian dancing in the Sofitel la Ora's **La Pérouse Restaurant** (tel. 56-17-61) on Tuesday, Thursday, and Saturday at 2000. At **Hôtel Bali Hai** (tel. 56-13-59) there's Polynesian dancing Wednesday and Saturday at 1800, Sunday at 1200. The **Cook's Bay Resort Hôtel** (tel. 56-10-50) has Tahitian dancing Tuesday, Thursday, and Saturday after 1900. The **Moorea Village Hôtel** (tel. 56-10-02) presents Polynesian dancing Sunday at lunchtime. The Tahitian show at the **Moorea Beachcomber Parkroyal** (tel. 55-19-19) is on Wednesday and Saturday nights after 2000. **Club Med** (tel. 55-00-00) presents Tahitian dancing on Thursday (CFP 5,500 admission includes the buffet at 1930). These times often change, so check. The Tahitian feasts that come with the shows cost CFP 4,000 and up, but you can often observe the action from the bar for the price of a drink. It's well worth going.

Since 1986 Moorea has had its own instant culture village, the **Tiki Theater Village** (B.P. 1016, 98729 Papeete; tel. 56-18-97, fax 43-20-06) at PK 31, Haapiti. The doors are open Tues.-Sat. 1100-1500, with a charge of CFP 2,000 to visit the village and see the small dance show at 1300, plus CFP 500 if you want to visit the demonstration black pearl farm (or CFP 5,500 including the tour, lunch, and transfers). The guided tour of the recreated Tahitian village is informative and the 30 dancers and other staff members who live in the village year-round are enthusiastic, but sometimes they're a little disorganized so you might obtain some details about the show time before parting with your francs. Lunch is available in the à la carte restaurant. Line fishing from a *pirogue* is CFP 1,500 extra. Four or five nights a week at 1800 there's a big sunset show with a *tamaaraa* buffet and open bar (CFP 7,300, reservations required).It's possible to pay CFP 2,500 for the show alone at 2045 (plus CFP 1,000 for hotel transfers, if required). If you've got CFP 130,000 to spare, a "royal" Tahitian wedding can be arranged at the village (bring your own husband/wife). The ceremony lasts two hours, from 1600 to sunset. The bridegroom arrives by canoe and the newlyweds are carried around in procession by four "warriors." Otherwise there's the less extravagant "princely" wedding for CFP 99,000, photos included. Yes, it's kinda tacky, but that's show biz! (Such weddings are not legally binding.) Most readers say they really enjoyed Tiki Village.

SERVICES AND INFORMATION

Services
The Banque Socredo, Banque de Polynésie, and Banque de Tahiti are near the Hôtel Bali Hai at Maharepa. The Westpac Bank is in Le Petit Village shopping mall opposite Club Med. None of these banks are open on Saturday but Banque Socredo has an ATM outside.

The main post office (Mon.-Thurs. 0700-1500, Friday 0700-1400) is near the banks at Maharepa. Branch post offices are found at Afareaitu and Papetoai. The *gendarmerie* (tel. 56-13-44) is at PK 7.8, Paopao, just south of the Aquarium de Moorea.

The Tahiti Parfum shop (tel. 56-16-87; daily 0900-1300) in Le Petit Village will wash and dry six kg of laundry for CFP 1,600 (same-day service if you get your wash in early). Look for the Lav'matic sign.

Information
The Moorea Visitors Bureau (B.P. 1121, 98729 Papeete; tel./fax 56-29-09; closed Sunday) has a poorly marked but helpful kiosk next to the gas station in front of Le Petit Village. Activities and tours can be booked here, including day-trips to Tetiaroa.

There's also a tourist information counter at Vaiare ferry wharf but don't stop to visit them when you first arrive or you'll miss the bus to your hotel.

The boutique at the Hôtel Bali Hai offers a book-exchange service (on the top shelf above the new books).

Kina Maharepa (tel. 56-22-44), next to the post office at PK 5.5, Maharepa, sells books and magazines. There's also a newsstand in Le Petit Village opposite Club Med.

Health

The island's hospital (tel. 56-23-23) is at Afareaitu, on the opposite side of the island from most of the resorts, and it's much easier to see a private doctor or dentist in case of need.

The nearest to Cook's Bay is the Gabinet Medical (tel. 56-32-32) behind the Banque de Polynésie at PK 5.5, Maharepa, not far from the Hôtel Bali Hai. General practitioners Dr. Christian Jonville and Dr. Jean-Pierre Senechal share this clinic, which is open weekdays 0700-1200/1400-1800. Dr. Jonville is fluent in English. In the same building is the Cabinet Dentaire (tel. 56-32-44) of Dr. Jean-Marc Thurillet and Dr. Nadine Tremoulet, open weekdays 0800-1130/1500-1800.

General practitioner Dr. Hervé Paulus (tel. 56-10-09, in emergencies tel. 56-10-25) is conveniently located at Le Petit Village near Club Med. He sees patients weekdays 0800-1200/1500-1800, Saturday 0800-1200/1700-1800, Sunday 0900-1030. Dr. Dominique Barraille (tel. 56-27-07) has an office between Hôtel Hibiscus and Camping Chez Nelson. Also near Camping Chez Nelson and opposite Magasin Rene Junior at PK 27, Tiahura, is the joint office of Dr. Bernard Sztejnman (tel. 56-47-51; closed Thursday), a dentist, and Dr. Brigitte Busseuil (tel. 56-26-19, residence tel. 56-13-98), a medical doctor. Dr. Busseuil's clinic is open Monday, Tuesday, Thursday, and Friday 0800-1200/1515-1800, Wednesday 0800-1200, Saturday 0900-1200/1700-1800, and Sunday 0900-1030.

Pharmacie Fare Raau (tel. 56-10-51; weekdays 0730-1200/1400-1730, Saturday 0800-1200/1530-1800, Sunday 0800-1100) is at PK 6.5 between Maharepa and Paopao. There's a second branch of Pharmacie Fare Raau (tel. 56-38-37; Mon.-Sat. 0830-1200/1530-1830, Sunday 0900-1100) at PK 30.5, Haapiti, near Tiki Theater Village.

TRANSPORTATION AND TOURS

Air Moorea and **Air Tahiti** (both tel. 56-10-34) are based at Moorea Temae Airport. Details of the air and ferry services from Tahiti are given in the introduction to Tahiti-Polynesia.

Buses of 28 or 45 seats meet the ferries at Vaiare Wharf five times a day, charging CFP 100/200 child/adult to anywhere on the island. Although they don't go right around the island, the northern and southern routes meet at Le Petit Village opposite Club Med, so you could theoretically effect a circumnavigation by changing there, provided you caught the last bus back to Vaiare at 1545 from Le Petit Village.

Buses leave Le Petit Village for the ferry weekdays at 0445, 0545, 0645, 0945, 1145, 1345, 1445, and 1545, Saturday at 0445, 0545, 0645, 0845, 0945, 1130, 1345, 1445, and 1545, and Sunday at 0445, 0645, 1245, 1345, 1445, and 1645. If you have to catch a bus somewhere along its route, add the appropriate traveling time and ask advice of anyone you can. Some of the buses run 30 minutes early.

A taxi on Moorea is actually a minibus with a white letter **T** inside a red circle. In past, the taxi drivers have occasionally employed heavy-handed tactics to discourage visitors from using other means of transportation such as rental cars and the bus. A regular bus service along the north coast was launched in mid-1994 but the active opposition of taxi drivers managed to scuttle the service a year later. Some hotel staff will claim not to know about the ferry buses, and we've even heard of rental car tires being slashed! You should have no problem catching a bus when you arrive on Moorea from Tahiti by ferry, but be quick to jump aboard. Hitching is wearing thin with Moorea motorists, although it's still possible. If you really need the ride you'll probably get it; just be prepared to do some walking.

Car Rentals

Europcar (tel. 56-34-00, fax 56-35-05), with a main office opposite Club Med and branches at five other locations around the island plus various hotel desks, almost has the car rental business on Moorea wrapped up, and their dominant position is reflected in their lofty prices. Europcar's unlimited-mileage cars begin at CFP 5,000/6,000/7,000 for four/eight/24 hours. A weekend rate of CFP 13,000 is also offered. Scooters are CFP 4,500/5,000/ 5,500, bicycles CFP 1,200/1,500/2,000 (a ripoff).

Avis (tel. 56-12-58) at the ferry terminal and the airport has cars from CFP 7,400/13,100/19,200 for one/two/three days including kilometers and insurance. If you have limited time it's best to reserve an Avis or Europcar vehicle a day or two ahead at one of their offices in Papeete as all cars on Moorea are sometimes taken.

Rental cars and bicycles are also obtained at **Albert Activities Center** (B.P. 77, 98728 Temae; tel. 56-13-53, tel./fax 56-10-42), with locations opposite the Hôtel Bali Hai, Club Bali Hai, and Club Med. Unlimited-mileage cars begin at CFP 6,000/6,500/12,000 for eight/24/48 hours, including insurance. Some of their vehicles are of the "rent a wreck" variety, so before signing the credit card voucher look the car over and insist on a replacement if it's a high-mileage bomb. Otherwise, take your business elsewhere or just skip renting a car. Bicycles cost about CFP 800/1,200 for a half/full day.

There are five gasoline stations around Moorea: Mobil a km south of Vaiare Wharf, Shell opposite Vaiare Wharf, Total at the airport access road, another Mobil near Motel Albert at Paopao, and another Total opposite Club Med. The maximum speed limit is 60 kph.

Local Tours

Daily at 0900 **Albert Activities** (tel. 56-13-53) does a three-hour circle-island bus tour, including a visit to the Belvédère, for CFP 2,000 (lunch not included). Albert's five-hour 4WD jeep safari is CFP 3,500 pp (do it in the morning). Several other companies such as **Ben Tours** (Benjamin Teraiharoa, tel. 56-26-50), **Moorea Transports** (Greg Hardy, tel. 56-12-86), and **Inner Island Photo Tours** (tel. 56-20-09) offer the same.

Ron's Adventure Tours (Ronald Sage, B.P. 1097, 98729 Papetoai; tel. 56-42-43) specializes in hiking tours and mountain climbing, such as an ascent of Mt. Mouaputa at CFP 3,000 pp. Ron also does bicycle (CFP 2,500) and 4WD

jeep (CFP 4,500) tours. Contact him through the Moorea Visitors Bureau kiosk in front of Le Petit Village. **Derek Grell** (tel. 56-41-24) at Paopao also leads climbs up Mt. Rotui and to the Col des Trois Cocotiers.

Alexandre Haamaterii's **Inner Island Safari Tours** (tel. 56-20-09, fax 56-34-43) also offers an exhilarating 4WD tour to various viewpoints and around Moorea for CFP 4,500 pp.

Day Cruises

Albert Activities (tel. 56-13-53) runs a five-hour motorized aluminum canoe ride right around Moorea with a stop for snorkeling (gear provided), departing the Hôtel Bali Hai dock every Monday, Wednesday, and Friday at 0930 (CFP 4,000 pp, minimum of four). For a free pickup, inquire at one of the three Albert Activities centers around Moorea. You could see dolphins, whales, and human surfers on this trip. Others such as Hiro Kelley (tel. 56-13-59) also operate circle-island tours, so compare.

At 0930 and 1400 daily the **Moorea Beachcomber Parkroyal** (tel. 55-19-19) offers a three-hour cruise on the catamaran *Manu* at CFP 5,000 pp. The 1.5-hour sunset cruise is CFP 2,500 including drinks. You can take a one-hour ride in a glass-bottom motorboat called the *Aquascope* at CFP 2,500 pp and they'll go anytime between 0900 and 1500 even for only one person (the catamaran has a six-person minimum).

Other companies like **Moorea Transport** (tel. 56-12-87) run a variety of trips such a *motu* excursion by outrigger (CFP 2,500) or a *motu* picnic party (CFP 4,800) but the canoes are usually without radios, life jackets, or flotation devices and they can be frightening if you're not a good swimmer. The snorkeling itself is great.

Archipels Croisières (tel. 56-36-39) offers a day cruise around Moorea on a 34-meter classic schooner with various snorkeling and sightseeing stops, plus a buffet lunch (CFP 11,000 pp). They visit "Le Monde de Mu," an underwater sculpture garden in the lagoon off Papetoai with 10 large tikis created in 1998 by the renowned Tahitian stone carver Tihoti.

Dolphin Watching

The trendiest thing on Moorea these days is **Dolphin Quest,** at the Moorea Beachcomber Parkroyal (B.P. 1021, 98729 Papetoai; tel. 55-19-48, fax 56-16-67). Here tourists pay CFP 8,500 a head to spend 30 minutes wading around a shallow lagoon enclosure at the hotel with rough-toothed and bottlenose dolphins, and touching is allowed. These activities begin at 0930, 1330, and 1430. At 1030 and 1530 it's possible to don a mask and snorkel and actually swim with dolphins in a deeper part of the enclosure at CFP 9,500 for 30 minutes (the Parkroyal may tack on a CFP 1,000 surcharge in either case if you're not a hotel guest). This whole business has environmental implications. Dolphin Quest's brochure claims that part of the proceeds "helps fund education, research, and conservation programs around the world" without being specific. What is known is that in February 1997 "Tiani" became the second dolphin to die at Dolphin Quest, and seven months later two replacement dolphins had to be flown in from Hawaii. Two dolphins managed to escape from the enclosure in November 1997, and a month later one named "Aito" was recaptured at Bora Bora and returned to Moorea by helicopter. It's also clear that somebody is making a lot of money by exploiting these captive animals as a tourist attraction.

A quite different type of dolphin encounter is offered by Dr. Michael Poole of **Dolphin Watch** (B.P. 1013, 98729 Papetoai; tel. 56-28-44, 56-14-70, or 56-13-45, fax 56-28-15). Here small groups are taken out in speedboats to see acrobatic spinner dolphins—the only dolphins to spin vertically in the air like tops or ballerinas—in the wild. A Florida reader named Bonnie sent us this:

We were taken to Opunohu Bay and watched 45 spinner dolphins for a long time. It was exciting as several dolphins spun in the air, did tail slaps, and swam right next to the boat. We were all taking photos like crazy. Dr. Poole is very nice and off and on he will tell you what he has learned through his research.

You may also observe dolphins surfing (!) and from July to October humpback whales are often seen. These 3.5-hour trips go out early on Wednesday, Thursday, and Sunday mornings, and again on Wednesday and Sunday afternoons, costing CFP 4,650 pp with reductions for children 12 and under. Included in the price

are boat pickups at all hotels between the Bali Hai and Les Tipaniers (bus transfers arranged from the Sofitel). Space is quite limited, so reserve well ahead through one of the Moorea activities offices (but not Albert), a hotel tour desk, or by calling the numbers above. Be sure to state clearly that you want "Dr. Poole's boat" as several unscientific imitators are trying to do the same thing with varying success.

Dr. Poole is in charge of the marine mammal program at CRIOBE, a French biological research station on Moorea. He has been on Moorea researching dolphins since 1987 and it's possible to work alongside him as an expense-paying intern at US$895/1,695/2,495 for one/two/three weeks including room and board. Participants are expected to do two days of office work a week, but there are three boat days not connected with the tours just discussed, and it's said the internship fees are accepted as tax-deductible charitable donations in the U.S.!

Moorea Airport

Moorea Temae Airport (MOZ) is at the northeast corner of the island. No buses service the airport, so unless you rent a car you'll be stuck with a rip-off taxi fare in addition to the airfare: CFP 1,000 to Vaiare Wharf, CFP 1,150 to the Hôtel Bali Hai, CFP 2,100 to the Moorea Lagoon Hôtel, or CFP 3,500 to Club Med. Thanks to intimidation from the taxi drivers, none of the hotels are allowed to offer airport pickups and even the major tour companies are only authorized to carry tourists who have prebooked. (All of this is specifically aimed at foreign visitors: Moorea residents can obtain a card that provides them with ground transfers anywhere on Moorea for CFP 500 and flights for as little as CFP 1,000.) This considered, we suggest you give Air Moorea a miss and take the ferry to/from Moorea. At a third the price of the plane (CFP 800 compared to CFP 2,700), the scenic 30-minute catamaran ride to/from Tahiti may end up being one of the highlights of your visit.

If you do fly, be sure to sit on the left side of the aircraft on the way to Moorea and on the right on the way to Papeete. Avis and Europcar have counters at the airport but it's essential to reserve, otherwise they may not have a car for you and you'll be subjected to the scam described above.

M.G.L. DOMENY DE RIENZI

an early 19th-century view of Fare, Huahine

HUAHINE

Huahine, the first Leeward island encountered on the ferry ride from Tahiti, is a friendly, inviting island, sitting 170 km northwest of Papeete. In many ways, lush, mountainous Huahine (74 square km) has more to offer than overcrowded Bora Bora. The variety of gorgeous scenery, splendid beaches, deep bays, lush vegetation, archaeological remains, and charming main town all invite you to visit. Huahine is a well-known surfing locale, with consistently excellent lefts and rights in the two passes off Fare. Schools of dolphins often greet ships arriving through Avapeihi Pass.

It's claimed the island got its name because, when viewed from the sea, Huahine has the shape of a reclining woman—very appropriate for such a fertile, enchanting place. *Hua* means "phallus" (from a rock on Huahine-iti) while *hine* comes from *vahine* (woman). A narrow channel crossed by a concrete bridge slices Huahine into Huahine-nui and Huahine-iti (Great and Little

Huahine, respectively). The story goes that the demigod Hiro's canoe cut this strait.

The almost entirely Polynesian population numbers 5,500, yet some of the greatest leaders in the struggle for the independence of Polynesia, Pouvanaa a Oopa among them, have come from this idyllic spot. The artist Bobby Holcomb and poet Henri Hiro are also well remembered.

In recent years Huahine has been discovered by international tourism and deluxe hotels and bungalow-style developments are now operating on the island. Luckily Huahine has been able to absorb these new properties fairly painlessly, as it's a much larger island than Bora Bora and the resorts are well scattered and tastefully constructed in the traditional Tahitian style. It's an oasis of peace after Papeete or Bora Bora. The island has also become a major port of call for the yachts that anchor off the Hôtel Bali Hai. Backpackers pioneered Huahine in the mid-1980s, and good facilities still exist for them.

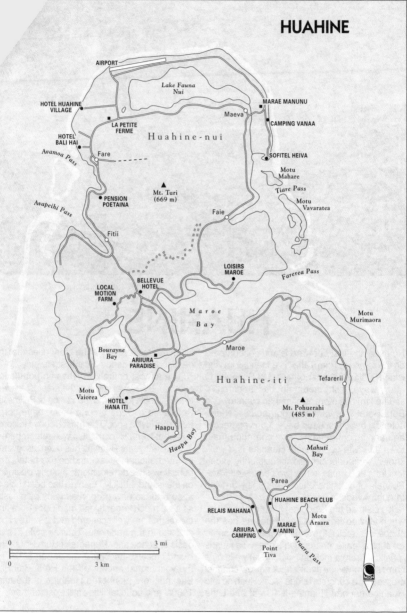

HUAHINE

AIRPORT

Lake Fauna Nui

HOTEL HUAHINE VILLAGE

MARAE MANUNU

Maeva

CAMPING VANAA

LA PETITE FERME

Huahine-nui

HOTEL BALI HAI

Avamoa Pass

Fare

SOFITEL HEIVA

Motu Mahare

Avapeihi Pass

PENSION POETAINA

Mt. Turi (669 m)

Faie

Tiare Pass

Motu Vavaratea

Fitii

LOISIRS MAROE

LOCAL MOTION FARM

BELLEVUE HOTEL

Farerea Pass

Maroe Bay

Motu Murimaora

Bourayne Bay

ARIIURA PARADISE

Maroe

Huahine-iti

Tefarerii

Motu Vaiorea

HOTEL HANA ITI

Mt. Pohuerahi (485 m)

Haapu

Haapu Bay

Mahuti Bay

Parea

HUAHINE BEACH CLUB

RELAIS MAHANA

Motu Araara

ARIIURA CAMPING

MARAE ANINI

Point Tiva

Araara Pass

0   3 mi

0   3 km

© DAVID STANLEY

Archaeology

Archaeologists have found that human habitation goes back 1,300 years on Huahine; Maeva village was occupied as early as A.D. 850. In 1925 Dr. Kenneth P. Emory of Hawaii's Bishop Museum recorded 54 *marae* on Huahine, most of them built after the 16th century. In 1968 Prof. Yosihiko H. Sinoto found another 40. Huahine-nui was divided into 10 districts, with Huahine-iti as a dependency. As a centralized government complex for a whole island, Maeva, on the south shore of Lake Fauna Nui, is unique in Tahiti-Polynesia. The great communal *marae* at Maeva and Parea have two-stepped platforms *(ahu)* that served as raised seats for the gods. Since 1967 about 16 *marae* have been restored, and they can be easily visited today. Like those of Raiatea and Bora Bora, the Huahine *marae* are constructed of large stone slabs, whereas comparable structures on Tahiti and Moorea are made of round stones. During construction of the Hôtel Bali Hai just north of Fare in 1972 a *patu* hand club was uncovered, proving that New Zealand's Maoris originated in this area.

History of the Leeward Islands

Huahine was settled by Polynesians around 850. Roggeveen, coming from Makatea in the Tuamotus, sighted (but did not land on) Bora Bora and Maupiti on 6 June 1722. Captain Cook "discovered" the other Leeward Islands in July 1769, which was quite easy since the Tahitians knew them well. In fact, Cook had the Raiatean priest Tupaia on board the *Endeavour* as a pilot. Cook wrote: "To these six islands, as they lie contiguous to each other, I gave the names of Society Islands." Later the name was extended to the Windward Islands. In 1773 a man named Omai from Huahine sailed to England with Cook's colleague, Captain Furneaux, aboard the *Adventure;* he returned to Fare with Cook in 1777.

During the 19th century, American whalers spent their winters away from the Antarctic in places like Huahine, refurbishing their supplies with local products such as sugar, vegetables, oranges, salted pork, and *aito,* or ironwood. These visits enriched the island economy, and the New England sailors presented the islanders with foreign plants as tokens of appreciation for the hospitality received. English missionaries arrived in 1808 and later Pomare II extended his power to Huahine, abolishing the traditional religion. In 1822 missionary law was imposed. Among the missionaries was William Ellis whose book, *Polynesian Researches,* published in London in 1829, has left us a detailed picture of the island at that time.

Though Tahiti and Moorea fell under French control in 1842, the Leeward Islands remained a British protectorate until 1887 when these islands were traded for fishing rights off Newfoundland and a British interest in what was then New Hebrides (today Vanuatu). Marines from the French warship *Uranie* had attacked Huahine in 1846, but they were defeated at Maeva. A year later France promised Britain that it would not annex the Leeward Islands, yet in 1887 it proceeded to do so. The local chiefs refused to sign the annexation treaty until 1895, and resistance to France, especially on Raiatea, was only overcome by force in 1897. The French then expelled the English missionary group that had been there 88 years; nonetheless, today 80% of the population of the Leewards remains Protestant.

In 1918 a Spanish influenza epidemic wiped out a fifth of the population including the last queen, Tehaapapa III. Only in 1945 was missionary law finally abolished and French citizenship extended to the inhabitants. In the 1958 referendum, 76% of the population of Huahine voted in favor of independence. Tourism began in 1973 with the building of the airstrip and the Hôtel Bali Hai.

FARE

The unsophisticated little town of Fare, with its tree-lined boulevard along the quay, is joyfully peaceful after the roar of Papeete. A beach runs right along the west side of the main street and local life unfolds without being overwhelmed by tourism. Local men play *pétanque* on the Fare waterfront around sunset. From here Bora Bora is visible in the distance to the left while the small twin peaks of Taha'a are to the right. The seven other villages on Huahine are linked to Fare by winding, picturesque roads. Despite the easy-going atmosphere it's unwise to leave valuables unattended on the beach anywhere between town and the Bali Hai (and beware of unperceived currents).

SIGHTS

After you've had a look around Fare, visit the beautiful *mape* (chestnut) forest up the Faahia valley. Walk inland 15 minutes along the road that begins two houses south of the house marked "Oliveti" near the Total service station. This road becomes a jungle trail that you can easily follow another 15 minutes up a small stream into a tropical forest laced with vanilla vines and the sweet smell of fermenting fruit. By the stream is a long bedlike rock known as Ofaitere, or "Traveling Rock," but you'd need to have someone point it out to you. A guide will certainly be required to continue right to the summit of Huahine's highest peak, Mt. Turi (669 meters), in about three hours, but it's rough going.

South of Fare

A side road from Hôtel Bellevue, six km south of Fare, leads one km west to **Local Motion Farm** (tel. 68-86-58; closed Sunday), a commercial tropical garden where lunch (from CFP 1,000) and fruit drinks (CFP 200-400) are served to visitors.

Ariiura Paradise (tel. 68-85-20) is a "Back to Eden" garden of herbal medicine, 800 meters west of the interisland bridge via the unpaved road along the north side of Bourayne Bay. It's a good place to learn about the local plants as all are clearly labeled (open weekdays 0900-1500, Saturday 0900-1200; admission CFP 250/500 children/adults including a coconut drink).

Sports and Recreation

Pacific Blue Adventure (Didier Forget, B.P. 193, 98731 Fare; tel. 68-87-21, fax 68-80-71) at Fare offers scuba diving at CFP 5,000/18,000 for one/four dives (night diving CFP 6,500), and PADI/CMAS certification courses for CFP 30,000 including four dives, texts, and documentation. Trips to sites like Avapeihi Pass, Fa'a Miti, Coral City, and Yellow Valley leave at 0915 and 1415, depending on demand. They'll take snorkelers only if things are really slow. They pick up at hotels around Fare.

Moana Tropical (tel./fax 68-74-01) in the car rental office on the wharf offers deep-sea fishing for blue marlin. They leave daily at 0700, charging CFP 8,500 pp (two-person minimum) for three hours.

La Petite Ferme (Pascale Le Diouris, B.P. 12, 98731 Fare; tel./fax 68-82-98), between Fare and the airport, offers riding with Pascale, Yvon, and their 16 small, robust Marquesan horses. A two-hour ride along the beach is CFP 3,500 pp, and they also offer a two-day ride and campout in the mountains or on the beach for CFP 17,500 pp, meals included. Call the day before to let them know you're coming. If riding is your main interest, it's possible to stay in their on-site guesthouse at CFP 3,600 double or CFP 1,500 pp dormitory (six beds), breakfast included. They also have a self-catering bungalow at CFP 5,000/7,500/9,500 single/double/triple (CFP 500 supplement for one night). This is the number-one horseback-riding operation in Tahiti-Polynesia—recommended.

ACCOMMODATIONS

Budget

Pension Guynette (Alain and Hélène Guerineau, B.P. 87, 98731 Fare; tel. 68-83-75), also known as "Club Bed," on the waterfront to the left as you get off the boat, is one of the nicest places to stay in the territory. The seven rooms, each with the name of a different Society island, are CFP 3,300/3,900/4,500 single/double/triple with fan and private bath (cold water). The eight-bed dorm at the back of the building is CFP 1,400 pp. There's a CFP 300 pp surcharge for a one-night stay and the maximum stay is one month. You can cook your own food in the communal kitchen here, and the meals prepared by the friendly staff are good value (order before 1400). It's a pleasant, clean place; no shoes are allowed in the house. Upon arrival peruse the list of rules and rates—applied rigorously (for example, it's lights out in the kitchen at 2200). On departure day the rooms must be vacated by 1000, but you can leave your bags at the reception until 1830 if catching a late boat. They don't mind at all if you sit on their terrace all afternoon and they'll even let you cook your dinner so long as you're gone by 1900. Most readers say they liked the efficiency. Thankfully, the management doesn't allow overcrowding and will turn people away rather than pack them in for short-term gain. Recommended.

Nearby on the waterfront is three-story **Hôtel Huahine** (B.P. 220, 98731 Fare; tel. 68-82-69), at CFP 3,500 single or double, CFP 4,500 triple, or CFP 1,200 in a dorm. The 10 bare rooms are large with their own toilet and shower, and there's no surcharge for a one-night stay (but no cooking facilities). Fish dishes on the menu are in the CFP 850-1,200 range. You may sit in the restaurant and watch TV for the price of a beer.

Stalwart surfers who don't care for the house rules at Pension Guynette often stay here. Love it or leave it.

Two more good budget places to stay are between Fare and the airport just beyond the Bali Hai, about 800 meters north of the wharf. **Pension Lovina** (Lovina Richmond, B.P. 173, 98731 Fare; tel./fax 68-88-06) has five small *fare* with TV and shared bath at CFP 3,000/4,500 single/double. For families and groups, there are four oversized thatched bungalows with cooking and bathing facilities at CFP 5,000/6,000/8,000 single/double/triple, CFP 12,000 for up to five persons, CFP 13,000 for seven people. Dormitory accommodations are CFP 1,500 pp, and camping is CFP 1,000 pp. All guests have access to communal cooking facilities (and mosquitoes). The minimum stay is two nights, and discounts may be negotiable. Airport pickups cost CFP 1,000 pp return; from the harbor it's CFP 500 pp.

In the same area is **Pension Vaihonu** (Etienne Faaeva, B.P. 302, 98731 Fare; tel./fax 68-87-33) with three *fare* at CFP 2,000/3,000 single/double and a six-bed dorm at CFP 1,200. A larger cottage with private bath, kitchen, and TV is CFP 6,500/10,000 double/quad. Camping is CFP 1,000 per person. There's an open communal kitchen in the small compound jammed with potted flowers. Unfortunately access to the nearby beach has recently been blocked by residential construction and you have to go back toward Fare to find a place to swim.

Fare *such as these are available at Ariiura Camping at the south end of Huahine.*

CAROLINE GREEN

Inexpensive

Pension Enite (Enite Temaiana, B.P. 37, 98731 Fare; tel./fax 68-82-37) is an eight-room boardinghouse at the west end of the waterfront beyond the snack bar. Rooms with shared bath are CFP 6,000 pp with half board (two-night minimum stay, no room rentals without meals). Enite also serves meals to guests in a thatched cookhouse on the beach and the food is good. In the event of a shortened stay, the pension will bill for the number of nights originally reserved. Middle-of-the-night arrivals mustn't knock on the door before 0700. French expats often stay here.

Just north of Fare is **Pension Meri** (Milton Brotherson, B.P. 35, 98731 Fare; tel./fax 68-82-44), past two doctor's offices down the road toward the lagoon from opposite the large Mormon church. Meri has two rooms with private bath and cooking facilities at CFP 5,500 single or double, CFP 6,500 for three or four (minimum stay three nights). There's direct access to the beach.

Chez Ella (Ella Mervin, B.P. 71, 98731 Fare; tel. 68-73-07), next to Motel Vanille at the air-

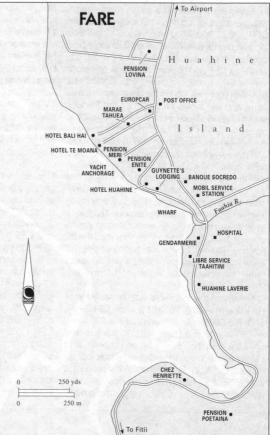

port turnoff, has three bungalows with kitchen, fridge, and TV at CFP 6,000 single or double, plus CFP 1,000 per additional person. You can ask to use the washing machine.

In a valley a km south of Fare (inland from the second bridge) is **Pension Poetaina** (Jean-Pierre Amo, B.P. 522, 98731 Fare; tel./fax 68-89-49), a large two-story building with spacious balconies and lounge. The four rooms with shared bath are CFP 6,000 single or double, CFP 7,500 triple, while one larger room with private bath is CFP 8,000/9,500 double/triple (two-night minimum stay). The 11-bed dormitory is CFP 2,000 pp. All rates include breakfast

and communal cooking facilities are provided. Boat trips around Huahine are arranged at CFP 5,000 pp including lunch and snorkeling. It's a bit overpriced.

Chez Henriette (B.P. 73, 98731 Fare; tel. 68-83-71) is beside the lagoon a few hundred meters beyond Pension Poetaina, a pleasant 15-minute walk south of Fare. The six thatched *fare,* each have basic cooking facilities. The three smaller units with double bed, mosquito net, fridge, hot plate, and shared bath are CFP 4,000 double, while the three larger *fare* with two double beds and private bath are CFP 7,500 for up to four persons—okay for two couples traveling together. It's sort of like staying in a local village while retaining a measure of privacy.

Moderate
Hôtel Te Moana (Moana Baumgartner, B.P. 195, 98731 Fare; tel. 68-88-63, fax 68-71-74), on the beach right beside Hôtel Bali Hai north of Fare, has five thatched bungalows with private bath and coral floors at CFP 5,500/6,500 single/double (minimum stay two nights). The large family bungalow capable of sleeping four is CFP 13,000 and only this unit has cooking facilities. The breakfast and dinner plan is CFP 3,000 pp. Mosquitos can be a problem here.

Fare Tehani (Frédéric Girard, B.P. 335, 98731 Fare; tel./fax 68-71-00) is on the beach down the road from the back entrance to Pension Lovina previously mentioned, between Fare and the airport. The two *fare* with kitchen and fridge are CFP 10,000/12,000 double/quad (expensive). Weekly and monthly rates are available. Ask about this place at the *Ono-Ono* office at the harbor. Nearby an American named Rande Vetterli (tel. 68-86-27) has a couple of self-catering units right on the beach at CFP 6,000 double (or CFP 4,000 if you stay a month). It's one heck of a deal.

In 1997 **Motel Vanille** (B.P. 381, 98731 Fare; tel./fax 68-71-77) opened on the corner of the airport access road and the Fare-Maeva highway. Their six thatched bungalows positioned around the swimming pool are CFP 13,000 double with breakfast, dinner, bicycles, and airport transfers included (credit cards not accepted). The meals are served at the host's table and it's all rather informal, but a kilometer from the beach.

The **Hôtel Huahine Village** (B.P. 295, 98731 Fare; tel. 68-87-00, fax 68-86-99) is on a rocky shore, 900 meters down an access road west from the airport road. It's a bit less than two km from the airport or three km from Fare. The thatched garden bungalows are CFP 8,000 single or double, beach bungalows cost CFP 10,000. Breakfast and dinner are CFP 4,000 pp. There's a swimming pool and Europcar desk. Airport transfers cost CFP 600 pp. It's rather lifeless and not the best value.

The **Hôtel Bellevue** (B.P. 21, 98731 Fare; tel. 68-82-76, fax 68-85-35), six km south of Fare, offers nine bungalows without cooking facilities at CFP 5,400 single or double, CFP 6,400 triple, and three with cooking at CFP 7,000 single or double, CFP 8,000 triple. The poor lighting makes it hard to read in the evening. There's a figure-eight shaped swimming pool. The restaurant has a lovely view of Maroe Bay but the meals are pricey at CFP 1,600-3,500 each. Roundtrip airport transfers are CFP 1,000 pp. Considering the expense, isolation, and absence of a beach, the Bellevue has little going for it.

Premium
The American-owned **Hôtel Bali Hai** (B.P. 341, 98731 Fare; tel. 68-84-77, fax 68-82-77), just north of Fare, is tastefully placed between a lake and the beach. The 10 rooms in the main building begin at CFP 11,500 single or double plus tax; the 34 bungalows cost CFP 13,500-15,500 in the garden, CFP 19,900 facing the beach. Some of the rooms could use a facelift but prices are much lower than those at comparable accommodations on Bora Bora and the staff is helpful. Cooking facilities are not provided, but the restaurant serves excellent food and the largely French crowd is chic. The hotel restaurant (open daily 0700-0930/1200-1400/1900-2100) is reasonable for such a deluxe place, and you can get a breakfast and dinner plan at CFP 4,500 pp. A showcase in the lobby displays artifacts found here by Prof. Yosihiko H. Sinoto of the Bishop Museum, Hawaii, who excavated the site during construction of the hotel in 1973-75. Marae Tahuea has been reconstructed on the grounds. The snorkeling off the resorts beach is great although questions have been raised about their sewage disposal system. Airport transfers are CFP 1,200 pp return.

Long-term Rentals
Worth considering if you have a small group interested in spending seven days on Huahine is the **Residence Loisirs Maroe,** a colonial-style house on Maroe Bay, 11 km southeast of Fare, which goes for CFP 100,000 a Friday-to-Friday week. The house contains four bedrooms (up to eight persons total), three bathrooms, two living rooms, a kitchen, and deck. Tennis courts are adjacent, and a car and motor boat come with the rental. For reservations contact Mr. Frantz Vanizette, B.P. 2383, 98713 Papeete, Tahiti (tel. 42-96-09). Payment in cash in advance is required.

To rent a house by the month check the notices in the window at Libre Service Taahitini just south of Fare.

FOOD AND ENTERTAINMENT

Food Trailers

Food trailers congregate at Fare Wharf selling spring rolls, pastries, and long French sandwiches. Coffee and bread is CFP 200. At night you can get steak frites, chicken and chips, and *poisson cru* for CFP 700. Look for the trailer that parks next to a row of telephone booths as it has excellent fish brochettes for CFP 150.

Restaurants

Snack Temarara (tel. 68-86-61; closed Sunday) at the west end of the waterfront has a nice terrace built over the lagoon, fine for a sunset beer. During happy hour Friday 1600-1800 the place is crowded with Polynesians enjoying *kaina* (folkloric) music. It's quite elegant, with fish dishes costing CFP 950-1,400, meat dishes CFP 1,100-1,400. One reader's comment: "Overpriced food that is really lacking in quality."

The **Restaurant Bar Orio** (tel. 68-83-03; lunch 1100-1430, dinner 1830-2130), at the opposite end of the Fare waterfront, also has a terrace overlooking the lagoon but it has less class than Temarara. Fish dishes are in the CFP 1,000-1,600 range, lobster CFP 2,500-2,800, Chinese dishes CFP 900-1,200.

Opposite the car rental offices on the waterfront is **Restaurant Te Vaipuna** (tel. 68-70-45; Mon.-Sat. 1100-1430/1800-2130) with Chinese and French dishes. A cheaper snack bar is next door.

Pension Guynette (tel. 68-83-75) serves an inexpensive breakfast and lunch on its waterfront terrace, and this is also a good choice for only coffee and a snack.

The **Tiare Tipanier Restaurant** (tel. 68-80-52; Monday 1800-2045, Tues.-Sat. 1130-1345/1800-2045), next to the *mairie* (town hall) at the north entrance to Fare from the Bali Hai, is a typical French rural restaurant without the tourist touches of some of the others. They serve meat and fish dishes in the CFP 1,150-1,600 range, fondue bourguignone at CFP 1,500 (two-person minimum), and a set menu for CFP 1,900 including wine. A large Hinano is CFP 480.

Also check thatched **Restaurant Te Moana** (tel. 68-88-63), facing the beach next to Hôtel Bali Hai. Complete meals (without drinks) are CFP 2,500, 3,000, and 3,800.

Groceries

Super Fare-Nui (tel. 68-84-68; weekdays 0600-1200/1300-1800, Saturday 0600-1200, Sunday 0600-1100), on the Fare waterfront, sells groceries and cold beer. An alternative place to shop is **Libre Service Taahitini** (tel. 68-89-42; weekdays 0600-1200/1330-1900, Saturday 0600-1200/1600-1900, Sunday 0600-1100/1700-1900), just beyond the *gendarmerie* south of town. **Magasin Matehau** at Fitii also has groceries.

If you see a cruise ship tied up at Fare one morning, pop into the supermarket quickly to buy your daily bread before the ship's cook comes ashore to snap up the day's entire supply, leaving the townspeople to eat cake (a classic example of how tourism exploits small island communities).

The tap water on Huahine can be clouded after heavy rains.

Cultural Shows for Visitors

If you're staying in budget accommodations around Fare, you'll be able to witness the Polynesian dancing at the **Hôtel Bali Hai** (tel. 68-84-77) on Friday evening at 2000 for the price of a drink from the bar, although the regular dinner menu isn't outrageous (CFP 1,100-1,700 entrees). Drop by beforehand to check the program.

There's also traditional dancing at the **Sofitel Heiva Huahine** (tel. 68-88-88) at Maeva on Monday, Thursday, and Saturday nights, but you'll need motorized transportation to get there.

SERVICES AND INFORMATION

Services

ATM machines are outside the Banque de Tahiti (tel. 68-82-46; weekdays 0745-1145/1330-1630), facing the Fare waterfront, and the Banque Socredo (tel. 68-82-71; weekdays 0730-1130/1330-1600), on the first street back from the waterfront.

The post office (Mon.-Thurs. 0700-1500, Friday 0700-1400), opposite the access road to the Hôtel Bali Hai, has a convenient Coca Cola vending machine. The *gendarmerie* (tel. 68-82-61) is opposite the hospital over the bridge at the south end of town.

The laundromat (no phone) just south of Fare charges CFP 750 to wash and CFP 750 to dry (Mon.-Thurs. 0730-1600, Friday 0730-1500).

Public toilets and washbasins are in one of the yellow buildings on the waterfront (if open).

Information

The Comité du Tourisme information office (B.P. 54, 98731 Fare; tel./fax 68-89-49; weekdays 0800-1500) shares a pavilion on the waterfront with Europcar, Pacifique Car Rental, the *Ono-Ono* office, and Pacific Blue Adventure.

Health

A Gabinet Medical-Dentaire (tel. 68-82-20) is next to the Mobil service station on the next street back from the wharf. Dr. Hervé Carbonnier and Dr. Pascal Matyka, general practitioners, see patients 0730-1200/1400-1600.

Dr. Caroline Veyssiere and Dr. Isabelle Damery-Beylier (tel. 68-70-70; weekdays 0700-1200/1330-1700, Saturday 0800-1200), have small offices opposite the large Mormon church just north of Fare.

La Pharmacie de Huahine (tel. 68-80-90; weekdays 0730-1130/1400-1700, Saturday 0730-1130), is behind the yellow warehouse facing the waterfront.

TRANSPORTATION

Getting There

The **Air Tahiti** agent (tel. 68-82-65) is at the airport. For information on flights to Huahine from Papeete, Moorea, Raiatea, and Bora Bora see the introduction to Tahiti-Polynesia. Air Tahiti's direct flight between Huahine and Moorea would be great if it didn't cost CFP 11,000 when the flight to Papeete is only CFP 8,800.

The jet cruiser *Ono-Ono* departs Huahine for Raiatea (45 minutes, CFP 1,778), Taha'a (two hours, CFP 2,111), and Bora Bora (three and a half hours, CFP 3,111) Monday and Wednesday at 1245, Friday at 2000, and Saturday at 1500. To Papeete (three and a half hours, CFP 4,895)

it leaves Huahine Tuesday and Thursday at 1015, Sunday at 1515. The Tuesday and Thursday services connect to the Moorea ferries at Papeete.

The Papeete cargo ships tie up to the wharf in the middle of town. If you arrive in the middle of the night you can sleep in the large open pavilion until dawn. *Taporo VI* arrives from Papeete bound for Raiatea, Taha'a, and Bora Bora around 0200 on Tuesday, Thursday, and Saturday, returning from Raiatea on its way to Papeete Tuesday, Thursday, and Saturday evenings. Northbound, the *Vaeanu* calls at Huahine on Tuesday, Thursday, and Saturday at 0230; southbound on Tuesday and Sunday at 1700 and Thursday at 1800. The *Raromatai Ferry* arrives from Papeete very early Wednesday and Saturday mornings, departing for Papeete again on Wednesday at 1530 and Sunday at 2000 (nine hours, CFP 3,200 deck). You can also take this ship to Raiatea, Taha'a, and Bora Bora (all CFP 1,000) Wednesdays and Saturdays in the very early morning.

Tickets for *Vaeanu* go on sale at their office adjoining the yellow warehouse on the wharf four hours before sailing or you can buy one as the ship is loading. Tickets for the *Taporo VI* are sold on board upon arrival. The office of the *Raromatai Ferry* is next to the public washrooms on the mountain side of the yellow warehouse on the wharf. The *Ono-Ono* office (tel./fax 68-85-85) is next to Pacifique Car Rental on the wharf.

Getting Around

Getting around Huahine is not easy. Only one *truck* a day runs to Maeva, leaving Fare weekdays at 0900 (CFP 150). However, it's fairly easy to hitch back to Fare from Maeva. The bus to Parea leaves Fare on weekdays at 1100, returning from Parea to Fare at 0500 and 1400 (CFP 250 one-way). Other *trucks* run to Haapu and Tefarerii.

Car Rentals

Pacifique Car Rental/Hertz (tel./fax 68-73-37; daily 0800-1200/1400-1800) on the wharf has Peugeot cars from CFP 4,600/6,000/6,900 for five/10/24 hours with unlimited kms. Insurance with CFP 50,000 deductible is included and the deductible can be waved for CFP 1,000 a day.

The minimum age is 18. The manager Serge is very helpful.

Avis (tel. 68-73-34, fax 68-73-35) is at the Mobil service station a street back from the waterfront. Their cars start at CFP 7,300/13,600/18,900 for one/two/three days all inclusive.

Europcar (tel. 68-82-59, fax 68-80-69) is beside the entrance to the Hôtel Bali Hai. The smaller Europcar office on the wharf is often closed. Their smallest car is CFP 2,000 a day plus CFP 44 a kilometer plus CFP 700 insurance, or CFP 7,000/13,000 for one/two days with unlimited kilometers (insurance extra). Their older cars have transmission problems.

Tropic 2000 Rent a Car (tel. 68-70-84, fax 68-70-96), between La Petite Ferme and Motel Vanille north of town, has slightly cheaper rates than Avis and Europcar with CFP 30,000 deductible insurance included. You must be 24 or over to rent from them.

Huahine has only two gas stations, both in Fare: Mobil (tel. 68-81-41) is open weekdays 0630-1745, Saturday 0700-1100, Sunday 0630-0930, while Total (tel. 68-71-25) is open weekdays 0630-1700, Saturday 0630-1100, Sunday 0630-0930.

Huahine Lagoon (tel. 68-70-00), next to Snack Bar Te Marara at the north end of the Fare waterfront, rents small aluminum boats with outboard motor for CFP 3,000/5,000/8,000 for two/four/eight hours (gas not included). Masks, snorkels, life jackets, anchor, and oars come with the boat. Bicycles are for rent here at CFP 1,200 a day.

Boutique Photo Jojo (tel. 68-89-16), next to Pension Guynette, also has bicycles but they're more expensive because they charge the full Europcar tariff.

Local Tours

Jacques and Sylvie at **Huahine Land** (B.P. 140, 98731 Fare; tel. 68-89-21, fax 68-86-84) offer 3.5-hour 4WD safaris at CFP 4,000 pp, which is a good alternative to renting a car (and the guides are highly knowledgeable). **Piteta Tour** (tel. 68-82-31 or 68-87-00) at the Hôtel Huahine Village offers the same.

Félix Tours (tel. 68-81-69) does a three-hour morning archaeological tour at CFP 3,000 daily except Sunday.

Héli-Inter Polynésie (tel. 68-86-86) at the Sofitel Heiva offers 20-minute helicopter tours of Huahine-nui at CFP 15,000 pp (minimum of four).

Boutique Photo Jojo (tel. 68-89-16) runs a seven-hour boat trip Mon.-Sat. at 1000 for CFP 5,000 pp including lunch.

Airport

The airport (HUH) is three km north of Fare. Make arrangements for the regular airport minibus (CFP 500 pp) at Pension Enite. Avis, Europcar, and Pacifique Car Rental have counters at the airport.

MAEVA

At Maeva, six km east of Fare, you encounter that rare combination of an easily accessible archaeological site in a spectacular setting. Here each of the 10 district chiefs of Huahine-nui had his own *marae,* and huge stone walls were erected to defend Maeva against invaders from Bora Bora (and later France). The plentiful small fish in Lake Fauna Nui supported large chiefly and priestly classes (ancient stone fish traps can still be seen near the bridge at the east end of the village). In the 1970s Prof. Y.H. Sinoto of Hawaii restored many of the structures strewn along the lakeshore and in the nearby hills. Once a day Maeva is accessible by *le truck* from Fare (CFP 150), and there are two small stores in the village where you can get cold drinks.

On the shores of the lake is round-ended **Fare Pote'e** (1974), a replica of an old communal meeting house. This now contains an **Eco-Museum** operated by the Opu Nui Association, B.P. 150, 98731 Fare. Half the museum consists of historical explanations through texts, old photos, and replicas of traditional paddles, fishhooks, adzes, stilts, and tapa cloth. The other part is a shop selling quality handicrafts such as *tifaifai* quilts, pottery, woven hats and bags, and pareus. Prices are clearly marked and all income goes to supporting the museum. You can also buy music cassettes and compact discs, cards, books, and T-

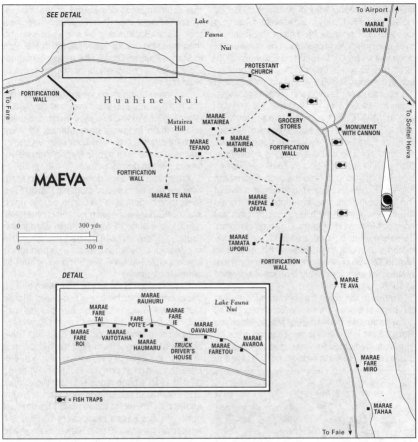

© DAVID STANLEY

MAEVA VILLAGE

In ancient times all the district chiefs on Huahine Nui lived side by side and worshipped their ancestors at their respective *marae*. *Marae* on Matairea Hill behind Maeva are older than the ones on the shores of the lagoon. Twenty-eight *marae* are recorded here, 16 of which have been restored. A *fare pote'e* (round-ended house), which had been used as a chiefly meeting house for over 100 years, was finally judged beyond repair in 1972. A replica of this house—in size and use of local materials—was built in 1974, and in 1997 it was turned into a museum. The fish traps in the lagoon, recently repaired, are still being used. Fish enter the stone traps with the incoming and outgoing tides.

shirts. The reproductions of paintings by Bobby Holcomb (CFP 1,200) are excellent. Changing exhibitions of artifacts from other Pacific countries are presented regularly. The museum of open weekdays 0900-1500 and Saturday 0900-1200. Admission is free but there's a donation box at the door. This is a visit not to miss. Guided 1.5-hour tours of the ruins and gardens of Maeva leave here weekdays at 1000 and 1300, Saturday at 1000 (CFP 1,200 pp). **Marae Rauhuru** next to Fare Pote'e bears petroglyphs of turtles.

From Fare Pote'e, walk back along the road toward Fare about 100 meters, to a **fortification wall** on the left, built in 1846 with stones from the *marae* to defend the area against the French. Follow this inland to an ancient well at the foot of the hill, then turn right and continue around the base of the hill until you find the trail up onto Matairea Hill (opposite a stone platform). Twenty meters beyond a second, older fortification wall along the hillside is the access to **Marae Te Ana** on the right. The terraces of this residential area for chiefly families, excavated in 1986, mount the hillside.

Return to the main trail and continue up to the ruins of **Marae Tefano,** which are engulfed by an immense banyan tree. **Marae Matairea Rahi,** to the left, was the most sacred place on Huahine, dedicated to Tane, god of light. The backrests of Huahine's principal chiefs are in

the southernmost compound of the *marae,* where the most important religious ceremonies took place. Backtrack a bit and keep straight, then head up the fern-covered hill to the right to **Marae Paepae Ofata,** which gives a magnificent view over the whole northeast coast of Huahine.

Continue southeast on the main trail past several more *marae* and you'll eventually cross another fortification wall and meet a dirt road down to the main highway near **Marae Te Ava.** Throughout this easy two-hour hike, watch for stakes planted with vanilla by the present villagers (please don't touch).

When you get back down to the main road, walk south a bit to see photogenic **Marae Fare Miro,** then backtrack to the bridge, across which is a **monument** guarded by seven cannon. Beneath it are buried French troops killed in the Battle of Maeva (1846), when the islanders successfully defended their independence against marauding French marines sent to annex the island.

Seven hundred meters farther along toward the ocean and to the left is two-tiered **Marae Manunu,** the community *marae* of Huahinenui, dedicated to the gods Oro and Tane. According to a local legend, Princess Hutuhiva arrived at this spot from Raiatea hidden in a drum. In the base of the *marae* is the grave of Raiti, the last great priest of Huahine. When he died in 1915 a huge stone fell from the *marae.* The coral road passing Marae Manunu runs another six km along the elevated barrier reef north of Lake Fauna Nui directly to Huahine Airport, an alternative route back to Fare. White beaches line this cantaloupe- and watermelon-rich north shore.

Faie

Below the bridge in the center of **Faie,** five km south of Maeva on a good paved road, is a river populated by sacred blue-eyed eels. Legend holds that it was the eels who brought fresh water to the village. You can buy fish to feed them at the red kiosk for CFP 100. From Faie the very steep Route Traversiere crosses the mountains to Maroe Bay (2.5 km), making a complete circuit of Huahine-nui possible. Two hundred meters up this road from the bridge is **Faie Glaces** (tel. 68-87-95; closed weekends), which

Marae Fare Miro at Huahine's Maeva

DAVID STANLEY

BOBBY HOLCOMB

Dancer, choreographer, musician, composer, singer, and painter, Bobby Holcomb (1947-1991) personified the all-round artist. He was born in Honolulu, child of a half Hawaiian, half Portuguese prostitute and an American sailor. Later he traveled widely, with periods as a rock musician in France and an actor in Venice. From Salvador Dalí he absorbed surrealism. In 1976 Holcomb arrived at Huahine aboard a friend's yacht and there he established his studio at Maeva. Prints of his colorful painting of Polynesian mythology and legends are widely available in the islands, as are recordings of his joyful Tahitian music. With his dreadlocks and tattoos on arms and legs Holcomb personified living theater. He's buried near Marae Fare Miro at Maeva.

manufactures ice cream from natural ingredients. If continuing south by bicycle don't begin coasting too fast on the other side as you may not be able to stop.

Accommodations
On the road to the Sofitel Heiva Huahine, a km from the bridge at Maeva, is **Camping Vanaa** (Vanaa Delord, tel. 68-89-51) with 13 small thatched *fare* on the beach at CFP 5,000 double including breakfast. Camping is CFP 1,000 pp. Meals in the restaurant are in the CFP 1,300-2,000 range. It's a shady spot, conveniently located for exploring the *marae*. The huts are a bit better than those at Ariiura Camping (see below) but the beach isn't as good as the one at Parea. The bar broadcasts loud music all afternoon.

In 1989 the exclusive **Sofitel Heiva Huahine** (B.P. 38, 98731 Fare; tel. 68-86-86, fax 68-85-25), part of the French-owned Accor chain, opened in a coconut grove on a *motu* two km southeast of Maeva along a rough road. The 24 rooms in long blocks are CFP 22,500 single or double, the 12 thatched garden bungalows CFP 32,000, the 18 beach bungalows CFP 48,000 plus tax. Six overwater suites are CFP 60,000 single or double. For a third person add CFP 4,500 (children under 12 free). Some of the more expensive bungalows are exposed to the southeast trades and can be dark and unpleasant in windy weather when you're forced to keep the windows shut. The breakfast and dinner plan is CFP 5,600 pp and it's prudent to be punctual at mealtime as the staff will refuse service to latecomers. Happy hour at the Manuia Bar is 1700-1800 (drinks two for one). The architecture is impressive and one of the best Polynesian cultural shows you'll ever see usually takes place here on Monday, Thursday, and Saturday nights at 2000, complete with fire dancing, acrobatics, and coconut tree climbing.

Evocative neo-Polynesian paintings by the late artist/singer Bobby Holcomb highlight the decor in the public areas, and ancient *marae* are preserved in the gardens. Unspoiled white beaches stretch all along this section of the lagoon and there's passable snorkeling off the oceanside beach. A swimming pool is available. The hotel tacks a hefty surcharge on any tours or activities arranged through their reception but the Maeva archaeological area is only a 30-minute walk away. Europcar has a desk at this hotel. Return airport transfers are CFP 1,800 pp extra. Luxury.

HUAHINE-ITI

Though the concrete "July Bridge" joins the two islands, Huahine-iti is far less accessible than Huahine-nui. *Le truck* only runs to **Parea** village once a day (CFP 250), so you'll have to stay the night unless you rent a bicycle or car. The 24 km from Fare to Parea via Haapu is paved, but only four of the 16 km from Parea back to the bridge via Maroe are paved: a km or so around Tefarerii, then the two km from Maroe to the bridge.

Haapu village was originally built entirely over the water, for lack of sufficient shoreline to house it. The only grocery store on Huahine-iti is at Haapu, otherwise three grocery trucks circle the island several times daily; the locals will know when to expect them. There's a wide white beach along Avea Bay with good swimming right beside the road as you approach the southern end of the island. Yachts can follow a protected channel inside the barrier reef down the west coast of Huahine to the wonderful (if occasionally rough) anchorage at Avea Bay but shallows at Point Tiva force sailboats to return to Fare.

On another white beach on the east side of Point Tiva, one km south of Parea, is **Marae Anini,** the community *marae* of Huahine-iti. It was built toward the end of the 18th century by Ta'aroari, son of grand chief Mahine. Look for petroglyphs on this two-tiered structure, dedicated to the god of war Oro, where human sacrifices once took place. The *marae* is unmarked and hard to find. Go down the track without a bread delivery box, 900 meters north of Ariiura Camping or 500 meters south of the Huahine Beach Club. After 200 meters this track reaches the beach, which you follow 100 meters to the right (south) to the huge stones of the *marae*. Surfing is possible in Araara Pass, beside the *motu* just off Marae Anini. If snorkeling here, beware of an outbound current in the pass.

Accommodations
The only low-cost place to stay on Huahine-iti is **Ariiura Camping** (Hubert Bremond, B.P. 145, 98731 Fare; tel. 68-83-78 or 68-85-20), 22 km south of Fare via the paved road. It's 1,400 meters from the upmarket Hôtel Huahine at Parea and shares the same lovely white beach with Relais Mahana, 800 meters northwest. There are 12 small open *fare,* each with a double bed, at CFP 2,000/3,500 single/double. Camping is CFP 1,200 pp a day, and a communal kitchen and pleasant eating area overlooks the turquoise lagoon. Bring food as no grocery stores are near-

This bridge links Huahine-nui to Huahine-iti.

DAVID STANLEY

by, although grocery trucks pass daily, once in the morning and twice in the afternoon Mon.-Sat. and twice in the morning on Sunday. Also bring insect repellent and coils. An outrigger canoe is available, and you may be able to rent bicycles at Relais Mahana. The snorkeling here is superb. The owner will pick you up at the airport or wharf if you stay three nights or more; watch for his pickup truck on the wharf if you arrive by boat from Papeete. Otherwise take *le truck,* which leaves Fare at 1030 Mon.-Sat. (CFP 250 pp). Budget.

If Ariiura Camping is too primitive for you, the only other choice apart from the luxury hotels is **Pension Mauarii** (Marcelle Flohr, tel. 68-86-49), 20 km south of Fare. It's on the same long white beach as Relais Mahana but a bit back toward Fare. Rooms in the main building are CFP 6,500/7,500 single/double, or CFP 9,000 in the mezzanine. The three garden bungalows are CFP 9,000/10,000 single/double, or CFP 15,000 for four persons. A beach bungalow is CFP 35,000, while the 10-mattress dormitory is CFP 2,400 pp. No cooking facilities are provided and the breakfast/dinner plan is CFP 3,000 pp. Every Friday 1900-2300 there's a buffet dinner (CFP 2,500 pp) with local music. Moderate to expensive.

The US$12-million **Hôtel Hana Iti** (B.P. 185, 98731 Fare; tel. 68-85-05, fax 68-85-04) opened in 1992 on a verdant ridge high above Bourayne Bay with stunning views of lagoon, reef, and Raiatea beyond. The Hana Iti is a little over a km off the main road, 12 km south of Fare. Vehicles are left at the reception and visitors board a shuttle to their units. A three-room thatched bungalow complete with whirlpool spa will set you back CFP 54,000/59,000 double/triple or more plus tax. Breakfast and dinner are another CFP 7,800 pp, return airport transfers CFP 2,400 pp. Each of the 24 traditional *fare* units is unique. Some

perch on rocks, more stand on stilts, and a few are built into huge trees. The Hana Iti is owned by American meat-packing millionaire Thomas C. Kurth, who bought the 34-hectare property from Spanish singer Julio Iglesias. If you're a Hollywood star in search of an exotic hideaway, this is it. Europcar is represented here. (The Hana Iti was badly damaged by a hurricane in April 1998 and you could arrive to find them closed.)

Relais Mahana (B.P. 30, 98731 Fare; tel. 68-81-54, fax 68-85-08) sits on Avea Bay's lovely shaded white beach, a little over two km west of Parea. The 22 units are CFP 16,000 single or double, CFP 19,000 triple for a garden bungalow, CFP 2,000 more for a beach bungalow, plus tax. For breakfast and dinner add another CFP 3,700 pp. Recreational activities and the pool/beach are strictly for hotel guests only but the restaurant/bar is open to all, with meals in the CFP 1,500-2,600 range. Roundtrip airport transfers are CFP 2,000 pp and a Europcar agency is here. This French-operated hotel seems to embody an odd mix of Parisian snobbery and military-style discipline you may or may not appreciate. It closes each year from mid-November to mid-December.

The 17-unit **Huahine Beach Club** (B.P. 39, 98731 Fare; tel. 68-81-46, fax 68-85-86) at Parea is overpriced at CFP 18,500 plus tax for a large garden bungalow, CFP 4,500 more for a beachfront bungalow. In late 1998 another 12 rooms were added to this hotel. Breakfast and dinner are CFP 4,000 pp, airport transfers CFP 1,800 pp. This resort squats on a small beach between Parea village and Marae Anini. Windsurfing, snorkeling, and fishing gear are loaned free. The Club can arrange cars through Europcar, a necessity due to the paucity of public transport. On Sundays cock fights are held in a pit near the hotel.

M.G.L. DOMENY DE RIENZI

an early 19th-century view of Raiatea

RAIATEA AND TAHA'A

RAIATEA

At 171 square km, Raiatea is the second-largest island of Tahiti-Polynesia. Its main town and port, Uturoa, is the business, educational, and administrative center of the Leeward Islands or Îles Sous-le-Vent (Islands under the Wind). The balance of Raiatea's population of about 10,000 lives in eight flower-filled villages around the island: Avera, Opoa, Puohine, Fetuna, Vaiaau, Tehurui, Tevaitoa, and Tuu Fenua. The west coast of Raiatea south of Tevaitoa is old Polynesia through and through.

Raiatea is traditionally the ancient Havai'i, the "sacred isle" from which all of eastern Polynesia was colonized. It may at one time have been reached by migrants from the west as the ancient name for Taha'a, Uporu, corresponds to Upolu, just as Havai'i relates to Savai'i, the largest islands of the Samoan chain. A legend tells how Raiatea's first king, Hiro, built a great canoe he used to sail to Rarotonga. Today Raiatea and Taha'a are mostly worth visiting if you want to get off the beaten tourist track. Though public transportation is scarce, the island offers good possibilities for scuba diving, charter yachting, and hiking, and the varied scenery is worth a stop.

The Land
Raiatea, 220 km northwest of Tahiti and 45 km west of Huahine, shares a protected lagoon with Taha'a three km away. Legends tell how the two islands were cut apart by a mythical eel. About 30 km of steel-blue sea separates Raiatea from both Huahine and Bora Bora. Mount Temehani on mountainous Raiatea rises to 772 meters, and some of the coastlines are rugged and narrow. The highest mountain is Toomaru (1,017 meters). All of the people live on a coastal plain planted in coconuts, where cattle also graze.

No beaches are found on big, hulking Raiatea itself. Instead, picnickers are taken to picture-postcard *motu* in the lagoon. Surfing is possible at the 10 passes that open onto the Raiatea/Taha'a lagoon, and windsurfers are active. The Leeward Islands are the most popular sailing area in Tahiti-Polynesia, and most of the charter boats are based at Raiatea.

History

Originally called Havai'i, legend holds that the island was rechristened by Queen Rainuiatea in honor of her parents, Rai, a warrior from Tahiti, and Atea, queen of Opoa. Before European encroachment, Raiatea was the religious, cultural, and political center of Tahiti-Polynesia. Tradition holds that the great Polynesian voyages to Hawaii and New Zealand departed from these shores.

Raiatea was Captain Cook's favorite island; he visited three times. During his first voyage in 1769 he called first at Opoa from 20 to 24 July. After having surveyed Bora Bora from the sea, he anchored for a week in the Rautoanui Pass on the northwest coast of Raiatea, near the village of Tuu Fenua. During his second voyage Cook lay at anchor twice, first from 8 to 17 September 1773 and again from 25 May to 4 June 1774, both times at Rautoanui. His third visit was from 3 November to 7 December 1777, again at Rautoanui. It can therefore be said that Rautoanui (which he calls "Haamanino Harbour" in his journals) was one of Cook's favorite anchorages.

These islands accepted Christianity soon after the Tahitians were converted. The noted Protestant missionary John Williams arrived in 1818, as a monument in the form of a black basalt pillar standing in front of the Protestant church just north of Uturoa recalls. From Raiatea, Williams carried the gospel to Rarotonga in 1823 and Samoa in 1830. Later Queen Pomare IV spent the years 1844-1847 in exile on Raiatea. When France annexed the island in 1887 Chief Teraupoo launched a resistance campaign that lasted until 1897, when French troops and warships conquered the island. Teraupoo was captured after six weeks of fighting and deported to New Caledonia where he remained until 1905. The Queen of Raiatea and 136 of her followers were exiled to remote Eiao Island in the Marquesas.

UTUROA

Uturoa (pop. 3,500) is an easy place to find your way around. The double row of Chinese stores along the main drag opens onto a colorful market built in 1946 (the Sunday market is over by 0800). Beyond the market is the harbor, with a pleasant park alongside. All of the ferries plying between Tahiti and Bora Bora call here and there's a frequent shuttle to Taha'a. The island's airport is three km west of town with the main yacht charter base, Marina Apooiti, a km beyond that. This is the territory's second city and the first stop on any exploration of the island.

Sights

For a view of four islands, climb **Tapioi Hill** (294 meters), the peak topped by a TV antenna behind Uturoa—one of the easiest and most satisfying climbs in Tahiti-Polynesia. Take the road beside the *gendarmerie* up past the Propriété Privé sign. This is private property, and although the owners allow visitors to climb the hill on foot, they've posted a sign just before the cattle grid at the bottom of the hill asking that private cars not be used, and this request should be respected. The fastest time on record for climbing Tapioi is 17 minutes, but it's best to allow two or three hours to hike up and down.

Sports and Recreation

The coral life at Raiatea is rather poor, but there's ample marinelife, including gray sharks, moray eels, barracudas, manta rays, and countless tropical fish. Experienced divers will appreciate the shark action in Teavarua Pass, while beginners and others will enjoy diving near Motu Taoru. South of Uturoa is the century-old wreck of a 50-meter Dutch coal boat, the top of which is 18 meters down.

Hémisphère Sub (Hubert Clot, B.P. 985, 98735 Uturoa; tel. 66-12-49, fax 66-28-63, VHF channel 68), at the Marina Apooiti, offers scuba diving at CFP 5,000 per dive. The second to fifth dives are CFP 4,500 each, the sixth to tenth CFP 4,300. Night dives cost CFP 5,500.

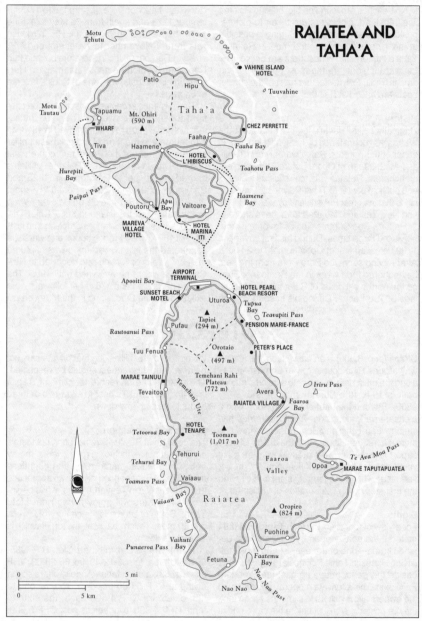

RAIATEA AND
TAHA'A

Motu Tehutu

VAHINE ISLAND HOTEL

Tuuvahine

Patio   Hipu

Motu Tautau   Tapuamu   Taha'a

Mt. Ohiri
(590 m)

WHARF   CHEZ PERRETTE

Tiva   Haamene   Faaha

Faaha Bay

HOTEL
L'HIBISCUS

Toahotu Pass

Hurepiti Bay

Paipai Pass   Haamene
                                        Bay

Poutoru   Apu
            Bay   Vaitoare

MAREVA
VILLAGE
HOTEL   HOTEL
               MARINA
               ITI

AIRPORT
TERMINAL

Apooiti Bay   HOTEL PEARL
                                        BEACH RESORT
SUNSET BEACH
MOTEL   Uturoa   Tupua
                               Bay   Teavapiti Pass

Pufau   Tapioi
          (294 m)   PENSION MARIE-FRANCE

Rautoanui Pass

Tuu Fenua   Orotaio   PETER'S PLACE
                   (497 m)

MARAE TAINUU   Temehani Rahi
                      Plateau
Tevaitoa   (772 m)   Avera   Iriru Pass

                                        RAIATEA VILLAGE   Faaroa
                                                            Bay
HOTEL
TENAPE
Tetooroa Bay   Toomaru
                      (1,017 m)   Faaroa
Tehurui Bay   Tehurui   Valley
                                                            Opoa   Te Ava Moa Pass
Toamaro Pass   Vaiaau   MARAE TAPUTAPUATEA

Vaiaau Bay   Raiatea

                               Oropiro
                               (824 m)

Vaihuti   Puohine
Bay

Punaeroa Pass   Fetuna   Faatemu
                                        Bay

                      Nao Nao   Nao Nao Pass

0   5 mi
0   5 km

© DAVID STANLEY

They go out daily at 0830 and 1430 and offer free pickups. A five-dive CMAS certification course is CFP 30,000 but to enroll you'll need a medical certificate, which can be obtained locally for CFP 3,000.

Raiatea Plongée (B.P. 272, 98735 Uturoa; tel. 66-37-10, fax 66-26-25, VHF channel 18) is run by Patrice Philip, husband of the Marie-France mentioned under **Accommodations,** below. He also charges CFP 5,000 for a one-tank dive. A trip right around Taha'a by motorized canoe with visits to two *motu* is CFP 5,500 (eight-person minimum), snorkeling in a pass is CFP 3,500. PADI scuba certification (four dives) is

CFP 50,000. A swimming pool on the premises is used for the lessons. We've had varying reports about Patrice's operation.

Nauti-Sport (tel./fax 66-35-83), next to the Kuomintang building at the south end of Uturoa, sells quality snorkeling gear.

There's good swimming in a large pool open to the sea at the **Centre Nautique** *("la piscine")* on the coast just north of Uturoa, beyond the new yacht harbor. The local Polynesians keep their long racing canoes here.

The **Kaoha Nui Ranch** (Patrick Marinthe, B.P. 568, 98735 Uturoa; tel./fax 66-25-46) at PK 6, Avera, a few hundred meters north of Pension

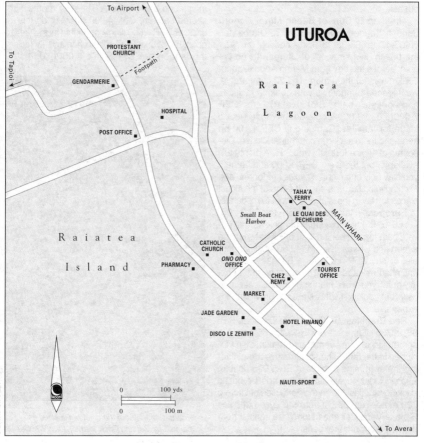

Manava, charges CFP 3,500 for horseback riding (an hour and a half). You must reserve 24 hours in advance, and there's a two-person minimum.

Turn to **Transportation** in the Tahiti-Polynesia introduction for information on yacht charters.

PRACTICALITIES

Accommodations

Most of the places to stay are on the northeast side of Raiatea and we've arranged them here from north to south. The proprietors often pick up guests who call ahead for reservations at the airport or harbor. The transfers are usually free, but ask.

The friendly **Sunset Beach Motel Apooiti** (Moana Boubée, B.P. 397, 98735 Uturoa; tel. 66-33-47, fax 66-33-08) is in a coconut grove by the beach, five km west of Uturoa. It's on the point across the bay from Marina Apooiti, about 2.5 km west of the airport. The 22 comfortable, well-spaced bungalows with cooking facilities and private bath (hot water) are CFP 7,000/8,000/9,000 single/double/triple—good value for families. Camping is CFP 1,100 pp here, and there's a large communal kitchen. Discounts of 10% a fortnight and 20% a month are available, but there's a CFP 1,000 surcharge if you stay only one night. Bicycles are for rent and hitching into Uturoa is easy. It's one of the nicest places to stay in the islands. Budget to moderate.

Europcar (Raiatea Location, tel. 66-34-06, fax 66-16-06) has four small bungalows with private bath for rent behind their office between the airport and Uturoa. It's CFP 4,500 single or double, or pay CFP 9,000 for a bungalow and an unlimited mileage car. It's a deal worth checking out if you were planning to rent a car anyway (but cooking facilities are not provided). Inexpensive.

Bed-Breakfast Bellevue (Max Boucher, B.P. 98, 98735 Uturoa; tel. 66-15-15, fax 66-14-15) is something of a misnomer as breakfast isn't included in the tariff. The six attractive rooms facing the swimming pool are CFP 5,900 double. Each includes private bath, fridge, and TV, but no cooking facilities. It's on the north side of Uturoa, 700 meters up the hill from the Lycée des Îles Sous-le-Vent. Call ahead for a free transfer from the wharf/airport. Inexpensive.

The **Hôtel Hinano** (Georges Moulon, B.P. 196, 98735 Uturoa; tel. 66-13-13; fax 66-14-14), conveniently located on the main street in the center of Uturoa, has 10 rooms at CFP 4,500/5,500 single/double (CFP 1,000 extra for one of the four a/c rooms). Cooking facilities are not available. The Hinano would be a good choice if you were interested in Uturoa's bar/disco scene or only wanted to spend one night here between boats. Inexpensive.

Pension Marie-France (Patrice and Marie-France Philip, B.P. 272, 98735 Uturoa; tel. 66-37-10, fax 66-26-25), by the lagoon just beyond Magasin Andre Chinese store, 2.5 km south of Uturoa (yellow sign), caters to scuba divers and misplaced backpackers. The four rooms with shared bath are CFP 4,000 single or double in back, or CFP 4,500 single or double facing the lagoon. Five bungalows with kitchen and TV facing the lagoon are CFP 7,000/8,000/9,000 sin-

Poetua, daughter of the chief of Raiatea, as painted by Captain Cook's artist, John Webber

JOHN WEBBER

gle/double/triple. There's also a six-bed dormitory with cooking facilities at CFP 1,200 pp (sheets provided on request). A supplement of up to CFP 1,000 is charged if you stay only one night. Bicycles (CFP 1,000 daily) and a washing machine are for rent, and there's sometimes hot water. The lagoon off Pension Marie-France is good for windsurfing and there's surfing off Taoru Island in nearby Teavapiti Pass. Unfortunately they're a little pushy in the way they try to convince you to sign up for the half-day minibus tour of the island (CFP 4,000), so don't come expecting to rest. As soon as Marie-France senses that you're not interested in taking any of her trips, she becomes rather abrupt. The food in the restaurant is satisfactory and the accommodations okay, but Marie-France's unhelpful management style means bad vibes all around. Airport transfers are CFP 600 pp each way (nothing is free here). Inexpensive to moderate.

Three of the best value places to stay on Raiatea are close together six km south of Uturoa, a CFP 1,500 taxi ride from Uturoa. **Kaoha Nui Ranch** (B.P. 568, 98735 Uturoa; tel./fax 66-25-46) has two rooms with private bath at CFP 5,500 single or double, CFP 6,500 triple. Otherwise there are four double "dormitory" rooms with shared bath at CFP 1,800 per bed (plus CFP 500 for one-night stays). Communal cooking facilities are provided. It's the obvious selection if you have an interest in riding. Airport transfers are free. Inexpensive.

Pension Manava (B.P. 559, 98735 Uturoa; tel. 66-28-26, fax 66-16-66), right next door to Kaoha Nui Ranch at PK 6, Avera, is run by Andrew and Roselyne Brotherson. This warm, sympathetic couple has four Polynesian-style bungalows with cooking facilities and private bath at CFP 4,500 or CFP 5,500 single or double, depending on the unit. Two rooms in a separate building are CFP 3,500 single or double with shared kitchen and bath. A half-day boat trip to southern Raiatea is CFP 2,500 pp, and they also do a full-day boat trip right around Taha'a at CFP 3,750 including lunch (five-person minimum)—these trips are also open to nonguests. Bicycles are CFP 1,000. Inexpensive.

The backpacker's number-one choice on Raiatea is **Peter's Place** (Peter Brotherson, tel. 66-20-01) at Hamoa, six km south of Uturoa and just beyond Pension Manava. The eight neat double rooms in a long block are CFP 1,400 pp, or you can pitch a tent in the large grassy area facing the rooms at CFP 700 pp. A large open pavilion is used for communal cooking but there are no grocery stores nearby, so bring food. The pavilion doubles as a traveler's library with good lighting and it's very pleasant to sit there on a rainy night as torrents of water beat on the tin roof. Bicycles rent for CFP 800 a day. Peter is the progeny of a Danish sea captain named Brotherson who left hundreds of descendants on Raiatea. He or his son Frame take guests on a hike up the valley to a picturesque waterfall with swimming in the river, fish feeding, and a tour of a vanilla plantation included at CFP 3,000 per group. They can also guide you directly to the Temehani Plateau, taking about three hours up and two hours down (CFP 5,000 per group). Peter's boat trips cost around CFP 1,000 pp when a few people are interested, and he'll also loan you a dugout canoe free to paddle yourself around the lagoon. Budget.

Coco Beach Houses (Marie-Isabelle Chan, B.P. 598, 98735 Uturoa; tel./fax 66-37-64) sits on an artificial lagoon beach behind the rectangular sports stadium with the green roof at Avera, 8.5 km south of Uturoa. There are six self-catering bungalows with living room and terrace. At last report, this place was closed, so check.

Pension Yolande Roopinia (Yolande Roopinia, B.P. 298, 98735 Uturoa; tel. 66-35-28) is in an attractive location facing the lagoon at PK 10, Avera. The four rooms are CFP 5,000 single or double (private bath). Cooking facilities are provided, but you may be asked to take half pension (CFP 7,000/13,000 single/double). You'll like the family atmosphere. Inexpensive.

A hundred meters beyond Chez Yolande is the 12-unit **Raiatea Village Hôtel** (Philippe Roopinia, B.P. 282, 98735 Uturoa; tel. 66-31-62, fax 66-10-65), at the mouth of Faaroa Bay (PK 10). A garden bungalow with kitchenette and terrace is CFP 5,400/6,480/7,560/8,640 single/double/triple/quad. Airport transfers are CFP 1,000 pp extra. Moderate.

On the hillside a little beyond is **La Croix du Sud** (Annette and Eric Germa, B.P. 769, 98735 Uturoa; tel./fax 66-27-55). The three rooms with bath are CFP 6,350/9,090 single/double including breakfast and dinner (no cooking facilities). Facilities include a swimming pool, bicycles, and free airport pickups.

Luxury

The 32-unit **Hôtel Raiatea Pearl Beach Resort** (B.P. 43, 98735 Uturoa; tel. 66-20-23, fax 66-20-20), 1.5 km south of Uturoa, is Raiatea's only luxury hotel. This is the former Raiatea Bali Hai, destroyed by a kitchen fire in 1992 and completely rebuilt in 1994 as the Hôtel Hawaiki Nui. In 1998 it became the Pearl Beach Resort, changing CFP 17,000 single or double for one of the eight thatched garden bungalows, CFP 21,000 for the 12 lagoonside bungalows, or CFP 29,000 for the 12 overwater bungalows, plus tax. The layout is attractive with a swimming pool overlooking the lagoon. A Europcar desk is here. Airport transfers are CFP 1,400 pp.

Food

To escape the tourist scene, try **Bar Restaurant Maraamu,** also known as Chez Remy, in what appears to be an old Chinese store between the market and the wharf. The few minutes it takes to locate the place will net you the lowest prices in town. Coffee and omelettes (CFP 600) are served in the morning, while the lunch menu tilts toward Chinese food. There's also excellent *poisson cru* (CFP 350, sold out by 1400) and a good selection of other dishes. Hinano beer is on tap.

Snack Moemoea (tel. 66-39-84; weekdays 0600-1700, Saturday 0600-1300, closed Sunday), on the harbor, serves hamburgers plus a range of French and Chinese dishes on their terrace. Despite the name it's rather upmarket.

Le Quai des Pécheurs (tel. 66-36-83), closer to the wharf, offers a view of the port.

Unpretentious **Restaurant Michele** (tel. 66-14-66; weekdays 0500-1530/1800-2100, Saturday 0500-1530) below Hôtel Hinano (rear side of the building) is a good place for breakfast with coffee, bread, and butter at CFP 250. Chinese meals are around CFP 800, otherwise take one of the French dishes costing CFP 1,000-1,200 listed on the blackboard at the door. Their *poisson cru* is CFP 400, a small glass of beer CFP 250.

A more upmarket choice would be the **Jade Garden Restaurant** (tel. 66-34-40; open Wed.-Sat. 1100-1300/1830-2100) on the main street, offering some of the tastiest Chinese dishes this side of Papeete.

The upstairs dining room at **Restaurant Moana** (tel. 66-27-49; open Tues.-Sun. 1030-1330/1830-2130) opposite Uturoa Market also serves Chinese dishes. Weekdays the lunch specials are listed on a blackboard downstairs, costing around CFP 1,000 including a beer. If you have a late dinner on weekends and wish to stay for the disco you won't have to pay the CFP 1,000 cover charge provided you don't go out.

The largest supermarket is **Champion** facing the small boat harbor, open weekdays 0700-1200/1330-1830, Saturday 0700-1200/1430-1800. Whole barbecued chickens are CFP 700.

All of the stores in Uturoa close for lunch 1200-1330.

Entertainment

Friday, Saturday, and Sunday at 2200 Restaurant Moana (tel. 66-27-49) opposite Uturoa Market becomes **Discothèque Le Zénith.** They begin collecting a CFP 1,000 cover charge at 2200, but if you arrive around 2100 and have a few drinks at the bar you won't have to pay it.

The nicest place for a drink is Le Quai des Pécheurs, which transforms itself into **Disco Quaidep** on Friday and Saturday from 2200 (CFP 1,000 cover).

Services and Information

None of Uturoa's four banks open on Saturday but ATMs accessible 24 hours are outside the market and in front of the Banque de Tahiti.

The large modern post office (Mon.-Thurs. 0730-1500, Friday 0700-1400, Saturday 0800-1000) is opposite the new hospital just north of town, with the *gendarmerie* (tel. 66-31-07) about 50 meters beyond on the left.

There are free public toilets *(sanitaires publics)* on the wharf behind Le Quai des Pécheurs.

A km west of the Sunset Beach Motel is Raiatea Carenage Services (B.P. 165, 98735 Uturoa; tel. 66-22-96), a repair facility often used by cruising yachts. The only easily accessible slip facilities in Tahiti-Polynesia are here (maximum 22 tons).

Beside the souvenir stalls opposite the wharf is a tourist information stand (B.P. 707, 98735 Uturoa; tel. 66-23-33), open Mon.-Fri. 0800-1130/1330-1600. They can supply a few brochures but are not very helpful.

Health

Uturoa's public hospital (tel. 66-35-03) is on the north side of town.

Dr. Patrick Lazarini (tel. 66-23-01), general practitioner, and Dr. Françis Falieu (tel. 66-35-95), dentist, have adjacent offices above La Palme d'Or in the center of Uturoa. Both are open weekdays 0730-1145/1330-1700, Saturday 0800-1130.

Several private doctors and dentists have offices above the pharmacy opposite the Catholic church in central Uturoa. Among them are Dr. Alain Repiton-Préneuf and Dr. Bruno Bataillon, general practitioners, and Dr. Frederic Koutzevol (tel. 66-31-31; weekdays 0730-1130/1400-1700, Saturday 0730-1000), a dentist.

The Pharmacy (tel. 66-35-48), opposite the Catholic church, is open weekdays 0730-1130/1400-1730, Saturday 0730-1130, Sunday 0930-1030.

TRANSPORTATION

Getting There and Away

The **Air Tahiti** office (tel. 66-32-50) is at the airport. Flights from Raiatea to Maupiti (CFP 5,600) operate three times a week. For information on flights from Papeete, Huahine, and Bora Bora see the introduction to Tahiti-Polynesia.

The jet cruiser *Ono-Ono* departs Raiatea for Taha'a (45 minutes hours, CFP 667) and Bora Bora (2.5 hours, CFP 1,778) Monday and Wednesday at 1400, Friday at 2100, and Saturday at 1615. To Huahine (one hour, CFP 1,778) and Papeete (4.5 hours, CFP 5,499) it leaves Tuesday and Thursday at 0900, Sunday at 1430. There's an extra trip to Huahine Saturday at 1000. Check the departure information carefully as they often leave earlier than the time printed in their timetable. The *Ono-Ono* office (tel. 66-24-25, fax 66-39-83; open Mon.-Sat. 0630-1730, Sunday 0900-1400) is on waterfront between Snack Moemoe and Champion Supermarket. A Europcar desk is in the same office.

You can catch the *Vaeanu, Taporo VI,* and *Raromatai Ferry* to Taha'a, Bora Bora, Huahine, and Papeete twice weekly. Consult the schedule in the introduction to Tahiti-Polynesia. Tickets for the *Vaeanu, Taporo VI,* and *Raromatai Ferry* are sold when the ships arrive.

A government supply barge, the *Meherio III,* shuttles twice a month between Raiatea and Maupiti, usually departing Raiatea on Thursday (CFP 1,058 deck). The exact time varies, so check with the Capitainerie Port d'Uturoa (tel. 66-31-52) on the wharf.

The yellow and blue *Maupiti Express,* a fast ferry with 62 airline type seats, charges CFP 2,500 each way between Raiatea and Bora Bora, departing Uturoa for Bora Bora Wednesday and Friday afternoons. Inquire at Agence Blue Lagoon (tel. 66-17-74) next to Snack Moemoe on the waterfront.

Blue Lagoon should also have information about **Les Navettes des Îles** (B.P. 158, 98735 Uturoa; tel. 65-67-10, fax 65-67-11), which shuttle between Raiatea and Taha'a at CFP 750 pp each way (bicycles CFP 500). The fleet consists of two 57-seat ferries painted yellow and blue. The *Uporu* serves Taha'a's west coast (Marina Iti, Poutoru, Patii, Tiva, Tapuamu) while the *Iripau* serves the east coast (Haamene, Faaha Quai Amaru). Both leave Uturoa three times daily on weekdays, but one of the *Uporu's* trips terminates at Marina Iti. On Monday, Wednesday, and Friday one of the *Iripau* trips has a bus connection between Faaha Quai Amaru and Patio. On Saturday only the west coast service operates—once. There's no schedule at all on Sunday and holidays.

Getting Around

Getting around Raiatea by *le truck* isn't practical as they only leave Uturoa in the afternoon (except Sunday) to go to Fetuna, Vaiaau, and Opoa. You might be able to use them to get to town in the morning, however, and the people where you're staying will know what time you have to be waiting. In Uturoa the *trucks* are usually parked in front of Restaurant Michele and the drivers are the only reliable source of departure information.

Raiatea Location Europcar (tel. 66-34-06, fax 66-16-06), between the airport and Uturoa, is the main car rental operator on Raiatea. Their cars begin around CFP 7,000 a day, including mileage and insurance (minimum age 18). Ask about the package that gives you a small car and a bungalow behind their main office between Uturoa and the airport at CFP 9,000. Bicycles are CFP 1,200/1,500/2,000 for four/eight/24 hours (expensive). Apart from cars and bikes, Raiatea Location rents a four-meter boat with a six-horsepower motor at CFP 6,000/8,000 a four/eight hours. Scooter rentals are generally unavailable.

Avis (tel. 66-15-59) is at the airport only. Their cars start at CFP 6,900/12,500/16,900 for one/two/three days all inclusive.

Garage Motu Tapu (Guirouard Rent-a-Car, B.P. 139, 98735 Uturoa; tel. 66-33-09), in a poorly marked building a few hundred meters east of the airport, has cars at CFP 6,500 for eight hours, insurance and mileage included.

Many of the hotels and pensions run circle-island bus tours and boat trips to a *motu* or Taha'a. **Raiatea Safari Tours** (tel. 66-37-10) and **Raiatea 4X4** (tel. 66-24-16) offer 4WD excursions into the interior, which you can't do on your own by rental car at CFP 4,000 and up. **Almost Paradise Tours** (tel. 66-23-64), run by Faaroa Bay resident Bill Kolans, offers a very good three-hour minibus tour in American English for CFP 3,000.

Airport

The airport (RFP) is three km northwest of Uturoa. A taxi from the Uturoa market taxi stand to the airport is CFP 800 (double tariff late at night). Most of the hotels pick up clients at the airport free of charge upon request. Avis and Europcar both have car rental desks inside the terminal. The Air Tahiti reservations office is in a separate building adjacent to the main terminal. The friendly but unknowledgeable Tourist Board information kiosk at the airport is open at flight times only. The airport restaurant offers a good *plat du jour* at lunchtime.

AROUND RAIATEA

It takes five to 10 hours to ride a bicycle the 97 km around Raiatea, depending on how fast you go; by car you can take anywhere from a couple of hours to a leisurely day. The road down the east coast is paved to the head of Faaroa Bay, then the paved road cuts directly across the island to the south coast. Down the west coast, the road is paved as far as Tehurui. The bottom half of the circuminsular road is unpaved, but no problem for a car.

The road down the east coast circles fjordlike **Faaroa Bay,** associated with the legends of Polynesian migration. Stardust Marine has a yacht charter base on the north side of the bay, and from the anchorage there's a fine view of Toomaru, highest peak in the Leeward Islands. The Apoomau River drains the Faaroa Valley. (The boat trips occasionally offered up this river are not recommended, as the boat can only proceed a couple of hundred meters. However, if you're off a yacht you could explore it with your dingy.)

Instead of crossing the island on the paved road, keep left and follow the coast around to a point of land just beyond Opoa, 32 km from Uturoa. Here stands **Marae Taputapuatea,** one of the largest and best preserved in Polynesia, its mighty *ahu* measuring 43 meters long, 7.3 meters wide, and between two and three meters high. Before it is a rectangular courtyard paved with black volcanic rocks. A small platform in the middle of the *ahu* once bore the image of Oro, god of fertility and war (now represented by a reproduction); backrests still mark the seats of high chiefs on the courtyard. Marae Taputapuatea is directly opposite Te Ava Moa Pass, and fires on the *marae* may once have been beacons to ancient navigators. Human sacrifices and firewalking once took place on the *marae.*

In 1995 a fleet of traditional Polynesian voyaging canoes, including three from Hawaii and two each from Cook Islands and Tahiti, plus an Easter Island raft, gathered at Taputaputea to lift a 650-year-old curse and rededicate the *marae.* The seven canoes then left for the Marquesas, navigating by the stars and swells. Some carried on to Hawaii and the west coast of the U.S. in an amazing demonstration of the current revival of this aspect of traditional culture.

Marae Taputapuatea is said to retain its psychic power. Test this by writing down all your negative emotions, bad habits, unhappy memories, and self-doubts on a piece of paper. Then burn the paper(s) on the *marae.* The catharsis works best when done solo, beneath a full moon or on one of the three nights following it. The *tupapau* (spirits) are most active at this time, often taking the forms of dogs, cats, pigs, etc.

The only places to buy food in the southern

Marea Taputapuatea on Raiatea is among the most sacred sites in Polynesia.

DAVID STANLEY

part of Raiatea are the two Chinese grocery stores at **Fetuna** and another at **Vaiaau,** on the west side of Raiatea. Vaiaau Bay marks the end of the protected inner channel from Uturoa around Raiatea clockwise and yachts must exit the lagoon through Toamaro Pass in order to continue northward. At Rautoanui Pass sailboats can come back in behind the barrier reef to continue the circumnavigation, with the possibility of a sidetrip south to Tevaitoa.

Behind Tevaitoa church is **Marae Tainuu,** dedicated to the ancient god Taaroa. Petroglyphs on a broken stone by the road at the entrance to the church show a turtle and some other indistinguishable figure. At Tevaitoa Chief Teraupo and his people fought their last battles against the French invaders in early 1897.

The territory's largest yacht charter base is the **Marina Apooiti,** which opened in 1982 one km west of the airport. Aside from The Moorings and Tahiti Yacht Charter, there's a large restaurant here, a dive shop, and the **Musée de la Mer** (tel. 66-27-00; closed Sunday), whose collection you can peruse for CFP 500. Otherwise check out the polished seashells in their souvenir shop for free.

Hiking

According to Polynesian mythology the god Oro was born from the molten rage of **Mt. Temehani** (772 meters), the cloud-covered plateau that dominates the northern end of the island. *Tiare apetahi,* a sacred white flower that exists nowhere else on earth and resists transplantation, grows above the 400-meter level on the slopes around the summit. The fragile one-sided blossom represents the five fingers of a beautiful Polynesian girl who fell in love with the handsome son of a high chief, but was unable to marry him due to her lowly birth. The petals pop open forcefully enough at dawn to make a sound and local residents sometimes spend the night on the mountain to be there to hear it. These flowers are protected and there's a minimum CFP 50,000 fine for picking one. Small pink orchids also grow here.

Temehani can be climbed from Pufau, the second bay south of Marina Apooiti. Note a series of old concrete benches by the road as you come around the north side of the bay (which offers good anchorage for yachts). The track inland begins at a locked gate, 700 meters south of the bridge, beyond the concrete benches. It's private property, so ask permission to proceed of anyone you meet. You hike straight up through an area reforested in pine until you have a clear view of Temehani Rahi and Temehani Ute, divided by a deep gorge. Descend to the right and continue up the track you see on the hillside opposite. It takes about three hours to go from the main road to the Temehani Rahi Plateau. Friday and Saturday are the best days to go, and long pants and sturdy shoes are required. A guide up Temehani should charge about CFP 5,000 for the group.

Reader Will Paine of Maidstone, England, sent us this:

The through hike from Pufau to Uturoa takes five or six hours on foot with beautiful views from high vantage points where the difficultly manageable jeep track becomes a path. The same trail is shared by the Temehani route until it splits up shortly after the ford/bathing pool on the higher reaches. Here take the left branch. Follow it down across a water catchment and up to a ridge. The Orotaio cone will come into view to the east and the path drops to a better four-wheel-drive track. From here it's just under two hours down to a gas station on the coastal road a few km south of Uturoa.

Accommodations around Raiatea

The **Hôtel Atiapiti** (Marie-Claude Rajaud, B.P. 884, 98735 Uturoa; tel./fax 66-16-65), on the beach next to Marae Taputapuatea at Opoa, 35 km from Uturoa, has seven tastefully decorated bungalows from CFP 8,500/9,500 double/triple, plus CFP 3,500 pp for half board (good seafood). The managers organize excursions to a *motu* and around the island, and there's good snorkeling off their wharf. The hotel's biggest drawback is its isolation, but they'll pick you up at the port or airport if you call ahead (CFP 2,000 pp roundtrip). It's good for a couple of days of relaxation. Moderate.

In 1999 the two-story, 16-room **Hôtel Le Maitai Tenape** (Marie-Hélène Viot, B.P. 717, 98735 Uturoa; tel. 66-14-50, fax 66-40-50) was under construction at PK 10, Pufau, on the west coast.

TAHA'A

Raiatea's 90-square-km lagoonmate Taha'a is shaped like a hibiscus flower with four long bays cutting into its rugged south side. Mount Ohiri (590 meters), highest point on the island, got its name from Hiro, god of thieves, who was born here. Taha'a is known as the "vanilla island" for its plantations that produce 70% of the territory's "black gold." The Taha'a Festival in late October includes stone fishing, with a line of people in canoes herding the fish into a cove by beating stones on the surface of the lagoon. In November the Hawaiki Nui Outrigger Canoe Race passes Taha'a on its way from Huahine to Bora Bora.

It's a quiet island, with little traffic and few tourists. Most families use speedboats to commute to their gardens on the reef islets or to fishing spots, or to zip over to Raiatea on shopping trips, so they don't really need cars. Beaches are scarce on the main island but the string of *motu* off the northeast side of Taha'a have fine white-sand beaches. The pension owners and tour operators arrange picnics on a few of these, such as Tautau off Tapuamu, and pearl farms have been established on some. This is the only Society island you can sail a yacht right around inside the barrier reef, and the many anchorages and central location between Raiatea, Huahine, and Bora Bora make Taha'a a favorite of both cruisers and charterers.

There aren't many specific attractions on Taha'a, and the dearth of inexpensive places to stay and lack of public transportation has kept this island off the beaten track. The easy way to visit Taha'a is still an all-day outrigger canoe tour from Raiatea. This could change but meanwhile the isolation has made the 4,500 Taha'a islanders rather wary of outsiders.

Orientation

The administrative center is at Patio (or Iripau) on the north coast, where the post office, *mairie*, and *gendarmerie* (tel. 65-64-07) share one compound. A second post office is at Haamene where four roads meet. The ship from Papeete ties up to a wharf at Tapuamu, and there's a large covered area at the terminal where you could spread a sleeping bag in a pinch. The Banque Socredo branch is also at Tapuamu.

The 70-km road around the main part of the island passes six of the eight villages; the other two are south of Haamene. Only the scenic road over the 141-meter Col Taira between Haamene and Tiva, and a stretch around Patio, are paved. Ferries run from Raiatea to Tapuamu and Haamene but there's no regular public transportation.

VANILLA

Vanilla, a vine belonging to the orchid family, is grown on small family plantations. Brought to Tahiti from Manila in 1848, the Tahitensis type, which has a worldwide reputation, originated from a mutation of Fragrans vanilla. The plants must be hand pollinated, then harvested between April and June. The pods are then put out to dry for a couple of months—an exceptionally time-consuming process generally entrusted to the Chinese. Between 1915 and 1933 Tahiti produced 50-150 tons of vanilla a year, peaking in 1949 at 200 tons. Production remained high until 1966, when a steady decline began due to the producers leaving for paid employment in Papeete related to nuclear testing. By 1990 production had fallen to only 39 metric tons, though things have picked up since then.

Sights

The mountain pass between Haamene and Tiva offers excellent views of Hurepiti and Haamene Bays, two of the four deep fjords cutting into the southern side of the island. You could also follow the rough track from Haamene up to the Col Vaitoetoe for an even better view. This track continues north, coming out near the hospital in Patio.

Rarahu, the girl immortalized in Pierre Loti's 1880 novel *The Marriage of Loti,* is buried near Vaitoare village at the south end of Taha'a, east of the Marina Iti.

PRACTICALITIES

Accommodations

Unfortunately, there aren't any budget accommodations on Taha'a. The most convenient and least expensive place is **Chez Pascal** (Pascal Tamaehu, tel. 65-60-42). From the Tapuamu ferry wharf you'll see a small bridge at the head of the bay. Turn left as you leave the dock and head for this. Chez Pascal is the first house north of the bridge on the inland side. The rate is CFP 5,000 pp for bed, breakfast, and dinner, or CFP 3,000 pp with breakfast only. Boat trips to a *motu* are CFP 4,000 pp, and the loan of the family bicycle is possible. Inexpensive.

The **Mareva Village Hôtel** (B.P. 214, 98734 Haamene; tel. 65-61-61, fax 65-68-67) on Apu Bay is easily accessible weekdays on the ferry *Uporu* to Poutoru. Standing in a row between the road and the lagoon are six large bungalows with kitchen, bath, TV, and porch at CFP 7,000 single or double, CFP 8,500 triple, CFP 10,000 quad. The cooking facilities allow you to avoid the expensive meals you're forced to take in some of the other hotels, but bring groceries from Raiatea. Moderate.

Also at Poutoru and a bit northwest of the Mareva Village is **Pension Herenui** (B.P. 148, Haamene; tel./fax 65-62-60) with three *fare* at CFP 7,000 single or double (children under 12 free), plus CFP 3,500 pp for half board. A communal kitchen is provided in the club house and there's a circular swimming pool. Moderate.

The **Hôtel Marina Iti** (B.P. 888, 98735 Uturoa, Raiatea; tel. 65-01-01, fax 65-63-87, VHF channel 12) sits at the isolated south tip of Taha'a, opposite Raiatea on Taha'a's only sandy beach. The five tidy bungalows by the lagoon are CFP 16,000 double, or pay CFP 12,000 for a room in a duplex garden bungalow. Third persons pay CFP 2,000. Cooking facilities are not provided and meals are CFP 5,000 pp extra for breakfast and dinner. Use of bicycles, canoe, and snorkeling gear is included, and scuba diving is available. As you'll have guessed, the Marina Iti caters to an upmarket crowd on yacht charters from Raiatea, and numerous cruising yachts anchor in the calm waters offshore. The ferry *Uporu* from Raiatea stops here. (In 1998 the Marina Iti changed hands for just over a million dollars.) Premium.

The **Hôtel L'Hibiscus** (B.P. 184, 98734 Haamene; tel. 65-61-06, fax 65-65-65, VHF channel 68), also know as the Hôtel Taha'a Lagon, is run by Léo and Lolita on the northeast side of windy Haamene Bay. L'Hibiscus has two classes of accommodations: two plain rooms with shared bath at CFP 5,750 for up to three people, and four small bungalows with private bath at CFP 8,000/9,350 double/triple. Virtually everything you consume here—even the water you drink—is charged extra at resort prices. Common drinking water is not available at L'Hibiscus; bottled water must be purchased. The prices of the meals are fixed at CFP 3,500 pp half pension, CFP 5,500 full pension (not possible to order à la carte). Don't accept a "free welcome drink" unless you don't mind having it added to your bill ("misunderstandings" about prices are routine here). There are no cooking facilities, and the nearest store is three km away in Haamene (bring food and bottled water). L'Hibiscus has 10 yachts moorings that are "free" to those who patronize the restaurant and bar. However, Haamene Bay catches the full force of the southeast trades and there's far better anchorage off the Marina Iti. The ferry *Iripau* will drop you at Faaha Quai Amaru near here. We have received several convincing complaints about this place. Moderate.

Nearby on Haamene Bay is **Pension Patricia et Daniel** (Daniel Amaru, B.P. 104, 98734 Haamene; tel./fax 65-60-83) with three thatched bungalows at CFP 6,000/7,000 double/triple, plus CFP 2,500 pp for breakfast and dinner.

Chez Perrette (Perrette Tehuitua, tel. 65-65-78) is in an isolated location at Faaopore, 10 km east of Haamene. At CFP 2,500 for a mattress in an eight-bed dorm or CFP 15,000 double with breakfast and dinner in a self-catering bungalow, it's not worth the trip.

In 1998 the **Tupena Village** pension opened at Patio. It offers three rooms downstairs and two upstairs with plans for four bungalows, but prices were still unknown.

Taha'a's most upscale place is the **Vahine Island Private Resort** (B.P. 510, 98735 Uturoa, Raiatea; tel. 65-67-38, fax 65-67-70, VHF channel 70) on lovely Motu Tuuvahine off the northeast side of the island. The six seafront bungalows are CFP 30,000 single or double while the three overwater units cost CFP 45,000 plus tax. (Local French pay only CFP 12,000 seafront, CFP 18,000 overwater, an indication of the true value.) For breakfast/lunch/dinner add CFP 1,600/3,200/4,200 pp, for airport transfers CFP 5,000 pp. Outrigger canoes, windsurfing, snorkeling, and fishing gear are free, and moorings are provided for yachts. Luxury.

Food

Village stores are at Tapuamu, Tiva, Haamene, and Patio. A grocery truck passes L'Hibiscus around 1000 on Monday, Tuesday, Thursday, and Saturday; the same truck calls at the Marina Iti about noon daily except Sunday. The only nonhotel restaurant on Taha'a is at **Magasin Tissan** (tel. 65-64-15) in Patio.

Health

There's a medical center (tel. 65-63-31) at Patio and a dispensary (tel. 65-61-03) at Haamene. Dr. Marc Chabanne (tel. 65-60-60) is also at Haamene.

Transportation

There's no airport on Taha'a. The *Le Navette des Îles* shuttles between Raiatea and Taha'a three times daily on weekdays and once on Saturday (CFP 750 pp each way, bicycles CFP 500). Make sure your boat is going exactly where you want to go. For more information see **Raiatea,** above.

Large ships and ferries call at Tapuamu Wharf on the west side of Taha'a behind the Total service station. There's a telephone booth on the wharf that you could use to call your hotel to have them pick you up. The *Ono-Ono* leaves Taha'a for Bora Bora (CFP 1,333) Monday and Wednesday at 1445 and Saturday at 1700. Toward Raiatea (CFP 667), Huahine (CFP 2,111), and Papeete (CFP 6,050) it leaves Tuesday and Thursday at 0815, Saturday at 0915, and Sunday at 1315.

Taporo VI arrives from Papeete, Huahine, and Raiatea Tuesday, Thursday, and Saturday at 0700, and continues on to Bora Bora (southbound it doesn't stop at Taha'a). The *Vaeanu* departs Taha'a for Raiatea, Huahine, and Papeete Tuesday and Sunday at noon; Saturday at 0800 it goes to Bora Bora. The *Raromatai Ferry* visits Taha'a on Wednesday and Saturday mornings northbound, and Sunday afternoon southbound. The *Maupiti Express* leaves Taha'a for Bora Bora Wednesday and Friday at 1615.

Trucks on Taha'a are for transporting schoolchildren only, so you may have to hitch to get around. It's not that hard to hitch a ride down the west coast from Patio to Haamene, but there's almost no traffic along the east coast.

Rental cars are available from **Europcar** (tel. 65-67-00, fax 65-68-08) at the Total station next to Tapuamu Wharf, **Taha'a Transport Services** (tel. 65-67-10) at the Marina Iti, and **Monique Location/Avis** (tel. 65-62-48) at Haamene Wharf. Marina Iti also rents bicycles. Avis charges CFP 7,900 a day with 100 kilometers (extra kms CFP 40 each); Europcar is CFP 7,000 a day with unlimited kilometers and insurance. It's smart to book ahead if you want to be sure of a car.

M.G.L. DOMENY DE RIENZI

BORA BORA

Bora Bora, 260 km northwest of Papeete, is everyone's idea of a South Pacific island. Dramatic basalt peaks soar 700 meters above a gorgeous, multicolored lagoon. Slopes and valleys blossom with hibiscus. Some of the most perfect beaches you'll ever see are here, complete with topless sunbathers. Not only are the beaches good but there's plenty to see and do. The local population of 6,000 includes many skilled dancers. To see them practicing in the evening, follow the beat of village drums back to their source.

Bora Bora is the only island of Tahiti-Polynesia that can be said to have reached a tourist glut. The relentless stream of cars, pickups, hotel *trucks,* and scooters up and down the main road from Vaitape to Matira Point approaches Tahitian intensity at times. The uncontrolled expansion of tourism continues as luxury resorts are thrown up around the island, creating the illusion of being in Hawaii or some West Indies hot spot. Yet many of the US$500-a-night hotels stand almost empty. Construction of a huge Hyatt Regency on

a swampy shore at the far north end of the island was halted by a land dispute. Today the crumbling Hyatt ruins stand as a monument to bad planning and the perils of high-impact development. Other problems for Bora Bora include an upsurge of petty theft from visitors and improper garbage disposal by almost everyone. You may also find the swarms of young honeymooners from Chicago milling around Matira rather anticlimactic.

The Land

Seven-million-year-old Bora Bora (29 square km) is made up of a 10-km-long main island, a few smaller high islands in the lagoon, and a long ring of *motu* on the barrier reef. Pofai Bay marks the center of the island's collapsed crater with Toopua and Toopuaiti as its eroded west wall. Mount Pahia's gray basalt mass rises 649 meters behind Vaitape, and above it soar the sheer cliffs of Otemanu's mighty volcanic plug (727 meters). The wide-angle scenery of the main island is complemented by the surrounding coral reef and numerous *motu,* one of which bears the airport. Motu Tapu of the travel brochures was featured in F.W. Murnau's classic 1931 silent movie *Tabu* about two young lovers who escape to this tiny island. Te Ava Nui Pass is the only entry through the barrier reef. Watch for dolphins near this channel as your ship enters Bora Bora's lagoon; whole colonies sometimes race the boats. However these days you're more likely to be met by a line of tourists on jet skis following their guide.

History

The letter *b* doesn't exist in Tahitian, so Bora Bora is actually Pora Pora, meaning "first born" since this was the first island created after Raiatea. The island's traditional name, Vava'u, suggests Tongan voyagers may have reached here centuries ago. It's believed Bora Bora has been inhabited since the year 900 and 42 *marae* ruins can still be found around the island. The Bora Borans of yesteryear were indomitable warriors who often raided Maupiti, Taha'a, and Raiatea.

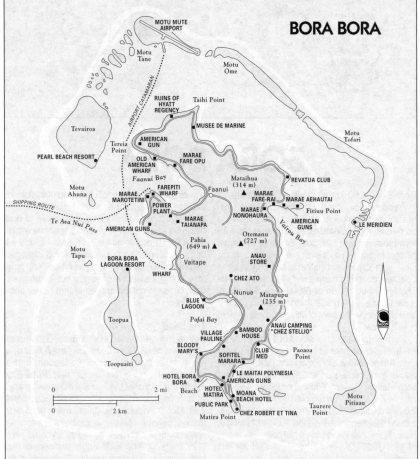

BORA BORA

MOTU MUTE AIRPORT

Motu Tane

Motu Ome

RUINS OF HYATT REGENCY

Taihi Point

Tevairoa

MUSEE DE MARINE

Motu Tofari

AMERICAN GUN

Tereia Point

MARAE FARE OPU

PEARL BEACH RESORT

OLD AMERICAN WHARF

Faanui Bay

Mataihua (314 m) ▲

REVATUA CLUB

Motu Ahuna

MARAE MAROTETINI

FAREPITI WHARF

Faanui

MARAE FARE-RAI

MARAE AEHAUTAI

POWER PLANT

Fitiiu Point

SHIPPING ROUTE

MARAE TAIANAPA

MARAE NONOHAURA

AMERICAN GUNS

Te Ava Nui Pass

AMERICAN GUNS

Vairou Bay

LE MERIDIEN

Pahia (649 m) ▲

Otemanu (727 m) ▲

Motu Tapu

BORA BORA LAGOON RESORT

ANAU STORE

Vaitape

WHARF

CHEZ ATO

Nunue

Matapupu (235 m) ▲

Toopua

BLUE LAGOON

Pofai Bay

ANAU CAMPING "CHEZ STELLIO"

VILLAGE PAULINE

BAMBOO HOUSE

Toopuaiti

BLOODY MARY'S

SOFITEL MARARA

CLUB MED

Paoaoa Point

HOTEL BORA BORA

LE MAITAI POLYNESIA

AMERICAN GUNS

Beach

HOTEL MATIRA

MOANA BEACH HOTEL

PUBLIC PARK

Motu Pitiaau

CHEZ ROBERT ET TINA

Matira Point

Taurere Point

0   2 mi

0   2 km

AIRPORT CATAMARAN

© DAVID STANLEY

"Discovered" by Roggeveen in 1722, Bora Bora was visited by Capt. James Cook in 1769 and 1777. The first European to live on the island was James O'Connor, a survivor of the British whaler *Matilda* wrecked at Moruroa atoll in 1793. O'Connor made his way to Tahiti where he married into the Pomare family, and eventually ended up living in a little grass shack on "Matilda Point," later corrupted to Matira Point. In 1895 the island was annexed by France.

In February 1942 the Americans hastily set up a refueling and regrouping base, code-named "Bobcat," on the island to serve shipping between the U.S. west coast or Panama Canal and Australia/New Zealand. You can still see remains from this time, including eight huge naval guns placed here to defend the island against a surprise Japanese attack that never materialized. The big lagoon with only one pass offered secure anchorage for as many as 100 U.S. Navy transports at a time. A road was built around the island and by April 1943 the present airfield on Motu Mute had been constructed. The 4,400 American army troops also left behind 130 half-caste babies, 40% of whom died of starvation when the base closed in June 1946 and the abandoned infants were forced to switch from their accustomed American baby formulas to island food. The survivors are now approaching ripe middle age. Novelist James A. Michener, a young naval officer at the time, left perhaps the most enduring legacy by modeling his Bali Hai on this "enchanted island," Bora Bora.

Orientation

You can arrive at Motu Mute airport and be carried to Vaitape Wharf by catamaran, or disembark from a ship at Farepiti Wharf, three km north of Vaitape. Most of the stores, banks, and business offices are near Vaitape Wharf. The finest beaches are along Matira Point at the island's southern tip.

SIGHTS

Vaitape

Behind the Banque de Tahiti at Vaitape Wharf is the **monument to Alain Gerbault,** who sailed his yacht, the *Firecrest,* solo around the world from 1923 to 1929—the first Frenchman to do so. Gerbault's first visit to Bora Bora was from 25 May to 12 June 1926. He returned to Polynesia in 1933 and stayed until 1940. A supporter of the Pétian regime in France, he left Bora Bora when the colony declared its support for General de Gaulle and died at Timor a year later while trying to return to Vichy France.

To get an idea of how the Bora Borans live, take a stroll through Vaitape village: go up the road that begins beside the Banque Socredo.

Around the Island

The largely paved and level 32-km road around the island makes it easy to see Bora Bora by rented bicycle (it's unnecessary to rent a car). At the head of **Pofai Bay** notice the odd assortment of looted war wreckage across the road from Alain Linda Galerie d'Art. Surrounded by a barbed wire fence are a seven-inch American gun dragged here from Tereia Point in 1982 and two huge anchors. On the hillside above is an abandoned A-frame museum, which didn't prove as profitable as its promoters had hoped. The locations of seven other MK II naval guns that have thus far escaped desecration are given below.

Stop at **Bloody Mary's Restaurant** to scan the goofy displays outside their gate, but more importantly to get the classic view of the island's soaring peaks across Pofai Bay as it appears in countless brochures. For an even better view go inland on the unmarked road that begins at a double electricity pole 100 meters north of Bloody Mary's. This leads to a jeep route with two concrete tracks up the 139-meter-high hill to a **radio tower,** a 10-minute hike. From the tower you get a superb view of the south end of the island.

The finest beach on the island stretches east from **Hôtel Bora Bora** to Matira Point. Some of the best snorkeling on the island, with a varied multitude of colorful tropical fish, is off the small point at Hôtel Bora Bora. Enter from east of the hotel grounds (such as via the Bora Diving Center or the beach beyond) and let the current pull you toward the hotel jetty, as the hotel staff don't appreciate strangers who stroll through their lobby to get to the beach. From the way they approach you, the small fish are quite obviously accustomed to being fed here, and for a more natural scene you could snorkel due south to the northern edge of the barrier reef. Just beware of getting run over by a glass-bottom boat! If you stay on the east side of the point, the hotel employees will leave you alone.

Two **naval guns** sit on the ridge above Hôtel Matira. Take the track on the mountain side of the road that winds around behind the bungalows from the east end of the property and keep straight ahead on a trail to the top of the ridge (10 minutes).

Bora Bora's most popular public beach is **Matira Beach Park** directly across the street from the Moana Beach Hôtel on Matira Point. At low tide you can wade from the end of Matira Point right out to the reef. These same shallows prevent yachts from sailing around the island inside the barrier reef.

Proceed north to the **Sofitel Marara,** a good place for a leisurely beer. Visitors are unwelcome at the new Club Med, which the road climbs over a hill to avoid. The two general stores at **Anau** can supply a cold drink or a snack.

On the north side of Vairou Bay the road begins to climb over a ridge. Halfway up the slope, look down to the right and by the shore you'll see the *ahu* of **Marae Aehautai,** the most intact of the three *marae* in this area. From the *marae* there's a stupendous view of Otemanu and you should be able to pick out Te Ana Opea cave far up on the side of the mountain. To visit the two American **seven-inch guns** on Fitiuu Point, follow the rough jeep track to the right at the top of the ridge a few hundred meters east (on foot) to a huge black rock from which you can see the guns. The steep unpaved slope on the

other side of this ridge can be dangerous on a bicycle, so slow down or get off and walk. There's a municipal dump in this area and you could catch the stench of burning garbage.

Just before Taihi Point at the north end of the main island is a **Musée de Marine** (tel. 67-75-24, donations accepted) on the right, which is usually closed. Just beyond Taihi Point you'll notice a concrete trestle running right up the side of the hill from the ruins of a group of platforms meant to be the overwater bungalows. This is all that remains an undercapitalized **Hyatt Regency hotel** project that went broke in the early 1980s.

One American **naval gun** remains on the hillside above the rectangular concrete water tank with a transformer pole alongside at Tereia Point. The housing of a second gun, vandalized in 1982, is nearby. The remains of several American concrete wharves can be seen along the north shore of **Faanui Bay.** Most of the wartime American occupation force was billeted around here and a few Quonset huts linger in the bush. Just beyond the small boat harbor (a wartime American submarine base) and the Service de l'Equipment is **Marae Fare Opu,** notable for the petroglyphs of turtles carved into the stones of the *ahu.* Turtles, a favorite food of the gods, were often offered to them on the *marae.* (Mindless guides sometimes highlight the turtles in chalk for the benefit of tourist cameras.)

Between Faanui and Farepiti Wharf, just east of the Brasserie de Tahiti depot and the electricity-generating plant, is **Marae Taianapa;** its long *ahu,* restored in 1963, is clearly visible on

one of eight U.S. naval guns left behind in 1945

the hillside from the road. The most important *marae* on Bora Bora was **Marae Marotetini,** on the point near Farepiti Wharf—west of the wharf and accessible along the shore at low tide. The great stone *ahu,* 25 meters long and up to 1.5 meters high, was restored by Professor Sinoto in 1968 and is visible from approaching ships.

The last two **American guns** are a 10-minute scramble up the ridge from the main road between Farepiti Wharf and Vaitape. Go straight up the concrete road a bit before you reach Otemanu Tours (where you see several *trucks* parked). At the end of the ridge there's a good view of Te Ava Nui Pass, which the guns were meant to defend, and Maupiti is farther out on the horizon. This is private property so ask permission to proceed of anyone you meet.

Hiking

If you're experienced and determined, it's possible to climb **Mount Pahia** in about four hours of rough going. Take the road inland beside the Banque Socredo at Vaitape and go up the depression past a series of mango trees, veering slightly left. Circle the cliffs near the top on the left side, and come up the back of Snoopy's head and along his toes. (These directions will take on meaning when you study Pahia from the end of Vaitape's Wharf.) The trail is unmaintained and a local guide would be a big help. The coordinator at CETAD at the Collège de Bora Bora in Vaitape arranges guides for groups of five or more. Avoid rainy weather, when the way will be muddy and slippery.

Despite what some tourist publications claim, slab-sided **Otemanu,** the high rectangular peak next to pointed Pahia, has *never* been climbed. It's possible to climb up to the shoulders of the mountain, but the sheer cliffs of the main peak are inaccessible because clamps pull right out of the vertical, crumbly cliff face. Helicopters can land on the summit, but that doesn't count. Otemanu's name means "It's a bird."

SPORTS AND RECREATION

The **Bora Diving Center** (Anne and Michel Condesse, B.P. 182, 98730 Nunue; tel. 67-71-84, fax 67-74-83, VHF channel 8), just east of Hôtel Bora Bora, offers scuba diving daily at 0830, 1330, 1930. Prices are CFP 5,500/9,000 for one/two

tanks, CFP 25,000 for a five-dive package, or CFP 6,500 for night dives, plus 3% tax. Snorkelers are welcome to tag along for CFP 1,500. Both PADI and CMAS open-water certification courses are offered at CFP 35,000 (three days). Otherwise try a one-tank initiation shore dive at CFP 5,500 (no experience required). Gear is included. Ten different sites are visited (those around Toopua Island are recommended for snorkelers). They also have a new activity called "Aqua Safari" in which participants put on a funny yellow diving helmet and walk along the lagoon floor (no experience required), also CFP 5,500. Bookings for any of this can be made through their dive shop on Matira Beach (which is closed while their five boats are out but usually staffed at 1030 and 1530), or at Aqua Safari inside the Bora Bora Beach Club. If you book through your hotel reception a surcharge may be added. Hotel pickups are available to divers who have booked ahead.

Scuba diving can also be arranged through Ben Heriteau's **Nemo World Diving** (B.P. 503, 98730 Vaitape; tel. 67-63-00, fax 67-63-33 near the Sofitel Marara. They charge CFP 6,000/11,000/26,250 for one/two/five dives, gear included, and they go out daily at 0900 and 1400 (hotel pickups available). Snorkelers can go along at CFP 2,000 pp. Nemo's specialty is diving with manta rays (worth doing to see the mantas, though you won't see much else in that area as the coral is all dead and the waters fished out). Since it's a long way around to the single pass, most scuba diving at Bora Bora is within the lagoon and visibility is sometimes limited.

Sportfishing from a luxury catamaran is a Bora Bora eccentricity invented by ex-Californian Richard Postma of **Island Sport Charters** (B.P. 186, 98730 Vaitape; tel./fax 67-77-79). His 15-meter *Tara Vana* based at Hôtel Bora Bora is fitted with a flybridge and two fighting chairs, and the sails and multihull stability make for a smooth, quiet ride. Any doubts you may have about fishing from a sailboat can be laid aside as this prototype vessel ranks among the best. A half-day fishing charter is CFP 60,000 for up to 10 people.

Horseback riding is available at **Ranch Reva Reva** (Olivier Ringeard, B.P. 117, 98730 Vaitape; tel. 67-63-63) on Motu Pitiaau, the long coral island east of Matira Point. Organized riding is four times at CFP 5,500 for 1.5 hours. Book through Miki Miki Jet Ski (tel. 67-76-44) at Matira, which arranges free transfers to the *motu.*

PRACTICALITIES

ACCOMMODATIONS

There's an abundance of accommodations on Bora Bora and, except at holiday times (especially during the July festivities), it's not necessary to book a room in advance. When things are slow, the hotel owners meet the interisland boats in search of guests. If someone from the hotel of your choice isn't at the dock when you arrive, get on the blue *truck* marked Vaitape-Anau and ask to be taken there. This should cost CFP 500 pp from Farepiti Wharf, CFP 300 pp from Vaitape Wharf, plus CFP 100 for luggage. However, if you're staying at a luxury resort you could be charged CFP 1,800 pp return for airport transfers. A daily CFP 150 pp municipal services tax is collected at all accommodations.

The luxury hotels add an eight percent tax to their room rates (often not included in the quoted price) but most of the budget places include the tax in their price. Be aware that the hotels frequently tack a CFP 1,000 commission onto rental cars, lagoon excursions, and scuba diving booked through their front desks. Bora Bora suffers from serious water shortages, so use it sparingly, and protect yourself against theft from the room by locking up when you go out.

Budget

Backpackers often stay at **Chez Stellio** (B.P. 267, 98730 Vaitape; tel. 67-71-32), also known as "Camping Chez Henriette," at Anau on the east side of the island. The nine shared-bath rooms in a long tin-roofed block at CFP 4,000 double and two smaller rooms in a separate unit in the garden are CFP 5,000. A room with private bath is CFP 8,000. There's a refundable CFP 2,000 key deposit. To stay in a 10-bed dormitory next to the lagoon is CFP 1,500 pp, but a majority of guests pay CFP 1,000 pp to camp. Communal cooking facilities are provided (shortage of utensils). The nearest grocery stores are 2.5 km north (the second store you reach is the better) or opposite Motel Bora Bora at Matira. Although Chez Stellio is not on a natural beach it is right beside the lagoon and the

kitchen and picnic area are at the waterside. It's nice and breezy when the southeast trades are blowing. Stellio owns land on idyllic Motu Vaivahia and he's planning to build another 10 thatched bungalows over there, so ask. In any case, you can go over for the day by paying CFP 500 pp each way for boat transfers. Stellio has also built a Seventh-Day Adventist Church in the campground and interminable sermons are presented most evenings (no problem if you're sitting down by the shore). Yelping dogs take over at night followed by roosters in the morning, each adding their own flavor. Bring mosquito repellent. A neighbor rents bicycles at CFP 500 per half day (reserve ahead if possible). Stellio's own *le truck* runs from the campground into Vaitape twice a day, but let the staff know in advance if you're going as they often leave ahead of the scheduled departure time. It's a free ride for Stellio's guests. It's also possible to hike straight across the island to Pofai Bay. Go up the overgrown dirt road directly across the street from Stellio's. As you approach the ridge you'll see a Private Property sign and a house ahead on the left. Here cut straight up the hill to the right toward a radio transmitter from which a concrete road runs down to the west coast. As you disembark on Bora Bora look for Stellio's blue Vaitape-Anau *truck* with "Vaiho" on the door at the wharf or a green Land Rover marked Bora Safari Land. They'll give you a free ride to the camping ground when you first arrive, although upon departure everyone must pay CFP 300 pp for the transfer back to the wharf.

Inexpensive

Pension Au Lait de Coco (B.P. 626, 98730 Vaitape; tel. 67-61-48, fax 45-37-15) is between Magasin Chin Lee and the Total station on the north side of Vaitape, a 10-minute walk from the ferry wharf. It's in the village on the mountain side of the road near the landing for the Bora Bora Lagoon Resort. The two rooms with shared bath in this pleasant local house are CFP 6,000 single or double. The one room with private bath is CFP 7,500. Cooking facilities are provided, and there's

TAHITI TOURISME

a shaded porch and lounge in which to sit. The son of the family, Hinano, guides visitors up Mt. Pahia at CFP 4,000 pp (minimum of two).

CETAD (B.P. 151, 98730 Vaitape; tel. 67-71-47, fax 67-78-30), at the Collège de Bora Bora on the lagoon just north of Magasin Chin Lee in the center of Vaitape, rents a small five-bed bungalow with kitchenette and private bath at CFP 5,000 for the first person, plus CFP 1,000 for each additional person.

At the entrance to Pofai Bay three km south of Vaitape is **Blue Lagoon** (B.P. 467, 98730 Vaitape; tel./fax 67-65-64) with five rooms at CFP 6,000/10,000/13,000 single/double/triple. It's a lot to pay for a place without cooking facilities, with shared bath, and no beach.

At Nunue, right up below Otemanu's soaring peak is **Pension Chez Ato** (B.P. 49, 98730 Vaitape; tel. 67-77-27), a secluded little hideaway with five rooms at CFP 4,000 double. You can use a small kitchen to cook and Ato can arrange guides for mountain hikes at CFP 4,000 pp. Ato is a member of the environmental group *atu atu te natura* and he takes the concept of ecotourism seriously. He's also a defender of Polynesian tradition, and in 1987 and 1994 he organized firewalking rituals here, the first time this had happened in decades. Staying with Ato is a good way to experience a slice of old Tahitian life, so long as you don't mind being away from the beach. Look for a paved road running inland from opposite a large stone engraved Bora 2000 at the head of Pofai Bay and follow it right up to the end past a water pumping station (there's no sign).

Chez Rosina (B.P. 51, 98730 Vaitape; tel./fax 67-70-91), next to Honeymoon Boutique a few hundred meters north of Village Pauline on Pofai Bay, has four rooms at CFP 4,500/6,000 single/double with private bath and shared cooking facilities. Breakfast and transfers are included. Rosina is friendly and her place is less crowded and less touristy than Pauline's but there's no beach.

In 1997 **Village Pauline** (Pauline Youssef, B.P. 215, 98730 Vaitape; tel. 67-72-16, fax 67-78-14) moved from the white beach where the Hôtel Le Maitai Polynesia now stands to a hot interior location (no breeze, many mosquitos) on Pofai Bay. Despite the downgrade, prices went up and you'll now pay CFP 1,800 pp to camp (own tent), CFP 2,500 in the eight-bed dormitory, or CFP 6,000 single or double for a room with shared bath. The thatched bungalows are CFP 9,000. Children under 11 are free. Communal cooking facilities are provided for campers but don't leave too much in their fridge as things tend to disappear. Bicycles rent for CFP 500/800/1,000 for two/four/eight hours. These accommodations are grossly overpriced and not recommended.

Chez Reva Pension (tel. 67-78-09) is a small pension near Ben's Snack across the road from Matira Beach. The two rooms are CFP 5,000/6,000 single/double.

On the Matira Point peninsula are two excellent alternatives to the upmarket hotels. **Chez Nono** (Noël Leverd, B.P. 282, 98730 Vaitape; tel. 67-71-38, fax 67-74-27) faces the beach across from the Moana Beach Hôtel. They have one large bungalow with cooking facilities (CFP 10,000), two smaller bungalows with private bath (CFP 8,000), and a six-bedroom thatched guesthouse with shared kitchen at CFP 5,000/6,000 single/double per room. Ventilation spaces between the ceilings and walls mean you hear *everything* in the other rooms, but the atmosphere is amiable and all guests soon become good friends. Tahitians from other islands and local French often stay here. Their garden is a pleasant place to sit, but the bungalows occasionally experience a lot of noise from beach parties. The solar hot water heating only works when the sun is shining. Their boat tour around the island 0930-1600 includes shark feeding and an excellent fish lunch (CFP 5,000 including lunch).

Also good is **Chez Robert et Tina** (tel. 67-72-92), two European-style houses with cooking facilities down the road from Chez Nono at the tip of Matira Point (CFP 4,000/6,000 single/double). Robert offers excellent low-key lagoon trips at CFP 4,000 pp without lunch (the savings are passed on to you). You'll enjoy it more if you know a little French.

On the beach near the Moana Beach Parkroyal and just north of the junction to Matira Point is **Chez Maeva Masson** (Rosine Temauri-Masson, B.P. 33, 98730 Vaitape; tel. 67-72-04). There's no sign, but this large house has four rooms with shared bath at CFP 6,000 double, plus dorm beds at CFP 2,500 pp (CFP 1,000 pp surcharge for stays of only one night). Communal cooking facilities are provided and there's a picturesque lounge decorated with bright paintings by Rosine's late husband, the noted artist Jean Masson. It's one of the most colorful places to stay on the island, if you don't mind sharing the facilities.

Moderate

In Anau village to the north of Club Med is **Pension Chez Teipo** (B.P. 270, 98730 Vaitape; tel. 67-78-17, fax 67-73-24), also known as Pension Anau, with three neat little thatched bungalows by the lagoon at CFP 6,000/7,000/8,000 single/double/triple (children under 12 free). Cooking facilities are provided and it's a step up from Chez Stellio, a stone's throw away in the same village. There's no sign, so ask. Transfers are free.

Expensive

The colonial-style **Revatua Club** (B.P. 159, 98730 Vaitape; tel. 67-71-67, fax 67-76-59), on the northeast side of the island, has 16 rooms at CFP 8,900/10,400/11,700 single/double/triple, plus CFP 3,800 pp for breakfast and dinner. There's no beach but a salt-water swimming pool has been built out in the lagoon and you can snorkel off their dock. The overwater French restaurant/bar **L'Espadon** makes the most of the attractive location and the mock-Victorian architecture is right out of Hollywood. It's also isolated, and airport transfers are CFP 800 pp.

The **Yacht Club de Bora Bora** (B.P. 17, 98730 Vaitape; tel. 67-70-69), near Farepiti Wharf and opposite Te Ava Nui Pass, has two garden bungalows at CFP 9,000 for up to four persons and three overwater bungalows at CFP 10,000 double. No cooking facilities are provided and there's no beach. During the night you could be visited by mosquitoes and burglars. Cruising yachties may use the moorings, and fresh water and showers are provided. These services are free to cruisers who splash out in the outstanding seafood restaurant, otherwise they're CFP 2,500 per day per group, plus CFP 300 per shower (drinks at the bar are not good enough for free mooring). Yachties are asked not to carry bicycles through the restaurant. Beware of theft off yachts anywhere around this island.

Premium

Hôtel Matira (B.P. 31, 98730 Vaitape; tel. 67-70-51, fax 67-77-02) near Matira Point is one of the few medium-priced places offering cooking facilities. Their nine thatched bungalows with kitchenettes on the mountain side of the road are CFP 12,960/17,280 double/triple. The 16 deluxe thatched bungalows without kitchenettes in the annex right facing the lagoon at the neck of Matira Point peninsula are CFP 20,520/24,840 and up. The Matira's Chinese restaurant (closed Monday) is reasonable, and the beach is excellent. Airport transfers are CFP 1,000 pp return.

Motel Bora Bora (Jean Vanfau, B.P. 180, 98730 Vaitape; tel. 67-78-21, fax 67-77-57), on the main hotel strip across the street from Vairupe Villas, shares a white beach with the Sofitel Marara at Matira. Their four studios with bedroom, living room, dining room, kitchen, and fridge are CFP 13,000 double, while the three slightly larger apartments are CFP 17,000 double, extra persons CFP 3,000 each (children under 13 years CFP 1,500, under age six free). You'll probably have a great ocean view from your deck. These units built in 1991 are comfortable and spacious, a good compromise if you want to go upmarket while controlling expenditure. The cooking facilities make the motel ideal for families and there's a mini-market across the street. Transfers are CFP 1,500 pp return. Unfortunately mosquitos can be a real nuisance.

Next to the Hyatt Regency ruins at the north end of the island is **Bora Bora Condominiums** (B.P. 98, 98730 Vaitape; tel./fax 67-71-33) with 14 large thatched bungalows for rent. Those on the mountainside cost CFP 15,000 a day for up to five people, whereas the overwater bungalows are CFP 20,000. Each unit has a kitchen, living room, and private bath, and there's a communal laundry room on the premises. The monthly rates of CFP 150,000 and 200,000 respectively make this place interesting for anyone considering a long stay (and the absence of a restaurant indicates that you're expected to use your kitchen). It's a bit out of the way (and a favorite of visiting celebrities like Jack Nicholson and entourages).

Luxury

The Japanese-owned **Bora Bora Lagoon Resort** (B.P. 175, 98730 Vaitape; tel. 60-40-00, fax 60-40-01) is perched on Toopua Island opposite Vaitape. Opened in 1993, this place offers wonderful views of Mount Pahia, and the large swimming pool compensates for the average beach and shallow lagoon. The 12 garden bungalows are CFP 52,000/60,500 double/triple, the 16 beach bungalows CFP 55,000/63,500, the 50 overwater bungalows CFP 71,000/79,500, plus tax and another CFP 12,500 pp for all meals (it's forbidden to bring your own food and drink into the resort). Of course, few pay those outlandish prices as the vast majority of guests at all of the luxury resorts arrive on all-inclusive packages. Check-in time is 1500. Free activities include tennis, sailing, windsurfing, canoeing, pedal boating, the fitness center, and the launch to the main island.

Hôtel Bora Bora (B.P. 1, 98730 Vaitape; tel. 60-44-60, fax 60-44-66), which opened on a spectacular point in 1961, was the island's first large hotel. At CFP 70,000 single or double without meals for a deluxe overwater bungalow, it's one of the most exclusive millionaire's playgrounds in the South Pacific. Garden rooms in this ostentatious 55-unit resort begin at CFP 39,500 single or double, CFP 47,000 triple. Rather than pay CFP 65,000 for a rather poorly situated overwater bungalow, for the same price take one of the eight deluxe bungalows each with its own private swimming pool, but beware of noisy rooms near the road. Breakfast and dinner are CFP 7,200 pp extra. Their beach is superb and the hotel restaurant's cuisine exceptional.

Japanese-owned **Hôtel Moana Beach Parkroyal** (B.P. 156, 98730 Vaitape; tel. 60-49-00, fax 60-49-99), on a superb white-sand beach at Matira Point, opened in 1987. One of the 10 beachfront bungalows here will set you back CFP 49,800 single or double plus tax; the 41 posh overwater bungalows are CFP 63,800 (children under 14 free). It's CFP 6,800 pp extra for breakfast and dinner. We've had reports of unpleasant sewer smells around the overwater bungalows.

Hôtel Le Maitai Polynesia (B.P. 505, 98730 Vaitape; tel. 60-30-00, fax 67-66-03) is on the site of the former Camping Chez Pauline at Matira. In 1997 the backpackers were bumped from this piece of prime real estate and in 1998 a new three-story hotel was opened. The 28 a/c rooms in the main complex are CFP 21,900 single or double, CFP 27,990 triple, plus tax (children under 12 free). The six beach bungalows go for CFP 31,620, while the 11 overwater bungalows are CFP 39,180. Although the prices indicate otherwise, this place still has a budget feel. A hundred meters north and on the inland side of the road is **Vairupe Villas** which is under the same management. The 10 spacious thatched villas with kitchen and TV are CFP 29,460 for up to four people. Although the cooking facilities are useful, the villas are not on the beach and seem rather exorbitant compared to the places in the premium category above.

The **Bora Bora Beach Club** (B.P. 252, 98730 Nunue; tel. 67-71-16, fax 67-71-30), part of the Tahiti Resort Hotels chain, is between the Bora Bora Motel and the Sofitel Marara. The nine four-unit, single-roof blocks total 36 smallish rooms beginning at CFP 18,000 single, double, or triple (garden) or CFP 20,000 (beach) plus 8% tax—

about double what it should cost, and air conditioning is CFP 2,500 extra. Not all rooms have a fridge (check), and if your room is without a/c make sure your neighbors are in the same predicament, otherwise you could get the noise without the chill. There are no cooking facilities. In 1999 another 48 rooms were to be added to this hotel. Windsurfing, fishing, and snorkeling gear are loaned free to guests (that's why they call it a "club"). Airport transfers are CFP 1,750 pp return. The Beach Club generally gets unfavorable reviews from readers and it's only the high price that puts it in the "luxury" category.

Somehow the **Hôtel Sofitel Marara** (B.P. 6, 98730 Vaitape; tel. 67-70-46, fax 67-74-03) is less pretentious than most of the other luxury places. The Sofitel Marara (the name means "Flying Fish") was built in 1978 to house the crew filming Dino de Laurentiis's *Hurricane* (based on a novel by Nordhoff and Hall); the film flopped but the hotel has been going strong ever since. The 32 garden bungalows are CFP 30,000 single or double plus tax, the 11 beach bungalows CFP 39,000, and the 21 larger overwater units, arranged along the shore rather than far out in the lagoon, are CFP 50,000. This is less than what some of the other top-end hotels charge and you shouldn't expect quite the same degree of opulence. Still, it's open and informal, and instead of the Americans you hear at Hôtel Bora Bora and the Japanese you see at the Moana Beach, the Marara caters to an international mix of tourists. The beach doesn't have the policed feel of the Bora Bora's, and this is the only hotel on the main island with a swimming pool. The Marara's bar is fairly reasonable for such a swank place but the restaurant isn't highly rated (and the service is incredibly slow). Luckily there are lots of other restaurants nearby.

In late 1993 a 150-bungalow **Club Méditerranée** (B.P. 34, 98730 Vaitape; tel. 60-46-04, fax 60-46-11) opened on the southeast side of Bora Bora to replace an earlier Club Med north of Vaitape. The circuminsular road had to be rerouted around this US$30-million enclave just north of the Sofitel, and as usual, security is tight. You can't just stroll in and rent a room at Club Med, as only prepackaged guests are allowed to set foot on these sanctified premises, so book in advance at the Club Med office in Papeete's Vaima Center (tel. 42-96-99) or at any travel agency

(two-night minimum stay). The Bora Bora Club Med is more chic than the larger Club Med on Moorea, and as usual, lavish buffet meals and a range of nonmotorized nautical activities are included in the basic price. The gaudy orange and yellow bungalows go for CFP 19,000 pp in the garden or CFP 22,800 pp on the beach, double occupancy (singles can be matched with other same-sex singles). Some of the "oceanview" units are far from the water. Club Med is good value for Bora Bora when you consider how much you save on food. There's a dazzling beach and a canoe shuttle out to a fabulous snorkeling spot. Club's disco is the wildest nightspot on the island. For just a taste of paradise, the CFP 5,500 day pass includes a splendid lunch with drinks plus unlimited sporting activities and *motu* transfers. Unfortunately, bicycles are not available (Boutique Hibiscus on the hill behind the resort rents them).

In June 1998 **Le Méridien Bora Bora** (B.P. 190, 98730 Vaitape; tel. 60-51-51, fax 60-51-52) opened on a 10-km-long *motu* opposite Fitiuu Point on the east side of the island. The 85 thatched overwater bungalows are CFP 71,000 single or double plus tax, while the 15 beach bungalows are CFP 58,000 (children under 12 free). Add CFP 7,000/10,800 pp for two/three meals. All the usual sporting activities are offered including scuba diving (CFP 6,000). A day tour to Tupai Atoll is CFR 15,000 pp. When the wind is blowing in the wrong way you may get a whiff of the smoldering debris at the horrendous municipal dump on the north side of Fitiuu Point.

Also new is the **Hôtel Bora Bora Pearl Beach Resort** (tel. 43-90-04, fax 43-08-93), on Teveiroa Island between the airport and Vaitape, with 10 beach bungalows at CFP 42,000 double and 50 overwater bungalows at CFP 52,000 (third person CFP 4,000). Half/full pension is an extra CFP 6,200/8,500 pp. All units have a TV, fridge, jacuzzi, safe, and sundeck, and the meals received good reviews. There's a swimming pool, dive center, and a full range of activities, including a complimentary shuttle to Vaitape. The mini-cruiseship *Haumana* is owned by the same company.

As if to disprove the theory that Bora Bora is already overbuilt, Outrigger Hotels of Hawaii is to erect a 79-unit hotel with hillside and overwater bungalows on the site of the old Club Méditerranée near Vaitape.

FOOD

Vaitape

Pâtisserie-Bar Le Vaitape, across the street from the Banque de Polynésie in Vaitape, has reasonable beer prices and the *poisson cru* (CFP 700) is excellent, but they don't have it every day (ask). Their coffee is terrible.

Snack Michel (no phone; weekdays 0630-1600, Sunday 0730-1500, closed Saturday), opposite the college just north of Magasin Chin Lee, serves filling meals for CFP 700 (but no alcohol). Try the *ma'a tinito.* You eat at picnic tables behind a thatched roof. This good local place is a little hard to find as the sign is not visible from the street.

The **Restaurant Manuia** at the Collège de Bora Bora (tel. 67-71-47), just north of Magasin Chin Lee in Vaitape, is used to train students for employment at the large hotels. Since their aim is not profit, you can get a three-course meal for CFP 1,200 here, but only on Wednesday and Friday 1130-1330 during the school year (mid-January to June and August to mid-December). It's a nice change of pace and excellent value.

Cold Hinano beer is available for a reasonable price at the **Jeu Association Amical Tahitien Club** (tel. 43-48-63) next to Farepiti Wharf. You must consume your beer at one of their picnic tables as they don't want to lose any bottles. It's a good stop on your way around the island and the perfect place to sit and wait for your boat.

Pofai Bay

Bloody Mary's (closed Sunday; tel. 67-72-86) on Pofai Bay is the longest established non-hotel restaurant on the island with a tradition dating back to 1979. A board outside lists "famous guests," including Jane Fonda and Baron George Von Dangel. Other than pizza the lunch menu (available 1100-1500) includes fish and chips (CFP 900) and poisson cru (CFP 1,000). Upmarket seafood is served at dinner (1830-2100). For ambience, menu, service, and staff it's hard to beat. Free hotel pickups for diners are available at 1830 if you call ahead.

The **Bamboo House Restaurant** (tel. 67-76-24), next to Le Jardin Gauguin nearby, tries to challenge Bloody Mary's famous seafood but

doesn't quite succeed. In the South Pacific, one should get a slab of mahimahi, not cubes—those could be anything. It's also a bit cramped.

The **Blue Lagoon Restaurant** (tel. 67-65-64; daily 1000-0200), south of Vaitape by the lagoon at the entrance to Pofai Bay, offers things like pizza (CFP 1,000) and lobster (from CFP 1,500). Free hotel pickups are available.

Matira

Facing the beach just east of Hôtel Bora Bora are two reasonable places to eat. **Ben's Snack** (tel. 67-74-54) manages to turn out surprisingly good home-cooked pizza (CFP 1,000), lasagna, pasta, and omelettes, and the colorful American-Tahitian owners, Robin and Ben, add a Bohemian air to the place. Lunch here would be a great change of pace if you're staying at one of the fancy resorts. **Snack Matira** (tel. 67-77-32; closed Monday), across the street and a bit east, offers hamburgers and *poisson cru* for slightly lower prices.

Snack-Restaurant Le Temanuata (tel. 67-75-61), near the turnoff to the Moana Beach Parkroyal, offers meats, seafood, fish, and Chinese dishes. The dinner menu is expensive so you might come for lunch (1200-1430).

Snack Kaina Beach serves hamburgers and various types of fish including *poisson cru* in their garden between the Moana Beach and Sofitel (daily until 2200).

In 1995 **Restaurant Le Tiare** (tel. 67-61-39) opened across the street from the Bora Bora Motel. In the evening the tables are all taken, which perhaps says something about the restaurants in the nearby Bora Bora Beach Club and Sofitel Marara. You've a choice of pasta, meat, fish, lobster, and other seafood.

Groceries

Bora Bora's largest supermarket is **Magasin Chin Lee** (tel. 67-63-07; open Mon.-Sat. 0500-1800), opposite the island's Mobil gas station north of Vaitape Wharf. Takeaway meals at the checkout counters are CFP 500. It and another well-stocked grocery store in Vaitape are open Mon.-Sat. 0500-1800. The Total service station is farther north.

Tiare Market (tel. 67-61-38; daily 0630-1300/1500-1830), opposite Motel Bora Bora at Matira, is very well stocked with a good wine section and even some fresh vegetables. It's always crowded with tourists from the upmarket hotels.

Other places to buy groceries are the two general stores (closed Sunday) at Anau, halfway around the island, and a small grocery store at the head of Pofai Bay. A grocery truck passes Matira between 1000 and 1100 daily except Sunday.

The **Pofai Shoppe** on the road near Hôtel Bora Bora sells cold fruit drinks and takeaway beer at normal prices (open daily).

ENTERTAINMENT AND EVENTS

Disco
Le Récife Bar (B.P. 278, 98730 Vaitape; tel. 67-73-87), between Vaitape and Farepiti Wharf, is Bora Bora's after-hours club, open Friday and Saturday from 2230. Disco dancing continues almost until dawn, but expect loud, heavy-on-the-beat music with few patrons. Steer clear of the local drunks hanging around outside who can't afford the CFP 500 cover charge.

Cultural Shows for Visitors
To see Polynesian dancing on the beach at **Hôtel Bora Bora** (tel. 60-44-60) grab a barside seat before it starts at 2030 on Wednesday and Sunday nights (buffet CFP 5,500).

Additional Tahitian dancing occurs after dinner Tuesday, Thursday, and Saturday nights at 2030 at the **Moana Beach Parkroyal** (tel. 60-49-00).

Another Tahitian dance show takes place at the **Hôtel Sofitel Marara** (tel. 67-74-01) every Tuesday, Friday, and Saturday night at 2030; see it all for the price of a draft beer. On Saturday at 1830 they open the earth oven and a Tahitian feast begins.

Events
The **Fêtes de Juillet** are celebrated at Bora Bora with special fervor. The canoe and bicycle races, javelin throwing, flower cars, singing, and dancing competitions run until 0300 nightly. A public ball goes till dawn on the Saturday closest to 14 July. Try to participate in the 10-km foot race to prove that all tourists aren't lazy, but don't take the prizes away from the locals. If you win, be sure to give the money back to them for partying. You'll make good friends that way and have more fun dancing in the evening. The stands are beautiful because the top decorations win prizes, too.

SHOPPING AND SERVICES

Shopping
Plenty of small boutiques around Vaitape sell black coral jewelry, pearls, pareus, T-shirts, designer beachwear, etc. The **Centre Artisanal** near Vaitape Wharf is a good place to buy a shell necklace or a pareu directly from the locals.

A cluster of shops on Pofai Bay offers some of Bora Bora's best tourist shopping. **Boutique Gauguin** (tel. 67-76-67) has tropical clothing, T-shirts, souvenirs, and jewelry. Next door is an upmarket black pearl showroom called **O.P.E.C.** (tel. 67-61-62) where numbered black pearls complete with X-ray and certificate go for US$400-900. The pearls can be set in gold as earrings or necklaces in one day. A full pearl necklace will cost US$12,000—the gift of a lifetime. Alongside O.P.E.C. is **Art du Pacifique** (tel. 67-63-85) with a display of woodcarvings from the Marquesas Islands, and behind it is another shop selling shell jewelry and photographic supplies. These shops surround a small garden called *Le Jardin Gauguin* with a series of tacky plaster sculptures of scenes from Gauguin's paintings. A few hundred meters south of here is **Honeymoon Boutique** (tel. 67-78-19) with more clothing, jewelry, and souvenirs.

At photographer Erwin Christian's **Moana Art Boutique** (tel. 67-70-33) just north of Hôtel Bora Bora you can buy striking postcards and other souvenirs. **Martine's Créations** (tel. 67-70-79) east of Hôtel Bora Bora has finely crafted black-pearl jewelry and designer beachwear.

Services and Information
The four main banks all have offices near Vaitape Wharf, but none are open on Saturday (open weekdays 0730-1130/1330-1600). Many yachties "check out" of Tahiti-Polynesia at Bora Bora and reclaim their bond or *caution* at these banks. It's wise to check a few days ahead to make sure they'll have your cash or traveler's checks ready.

The post office (Monday 0800-1500, Tues.-Fri. 0730-1500, Saturday 0800-1000), *gendarmerie* (tel. 67-70-58), and health clinic *(Santé Publique)* are within a stone's throw of the wharf.

The helpful tourist information office (B.P. 144, 98730 Vaitape; tel./fax 67-76-36; weekdays 0730-1200, Saturday 0800-1130) and public toilets are in the Centre Artisanal next to Vaitape Wharf. The **Air Tahiti** office (tel. 67-70-35) is beside the Banque de Tahiti on Vaitape Wharf.

Health

The private Cabinet Médical (tel. 67-70-62) behind the Banque de Polynésie is open weekdays 0700-1200 and 1500-1800, Saturday 0700-1200.

Dr. François Macouin's Cabinet Dentaire (tel. 67-70-55; weekdays 0730-01130/1600-1800, Saturday 0730-1130) is in the Centre Commercial Le Pahia opposite Magasin Chin Lee and the large Protestant church.

Pharmacie Fare Ra'au (tel. 67-70-30; weekdays 0800-1200/1530-1800, Saturday 0800-1200/1700-1800, Sunday 0900-0930) is north of the wharf.

TRANSPORTATION

Getting There

Air Tahiti (tel. 67-70-35) has a useful transversal flight direct from Bora Bora to Rangiroa (CFP 20,700) and Manihi (CFP 23,400) three times a week. For information on flights to Bora Bora from Papeete, Huahine, and Raiatea, see the introduction to Tahiti-Polynesia.

The high-speed cruiser *Ono-Ono* (tel./fax 68-85-85), with an office at Farepiti Wharf, departs Bora Bora for Taha'a (one hour, CFP 1,333), Raiatea (two hours, CFP 1,778), Huahine (3.5 hours, CFP 3,111), and Papeete (seven hours, CFP 6,610) on Tuesday and Thursday at 0700, Sunday at 1200. On Saturday there's a trip to Taha'a, Raiatea, and Huahine alone at 0800. Consider calling to check the schedule the afternoon before, as departures are often abruptly canceled.

Ships from Raiatea and Papeete tie up at Farepiti Wharf, three km north of Vaitape. The shipping companies have no representatives on Bora Bora, so for departure times just keep asking. Drivers of the *trucks* are the most likely to know. You buy your ticket when the ship arrives. Officially the *Taporo VI* leaves for Raiatea, Huahine, and Papeete on Tuesday, Thursday, and Saturday at 1130. The *Vaeanu* departs Bora Bora for Raiatea, Huahine, and Papeete Tuesday at 1030, Thursday at noon, and Sunday at 0900. The *Raromatai Ferry* leaves for Taha'a, Raiatea, Huahine, and Papeete Wednesday at 1000 and Sunday at 1400. Beware of ships leaving early.

A fast yellow-and-blue passenger ferry, the *Maupiti Express* (tel./fax 67-66-69), departs Vaitape Wharf for Maupiti, Taha'a, and Raiatea. It leaves for Maupiti on Thursday and Saturday at 0830 (CFP 3,000), for Taha'a and Raiatea on Wednesday and Friday at 0700 (CFP 2,500). Tickets are sold on board.

Getting Around

Getting around is a bit of a headache, as *le truck* service is irregular and at lunchtime everything stops. Public *trucks* usually meet the boats, but many of the *trucks* you see around town are strictly for guests of the luxury hotels. If you do

Mount Otemanu, Bora Bora

find one willing to take you, fares between Vaitape and Matira vary from CFP 300-500, plus CFP 100 for luggage. Taxi fares are high, so check before getting in. If you rent a bicycle, keep an eye on it when you stop to visit sights.

Farepiti Rentacar (B.P. 53, 98730 Vaitape; tel. 67-71-58, fax 67-65-29), opposite Farepiti Wharf, has cars from CFP 4,500/5,500/6,500/7,500 for two/four/eight/24 hours with unlimited kms. Scooters are CFP 2,500/3,500/4,500/5,000 (CFP 3,000 deposit—no license required). Bicycles cost CFP 500/800/1,000/1,500. Third party insurance is included with the cars but collision insurance is not available. They can deliver cars to any hotel.

Europcar (tel. 67-70-15, fax 67-79-95; daily 0730-1800), next to the *gendarmerie* opposite Vaitape Wharf and with desks at 15 hotels around the island, has Fiats at CFP 6,000 for a 0800-1700 day, CFP 7,000 for 24 hours. The price includes insurance and unlimited km; a valid driver's license is required. They also have motor scooters for CFP 5,000 0800-1700 or CFP 5,500 for 24 hours (license required). Two-seater "fun cars" are CFP 4,500 for four hours and no helmet or driver's licence is required.

Avis (B.P. 99, 98730 Vaitape; tel. 67-70-31, fax 67-62-07), on the inland side of the road south of Vaitape (where you see a lot of long blue trucks parked), is also known as Fredo Rent a Car. Cars/scooters/bicycles are available at CFP 6,800/5,500/1,500 for eight hours.

Mataura Rent-A-Bike (tel. 67-73-16) just south of Vaitape rents bicycles (if you can find anyone around). At **Chez Pauline** bicycles are CFP 800 half day, CFP 1,000 full day.

Taahana Tourisme (tel. 67-64-04, fax 67-64-44), almost opposite the Sofitel Marara, rents scooters at CFP 2,500/3,500/4,500/5,000 for two/four/eight/24 hours and bicycles at CFP 500/800/1,000 two/four/eight hours. They also have jet skis, motor boats, and pedal boats.

Boutique Hibiscus (tel. 67-72-43), on the hill behind Club Med, rents well-maintained bicycles with baskets at CFP 400/600/800/1,000 for two/four/eight/24 hours. (Their T-shirts and pareus are also good value.)

If you rent a car and drive at night, watch out for scooters and bicycles without lights. However, to better enjoy the scenery and avoid disturbing the environment, we suggest you dispense with motorized transport here. Little Bora Bora is perfect for cycling as there's an excellent paved road right around the island (with only one unpaved stretch on the incline at Fitiuu Point), almost no hills, and lots of scenic bays to shelter you from the wind. Do exercise caution with fast-moving vehicles between Vaitape and Matira Point, however.

Land Tours

Otemanu Tours (tel. 67-70-49), just north of Vaitape, offers a two-and-a-half-hour minibus tour around Bora Bora daily except Sunday at 1400 (CFP 2,000). **Jeep Safaris** (tel. 67-70-34) and **Tupuna 4WD Expeditions** (tel. 67-75-06) offer Land Rover tours up a steep ridge opposite Otemanu at CFP 5,500. You can book these and many other activities through **Taahana Tourisme** (tel. 67-64-04, fax 67-64-44), almost opposite the Sofitel Marara.

Day Cruises

Like Aitutaki in the Cook Islands, Bora Bora is famous for its lagoon trips. Prices vary depending on whether lunch is included, the length of the trip, the luxury of boat, etc., so check around. A seafood picnic lunch on a *motu,* reef walking, and snorkeling gear are usually included, and you get a chance to see giant clams, manta rays, and shark feeding. For the latter you don a mask and snorkel, jump into the shark-infested waters, and grasp a line as your guide shoves chunks of fish at a school of generally innocuous reef sharks in feeding frenzy. It's an encounter with the wild you'll never forget. See the Chez Nono and Chez Robert accommodations listings for two possibilities. Motorized canoe trips right around Bora Bora are also offered. An excursion of this kind is an essential part of the Bora Bora experience, so splurge on this one. (Several readers have written in to say they agree completely.)

Taahana Tourisme (tel. 67-64-04, fax 67-64-44), almost opposite the Sofitel Marara, operates a circle-island boat tour lasting 0900-1630 daily. The CFP 5,300 price includes a barbecue lunch, snorkeling with sting rays, and shark feeding. Half day boat trips are CFP 3,500. The same company also organizes catamaran cruises, one-day yacht charters, and deep-sea fishing.

Three-hour tours to the so-called **Bora Lagoonarium** (B.P. 56, 98730 Vaitape; tel. 67-71-34, fax 67-60-29) on a *motu* off the main island occur daily except Saturday at 0900 or 1400 (CFP 4,000). You'll see more colorful fish than you ever thought existed. Call for a free hotel pickup.

The activities people at the Sofitel Marara will ferry non-guests over to a *motu* for a day of snorkeling at CFP 1,500 return (take food, water, and sunscreen).

René et Maguy Boat Rental (B.P. 196, 98730 Vaitape; tel. 67-60-61, fax 67-61-01), next to Le Tiare Restaurant at Matira, rents small boats with motor at CFP 4,500/5,500/6,500/9,500 two hours/three hours/half day/full day. Pedal boats are CFP 3,500 for two hours, plus CFP 1,500 each for additional hours. *Motu* transfers are CFP 1,500 pp return. Free hotel pickups are available if you call.

Airport

Bora Bora's vast airfield (BOB) on Motu Mute north of the main island was built by the Americans during WW II. The first commercial flight from Paris to Tahiti-Polynesia landed here in October 1958, and until March 1961 all international flights used this airstrip; passengers were then transferred to Papeete by Catalina amphibious or Bermuda flying boat seaplanes. Today, a 25-minute catamaran ride brings arriving air passengers to Vaitape Wharf (included in the plane ticket).

When the catamaran from the airport arrives at Vaitape Wharf, all of the luxury hotels will have guest transportation waiting, but the budget places don't always meet the flights (the deluxe places don't bother meeting the interisland boats). As you arrive at the wharf, shout out the name of your hotel and you'll be directed to the right *truck* (they don't have destination signs).

The airport cafe serves a very good cup of coffee.

If you're flying to Bora Bora from Papeete go early in the morning and sit on the left side of the aircraft for spectacular views—it's only from the air that Bora Bora is the most beautiful island in the world!

M.G.L. DOMENY DE RIENZI

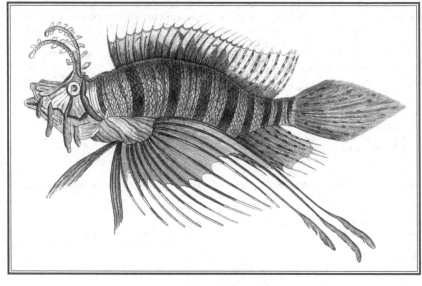

M.G.L. DOMÉNY DE RIENZI

MAUPITI

Majestic Maupiti (Maurua), 44 km west of Bora Bora, is the least known of the accessible Society Islands. Maupiti's mighty volcanic plug soars above a sapphire lagoon, and the vegetation-draped cliffs complement the magnificent *motu* beaches. Almost every bit of level land on the main island is taken up by fruit trees, while watermelons thrive on the surrounding *motu.* Maupiti abounds in native seabirds, including frigate birds, terns, and others. The absence of Indian mynahs allows you to see native land birds that are almost extinct elsewhere.

The 1,125 people live in the adjacent villages of Vai'ea, Farauru, and Pauma. Tourism is not promoted because there aren't any regular hotels, which is a big advantage! It's sort of like Bora Bora was 25 years ago before being "discovered" by the world of package tourism. Maupiti was once famous for its black basalt stone pounders and fishhooks made from the seven local varieties of mother-of-pearl shell. In late November 1997 Hurricane Oséa devastated Maupiti.

Sights

It takes only three hours to walk right around this 11-square-km island. The nine-km crushed-coral road, lined with breadfruit, mango, banana, and hibiscus, passes crumbling *marae,* freshwater springs, and a beach.

Marae Vaiahu, by the shore a few hundred meters beyond Hotuparaoa Massif, is the largest *marae.* Once a royal landing place opposite the pass into the lagoon, the *marae* still bears the king's throne and ancient burials. Nearby is the sorcerers' rock: light a fire beside this rock and you will die. Above the road are a few smaller *marae.*

Terei'a Beach, at the west tip of Maupiti, is the only good beach on the main island. At low tide you can wade across from Terei'a to Motu Auira in waist-deep water. **Marae Vaiorie** is a double *marae* with freshwater springs in between. As many as two dozen large *marae* are hidden in Maupiti's mountainous interior, and the island is known for its ghosts.

It's possible to climb to the 380-meter summit of Maupiti from the 42-meter-high saddle where the road cuts across Terei'a Point. You follow the ridge all the way to the top and the whole trip shouldn't take over three hours return.

PRACTICALITIES

Accommodations

Several of the inhabitants are willing to take paying guests, and they usually meet the flights and boats in search of clients. The absence of a regular hotel on Maupiti throws together an odd mix of vacationing French couples, backpackers, and "adventuresome" tourists in the guesthouses (none of which have signs). Agree on the price beforehand and check your bill when you leave. You could camp on the white sands of Terei'a Beach, but water and *no-nos* (insects) would be a problem. If you're set on camping, get across to the airport *motu,* hike south, and look for a campsite there—you'll have to befriend someone to obtain water. Otherwise check with Pension Auira, which allows camping on their grounds. Like Bora Bora, Maupiti experiences serious water shortages during the dry season.

Chez Mareta (Mareta and Anua Tinorua, tel. 67-80-25), in the center of Vai'ea village, is the house with the sloping blue roof a few minutes' walk from the *mairie.* They offer mattresses on the floor in the upstairs double rooms for CFP 1,000 pp. You can cook your own food or pay CFP 3,000 pp for breakfast and dinner. An agreeable sitting room faces the lagoon downstairs. Upon request, they'll drop you on a *motu* for the day (beware of sunburn). Chez Mareta is okay for a couple of days, but not an extended stay. The church choir in the next building practices their singing quite loudly each night.

Next door to Chez Mareta is **Chez Floriette Tuheiava** (B.P. 43, 98732 Maupiti; tel. 67-80-85), an island-style house with four pleasant shared-bath rooms at CFP 5,000/7,800 single/double including breakfast, dinner, activities, and airport transfers. Other places of the same type include **Pension Eri** (Eri Mohi, tel. 67-81-29), south of Chez Floriette, with four rooms in a separate house at CFP 4,500 pp with breakfast and dinner, and **Pension Marau** (Tino and Marau Tehahe, tel. 67-81-19), on the hillside

north of the *mairie,* with three rooms at CFP 4,500 pp including half board and transfers.

Pension Tamati (Ferdinand and Etu Tapuhiro, tel. 67-80-10), a two-story building at the south end of Vai'ea, rents eight bleak rooms at CFP 2,000 pp with breakfast or CFP 4,000 pp with half board. Unfortunately, tourists are usually given the inside rooms without proper ventilation, but communal cooking facilities are available.

Fare Pae'ao (Janine Tavaearii, B.P. 33, 98732 Maupiti; tel./fax 67-81-01) on Motu Pae'ao is quiet and offers a superb white beach with some of the finest snorkeling on Maupiti. The three thatched bungalows with bath are CFP 6,000 single or double, CFP 7,500 triple. Meals cost CFP 3,000/5,000 pp for two/three meals (children under 13 half price). Reservations are required to ensure an airport pickup (CFP 1,000 pp roundtrip for everyone over the age of three). (In 1962 Kenneth Emory and Yosihiko Sinoto excavated a prehistoric cemetery on Pae'ao and found 15 adzes of six different types, providing valuable evidence for the study of Polynesian migrations.)

Pension Auira (Edna Terai and Richard Tefaatau, B.P. 2, 98732 Maupiti; tel./fax 67-80-26) on Motu Auira, the *motu* opposite Terei'a Beach, has seven thatched bungalows with private bath. The garden variety are CFP 6,000 pp a day including breakfast and dinner; the better quality beach bungalows are CFP 7,000 pp. At those prices you'd expect fans in the rooms, reading lights, beach furniture, and nautical activities, but no such luck. Camping is CFP 1,000 pp. The food is good but the beach could use a cleaning. Boat transfers from the airport are CFP 2,000 pp return. In sum, Pension Auira is a wonderful experience, but not for everyone.

In addition, there are two small resorts on Motu Tiapa'a, one of the islands framing Onoiau Pass. **Pension Papahani** (Vilna Tuheiava, B.P. 1, 98732 Maupiti; tel. 67-81-58, fax 67-80-11) has a four-room house with shared bath at CFP 5,000 pp and two thatched bungalows with private bath at CFP 6,500 pp, both including breakfast and dinner. Excursions and return airport transfers are CFP 2,000 pp. The four *fare* with bath at the **Kuriri Village** (Gérard Bede, B.P. 23, 98732 Maupiti; no phone; fax 67-82-00), also on Tiapa'a, are Maupiti's most expensive at CFP 10,000/12,000 pp with half/full board, transfers included.

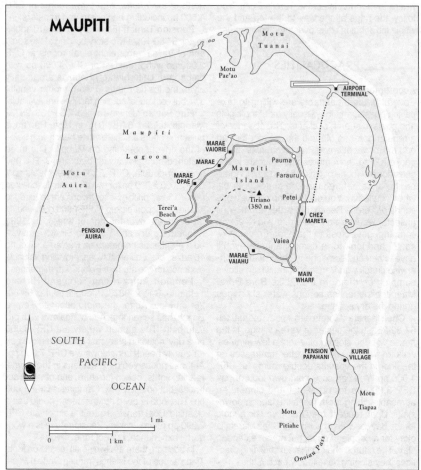

MAUPITI

Motu Tuanai

Motu Pae'ao

AIRPORT TERMINAL

Maupiti Lagoon

MARAE VAIORIE

MARAE

MARAE OPAE

Pauma

Farauru

Maupiti Island

Petei

CHEZ MARETA

Tiriano (380 m)

Terei'a Beach

Motu Auira

PENSION AUIRA

Vaiea

MARAE VAIAHU

MAIN WHARF

SOUTH

PACIFIC

OCEAN

0   1 mi
0   1 km

PENSION PAPAHANI

KURIRI VILLAGE

Motu Tiapaa

Motu Pitiahe

Onoiau Pass

© DAVID STANLEY

Services

Banque Socredo (tel. 67-81-95) has a branch on Maupiti, but it's not always operating, so change beforehand and don't count on using your credit cards. The post office and *mairie* are nearby. The bakery is in the power plant on the edge of town. It's important to check when the baguettes come out of the oven and to be punctual, as they sell out fast. The island youths come here an hour before and hang around waiting. Not all stores sell beer and the island's supply does run out at times.

Getting There

Maupiti's airport (MAU) is on a small *motu* and you must take a launch to the main island (CFP 400 pp). **Air Tahiti** has flights to Maupiti from Raiatea (CFP 5,600 one-way) and Papeete (CFP 12,700) three times a week, from Bora Bora twice a week (CFP 5,300). Reconfirm with the Air Tahiti agent (tel. 67-80-20) near the *mairie*.

The 62-seat fast ferry *Maupiti Express* arrives from Bora Bora (CFP 3,000 each way) on Thursday and Saturday mornings, returning to Bora Bora the same afternoon.

The government supply barges *Meherio III* or *Maupiti Tou Ai'a* depart Papeete for Raiatea and Maupiti Wednesday at 1900, departing Maupiti for the return Friday at 0800. Deck fares from Maupiti are CFP 1,058/2,221 to Raiatea/Papeete. See the Tahiti-Polynesia introduction for more information.

Ships must enter the channel during daylight, thus the compulsory morning arrival, and the boat usually returns to Raiatea from Maupiti on the afternoon of the same day. Onoiau Pass into Maupiti is narrow, and when there's a strong southerly wind it can be dangerous—boats have had to turn back. At low tide a strong current flows out through this pass and the optimum time for a yacht to enter is around noon.

OTHER LEEWARD ISLANDS

Tupai

Tupai or Motu Iti (Small Island), 13 km north of Bora Bora, is a tiny coral atoll measuring 1,100 hectares. The facing horseshoe-shaped *motu* enclose a lagoon that small boats can enter through a pass on the east side. A small airstrip is in the northwest corner of the atoll. In 1860 the king of Bora Bora gave the atoll to a planter named Stackett and for decades a few dozen people were employed to make copra from coconuts off the 155,000 trees on Tupai. In 1997 the territorial government bought Tupai from its last owner, a Mr. Lejeune, for US$8 million with an eye to resort development. Although there are no permanent inhabitants at the moment, the 1,000 traditional landowners are contesting the title.

Maupihaa

Tiny 360-hectare Maupihaa (Mopelia), 185 km southeast of Maupiti, is the only Society Islands atoll that can be entered by yachts but to attempt to do so in stormy weather is dangerous. Narrow, unmarked Taihaaru Vahine Pass on Maupihaa's northwest side can only be found by searching for the strong outflow of lagoon water at low tide. Despite this, cruising yachts traveling between Bora Bora and Cook Islands or Samoa often anchor in the atoll's lagoon. About 50 people from Maupiti live on Maupihaa.

In July 1917 the notorious German raider *Seeadler* was wrecked at Maupihaa after capturing 15 Allied ships. The three-masted schooner was too large to enter lagoon, and while being careened outside the pass, a freak wave picked the vessel up and threw it onto the reef. Eventually the ship's chivalrous captain, Count Felix von Luckner, was able to carry on to Fiji in a small boat, where he was captured at Wakaya Island. Count von Luckner's journal, *The Sea Devil,* became a best-seller after the war.

In 1983 the pro-independence Pomare Party filed claim to Maupihaa on the ancestral rights

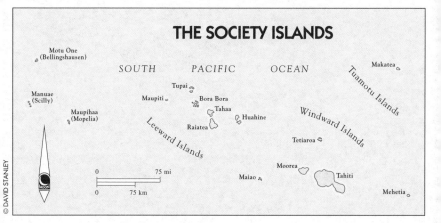

THE SOCIETY ISLANDS

Motu One
(Bellingshausen)

SOUTH   PACIFIC   OCEAN

Makatea

Tuamotu Islands

Tupai

Manuae
(Scilly)

Maupiti   Bora Bora

Maupihaa
(Mopelia)   Tahaa

Huahine

Windward Islands

Leeward Islands   Raiatea

Tetiaroa

Moorea

Maiao   Tahiti

0   75 mi

0   75 km

Mehetia

© DAVID STANLEY

of their leader, Joinville Pomare, a descendent of Queen Pomare IV. Party members occupied the atoll, and declared it and neighboring Manuae and Motu One to be an independent state. On Maupihaa they established a successful operation to supply oysters to black pearl farms in the Tuamotus. In 1991 the French colonial government took advantage of the chance to play one group of Polynesians against another by granting land concessions on Maupihaa to the Maupiti people, and on 5 September 1992 the eight Pomare oyster farmers were evicted from the atoll by 40 French *gendarmes* backed by a helicopter and a frigate. A day later settlers from Maupiti arrived on Maupihaa with the blessing of the French and took over the Pomare's oyster nursery.

Sea turtles come to Maupihaa to lay their eggs only to be illegally butchered for their flesh by poachers. Large numbers of terns, boobies, and frigate birds nest on the small *motu* and seabird fledglings are slaughtered for their meager meat or the unhatched eggs collected according to need. All this is supposed to be prohibited but it's hard to control what goes on in such an isolated place. (In August 1996, the municipal boat *Maupiti Tou Ai'a* was seized with a cargo of 1,500 kilos of turtle meat on board. At the trial 10 months later, the captain and 30 others were fined and each given a one-month suspended sentence over the affair.)

Manuae

Manuae (Scilly), 75 km northwest of Maupihaa, is the westernmost of the Society Islands. This atoll is 15 km in diameter but totals only 400 hectares. Pearl divers once visited Manuae. In 1855 the three-masted schooner *Julia Ann* sank on the Manuae reef. It took the survivors two months to build a small boat, which carried them to safety at Raiatea.

Motu One

Motu One (Bellingshausen), 65 km north of Manuae, got its second name from the Russian explorer Thadeus von Bellingshausen who visited Tahiti in 1820. Tiny 280-hectare Motu One is circled by a guano-bearing reef, with no pass into the lagoon. Of the 10 persons present on Motu One when Hurricane Martin swept through in November 1997, the sole survivor was a woman named Alice Haano who tied herself to a coconut tree.

M.G.L. DOMENY DE RIENZI

THE AUSTRAL ISLANDS

The inhabited volcanic islands of Rimatara, Rurutu, Tubuai, Raivavae, and Rapa, plus uninhabited Maria (or Hull) atoll, make up the Austral group. This southernmost island chain in the South Pacific is a 1,280-km extension of the same submerged mountain range as the southern Cook Islands, 900 km northwest. The islands of the Australs seldom exceed 300 meters, except Rapa, which soars to 650 meters. The southerly location makes these islands notably cooler and drier than Tahiti. Collectively the Australs are known as Tuhaa Pae, the "Fifth Part" or fifth administrative subdivision of Tahiti-Polynesia. It's still a world apart from tourism.

History
Excavations carried out on the northwest coast of Rurutu uncovered 60 round-ended houses arranged in parallel rows, with 14 *marae* scattered among them, demonstrating the presence of humans here as early as A.D. 900. Ruins of *marae* can also be seen on Rimatara, Tubuai,

and Raivavae. Huge stone tikis once graced Raivavae, but most have since been destroyed or removed. The terraced mountain fortifications, or *pa,* on Rapa are unique.

The Australs were one of the great art areas of the Pacific, represented today in many museums. The best-known artifacts are sculpted sharkskin drums, wooden bowls, fly whisks, and tapa cloth. Offerings that could not be touched by human hands were placed on the sacred altars with intricately incised ceremonial ladles. European contact effaced most of these traditions and the carving done today is crude by comparison.

Rurutu was spotted by Capt. James Cook in 1769; he found Tubuai in 1777. In 1789 Fletcher Christian and the *Bounty* mutineers attempted to establish a settlement at the northeast corner of Tubuai. They left after only three months, following battles with the islanders in which 66 Polynesians died. The European discoverer of Rapa was Capt. George Vancouver in 1791. Rimatara wasn't contacted until 1813, by the Australian captain Michael Fodger.

English missionaries converted most of the people to Protestantism in the early 19th century. Whalers and sandalwood ships introduced diseases and firearms, which decimated the Austral islanders. The French didn't complete their annexation of the group until 1901. Since then the Australs have gone their sleepy way.

The People

The 6,500 mostly Polynesian inhabitants are fishermen and farmers who live in attractive villages with homes and churches built of coral limestone. The rich soil and moderate climate stimulate agriculture with staple crops such as taro, manioc, Irish potatoes, sweet potatoes, leeks, cabbage, carrots, corn, and coffee. The coconut palm also thrives, except on Rapa. Today many Austral people live in Papeete.

Getting There

Air Tahiti has four flights a week to Rurutu and Tubuai, the only islands with airports. Two operate Papeete-Tubuai-Rurutu-Papeete, the other two Papeete-Rurutu-Tubuai-Papeete. One-way fares from Tahiti are CFP 17,700 to Rurutu and CFP 19,800 to Tubuai. Rurutu-Tubuai is CFP 8,300.

All the other Austral Islands are accessible only by boat. For information on the twice-monthly sailings of the *Tuhaa Pae II* from Papeete, see the introduction to Tahiti-Polynesia.

RURUTU

This island, 572 km south of Tahiti, is shaped like a miniature replica of the African continent. For the hiker, 32-square-km Rurutu is a more varied island to visit than Tubuai. Grassy, fern-covered Taatioe (389 meters) and Manureva (384 meters) are the highest peaks and coastal cliffs on the southeast side of the island drop 60 meters to the sea. A narrow fringing reef surrounds Rurutu, but there's no lagoon. The climate of this northernmost Austral island is temperate and dry. The recent history of Rurutu revolves around four important dates: 1821, when the gospel arrived on the island; 1889, when France declared a protectorate over the island; 1970, when Cyclone Emma devastated the three villages; and 1975, when the airport opened.

In January and July Rurutuans practice the ancient art of stone lifting or *amoraa ofai*. Men get three tries to hoist a 150-kg boulder coated with *monoï* (coconut oil) up onto their shoulders, while women attempt a 60-kg stone. Dancing and feasting follow the event. The women of Rurutu weave fine pandanus hats, bags, baskets, fans, lamp shades, and mats. A fine handicraft display is laid out for departing passengers. Rurutu's famous Manureva (Soaring Bird) Dance Group has performed around the world. The main evening entertainment is watching dancers practice in the villages.

Orientation

The pleasant main village, Moerai, boasts a post office, medical center, four small stores, two bakeries, and a bank. Two other villages, Avera and Hauti, bring the total island population to about 2,000. Neat fences and flower gardens surround the coral limestone houses. This is the Polynesia of 50 years ago: though snack bars have appeared and electricity functions 24 hours a day, there's almost none of the tourism development you see in the Society Islands nor the pearl farms common in the Tuamotus.

Public transportation is also lacking on the 36-km road around Rurutu, and even by bicycle it can be quite an effort to circle the island as the route climbs away from the coast on four occasions to avoid high cliffs. South of Avera the road reaches 190 meters, dropping back down to sea level at the southern tip, then rising again to 124 meters on the way up to Hauti. The direct road from Moerai to Avera also climbs to 168 meters. For hikers a three-km foot trail across the center of the island between Avera and Hauti makes a variety of itineraries possible. Beaches, waterfalls, valleys, bluffs, and limestone caves beckon the undaunted explorer.

One of the nicest spots is near **Toataratara Point** where a side road cuts back up the east coast to a *marae* and a few small beaches. It's quite easy to hike to the TV tower on the summit

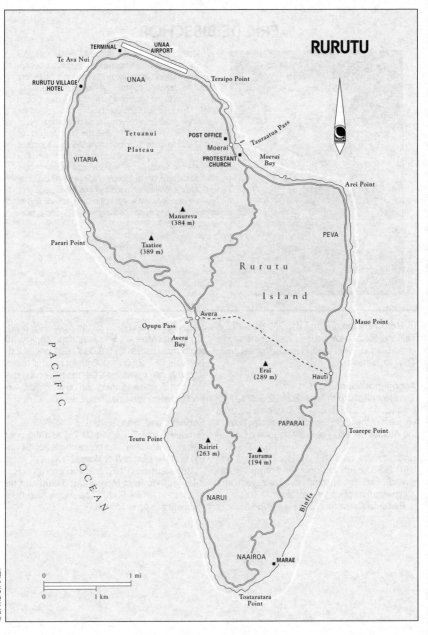

RURUTU

TERMINAL

UNAA AIRPORT

Te Ava Nui

RURUTU VILLAGE HOTEL

UNAA

Teraipo Point

Tetuanui

Plateau

POST OFFICE

Moerai

PROTESTANT CHURCH

Tauraatua Pass

Moerai Bay

Arei Point

VITARIA

Manureva
(384 m)

Taatioe
(389 m)

PEVA

Parari Point

R u r u t u

I s l a n d

Avera

Mauo Point

Opupu Pass

Avera Bay

Erai
(289 m)

Hauti

P A C I F I C

PAPARAI

Toarepe Point

Teutu Point

Rairiri
(263 m)

Taurama
(194 m)

O C E A N

NARUI

Bluffs

NAAIROA

MARAE

0   1 mi

0   1 km

Toataratara Point

© DAVID STANLEY

ÉRIC DE BISSCHOP

BENGT DANIELSSON

At Moerai village lies the tomb of French navigator Éric de Bisschop, whose exploits equaled, but are not as well known as, those of Thor Heyerdahl. Before WW II de Bisschop sailed a catamaran, the *Kaimiloa,* from Hawaii to the Mediterranean via the Indian Ocean and the tip of Africa. His greatest voyage was aboard the *Tahiti Nui,* a series of three rafts, each of which eventually broke up and sank. In 1956 the *Tahiti Nui* set out from Tahiti to Chile to demonstrate the now-accepted theory that the Polynesians had visited South America in prehistoric times. There, two of his four crewmembers abandoned ship, but de Bisschop doggedly set out to return. After a total of 13 months at sea the expedition's final raft foundered on a reef in the Cook Islands and its courageous leader, one of the giants of Pacific exploration, was killed.

of **Manureva** from either the 200-meter-high Tetuanui Plateau toward the airport or the saddle of the Moerai-Avera road. Rurutu's highest peak, Taatioe, is nearby.

Accommodations

The **Hôtel Rurutu Village** (B.P. 22, 98753 Moerai; tel. 94-03-92, fax 94-05-01), on a beach a km west of the airport, is the only regular hotel in the Austral Islands. The eight tin-roofed bungalows with bath go for CFP 3,500/4,500 single/double, plus CFP 500 for breakfast and CFP 2,500 each for lunch and dinner (if required). Facilities encompass a restaurant, bar, and swimming pool. Inexpensive.

Pension Catherine (B.P. 11, 98753 Moerai;

tel. 94-02-43, fax 94-06-99), in a concrete building behind Moerai's Protestant church, has 10 rooms with bath at CFP 3,000/4,000 single/double, plus CFP 2,500/4,000 pp for half/full board (monthly rates available). Car rentals, scuba diving, and deep-sea fishing can be arranged. Airport transfers are free. Inexpensive.

Services and Transportation

Banque Socredo (tel. 94-04-75) and the post office are at Moerai. The *gendarmerie* (tel. 94-03-61) is at the east end of Moerai.

Unaa Airport (RUR) is at the north tip of Rurutu, four km from Moerai. **Air Tahiti** can be reached at tel. 94-03-57. The supply ship from Papeete ties up at Moerai.

TUBUAI

Ten-km-long by five-km-wide Tubuai, largest of the Australs, is 670 km south of Tahiti. Hills on the east and west sides of this oval 45-square-km island are joined by lowland in the middle; when seen from the sea Tubuai looks like two islands. Mount Taitaa (422 meters) is its highest point. Tubuai is surrounded by a barrier reef; a pass on the north side gives access to a wide turquoise lagoon bordered by brilliant white-sand beaches. Picnics are often arranged on the small reef *motu,* amid superb snorkeling grounds, and surfers are just discovering Tubuai's possibilities.

Tubuai has a mean annual temperature 3°C lower than Tahiti and it's at its driest and sunniest Sept.-November. The brisk climate permits the cultivation of potatoes, carrots, oranges, and coffee, but other vegetation is sparse. Several *marae* are on Tubuai, but they're in extremely bad condition, with potatoes growing on the sites. The *Bounty* mutineers attempted unsuccessfully to settle on Tubuai in 1789 (though nothing remains of their Fort George, southeast of Taahuaia). Mormon missionaries arrived as early as 1844, and today there are active branches of the Church of Latter-day Saints in all the villages. The islanders weave fine pandanus hats, and some woodcarving is done at Mahu.

Most of the 2,050 inhabitants live in Mataura and Taahuaia villages on the north coast, though houses and hamlets are found all along the level 24-km road around the island. An eight-km road cuts right across the middle of Tubuai to Mahu village on the south coast, but even this presents no challenges for bicyclists (it's an easy hike to the summit of Mount Taitaa from this road). Mataura is the administrative center of the Austral Islands, and the post office, hospital, dental clinic, *gendarmerie* (tel. 95-03-33), and the branches of two banks are here. The two stores at Mataura bake bread. There's no public transportation so plan on doing a lot of walking.

Accommodations and Food
Pension Vaiteanui (Mélinda Bodin, B.P. 141, 98754 Mataura; tel./fax 95-04-19), near a small beach between the airstrip and Mataura, has five rooms with bath in a long block at CFP 2,500/4,000 single/double, plus CFP 2,500 pp for half board (no cooking facilities). Inexpensive.

Nearby is **Chez Sam et Yolande** (Yolande Tahuhuterani, B.P. 77, 98754 Mataura; tel./fax 95-05-52) with five rooms at CFP 2,500/4,000 single/double and you can cook.

Also in Mataura, **Chez Doudou** (B.P. 64, 98754 Mataura; tel. 95-06-71) has 20 rooms with bath in a long two-story building at CFP 3,000/4,500 single/double. Cooking facilities are not provided, and breakfast and dinner are CFP 2,300 pp extra.

At the west end of Taahueia village, just under three km east of Mataura, is **Chez Karine** (Karine Tahuhuterani, B.P. 34, 98754 Mataura; tel./fax 95-04-52) with one pleasant self-catering bungalow at CFP 5,000/7,500 single/double. Moderate.

A few minutes east of Chez Karine is **Pension Manu Patia** (Vahinetua Turina, B.P. 7, 98754 Mataura; tel. 95-03-27) with two self-catering apartments at CFP 2,500 pp a day or CFP 55,000 a month. Reasonable meals are served on their restaurant's nice veranda and bicycles are for rent. Inexpensive.

Le Bounty (Jean Duday, B.P. 74, 98754 Tubuai; tel. 95-03-32, fax 95-05-58), at the Collège de Mataura also at Taahuaia, has two self-catering rooms at CFP 3,000/4,000 single/double. Lunch is sometimes available in the student restaurant.

The **Ermitage Sainte Hélène** (Tihinarii Ilari, B.P. 79, 98754 Mataura; tel. 95-04-79) is at Mahu, eight km from both Mataruru and the airport. There are three quiet bungalows with cooking facilities at CFP 4,000 pp a day or CFP 50,000 pp a month, airport transfers CFP 3,000 return, and bicycles are for rent. The Ermitage, named for Napoleon's isle of exile, is the former home of Noel Ilari, a local politician falsely imprisoned by the French government during the 1950s (details posted on his grave in front of the house). The Ermitage is a nice place for an extended stay if you don't mind preparing your own meals. Moderate.

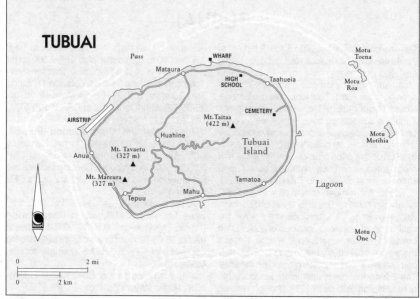

Getting There
Tubuai Airport (TUB), in the northwest corner of the island, opened in 1972. The best beach on the main island is beside the five-km road from the airport to Mataura. **Air Tahiti** (tel. 95-04-76) arrives from Rurutu and Papeete several times a week. Ships enter the lagoon through a passage in the barrier reef on the north side and proceed to the wharf a km east of Mataura. Otherwise, the lagoon is too shallow for navigation.

OTHER AUSTRAL ISLANDS

Rimatara

Without airport, harbor, wharf, hotels, restaurants, bars, and taxis, Rimatara is a place to escape the world. Only a narrow fringing reef hugs Rimatara's lagoonless shore; arriving passengers are landed at Amaru or Mutua Ura by whaleboat. It's customary for newcomers to pass through a cloud of purifying smoke from beachside fires. The women of Rimatara make fine pandanus hats, mats, and bags, and shell necklaces. *Monoï* (skin oil) is prepared from gardenias and coconut oil.

This smallest (nine square km) and lowest (84 meters) of the Australs is home to fewer than 1,000 people. Dirt roads lead from Amaru, the main village, to Anapoto and Mutua Ura. **Pension Umarere** (Tama Aténi Tereopa, tel. 83-25-84), at Mutua Ura, five km southwest of Amaru, has two rooms with shared bath at CFP 2,500/4,000 single/double or CFP 60,000 a month. Cooking is possible but bring food and drink to Rimatara. Water is short in the dry season.

Uninhabited Maria (or Hull) is a four-islet atoll 192 km northwest of Rimatara, visited once or twice a year by men from Rimatara or Rurutu for fishing and copra making. They stay on the atoll two or three months, among seabirds and giant lobsters.

Raivavae

This appealing, nine-km-long and two-km-wide island is just south of the tropic of Capricorn, and

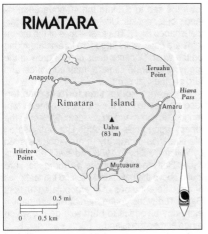

cal vegetation is rich: rose and sandalwood are used to make perfumes for local use.

A malignant fever epidemic in 1826 reduced the people of Raivavae from 3,000 to 120. The present population of around 1,050 lives in four coastal villages, Rairua, Mahanatoa, Anatonu, and Vaiuru, linked by a dirt road. A shortcut route direct from Rairua to Vaiuru crosses a 119-meter saddle, with splendid views of the island. The post office is in Rairua.

Different teams led by Frank Stimson, Don Marshall, and Thor Heyerdahl have explored the ancient temples and taro terraces of Raivavae. Many two- to three-meter-high stone statues once stood on the island, but most have since been destroyed, and two were removed to Tahiti where they can be seen on the grounds of the Gauguin Museum. One big tiki is still standing by the road between Rairua and Mahanatoa villages.

Annie Flores (tel./fax 95-43-28) runs a two-bedroom guesthouse with cooking facilities next to the *gendarmerie* in Rairua, the main village. The charge is CFP 2,000 pp a day or CFP 35,000 a month for the house. A Chinese shop is nearby, but bring your own bread.

If it's taken, try one of the two more expensive places to the east at Mahanatoa. **Chez Vaite** (B.P. 55, 98750 Raivavae; tel. 95-42-85, fax 92-42-00) has three rooms with shared bath at CFP

thus outside the tropics. It's the third most southerly island in the South Pacific (only Rapa and Easter Island are farther south). For archaeology and natural beauty, this is one of the finest islands in Polynesia. Fern-covered Mt. Hiro (437 meters) is the highest point on 18-square-km Raivavae. A barrier reef encloses an emerald lagoon, but the 20 small coral *motu* are all located on the southern and eastern portions of the reef. The tropi-

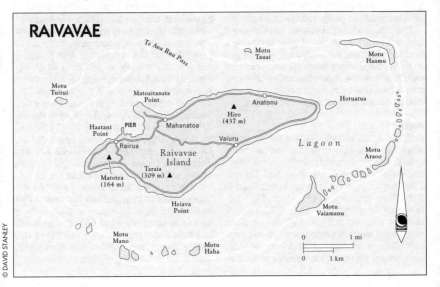

DAVID STANLEY

the famous tiki from Raivavae, now at Tahiti's Gauguin Museum

4,000/7,000 single/double including meals. **Pension Moana** (Teehu Haamoeura, tel. 95-42-47, fax 95-42-00) has two rooms with private bath at CFP 5,500/10,000 single/double. It might be possible to get a room without meals and use their kitchen.

The inhabitants of Raivavae have decided they don't want an airport. If you'll be taking a boat to the Australs anyway, you may as well go to Raivavae, where airborne tourists can't follow! Ships enter the lagoon through a pass on the north side and tie up to the pier at Rairua. A boat calls at the island about every 10-14 days.

Rapa

At 27°38' south latitude, Rapa is the southernmost island in the South Pacific, and one of the most isolated and spectacular. Its nearest neighbor is Raivavae, 600 km away, and Tahiti is 1,300 km north. It's sometimes called Rapa Iti (Little Rapa) to distinguish it from Rapa Nui (Easter Island). Soaring peaks reaching 650 meters surround magnificent Haurei Bay, Rapa's crater harbor, the western portion of a drowned volcano. This is only one of 12 deeply indented bays around the island; the absence of reefs allows the sea to cut into the 40-square-km island's outer coasts. Offshore are several sugar-loaf-shaped islets. The east slopes of the mountains are bare, while large fern forests are found on the west. Coconut trees cannot grow in the foggy, temperate climate. Instead coffee and taro are the main crops.

A timeworn **Polynesian fortress** with terraces is situated on the crest of a ridge at Morongo Uta, commanding a wide outlook over the steep, rugged hills. Morongo Uta was cleared of vegetation by a party of archaeologists led by William Mulloy in 1956 and is still easily visitable. Half a dozen of these *pa* (fortresses) are found above the bay, built to defend the territories of the different tribes of overpopulated ancient Rapa. Today the young men of Rapa organize eight-day bivouacs to hunt wild goats, which range across the island.

During the two decades following the arrival of missionaries in 1826, Rapa's population dropped from 2,000 to 300 due to the introduction of European diseases. By 1851 it was down to just 70, and after smallpox arrived on a Peruvian ship in 1863 it was a miracle that anyone survived at all. The present population of about 550 lives at Area and Haurei villages on the north and south sides of Rapa's great open bay, connected only by boat.

If you're planning to stay on Rapa, it might be useful to write Le Maire, Rapa, Îles Australes, well in advance, stating your name, nationality, age, and profession. Information may also be available from the Subdivision Administrative des Îles Australes (tel. 46-86-77, fax 46-86-79), rue des Poilus Tahitiens, Papeete. A number of local residents rent rooms in their homes at CFP 4,500 pp including meals. In Haurei there's Cerdan Faraire (tel. 95-72-84), Teni Faraire (tel. 95-72-37), and Freddy Riaria (tel. 95-72-27); near the landing at Pararaki are Tihoni Faraire (tel. 95-72-39) and Jean Tehau (tel. 95-72-42). The *Tuhaa Pae II* calls at Rapa every four to six weeks, so that's how long you'll be there.

Marotiri, or the "Bass Rocks," are 10 uninhabited islets totaling just four hectares, 74 km southeast of Rapa. Amazingly enough, some of these pinnacles are crowned with man-made stone platforms and round "towers." One 105-meter-high pinnacle is visible from Rapa in very clear weather. Landing is difficult.

a Tuamotu outrigger

THE TUAMOTU ISLANDS

Arrayed in two parallel northwest-southeast chains scattered across an area of ocean 600 km wide and 1,500 km long, the Tuamotus are the largest group of coral atolls in the world. Of the 78 atolls in the group, 21 have one entrance (pass), 10 have two passes, and 47 have no pass at all. A total of around 14,500 people live on the 48 inhabited islands. Although the land area of the Tuamotus is only 726 square km, the lagoons of the atolls total some 6,000 square km of sheltered water. All are atolls: some have an unbroken ring of reef around the lagoon, while others appear as a necklace of islets separated by channels.

Variable currents, sudden storms, and poor charts make cruising this group by yacht extremely hazardous—in fact, the Tuamotus are popularly known as the Dangerous Archipelago, or the Labyrinth. Wrecks litter the reefs of many atolls. The breakers only become visible when one is within eight km of the reef, and once in, a yacht must carry on through the group.

The usual route is to sail either between Rangiroa and Arutua after a stop at Ahe, or through the Passe de Fakarava between Toau and Fakarava. Winds are generally from the east, varying to northeast Nov.-May and southeast June-October. A series of hurricanes devastated these islands between 1980 and 1983.

The resourceful Tuamotu people have always lived from seafood, pandanus nuts, and coconuts. They once dove to depths of 30 meters and more, wearing only tiny goggles, to collect mother-of-pearl shells. This activity has largely ceased as overharvesting has made the oysters rare. Today, cultured-pearl farms operate on Ahe, Aratika, Arutua, Fakarava, Hao, Hikueru, Katiu, Kaukura, Kauehi, Manihi, Marutea South, Nengonengo, Raroia, Takapoto, Takaroa, Takume, Taenga, and others. Cultured black pearls *(Pinctada margaritifera)* from the Tuamotus and Gambiers are world famous. The pearl industry has reversed the depopulation of the atolls and spread prosperity through this remote region.

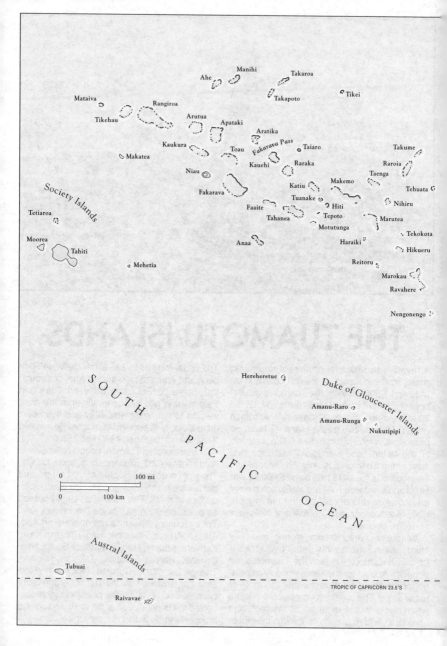

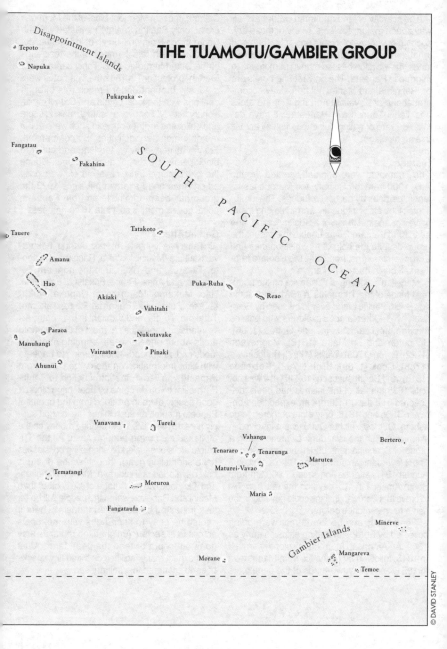

THE TUAMOTU/GAMBIER GROUP

Disappointment Islands

Tepoto

Napuka

Pukapuka

Fangatau

Fakahina

SOUTH PACIFIC OCEAN

Tauere

Tatakoto

Amanu

Hao

Puka-Ruha

Reao

Akiaki

Vahitahi

Paraoa

Nukutavake

Manuhangi

Vairaatea

Pinaki

Ahunui

Vanavana

Tureia

Vahanga

Bertero

Tenararo

Tenarunga

Marutea

Maturei-Vavao

Tematangi

Moruroa

Maria

Fangataufa

Minerve

Gambier Islands

Morane

Mangareva

Temoe

© DAVID STANLEY

The scarcity of land and fresh water have always been major problems. Many of these dry, coconut-covered atolls have only a few hundred inhabitants. Although airstrips exist on 26 islands, the isolation has led many Tuamotuans to migrate to Papeete. The only regular hotels are on Rangiroa and Manihi but homestay accommodations are available on most of the atolls and Tahiti Tourisme in Papeete will have details. Beware of eating poisonous fish all across this archipelago.

History

The Tuamotus were originally settled around A.D. 1000 from the Society and Marquesas Islands, perhaps by political refugees. The inhabitants of the atolls frequently warred among themselves or against those of a Society island, and even King Pomare II was unable to conquer the group despite the help of the missionaries and European firearms. Ironically, the Pomare family itself originated on Fakarava.

Magellan's sighting of Pukapuka on the northeast fringe of the Tuamotus in 1521 made it the first South Pacific island ever to be seen by European eyes. Other famous explorers who passed through the Tuamotus include Quirós (1606), Schouten and Le Maire (1616), Roggeveen (1722), Byron (1765), Wallis (1767), Bougainville (1768), Cook (1769), Bligh (1792), Kotzebue (1816), and Bellingshausen (1820), yet it was not until 1835 that all of the islands had been "discovered." Of the 14 European expeditions between 1606 and 1816, only eight bothered to go ashore. Of these, all but Quirós were involved in skirmishes with the islanders. Centuries later, a group of Scandinavians under the leadership of Thor Heyerdahl ran aground on Raroia atoll on 7 August 1947, after having sailed 7,000 km from South America in 101 days on the raft *Kon Tiki* to prove that Peruvian Indians could have done the same thing centuries before.

Pearl shells and bêche-de-mer were being collected by European trading ships as early as 1809. An American Mormon missionary arrived in 1845, followed by Catholics from Mangareva in 1851, and today two-thirds of the people are

Catholic, the rest Mormon. Most of the Mormons are actually Sanitos ("saints") affiliated with the Reorganized Mormon Church of Independence, Missouri, which rejects many of the teachings of the Utah Mormons. After Tahiti came under French "protection" in 1842 the Tuamotus were gradually brought under French rule through dealings with the local chiefs and Catholic missionary activity. For over a century, making copra and collecting mother-of-pearl shell were about the only monetary activities. By comparison, French military activity, tourism, and cultured black pearls are recent developments. During the 19th century French naval officers were posted on Anaa and Fakarava but since 1923 the group has been administered from Papeete. Local government is split into 16 communes.

Getting There

Air Tahiti has flights to Apataki, Arutua, Fakarava, Kaukura, Manihi, Mataiva, Rangiroa, Takapoto, Takaroa, and Tikehau in the northern Tuamotus, and Anaa, Faaite, Fakahina, Fangatau, Hao, Makemo, Mangareva, Napuka, Nukutavake, Pukapuka, Pukarua, Reao, Takume, Tatakoto, Tureia, and Vahitahi in the south.

Interisland boats call at most of the Tuamotu atolls about once a week, bringing imported foods and other goods and returning to Papeete with fish. Information on the cargo boats from Papeete is given in the introduction to Tahiti-Polynesia. If you do come by boat, bring along a good supply of fresh produce from the bountiful Papeete market, as such things are in short supply here. It's very difficult to change money on the atolls, so also bring enough cash. All the Tuamotu atolls offer splendid snorkeling possibilities (take snorkeling gear), though scuba diving is only developed on Fakarava, Manihi, Rangiroa, and Tikehau. The advantage of atolls other than Manihi and Rangiroa is that the people will be far less impacted by packaged tourism. There it should be easy to hitch rides with the locals across to *le secteur* (uninhabited *motu*) as they go to cut copra or tend the pearl farms. Just don't expect many facilities on these tiny specks of sand scattered in a solitary sea.

RANGIROA

Rangiroa, 350 km northeast of Papeete, is the Tuamotus' most populous atoll and the largest in Polynesia. Its 1,020-square-km aquamarine lagoon is 78 km long, 24 km wide (too far to see), and 225 km around—the island of Tahiti would fit inside its reef. The name Rangiroa means "extended sky." Some 240 *motu* sit on this reef.

Two deep passages through the north side of the atoll's coral ring allow a constant exchange of water between the open sea and the lagoon, creating a most fertile habitat. While lagoons in the Society Islands are often murky due to runoff from the main volcanic islands and pollution from coastal communities, the waters of the Tuamotus are clean and fresh, with some of the best swimming, snorkeling, and scuba diving in the South Pacific. You've never seen so many fish! However in May 1998 it was revealed that 80% of the reefs at Rangiroa had suffered bleaching due to the El Niño phenomenon, completing the destruction wrought earlier by hurricanes. What draws people to Rangi (as everyone calls it) is the marinelife in the lagoon, not the coral. For this one of the prime shark-viewing locales of the world.

Orientation

Rangiroa's twin villages, each facing a pass 500 meters wide into the lagoon, house 2,700 people. Avatoru village on Avatoru Pass is at the west end of the airport island, about six km from the airport itself. A paved 10-km road runs east from Avatoru past the airport and the Kia Ora Village Hôtel to Tiputa Pass. Tiputa village is just across the water. The accommodations listings below are arranged by category from west to east along this road.

Both villages have small stores; the town hall, *gendarmerie* (tel. 96-03-61), and hotel school are at Tiputa, and the medical center, college, and marine research center are at Avatoru. Avatoru has better commercial facilities, but Tiputa is less touristed and offers the chance to escape by simply walking and wading southeast. **Gauguin's Pearl** (tel. 96-05-39; Mon.-Sat. 0830-1400), a pearl farm between Avatoru and the airport, can be visited at no charge. There are no real restaurants outside the hotels and unless you get a place with cooking facilities it's better to take half board. Lunch can be obtained at one of the small snack bars or you can buy picnic fare.

Most of the accommodations face the tranquil lagoon rather than the windy sea and large ships can enter the lagoon through either pass. For yachts, the sheltered anchorage by the Kia Ora Village Hôtel near Tiputa Pass is recommended (as opposed to the Avatoru anchorage, which is exposed to swells and chop). Far less English is spoken on Rangiroa than in the Society Islands.

SPORTS AND RECREATION

The strong tidal currents *(opape)* through Avatoru and Tiputa passes generate flows of three to six knots. It's exciting to shoot these 30-meter-deep passes on an incoming tide, and the three dive shops offer this activity using small motorboats or Zodiacs. Some of the dives tend to be longer and deeper than the norm. The Tiputa Pass current dive begins 27.5 meters down and is only for advanced divers; even the Tiputa Pass right side dive to 18 meters calls for some experience. Beginners should ask for the Motu Nuhi Nuhi dive. On all, the marinelife is fantastic, and humphead wrasses, manta rays, barracudas, and lots of sharks (including hammerheads) are seen in abundance. Most of the time they're harmless black-tip or white-tip reef sharks (but don't risk touching them even if you see other divers doing so). The dive schedules vary according to the tides, winds, and number of tourists on the atoll, and

The relatively harmless black-tip reef shark (Carcharhinus melanopterus) *may be seen in shallow lagoon waters.*

DIANA LASICH HARPER

it's wise to book ahead. Free hotel pickups are offered.

Rangiroa's original scuba operator is arranged by the friendly **Raie Manta Club** (Yves and Brigette Lefèvre, B.P. 55, 98775 Avatoru; tel. 96-84-80, fax 96-85-60), with three branches at Rangiroa: near Rangiroa Lodge in Avatoru village, next to Pension Teina et Marie on Tiputa Pass, and at the Kia Ora Village Hôtel. Diving costs CFP 5,500 pp for one tank, including a float through the pass (night diving CFP 6,000). For the more enthusiastic, a 10-dive package is CFP 49,500. Every dive is different (falling, pass, cave, undulating bottom, hollow, and night). Snorkelers can go along when practical, otherwise an introductory dive is CFP 6,000. PADI and CMAS certification courses are offered at CFP 35,000 (five days, medical examination required). Divers come from all parts of the world to dive with Yves and his highly professional seven-instructor team.

Rangiroa Paradive (Bernard Blanc, B.P. 75, 98775 Avatoru; tel. 96-05-55, fax 96-05-50) is next to Chez Glorine at Tiputa Pass. It's CFP 5,500/10,000 for a one/two-tank dive; the package prices are CFP 26,500/50,000 for five/10 dives. Night dives are CFP 2,000 extra (minimum of four). Bernard isn't as aggressive about shark feeding as Yves but he does explore the shark caves and you'll see legions of sharks on his drift dives. He's obliging, hospitable, and one of the most highly qualified instructors in Polynesia. Both PADI and CMAS certification courses are offered at CFP 40,000 (three days, medical examination not necessary). There's no provision for snorkelers here and divers must show their cards. Without a card you could still do an introductory dive for CFP 6,000.

The Six Passengers (Frédéric Aragones, B.P. 128, 98775 Avatoru; tel./fax 96-02-60), in a hut between Chez Glorine and the Kia Ora, is Rangiroa's newest dive shop. Frédéric charges about the same as Yves and Bernard. Diving from a Zodiac is CFP 5,500/11,000/50,000 for one/two/10 tanks, night dives CFP 7,500, gear and pickups included. An all-day boat trip with two divers at the far end of the lagoon costs CFP 16,000 pp (minimum of six passengers). Snorkelers are not accepted, but a five-day CMAS certification course is offered at CFP 38,000.

Popular lagoon excursions include picnics to the slightly overrated **Blue Lagoon,** a fish-filled pool at Motu Taeoo (CFP 7,000 pp), to the **Île aux Récifs,** a number of uplifted coral formations on the south side of the lagoon (CFP 6,500), to the **Sables Roses,** a stretch of pink sand at the southeast end of the lagoon (CFP 9,000), and to tiny Motu Paio, a mid-lagoon bird sanctuary. Several companies offer a snorkel

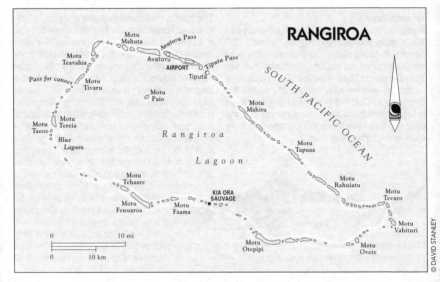

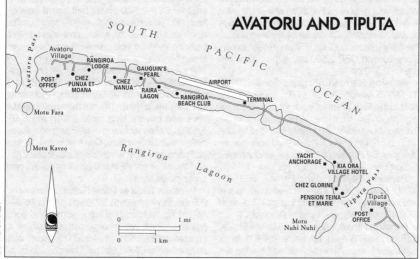

AVATORU AND TIPUTA

SOUTH PACIFIC OCEAN

Avatoru Pass

Avatoru Village

RANGIROA LODGE

POST OFFICE ■ CHEZ PUNUA ET MOANA

GAUGUIN'S PEARL

CHEZ NANUA

AIRPORT

RAIRA LAGON

RANGIROA BEACH CLUB

TERMINAL

Motu Fara

Motu Kaveo

Rangiroa Lagoon

YACHT ANCHORAGE ■ KIA ORA VILLAGE HOTEL

CHEZ GLORINE

PENSION TEINA ET MARIE

Tiputa Pass

Tiputa Village

POST OFFICE

Motu Nuhi Nuhi

© DAVID STANLEY

0   1 mi

0   1 km

---

through the pass at CFP 4,000 (or do it in a glass-bottom boat for CFP 2,000). **Sharky Parc Excursions** (tel. 96-84-73), at Chez Punua et Moana in Avatoru, organizes some better value trips starting at CFP 2,500.

PRACTICALITIES

Budget Accommodations
Chez Nanua (Nanua and Marie Tamaehu, B.P. 54, 98775 Avatoru; tel. 96-83-88), between the airport and Avatoru village, is an old favorite of budget travelers who are allowed to pitch their tents here at CFP 1,000 pp (CFP 2,000 pp with two meals). The four simple thatched bungalows with shared/private bath are CFP 3,000/4,000 pp including two meals. The six-bed dorm is CFP 3,000 pp including food. You eat with the owners—a little fish and rice every meal. There's no electricity, communal cooking, or running water, but you're right on the beach. Ask about bicycle and scooter rentals at Carole Pareo nearby.

Inexpensive
Chez Henriette (Henriette Tamaehu, tel. 96-85-85), by the lagoon in Avatoru village, is a

four-bungalow place charging CFP 2,500 pp for a bed, CFP 5,000 with half pension, CFP 6,000 full pension. It can be a little noisy here but the food is excellent (especially the banana crêpes) and it's possible stop by for lunch even if you're staying elsewhere. They organize their own Blue Lagoon excursions.

Rangiroa Lodge (Jacques and Rofina Ly, tel. 96-82-13) in Avatoru has four rooms at CFP 4,000 double with shared bath or CFP 5,000 with private bath (plus CFP 200 for a fan, if desired). A place in the six-bed dorm is CFP 1,500 pp. This is one of the few places with communal cooking facilities, though the proprietors also prepare meals upon request. The snorkeling just off the lodge is outstanding and they'll loan you gear if you need it. Divers from the adjacent Raie Manta Club often stay here.

Moderate
The son and daughter-in-law of the folks mentioned at Chez Nanua above operate **Chez Punua et Moana** (Punua and Moana Tamaehu, B.P. 54, 98775 Avatoru; tel. 96-84-73) in Avatoru village. The four thatched bungalows with shared bath are CFP 3,500 pp with breakfast, or CFP 4,500 pp with half board. Camping is CFP 1,500 pp. It's right by the road and can be a little noisy

due to the activities of the surrounding village. Watch your gear here. For those who really want to get away, Punua can arrange overnight stays on Motu Teavahia. Otherwise all are welcome on the daily lagoon tours and "Sharky Parc" excursions costing CFP 2,500 pp. Airport transfers are CFP 500 pp.

Pension Herenui (Victorine Sanford, B.P. 31, 98775 Avatoru; tel. 96-84-71, fax 96-85-60), next to the Raie Manta Club right in Avatoru village, four km from the airport, offers three thatched bungalows with private bath and terrace (but no cooking) at CFP 3,500 pp with breakfast, plus CFP 1,000/1,500 pp for lunch/dinner. Airport transfers are CFP 500 pp.

Pension Loyna (Loyna Fareea, B.P. 82, 98775 Avatoru; tel. 96-82-09) near Avatoru has three rooms with shared bath in a main house at CFP 4,500/5,500 pp with half/full board.

Pension Hinanui (René and Mareta Bizien, B.P. 16, 98775 Avatoru; tel. 96-84-61), on a quiet beach near Avatoru, four km from the airport, has three bungalows with private bath at CFP 4,000/7,000/8,000 single/double/triple, plus CFP 2,000/3,500 pp with half/full board.

On the lagoon between the airport and Avatoru is **Pension Cécile** (Alban and Cécile Sun, B.P. 98, 98775 Avatoru; tel./fax 96-05-06) where the four self-contained bungalows are CFP 4,000 pp, plus CFP 2,000 pp for half board (no cooking). (Reader Rowland Burley writes that "this was the friendliest accommodation I found in Tahiti-Polynesia. Cécile speaks excellent English, the units are spotlessly clean, and dinner is superb.) Alban does lagoon tours in his boat upon request at CFP 6,000 pp.

The **Turiroa Village** (Olga Niva, B.P. 26, 98775 Avatoru; tel./fax 96-04-27), less than a km west of the airport terminal, has four bungalows with cooking facilities at CFP 8,000 for up to four persons. If required, half/full board is CFP 3,000/3,500 pp.

A five-minute walk west of the airport terminal is **Pension Félix** (Félix and Judith Tetua, B.P. 18, 98775 Avatoru; tel. 96-04-41) with six bungalows with bath at CFP 2,500 pp, plus another CFP 3,000 pp for breakfast and dinner.

Pension Martine (Martine and Corinne Tetua, B.P. 68, 98775 Avatoru; tel. 96-02-53, fax 96-02-51), by the lagoon near the airport terminal, has four fan-cooled bungalows with private bath and terrace (but no cooking) at CFP 3,000 pp, plus another CFP 2,500 pp for half board (lots of fresh fish). There's no single supplement if you're alone and it's friendly, clean, and relaxed. Ask Corinne to show you around the family pearl farm.

A sister of the Henriette mentioned previously runs the popular **Chez Glorine** (Glorine To'i, tel. 96-04-05, fax 95-03-58) at Tiputa Pass, four km from the airport. The six thatched bungalows with private bath (cold water) are CFP 5,500/6,500 pp including two/three meals (specialty fresh lagoon fish). Children under 13 are half price and bicycle rentals are available. Airport transfers are CFP 800 pp. Non-guests can order meals here.

Pension Teina et Marie (Tahuhu Maraeura, B.P. 36, 98775 Avatoru; tel. 96-03-94, fax 96-84-44), at Tiputa Pass four km east of the airport, has two rooms with shared bath upstairs in a concrete house and six thatched bungalows with private bath at CFP 2,500 pp. There are no communal cooking facilities but half board is available at another CFP 3,000 pp. Transfers are CFP 500 pp. This place gets mixed reviews.

Pension Lucien (Lucien and Esther Pe'a, B.P. 69, 98776 Tiputa; tel. 96-73-55), near the pass in Tiputa village, offers three beach bungalows with private bath at CFP 5,000 pp with half board. Airport transfers are CFP 1,000 pp.

Pension Estall (Ronald Estall, B.P. 13, 98776 Tiputa; tel. 96-73-16), also in Tiputa village, has four Polynesian-style bungalows with private bath, CFP 4,500/6,000 pp half/complete pension. Add CFP 1,000 pp for transfers. It's overpriced for what you get.

Expensive

The **Miki Miki Village** (B.P. 5, 98775 Avatoru; tel./fax 96-83-83), also known as the Rangiroa Village, is an 11-bungalow resort near Avatoru: CFP 8,000/14,000 single/double, including breakfast and dinner. Reader comment about this place has been favorable. Lagoon tours are offered and it's possible to stop by for lunch or drinks.

Pension Tuanake (Roger and Iris Terorotua, B.P. 21, 98775 Avatoru; tel. 96-04-45, fax 96-03-29), by the lagoon next to Gauguin Pearls two km west of the airport, has four thatched bungalows with bath at CFP 5,000/8,000/10,000 single/double/quad. Breakfast/lunch/dinner are CFP 800/2,000/2,200 pp (no cooking facilities). Bicycles rent for CFP 500 a day.

The **Relais Mihiroa** (Maurice and Monique Guitteny, B.P. 51, 98776 Tiputa; tel. 96-72-14, fax 96-75-13), in a coconut grove on Tiputa Island four km from the village, has four cubical bungalows with bath and terrace at CFP 7,200 for up to three people, plus CFP 2,400/3,900 pp for half/full board. Boat transfers from the airport are CFP 1,500 pp.

The **Village Sans Souci** (Sara Nantz, B.P. 22, 98775 Avatoru; tel. 96-83-72) is an escapist's retreat on Motu Mahuta, an islet to the west of Avatoru Pass. The package price is CFP 7,500 pp per night including all meals, with a minimum stay of three nights. The breakfast and desserts offered here are meager and they make you wait until 1930 for dinner. Add CFP 13,000/16,000 single/double for return boat transfers from the airport. Despite the price, the nine thatched bungalows are very simple, with communal shower and toilet stalls (cold water). Scuba diving is possible, but it's remarkably overpriced and not recommended.

Premium

The **Raira Lagon** (Maxime Boetsch, B.P. 87, 98775 Avatoru; tel. 96-04-23, fax 96-05-86), a bit over a km west of the airport terminal, offers 10 thatched bungalows with private bath and fridge (but no cooking facilities or hot water) at CFP 8,000/10,000 pp with half/full board. A few well-used bicycles are loaned free and it's right on the beach. Their beachfront restaurant is open to the public.

Just west of the airport is the friendly 20-unit **Rangiroa Beach Club** (B.P. 17, 98775 Avatoru; tel. 96-03-34, fax 96-02-90), next to the Raira Lagon. A thatched garden bungalow will set you back CFP 13,000 single, double, or triple plus tax, and for CFP 2,000 more you can have a beach bungalow. Children under 12 sharing a room with their parents are free. Additional units were being added in late 1998 and most guests arrived on prepaid packages. The restaurant serves excellent food (compulsory CFP 4,700 pp breakfast and dinner plan). The beach here is poor, so protective footwear should be used. Snorkeling and fishing gear are loaned free, and all land and water tours are arranged.

Luxury

Rangiroa's top resort is the snobbish **Kia Ora Village** (B.P. 1, 98776 Tiputa; tel. 96-03-84, fax 96-02-20), established in 1973 near Tiputa Pass, a bit over two km east of the airport by road. The 30 beach bungalows and five larger garden bungalows are CFP 32,000/36,500 double/triple plus tax, while the 10 overwater units go for CFP 49,000 single or double, plus another CFP 5,500 pp for breakfast and dinner. Yachties anchored offshore are certainly not welcome to dingy in and use the facilities but the pricey seafood restaurant is open to all. A wide range of lagoon excursions and activities are offered at higher than usual prices. In 1991 the Kia Ora Village began offering accommodation in five thatched bungalows at "Kia Ora Sauvage" on Motu Avaerahi on the far south side of the lagoon. It's CFP 32,000 single or double plus a compulsory three-meal plan at CFP 7,000 pp, plus CFP 7,500 pp for return boat transfers (two-night minimum stay). The boat leaves at 0900 daily so you'll probably have to wait one night to go. Both Kia Ora's cater mostly to the package tour market.

Services

The Banque de Tahiti (tel. 96-85-52) has a branch at Avatoru, while Banque Socredo (tel. 96-85-63) has branches at the *mairies* in both Avatoru and Tiputa. All branches are open limited hours according to a variable timetable (in Tiputa only on Monday, Tuesday, and Thursday). Post offices are found in Avatoru, Tiputa, and the airport. There's a medical center (tel. 96-03-75) two km east of Avatoru and an infirmary (tel. 96-73-96) at Tiputa. It's prudent to drink bottled water on Rangiroa.

Getting There

Air Tahiti (tel. 96-03-41) flies Tahiti-Rangiroa daily (CFP 13,600 one-way). Three times a week a flight arrives direct from Bora Bora (CFP 20,700), but from Rangiroa to Bora Bora there's only a weekly flight. There's service five times a week from Rangiroa to Manihi (CFP 8,800). From Rangiroa to the Marquesas (CFP 24,500), there's a weekly ATR 42 flight (48 passengers) to Nuku Hiva and a weekly Dornier 228 flight (19 passengers) to Hiva Oa. Seats on flights to the Marquesas should be booked well in advance.

Schooners *(goélettes)* from Papeete take 23 hours to get there from Tahiti, but 72 hours to return (not direct). One cargo boat, the *Dory*, departs Papeete for Rangiroa every Monday at 1300 (CFP 2,500), the most regular connection. To return, ask about the copra boat *Rairoa Nui*, which is supposed to leave Rangiroa Wednesday at 0230 and arrive at Papeete Thursday at 0500 (CFP 3,000 including meals and a bunk—men only). The *Manava II, Saint Xavier Maris Stella*, and *Vai Aito* also call here regularly. They may dock at either Avatoru or Tiputa. The *Aranui* stops at Rangiroa on the way back to Papeete from the Marquesas and you could disembark here. For more information on transport to the Tuamotus, see the introduction to Tahiti-Polynesia.

Archipels Croisieres (B.P. 1160, 98729 Papetoai, Moorea; tel. 56-36-39, fax 56-35-87) offers two/three-night cruises around the Rangiroa lagoon on the 18-meter, eight-passenger catamaran *Motu Iti* at US$790/1,030 pp double occupancy (excluding airfare). It's a great way to explore the atoll and they'll go even if only two people reserve. When you consider that all meals and activities are included, it's no more expensive than staying at the Kia Ora. The entire vessel can be chartered at CFP 250,000 a day including meals. Tahiti Vacations handles North American bookings.

Getting Around

There's no public transportation on Rangiroa although the scuba operators offer shuttles to their clients. To reach Tiputa village across Tiputa Pass from the airport island wait for a lift on the dock next to Chez Glorine (watch for dolphins in the pass).

Europcar (tel./fax 96-03-28) with an office near Avatoru and a desk at the Kia Ora Village has cars beginning at CFP 5,500/6,500/7,500 for four/eight/24 hours, scooters at CFP 4,000/5,000/5,500, bicycles CFP 800/1,200/1500. Two-person "fun cars" are slightly cheaper than regular cars.

Arenahio Locations (tel./fax 96-82-85), at Carole Pareo between the airport and Avatoru village, rents bicycles at CFP 500/1,000 a half/full day and scooters at CFP 3,000/4,000. Many of the pensions also rent bicycles.

Airport

The airstrip (RGI) is about six km from Avatoru village by road, accessible to Tiputa village by boat. Most of the Avatoru pensions offer free airport transfers to those who have booked ahead (ask).

OTHER ISLANDS AND ATOLLS

MANIHI

Manihi, 175 km northeast of Rangiroa, is the other Tuamotu atoll on the package tour circuit with visions of white-sand beaches and cultured black pearls radiating from glossy brochures. You can see right around Manihi's six-by-30-km lagoon and the 50,000 resident oysters on the 60 commercial pearl farms outnumber the 1,000 human inhabitants 50 to one. Due to the pearl industry the people of Manihi have become more affluent than those on some of the other Tuamotu islands.

Turipaoa (or Paeua) village and its 50 houses shaded by flowers and trees face Tairapa Pass at the west end of a sandy strip just over a kilometer long. The airport island and main resort are just across the pass from Turipaoa, and many of the other *motu* are also inhabited.

Scuba Diving

Gilles Pétré of **Manihi Blue Nui** (B.P. 2460, 98713 Papeete; tel./fax 96-42-17) at the Manihi Pearl Beach Resort offers year-round scuba diving on the outer reef walls. A one-tank dive is CFP 6,000 (plus CFP 7,000 for night diving). Five/10-dive packages are CFP 27,500/50,000. Rental of a wetsuit or waterproof light is CFP 500. Gilles will also take snorkelers on the boat at CFP 1,500 pp including mask and snorkel. Both PADI and CMAS certification courses are offered, otherwise a one-dive resort course is CFP 7,000.

It's exciting to shoot Tairapa Pass on the incoming tide, and since it's shallower than the passes at Rangiroa, you see more. Reef sharks are less common here but manta rays are often seen, as are countless Moorish idols. Just inside the lagoon at the mouth of the pass is a site called "The Circus" frequented by huge, sci-

ence fiction-like rays with enormous socket eyes, and it's a fantastic experience to swim near them (also possible at Rangiroa).

The ocean drop-off abounds in gray sharks, Napoleon fish, giant jack fish, and huge schools of snappers, barracudas, and tuna. Each year, around late June or early July, thousands of groupers gather here to breed in one of the most fascinating underwater events in the world. Among Gilles' other favorite spots are "West Point" with fire, antler, and flower petal coral in 65-meter visibility, and "The Break," where he feeds black-tip, white-tip, gray, and occasionally hammerhead sharks.

Accommodations

Air Tahiti owns and heavily promotes the **Manihi Pearl Beach Resort** (B.P. 2460, 98713 Papeete; tel. 96-42-73, fax 96-42-72), by the lagoon near the airport. This place was known as the Kaina Village until a hurricane blew it away in 1993. Now rebuilt, the eight beach bungalows are CFP 26,000 single or double, while the 22 overwater bungalows go for CFP 46,000 plus tax. Add CFP 5,950 pp for breakfast and dinner, or CFP 8,250 full board. Roundtrip airport transfers are a ripoff at CFP 1,200 pp. Almost all guests arrive on prepaid packages. There's a beachfront saltwater swimming pool and floodlit tennis courts at the Manihi Pearl. Luxury.

Nine km northeast of the airport by road is **Chez Jeanne** (Jeanne Huerta, tel. 96-42-90, fax 96-42-91), formerly known as Le Keshi, at Motu Taugaraufara. The two self-catering beach bungalows here are CFP 8,000 for up to three people, while the overwater unit is CFP 12,000 double (minimum stay two nights). Food, water, and excursions are extra. Moderate.

The **Vainui Pearls Resort Lodge** (Edmond and Vaiana Buniet, B.P. 10, 98771 Manihi; tel. 96-42-89, fax 96-42-00) is across the lagoon on Motu Marakorako. The three rooms with shared bath in the main house and the one beach bungalow go for CFP 7,000 pp a day including airport transfers, activities, and all meals. A free tour of the owner's pearl farm is offered and it's obviously the place to stay if your main interest is pearls. Reservations are recommended. Moderate.

In Turipaoa village you can rent a *fare* from Madame Puahea Teiva (no phone), but they're decrepit and remarkably overpriced at CFP 3,500 pp with two miserable meals. Itinerant pearl industry workers are the target clientele.

Getting There

Manihi airport (XMH) is 2.5 km north of Turipaoa village by boat. Most Air Tahiti (tel. 96-43-34) flights to Manihi from Papeete (CFP 17,100) or Bora Bora (CFP 23,400) are via Rangiroa. Flights between Manihi and Rangiroa are also expensive at CFP 8,800. Boats from Papeete enter the lagoon and tie up to a wharf at Turipaoa.

OTHERS

Ahe

Ahe, 13 km west of Manihi, is often visited by cruising yachts, which are able to enter the 16-km-long lagoon through Tiarero Pass on the northwest side of the atoll. Tenukupara village is south across the lagoon. Facilities include two tiny stores, a post office, and a community center where everyone meets at night. Despite the steady stream of sailing boats, the 400 people are very friendly. All of the houses have solar generating panels supplied after a hurricane in the early 1980s.

Only a handful of small children are seen in the village; most are away at school on Rangiroa or Tahiti. Many families follow their children to the main islands while they're at school, so you may even be able to rent a whole house. As well as producing pearls, Ahe supplies oysters to the pearl farms on Manihi. In March 1998 an airport constructed by the Foreign Legion opened on Ahe.

Anaa

Anaa is 437 km due east of Tahiti and it receives an Air Tahiti flight from Papeete (CFP 15,000) twice a week with one service continuing to Makemo (CFP 7,700) and the other to Hao (CFP 14,600). Unlike most of the other atolls covered here, Anaa is part of the southern Tuamotu group that was forbidden to non-French during the nuclear testing era.

The 450 inhabitants live in five small settlements scattered around Anaa's broken coral ring and there's no pass into the shallow elongated lagoon. Anaa's tattooed warriors were once widely feared, yet this was the first Tuamotuan atoll to accept Christianity after a local missionary returned from training on Moorea in 1817. In 1845 an American named Benjamin Grouard converted the inhabitants to Mormonism. Catholic missionaries followed in 1851, leading to a mini-religious war and the banning of Mormon missionaries from the colony by the French authorities (they were not allowed to return until 1892). From 1853 to 1878 the French colonial administration of the Tuamotus was based here.

Accommodations are available at **Te Maui Nui** (François Mo'o, tel. 98-32-75) at Tokerau village, 400 meters from the airstrip on the north side of Anaa. The one bungalow is CFP 6,000 pp including all meals, while a room in a three-room *fare* is CFP 4,000 pp with two meals. François used to run a snack bar in Papeete and speaks a little English.

Joél Teaku operates **Toku Kaiga** (tel. 98-32-69) in Tokerau village, 400 meters from the airport. The two bungalows here go for CFP 4,500 pp or CFP 5,000 pp, both including meals.

Arutua

Numerous black pearl farms grace the 29-km-wide lagoon of this circular atoll between Rangiroa and Apataki. Rautini village near the only pass was rebuilt after devastating hurricanes in 1983, and among the 500 inhabitants are some locally renowned musicians and storytellers. Mr. Nerii Fau'ura (tel. 96-52-55) at Rautini has one room set aside for visitors at CFP 6,000 pp including all meals, excursions, and transfers. Arutua receives Air Tahiti flights from Papeete (CFP 14,000) three times a week with two carrying on to Rangiroa. The airstrip is 30 minutes by boat from the village.

Fakarava

Fakarava is the second-largest Tuamotu atoll, about 250 km southeast of Rangiroa and 450 km northeast of Tahiti. A pass gives access to each end of this rectangular 60-by-25-km lagoon, which is dotted and flanked by 80 coconut-covered *motu*. There's spectacular snorkeling and drift diving in the passes or along the vertical dropoffs. Passe Garuae on the north is a km wide, nine meters deep, and the haunt of countless sharks, dolphins, barracuda, and rays.

French colonial administration for the Tuamotus moved here from Anaa in 1878 and Fakarava's Catholic church is one of the oldest in the group. Robert Louis Stevenson visited Fakarava aboard the yacht *Casco* in 1888 and spent two weeks living in a house near the church in the center of the village, Rotoava. The present airstrip, eight km from village, only opened in 1995. About 500 people live on the atoll and a number of pearl farms have been established around the lagoon.

The least expensive place to stay is the **Relais Marama** (Marama Teanuanua, tel. 98-42-25), in Rotoava village, four km from the airstrip. The three rooms with shared bath in the main house are CFP 2,500/4,000 single/double, otherwise it's CFP 5,000 double for the garden bungalow. Cooking facilities are available.

The **Kiritia Village** (Marcelline Kachler, tel. 98-42-37), also in Rotoava, offers two bungalows and four *fare* with shared bath at CFP 8,500/15,000 single/double including all meals and transfers. Bicycles are for rent.

Marc-Antoine Baudart runs a scuba diving operation called **Club Aventure** or **CPSM Rotoava** (B.P. 330002, 98711 Paea, Tahiti; fax 43-07-54) next to the Kiritia Village. Diving is CFP 6,000 a tank day or night, or CFP 27,000 for five dives, gear included. He also takes snorkelers out at CFP 3,800 pp (black pearl farm visits possible). Otherwise sign up for his four-day CMAS certification course at CFP 20,000 (medical certificate required). An excursion to uninhabited Toau Atoll is CFP 5,000 pp (five person minimum), plus the diving or snorkeling charges. Don't bother asking about shark feeding as that's not his thing.

At the other end of the atoll is the **Tetamanu Village** (Sane Richmond, B.P. 951, 98713 Papeete; tel. 45-20-30, fax 45-47-70). The four wa-

THE LOST TREASURE OF THE TUAMOTUS

During the War of the Pacific (1879-83) four mercenaries stole 14 tons of gold from a church in Pisco, Peru. They buried most of the treasure on Pinaki or Raraka atolls in the Tuamotus before proceeding to Australia where two were killed by aboriginals and the other two were sentenced to 20 years imprisonment for murder. Just prior to his death the surviving mercenary told prospector Charles Howe the story.

In 1913 Howe began a 13-year search, which finally located part of the treasure on an island near Raraka. He reburied the chests and returned to Australia to organize an expedition that would remove the gold in secret. Before it could set out, however, Howe disappeared. But using Howe's treasure map, diver George Hamilton took over the recovery in 1934. Hamilton thought he found the cached gold in a pool but was unable to extract it. After being attacked by a giant octopus and moray eel, Hamilton abandoned the search and the expedition dissolved.

In 1994 a descendant of Hamilton chartered a boat at Fakarava and headed for Tepoto atoll, which had been identified from an old photograph as the site of the treasure. Soon after their arrival at Tepoto, the weather turned nasty and the expeditionaries turned back after narrowly escaping death on the reef.

As far as is known, the US$1.8 million in gold has never been found, but the legend is still very much alive and traces of old diggings can be seen in a dozen places, mostly around Pinaki's only passage (which is too shallow for even dinghies to enter). Only landowners are allowed to dig for treasure, so a foreigner would have to marry a local first. At night the treasure is guarded by the spirits of two whites and a black (who were killed after burying the gold).

Some claim the islanders found the gold long ago and, believing it cursed, dumped it into the sea. Most scholars say the whole thing is a hoax, yet treasure hunters still dream of locating this elusive treasure!

---

terfront *fare* here are CFP 75,000 pp a week including all meals, activities, and airport transfers (three hours each way by boat). A private bathing pontoon in the adjacent Tumakohua Pass facilitates snorkeling at slack tide. Tanks and weights are available to scuba divers who bring their own gear. Ask Sane to show you around his pearl farm. Premium.

Air Tahiti flies from Papeete to Fakarava (CFP 14,700) twice a week with one flight going on to Rangiroa (CFP 4,400).

Hao

Hao Atoll was visited by the Spaniard Quirós in 1606. Kaki Pass gives access to the 50-km-long lagoon from the north. The pass has been dredged to a depth of seven meters and medium-sized ships can enter and proceed eight km to the anchorage off Otepa village on the northeast side of the atoll.

From 1966 to 1996 the giant French air base on Hao (population 1,400) served as the main support base for nuclear testing on Moruroa, 500 km southeast, allowing the French military to fly materials directly into the area without passing through Faa'a Airport. The formidable airstrip on Hao is over three km long, big enough to be considered a possible emergency landing site for NASA space shuttles. In 1986, after economic blackmail from France, the convicted *Rainbow Warrior* bombers Captain Dominique Prieur and Major Alain Mafart were sent from New Zealand to Hao where it was formally agreed they would remain in seclusion for three years to complete their 10-year sentences for manslaughter. Yet after only 18 months Mafart was flown to Paris for "medical reasons" and Prieur followed five months later, a good example of how France honors its treaty obligations.

Hao is strategically situated in the heart of Tahiti-Polynesia, equidistant from Tahiti, Mangareva, and the Marquesas, and despite the windup of nuclear testing on Moruroa in 1996, France continues to project its military power from Hao, current home of the 5th Foreign Legion Regiment. There are no tourist accommodations on Hao and prior to 1996 non-French visitors were forbidden to even transit the atoll. Most Air Tahiti flights to Mangareva and the southern Tuamotus are via Hao, and it might be worth inquiring about the current situation before making too many plans.

Kaukura

A narrow pass gives limited access to Kaukura's shallow, 40-km-long lagoon, midway between Rangiroa and Fakarava. Air Tahiti has flights twice a week from Papeete to Kaukura (CFP 14,000) with a connection to/from Rangiroa. Accommodations are available at **Pension Rekareka** (Mrs. Titaua Parker, tel. 96-62-40) in Raitahiti village, two km from the airstrip at the west end of the atoll. It's CFP 5,000 pp including meals in a six-room house in the village and they also have four cabins on a *motu* at CFP 6,000 pp. Fewer than 400 people live on Kaukura.

Makatea

Unlike the low coral atolls of the Tuamotus, Makatea, 200 km northeast of Tahiti, is an uplifted limestone block with a lunar surface eight km long and 110 meters high. Gray cliffs plunge 50 meters to the sea. Phosphate was dug up here by workers with shovels from 1908 to 1966 and exported to Japan and New Zealand by the Compagnie française des Phosphates de l'Océanie. At one time 2,000 workers were present but fewer than 100 people are there today. Even though the mining has been abandoned, many buildings and a railway remain. Numerous archaeological remains were found during the mining. There are no flights to Makatea.

Mataiva

Tiny Mataiva, westernmost of the Tuamotus and 40 km from Tikehau, receives two Air Tahiti flights a week from Papeete (CFP 13,600). One continues to Rangiroa, the other to Tikehau (at CFP 4,400 to either), so with careful planning you could do some island hopping. The airstrip is 400 meters from Pahua village on the west side of the atoll. The village is divided into two parts by a shallow pass crossed by a wooden bridge.

Only nine km long and four km wide, Mataiva (population 225) is worth considering as an offbeat destination. A coral road covers most of the 35 km around the atoll with narrow concrete bridges over the nine shallow channels or "eyes" which gave the island its name (*mata* means eye, *iva* is nine). Exploratory mining of a phosphate deposit under the lagoon ended in 1982 and further mining has been strongly opposed by residents aware of the environmental devastation

that would be inflicted. In February 1998 Mataiva was struck by Hurricane Veli.

Mr. Aroma Huri of Pahua runs a small resort called **Mataiva Cool** (tel. 96-32-53) on a white beach south of the pass. To stay in one of the six *fare* with shared bath is CFP 4,500 pp a night including meals. The five larger bungalows with private bath are CFP 6,500 pp including all meals. For reservations from Tahiti, call 82-69-69.

Ava Hei Pension (Mahetau Lacour, tel. 96-32-39 or 96-32-58), by the lagoon at Tevaihi 3.5 km south of the airport, offers three *fare* at CFP 6,500 pp including all meals. Camping is possible at CFP 2,500 pp including meals. Airport transfers are provided.

Another place to stay is the **Mataiva Village** (Edgar Tetua, tel. 96-32-33), on a beach north of the pass, with seven bungalows with bath at CFP 6,500/12,000 single/double including all meals. The guesthouses rent bicycles at CFP 1,000 a day.

Niau

The shark-free lagoon at Niau, 50 km southeast of Kaukura, is enclosed by a circle of land. Low-grade phosphate deposits on the island were judged too poor to mine. This lonely island of 450 souls does not receive any Air Tahiti flights.

Reao

No pass gives access to the lagoon of this easternmost inhabited Tuamotu atoll. In 1865 Catholic missionaries from Mangareva arrived on Reao and in 1901 they established a leper colony here that accepted patients from all over the Tuamotus and Marquesas until it was moved to Tahiti in 1914. Some 300 people live on the atoll today. Reao receives two Air Tahiti flights a month from Papeete (CFP 30,000) via Hao. On the way back to Tahiti the plane calls at Fangatau, Takume, and Makemo.

Taiaro

In 1972 the private owner of Taiaro, Mr. W.A. Robinson, declared the atoll a nature reserve and in 1977 it was accepted by the United Nations as a biosphere reserve. Scientific missions studying atoll ecology sometimes visit tiny Taiaro, the only permanent inhabitants of which are a caretaker family. There are no flights to this isolated island northeast of Kauehi and Raraka.

Takapoto

Takapoto and Takaroa atolls are separated by only eight km of open sea, and on both the airstrip is within walking distance of the village. Air Tahiti flies three times a week from Papeete to Takapoto (CFP 17,800) and Takaroa (CFP 18,800) with a westward connection to Manihi. The freighter *Taporo IV* carries passengers from Papeete to Takapoto (36 hours, CFP 9,000/13,000 deck/cabin including meals) every two weeks, continuing on to the Marquesas. The more upmarket *Aranui* also calls at Takapoto.

There's no pass into the lagoon but landing by whaleboat is easy. Jacob Roggeveen lost one of his three ships on Takapoto's reef in 1722. Today the 16-km-long lagoon is a nursery for black pearl oysters and over 600 people live here.

Two families in Fakatopatere village near the airport at the southwest end of the atoll take guests at CFP 6,000 pp full board: Pimati and Marie Toti (tel. 98-65-44), and Clotilde and Opeta Bellais (tel. 98-65-42). Inexpensive.

Takaroa

This northeasterly atoll is 24 km long and up to eight km wide. The 30-meter-wide pass is barely three meters deep and the snorkeling here is second to none. On the outer reef near Takaroa's airstrip are two wrecks, one of a four-masted sailing ship here since 1906. Pearl farming flourishes in the Takaroa lagoon, which offers good anchorage everywhere. Since the appearance of this industry, visits by cruising yachts have been discouraged due to the danger of boats hitting poorly marked oyster platforms in the lagoon. Most of the 450 inhabitants of Teavaroa village belong to the Mormon church and their village is often called "little America." Tea, coffee, alcohol, and cigarettes are all frowned on but dog is considered a delicacy. *Marae* remains lurk in the bush.

Accommodations are available at **Chez Vahinerii** (Mrs. Vahinerii Temanaha, tel. 98-23-59), between the airport and the village, where the one bungalow with cooking facilities is CFP 6,000 double. If it's full you may be able to rent a room in the Temanaha family residence in the village, or ask if Eugénie Ennemoser or Hiriata Tehina could put you up.

It's also possible to stay at a pearl farm on Motu Vaimaroro at the **Poerangi Village** (Eléonore Parker, tel. 98-23-65, fax 98-22-65). The three self-catering beach bungalows here are CFP 2,500/4,000 single/double plus CFP 1,000 pp for transfers.

Tikehau

Rangiroa's smaller and less commercialized neighbor, Tikehau (400 inhabitants), is an almost circular atoll 26 km across with the shallow Passe de Tuheiava on its west side. Tuherahera village and the airstrip share an island in the southwest corner of the atoll. Five pearl farms operate on Tikehau. Plans exist to build a five-star resort called "Eden Beach" on Tikehau but the project has been delayed due to a lack of funds.

an early 19th-century chief of Tikei atoll near Takapoto

M.G.L. DOMENY DE RIENZI

A variety of places to stay are found on Tikehau, beginning with the **Panau Lagon** (Arai and Lorina Natua, tel./fax 96-22-99) on a white beach a few minutes walk from the airport. The six simple bungalows with bath are CFP 2,500 pp, plus CFP 3,000 pp for breakfast and dinner. Camping is possible. Inexpensive.

Also in the direction away from the village and a few minutes beyond Panau Lagon is **Chez Justine** (Justine and Laroche Tetua, tel. 96-22-37, fax 96-22-26) with two *fare* at CFP 5,000 pp with half board. **Pension Kahaia** (Merline Natua, tel. 96-22-77), on an adjacent *motu,* has three *fare* at CFP 5,000 pp with half board. The **Tikehau Village** (Caroline and Pa'ea Tefaiao, tel. 96-22-86, fax 96-22-91), on the beach between the airstrip and the village, has eight *fare* at CFP 7,000 pp including all meals. Moderate.

All of the other accommodations are in Tuherahera village, a bit over a km from the airstrip. At these you'll usually get a room with shared bath in a family home at CFP 2,000-2,500 pp for the room only or CFP 4,000 pp and up with two meals. Among the people offering this are Isidore and Nini Hoiore (tel. 96-22-89), Colette Huri (tel. 96-22-47), Maxime Metua (tel. 96-22-38), and Hélène Teakura (tel. 96-22-52). Some places such as Chez Maxime or Chez Colette may allow you to cook your own food (ask). Inexpensive.

All of these organize boat trips to bird islands such as Puarua, picnics on a *motu,* snorkeling in the pass, visits to Eden Point, etc, costing CFP 3,000-6,000 pp. Scuba diving is available with the **Raie Manta Club** (Alex Vaure, B.P. 9, 98778 Tikehau; tel. 96-22-53, fax 96-85-60) in Tuherahera. Alex will show you huge manta rays, sea turtles, shark-infested caves, great schools of barracuda, and fabulous red reefs.

Air Tahiti flies from Papeete to Tikehau (CFP 13,600) four times a week and from Rangiroa (CFP 4,400) twice a week. The supply boat *Dory* sails direct from Papeete to Tikehau (CFP 2,500) once a week.

Toau

Yachts can enter the lagoon at Toau, between Kaukura and Fakarava, though the pass is on the windward side. No flights land on Toau.

THE NUCLEAR TEST ZONE

The former French nuclear test site operated by the Centre d'Expérimentations du Pacifique until 1996 is at the southeastern end of the Tuamotu group, 1,200 km from Tahiti. The main site was 30-km-long Moruroa atoll, but Fangataufa atoll 37 km south of Moruroa was also used. In 1962 the French nuclear testing facilities in the Algerian Sahara had to be abandoned after that country won its independence, so in 1963 French president Charles de Gaulle officially announced that France was shifting the program to Moruroa and Fangataufa. Between 1966 and 1996 a confirmed 181 nuclear bombs, reaching up to 200 kilotons, were set off in the Tuamotus at the rate of six a year. By 1974 the French had conducted 41 *atmospheric* tests, 36 over or near Moruroa and five over Fangataufa. Five of these were megaton hydrogen bombs.

Way back in 1963, the U.S., Britain, and the USSR agreed in the Partial Test Ban Treaty to halt nuclear tests in the atmosphere. France chose not to sign. On 23 June 1973, the World Court urged France to discontinue the nuclear tests, which might drop radioactive material on surrounding territories. When the French government refused to recognize the court's jurisdiction in this matter, New Zealand Prime Minister Norman Kirk ordered the New Zealand frigate *Otago* to enter the danger zone off Moruroa, and on 23 July Peru broke diplomatic relations with France. On 15 August French commandos boarded the protest vessels *Fri* and *Greenpeace III,* attacking and arresting the crews.

In 1974, with opposition mounting in the Territorial Assembly and growing world indignation, French President Giscard D'Estaing ordered a switch to *underground* tests. Eighteen years and 134 tests later, as the Greenpeace *Rainbow Warrior II* confronted French commandos off Moruroa, French prime minister Pierre Bérégovoy suddenly announced on 8 April 1992 that nuclear testing was being suspended. President Boris Yeltsin had already halted Russian nuclear testing in October 1991, and in October 1992 U.S. president George Bush followed suit by halting underground testing in Nevada. Despite the French moratorium, the testing facilities in the Tuamotus were maintained at great expense, and in June 1995 newly elected President Jacques Chirac ordered the testing to resume without bothering to consult the Polynesians.

On 31 August 1995, with the first test imminent, the Greenpeace ship *Rainbow Warrior II* reached Moruroa just over 10 years after its predecessor had been sunk by French terrorists at Auckland, New Zealand. As the ship crossed the 12-mile limit and launched six Zodiacs toward the French drilling rigs in the lagoon, the *Rainbow Warrior* was boarded by French commandos who fired tear gas at the unresisting crew and smashed computers, generators, and the ship's engine. The MV *Greenpeace* was nearby in international waters at the time, and the French seized it too on the pretext that it had launched a helicopter that crossed the territorial limit. With the main protest vessels impounded and their crews deported, the French hoped they could carry on with the tests without further interference.

So on 5 September 1995, despite opposition from 63% of the French public and a large majority of Polynesians, the French military exploded the first of a planned series of eight bombs under Moruroa. This led to the worst rioting ever seen in Polynesia as thousands of enraged Tahitians ran amok, ransacking Faa'a Airport and much of Papeete. The independence leader Oscar Temaru managed to calm the crowd, and the French brought in additional riot police to guard the capital. After a second blast on 2 October the South Pacific Forum carried out its threat to suspend France as a "dialogue partner."

In an attempt to deflect mounting worldwide condemnation, Chirac announced that the number of tests would be reduced from eight to six. Additionally, France, the U.S., and Britain said they would finally sign the protocols of the 1985 South Pacific Nuclear-Free Zone Treaty. The sixth and last test was carried out below Fangataufa atoll on 27 January 1996. Since then

the facilities on Moruroa have been demolished and it's very unlikely there will ever be another nuclear test in this area.

Moruroa

Obviously, an atoll, with its porous coral cap sitting on a narrow basalt base, is the most dangerous place in the world to stage underground nuclear explosions. It's doubtful this was ever considered. Moruroa was chosen for its isolated location, far from major population centers that might be affected by fallout. By 1974, when atmospheric testing had to cease, the French military had a huge investment in the area. So rather than move to a more secure location in France or elsewhere, they decided to take a chance. Underground testing was to be carried out in Moruroa's basalt core, 500-1,200 meters below the surface of the atoll. Eventually 130 bombs were exploded below Moruroa and 10 below Fangataufa, making France the only nuclear state that conducted tests *under* a Pacific island.

On 10 September 1966 President Charles de Gaulle was present at Moruroa to witness the atmospheric test of a bomb suspended from a balloon. Weather conditions caused the test to be postponed, and the following day conditions were still unsuitable, as the wind was blowing in the direction of inhabited islands to the west instead of toward uninhabited Antarctica to the south. De Gaulle complained that he was a busy man and could afford to wait no longer, so the test went ahead, spreading radioactive fallout across the Cook Islands, Niue, Tonga, Samoa, Fiji, and Tuvalu. Tahiti itself was the most directly affected island, but the French authorities have never acknowledged this fact.

Archive documentation published by the French weekly *Nouvel Observateur* in February 1998 has confirmed that French defense officials knew very well that nearby islands such as Mangareva, Pukarua, Reao, and Tureia were receiving high doses of radiation during the 1966 texts, even as spokespersons publicly described

VOYAGES OF THE *RAINBOW WARRIOR*

Beginning in 1978 the *Rainbow Warrior* confronted whalers, sealers, and nuclear waste dumpers in the North Atlantic. In 1980 the ship was seized in international waters by the Spanish navy while interfering with the Spanish whale kill. After five months under arrest in Spain the ship made a dramatic escape. In 1981-82 *Rainbow Warrior* led the struggle against the Canadian harp seal slaughter, bringing about a European Economic Community ban on the import of all seal products. The next year the ship battled Soviet whalers in Siberia, finally escaping to Alaska with naval units in hot pursuit. A confrontation with Peruvian whalers led to the termination of that whale hunt. In 1985, fresh from being fitted with sails in Florida, the *Rainbow Warrior* reentered the Pacific to rescue nuclear victims from Rongelap in the Marshalls. In July, 1985, as the valiant little ship lay at anchor in Auckland Harbor, New Zealand, externally attached terrorist bombs tore through the hull in the dead of night to prevent a voyage to Moruroa to protest French nuclear testing in the Pacific.

Rainbow Warrior, *onetime flagship of the Greenpeace fleet*

BOB RACE

the tests as "innocuous." France's radiological security service recommended at the time that the four islands be evacuated, but the newly discovered documents only note that "the hypothesis of an evacuation was excluded for political and psychological reasons."

A serious accident occurred on 25 July 1979 when a nuclear device became stuck halfway down an 800-meter shaft. Since army engineers were unable to move the device, they exploded it where it was, causing a massive chunk of the outer slope of the atoll to break loose. This generated a huge tsunami, which hit Moruroa, overturning cars and injuring seven people. After the blast, a crack 40 cm wide and two km long appeared on the surface of the island. As a precaution against further tsunamis and hurricanes, refuge platforms were built at intervals around the atoll. For an hour before and after each test all personnel had to climb up on these platforms.

By 1981 Moruroa was as punctured as a Swiss cheese and sinking two centimeters after every test, or a meter and a half between 1976 and 1981. In 1981, with the atoll's 60-km coral rim dangerously fractured by drilling shafts, the

French switched to underwater testing in the Moruroa lagoon, in order to be closer to the center of the island's core. In 1987 the famous French underwater explorer Jacques Cousteau filmed spectacular cracks and fissures in the atoll as well as submarine slides and subsidence, and described the impact of testing on the atoll as creating "premature and accelerated aging." By 1988 even French officials were acknowledging that the 108 underground blasts had severely weakened the geological formations beneath Moruroa, and it was announced that, despite the additional cost involved, the largest underground tests would take place henceforth on nearby Fangataufa atoll. The military base remained on Moruroa, and small groups of workers and technicians were sent over to Fangataufa every time a test was made there.

The French government always claimed that it owned Moruroa and Fangataufa because in 1964 a standing committee of the Territorial Assembly voted three to two to cede the atolls to France for an indefinite period. This was never ratified by the full assembly, and French troops had occupied the islands before the vote was taken anyway. The traditional owners of Moruroa, the people of Tureia atoll, 115 km north, were not consulted and have never been compensated.

Impact

In 1983 the French government invited a delegation of scientists from Australia, New Zealand, and Papua New Guinea to visit Moruroa. Significantly, they were not permitted to take samples from the northern or western areas of the atoll, nor of lagoon sediments. The scientists reported that "if fracturing of the volcanics accompanied a test and allowed a vertical release of radioactivity to the limestones, specific contaminants would, in this worst case, enter the biosphere within five years."

On 21 June 1987 Jacques Cousteau was present for a test at Moruroa and the next day he took water samples in the lagoon, the first time such independent tests had been allowed. Two samples collected by Cousteau nine km apart contained traces of cesium-134, an isotope with a half-life of two years. Though French officials claimed the cesium-134 remained from atmospheric testing before 1975, a 1990 study by American radiologist Norm Buske proved that this is not scientifically feasible, and that leakage from underground testing is the only possible explanation. In 1990 a computer model of Moruroa developed by New Zealand scientists indicated that radioactive groundwater with a half-life of several thousand years may be seeping through fractures in the atoll at the rate of 100 meters a year and, according to Prof. Manfred Hochstein, head of Auckland University's Geothermal Institute, "in about 30 years the disaster will hit us." In December 1990 Buske found traces of cesium-134 in plankton collected in the open ocean, outside the 12-mile exclusion zone. Buske's findings indicate that the release of contamination into the Pacific from the numerous cracks and fissures has already started.

Unlike the U.S., which has paid millions of dollars in compensation money to the Marshallese victims of its nuclear testing program, the French government has refused to even acknowledge the already-apparent effects of its 41 atmospheric nuclear tests. From 1963 to 1983, no public health statistics were published in the colony. Now the rates of thyroid cancer, leukemia, brain tumors, and stillbirths are on the upswing in Tahiti-Polynesia, and the problem of seafood poisoning (ciguatera) in the nearby Gambier Islands is clearly related. Before being employed at the base, all workers at Moruroa had to sign contracts binding them to eternal silence and waiving access to their own medical records or to any right to compensation for future health problems. Surveys conducted by the Tahitian NGO Hiti Tau among 737 of the 12,000 Polynesians who worked at Moruroa between 1966 and 1996 have demonstrated that many have experienced adverse health effects, yet no official studies of this impact have been carried out.

In July 1998 the pro-nuclear International Atomic Energy Agency issued a report commissioned by the French government that claims there has been no adverse effect on human health or the environment that can be attributed to radiation from radioactive residue. The study only dealt with the 1995 test series and made no attempt to investigate the previous testing. The report does admit that about eight kilograms of plutonium and other dangerous elements still rest in sediments in the Moruroa and Fangataufa lagoons as a result of the atmospheric testing and plutonium safety trials. More worrisome are the tritium levels in the Moruroa lagoon, which are 10 times higher than those of the surrounding sea, a result of leakage from cavities created by the underground tests. A detailed geological examination of Moruroa's fragile basalt base was not carried out, yet the IAEA report concludes that "no remedial action is needed" and "no further environmental monitoring" is required for purposes of radiological study.

A detachment of 30 foreign legionnaires now keeps watch over the abandoned wharf, airstrip, and concrete bunkers at the dismantled Moruroa test site (Fangataufa has been abandoned). No one is allowed in without official approval. One can only hope the IAEA is right and that there's nothing to worry about, although based on the experience of previous official pronouncements on Moruroa, the credibility of this French-funded study is open to question. Without ongoing monitoring Moruroa remains wrapped in the same sinister mystery that has dogged it since 1966. Nothing will ever change the fact that even with the testing over, French radioactivity will remain in the Tuamotus for thousands of years, and the unknown future consequences of the tests remain as uncertain as ever. The story definitely isn't over yet.

an early 19th-century engraving of Mangarevans aboard a craft with sail

M.G.L. DOMENY DE RIENZI

THE GAMBIER ISLANDS

The Gambier (or Mangareva) Islands are just north of the tropic of Capricorn, 1,650 km southeast of Tahiti. The southerly location means a cooler climate. The archipelago, contrasting sharply with the atolls of the Tuamotus, consists of 10 rocky islands enclosed on three sides by a semicircular barrier reef 65 km long. In all, there are 46 square km of dry land. The Polynesian inhabitants named the main and largest island Mangareva, or "Floating Mountain," for 482-meter-high Mount Duff. Unlike the Marquesas, where the mountains are entirely jungle-clad, the Gambiers have hilltops covered with tall *aeho* grass. Black pearls are cultured on numerous platforms on both sides of the Mangareva lagoon. A local seabird, the *karako,* crows at dawn like a rooster.

History

Mangareva, which was originally settled from the Marquesas Islands around A.D. 1100, was shortly afterwards the jumping-off place for small groups that discovered and occupied Pitcairn and Henderson islands. In 1797 Capt. James Wilson of the London Missionary Society's ship *Duff* named the group for English Admiral James Gambier (1756-1833), a hero of the Napoleonic wars who had helped organize the expedition. France made the Gambiers a protectorate in 1871 and annexed the group in 1881.

Mangareva was the area of operations for a fanatical French priest, Father Honoré Laval of the Congregation for the Sacred Hearts. Upon hearing whalers' tales of rampant cannibalism and marvelous pearls, Laval left his monastery in Chile and with another priest reached the Gambiers in 1834. An old Mangarevan prophecy had foretold the coming of two magicians whose god was all-powerful and Laval himself toppled the dreaded stone effigy of the god Tu on the island's sacred *marae*. He then single-handedly imposed a ruthless and inflexible moral code on the islanders, recruiting them as virtual slaves to build a 1,200-seat cathedral, convents, and triumphal arches—116 stone buildings in all—with the result that he utterly destroyed this once vigorous island culture and practically wiped out its people. During Laval's 37-year reign the population dropped from 9,000 to 500. You can still see his architectural masterpiece—the Cathedral of St. Michael with its twin towers of white coral rock from Kamaka and altar shining with polished mother-of-pearl—a monument to horror and yet another lost culture. The cathedral was built between 1839 and 1848 on the *ahu* of the island's principal *marae,* and Laval's colleague, Father François Caret, who died in 1844, lies buried in a crypt before the altar. In 1871 Laval was removed from Mangareva by a French warship, tried for murder on Tahiti, and declared insane.

For a glimpse of the Gambiers half a century ago and a fuller account of Père Laval, read Robert Lee Eskridge's *Manga Reva, The Forgotten Islands.*

The Nuclear Impact
A dramatic intensification of the ciguatera problem in the Gambiers since the late 1960s is believed to be linked to reef damage or pollution originating at the former nuclear-testing base on Moruroa, 400 km northwest. During the atmospheric testing series (until 1974), Mangarevans had to take refuge in French-constructed fallout shelters whenever so advised by the military. Before each of the 41 atmospheric tests, French warships would evacuate the 3,000 persons from Moruroa, usually to Mangareva, Hao, and Fakarava. Upon arrival the ships were washed down with seawater, spreading radioactive contamination into the lagoons, yet the French never made the slightest attempt to clean up after themselves. Between 1971 and 1980 the annual incidence of ciguatera remained above 30%, peaking at 56% in 1975. Each of the inhabitants has suffered five to seven excruciating attacks of seafood poisoning and lagoon fish can no longer be eaten.

Now, increases in birth defects, kidney problems, and cancer among the inhabitants are being covered up by the authorities. It's believed that a deciding reason for the French decision to launch a terrorist attack on Greenpeace's *Rainbow Warrior* in 1985 was an intelligence report indicating that the ship intended to proceed to Mangareva with doctors aboard to assess the radiation exposure of residents.

Orientation
Most of the current 1,100 inhabitants of the Gambiers live on eight-by-1.5-km Mangareva, of which Rikitea is the main village. A post office, seven small shops, a *gendarmerie* (tel. 97-82-68), an infirmary, schools, and a cathedral three times as big as the one in Papeete make up the infrastructure of this administrative backwater.

Sights
The tomb of Grégoire Maputeoa, the 35th and last king of Mangareva (died 1868), is in a small chapel behind the cathedral. Follow the path be-

The Cathedral of St. Michael at Rikitea village overlooks Mangareva's Harbor.

ANSELM ZÄNKERT

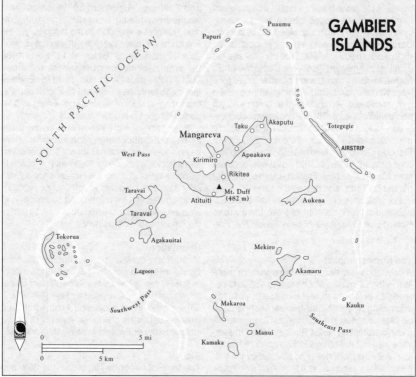

© DAVID STANLEY

hind the church to the top of the hill and through the gate on the left (close it after you as dogs dig up the graves). Among the walled ruins of Rouru convent in Rikitea one can pick out the chapel, refectory, infirmary, and a dormitory for 60 local nuns. On the opposite side of Rikitea is a huge nuclear-fallout shelter built during the French atmospheric testing at Moruroa.

A 28-km road runs around Mangareva offering ever-changing views. At the north end of the island it passes St. Joseph's Chapel (1836) at Taku, place of worship of the Mangarevan royal family. The south coast of Mangareva is one of the most beautiful in Polynesia, with a tremendous variety of landscapes, plants, trees, smells, and colors.

The white sands of **Aukena** make a good daytrip destination by boat. The Church of St. Raphael here is the oldest in the Gambier Islands and to the south are the ruins of the Rehe Seminary (1840). The Church of Notre-Dame-de-la-Paix (1844) on abandoned **Akamaru** has twin towers added in 1862. Solitary **Makaroa** is a barren, rugged 136-meter-high island.

St. Gabriel Church (1868) on **Taravai** has a neo-Gothic facade decorated with seashells. In a cliffside cave on the uninhabited island of **Agakauitai** the mummies of 35 generations of cannibal kings are interred.

PRACTICALITIES

Accommodations

Although it costs an arm and a leg to fly here, staying is inexpensive. The four guest houses on Mangareva each charge around CFP 2,000/3,000/3,500 single/double/triple for a room with shared bath. Cooking facilities are provided, or you can order food at CFP 2,000/4,000 pp for half/full board. All offer boat transfers from the airport at CFP 1,000 pp return and children under 13 are half price for all services.

Chez Bianca et Benoit (B.P. 19, 98755 Rikitea; tel. 97-83-76) is a modern two-story house with three rooms. It's just above Rikitea and the view across to Aukena is lovely.

Chez Pierre et Mariette (B.P. 28, 98755 Rikitea; tel. 97-82-87), near the wharf, also has three rooms. **Chez Terii et Hélène** (tel. 97-82-80) nearby has two rooms.

Farther north is **Chez Jojo** (Jocelyne Mamatui, B.P. 1, 98755 Rikitea; tel. 97-82-61) with two rooms. Camping space here is CFP 1,000 pp.

Transportation

The airstrip (GMR) is on Totegegie, a long coral island eight km northeast of Rikitea. Arriving passengers pay CFP 500 pp each way for the boat ride to the village. The Air Tahiti flights from Papeete (CFP 30,000 one way) are either nonstop or via Hao. The monthly supply ship from Papeete, the *Manava IV,* also travels via Hao. The one-way fare from Papeete is CFP 7,500/13,101 deck/couchette (no cabins), plus CFP 2,575 a day for three meals. Large vessels can enter the lagoon through passes on the west, southwest, and southeast. Mr. Jean Anania (nicknamed "Siki") offers speedboat charters and fishing trips.

M.G.L. DOMENY DE RIENZI

a Marquesan me'ae *at Nuku Hiva in the early 19th century*

THE MARQUESAS ISLANDS

The Marquesas Islands are the farthest north of the high islands of the South Pacific, on the same latitude as the Solomons. Though the group was known as Te Henua Enata (The Land of Men) by the Polynesian inhabitants, depopulation during the 19th and 20th centuries has left many of the valleys empty. Ten main islands form a line 300 km long, roughly 1,400 km northeast of Tahiti, but only six are inhabited today: Nuku Hiva, Ua Pou, and Ua Huka in a cluster to the northwest, and Hiva Oa, Tahuata, and Fatu Hiva to the southeast. The administrative centers, Atuona (Hiva Oa), Hakahau (Ua Pou), and Taiohae (Nuku Hiva), are the only places with post offices, banks, *gendarmes,* etc.

The expense and difficulty in getting there has kept many potential visitors away. Budget accommodations are scarce and public transport is nonexistent, which makes getting around a major expense unless you're really prepared to rough it. Of the main islands, getting to and from Hiva Oa airport is easier but Nuku Hiva has

more variety. Cruising yachts from California often call at the Marquesas on their way to Papeete, and yachties should also steer for Hiva Oa first to enjoy the smoothest possible sailing through the rest of the group. For hikers, the Marquesas are paradise. Multitudes of waterfalls tumble down the slopes, and eerie overgrown archaeological remains tell of a golden era long gone. If you enjoy quiet, unspoiled places, you'll like the Marquesas, but one month should be enough. The Marquesas have been left behind by their remoteness.

The Land

These wild, rugged islands feature steep cliffs and valleys leading up to high central ridges, sectioning the islands off into a cartwheel of segments, which creates major transportation difficulties. Large reefs don't form due to the cold south equatorial current though there are isolated stretches of coral. The absence of protective reefs has prevented the creation of coastal plains, so no roads go around any of the islands. Most of the people live in the narrow, fertile river valleys. The interiors are inhabited only by hundreds of wild horses, cattle, and goats, which have destroyed much of the original vegetation. A Catholic bishop introduced the horses from Chile in 1856, and today they're almost a symbol of the Marquesas. The islands are abundant with lemons, tangerines, oranges, grapefruit, bananas, mangoes, and papayas. Taro and especially breadfruit are the main staples. Birdlife is rich, and the waters around the Marquesas teem with lobster, fish, and sharks.

The subtropical climate is hotter and drier than that of Tahiti. July and August are the coolest months. The deep bays on the west sides of the islands are better sheltered for shipping, and the humidity is lower there than on the east sides, which catch the trade winds. The precipitation is uneven, with drought some years, heavy rainfall the others. The southern islands of the Marquesas (Hiva Oa, Tahuata, Fatu Hiva) are green and humid; the northern islands (Nuku Hiva, Ua Huka, Ua Pou) are brown and dry.

HISTORY AND EVENTS

Pre-European Society

Marquesan houses were built on high platforms *(paepae)* scattered through the valleys (still fairly easy to find). Each valley had a rectangular ceremonial area *(tohua)* where important festivals took place. Archaeologists have been able to trace stone temples (*me'ae,* called *marae* elsewhere in Tahiti-Polynesia), agricultural terraces, and earthen fortifications *(akaua)* half hidden in the jungle, evocative reminders of a vanished civilization. Then as now, the valleys were isolated from one another by high ridges and turbulent seas, yet warfare was vicious and cannibalism an important incentive. An able warrior could attain great power. Local hereditary chiefs exercised authority over commoners.

The Marquesans' artistic style was one of the most powerful and refined in the Pacific. The ironwood war club was their most distinctive symbol, but there were also finely carved wooden bowls, fan handles, and tikis of stone and wood, both miniature and massive. The carvings are noted for the faces: the mouth with lips

parted and the bespectacled eyes. Both men and women wore carved ivory earplugs. Men's entire bodies were covered with bold and striking tattoos, a practice banned by the Catholic missionaries. Stilts were used by boys for racing and mock fighting. This was about the only part of Polynesia where polyandry was common. There was a strong cult of the dead: the bodies or skulls of ancestors were carefully preserved. Both Easter Island (around A.D. 500) and Hawaii (around A.D. 700) were colonized from here.

European Contact

The existence of these islands was long concealed from the world by the Spanish, to prevent the English from taking possession of them. The southern group was found by Álvaro de Mendaña in July 1595 during his second voyage of exploration from Peru. He named them Las Marquesas de Mendoza after his benefactor,

The Marquesans once staged races and mock battles on stilts such as these; the participants attempted to knock one another off balance.

FIELD MUSEUM OF NATURAL HISTORY, CHICAGO

The Marquesans preserved the skulls of their ancestors

FIELD MUSEUM OF NATURAL HISTORY, CHICAGO

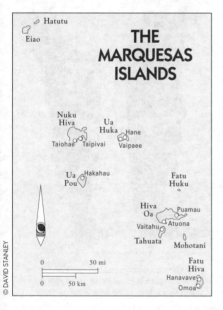

THE MARQUESAS ISLANDS

Hatutu
Eiao

Nuku Hiva
Taiohae Taipivai
Ua Huka Hane
Vaipaee

Ua Pou Hakahau

Fatu Huku

Hiva Oa Puamau
Vaitahu Atuona
Tahuata Mohotani

Fatu Hiva
Hanavave
Omoa

0   50 mi
0   50 km

© DAVID STANLEY

the Spanish viceroy. The first island sighted (Fatu Hiva) seemed uninhabited, but as Mendaña's *San Jerónimo* sailed nearer, scores of outriggers appeared, paddled by about 400 robust, light-skinned islanders. Their hair was long and loose, and they were naked and tattooed in blue patterns. The natives boarded the ship, but when they became overly curious and bold, Mendaña ordered a gun fired, and they jumped over the side.

Then began one of the most murderous and shameful of all the white explorers' entries into the South Pacific region. As a matter of caution, Mendaña's men began shooting natives on sight, in one instance hanging three bodies in the shore camp on Santa Cristina (Tahuata) as a warning. They left behind three large crosses, the date cut in a tree, and over 200 dead Polynesians. When Captain Cook arrived at Tahuata in 1774 it soon became obvious that knowledge of the earlier Spanish visit had remained alive in oral traditions, and Cook and his crew were shunned.

The northern Marquesas Islands were "discovered" by Joseph Ingraham of the American trading vessel *Hope* on 19 April 1791. After that, blackbirders, firearms, disease, and alcohol reduced the population. American whalers called frequently from 1800 onwards. Although France took possession of the group in 1842, Peruvian slavers kidnapped some Marquesans to South America in 1863 to work the plantations and mines. Those few able to return thanks to diplomatic lobbying by their French protectors brought a catastrophic smallpox epidemic. The Marquesans clung to their warlike, cannibalistic ways until 95% of their number had died—the remainder adopted Catholicism. (The Marquesas today is the only island group of Tahiti-Polynesia with a Catholic majority.) From 80,000 at the beginning of the 19th century, the population fell to about

15,000 by 1842, when the French "protectors" arrived, and to a devastated 2,000 by 1926. Even today the total population is just 8,000.

The Marquesas Today

Slowly the Marquesas are catching up with the rest of the world—VCRs are the latest introduced species. Cruise ships are also finding their ways into the group. Yet the islands remain very untouristy. Though there are many negative attitudes toward the French and on Tahiti talk for independence is heard, the Marquesans realize that without French subsidies their economy would collapse and they would become even more distant from the Tuamotus, Tahiti, and "civilization." Making copra would no longer be an economically viable activity and far fewer supply ships would call at the islands. Hospitalization, drugs, and dental care are provided free by the government and a monthly family allowance of US$100 is paid for each child under 16—quite a bundle if you have eight kids, as many do! If the Marquesans had to give up their cars, videos, and U.S. frozen chicken, many would abandon the already underpopulated islands.

The Marquesan language, divided into north and south dialects, is only about 50% comprehensible to a Tahitian and is actually a bit closer to Rarotongan and Hawaiian. There's a small separatist movement here which believes the Marquesas will receive more benefits as a distinct colony of France, or failing that, as a country independent of Tahiti. And just to complicate matters, twice as many Marquesans live in Papeete as in the Marquesas itself.

Events

The Marquesas Islands Festival or *Matava'a o te Henua Enata* is a major cultural event celebrated every few years in December with dancing, singing, drumming, and sports, plus handicraft displays and feasts. Aside from strengthening and reviving traditional knowledge and skills, numerous archaeological sites have been restored or rebuilt in preparation for these events. Previous festivals have been at Ua Pou (1987), Nuku Hiva (1989), Hiva Oa (1991), and Ua Pou (1995), and the next will be on Nuku Hiva again in 1999, just in time for the millennium.

UNINHABITED ISLANDS

Motane (Mohotani) is an eight-km-long island rising to 520 meters about 18 km southeast of Hiva Oa. The depredations of wild sheep on Motane turned the island into a treeless desert. When the Spaniards "discovered" it in 1595, Motane was well-wooded and populated, but today it's uninhabited.

Uninhabited Eiao and Hatutu islands, 85 km northwest of Nuku Hiva, are the remotest (and oldest) of the Marquesas. Eiao is a 40-square-km island, 10 km long and 576 meters high, with rather difficult landings on the northwest and west sides. The French once used Eiao as a site

M.G.L. DOMENY DE RIENZI

Madisonville, Nuku Hiva: On 19 November 1813, Captain David Porter of the U.S. frigate Essex took possession of Nuku Hiva, Marquesas Islands, for the United States.

of deportation for criminals or "rebellious" natives. The Queen of Raiatea and 136 Raiateans who had fought against the French were interned here from 1897 to 1900. In 1972 the French Army drilled holes 1,000 meters down into Eiao to check the island's suitability for underground nuclear testing but deemed the basalt rock too fragile for such use. Wild cattle, sheep, pigs, and donkeys forage across Eiao, ravaging the vegetation and suffering from droughts. In contrast, the profusion of fishlife off Eiao is incredible.

Hatutu, the northernmost of the Marquesas, measures 7.5 square km. Thousands of birds nest here.

TRANSPORTATION

A visit to the Marquesas requires either lots of money or lots of time, or both. An **Air Tahiti** ATR flies from Papeete to Nuku Hiva five times a week (three hours, CFP 28,700). One of these ATR flights is via Manihi and Rangiroa. There's also a weekly Dornier 228 flight from Rangiroa to Hiva Oa via Napuka or Puka Puka (CFP 24,500), but the plane is always full. Ask about Air Tahiti's "Decouverte Marquises" ticket, which allows a return flight from Papeete to Nuku Hiva for CFP 49,900, to Atuona, Ua Pou, or Ua Huka for CFP 54,900. It's valid for a stay of 7-15 days and you may only use off-peak "blue" flights (not available in March, July, August, or around Christmas).

Dornier flights between Nuku Hiva and Ua Huka and Ua Pou operate weekly, connecting with one of the ATR flights from Papeete. Fares from Nuku Hiva are CFP 5,100 to Ua Pou, CFP 5,100 to Ua Huka, and CFP 8,800 to Atuona. No flight goes straight from Ua Pou to Ua Huka—you must backtrack to Nuku Hiva. Get a through ticket to your final destination, as flights to Hiva Oa, Ua Pou, and Ua Huka are all the same price from Papeete (Nuku Hiva is CFP 1,300 cheaper). Tahuata and Fatu Hiva are without air service. All flights are heavily booked. Coming or going, remember the 30-minute time difference between Tahiti and the Marquesas.

Three ships, the *Aranui, Tamarii Tuamotu,* and *Taporo IV,* sail monthly from Papeete, calling at all six inhabited Marquesas Islands. The *Aranui* and *Taporo IV* are the easiest to use, as they follow a regular schedule. For more information turn the Tahiti-Polynesia introduction.

The freighter *Aranui* is the more convenient and comfortable, if you can afford it. The round-trip voyages designed for tourists flown in from Europe and the U.S. cost cruise-ship prices (from US$3,000 pp return). See the introduction to Tahiti-Polynesia for details. The other main interisland boat, *Taporo IV,* is cheaper at CFP 20,000/30,000 deck/cabin one-way from Papeete to any Marquesan port, but it's basic. Food is included in the passages and it's not necessary to reserve deck passage on these boats. The ships tie up to the wharves at Taiohae, Atuona, Vaipae'e, and Hakahau; at Tahuata and Fatu Hiva, passengers must go ashore by whaleboat. In stormy weather, the landings can be dangerous.

Archipels Croisieres (B.P. 1160, Papetoai, Moorea; tel. 56-36-39, fax 56-35-87) offers seven-night catamaran cruises around the Marquesas at US$2,050 pp double occupancy, airfare not included. The eight passengers sleep in four cabins and visit five of the six inhabited islands with shore excursions and airport transfers included. Departures are guaranteed even if only two people book. In the U.S. and Canada, Tahiti Vacations handles bookings for both Archipels and the *Aranui.*

To island hop within the Marquesas you could try using any of the three ships mentioned above, if they happen to be going where you want to go, or ask at local town halls about the government boat *Ka'oha Nui,* which circulates among the islands on official business. Private boats run from Taiohae to Ua Pou fairly frequently, and there are municipal boats from Atuona to Tahuata and Fatu Hiva at least once a week. Chartering boats interisland is extremely expensive, and to join a regular trip you just have to be lucky, persistent, and prepared to wait. You can also island-hop by helicopter if you've got tons of money to throw around.

Getting around the individual islands can be a challenge as there's no organized public transportation other than expensive airport transfers, and due to the condition of the roads rental cars are limited to a few pricey vehicles at Taiohae and Atuona. It's fairly easy to hire a chauffeur-driven vehicle on Hiva Oa, Nuku Hiva, Ua Huka, and Ua Pou, but expect to pay CFP 15,000 a day and up. Since this amount can be shared among as many people as can fit inside, you'll want to join or form a group. While making your inquiries, keep your ears open for any mention of boat tours as these are often no more expensive than land tours.

Hitchhiking is complicated because many of the private vehicles you see out on the roads double as taxis and drivers who depend on tourists for a large part of their incomes are unlikely to be eager to give rides for free. In small communities like these you'll soon become known if you hitchhike, and it may not work to your advantage (for example, the driver who passes you may be the owner of the guest house where you intended to stay). The safest option for hardy backpackers is just to count on having to walk the whole way and accept any lifts that happen to be offered. It's too far to walk from Nuku Hiva airport to Taiohae or from Atuona to Puama'u in one day, but many other stretches can be covered on foot. If you're fit you can easily walk from Taiohae to Taipivai and from Taipivai to Hatiheu on Nuku Hiva, and from Atuona to Ta'aoa or the airport on Hiva Oa. Almost everywhere on Fatu Hiva, Tahuata, Ua Huka, and Ua Pou is accessible on foot, provided you have the time. If you pack a tent, food, and water, you'll be self sufficient and able to see the islands on a shoestring budget.

NUKU HIVA

Nuku Hiva is the largest (339 square km) and most populous (2,375 inhabitants) of the Marquesas. Taiohae (population 1,700) on the south coast is the administrative and economic center of the Marquesas. It's a modern little town with a post office, a hospital, a town hall, a bank, five grocery stores, street lighting, and several hotels. Radio Meitai broadcasts over 101.3 MHz. Winding mountain roads lead northeast from Taiohae to Taipivai and Hatiheu villages or northwest toward the airport. In the center of the island Mt. Tekao (1,224 meters) rises above the vast, empty Toovii Plateau.

Taiohae Bay is a flooded volcanic crater guarded by two tiny islands called The Sentinels. Though open to the south, Taiohae's deep harbor offers excellent anchorage. Cruising yachts toss in the hock on the west side of the bay below the Keikahanui Inn, while the *Aranui* and *Taporo* tie up to a wharf at the southeast end of town. Take care with the drinking water at Taiohae. Unfortunately, many beaches around Nuku Hiva are infested with sandflies called *no-nos* that give nasty bites (the bugs disappear after dark).

History
In 1813 Capt. David Porter of the American frigate *Essex* annexed Nuku Hiva for the United States, though the act was never ratified by Congress. Britain and the U.S. had gone to war in 1812 and Porter's mission was to harass British shipping in the Pacific. After capturing a dozen ships off South America, Porter arrived at Nuku Hiva and built a fort at the present site of Taiohae, which he named Madisonville for the U.S. president of his day. Porter allowed himself to be drawn into local conflicts among the Polynesian tribes. A few months later he left to continue his raiding and was defeated by two British warships off Chile. In 1842 the French erected Fort Collet on the site of Porter's fort, near the marina at the east end of Taiohae.

Sandalwood traders followed Porter, then whalers. Herman Melville arrived on the American whaling ship *Acushnet* in 1842, and his book *Typee*, written after a one-month stay in the Taipivai Valley, is still the classic narrative of Marquesan life during the 19th century. A half century later Scottish writer Robert Louis Stevenson visited the island.

SIGHTS

Sights of Taiohae
Many stone- and woodcarvers continue to work on Nuku Hiva, making wooden tikis, bowls, ukuleles, ceremonial war clubs, paddles, and ukuleles. Some items are on display at the **Banque Socredo** near the *mairie*. The **Monument to the Dead** obelisk is on the waterfront a bit west.

More woodcarvings, including a massive wooden pulpit bearing the symbols of the four

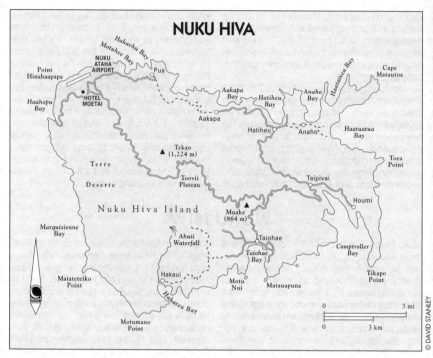

NUKU HIVA

evangelists, may be viewed in **Notre-Dame Cathedral** (1974) on the west side of central Taiohae. Two towers retained from an earlier church give access to the cathedral's open courtyard. Ask to see the small collection of artifacts at the bishop's residence.

The road inland just west of the cathedral leads up the Meau Valley. About a kilometer up this way and to the right of the road is the restored **Mauia Paepae** graced by a contemporary tiki.

Return to the bayside road and continue west past the **Temehea Tohua,** created for the Marquesas Islands Festival in 1989. Among the modern tikis on this platform are the figures of Temoana and Vaekehu who were designated king and queen of the island by the French in 1842. Also on the left and 600 meters further along is the wooden **Typee Memorial** (1842-1992) by Séverin Kahe'e Taupotini (who also carved the cathedral pulpit). At the southwest end of the bay the track climbs inland from the Nuku Hiva Village Hôtel and continues two km

over the ridge to secluded **Haaotupa Bay,** a nice picnic spot.

West of Taiohae

At Hakaui, 15 km west of Taiohae, a river runs down a narrow steep-sided valley. Fantastic 350-meter **Ahuii Waterfall,** highest in the territory, drops from the plateau at the far end of the valley, four km from the coast. It's a two-hour walk from Hakaui to the waterfall with a few thigh-high river crossings after rains (guide not required). The trail passes many crumbling platforms, indicating that the valley was once well populated. If you swim in the pool at the falls beware of falling pebbles. A boat from Taiohae to Hakaui would cost CFP 12,500 and up return, but an overgrown 12-km switchback trail also crosses the 535-meter ridge from above Haaotupa Bay to uninhabited Hakaui. You'll need to be adventurous and good at finding your own way to follow it (allow four hours each way between Taiohae to Hakaui).

Across the Island

For a good view of Taiohae Bay, hike up to **Muake** (864 meters) in half a day there and back. After seven km turn left where the airport and Taipivai roads divide, then left again into the forest another four km along. The remains of an old Marquesan fort can be found in the vicinity of the modern radio tower two km down this road. From up here lifts are possible with market gardeners headed for the agricultural station on the 900-meter-high **Toovii Plateau** to the west. Herds of cattle range across the pine-covered plateau.

Several hundred people live at **Taipivai,** a five-hour, 16-km walk from Taiohae over the Col Teavanui (576 meters). Vanilla grows wild throughout this valley. At Hooumi, on a fine protected bay near Taipivai, is a truly magical little church. The huge *tohua* of Vahangeku'a at Taipivai is a whopping 170 by 25 meters. Eleven great stone tikis watch over the *me'ae* of Pa'eke, a couple of km up the Taipivai Valley toward Hatiheu then up the slope to the right. About two km farther up the road to Hatiheu is a monument to the left of the road marking the spot where Herman Melville spent a month with his tattooed sweetheart Fayaway in 1842. In his novel, *Typee* (his spelling for Taipi), he gives a delightful account of the life of the great-grandparents of the present forlorn and decultured inhabitants.

From Taipivai it's another 12 km via the Col Teavaitapuhiva (443 meters) to **Hatiheu** on the north coast. Some spectacular falls are seen in the distance to the left of the road near the mountain pass. A statue of the Virgin Mary stands on a green peak 300 meters above Hatiheu Bay and its black sand beach. (Yachties are better off anchoring in protected Anaho Bay than here.) Hatiheu was destroyed by a tsunami in 1946 but 350 people still live there today. The restored Hikoku'a Tohua is a bit over a kilometer from Hatiheu back toward Taipivai. Several of the tikis on the structure were added during the 1989 Marquesas Islands Festival while others are old (notice the phallic fertility statue on the left). In the jungle a kilometer farther up the valley and across the road is the Te I'ipoka Me'ae where many human sacrifices were made to the goddess Te Vana'uau'a. The victims were kept in a pit beneath a huge sacred banyan tree until their turn to be consumed at cannibal feasts arrived. Up the steep wooded slope from here is the overgrown Kamuihei Tohua with petroglyphs.

Anaho is two km east of Hatiheu over a 217-meter pass. It's one of the most beautiful of Nuku Hiva's bays, with a fine white beach and some of the finest snorkeling in the Marquesas (lovely coral and the possibility of seeing turtles or reef sharks). Even better white-sand beaches face Ha'atuatua and Haataivea bays beyond Anaho. No one lives there, though wild horses are seen.

Sports and Recreation

Scuba diving is offered by Xavier Curvat's **Centre Plongée Marquises** (B.P. 100, 98742 Taiohae; tel./fax 92-00-88) at the old marina in Taio-

Hakaui on Nuku Hiva's south coast, home of the Taioa tribe

M.G.L. DOMENY DE RIENZI

LES MARQUISES

Ils parlent de la morte comme tu parles d'un fruit
They talk about death like you discuss fruit
Ils regardent la mer comme tu regardes un puits
They gaze at the sea as you'd look down a well
Les femmes sont lascives au soleil redouté
The women are wanton in the dreaded sunlight
Et s'il n'y a pas d'hiver cela n'est pas l'été
And if it weren't for winter, there would be no summer
La pluie est traversière elle bat de grain en grain
The rain falls crosswise, beating heavier and heavier
Quelques vieux chevaux blancs qui fredonnent Gauguin
On some old white horses humming the name Gauguin
Et par manque de brise le temps s'immobilise
And, without a breeze, the weather remains the same
Aux Marquises.
In the Marquesas.

Du soir montent des feux et des points de silence
From the darkness rise fires and moments of silence
Qui vont s'élargissant et la lune s'avance
Which keep growing as the moon crosses the sky
Et la mer se déchire infiniment brisée
And the sea breaks, shattered infinitely
Par des rochers qui prirent des prénoms affolés
By rocks with terror-stricken names
Et puis plus loin des chiens des chants de repentance
And then, further off, the dogs' penitent songs
Et quelques pas de deux et quelques pas de danse
And some two-steps and some dance steps
Et la nuit est soumise et l'alizé se brise
And the night is subdued and the trade winds relent
Aux Marquises.

Leur rire est dans le coeur le mot dans le regard
They laugh from the heart and speak with their eyes
Le coeur est voyageur l'avenir est au hasard
Their heart is a wanderer, the future left to fate
Et passent des cocotiers qui écrivent des chants d'amour
And the coconut groves lose those who wrote love songs
Que les soeurs d'alentours ignorent d'ignorer
Which the local women don't realize they don't know
Les pirogues s'en vont les pirogues s'en viennent
The canoes paddle out, the canoes paddle in
Et mes souvenirs deviennent ce que les vieux en font
And my memories become whatever the old people make of them
Veux-tu que je te dise gémir n'est pas de mise
Maybe I should say to you that moaning has its place
Aux Marquises.

—JACQUES BREL

hae. A 10-dive package is CFP 45,000 including gear. Snorkelers are welcome and scuba certification is offered. Xavier has explored the archipelago thoroughly during his 20 years in the Marquesas and his local knowledge is unequaled. There's not much coral to be seen here but the underwater caves and spectacular schools of hammerhead sharks or pygmy orcas compensate. Dive trips to Ua Pou are offered weekly.

Horseback riding is offered by Sabine Teikiteetini (B.P. 171, 98742 Taiohae), who can be contacted through the *mairie* in Taiohae. Rides from Taiohae to Taipivai are possible.

PRACTICALITIES

Accommodations in Taiohae

The least expensive place to stay is **Chez Fetu** (Cyprien Peterano, B.P. 22, 98742 Taiohae; tel. 92-03-66), on a hill behind Magasin Kamake, an eight-minute walk from the wharf in Taiohae. The four rooms with shared bath in the family residence and one bungalow are CFP 2,000/4,000/6,000 single/double/triple, or CFP 50,000 a month. Communal cooking facilities are available and there's a terrace, but the children can be loud. Inexpensive.

Andy's Dream (André Teeikiteetini, B.P. 111, 98742 Taiohae; tel. 92-00-80, fax 92-04-05) is at Hoata about a kilometer from the wharf. A room with breakfast in an island house is CFP 3,000 pp and you may be able to cook. Inexpensive.

The friendly, two-story **Hôtel Moana Nui** (Charles Mombaerts, B.P. 33, 98742 Taiohae; tel. 92-03-30, fax 92-00-02), on the waterfront in the middle of Taiohae, has seven clean rooms with private bath (hot water) above their popular restaurant/bar. Bed and breakfast is CFP 4,000/4,500 single/double, other meals CFP 2,500 each. The Moana Nui is famous for its pizza. Mosquitos and bar noise are drawbacks, the excellent views from the terrace a plus. Cars are for rent at CFP 8,000 a day and boat excursions can be arranged. Inexpensive.

In 1993 the **Nuku Hiva Village Hôtel** (Bruno and Gloria Gendron, B.P. 82, 98742 Taiohae; tel. 92-01-94, fax 92-05-97) opened in Taiohae village with 15 thatched *fare* with private bath arrayed along the west side of Taiohae Bay op-

posite the yacht anchorage. The rates are CFP 6,500/7,500/8,500 single/double/triple, plus CFP 3,500 pp a day for breakfast and dinner. A local band plays in the restaurant Saturday nights. Excursions by 4WD, horseback riding, and scuba diving can be arranged. Moderate.

The **Keikahanui Inn** (B.P. 21, 98742 Taiohae; tel. 92-03-82, fax 92-00-74), just up the hill from the Nuku Hiva Village, is named after a tattooed chief but owned by ex-American yachtie Rose Corser (ask to see Maurice McKittrick's logbooks). They have five screened Polynesian bungalows with private bath: CFP 8,500/12,000/14,000 single/double/triple plus tax. In early 1999 it was reported that the Inn was being completely rebuilt as "Pearl Lodge" with a swimming pool and 20 new a/c bungalows costing CFP 18,000 to 22,000 double plus tax. Cooking facilities are not provided, so for breakfast and dinner add CFP 5,300 pp. Rose's restaurant/bar is Nuku Hiva's unofficial yacht club (rinse the sand off your feet before entering). You can buy Fatu Hiva tapa at the inn. Premium to luxury.

Accommodations around the Island

The **Hôtel Moetai Village** (Guy Millon, tel. 92-04-91), a five-minute walk from Nuku Ataha Airport, has five bungalows with private bath (cold water): CFP 2,500/3,500/4,500 single/double/triple for bed and breakfast, other meals CFP 2,500. Budget.

At Taipivai village, **Chez Martine Haiti** (B.P. 60, 98742 Taiohae; tel. 92-01-19, fax 92-05-34) has two bungalows at CFP 2,000/3,500 single/double. You can cook for yourself or order dinner at CFP 2,000 pp. It's also possible to camp on Taipivai's football field (ask). Inexpensive.

In Hatiheu village, **Chez Yvonne Katupa** (B.P. 199, 98742 Taiohae; tel. 92-02-97, fax 92-01-28) offers five pleasant bungalows without cooking facilities or hot water at CFP 2,500/4,800 single/double, breakfast included. The bungalows are set in their own garden with views of Hatiheu Bay. A small restaurant nearby serves fried fish and lobster. Ask to see Yvonne's collection of artifacts from Ha'atuatua. It's possible to hire horses here. Inexpensive.

You can also stay on the white-sand beach at Anaho Bay, two km east of Hatiheu, accessible on horse or foot. **Te Pua Hinako** (Juliette and André Vaianui, B.P. 202, 98742 Taiohae; tel.

92-04-14), also known as Chez Juliette, has two rooms with shared bath at CFP 2,000 pp with breakfast, or CFP 5,000 pp with all meals. Yachties often come ashore to buy fresh vegetables from Teiki Vaianui's garden. Inexpensive.

In 1998 a new place opened at Anaho Bay, the **Kaoha Tiare** (Raymond Vaianui, B.P. 290, 98742 Taiohae; tel. 92-00-08 or 92-02-66). The five bungalows with bath are CFP 3,000/4,000 single/double, plus CFP 3,000 pp for all meals.

Services and Information
Central Taiohae boasts a Banque Socredo branch (tel. 92-03-63). The post office on the east side of town sells telephone cards that you can use at the public phone outside and several other locations around the island. The *gendarmerie* (tel. 92-03-61) is just up the road to the left of the post office, while the public hospital (tel. 92-03-75) is to the right. A private dentist, Dr. Jean-Michel Segur (tel. 92-00-83), is in the *mairie.* Tourist information is available from Déborah Kimitete's Nuku Hiva Visitors Bureau (tel. 92-03-73) in the old jail between the *mairie* and the post office. Air Tahiti (tel. 92-01-45) is next to the *mairie.*

Don't have your mail sent c/o poste restante at the local post office as it will be returned via surface after 15 days. Instead have it addressed c/o the Keikahanui Inn, B.P. 21, 98742 Taiohae, Nuku Hiva. From 1600 to 1800 you can also receive telephone calls and faxes through the inn (tel. 92-03-82, fax 92-00-74), but remember that Rose Corser is running a restaurant and your patronage will be appreciated.

Getting Around
There's no public transportation from Taiohae to other parts of the island, though it's possible to hike across the island if you're fit. From Taiohae you could walk to Taipivai and Hatiheu in two days, camping or staying at local pensions along the way. The helicopter to the airport will pick up pre-booked passengers at Hatiheu for the usual CFP 6,900, so it's not necessary to return to Taiohae. Check with Héli-Inter Marquises (tel. 92-02-17) at the Air Tahiti office in Taiohae. Also ask about the new road from Hatiheu to the airport via Aakapa and Pua, which may be open by the time you get there.

Island tours by Land Rover or speedboat can be arranged, but get ready for some astronomical charges (for example, CFP 15,000 for a visit to Hatiheu). Most car rentals are with driver only and thus cost taxi prices. To rent a car without driver for something approaching normal prices, ask at the Hôtel Moana Nui (tel. 92-03-30) or check with Alain Bigot (B.P. 51, 98742 Taiohae; tel. 92-04-34, fax 92-02-27) who has a store on the road inland from the beach. **Teiki Transports** (Mr. Teikivaini Puhetini, tel. 92-03-47) arranges chauffeur-driven cars.

Airport
Nuku Ataha Airport (NHV) is in the arid Terre Déserte at the northwest corner of Nuku Hiva, 32 km from Taiohae along a twisting dirt road over the Toovii Plateau. Upon arrival from Papeete or Rangiroa turn your watch ahead 30 minutes. A restaurant and hotel are near the terminal. The main drawback to flying into Nuku Hiva is the cost of airport transfers, which run CFP 3,500 each way by 4WD Toyota Landcruiser by day (CFP 5,000 pp by night), or CFP 6,900 pp each way by helicopter. Air Tahiti weight limits also apply on the 10-minute helicopter ride, so the 2.5-hour drive should be your choice if you're not traveling light. When shopping for woodcarvings during your stay on Nuku Hiva keep in mind the problem of getting the stuff back to Papeete. The excellent Marquesan low-relief woodcarvings made to decorate the airport's bar and shop when the airport was built in 1979 are worth examining while waiting for your flight.

OTHER NORTHERN ISLANDS

UA POU

This spectacular, diamond-shaped island lies about 40 km south of Nuku Hiva. Several jagged volcanic plugs loom behind Hakahau, the main village on the northeast coast of 105-square-km Ua Pou, the third-largest Marquesan island. One of these sugarloaf-shaped mountains inspired Jacques Brel's song "La Cathédrale" and the name Ua Pou itself means "the pillars." Mount Oave (1,203 meters), highest point on Ua Pou, is often cloud-covered. The population of 2,000 plus is larger than Hiva Oa's. In 1988, 500 French foreign legionnaires rebuilt the breakwater at Hakahau, and the *Aranui* can now tie up to the concrete pier.

Sights

The first stone church in the Marquesas was erected at Hakahau in 1859, and the present **Church of Saint-Etienne** (1981) has a pulpit shaped like a boat carved from a single stump. The **Tenai Paepae** in the center of the village was restored for the 1995 Marquesas Islands Festival, the same occasion that saw the inauguration of the small **museum** at the south end of Hakahau.

Anahoa Beach is a scenic 30-minute walk east of the marina, and from the ridge halfway there you can climb up to the cross overlooking Hakahau for a superlative bird's-eye view.

A road leads south from Hakahau to a beach beyond Hohoi. Three km along this road turn left and halfway down the track to **Hakamoui Bay** you'll find several *paepae* on the right. The stones bear carvings of faces and a tiki is nearby. On 88-meter-high **Motu Oa** off the south coast, millions of seabirds nest. The villages of Hakatao and Hakamaii on the west coast are only accessible by foot, hoof, or sea.

Accommodations in Hakahau

Right beside the post office and just back from the beach is **Chez Marguerite Dordillon** (B.P. 87, 98745 Hakahau; tel. 92-51-36). Here guests are accommodated in a modern two-room house

with cooking facilities at CFP 2,000/3,500 single/double (CFP 500 pp surcharge for one or two nights). Marguerite herself lives in the southern part of town up the hill from the museum. Budget.

Pension Pukuéé (Hélène and Doudou Kautai, B.P. 31, Hakahau; tel./fax 92-50-83) is on a hill overlooking the village, just a few minutes walk from the wharf on the road to Anahoa Beach. The six shared-bath rooms are CFP 3,000 pp with breakfast, plus CFP 1,000/2,000 for lunch/dinner. Yachties often order seafood meals here. Inexpensive.

Chez Sam Teikiehuupoko (Samuel and Jeanne-Marie Teikiehuupoko, B.P. 19, 98745 Hakahau; tel. 92-53-16), opposite the Air Tahiti agent in the center of the village, has a pair of two-room houses with cooking facilities at CFP 2,500 pp with reductions for stays of three days or more. Inexpensive.

Pension Vaikaka (Valja Klima, B.P. 16, 98745 Hakahau; tel. 92-53-37), two km south of Hakahau Wharf, is CFP 2,500/4,500 single/double including breakfast in the one bungalow. Inexpensive.

You could also inquire at the Collège de Ua Pou opposite the beach not far from the wharf in Hakahau where **CETAD** (B.P. 9, 98745 Hakahau; tel. 92-53-83) has a bungalow that is sometimes rented to visitors. There's also a culinary school here where you can have an excellent lunch prepared by the students for CFP 1,200 if you reserve ahead.

Accommodations around the Island

In Hakahetau you can stay at **Chez Étienne Hokaupoko** (tel. 92-51-03), next to a small Protestant church, for CFP 2,000 pp. Meals (CFP 600 each) are served under a huge mango tree in the front yard and yachties often drop in to sign Étienne's guest book. He's working on an Marquesan-English dictionary and knows many old stories that he's only too happy to share. Inexpensive.

Farther afield, **Pension Paeaka** (Marie-Augustine Aniamioi, B.P. 27, 98745 Hakahau; tel. 92-53-96) is at Haakuti village, 12 km southwest of the airport. To stay in the one-room house with cooking facilities is CFP 1,000 pp a day or CFP 25,000 a month. Budget.

Shopping

A craft shop near the wharf at Hakahau sells local carvings, goatskin ukuleles, and beautiful hand-painted pareus. Four woodcarvers work in Hakahau village—just ask for *les sculpteurs*. If you're buying, shop around at the beginning of your stay, as many items are unfinished and there'll be time to have something completed for you.

Services and Information

The Banque Socredo (tel. 92-53-63), *mairie,* and a post office are all adjacent opposite the market and not far from the beach. The *gendarmerie* (tel. 92-53-61) is a bit south. Infirmaries are in Hakahau, Hakatao, and Hakamaii. Six or seven stores are to be found in Hakahau.

Motu Haka (Georges Teikiehuupoko, B.P. 54, 98745 Hakahau; tel. 92-53-21) is a cultural organization that promotes Marquesan language instruction, archaeological projects, and traditional arts while rejecting cultural domination by Tahiti. The Marquesas Islands Festival is one of Motu Haka's projects.

Getting There

Ua Pou's Aneou airstrip (UAP) is on the north coast, 10 km west of Hakahau on a rough road over a ridge. The pensions in Hakahau offer air-

tattooed man,
Marquesas Islands

M.G.L. DOMENY DE RIENZI

port transfers for CFP 1,000 pp return. You can reach Air Tahiti in Hakahau at tel. 92-53-41.

Xavier Curvat's Centre Plongée Marquises (tel./fax 92-00-88) in Taiohae generally has a launch from Nuku Hiva to Hakahau Friday at 0700, departing Hakahau for the return to Taiohae the same afternoon at 1600 (1.5 hours each way, CFP 4,000 one-way or CFP 6,000 for a roundtrip the same day). It's better to check on this a few days before.

UA HUKA

Ua Huka lies 35 km east of Nuku Hiva and 56 km northeast of Ua Pou. Crescent-shaped Ua Huka is the surviving northern half of an ancient volcano and the 575 inhabitants reside in the truncated crater in the south. Goats and wild horses range across this arid, 83-square-km island, while the tiny islands of Teuaua and Hemeni, off the southwest tip of Ua Huka, are a breeding ground for millions of *kaveka* (sooty terns). Sadly, local residents use these islands as a source of eggs. Mount Hitikau (884 meters) rises northeast of Hane village. Vaipae'e is the main village of the island, although the clinic is at Hane.

Archaeological excavations by Prof. Y.H. Sinoto in 1965 dated a coastal site on Ua Huka to A.D. 300, which makes it the oldest in Tahiti-Polynesia; two pottery fragments found here

UA POU

ANEOU AIRSTRIP
WHARF
Motu Mokohe
Hakahetau
Hakahau
Point Punahu
Haakuti
Oave (1,203 m)
Hakamoui Bay
Vaiehu Bay
Ua Pou
Island
Paaumea Bay
Hakamaii
Hohoi
Hohoi Bay
Hakatao
Motutakaae
Motu Oa

0   2 mi
0   2 km

© DAVID STANLEY

suggest that the island was probably a major dispersal point for the ancient Polynesians. Sinoto believes the migratory paths of Ua Huka's terns may have led the ancient Polynesians on their way to new discoveries.

Three small tikis cut from red rock may be visited in the valley behind Hane. Between Hane and Vaipae'e is a plantation that has been converted into a botanical garden complete with an aviary (open weekday mornings). Near the post office in Vaipae'e is a small but admirable **Musée Communal** of local artifacts and seashells, and replicas made by local artist Joseph Tehau Va'atete. Many other woodcarvers are active here.

Accommodations

Chez Alexis (Alexis Scallamera, tel. 92-60-19) in Vaipae'e village, six km from the airport, is a two-room house with shared bath at CFP 1,500 pp, or CFP 5,000 with full board. You're welcome to cook your own food. Alexis can arrange horseback riding and boat excursions. Budget.

Also in Vaipae'e is **Chez Christelle** (Christelle Fournier, tel. 92-60-85), a four-room house with shared bath at CFP 2,000 pp with breakfast, plus CFP 1,000/2,000 for lunch/dinner. It's run by the Air Tahiti agent. Inexpensive.

The **Mana Tupuna Village** (Raphael Taiaapu, tel./fax 92-60-08) in Vaipae'e offers three bungalows on a hill at CFP 5,500/10,000 single/double including all meals.

A more isolated place to stay is **Chez Joseph Lichtle** (tel. 92-60-72) at Haavei Beach, 12 km west of the airport (CFP 1,000 pp return). There's a white sandy beach with good swimming, and few other families live here. The pension consists of two bungalows with bath and two houses with two or three rooms at CFP 2,500 pp with breakfast, or CFP 5,500 pp with full board. Communal cooking facilities should also be available. Joseph and Laura are reputedly the most skillful cooks in the Marquesas, and their son Leon, mayor of Ua Huka, is extremely helpful. You can also rent a horse from Joseph. Inexpensive.

In Hane village, the **Auberge Hitikau** (Céline and Jean Fournier, tel. 92-60-68) offers four rooms with shared bath in a concrete building at CFP 2,000/3,500 single/double with breakfast. Lobster is served in their restaurant at CFP 2,000. Jean has a car and boat for rent. Inexpensive.

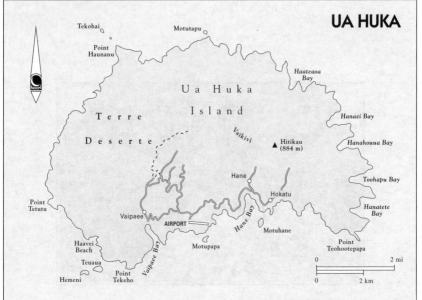

© DAVID STANLEY

Also worth checking is **Chez Maurice et Delphine** (Maurice and Delphine Rootuehine, tel./fax 92-60-55) at Hokatu village, 13 km from the airport. The two bungalows with private bath are CFP 2,500 pp with breakfast or CFP 4,400 pp with all meals. The three rooms with shared bath in the main house are CFP 1,700 pp with breakfast or CFP 3,600 pp with all meals. Maurice can arrange a rental car. Inexpensive.

Getting There

The airstrip (UAH) is on a hilltop between Hane and Vaipae'e, slightly closer to the latter. The Vaipae'a pensions generally provide free airport transfers, while those at Hane and Hokatu want CFP 2,000-3,000 for the car. The Air Tahiti number is tel. 92-60-85. The *Aranui* enters the narrow fjord at Vaipae'e and ties up to a wharf. It's quite a show watching the ship trying to turn around.

M.G.L. DOMENY DE RIENZI

HIVA OA

Measuring 40 by 19 km, 315-square-km Hiva Oa (population 1,900) is the second largest of the Marquesas and the main center of the southern cluster of islands. Mount Temetiu (1,276 meters) towers above Atuona to the west. Steep ridges falling to the coast separate lush valleys on the long crescent-shaped island. Ta'aoa, or "Traitors'," Bay is a flooded crater presently missing its eastern wall, while Puama'u sits in a younger secondary crater. The administrative headquarters for the Marquesas group has switched back and forth several times: Taiohae was the center until 1904, then it was Atuona until 1944, when Taiohae took over once more.

The tomb of Gauguin at Atuona. Gauguin's wish that his ceramic figure of Oviri, goddess of death, mourning, and destruction, be erected over his tomb has finally been granted, if only in the form of a copy. The name Oviri also means "the savage."

SIGHTS

Atuona

Along with exhibits on the life of Atuona's most famous resident, the **Musée Ségelin-Gauguin** (admission CFP 400) in central Atuona is dedicated to the life of French writer Victor Ségelin who visited Atuona just after Gauguin's death. In 1991 Gauguin's thatched "Maison du Jouir" (House of Pleasure) was reconstructed next to the museum and it's presently used as a place for local artists to display their works. Jacques Brel's aircraft is on display here. The *paepae* platforms near the museum were also built for the Marquesas Islands Festival in December 1991.

Back on the main street is **Magasin Pierre Shan** where Gauguin left an unpaid wine bill when he died. Go up the hill from just past the nearby *gendarmerie* and take the first fork in the road to the left to reach **Calvary Cemetery**, which hosts the graves of Brel and Gauguin. The views of Atuona from here are excellent.

The beach at Atuona is poor and for better swimming, take the road six km southwest along the bay to the black beach at **Ta'aoa.** A big restored *tohua* with several *me'ae* platforms and a basalt tiki is found a bit over a kilometer up the river from there.

Across the Island

A second village, **Puama'u,** is on the northeast coast, 30 km from Atuona over a winding mountain road. It's a good eight-hour walk from Atuona to Puama'u, up and down all the way. A few descendants of Gauguin are among the 300 people who live there today. Aside from the village's golden beach, the main reason for coming are the five huge stone tikis to be seen on the Te I'ipona Me'ae in the valley behind Puama'u, a 15-minute walk from the village soccer field. One stands almost three meters high—the largest old stone statue in Polynesia outside of Easter Island. Notice the statue of the priestess who died in childbirth and the sculpted heads of victims of human sacrifice. The site was restored in 1991

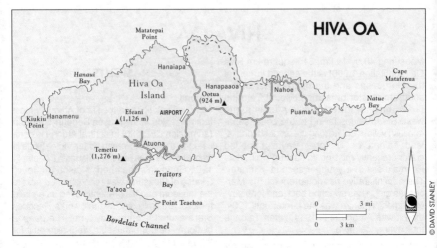

© DAVID STANLEY

and an admission of CFP 300 is charged (previous thefts from the site have necessitated the presence of a custodian).

At **Hanaiapa** on the north coast, ask for William who keeps a yachties' log. He's happy to have his infrequent visitors sign and is generous with fresh fruit and vegetables. Barren **Hanamenu Bay** in the northwest corner of Hiva Oa is now uninhabited, but dozens of old stone platforms can still be seen. If you'd like to spend some time as a hermit in the desert, ask for Ozanne in Atuona (see below), who has a house at Hanamenu he might be willing to rent. To the right of Ozanne's house is a small, crystal-clear pool. The trails into this area have become overgrown and it's now accessible only by boat (CFP 15,000 charter).

PRACTICALITIES

Accommodations and Food

The **Mairie de Atuona** (B.P. 18, 98741 Atuona; tel. 92-73-32, fax 92-74-95) rents five well-equipped bungalows behind the town hall and post office at CFP 2,500/3,000 single/double. These have cooking facilities and private bath but can only be booked directly at the *mairie* during business hours. Budget.

Pension Gauguin (André Teissier, B.P. 34, 98741 Atuona; tel./fax 92-73-51), a bit east of the post office and up, has four rooms with shared bath at CFP 5,500/10,000 single/double with half board. It may be possible to get a room without meals at CFP 3,000 pp, and a kitchen and common room are provided. Deep-sea fishing and excursions can be arranged. Moderate.

Chez Ozanne (Ozanne and Marie Rohi, B.P. 43, 98741 Atuona; tel./fax 92-73-43), up the hill from Pension Gauguin, offers two rooms with shared bath at CFP 1,500/2,500 single/double. There's also a two-story bungalow in the yard at CFP 2,000/3,500. Cooking facilities are provided in the bungalow, or you can order breakfast/dinner at CFP 500/2,000. Ozanne has a 12-meter boat he uses for excursions and trips to Tahuata. He also organizes garden parties for yachties at CFP 1,000 pp, which includes transportation from the harbor and plenty of good local food (bring your own drinks). Ask to see Ozanne's log books that date back to the 1970s and contain dozens of entries by cruisers who have passed this way over the years. Budget.

Overlooking Tahauku Bay is the **Temetiu Village** (Gabriel Heitaa, B.P. 52, 98741 Atuona; tel. 92-73-02), a km east of Atuona on the way to the airport, then up the hill. The three bungalows with bath (cold water) are CFP 5,500/10,000 single/double with half pension (no cooking facilities). Nonguests are welcome at their terrace restaurant. Gabriel also has an eight-passenger boat for rent. Moderate.

Atuona's upmarket place, the **Hôtel Hanakéé** (Serge Lecordier, B.P. 57, 98741 Atuona; tel. 92-71-62, fax 92-72-51), has five stylish A-frame bungalows on the hillside above Tahauku wharf, two km east of the center. Accommodations run CFP 12,000/18,000/20,000 single/double/triple plus tax. Breakfast and dinner are CFP 3,360 pp extra, airport transfers CFP 3,600 pp return. Each bungalow contains a TV, VCR, washing machine, kitchen, fridge, and bathtub. A path behind the hotel leads up to the Jacques Brel Memorial on the spot where the singer had wished to build his home. There's a splendid view from there. Luxury.

In Puama'u village on northeastern Hiva Oa, you can stay at **Chez Heitaa** (Bernard and Marie-Antoinette Heitaa, tel. 92-72-27). The two rooms with cooking facilities and shared bath are CFP 3,000 pp including half board (or CFP 1,000 pp without meals). Airport transfers are CFP 20,000 for up to four people. Horses are for hire. Inexpensive.

For a juicy hamburger, *poisson cru,* or grilled fish with a cold beer try **Snack Make Make** (tel. 92-74-26), 100 meters east of the post office and on the opposite side of the street.

Services and Information

Banque Socredo (tel. 92-73-54) is located next to the Air Tahiti office, which is opposite the museum. The post office, town hall, dental center, and hospital (tel. 92-73-75) are two blocks east with the *gendarmerie* (tel. 92-73-61) diagonally opposite.

The Hiva Oa Comité du Tourisme (B.P. 62, 98741 Atuona; tel./fax 92-75-10) is in the craft shop at the museum.

Transportation

Yachts anchor behind the breakwater in Tahauku harbor, two km east of the center of town. Copra boats and the *Aranui* also tie up here. A lighthouse on the point between Tahauku and Atuona looks across the bay.

Location David (Augustine Kaimuko, tel. 92-72-87), next to Magasin Chanson up from the museum, rents cars at around CFP 10,000 a day all inclusive. To hire a four-passenger Land

Marquesan model Tohotaua (left) served as the model for Gauguin's Girl with a Fan. *Gauguin's friend Louis Grelet took the photo.*

FAMOUS RESIDENTS OF ATUONA

Atuona was made forever famous when Paul Gauguin came to live here in 1901. Despite the attentions of his 14-year-old mistress, Vaeoho, he died of syphilis a year later at age 55 and is buried in the cemetery above the town. When Tioka, Gauguin's neighbor, found him stretched out with one leg hanging over the side of his bed, he bit him on the head as the Marquesans do to see if he really was dead. No, there was no doubt. *"Ua mate Koke!"* he cried, and disappeared. Gauguin was constantly in conflict with the colonial authorities, who disapproved of his heavy drinking sessions with the locals. Just a week before his death, Gauguin was summarily convicted of "libel of a *gendarme* in the course of his official duties," fined, and sentenced to three months in prison.

The famous Belgian *chanson* singer Jacques Brel and his companion Maddly Bamy came to the Marquesas aboard his 18-meter yacht, the *Askoy II*, in 1975. Jaques decided to settle at Atuona and sold his boat to an American couple. Maddly, who had been a dancer on her native Guadeloupe, gave dancing lessons to local girls, while Jacques ran an open-air cinema. His plane, nicknamed *Jojo*, was kept at Hiva Oa airport for trips to Papeete, 1,500 km southwest. The album *Brel 1977* on the Barclay label includes one of his last songs, "Les Marquises." In 1978, chain-smoker Brel died of lung cancer and was buried in Atuona cemetery near Gauguin.

Rover with driver from Atuona to Puama'u will run you CFP 20,000 for the vehicle.

Airport

The airstrip (AUQ) is on a 441-meter-high plateau, eight km northeast of Atuona. In 1991 the runway was upgraded to allow it to receive direct ATR 42 flights from Papeete (via Nuku Hiva).

Weekly flights by the smaller Dornier 228 aircraft continue to arrive from Rangiroa. Air Tahiti is at tel. 92-73-41.

It's a two-hour downhill walk from the airport to Atuona. The normal taxi fare from the airport to Atuona is CFP 1,800 pp each way, but the actual amount collected by the various hotels seems to vary, so check when booking.

OTHER SOUTHERN ISLANDS

TAHUATA

Tahuata (population about 650) is just six km south of Hiva Oa across Bordelais Channel. Fifteen km long by nine km wide, 69-square-km Tahuata is the smallest of the six inhabited islands of the Marquesas. A 17-km track crosses the island from Motopu to Vaitahu.

On the west coast is the main village, Vaitahu, where a new Catholic church was completed in 1988 to mark the 150th anniversary of the arrival here of Catholic missionaries. Archaeological sites exist in the Vaitahu Valley and there's a small collection of artifacts in the school opposite the post office in Vaitahu. Mendaña anchored in Vaitahu Bay in 1595, followed by Captain Cook in 1774. Here too, Admiral Abel Dupetit-Thouars took possession of the Marquesas in 1842 and established a fort, despite strong resistance led by Chief Iotete. The anchorage at Hana Moe Noa north of Vaitahu is protected from the ocean swells. There's a lovely white beach and the water here is clear, as no rivers run into this bay.

Hapatoni village, farther south, is picturesque, with a century-old *tamanu*-bordered road and petroglyphs in the Hanatahau Valley behind. Coral gardens are found offshore and white-sand beaches skirt the north side of the island.

Accommodations

The only official place to stay is **Chez Naani** (François and Lucie Barsinas, tel. 92-92-26) in Vaitahu village. A room in this four-room concrete house with communal cooking facilities is CFP 1,500 pp (or CFP 4,850 pp with full board). Budget.

Getting There

There's no airport on Tahuata. To charter a six-passenger boat to/from Atuona is CFP 15,000-25,000 (one hour). Small boats leave Hiva Oa for Tahuata almost daily, so ask around at the harbor on Takauku Bay near Atuona.

The launch *Te Pua O Mioi*, belonging to the Commune of Tahautu (tel. 92-92-19), shuttles between Atuona and Vaitahu on Tuesday and Thursday (one hour, CFP 1,000 pp each way). It leaves Tahuatu around dawn, departing Hiva Oa for the return at noon. Southbound, take groceries with you.

FATU HIVA

Fatu Hiva is the southernmost (and youngest) of the Marquesas Islands, 56 km southeast of Tahuata. It was the first of the Marquesas to be seen by Europeans (Mendaña passed by in 1595). None landed until 1825 and Catholic missionaries couldn't convert the inhabitants until 1877. In 1937-38 Thor Heyerdahl spent one year on this island with his young bride Liv and wrote a book called *Fatu Hiva,* describing their far from successful attempt "to return to a simple, natural life." Fatu Hiva (84 square km) is far wet-

the Cannilie Kai *at Bay of Virgins, Fatu Hiva*

FATU HIVA

Point Tevaii

Fatu Hiva

Bay of Virgins — Hanavave

Cape Matautu

Island

Ouia

Matakoo Point

Tauaouoho (960 m) ▲

Omoa

0   2 mi
0   2 km

Point Teae

© DAVID STANLEY

ter than the northern islands, and the vegetation is lush. Mount Tauaouoho (960 meters) is the highest point.

This is the most remote of the Marquesas, and no French officials are present. With 650 inhabitants, Fatu Hiva has only two villages, Omoa and Hanavave, in the former crater on the western side of the island. It takes about five hours to walk the 17-km track linking the two, up and down over the mountains amid breathtaking scenery. Surfing onto the rocky beach at Omoa can be pretty exciting! Hanavave on the Bay of Virgins offers one of the most fantastic scenic spectacles in all of Polynesia, with tiki-shaped cliffs dotted with goats. Yachts usually anchor here. Horses and canoes are for hire in both villages.

Today a revival of the old crafts is taking place in Fatu Hiva, and it's again possible to buy not only wooden sculptures but painted tapa cloth. Hats and mats are woven from pandanus. *Monoï* oils are made from coconut oil, gardenia, jasmine, and sandalwood. Yachties trade perfume, lipstick, and cosmetics for the huge Fatu Hiva grapefruits. Fatu Hiva doesn't have any *no-nos,* but lots of mosquitoes. If you plan on staying over four months, get some free anti-elephantiasis pills such as Notézine at any clinic.

Accommodations and Food

Several families in Omoa village take paying guests. **Norma Ropati** (tel. 92-80-13) has four rooms at CFP 2,000 pp with breakfast or CFP 5,500 with all meals. **Albertine Tetuanui** (tel. 92-80-58) has two rooms at CFP 2,500 pp with breakfast, plus CFP 1,500 each for other meals. **Marie-Claire Ehueinana** (tel. 92-80-75) takes guests in her two-room house at CFP 3,000 pp a day or CFP 50,000 a month. **Cécile Gilmore** (tel. 92-80-54) has two rooms with shared bath at CFP 3,500 pp or CFP 5,000 with all meals. A bakery and four or five small stores are also in Omoa.

Getting There

There's no airstrip on Fatu Hiva but the Mairie de Fatu Hiva (tel. 92-80-23) operates the 30-passenger catamaran *Atuona II,* once a week between Atuona and Omoa. It usually leaves Atuona Tuesday or Friday at 1400 (ask) and on the return trip they may agree to drop you on Tahuata. The trip takes just over three hours and costs CFP 4,000 pp each way.

EASTER ISLAND
Rapa Nui

birdman with the first egg

BOB RACE

EASTER ISLAND

INTRODUCTION

The mystery of Easter Island (Isla de Pascua) and its indigenous inhabitants, the Rapanui, has intrigued travelers and archaeologists for many years. Where did these ancient people come from? How did they transport almost 1,000 giant statues from the quarry to their platforms? What cataclysmic event caused them to overthrow all they had erected with so much effort? And most importantly, what does it all mean? With the opening of Mataveri airport in 1967, Easter Island became more easily accessible, and many visitors now take the opportunity to pause and ponder the largest and most awesome collection of prehistoric monuments in the Pacific. This is one of the most evocative places you will ever visit.

The Land

Barren and detached, Easter Island lies midway between Tahiti and Chile, 4,000 km from the former and 3,700 km from the latter. Pitcairn Island, 1,900 km west, is the nearest inhabited land. No other populated island on earth is as isolated as this. At 109°26' west longitude and 27°9' south latitude, it's the easternmost and almost the southernmost island of the South Pacific (Rapa Iti in Tahiti-Polynesia is a bit farther south). Easter Island is triangular, with an extinct volcano at each corner. It measures 23 by 11 km, totaling 171 square km.

The interior consists of high plateaus and craters surrounded by coastal bluffs. Ancient lava flows from Maunga Terevaka (507 meters), the highest peak, covered the island, creating a rough, broken surface. Maunga Pukatikei and Rano Kau (to the east and south respectively) are nearly 400 meters high. Many parasitic craters exist on the southern and southeast flanks of Maunga Terevaka. Three of these, Rano Aroi, Rano Raraku, and Rano Kau, contain crater lakes, with the largest (in Rano Kau) over a kilometer across. Since 1935 about 42% of the island, including the area around Rano Kau and much of the island's shoreline, has been set aside as **Parque Nacional Rapa Nui** administered by the Corporación Nacional Forestal (CONAF). In 1995 the park was added to UNESCO's World Heritage List, the first place in Chile to be so honored.

The forests of Easter Island were wiped out by the indigenous inhabitants long ago, and during the 19th century sheep finished off most of the remaining native vegetation. The last indigenous *toromiro* tree died in the 1960s and attempts have been made to reintroduce the species from overseas botanical gardens without success. Grasslands now envelop the green, windswept landscape; few endemic plants and no native land birds survive. The lakes feature thick, floating bogs of peat; *totora* reeds related to South American species surround and completely cover their surfaces. Pollen studies have determined that these reeds have existed here for at least 30,000 years. Large tracts of eucalyptus have been planted in recent years.

Small coral formations occur along the shoreline, but the lack of any continuous reef has allowed the sea to cut cliffs around much of the island. These bluffs are high where the waves encountered ashy material, low where they beat upon lava flows. Lava tubes and volcanic caves are other peculiarities of the coastline. The only sandy beaches are at Ovahe and Anakena, on the northeast coast.

Climate

The climate is moderated by the cool Humboldt current and the annual average temperature is 20.3°C. The hottest month is February; the coolest are July and August. Winds can make the island feel much cooler. The climate is moist and some rain falls 200 days a year. March to June are the rainiest months; July to October are generally the driest and coolest, although heavy rains are possible year-round. Drizzles and mist are common, and a heavy dew forms overnight. Snow and frost are unknown, however. The porous volcanic rock dries out quickly, so the dampness need not deter the well-prepared hiker/camper.

HISTORY

Polynesian Genesis

It's believed that Easter Island was colonized around A.D. 400 by Polynesians from the Marquesas Islands, as part of an eastward migratory trend that originated in Southeast Asia around 1500 B.C. Here they developed one of the most remarkable cultures in all of Polynesia.

Long platforms or *ahu* bearing slender statues known as *moai* were built near the coasts, with long retaining walls facing the sea. Each *ahu* carried four to six *moai* towering four to eight meters high. These statues, or *aringa ora* (living faces), looked inland towards the villages, to project the mana (protective power) of the *aku-aku* (ancestral spirits) they represented.

The *moai* were all cut from the same quarry at Rano Raraku, the yellowish volcanic tuff shaped by stone tools. Some writers have theorized that the statues were "walked" to their platforms by a couple of dozen men using ropes to lean the upright figures from side to side while moving forward; others claim they were pulled along on a sledge or log rollers. Some statues bore a large cylindrical topknot *(pukao)* carved from the reddish stone of Punapau. Eyes of cut coral were fitted into the faces.

Other unique features of Easter Island are the strange canoe-shaped house foundations with holes for wall supports, and the incised wooden tablets *(rongorongo)*, the only ancient form of writing known in Oceania. Only 25 examples survive, and Dr. Steven Roger Fischer, Director of the Institute of Polynesian Languages and Literatures in Auckland, has shown how the neat rows of symbols on the boards record procreation chants.

In 1774 Captain Cook reported internecine fighting among the islanders, with statues toppled and their platforms damaged, and by 1840 all of the *moai* had been thrown off their *ahu*, either by earthquakes or rival tribes.

Fantasy and Fact

The first comprehensive explorations of Easter Island were carried out by Katherine Routledge in 1914-15, Alfred Metraux in 1934, and Thor Heyerdahl in 1955-56. Earlier, in 1947, Heyerdahl had achieved notoriety by sailing some

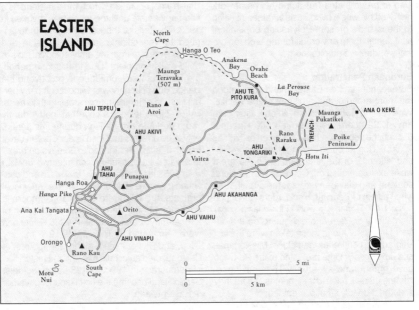

© DAVID STANLEY

6,500 km from South America to the Tuamotu Islands in a balsa raft, the *Kon Tiki*. His 1955 Norwegian Archaeological Expedition was intended to uncover proof that Polynesia was populated from South America, and Heyerdahl developed a romantic legend that still excites the popular imagination today.

Heyerdahl postulated that Easter Island's first inhabitants (the "long ears") arrived from South America around A.D. 380. They dug a three-km-long defensive trench isolating the Poike Peninsula and built elevated platforms of perfectly fitted basalt blocks. Heyerdahl noted a second wave of immigrants, also from South America, who destroyed the structures of the first group and replaced them with the *moai*-bearing *ahu* mentioned above. Heyerdahl sees the toppling of the *moai* as a result of the arrival of Polynesian invaders (the "short ears") who arrived from the Marquesas and conquered the original inhabitants in 1680. According to Heyerdahl, the birdman cult, centering on the sacred village of Orongo, was initiated by the victors.

Modern archaeologists discount the South American theory and see the statues as having de-

veloped from the typical backrests of Polynesian *marae*. The civil war would have resulted from over-exploitation of the island's environment, leading to starvation, cannibalism, and the collapse of the old order. Previous destruction of the forests would have deprived the inhabitants of the means of building canoes to sail off in search of other islands. The Poike trench was only a series of discontinuous ditches dug to grow crops, probably taro. Despite decades of study by some of the world's top archaeologists, no South American artifacts have ever been excavated on the island.

Heyerdahl argued that the perfectly fitted, polished stonework of the stone wall of Ahu Vinapu (Ahu Tahira) was analogous to Incan stone structures in Cuzco and Machu Picchu, but fine stonework can be found elsewhere in Polynesia (for example, the *langi,* or stone-lined royal burial mounds, of Mu'a on Tongatapu). Easter Island's walls are a facade holding in rubble fill, while Incan stonework is solid block construction. The timing is also wrong: the Incas were later than the stonework on Easter Island. In academic circles Heyerdahl has always been considered a maverick who started out with a conclusion to prove instead of doing his homework first. And his whole hypothesis is rather insulting to the island's present Polynesian population, as it denies them any credit for the archaeological wonders we admire today.

European Penetration

European impact on Easter Island was among the most dreadful in the history of the Pacific. When Jacob Roggeveen arrived on Easter Sunday, 1722, there were about 4,000 Rapanui (though the population had once been as high as 20,000). Roggeveen's landing party opened fire and killed 12 of the islanders; then the great white explorer sailed off. Contacts with whalers, sealers, and slavers were sporadic until 1862 when a fleet of Peruvian blackbirders kidnapped some 1,400 Rapanui to work in the coastal sugar plantations of Peru and dig guano on the offshore islands. Among those taken were the last king and the entire learned class. Missionaries and diplomats in Lima protested to the Peruvian government, and eventually 15 surviving islanders made it back to their homes, where they sparked a deadly smallpox epidemic.

French Catholic missionaries took up residence on Easter Island in 1865 and succeeded in converting the survivors; businessmen from Tahiti arrived soon after and acquired property for a sheep ranch. Both groups continued the practice of removing Rapanui from the island: the former sent followers to their mission on Mangareva, the latter sent laborers to their plantations on Tahiti. Returnees from Tahiti introduced leprosy. By 1870 the total population had been reduced to 110. One of the business partners, Jean Dutrou-Bornier, had the missionaries evicted in 1871 and ran the island as he wished until his murder by a Rapanui in 1877. The estate then went into litigation, which lasted until 1893.

The Colonial Period

In 1883 Chile defeated Peru and Bolivia in the War of the Pacific. With their new imperial power, the Chileans annexed Easter Island in 1888, erroneously believing that the island would become a port of call after the opening of the Panama Canal. Their lack of knowledge is illustrated by plans to open a naval base when no potential for harbor construction existed on the island. As this became apparent, they leased most of it to a British wool operation, which ran the island as a company estate until the lease was revoked in 1953. The tens of thousands of sheep devastated the vegetation, causing soil erosion, and stones were torn from the archaeological sites to build walls and piers. During this long period, the Rapanui were forbidden to go beyond the Hanga Roa boundary wall without company permission, to deter them from stealing the sheep. (A local joke tells of a cow that inadvertently wandered into Hanga Roa during this period, only to be arrested and tried under Chilean naval law as a "ship." Sentenced to 30 days on bread and water, it died of starvation after two weeks.)

In 1953 the Chilean Navy took over and continued the same style of paternal rule. After local protests, the moderate Christian Democratic government of Chile permitted the election of a local mayor and council in 1965. Elections were terminated by Pinochet's 1973 military coup, and Easter Island, along with the rest of Chile, suffered autocratic rule until the restoration of democracy in 1990. In 1984 archaeologist Sergio Rapu became the first Rapanui governor of Easter Island.

Captain Cook's illustrator, William Hodges, drew this image of a man on Easter Island.

GOVERNMENT

Easter Island is part of the Fifth Region of Chile, with Valparaíso (Chile) as capital. The Chilean government names the governor; the appointed mayor and council have little power. Many local leaders would like to see Easter Island made a separate region of Chile, a change that would greatly increase local autonomy. Chile heavily subsidizes services on the island, and a large military and official staff are present, mostly *continentales* (mainlanders). A five-member Comisión de Desarrollo (development committee) representing the 800 ethnic Rapanui was established in 1994 under Chile's Indigenous Law.

Politics

After the return to democracy in Chile an indigenous rights group, the Consejo de Ancianos (Council of Elders), was formed to represent the island's 36 original families. They called for the creation of a new electoral district giving Easter Island its own representative in the Chilean Congress. In 1994 the Consejo split into two rival factions over the question of land rights, the original Consejo No. 1 led by former Mayor Alberto Hotus and a radical Consejo No. 2 without any legal authority but representing a growing body of opinion. The second group has posted banners outside the church demanding the return of lands and has tried to collect "cultural taxes" from off-island filmmakers and archaeologists. There have even been attempts to "tax" tourists! The clash of the long ears and short ears is reenacted here.

Today most of Easter Island's land is held by the Chilean State but any local will be able to tell which part of the island originally belonged to his/her original clan. On several occasions Chilean governments have tried to give the Rapanui clear title to rocky, eucalyptus-covered areas unsuitable for agriculture or cattle grazing, but these offers have been refused. Only about 10% of the island has ever been offered, and the Rapanui want much more than that. Protesters from Consejo No. 2 demand that the government turn over most of the island, despite the very negative effect this would have on the environment. At the moment Hanga Roa is the only permanent settlement, but many locals wish to colonize other areas. Unserviced squatter shacks are already springing up around the island and fields are being plowed without any archaeological impact studies being carried out. In Hanga Roa, houses have even been constructed right on top of ancient *ahu* platforms. The national park authorities are very upset about all this, but hesitate to expel anyone out of fear of provoking major unrest.

At times officials in far-off Chile have come up with reckless development plans of their own, such as projects for a "monumental" lighthouse on a hill overlooking the airport flight path, a naval base to proclaim Chilean sovereignty, a huge container port at La Pérouse Bay to service shipping across the Pacific, and a new airport on the north side of the island to support a massive increase in tourism. The Sociedad Agrícola y Servicios Ltda. (SASIPA), which provides water and electricity to the island and operates a cattle ranch at Vaitea, has come with crazy ideas of its own, such as an elitist golf course, resort, and botanical garden at Vaitea (the island's richest agricultural land). As yet, none of these wild plans have been implemented, but "progress" is catching up with this remote island. Sadly, there is no coherent management plan for Easter Island as a whole, no long pants in Paradise. It's just one interest group clawing against another, the world on a small scale.

THE PEOPLE

The original name of Easter Island was Te Pito o Te Henua, "navel of the world." The Rapanui believe they are descended from Hotu Matua, who arrived by canoe at Anakena Beach from Te Hiva, the ancestral homeland. The statues were raised by magic. The original inhabitants wore tapa clothing and were tattooed like Marquesans; in fact, there's little doubt their forebears arrived from Eastern Polynesia. The language of the Rapanui is Austronesian, closely related to all the other languages of Polynesia, with no South American elements.

The Rapanui have interbred liberally with visitors for over a century, but the Polynesian element is still strong. Three-quarters of the almost 3,000 people on Easter Island are Rapanui or Rapanui-related. Some 1,000 Rapanui live abroad, most of them in Chile with a smaller number on Tahiti. Many of the local Rapanui made money during the 1993 filming of Kevin Costner's US$20 million epic *Rapa Nui,* and almost all of them bought a car. There's now one car for every two Rapanui and the newly paved streets of Hanga Roa are often jammed! Cars have replaced horses as status symbols and people cruise around town to show off. The sweet potato gardens around Hanga Roa have been abandoned, and frozen chickens, vegetables, and TV dinners are imported from Santiago in increasing quantities. Many people earn money from tourism as innkeepers, guides, and craftspeople, and lots more are employed by the Chilean government. About a thousand *continentales* also live on Easter Island, most of them government employees and newly arrived small shopkeepers.

The island receives around 10,000 tourists a year from Europe, Chile, the U.S., and Japan in that order. In 1997 Easter Island experienced a surge in tourism from the continent after Chilean TV ran a miniseries partly filmed on the island. According to the local Catholic priest, the sight of gorgeous bimbos in bikinis running topless into the surf at Anakena in slow motion had attracted the wrong sort of clientele to the island, but the local tourism operators weren't complaining.

Since 1966 the Rapanui have been Chilean citizens, and many have emigrated to the mainland. The locals generally speak Rapanui in private, Spanish in public, French if they've been to Tahiti, and English almost not at all. Spanish is gradually supplanting Rapanui among the young, and it's feared the language will go out of everyday use within a generation or two. Television is diluting the local culture. In general, the Rapanui are honest and quite friendly toward visitors.

Conduct

The archaeological sites of Easter Island are fragile and easily damaged by thoughtless actions, such as climbing on the fallen statues or walking on petroglyphs. The volcanic tuff is soft and easily broken off or scuffed. Incredibly, some people have scraped ancient rock carvings with stones to make them easier to photograph! Cruise ships can land hundreds of people a day,

and the large groups often spin out of control, swarming over the quarry at Rano Raraku or standing on the stone house tops at Orongo (several of which have collapsed in recent years). Local residents have had to organize voluntary projects to pick up trash discarded in the national park by tourists.

Though it may seem that these places are remote from the world of high-impact consumer tourism, they are in fact endangered by the selfishness of some visitors and those locals who would profit from them. It's strictly prohibited to remove any ancient artifacts (such as spear heads, fishhooks, or basalt chisels) from the island. The warning signs erected in the park are there for a reason, and the human bones often encountered on the *ahu* and in the caves deserve to be left in peace. For most of us these things go without saying, but it can be really upsetting to see the way some tourists behave.

Public Holidays and Festivals

Public holidays in Chile include New Year's Day (1 January), Easter Friday (March or April), Labor Day (1 May), Battle of Iquique Day (21 May), San Pedro and San Pablo Day (29 June), Assumption Day (15 August), Policarpo Toro Day (9 September), Military Coup Day (11 September), Independence Day (18 September), Army Day (19 September), Columbus Day (12 October), All Saints' Day (1 November), Conception Day (8 December), and Christmas Day (25 December). Policarpo Toro Day recalls the Chilean captain who annexed the island for Chile in 1888.

In late January or early February is the carnival-like Tapati Rapa Nui festival, with traditional dancing, sporting events, canoe races, a horse race, art shows, statue-carving contest, shell-necklace-stringing competition, body-painting contest, *kai-kai* (string figure) performances, mock battles, and the election of Queen Rapa Nui (who is dramatically crowned on a spotlit Ahu Tahai). A unique triathlon at Rano Raraku involves male contestants in body paint who paddle tiny reed craft across the lake, pick up bunches of bananas on poles and run around the crater and up the hill, where they grab big bundles of totara reeds to carry down and around the lake before a final swim across. There's also *haka pei,* which involves young men sliding down a grassy mountainside on banana-trunk sleds at great speed. Colored lights are strung up along the main street. Since 1994 Tapati Rapa Nui parades have displayed strong Hollywood influences in the floats and costumes, and you may even see topless young women riding on floats through Hanga Roa, just as they appeared in *Rapa Nui!* Needless to say, all flights immediately before and after the festival are fully booked far in advance.

Chilean Independence Day (18 September) is celebrated with parades and a *fonda* (carnival). Everybody takes three days off for this big fiesta. On the day of their patron saint, the main families stage a traditional feast *(curanto),* complete with an earth oven.

SIGHTS

Vicinity of Hanga Roa
The **Catholic church** in the center of town is notable for its woodcarvings. Buried next to the church is Father Sebastian Englert, who founded the one-room **Museo Antropólogico** (tel. 100-296, closed Sunday afternoon and all day Monday; US$1 admission) on the north side of Hanga Roa. Inside is kept the white coral and red scoria eye of the *moai* found at Anakena in 1978. The William Mulloy Research Library (e-mail: BiMulloy@entelchile.net), presently at the Museo Fonck in Viña del Mar, Chile, is to be relocated here when funding allows.

Nearby at **Ahu Tahai,** just outside the town, are three *ahu,* one bearing five restored *moai* and a large restored statue complete with a red 10-ton topknot reerected by the late Dr. William Mulloy in 1967. The statue's "eyes" are crude copies recently cemented in place for the benefit of tourists. The islanders launched their canoes from the ramp leading down to the water between the *ahu.*

Five km north along the rough coastal road is unrestored **Ahu Tepeu,** with the foundations of canoe-shaped and round houses nearby. Inland via a little-used track and 10 km from Hanga Roa is **Ahu Akivi** (Siete Moai), with seven statues restored in 1960 by Dr. Mulloy. The seven *moai* that once overlooked a village are visible from afar.

On the way back to Hanga Roa climb **Punapau,** where the topknots were quarried. About 25 red topknots are in or near Punapau, the largest weighing 11 tons. **Maunga Orito,** south of Punapau, contains black obsidian, which the islanders used for weapons and tools.

Five km from Hanga Roa via the road along the north side of the airstrip are the fine Inca-like stone walls of the two *ahu* at **Ahu Vinapu** (Ahu Tahira). According to Heyerdahl, the perfectly fitted stonework of one dates from the earliest period and is due to contact with South America. Most authorities dispute this claim and suggest it was a later development by the skilled Polynesian stonemasons.

Rano Kau and Orongo
From Hanga Roa, the brisk six-km uphill hike south to Orongo and the vast crater of Rano Kau (316 meters) is easily done in a morning, but take along a lunch and make a day of it if you have the time. On the way, just past the west end of the airstrip, at the foot of the cliff near the water, is **Ana Kai Tangata,** the Cannibal Cave. Paintings of birds grace the ceiling of this cave.

The road, which swings around and up the side of Rano Kau to Orongo, offers an exciting panorama of cliffs, crater lake, and offshore islands. An admission of US$10 is charged by the national park ranger, who also sells a few interesting publications about the island and an excellent map. The entry fee may seem stiff, but all the other sites on the island are free, and CONAF is desperately short of funds needed to protect and maintain Easter Island's monuments. Save your receipt if you plan a repeat visit up this way. (Beware of paying the money to unauthorized persons—check at the CONAF office if in doubt.)

At Orongo, the main ceremonial center on the island, are many high-relief carvings of bird-headed men on the rock outcrops. The 40 cavelike dwellings here (restored by Dr. Mulloy in 1974) were used by island chiefs and participants during the birdman festival. Each year a race was staged to the farthest offshore island, **Motu Nui,** to find the first egg of a species of migratory sooty tern *(manutara).* The winning swimmer was proclaimed birdman *(tangata manu)* and thought to have supernatural powers. You can hike right around the rim of Rano Kau. On the way back to town, it's possible to cut back toward Ahu Vinapu along the south side of the airstrip.

Around the Island

Although many of the enigmatic statues *(moai)* are concentrated at moss-covered Rano Raraku (the statue quarry), they are also found along the coast around the island. The stone walls seen at various places date from the English sheep ranch. Take the road along the south coast toward Rano Raraku, 18 km from Hanga Roa. Eight fallen *moai* lie facedown at **Ahu Vaihu.** The first king of the island, Hotu Matua, is buried at **Ahu Akahanga,** where four toppled statues are seen.

Work on the statues ended suddenly, and many were abandoned en route to their *ahu.* About 300 are still in the quarry at **Rano Raraku** in various stages of completion, allowing one to study the process; one unfinished giant measures 21 meters long. Others, visible from the top of Rano Raraku, lie scattered along the roadway to the coast. Some 70 statues stand on the slopes or inside the volcano; another 30 lie facedown on the ground. The kneeling statue, called Tukuturi, on the west side of Rano Raraku is unusual. A park ranger is posted in this area.

After climbing Rano Raraku, circle around to **Ahu Tongariki** at Hotu Iti, destroyed in 1960 by a huge tsunami that tossed the 15 statues around like cordwood. Between 1992 and 1994 Japanese archaeologists reconstructed the *ahu* and reerected the *moai* using an enormous crane donated by the Japanese crane manufacturer Tadano. Some extraordinary petroglyphs are at Tongariki, very close to the road.

Continue up along the ancient trench, which still isolates the **Poike Peninsula.** Legends maintain that the "long ears" filled the trench with wood to create a burning barrier between them and their "short-eared" adversaries, but were annihilated in the end. Heyerdahl claimed to have found a thick layer of red ash in the trench, but more recent excavations here have found no evidence of any battle.

The tallest *moai* ever to stand on Easter Island is at **Ahu Te Pito Kura** on the north coast by La Pérouse Bay. The toppled 10-meter-long statue lies facedown beside the *ahu,* awaiting restoration.

The inviting white sands of palm-fringed **Anakena Beach** are 20 km northeast of Hanga Roa via the paved central highway or 30 km via Rano Raraku. The National Parks Department has set up picnic tables, barbecue pits, toilets, and a campground here, and many locals come to swim or fish on Sunday (an easy time to hitch a ride). Anakena is the traditional disembarkation point of Hotu Matua, the legendary founder of the island. The one *moai* on **Ahu Ature Huki** here was reerected by Thor Heyerdahl in 1955, as is indicated on a bronze plaque—the first statue to be restored on the island. **Ahu Naunau** at Anakena bears seven *moai,* four with topknots. During the restoration of this *ahu* in 1978, archaeologist Sergio Rapu discovered the famous white coral eyes of the statues. Unfortunately this area is threatened by plans for a new major new port and fish freezing plant with all its attendant industrial development.

SPORTS AND RECREATION

The scuba diving off Easter Island is not for beginners as one must dive in the open sea and the water is cool (Nov.-April is warmest). On the plus side are the unique caves, walls, corals, and fish. Michel García's **Orca Diving Center** (tel. 100-375, fax 100-448) offers diving, but certification is mandatory.

Surfers will find a couple of consistent waves adjacent to town, such as the rights at Ahu Tahai and Hanga Roa Bay and the left at Hanga Mataveri Otai. On the south side of the island a powerful right plows into the lava at Hanga Poukura. Some of the highest walls are a couple of kilometers east at Cabo Koe Koe. Summer is the best season on the north coast, winter on the south (especially Mar.-Sept.). Ask for Carlos Lara, the local surf guide, who can provide vehicles and support.

Horseback riding is fun, and at about US$20/30 a half/full day, it's inexpensive. Guys on the street around Hanga Roa rent horses for less, but both animal and saddle may, sadly, be the worse for wear. Many of the island's hoofed animals look like the traditional woodcarvings of emaciated ancestor figures *(moai kavakava)* with their ribs sticking out. Anakena is a little far to go by horse and return in a day anyway, so look upon riding more as a change of pace than as a way of getting around. The area north of Hanga Roa can be explored by horse.

You can hike 60 km clockwise right around the island in three or four days, but take all the food and water you'll need. Camping is allowed at the national park attendant's post at Rano Raraku, and there's a regular campsite at Anake-na. The park rangers may deign to replenish your water supply, but on very dry years no water is available for campers, so ask. If you camp elsewhere, try to stay out of sight of motorized transport. This is not an easy trip, so only consider it if you're in top physical shape. Good boots and a wide-brimmed hat are musts, as the terrain is rough and there's absolutely no shade. There are no snakes but watch out for scorpions and black widow spiders.

PRACTICALITIES

ACCOMMODATIONS

The median price for guesthouse accommodation is US$35/50/75 single/double/triple with private bath—expensive for Chile. The rooms are clean and simple, often facing a garden, but the cheaper places don't always have hot water (ask if it's included). All rates include a light breakfast, but for a full English breakfast you'll have to add US$5-10 pp. Beware if something extra is "offered," as you could end up paying US$40 extra for one small frozen lobster. If you're asked to choose a meal plan, take only breakfast and dinner as it's a nuisance to have to come back for lunch. Picnic fare can be purchased at local stores. Unfortunately few places offer cooking facilities.

Room prices do fluctuate according to supply and demand, and when things are slow bargaining is possible everywhere except at the most upmarket places. Foreign tourists paying for rooms at the top hotels in U.S. dollars (cash or traveler's checks) rather than with pesos or by credit card may be exempt from the 18% value added tax, something to ask about. If you're on a very low budget, ask about camping at a *residencial*. The only organized campsite is the one left by the Norwegian archaeological expedition at Anakena Beach, and you'll need to carry all your own food and water if you go there.

If you haven't booked a package, accommodations are easily arranged upon arrival, as many of the *residencial* (guesthouse) owners meet the flights. Only members of the tourist association representing the more expensive hotels are allowed inside the arrivals area at the airport. Outside the terminal you'll find several peo-ple offering less-expensive accommodations, and you'll save money by waiting to deal with them. Try to speak to the owner in person rather than a tout who will take a commission. Once it's all arranged they'll give you a free lift to their place. Don't promise to stay more than one night until you've seen the place and are happy.

The peak season with the highest visitor levels is Dec.-Feb.; June is the slackest month. Rooms are always available and advance bookings are not required, except perhaps during the Tapati Rapa Nui festival. Reservations for the top hotels are handled by Chile Hotels (tel. 56-2/231-8181, fax 56-2/232-4299, www.chile-hotels.com, e-mail: massie@chile-hotels.com) in Santiago. The oldest and most reliable travel agency on Easter Island itself is **Mahinatur** (Benito Rapahango, tel. 100-220, fax 100-420, e-mail: mahina@entelchile.net) on Ave. Policarpo Toro near the airport. They can book hotel accommodations, excursions, and rental vehicles in advance, and their services are used by most overseas tour operators. Otherwise most of the properties listed below (or anybody on the island) can be faxed at 56-32/100-105, the Entel telephone office, which will call the hotel and ask them to come and get their fax.

If you do have reservations beware of touts who may come up to you as you're leaving the baggage area claiming that the hotel you booked is full and that your reservation has been transferred to another hotel. If you get this story insist on checking directly with the original hotel, otherwise you could end up with a worse room for a higher price. Japanese tourists who don't speak English or Spanish are often targeted in this way.

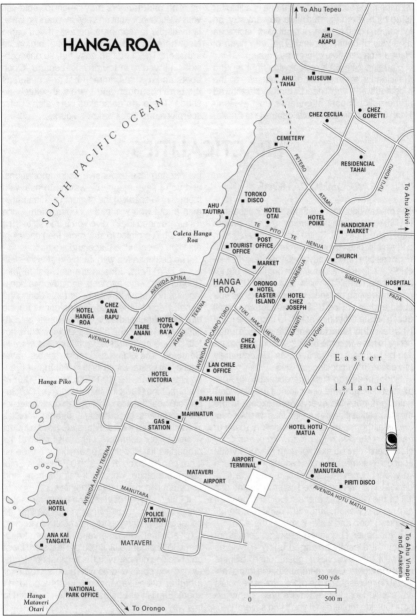

HANGA ROA

SOUTH PACIFIC OCEAN

To Ahu Tepeu

AHU AKAPU

MUSEUM

AHU TAHAI

CHEZ CECILIA

CHEZ GORETTI

CEMETERY

RESIDENCIAL TAHAI

PETERO

ATAMU

TU'U KOIHU

To Ahu Akivi

TOROKO DISCO

AHU TAUTIRA

HOTEL OTAI

HOTEL POIKE

HANDICRAFT MARKET

TE   PITO   TE   HENUA

Caleta Hanga Roa

TOURIST OFFICE

POST OFFICE

CHURCH

MARKET

SIMON

HOSPITAL

PAOA

HANGA ROA

ORONGO HOTEL EASTER ISLAND

HOTEL CHEZ JOSEPH

AVAREIPUA

AVENIDA APINA

CHEZ ANA RAPU

HOTEL HANGA ROA

TEKENA

TUKI HAKA HEVARI

MANNITI

TU'U KOIHU

TIARE ANANI

HOTEL TOPA RA'A

ATAMU

AVENIDA POLICARPO TORO

CHEZ ERIKA

Easter
Island

AVENIDA   PONT

Hanga Piko

HOTEL VICTORIA

LAN CHILE OFFICE

RAPA NUI INN

MAHINATUR

GAS STATION

HOTEL HOTU MATUA

AVENIDA ATAMU TEKENA

AIRPORT TERMINAL

HOTEL MANUTARA

PIRITI DISCO

MATAVERI AIRPORT

AVENIDA HOTU MATUA

MANUTARA

IORANA HOTEL

POLICE STATION

MATAVERI

ANA KAI TANGATA

To Ahu Vinapu
and Anakena

Hanga Mataveri Otari

NATIONAL PARK OFFICE

To Orongo

| 0 | | 500 yds |
| 0 | | 500 m |

© DAVID STANLEY

The listings that follow are not exhaustive because almost every family on the island is involved in tourism in some way. The prices given are those charged in the low season (May-Nov.), and one should expect basic conditions at the cheapest places and less than might be hoped for at the more expensive ones. All of the 10 hotels and 30 *residenciales* are in Hanga Roa, arranged here beginning with those closest to the airport.

Budget
Residencial Anna Rapu Briones (tel. 100-540), near Hotel Hanga Roa on Ave. Apina, offers eight rooms at US$30 double with shared bath, US$35 with private bath, or US$5 pp to camp in the garden. You can also wash clothes here and cook your own food. Ask for Anna at the airport.

Residencial Tekena Inn (tel. 100-289), on Policarpo Toro in the center of town, is US$30 double, plus US$10 pp for dinner.

Residencial Maorí (tel. 100-497), Calle Te Pito o Te Henua, is also US$30 double.

Inexpensive
Directly across Ave. Hotu Matua from the airport terminal is **Residencial Vinapu** (tel. 100-393) at US$50 double.

One of the island's best established guesthouses is the **Rapa Nui Inn** (tel. 100-228), Ave. Policarpo Toro at Ave. Hotu Matua near the airport. The 10 spacious rooms with bath begin at US$30/45 single/double.

West on Ave. Pont is **Residencial Tiare Anani** (tel. 100-580) at US$50 double. **Residencial Apina Nui** (tel. 100-292) on Atamu Tekena is US$25/45 single/double.

Residencial Chez Erika (tel. 100-474), on Calle Tuki Haka Hevari, offers 12 rooms with bath and TV at US$30 pp. **Residencial El Tauke** (tel. 100-253), on Calle Te Pito o Te Henua, charges US$50 double.

Martín and Anita Hereveri (tel. 100-593), on Simón Paoa opposite the hospital just east of the church, offer 10 double rooms at US$20 pp with shared bath, US$30 pp with private bath. Another US$10 pp nets you an ample three-course dinner. Camping on their lawn is also possible. Martín picks up guests at the airport and he's very helpful.

One of the least-expensive hotels easily booked from abroad through Chile Hotels is **Cabañas Vai Moana** (tel. 100-626) on Policarpo Toro just north of the center. The 10 large tin-roofed bungalows are US$40/60/90 single/double/triple, plus US$15 for a romantic dinner by candlelight. If you book locally upon arrival you'll probably pay US$25 pp (ask for Edgar inside the airport terminal). He rents bicycles, scooters, and jeeps at reasonable rates and is very helpful.

Residencial Chez Cecilia (tel. 100-499), also off Ave. Policarpo Toro north of center near Ahu Tahai, charges US$35/50/75 single/double/triple plus US$15 pp for dinner. Camping may be possible here. Cecilia is a good cook and there's hot water. A city tour is also included. Nearby on Pasaje Reimiro in this same quiet area a bit north of town is **Residencial Tahai** (tel. 100-395) at US$30/50 single/double.

Lucía Riroroko de Haoa runs **Mahina Taka Taka Georgia** (tel. 100-452, fax 100-282), near the museum and Ahu Tahai. The four clean, quiet rooms with private bath are US$25 pp (plus

Cabañas Vai Moana offers inexpensive accommodations on Easter Island.

US$20 for dinner). Sliding doors lead out to the garden and you're really made to feel like part of the family. If you book ahead she'll be waiting with a flower necklace at the airport.

Moderate

The 16-room **Hotel Victoria** (Jorge Edmunds, tel. 100-272), on Ave. Pont west of Policarpo Toro, is US$50/70 single/double. A terrace overlooks the sea.

The friendly, 18-room **Hotel Topa Ra'a** (tel. 100-225), Calle Hetereki at Atamu Tekena, is conveniently located right in town. It's US$45/78/90 single/double/triple with a good view from the patio. Ask to see the room before accepting. This place belongs to archaeologist and ex-governor Sergio Rapu, who also owns the Tumu Kai shopping mall and supermarket on Ave. Policarpo Toro.

The **Hotel Orongo Easter Island** (Juan Chávez, tel. 100-294), formerly the Hotel Easter Island International, is on Ave. Policarpo Toro in the center of town. The 12 rooms with private bath are US$60/80/100 single/double/triple, breakfast and dinner included.

The **Hotel Poike** (Carmen Cardinali, tel. 100-283), on Petero Atamu a bit north of the church, has 13 rooms with bath at US$80 double.

Hotel Chez Maria Goretti (tel./fax 100-459), on the north side of town near near Ahu Tahai, has 13 large rooms at US$50/70/90 single/double/triple, plus US$10 pp for dinner.

Expensive

Hotel Chez Joseph (tel. 100-281), on Calle Avareipua in the center of town, charges US$65/90/105 single/double/triple with breakfast and dinner for the 12 rooms with bath.

Hotel O'tai (Nico and Rosita Haoa, tel. 100-250, fax 100-482), also known as "Rosita's Pension," is on Calle Te Pito o Te Henua across from the post office. In 1993 the movers and shakers in Kevin Costner's team stayed here during the filming of *Rapa Nui,* and with her profits Rosita has increased the number of rooms to 31 (all with private bath). These cost US$68/104/134 single/double/triple with reductions April-September. The new swimming pool and jacuzzi also came out of movie money, and there's a nice garden. Unfortunately it's just around the corner from the noisy Toroko Disco.

Premium

Hotel Manutara (tel./fax 100-297), on Ave. Hotu Matua near the airport, is a single-story, L-shaped building facing a pool. The 18 rooms with bath are US$78/121/136 single/double/triple. Tours are arranged.

The **Iorana Hotel** (tel./fax 100-312), on Ave. Atamu Tekena south of town, is just below the west end of the runway, and the middle-of-the-night landings and takeoffs can be jarring. The 32 rooms with mini-fridge and cable TV begin at US$94/130/186 single/double/triple, but they're rather hot due to the thinness of the walls. At least there's a swimming pool and fine coastal views. The tennis court has a *low* wire fence around it.

Luxury

The **Hotel Hanga Roa** (tel. 100-299, fax 100-426), overlooking the bay at the west end of Ave. Pont, was occupied by Hollywood moviemakers for six months in 1993, and they really tore the place apart. A year later the Hanga Roa was taken over by the Panamericana hotel chain, which added 10 large bungalows, nine of them containing three a/c rooms with marble bathrooms and fake thatched roofs at US$180/200 single/double. The 10th unit is a deluxe suite at US$350. Lunch or dinner is US$25. The 60 older rooms with bath in the prefabricated main building are still US$90/110/130, but plans call for this section to be demolished and placed by additional bungalows, a shopping complex, oceanfront restaurant/bar, tennis courts, and a second swimming pool.

Top of the line on Easter Island is the **Hotel Hotu Matua** (tel. 100-444, fax 100-445), at the east end of Ave. Pont near the airport. The 57 rooms with private bath and mini-fridge are US$129/169 single/double including a buffet breakfast. This single-story, motel-style complex angles around a half-moon freshwater swimming pool, and there's a bar. The Hotua Matua is owned by local businessman Orlando Paoa who also owns the supply ship *Piloto Pardo.*

FOOD AND ENTERTAINMENT

Food

Although three supermarkets sell basic foodstuffs, a limited selection of postcards, Chilean news-

RAUTENSTRAUCH-JOEST-MUSEUM, COLOGNE, GERMANY

This expressive toromiro *woodcarving of an ancestral figure* (moai kavakava) *was done in the mid-19th century. The eyes are inlaid with circles of bone and obsidian.*

day (you can pay in dollars here, but will get your change in pesos). Fresh fish is available from fishermen who land their catch at the *caleta*. Watch for tasty local pastries called *empanadas*.

A growing number of snack bars and restaurants exist along Calle Te Pito o Te Henua and Ave. Policarpo Toro. For seafood try the restaurants down by the *caleta*. Insist on a menu with prices clearly listed, otherwise you'll be charged absurdly high tourist rates. The local lobsters *(langostas)* are becoming very scarce due to overharvesting. Many visitors take meals at their lodgings for a fixed price. The local water piped down from Rano Kao has a high magnesium content and is a little brown, but it's safe to drink.

Entertainment

The discos, **Toroko** in town and **PiRiTi** near the airport, crank up on Thursday, Friday, and Saturday nights: US$6 for a Coke. They open around 2200, but nothing much happens before midnight. Avoid taking a room near either of these or you'll be blasted until 0600 (numerous requests to have the Toroko moved out of earshot of the sleepless citizenry to new location have been ignored because the mayor gets a piece of the action).

Ask at the tourist office and the Hotel Hanga Roa about Polynesian dancing. Sunday there's church singing at 0900 and soccer in the afternoon. Otherwise it's pretty dead at night, with lots of private *pisco* (brandy) drinking by the locals (no problem). Expect everything except church to start late.

OTHER PRACTICALITIES

Shopping

Aside from shell necklaces, the main things to buy are *moai kavakava* (woodcarvings of emaciated ancestor figures), dance paddles, miniature stone *moai,* and imitation *rongorongo* tablets. The obsidian jewelry sold locally is imported from mainland Chile. Don't buy anything at all made from coral as you'll only be encouraging unscrupulous individuals to damage the island's small reefs.

The handicraft market near the church in Hanga Roa sells overpriced woodcarvings, and this is one of the only places in Polynesia where

papers a week or two old, and expensive recordings of local music, bring with you everything you're likely to need during your stay, especially film, PABA sunscreen, a canteen, and sturdy shoes. Supply ships only arrive every couple of months, meaning high prices and limited selection, so canned or snack foods might also be a good idea if you can spare the weight. It's prohibited to bring in fresh fruit and vegetables however, so get these at the *feria municipal* (market) held on Ave. Policarpo Toro (largest early Tuesday and Saturday mornings). **Tumu Kai Supermarket** on Ave. Policarpo Toro stays open all

bargaining is expected. The vendors at this market are always eager to trade woodcarvings for jeans, windbreakers, T-shirts, sneakers, toiletries, cosmetics, and rock music cassettes. But don't count on unloading old winter clothes just before leaving for Tahiti. The locals know that trick and won't give you much for them. Some of the shops sell truly beautiful carvings at astronomical prices.

A commercial art gallery, the **Galería Aukara** on Ave. Pont off Policarpo Toro, sells woodcarvings by Bene Tuki Aukara and paintings by Amaya.

Money

The local currency is the Chilean peso (approximately US$1 = 475 pesos), which comes in notes of 500, 1,000, and 10,000 pesos. Chilean currency is almost worthless outside Chile itself, so only change what you're sure you'll need, and get rid of the remainder before you leave. The shops at the airport will often sell you dollars.

The Banco del Estado, beside the tourist office in Hanga Roa, charges a rip-off 10% commission to change traveler's checks, so bring U.S. dollars in cash, which are accepted as payment at all tourist-oriented establishments (though not always at good rates). If coming from Santiago, bring an adequate supply of pesos. The Sunoco gas station west of the airport gives good rates for U.S. cash (posted in the office) and the Tumu Kai Supermarket gives a better rate for traveler's checks than the local bank. Currencies other than U.S. dollars can be difficult to exchange, and credit cards are rarely usable as those accepting them have to wait a long time to be paid.

Except for the most basic things, it's often hard to determine exactly what a service will cost and some islanders have an inflated idea of value. To avoid shocks, it's wise to make sure prices are clearly understood beforehand.

Post and Telecommunications

All mail is routed through Chile and Chilean postage stamps are used. The Entel telephone center (fax 56-32/100-105) is opposite the tourist office and bank. When calling Easter Island from abroad, dial your international access code plus 56 for Chile, 32 for Easter Island, and the six-digit local number (which always begins with 100).

Visas and Officialdom

Most visitors require only a passport valid three months ahead to visit Chile. Visas are not necessary for North Americans, Australians, and most Europeans, but New Zealanders do need a visa (NZ$90), which must be obtained beforehand. Check with any LanChile Airlines office, the Chilean Consulate in Papeete, or the Chilean Embassy in New Zealand (12/1 Willeston St., Wellington; tel. 64-4/471-6270, fax 64-4/472-5324). No vaccinations are required, and malaria is not present anywhere in Chile.

Yachting Facilities

Some 40 cruising yachts a year visit Easter Island between Galapagos or South America and Pitcairn/Tahiti. Due to Rapa Nui's remoteness, the boats will have been at sea two to four weeks before landfall. As Easter is well outside the South Pacific hurricane zone, they usually call between January and March, so as to time their arrival in Tahiti-Polynesia for the beginning of the prime sailing season there. The southeast trades extend south to Easter Island most reliably Dec.-May, allowing for the easiest entry/exit. The rest of the year, winds are westerly and variable.

Anchorages include Hanga Roa, Vinapu, Hotu Iti, and Anakena/Ovahi, and a watch must be maintained over yachts at anchor at all times as the winds can shift quickly in stormy weather. The anchorages are deep with many rocks to foul the anchor and little sand. Landing can be difficult through the surf. The frequent moves necessitated by changing winds can be quite exhausting, and crews often have only one or two days a week ashore. Luckily the things to see are quite close to these anchorages.

A pilot is required to enter the small boat harbor at Hanga Piko and US$100 is asked. Entry through the breakers and rocks is only possible in calm weather. Mooring to the concrete wharf here is stern to as at Tahiti (no charge), but there's little space and this is only supposed to be done by boats in need of repairs. The harbor has 2.8 meters of water at low tide.

Information

There's a Sernatur tourist office (tel. 100-255; open weekday mornings) on Calle Tuu Maheke a few doors west of the bank. Their airport branch opens only for flights. In Santiago, the **Servicio**

Nacional de Turismo (Ave. Providencia 1550, Santiago de Chile; tel. 56-2/236-1420, fax 56-2/236-1417, www.segegob.cl/sernatur/inicio2.html, e-mail: sernatur@ctc-mundo.net) can supply maps, brochures, and a complete list of hotels on Easter Island.

A very good 1:30,000 topographical map of Easter Island printed in Spain is sold locally at souvenir shops, such as Hotu Matua's Favorite Shoppe on Ave. Policarpo Toro. The CONAF office on the road to Orongo sells an even better map coated with rainproof plastic. It's called *Parque Nacional Rapa-Nui/Easter Island Chile, Corporación Nacional Forestal/World Monuments Fund* and is nice enough to frame. The Fund put up the money to print the map and all proceeds from sales go to CONAF's conservation efforts.

No newspapers or magazines are published on Easter Island, so the easiest way to keep in touch with what's happening is to subscribe to Georgia Lee's *Rapa Nui Journal* (Easter Island Foundation, Box 6774, Los Osos, CA 93412-6774, U.S.A.; tel. 1-805/528-6279, fax 1-805/534-9301, www.netaxs.com/~trance/rapanui.html, e-mail: rapanui@compuserve.com). The *Journal*

comes out four times a year, and contains an interesting mix of scientific studies, announcements, and local gossip—well worth the US$30 annual subscription price (US$40 airmail outside Canada and the U.S.).

Two basic books about the island are *The Island at the Center of the World* by Father Sebastian Englert and *Ethnology of Easter Island* by Alfred Metraux. *The Modernization of Easter Island,* by J. Douglas Porteous, concentrates on the postcontact period. Paul Bahn and John Flenley's 1992 book *Easter Island, Easter Island* presents the collapse of the island's civilization in environmental terms and warns that mankind is once again headed along that track. The most useful travel guides to the island are *An Uncommon Guide to Easter Island* by Georgia Lee (available through the Easter Island Foundation) and Alan Drake's *The Ceremonial Center of Orongo.* Both are the sort of books you can pick up and read from cover to cover without getting bored.

A quarterly newspaper called *Te Rapa Nui* contains articles in English and Spanish. Radio Manukena broadcasts locally over 580 kHz AM and 101.7 MHz FM.

TRANSPORTATION

Getting There

LanChile Airlines (www.lanchile.com) flies a Boeing 767 to Easter Island from Tahiti and Santiago three times a week, with an additional weekly flight between Easter Island and Santiago operating from November to March (summer holiday time for Chilean students). For North America and Europe, LanChile has direct flights to Santiago from Los Angeles, Miami, New York, Madrid, and Frankfurt. See the main Introduction to this book for sample fares and special deals (such as the "Pacific Circuit Fares"). Occasionally LanChile won't honor their own announced fares. In North America, call LanChile toll-free at 1-800/735-5526 for information.

In Santiago, check carefully which terminal you'll be using, as flights that turn around at

Easter Island and return to Santiago are classified "domestic" and leave from the old terminal, whereas flights continuing to Tahiti are "international" and use the new terminal. Occasionally you'll be sent to the wrong terminal, so allow a little extra time. The "international" flights are often inconveniently timed, with late-night arrivals common at all three points.

LanChile has a history of changing schedules or canceling flights at a moment's notice. Book and reconfirm your onward flight well ahead, as the plane is often overbooked between Easter Island and Santiago—a week is enough time to see everything. You'll occasionally witness heated arguments at Mataveri Airport as people who were careless with their bookings try desperately to get off Easter Island, and there have even been cases when the police had to intervene to restore order! Foreigners pay higher fares than local residents, so it's usually the locals who get bumped. The local Lan-

Chile office (tel. 100-279), on Ave. Pont at Policarpo Toro, is open mornings.

Package Tours
Nature Expeditions International (6400 East El Dorado Circle, Ste. 210, Tucson, AZ 85715, U.S.A.; tel. 1-800/869-0639 or 1-520/721-6712, fax 1-520/721-6719, www.naturexp.com, e-mail: Naturexp@aol.com) runs a comprehensive archaeology tour of Easter Island every other month (US$2,490 double occupancy, airfare extra). The groups spend seven of the tour's 15 days exploring Easter Island under the guidance of local archaeologists.

Far Horizons Trips (Box 91900, Albuquerque, NM 87199-1900, U.S.A.; tel. 1-800/552-4575 or 1-505/343-9400, fax 1-505/343-8076, www.farhorizon.com, e-mail: journey@farhorizon.com) organizes a 10-day tour to coincide with the Tapati Rapa Nui festival in early February (US$3,095 pp double occupancy, airfare extra). A noted archaeologist or scholar escorts the group.

Travel agencies around Papeete's Vaima Center offer cheap package tours from Tahiti to Easter Island, some of which are discussed in this book's Papeete section. The largest such agency is Tahiti Nui Travel (www.tahiti-nui.com). In the U.S., Tahiti Vacations (tel. 1-800/553-3477, www.tahitivacation.com) can add Easter Island extensions to all of their Tahiti tours at US$799. From Tahiti, low season fares apply from March to November.

From September to June **Azimut 360** (Montecarmelo 180, Depto. 36, Providencia, Santiago, Chile; tel. 56-2/735-8034, fax 56-2/777-2375) operates a five-night ride around Easter Island on horseback. The ground price without airfare is US$950/790 pp if two/three people go. Tents are supplied but you must bring your own sleeping bag.

The Surf Travel Company (Box 446, Cronulla, NSW 2230, Australia; tel. 61-2/9527-4722, fax 61-2/9527-4522, www.surftravel.com.au, e-mail: surftrav@ozemail.com.au) offers seven-night surfing tours to Easter Island, available year-round whenever at least three bookings come in.

Getting Around
There's no public transport but the locals are pretty good about giving lifts (a knowledge of Spanish is a big help here). On Sunday there's often a beach bus to Anakena from the vicinity of the church (ask). Several dozen taxis are available, charging the locals a bit over a dollar for a ride around town or US$15-25 to Anakena. Tourists are expected to pay more and bargaining may be required.

A day-long minibus tour around the island is US$25-50 pp—beware of two-hour "half day" tours. Boat tours to the *motu* off the southwestern tip of the island cost about US$30 pp a half day.

The top hotels rent vehicles at US$50 a half day, US$100 a full day, but you can usually get one for less than that. Lots of cars are available and to find one all you need to do is stroll down the main street watching for the signs. Do ask around, as prices vary (bargaining possible in the off season), and check to make sure the car has a spare tire *(neumático)* and a jack *(gata)*. We've received complaints about the condition of many of the cars. Sometimes the agency will throw in a driver for "free." Insurance is not available but gasoline is cheaper than on the mainland and the distances are small. An international driver's license is required. Scooters can be hired at US$30-45 a day, but a motorcycle license is mandatory. The gas tanks on some of the scooters are too small to visit both Rano Raraku and Anakena. The island's red cinder roads are gradually being paved and speeding on the central highway to Anakena has led to serious accidents. The improved roads have made bicycling a lot more practical and you should be able to rent a bike for no more than US$15 a day.

Airport
Mataveri Airport (IPC) is within half an hour on foot of most of the places to stay in Hanga Roa. Ask for the free map and hotel list at the tourist office to the right past customs. The departure tax is US$18 to Tahiti or US$6 to Santiago (check the amount when you reconfirm and have exactly that ready, otherwise you'll get your change in pesos). If you're headed for Tahiti, don't bother taking any fresh fruit as it will be confiscated at Papeete.

A rough airstrip was begun here in the early 1950s and improved by the U.S. Air Force as an "ionospheric observation center" in the 1960s. In fact, the Americans used the base to spy on French nuclear testing in the Tuamotus. It closed with the election of Salvador Allende in 1970, but in 1986 the Americans were back with permission from Pinochet to extend both ends of the airstrip for use as an emergency landing strip by NASA space shuttles. In late 1995 the older part of the runway was repaired and occasionally the Concorde lands with its nose down like a huge bird of prey. Passengers on these super luxury round-the-world tours spend 24 hours on the island.

Ahu Tongariki, Easter Island

COOK ISLANDS

The Southern Group,
The Northern Group

BOB RACE

INTRODUCTION

The Cook Islands lie in the center of the Polynesian triangle about 4,500 km south of Hawaii. They range from towering Rarotonga, the country's largest island, to the low oval islands of the south and the solitary atolls of the north. Visitors are rewarded with natural beauty and colorful attractions at every turn. There is motion and excitement on Rarotonga and Aitutaki, peaceful village life on the rest. Since few tourists get beyond the two main islands, a trip to Atiu, Mangaia, or Mauke can be a fascinating experience. After Tahiti, Cook Islands is inexpensive, and the local tourist industry is efficient and competitive. It's a safe, quiet place to relax and you feel right at home. The local greeting is *kia orana* (may you live on). Other words to know are *meitaki* (thank you), *aere ra* (goodbye), and *kia manuia!* (cheers!).

The Land

These 15 islands and atolls, with a land area of only 240 square km, are scattered over 1.83 million square km of the Pacific, leaving a lot of empty ocean in between. It's 1,433 km from

Penrhyn to Mangaia. The nine islands in the southern group are a continuation of the Austral Islands of Tahiti-Polynesia, formed as volcanic material escaped from a southeast/northwest fracture in the earth's crust. Five of the northern islands stand on the 3,000-meter-deep Manihiki Plateau, while Penrhyn rises directly out of seas 5,000 meters deep.

Practically every different type of oceanic island can be found in the Cooks. Rarotonga is the only high volcanic island of the Tahiti type. Aitutaki, like Bora Bora, consists of a middle-aged volcanic island surrounded by an atoll-like barrier reef, with many tiny islets defining its lagoon. Atiu, Mangaia, Mauke, and Mitiaro are raised atolls with a high cave-studded outer coral ring *(makatea)* enclosing volcanic soil at the center. It's believed these islands were uplifted during the past two million years due to the weight of Rarotonga on the earth's crust. There are low rolling hills in the interiors of both Atiu and Mangaia, while Mauke and Mitiaro are flat. The swimming and snorkeling possibilities at Atiu, Mangaia,

THE COOK ISLANDS

Penrhyn •

Rakahanga •
○ Manihiki

◄ Pukapuka
• Nassau

Northern Group

Suwarrow ◇

Palmerston •   Southern Group

Aitutaki •
Manuae •
Takutea •. •Mitiaro
Atiu   • Mauke

Rarotonga
○

Mangaia ○

0   250 mi
0   250 km

© DAVID STANLEY

mate. Rain clouds hang over Rarotonga's interior much of the year, but the coast is often sunny, and the rain often comes in brief, heavy downpours. The other islands are drier and can even experience severe water shortages. Winter evenings June-Aug. can be cool. On both Rarotonga and Aitutaki, the best combination of prolonged hours of sunshine, fresh temperatures, and minimal rainfall runs July-September.

May-Oct. the trade winds blow from the southeast in the southern Cooks and from the east in the more humid northern Cooks; the rest of the year winds are generally from the southwest or west. November to April is the summer hurricane season, with an average of one every other year, coming from the direction of Samoa. If you happen to coincide with one, you're in for a unique experience!

For weather information call the Meteorological Office (tel. 20-603) near Rarotonga Airport.

Flora and Fauna

The *au* is a native yellow-flowered hibiscus. The flower of the all-purpose plant is used for medicine, the leaves to cover the *umu* (earth oven), the fiber for skirts, reef sandals, and rope, and the branches for walling native cottages. The lush vegetation of the high islands includes creepers,

Mauke, and Mitiaro are limited, as there's only a fringing reef with small tidal pools. Aitutaki and Rarotonga have protected lagoons where snorkeling is relatively safe. The rich, fertile southern islands account for 89% of the Cooks' land area and population.

Manihiki, Manuae, Palmerston, Penrhyn, Pukapuka, Rakahanga, and Suwarrow are typical lagoon atolls, while tiny Takutea and Nassau are sand cays without lagoons. All of the northern atolls are so low that waves roll right across them during hurricanes, and you have to be within 20 km to see them. This great variety makes Cook Islands a geologist's paradise.

Climate

The main Cook Islands are about the same distance from the equator as Hawaii and have a similarly pleasant tropical cli-

THE ISLANDS OF THE COOKS

ISLAND	AREA IN HECTARES	POPULATION (1996)
Rarotonga	6,718	11,100
Mangaia	5,180	1,104
Atiu	2,693	960
Mitiaro	2,228	319
Mauke	1,842	646
Aitutaki	1,805	2,332
Penrhyn	984	600
Manuae	617	0
Manihiki	544	662
Pukapuka	506	780
Rakahanga	405	249
Palmerston	202	49
Takutea	122	0
Nassau	121	99
Suwarrow	40	4
COOK ISLANDS	24,007	18,904

ferns, and tall trees in the interior, while coconuts, bananas, grapefruit, and oranges grow on the coast. Avocados and papayas are so abundant that the locals feed them to their pigs. Taro and yams are subsistence crops. On the elevated atolls the vegetation in the fertile volcanic center contrasts brusquely with that of the infertile limestone *makatea.* November-Feb., the flamboyant trees bloom red.

The only native mammals are bats and rats. The mynah is the bird most often seen, an aggressive introduced species that drives native birds up into the mountains and damages fruit trees. By 1989 only about 29 examples of the Rarotonga flycatcher or *kakerori* remained due to attacks on the birds' nests by ship rats. Fortunately a local landowners group, the Takitumu Conservation Area, took an interest in the *kakerori's* survival and began laying rat poison in the nesting areas during the breeding season. By 1996 there were 134 *kakerori.* More common native birds are the Cook Islands fruit dove *(kukupa),* the Rarotonga starling *('i'oi),* and the Cook Islands warbler *(kerearako).*

Captain James Cook (1728-1779) as painted at the Cape of Good Hope by John Webber, 1776

The most interesting aspect of the natural environment is found among the fish and corals of the lagoons and reefs. Reef walks on Rarotonga and lagoon trips on Aitutaki display this colorful world to visitors. Humpback whales can sometimes be seen cruising along the shorelines July-Sept. having migrated 5,000 km north from Antarctica to bear their young. Pilot whales (up to six meters) are in the Cooks year-round. Sharks are not a problem in the Cook lagoons.

HISTORY AND GOVERNMENT

Discovery

Though peppered across a vast empty expanse of ocean, the Polynesians knew all these islands by heart long before the first Europeans happened on the scene. One of several legends holds that Rarotonga was settled about A.D. 1200 by two great warriors, Karika from Samoa and Tangiia-nui from Tahiti. The story goes that Karika and Tangiia-nui met on the high seas but decided not to fight because there would be no one to proclaim the victor. Instead they carried on to Rarotonga together and divided the island among themselves by sailing their canoes around it in opposite directions, with a line between their starting and meeting points becoming the boundary. Even today, tribes in the Cooks refer to themselves as *vaka* (canoes), and many can trace their ancestry back to these chiefs.

Archaeologists believe Rarotonga was reached much earlier, probably around A.D. 800 from Raiatea or the Marquesas. The mythical chief Toi who built the Ara Metua on Rarotonga is associated with this earlier migration. Recent excavations of a *marae* on a *motu* in the Muri Lagoon point to an even earlier date, perhaps A.D. 500. Atiu was a chiefly island that dominated Mauke, Mitiaro, Takutea, and sometimes Manuae.

The Spanish explorer Mendaña sighted Pukapuka in 1595, and his pilot, Quirós, visited Rakahanga in 1606. Some 500 inhabitants gathered on the beach to gaze at the strange ships. Quirós wrote, "They were the most beautiful white and elegant people that were met during the voyage—especially the women, who, if properly dressed, would have advantages over our Spanish women."

Then the islands were lost again to Europeans until the 1770s when Captain Cook contacted Atiu, Mangaia, Manuae, Palmerston, and Takutea—"detached parts of the earth." He named Manuae the Hervey Islands, a name that others applied to the whole group; it was not until 1824 that the Russian cartographer, Johann von Krusenstern, labeled the southern group the Cook Islands. Cook never saw Rarotonga, and the Pitcairn-bound *Bounty* is thought to be its first European visitor (in 1789). The mutineers gave the inhabitants the seeds for their first orange trees. Aitutaki was discovered by Captain Bligh just before the famous mutiny. Mauke and Mitiaro were reached in 1823 by John Williams of the London Missionary Society.

European Penetration

Williams stopped at Aitutaki in 1821 and dropped off two Tahitian teachers. Returning two years later, he found that one, Papeiha, had done particularly well. Williams took him to Rarotonga and left him there for four years. When he returned in 1827, Williams was welcomed by Papeiha's many converts. The missionaries taught an austere, puritanical morality and believed the white man's diseases such as dysentery, measles, smallpox, and influenza, which killed two-thirds of the population, were the punishment of God descending on the sinful islanders. The missionaries became a law unto themselves; today, the ubiquitous churches full to overflowing on Sunday are their legacy. (The missionaries arrived from Australia, and since they weren't aware of the idea of an international date line, they held Sunday service on the wrong day for the first 60 years of their presence!) About 63% of the population now belongs to the Cook Islands Christian Church (CICC), founded by the London Missionary Society. Takamoa College, the Bible school they established at Avarua in 1837, still exists.

Reports that the French were about to annex the Cooks led the British to declare a protectorate over the southern group in 1888. The French warship approaching Manihiki to claim the islands turned back when it saw a hastily sewn Union Jack flying and in 1889 the northern atolls were added to the protectorate. The local chiefs, well aware of how their counterparts on Tahiti had been marginalized by the French, petitioned the British to have their islands annexed to the British Crown, a position strongly endorsed by the missionaries. Thus on 11 June 1901 both the northern and southern groups were included in the boundaries of New Zealand. During WW II, the U.S. built air bases on Aitutaki and Penrhyn.

A legislative council was established in 1946, followed by an assembly with greater powers in 1957. After decolonizing pressure from the United Nations, a new constitution was granted in 1964 and the Cook Islands was made an internally self-governing state in free association with New Zealand on 4 August 1965. New Zealand has no veto over local laws; the Cook Islands also runs its own external affairs and operates as an independent country. The paper connection with New Zealand deprives the country of a seat at the U.N. but brings in millions of dollars in financial and technical assistance from Wellington that might otherwise be withheld. New Zealand citizenship, which the Cook Islanders hold, is greatly valued. The arrangement has been very successful and is looked upon as a model by many Tahitian leaders. In recent years Cook Islands has sought closer economic and cultural ties with Tahiti-Polynesia to balance their relationship with New Zealand.

Government

Cook Islands' 25-member Parliament operates on the Westminster system, with a prime minister as the head of government. The cabinet consists of seven ministers. While almost all members of parliament are men, most of the chiefly titles are held by women who are also the main landowners. In theory, the 15-member House of Ariki (chiefs) should be consulted on custom and land issues, but in practice this seldom happens.

On all the outer islands there's an appointed chief administrative officer (CAO), formerly known as the resident agent. Although each island also has an elected Island Council, the CAO runs the local administration on behalf of the local and central governments. In recent years the autonomy of the island councils has increased.

Politics

Party politics, often based on personalities, is vicious. The most dramatic event in the last few decades was the removal of Premier Albert Henry and the Cook Islands Party from office in 1978 by the chief justice of the High Court when it was proven that Henry had misused government funds to fly in his voters from New Zealand during the preceding election. Then, Queen Elizabeth II stripped Sir Albert of his knighthood. This was the first time in Commonwealth history that a court ruling had changed a government; the shock waves are still being felt in Rarotonga. Albert Henry died in 1981, it's said of a broken heart.

Albert Henry's successor, Sir Tom Davis of the Democratic Party, served as prime minister from 1978 until July 1987, when he was ousted by a vote of no confidence. The Cook Islands Party, led by Sir Geoffrey Henry, a cousin of Albert, won the 1989 and 1994 elections. The opposition is split between the Democratic Alliance, led by outspoken Atiu politician Norman George, and the New Alliance Party.

ECONOMY

Cook Islanders live beyond their means. Imports outweigh exports by 11 times, and food imports alone are nearly three times all exports. Tourism makes up for some of this, but without New Zealand aid (about NZ$12 million a year) Cook Islands would be bankrupt. The largest exports are cultured pearls, fish and seafood, fruits and vegetables (papaya, bananas, beans, taro), and clothing, in that order. Fresh fruit production is hindered by the small volume, uneven quality, inadequate shipping, poor marketing, and the unreliability of island producers.

The economy's small size is illustrated by the importance of the post office's Philatelic Bureau. Money remitted by Cook Islanders resident in N.Z. contributes about NZ$3 million a year to the local economy, and licensing fees from South Korean and other foreign fishing companies to exploit the exclusive economic zone bring in additional income. A number of small clothing factories in Avarua supply tropical beachware to the local and tourist markets and exports are picking up. Subsistence fishing and agriculture are important on the outer islands.

Things could change if mining of undersea deposits of cobalt, copper, and nickel inside the exclusive economic zone goes ahead. In 1997 Cook Islands signed a deal theoretically worth US$600 million with the American mining giant Bechtel Corporation. Royalties won't begin pouring in until actual mining is underway and that won't happen for another decade at least.

Finance

Since 1984 Cook Islands has operated as an "international finance center" providing offshore banking facilities to foreign corporations and individuals attempting to avoid taxation and regulation in their home countries. In contrast to local businesses, which are heavily taxed, some 3,000 Asian companies that don't operate in the Cooks are now registered in the Rarotonga "tax haven," bringing in over NZ$5 million a year in banking and licensing fees. Offshore "banks" can be owned by a single person and it's believed that millions of illicit dollars have been laundered through Rarotonga.

Such arrangements allow individuals in other jurisdictions to transfer revenue to "asset protection trusts" in the Cook Islands that are safe from creditors in the event of a subsequent bankruptcy. Thus unscrupulous individuals can plunder their own companies elsewhere in order to build up tax-free nest eggs on Rarotonga. Profits can be routed through tax havens to avoid taxation. Scams like these helped generate the Asian financial crisis of 1997, and teams of highly paid lawyers and accountants based on Rarotonga and abroad facilitate the process.

In 1987 the director of the Cook Islands Office of Audit and Inquiry was sacked after he warned the New Zealand and Australian governments that large corporations based in their countries were illegally evading taxation through the use of false tax withholding certificates issued by Cook Islands for a fraction their face value. The bogus certificates allowed the companies to claim deductions for overseas taxation; several large Japanese banks were also involved. In 1991 Australia and New Zealand revised their tax laws to restrict the use of tax havens by their citizens (penalties of up to 125% of the tax due and five years in prison).

In early 1995 *Islands Business* magazine reported that the Cook Islands government had guaranteed 12 letters of credit worth a total of US$1.2 billion in a scheme that Prime Minister Sir Geoffrey Henry had hoped would earn US$10 million in commissions. The worthless guarantees were quickly withdrawn when they came under scrutiny by the Reserve Bank of New Zealand.

The country has a NZ$200 million national debt, most of it incurred by tourism-related developments such as the Sheraton Hotel project, the National Cultural Center, power generation, and telecommunications since 1989 when Sir Geoffrey's administration took over. Much of the money is owed to the governments of Italy and

Nauru, which foolishly guaranteed huge unsecured loans to this tiny country, but NZ$23 million of it came from the Asian Development Bank, which has had to intervene several times to save Cook Islands from bankruptcy.

In mid-1994 local branches of the ANZ and Westpac banks began to severely restrict private credit after the government proved unable to service its heavy debt load. A few months later the banks stopped clearing checks drawn in Cook Islands dollars through the New Zealand banking system and announced that these would have to be collected locally. Local businesses began moving money offshore, and in late 1994 the Reserve Bank of New Zealand confirmed that it no longer guaranteed the convertibility of the Cook Islands dollar. The threat of imminent financial collapse forced the government to withdraw the currency from circulation in 1995. New Zealand banknotes are presently used.

Until 1996 Cook Islands had a bloated public service of 3,600 persons or 60% of the workforce. Then, after the Westpac Bank bounced official salary checks due to a US$5 million dollar overdraft in the government's current account, civil servants were forced to accept a 15% across the board pay cut. As interest on the unpaid government loans continued to mount, it became clear that harsher measures were required. Thus it was announced that government employee numbers would be reduced to 1,200 and the pay cut increased to 65%. From 1996 to 1998 some 6,000 Cook Islanders (30% of the population) voted with their feet and left for greener pastures in Australia and New Zealand. State assets (including four hotels and the telephone company) were hurriedly sold off and the number of government departments cut in half. Sir Geoffrey accurately concluded that by abruptly imposing a harsh structural adjustment program three years in advance of the next election, the worst of it would be over before he had to face the voters again and many of those most affected would already have left the country.

Cook Islands runs a discount "flag of convenience" ship registry that allows foreign shipping companies to avoid the more stringent safety and labor regulations of industrialized countries. Ominously, one of the first ships to sign up, the freighter *Celtic Kiwi,* sank off New Zealand in October 1991. After further sinkings and reports of gun running, most insurance companies won't touch ships registered in the Cooks.

The newest hustle is cyber-gambling over the internet with the world's fifth-largest online casino, Casinos of the South Pacific (www.cosp.com), based here since 1997. Blackjack, draw poker, roulette, and slots are all offered. The company operates under Rarotonga's financial center legislation, which means that taxation and regulation are minimal, but local punters are blocked from accessing the site and cosp.com's Avarua headquarters is unmarked. Of course, none of the profits go to charity. (Despite the political infighting and economic chicanery described above, Cook Islands is completely safe and stable for tourism. The Australian guidebooks conveniently leave out most of the above and are generally uncritical in order to boost sales on Rarotonga.)

Tourism

Since the opening of the international airport in 1973, tourism has been important, and directly or indirectly, it now employs a quarter of the workforce and accounts for over half the gross national product. Cook Islands has the highest tourist density in the South Pacific with three tourists a year for every local resident, compared to two Fijians, three Samoans, and four Tongans for every tourist visiting those countries. At times Rarotonga (with five tourists a year per Cook Islander) really has the feel of a little Hawaii.

About a third of the 50,000-odd arriving tourists are New Zealanders who spend all their time at resorts on Rarotonga and Aitutaki on prepaid packaged holidays. The rest are fairly evenly divided between Americans, Australians, Canadians, and Europeans. Few Asian tourists make it this far. Although arrival levels have stagnated since 1994, overdevelopment has led to ominous sewage disposal and water supply problems on Rarotonga.

The Rarotongan Resort Hotel was built in 1977 by the Cook Islands government, the Tourist Hotel Corporation of N.Z., and Air New Zealand, with each owning a third. In 1982, after the hotel proved to be a consistent money-loser, the Cook Islands government had to buy out its two partners to prevent closure. When the poorly planned Aitutaki Lagoon Hotel tottered on bankruptcy in 1989, the government was forced to take it over too. In the two decades to 1997 the

Rarotongan Resort Hotel lost millions of dollars, but that year it was privatized in a sweetheart deal that handed the property interest-free for 10 years to local businessman Tata Crocombe despite a better offer from an Australian company. A major refurbishment has now put the Rarotongan back on its feet.

In 1984 "experts" from the United Nations Development Program advised that the way to make tourism more "profitable" was to allow more large hotels and stop construction of the smaller, family-owned motels. Finding itself unable to attract the required foreign investment, the government itself decided to bankroll construction of a new four-star luxury hotel, and in 1987 NZ$52 million was borrowed from an Italian bank. A year later the Democratic Party government collapsed and in 1989 Sir Geoffrey Henry's Cook Islands Party was voted in after promising to stop the project. Once in office, however, Sir Geoffrey did an about-face and announced that he now backed the hotel. A management contract was signed with the Sheraton chain and in May 1990, despite many objections from local residents, construction began on the south side of Rarotonga using Italian building materials and contractors.

The 204-room Cook Islands Sheraton Resort was conceived as a cluster of two-story buildings, similar to the Fiji Sheraton, with the inevitable 18-hole golf course. The project suffered repeated delays, and then it was announced that the Italian construction company had gone broke after spending NZ$30 million of the government's loan money without getting much done. A second Italian construction company (Stephany SpA) was brought in, and the government borrowed another NZ$20 million so work could resume. In mid-1993 the Italian government began its "clean hands" crackdown on Mafia activities, and several people involved in the Sheraton project were arrested in Italy, causing the Italian insurers to freeze coverage on the loans, and work on the Sheraton stopped again.

The empty structure of the unfinished Sheraton now faces an uncertain future, and the full story of what went on behind the scenes has yet to be told. It's estimated that at least another NZ$18 million is required to finish the hotel, plus about NZ$4.5 million for the golf course. Incredibly, a monument bestowing full credit on

Sir Geoffrey for inaugurating the project still stands in front of the site! Meanwhile there are NZ$90 million and rising in accumulated Sheraton debts to repay. A recent report indicates that Japanese investors have finally put up enough money to complete the hotel, so it may actually be open under a new name by the time you get there! (Sheraton has had nothing to do with the construction scandal.)

Pearls

In 1982 research began at Manihiki into the possibility of creating a cultured-pearl industry similar to that of Tahiti-Polynesia. The first commercial farms were set up on Manihiki in 1989 and some 800,000 cultured oysters are presently held there. It's believed the Manihiki lagoon is approaching its maximum sustainable holding capacity and in 1994 farms began to be established on Penrhyn. These presently have 150,000 oysters and the Penrhyn hatchery is expected to increase those numbers considerably. Rakahanga and Suwarrow are now under consideration as prospective pearl-farming areas. Fluctuations in water temperature and overstocking can affect the amount of plankton available to the oysters and reduce the quality of the pearls. Rising temperatures can have an immediate impact.

To establish a farm, an investment of NZ$5,000 is required, and no return will be forthcoming for five years. In 1998 there were 300 farms with just 20% of them accounting for 80% of the oysters. The oysters are seeded once or twice a year by Japanese, Chinese, and Cook Islands experts screened by the Ministry of Marine Resources. Annual production is around 200 kilograms, with Japanese and Chinese dealers the big buyers. Black pearls are now Cook Islands' largest export, bringing in US$4 million a year and employing 700 people. Fortunately a major hurricane at Manihiki in November 1997 did little harm to the underwater oysters although surface facilities were destroyed.

THE PEOPLE

About 84% of the people are Polynesian Cook Island Maoris, most of whom also have some other ancestry. They're related to the Maoris of New Zealand and the Tahitians, although the

Cook Island schoolchildren

TOURISM COOK ISLANDS

Pukapukans are unique in that they are closer to the Samoans. Almost everyone on Rarotonga and most people on the outer islands speak flawless English while their mother tongue will be a form of Maori. Rarotongan and its dialects are spoken throughout the southern group. Penrhyn is closely related to Rarotongan, Rakahanga-Manihiki is more distantly related, and Pukapukan is related to Samoan.

Over half the population resides on Rarotonga; only 13% live in the northern group. Cook Islanders reside near the seashore, except on Atiu and Mauke, where they are interior dwellers. The old-style thatched *kikau* houses have almost disappeared from the Cook Islands, even though they're cooler, more esthetic, and much cheaper to build than modern housing. A thatched pandanus roof can last 15 years.

While 18,904 (1996) Cook Islanders live in their home islands, some 40,000 reside in New Zealand and another 20,000 in Australia. Emigration to New Zealand increased greatly after the airport opened in 1973 but New Zealanders do not have the reciprocal right to reside permanently in Cook Islands. During the 1980s the migratory patterns reversed and many ex-islanders returned from New Zealand to set up tourism-related businesses, but the steady flow of people to New Zealand and Australia has now resumed due to Cook Island's recent economic crisis. The loss of many teachers and students forced schools and classes to be amalgamated and led to an increase in the dropout rate among teenagers. Education is compulsory until the age of 15.

There are almost no Chinese in the Cooks due to a deliberate policy of discrimination initiated in 1901 by New Zealand Prime Minister Richard Seddon, although many islanders have some Chinese blood resulting from the presence of Chinese traders in the 19th century. About 14% of the population was born outside the South Pacific and the proportion of Americans, New Zealanders, Australians, and others is gradually increasing as expatriates arrive to set up businesses while Cook Island migrants move in the opposite direction.

Under the British and New Zealand regimes, the right of the Maori people to their land was protected, and no land was sold to outsiders. These policies continue today, although foreigners can lease land for up to 60 years. The fragmentation of inherited landholdings into scattered miniholdings hampers agriculture and many fine turn-of-the-century stone buildings have fallen into ruins because of ownership disputes.

The powerful *ariki,* or chiefly class, that ruled in pre-European times is still influential today. The *ariki* were the first to adopt Christianity, instructing their subjects to follow suit and filling leadership posts in the church. British and New Zealand colonial rule was established with the approval of the *ariki.* Now materialism, party politics, and emigration to New Zealand are eroding the authority of the *ariki.* Until self-government, Cook Islanders were only allowed to consume alcohol if they had a permit; now it's a serious social problem.

Dangers and Annoyances

There's been an increase in rape cases lately. Women should keep this in mind when stepping out at night and when choosing a place to stay. There's safety in numbers. Scanty dress outside the resorts will cause offense and maybe trouble. To go to church women should wear a dress with long sleeves and a hat, while men need long trousers. Be aware of petty theft, particularly if you're staying somewhere with young children running loose. Don't go off and leave things on the clothesline or beach. Never purchase pearls from people on the street and be wary of such vendors as black pearls have been used as a ruse to establish contact with visitors whose hotel rooms were later burglarized. Try to avoid being bitten by mosquitoes, as these are sometimes carriers of dengue fever (see **Health** in the main Introduction). Of the 15 islands of the Cooks, Rarotonga is the most affected by this painful disease and a serious epidemic occurred in April 1997.

ON THE ROAD

Highlights

Everyone will arrive on Rarotonga and the short-list of "musts" includes an island night dance show, a bicycle ride around the island, a swim in the Muri Lagoon, and a hike up to the Needle. The snorkeling at Aitutaki is even better and it's another nice place to hang loose. However, to get a real feel for the group, you must get beyond this rather touristy pair to an outer island like Mangaia, Mauke, or Atiu. All three have regular flights from Rarotonga and a few small hotels although other visitor facilities are scanty—they're that unspoiled.

Sports and Recreation

Most organized sporting activities are on Rarotonga and Aitutaki. Several professional scuba diving companies are based on these islands, and there are many snorkeling possibilities. Both islands offer lagoon tours by boat, with those at Aitutaki by far the better.

Several firms based on Rarotonga's Muri Beach rent water-sports equipment, including surfboards, sailboats, and kayaks, with training in their use available. The surfing possibilities are very limited in Cook Islands—windsurfing's the thing to do. Horseback riding and deep-sea fishing are other popular activities.

Most of the hiking possibilities are on mountainous Rarotonga, but uplifted islands such as Atiu, Mauke, and Mangaia are also fascinating to wander around, with many interesting, hidden features. The nine-hole golf courses on Aitutaki and Rarotonga aren't too challenging, but greens fees are low and the atmospheres amicable. Tournaments are held at both in September.

The spectator sports are cricket Dec.-March, with matches every Saturday afternoon, and rugby June-August. Rugby is the main team sport played in the Cooks; soccer is a more recent introduction. On Rarotonga, ask about rugby matches at Tereora National Stadium (built for the 1985 South Pacific Mini Games), on the inland side of the airport, and in the sports ground opposite the National Cultural Center in Avarua.

Music and Dance

Among main genres of Cook Islands music and dance are drum dancing *('ura pa'u),* choreographed group dancing *(kaparima)* to string band music, dance dramas *(peu tupuna)* based on island legends, religious pageants *(nuku),* formal chants *(pe'e),* celebratory song/chants *('ute),* and polyphonic choral music *('imene tapu)* or hymns.

Among the drums used are the small *pate* or *to'ere* slit drum used to guide the dancers, the *pa'u,* a double-headed bass drum that provides the beat, and the upright *pa'u mango* that accompanies the *pa'u.* The larger *ka'ara* slit drum and the conch shell accompany chanting. Tahitian drummers have often copied Cook Island rhythms. String band music is based on the ukulele although guitars are also used.

The top traditional dancing is seen during annual events on Rarotonga when the outer islanders arrive to compete. The drum dancing at hotel shows features the sensuous side-to-side hip movements of the women (differing somewhat from the circular movements seen on Tahiti) and the robust knee snapping of the men. In the *hura* (equivalent of the Hawaiian *hula)* the female dancers must keep their feet flat on the ground and shoulders steady as they sway in a stunning display.

Public Holidays and Festivals

Public holidays include New Year's Day (1 January), ANZAC Day (25 April), Good Friday, Easter Monday (March/April), Queen Elizabeth's Birthday (first Monday in June), Constitution Day (4 August), Gospel Day (26 October), Christmas Day (25 December), and Boxing Day (26 December). On Rarotonga, Gospel Day is celebrated on 26 July; elsewhere it's 26 October.

Cultural Festival Week, with arts and crafts displays, takes place in mid-February. The Dancer of the Year Competition is in late April. The 10-day Constitution Celebration, beginning on the Friday before 4 August, is the big event of the year. There are parades, dancing and singing contests, sporting events, and an agricultural fair. The Round Raro Run is a 31-km marathon held on the first Saturday of October (the record time is 98 minutes set by Kevin Ryan in 1979). Gospel Day (26 October) recalls 26 October 1821, when the Rev. John Williams landed on Aitutaki. Ask about itinerant religious plays *(nuku)* on that day. On All Souls Day (November 1st) Catholics visit the cemeteries to place candles and flowers on the graves of family members. The third or fourth week in November is Tiare Festival Week, with flower shows and floral parades. A food festival is also held in late November. On Takitumu Day (3 December), visits are made to historic *marae*.

ACCOMMODATIONS AND FOOD

Accommodations

There's an abundance of accommodations in all price categories on Rarotonga and Aitutaki, and many outer islands also have one or two regular places to stay. Local regulations prohibit visitors from staying in private homes, camping, living in rental cars, or sleeping on the beach, so have the name of a licensed hotel ready upon arrival.

As you come out of the airport terminal, someone may ask you which hotel you plan to stay at, and will direct you to the representative of that establishment (if he/she happens to be present). Repeat the name of the licensed accommoda-

tions you wrote on your arrival card, then go over and talk to the representative of that establishment if he/she is pointed out to you. It used to be necessary to make a hotel booking before you were allowed entry to Cook Islands, but this regulation is no longer enforced and you're now only required to stay at a licensed hotel, motel, or hostel.

In order to have the best choice of places to stay and maximum flexibility in your plans, it's better not to prepay any hotel accommodations at all. The backpacker places always have empty beds but accommodation is sometimes tight in the medium-price range. If you're sure you want to stay at a particular place and wish to play it safe, you can make an advance hotel booking through Air New Zealand offices in the South Pacific (but not overseas), Cook Islands Tourism Corporation (fax 21-435, e-mail: tourism@cookislands.gov.ck) in Avarua, or directly to the hostel or hotel. This service costs nothing extra and you can pay upon arrival. If you end up with something you don't like, it's always possible to move somewhere else later (although most places have a two-night minimum stay). If you do have a reservation, a representative of your hotel will be at the airport to take you to your assigned room for a fee of about NZ$20 roundtrip.

You'll save money and get closer to the people by staying at the smaller, locally owned "self-catering" motels and guesthouses. The fewer the rooms the motel has, the better. A "motel" in

DAVID STANLEY

the Cooks is styled on the New Zealand type of motel, which means a fully equipped kitchen is built into each unit. Some of them are quite attractive, nothing like the dreary roadside motels of the United States. The motels generally offer rooms with private bath and hot water, but some guesthouses and hostels do not, although communal cooking facilities are usually available. At the big resorts you not only pay a much higher price, but you're forced to eat in fancy dining rooms and restaurants.

All of the officially approved accommodations are listed herein. Hotel prices tend to fluctuate in Cook Islands and when things are slow some places cut their rates to attract guests, so in some cases you could end up paying less than the prices quoted herein. Outer islands without licensed accommodations, or where such accommodations are full, may be effectively closed to visitors. Ask Air Rarotonga about this before heading too far off the beaten track.

Booking Agencies

Three times a week **Stars Travel** (Box 75, Rarotonga; tel. 23-669; fax 21-569, e-mail: holidays@starstravel.co.ck), near the ANZ Bank in Avarua, has a seven-night package tour from Rarotonga to Atiu, Mitiaro, and Mauke for NZ$739 for one person, NZ$662 pp for two, NZ$615 pp for three, including airfare, accommodations (double occupancy), meals on Mitiaro, transfers, tax, and a full lei greeting on each island. These packages are for local sale on Rarotonga only. Other Stars Travel packages offer two nights on Aitutaki, Atiu, or Mauke. Stars Travel can also reserve rooms alone at any hotel or guesthouse in the Cook Islands. They also book entire houses on Aitutaki at NZ$200 a week.

Island Hopper Vacations (Box 240, Rarotonga; tel. 22-026, fax 22-036, e-mail: travel@islandhopper.co.ck), next to the Banana Court in Avarua, offers similar deals and arranges airport transfers to outer island flights. Other agencies specialized in booking rooms from overseas are **Hugh Henry & Associates** (Box 440, Rarotonga; tel. 25-320, fax 25-420, e-mail: hhenry@gatepoly.co.ck) and **Tipani Tours** (Box 4, Rarotonga; tel. 25-266, fax 23-266, e-mail: tours@tipani.co.ck), owned by the Tahitian tour company Tahiti Nui Travel. It's usually cheaper, however, to make your own arrangements.

Food and Drink

The Rarotonga restaurant scene has improved in recent years and you now have a good choice. A few restaurants are found on Aitutaki, but none exist on the outer islands. When ordering, keep in mind that an "entree" is actually an appetizer and not a main dish.

By law all bars are required to close at midnight, except Friday night when they can stay open until 0200. On Sunday no alcohol may be sold at grocery stores, and even restaurants are only allowed to serve alcohol with a meal that day, although this rule is not always followed. Wine is expensive at restaurants, due to high import duties, and drinking alcoholic beverages on the street is prohibited. Most of the motels and guesthouses offer cooking facilities and you'll save a lot on meals if you stay at one of them.

Rukau is Cook Islands *palusami,* made from spinachlike young taro leaves cooked in coconut cream. *Ika mata* is marinated raw fish with coconut sauce. Locals insist that slippery foods such as bananas lead to forgetfulness, while gluey foods like taro help one to remember. Dogs are sometimes eaten by young men on drinking sprees. Turn to the Atiu section for information on "bush beer" (called "home-brewed" on Rarotonga and Aitutaki).

SERVICES AND INFORMATION

Visas and Officialdom

No visa is required for a stay of up to 31 days, but you must show an onward ticket. For NZ$70 you can get extensions up to six months in the Cooks. Apply at the Immigration office on the top floor of the Government Office Building behind the post office. Actually, one week is plenty of time to see Rarotonga and 31 days is sufficient to visit all of the southern Cook Islands.

If you're thinking of taking a boat trip to the northern group, be sure to get a visa extension before you leave Rarotonga. Otherwise you could have problems with Immigration if your entry permit has expired by the time you get back.

For a foreigner to obtain permanent residency in Cook Islands is difficult and only allowed in exceptional circumstances (such as if you're willing to invest money). Cook Islands citizenship has never been extended to Europeans. For more information write: Principal Immigration Officer, Box 105, Rarotonga, Cook Islands (tel. 682/29-347, fax 682/21-247, e-mail: legaladv@foraffairs.gov.ck).

Rarotonga, Aitutaki, and Penrhyn are ports of entry for cruising yachts; the only harbors for yachts are at Aitutaki, Penrhyn, Suwarrow, and Rarotonga.

Money

The currency is the New Zealand dollar, which was valued at US$1 = NZ$1.94 at press time. After a financial crisis in 1995 the Cook Islands dollar, which had circulated at par with the New Zealand dollar since 1987, was withdrawn. Cook Islands coins are still in use, however, although these are worthless outside Cook Islands. The Cook Islands dollar coin bearing an image of the god Tangaroa makes an offbeat souvenir.

Traveler's checks are worth about three percent more than cash at the banks. Changing money on an outer island is difficult or impossible—do it before you leave Rarotonga. The upmarket hotels and restaurants accept the main credit cards, and the banks will give cash advances. The local American Express representative is Stars Travel (tel. 23-669). Unless otherwise indicated, all Cook Islands prices quoted in this book are in N.Z. dollars, currently worth about half as much as U.S. dollars, which makes the Cook Islands inexpensive.

A 12.5% value added tax (VAT) is added to all sales, services, activities, and rentals. Most places include it in the price, but some charge it extra, so ask. Bargaining has never been a part of the local culture and some locals find it offensive when tourists try to beat prices down. The way to do it is to ask for "specials." Thankfully tipping is still not widespread in the Cooks.

Telecommunications

Telecom Cook Islands (Box 106, Avarua; tel. 29-680, fax 26-174) charges a flat rate for international telephone calls with no off-hours discounts. Three-minute operator-assisted calls cost NZ$7.60 to New Zealand, NZ$10.90 to Australia, and NZ$18.50 to most other countries— very expensive. Person-to-person calls attract an additional two-minute charge.

It's a bit cheaper to use a local telephone card for international calls, and there's no three-minute minimum with a card (dial the international access code 00, the country code, the area code, and the number). More importantly, with a card you can't lose track of the time and end up being presented with a tremendous bill. The cards come in denominations of NZ$10, NZ$20, and NZ$50 and are good for all domestic and international calls. Calls to outer islands within Cook Islands cost NZ$1.20 a minute with a card. You'll probably also need a card to make local calls as very few coin phones remain on Rarotonga.

Collect calls can be placed to Australia, Canada, Fiji, Hong Kong, India, Netherlands, New Zealand, Niue, Sweden, Tahiti-Polynesia, Tonga, United Kingdom, U.S.A., and Vanuatu only. To call collect, dial the international/outer island operator at tel. 015. Directory assistance numbers within Cook Islands are tel. 010, international tel. 017. The **country code** of Cook Islands is 682.

For calls to the U.S., AT&T's "USADirect" service is more expensive than using a local telephone card, but perhaps useful in emergencies. To be connected to this service dial 09111 from any phone in the Cook Islands. The Telecom "New Zealand Direct" number is tel. 0964-09682.

Many local businesses now have e-mail and both www.ck and www.oyster.net.ck include directories of them. Gatepoly provides e-mail services only, while Telecom Cook Islands' more expensive Oyster service hosts both websites and e-mail.

Measurements and Time

The electric voltage is 240 volts DC, 50 cycles, the same as in New Zealand and Australia. American appliances will require a converter. The type of plug varies, but bring a three-pin adaptor. On outer islands other than Aitutaki electricity is only provided a few hours a day. Faxes to Atiu, Mauke, and some other outer islands don't go through between midnight and 0500 local time due to the central electricity supply being switched off at that time.

The time is the same as in Hawaii and Tahiti, two hours behind California and 22 hours behind New Zealand. "Cook Islands time" also runs a bit behind "Western tourist's time," so relax and let things happen. All travel agencies, banks, and offices are closed on Saturday, although most shops and restaurants are open until noon. In recent years regulations have been relaxed and many small shops on Rarotonga are now open early Sunday morning (until 0900) and again on Sunday evening (after 1700). The car rental places also open on Sunday.

Media

Be sure to pick up a copy of the *Cook Islands News* (Phil Evans, Box 15, Rarotonga; tel. 22-999, fax 25-303, www.cinews.co.ck), published daily except Sunday (70 cents). Its reporting on island affairs really gives you a feel for where you are, and local happenings are listed.

The *Cook Islands Press* (Jason Brown, Box 741, Rarotonga; tel. 24-865, fax 24-866), published weekly (NZ$2), provides outstanding coverage of domestic political issues. The *Cook Islands Sun* is a free tourist newspaper.

On Rarotonga Radio Ikurangi KCFM (tel. 23-203), a private commercial station, broadcasts over 103.3 MHz from 0530-2400 with overseas news at 0600 and 0700. Radio New Zealand International news is rebroadcast over this station at 0800, 0900, and 1200. The FM station can be difficult to pick up on the south side of Rarotonga but Radio Cook Islands at 630 kHz AM can be heard anywhere on the island (and even on nearby islands like Mauke in the evening).

Information

For advance information about the country, write to one of the branches of government-operated Cook Islands Tourism Corporation listed in the appendix, or to their head office at Box 14, Rarotonga (tel. 29-435, fax 21-435, www.cook-islands.com, e-mail: tourism@cookislands.gov.ck). Ask for their free magazine, *What's On In The Cook Islands,* and the color map *Jasons Passport Cook Islands.* Websites with useful information are listed in the appendix.

Elliot Smith's *Cook Islands Companion* is recommended for those who want more detailed information on the country than can be included here. Smith's book has much more of a "hands-

on" feel than other guides to the Cooks and it's possible to purchase a personally autographed copy directly from the author at Shangri-La Beach Cottages on Muri Beach.

TRANSPORTATION

Getting There

Air New Zealand (tel. 26-300), with an office at the airport, has direct services to Rarotonga from Auckland, Honolulu, Nadi, Papeete, and Los Angeles. Air services into Rarotonga are heavily booked, so reserve your inward and outward flights as far ahead as possible. If you try to change your outbound flight after arrival you could be put on standby.

In November 1998 the charter carrier **Canada 3000** began a weekly service between Vancouver and Rarotonga via Honolulu with connections to/from Toronto. Like Canada 3000's flights to Fiji, these flights only operate during the Nov.-April winter season in Canada. Polynesian Airlines has announced that it hopes to launch a weekly Apia-Rarotonga-Papeete service but these flights were still not operating at press time, so check.

Check in for your outgoing international flight at least one hour before the scheduled departure time, as the airlines are short of staff: if everyone is needed to attend to a flight arrival, they may simply close the check-in counter and you'll be out of luck.

Getting Around by Air

All of the main islands of the southern Cooks and a few of the northern group have regular air service from Rarotonga, although no flights operate on Sunday. **Air Rarotonga** (Box 79, Rarotonga; tel. 22-888, fax 23-288, e-mail: bookings@airraro.co.ck) serves Aitutaki (NZ$272 roundtrip) three times a day except Sunday. The "super saver" roundtrip excursion fare to Aitutaki is NZ$218 return provided you fly northbound on the afternoon flight and southbound on the morning flight for any length of time. There's no advance purchase requirement but seats cannot be booked over 14 days in advance. This pass is not available outside Cook Islands or in December and January (homecoming time for overseas Cook Islanders when many flights run

KILOMETERS BETWEEN ISLANDS

	Rarotonga	Aitutaki	Mauke	Mitiaro	Atiu	Mangaia	Palmerston	Pukapuka	Nassau	Manihiki	Rakahanga	Penrhyn
Aitutaki	259											
Mauke	278	296										
Mitiaro	263	241	59									
Atiu	215	209	93	235								
Mangaia	204	385	213	232	215							
Palmerston	500	367	657	611	574	704						
Pukapuka	1,324	1,089	1,361	1,304	1,296	1,470	843					
Nassau	1,246	1,000	1,278	1,217	1,209	1,382	756	89				
Manihiki	1,204	946	1,145	1,102	1,093	1,304	880	530	500			
Rakahanga	1,248	991	1,189	1,146	1,137	1,348	922	535	506	44		
Penrhyn	1,365	1,111	1,241	1,204	1,222	1,433	1,130	889	859	363	354	
Suwarrow	950	713	978	926	917	1,111	533	398	310	385	417	733

full). Air Rarotonga runs day trips to Aitutaki from Rarotonga, but these are expensive and rushed at NZ$329 including air tickets, transfers, a lagoon tour, lunch, and drinks. Northbound sit on the left side of the aircraft for the best views.

Every weekday Air Rarotonga flies to Atiu (NZ$244 roundtrip), Mangaia (NZ$244 roundtrip), and Mauke (NZ$272 roundtrip). Mitiaro (NZ$272 roundtrip) is served three times a week. The interisland connection Atiu-Mitiaro-Mauke only works twice a week and interisland flights Atiu-Mitiaro and Mitiaro-Mauke are NZ$110 each. There's no flight Atiu-Mauke and you must stop over on Mitiaro en route to make the connection.

Manihiki (NZ$1,092 roundtrip) and Penrhyn (NZ$1,210 roundtrip) receive Air Rarotonga flights weekly. Manihiki-Penrhyn costs NZ$160. Only charter flights operate to Pukapuka and the plane can't land at Rakahanga. Sitting in an 18-seat Bandierante for four hours from Rarotonga to Manihiki or Penrhyn can be quite an experience!

Children under 12 pay half price. Air Rarotonga's 30-day "Paradise Island Pass" allows unlimited flights in the southern group only at NZ$110 per sector but you must visit at least two islands. Advance reservations are required, as space is limited. Try to reconfirm your return flight, and beware of planes leaving early! Avoid scheduling your flight back to Rarotonga for the same day you're supposed to catch your international flight.

The baggage allowance is 16 kilos, though you can sometimes get by with more. On flights to Manihiki and Penrhyn the limit is 10 kilos. Overweight is not expensive, but if the plane is full and too heavy for the short outer-island runways they'll refuse excess baggage from all passengers. Thus it pays to stay below the limit.

Air Rarotonga offers 20-minute scenic flights (NZ$55 pp) around Rarotonga out of their hangar, 500 meters west of the main terminal. You can often arrange this on the spur of the moment if a pilot and plane are available.

Getting Around by Ship

Taio Shipping Ltd. (Teremoana Taio, Box 2001, Rarotonga; tel. 24-905, fax 24-906), in the Ports Authority Building on Rarotonga's Avatiu Harbor, operates the interisland vessels *Te Koumaru,* the former *Yrjar* from Trondheim, Norway, and the smaller *Maungaroa,* the former *Frida* from Svolver,

Norway. Taio tries to run a ship around the southern group once a week, around the northern group fortnightly. The schedule varies according to the amount of cargo waiting to move and the only way to find out is to ask at the office. Also ask about special trips to Apia in Samoa.

To do a four- to five-day roundtrip to the southern group costs NZ$90 deck, NZ$185-225 cabin. To sail around the northern group for 12-13 days costs NZ$600 deck, NZ$800-850 cabin. On a one-way basis it's NZ$50 deck or NZ$100-125 cabin from Rarotonga to any of the islands of the southern group, or NZ$20 deck between Atiu, Mauke, and Mitiaro only. One-way fares to the northern group are around NZ$280 deck or NZ$380-450 cabin.

Cabin prices include meals for the first two days but from the third day onwards cabin passengers must pay NZ$15 per day for meals. Deck passengers must bring their own food. The cheaper cabins are in a 10-berth dormitory cabin and it's better to try for one of the few double cabins that have private facilities. Deck passengers to the northern group must pay NZ$7 a day for tea/coffee and one meal, and considering the small price difference and long sailing times cabin passage is a much better deal.

Be forewarned that accommodations on this sort of ship are often next to noisy, hot engine rooms and are often cluttered with crates. Deck passengers sleep under a canvas awning, and although it may be a little crowded, the islanders are friendly and easy to get along with. On the outer islands, check with the radio operator in the post office to find out when a ship from Rarotonga might be due in. Delays of a few days are routine. In July 1998 the Taio vessel *Aroa Nui* was wrecked on the reef at Atiu.

Airport

Rarotonga International Airport (RAR) is 2.4 km west of Avarua. Immigration will stamp a 31-day entry permit onto your passport. Be sure to enter the name of a hotel in the relevant space on your arrivals card—to leave blank that space will prompt the Immigration clerk to ask you where you plan to stay.

As you come out of customs you'll find representatives from most of the backpacker's hostels waiting to the left, at a counter marked "budget accommodations." State the name of the establishment you think best suits your needs and their representative will inform you whether they have vacant rooms. Have a second choice ready in case your first choice is fully occupied. This will make it easier to deal with the drivers eagerly jostling for your business. Most offer a free transfer to their lodging on the understanding that you'll stay with them at least two nights. A taxi to Avarua will cost around NZ$5.

Hugh Henry Travel, Stars Travel, Cook Islands Tours, Island Hopper Vacations, Budget Rent-a-Car, and Avis all have offices outside arrivals at the airport. There's only a card telephone at Rarotonga Airport but you can use the public phone at the RSA Club across the street for 20 cents. If you're stuck here waiting for a flight the RSA Club is a much better place to relax than the dreary airport terminal.

The Westpac Bank at the airport charges NZ$2.50 commission per transaction. Cook Islands Tours & Travel (tel. 28-270) at the airport will store excess luggage at NZ$2 per piece per day. Clarify their hours to make sure they'll be there when you want to collect your bags. Several duty-free shops open for international arrivals and departures, and arriving passengers are allowed to duck into the duty-free liquor shop (tel. 29-322) to the right before clearing customs.

A NZ$25 departure tax is charged for international flights (children aged 2-11 pay NZ$10, and transit passengers staying fewer than 24 hours are exempt).

BOB RACE

RAROTONGA

The name Rarotonga means "in the direction of the prevailing wind, south," the place where the chief of Atiu promised early explorers they would find an island. It's fairly small, just 31 km around. Twisting valleys lead up to steep ridges covered with luxuriant green vegetation and towering mountains crowned in clouds. Yet, Te Manga (653 meters) is only a fraction of the height Rarotonga reached before the last volcanic eruption took place, over two million years ago.

Though Rarotonga is younger than the other Cook islands, continuous erosion has cut into the island, washing away the softer material and leaving the hard volcanic cones naked. The mountains are arrayed in a U-shaped arch, starting at the airport and then swinging south around to Club Raro, with Maungatea plopped down in the middle. Together they form the surviving southern half of the great broken volcanic caldera that became Rarotonga.

The reef circling the island defines a lagoon that is broad and sandy to the south, and narrow and rocky on the north and east. The finest beaches are on the southeast side near the Muri Lagoon, with crystal-clear water and a sandy bottom, but the best snorkeling is at Titikaveka. Elsewhere the water can be cloudy, with a lot of coral and shells that make wading difficult. Take care everywhere, as several snorkelers have drowned after being sucked out through the passes where a lot of water moves due to surf and tidal swings. Scuba diving on Rarotonga features coral dropoffs, canyons, caves, walls, sharks, wrecks, and swim throughs. All beaches on the island are public.

In recent years Rarotonga has become New Zealand's answer to Honolulu with 50,000 visitors to an island of 10,000 inhabitants, the same five-to-one visitor/resident ratio experienced in Hawaii. To find that "last heaven on earth" promised in the brochures you must escape to an outer island. Yet Raro remains one of the most beautiful islands in Polynesia, somewhat reminiscent of Moorea (though only half as big). If you enjoy the excitement of big tourist resorts with plenty of opportunities for shopping and eating out, you'll like Rarotonga.

SIGHTS

Avarua

This attractive town of around 5,000 inhabitants is strung along the north coast beneath the green, misty slopes of Maungatea. Somehow Avarua retains the air of a 19th-century South Seas trading post, and offshore in Avarua Harbor lies the boiler of the Union Steam Ship SS *Maitai*, wrecked in 1916. Near the bridge over Takuvaine Stream is the **Seven-in-One Coconut Tree** planted in 1906. In May 1992 a devastating fire swept through the old colonial buildings of the government complex south of the tree, badly damaging the post office, telephone exchange, and courthouse, all of which have since been demolished.

Just inland from the new post office is the privately owned **Rarotonga Brewery** (Box 814, Rarotonga; tel. 21-083, fax 21-089), which offers a free guided tour weekdays at 1400, during which participants get to taste the four-and-a-half-percent-alcohol draft beer (bottled beer is six percent alcohol). The Cooks Lager T-shirts sold at the brewery souvenir counter are hot items.

Inland again and a block south of the brewery is the stone on which in 1823 Papeiha preached the first Christian sermon on Rarotonga. It's set up on a pedestal in the middle of the crossing with the Ara Metua, Rarotonga's old interior road. Turn left and follow the Ara Metua 150 meters east to a small bridge and a gate leading into the original missionary compound, now **Takamoa Theological College.** You pass a row of student residences, and at the next crossroad you'll find a monument to the missionaries of the London Missionary Society who have served in the Cook Islands. Across the street is an impressive monument to Polynesian missionaries from the college who carried the Gospel to other Pacific islands. In 1837 the third LMS missionary, Rev. Aaron Buzacott, erected the two-story **Takamoa Mission House** facing

the monuments. It's now a government office. The adjacent lecture hall dates from 1890.

Follow the road north between the monuments and you'll reach the **Library and Museum of the Cook Islands** (Box 71, Rarotonga; tel. 20-748; open Mon.-Sat. 0900-1300, Tuesday also 1600-2000, NZ$2 admission) with assorted artifacts, many of them on loan from museums in New Zealand. Across the street from the museum is the **Cook Islands Center** (tel. 29-415) of the University of the South Pacific, which is worth entering for the interesting books in the showcase on the right.

The massive white walls and roof of the **Cook Islands Christian Church** (1853) are visible from here. Check out the massive wooden balcony inside. It's worth being here Sunday morning at 1000, if only to see the women arrive in their Sunday best and to stand outside and listen to the wonderful singing (only go inside and sit down if you're prepared to stay for the entire service). Near the front of the church is the tomb of Albert Henry (1907-81), topped by a lifelike statue of the man. American writer Robert Dean Frisbie (1895-1948), author of *The Book of Puka-puka* and *The Island of Desire,* is buried in the southwest corner of the cemetery.

Across the road, beyond some old graves, is the **Para O Tane Palace** of the Makea Takau Ariki, high chief of the landowning clan of most of the Avarua town area. **Marae Taputaputea** and a basalt investiture pillar are on the palace grounds.

Backtrack to the University Center and turn left along a wide road to the massive green and white **Are-Karioi-Nui National Auditorium** with 2,000 seats. The four huge buildings to the left of this road are hostels used to house outer islanders when they visit Rarotonga. The auditorium forms part of the **National Cultural Center,** erected for

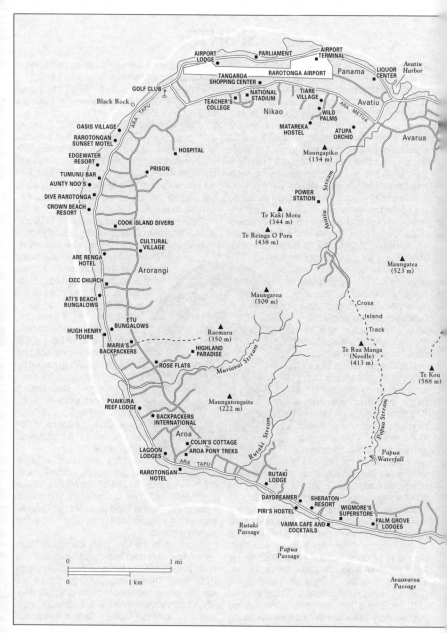

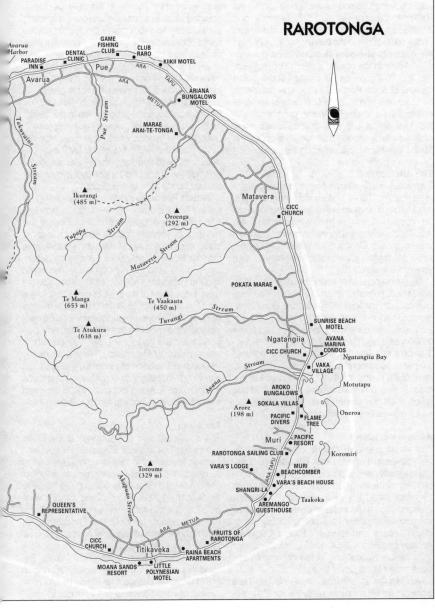

RAROTONGA

Avarua
Harbor

PARADISE
INN

DENTAL
CLINIC

GAME
FISHING
CLUB

CLUB
RARO

KIIKII MOTEL

Pue

ARA

TAPU

ARA

METUA

Avarua

ARIANA
BUNGALOWS
MOTEL

Takuvaine
Stream

Pue
Stream

MARAE
ARAI-TE-TONGA

Ikurangi
(485 m)

Oroenga
(292 m)

Matavera

CICC
CHURCH

Tupapa
Stream

Matavera Stream

Te Manga
(653 m)

Te Vaakauta
(450 m)

POKATA MARAE

Te Atukura
(638 m)

Turangi

Stream

SUNRISE BEACH
MOTEL

Ngatangiia

AVANA
MARINA
CONDOS

Avana

Stream

CICC CHURCH

Ngatangiia Bay

VAKA
VILLAGE

Motutapu

Arore
(198 m)

AROKO
BUNGALOWS

SOKALA VILLAS

Oneroa

PACIFIC
DIVERS

FLAME
TREE

Muri

PACIFIC
RESORT

Koromiri

RAROTONGA SAILING CLUB

ARA TAPU

VARA'S LODGE

MURI
BEACHCOMBER

Toroume
(329 m)

Akapuao Stream

VARA'S BEACH HOUSE

SHANGRI-LA

Taakoka

QUEEN'S
REPRESENTATIVE

AREMANGO
GUESTHOUSE

ARA

METUA

CICC
CHURCH

Titikaveka

FRUITS OF
RAROTONGA

RAINA BEACH
APARTMENTS

MOANA SANDS
RESORT

LITTLE
POLYNESIAN
MOTEL

© DAVID STANLEY

the 6th Festival of Pacific Arts in 1992. The two yellow buildings beyond the auditorium contain the **National Library** (tel. 20-725; Monday and Wednesday 0900-2000, Tuesday, Thursday, and Friday 0900-1600) in the building to the right, and the **National Museum** (tel. 20-725; weekdays 0800-1600) in the one on the left. The museum has a collection of model canoes and modern replicas of South Pacific artifacts. This outlandish complex was one of the pet projects of the Honorable Sir Geoffrey Henry who put his country NZ$11.6 million in debt to finance construction of the island's second museum and library (in 1996 Cook Islands defaulted on the loan).

The Ara Metua

Two roads circle Rarotonga: the new coastal road (the Ara Tapu) and an old inner road (the Ara Metua). The main sights are arranged below for a counterclockwise tour of the island on the Ara Tapu with the distances from Avarua shown in parentheses. On a scooter you should be able to do it in four hours with stops; by bicycle give yourself a leisurely day.

On your second time around try using the scenic Ara Metua, passable much of the way. You'll encounter lush gardens, orchards, and good viewpoints. This inner road is said to be the oldest in Polynesia, the coral-block foundation laid some 1,000 years ago by chief Toi. Up until the mid-19th century, when the missionaries concentrated the population around their churches on the coast, most of the people lived on the inland side of this road. During WW II the road was resurfaced and much of it is now paved. There's very little traffic, which makes it perfect for cycling.

Around the Island

Just under a km west of Rarotonga airport is the **Parliament of the Cook Islands** in a building originally used to house workers during construction of the airport in 1973. Parliament meets Feb.-March and July-Sept., and if you're properly dressed (no shorts or jeans), you can observe the proceedings from the public gallery (Monday, Tuesday, and Thursday 1300-1700, Wednesday and Friday 0900-1300). Call 26-500 for information. Notice how all the important positions here are occupied by men.

Across the street from the Golf Club (see **Sports and Recreation,** below) west of the air-

port is a beach park with toilets and outdoor showers. From here it's not far to **Black Rock** (6 km), standing alone in a coral lagoon (good snorkeling at high tide). This rock marks the spot where the spirits of deceased Rarotongan Polynesians pass on their way back to the legendary homeland, Avaiki. The Tahitian missionary Papeiha is said to have swum ashore here, holding a Bible above his head (in fact, he landed in a small boat).

Arorangi (8.5 km) was established by the Rev. Aaron Buzacott (who served in the Cooks 1828-57) as a model village, and Papeiha is buried in the historic white cemetery at the old CICC church (1849). It was the LMS missionaries who resettled the people near the coast and built the **Tinomana Palace** by the church for the last native ruler of this district.

Mount Raemaru (350 meters tall) rising up behind Arorangi has a flattened top—a local legend tells how Aitutaki warriors carried off the missing upper part. (To climb Raemaru, take the steep track off the Ara Metua when you see the sign for Maria's Backpackers Accommodation, then via a trail to the right up the fern-covered ridge to Raemaru's western cliffs. When you get close to the forest at the base of the cliffs, take the right fork of the trail up to the cliff itself. The final climb to the mountain's flat summit can be dangerous if the rocks on the cliff are wet and slippery, but once on top, you can see the whole western side of Rarotonga. There's an easier track down the back of Raemaru that you can use to return, but you'd probably get lost if you tried to climb it. Along this route you circle down a taro-filled valley back to the Ara Metua.)

Takitumu

The southeast side of Rarotonga is known as Takitumu. The skeletal **Sheraton Resort** with its ironic monument to the Honorable Sir Geoffrey A. Henry is the most visible physical reminder of the financial calamities that gripped these islands in the 1990s. The building with the flagpole a couple of kilometers east is the residence of the representative of Queen Elizabeth II (his NZ$120,000 annual salary comes out of local taxes). East again and on the corner before Kent Hall in **Titikaveka** is Te Pou Toru Marae. Beyond this another fine coral-block CICC church (1841) stands beside the road, 19 km from Avarua counterclockwise or 14 km clockwise.

Some of the finest **snorkeling** on Rarotonga is off the beach opposite Raina Beach Apartments, behind the cemetery with the radio mast next to TM Motors. There's not a lot of coral but plenty of small fish. Some of the scuba operators bring their clients here for diving.

Turn in at the Rarotonga Sailing Club, four km northeast, to see the lovely **Muri Lagoon,** with the nicest swimming and windsurfing area on the island. At low tide you can wade across to uninhabited Koromiri Island, where hermit crabs forage as bathers enjoy the oceanside beach. Full nautical gear is for rent at the club (open daily) and the restaurant serves a good lunch.

The road up the **Avana Valley** begins near the bridge over Avana Stream and runs along the south bank. You can cycle halfway up, then continue on foot.

On the right just beyond the Avana Stream bridge is **Vaka Village** with a monument marking the historic gathering of ocean voyaging and war canoes here during the 1992 Festival of Pacific Arts. Local fishing boats anchor on the spot today. A little beyond is another old white **CICC church** on the left, once the seat of the Rev. Charles Pitman who translated many works into Maori during his stay here from 1827 to 1854. Across the street from the church is a small park with a good view of the tiny islands or *motu* in the Muri Lagoon and **Ngatangiia Harbor.** Legend claims seven canoes departed from here in A.D. 1350 on a daring voyage to New Zealand, and the names of the canoes are inscribed on a monument. Cruising yachts sometimes anchor here, though it's rather exposed to the southeast trades.

Back near the bridge is a road in to the **Ara Metua.** On the right a short distance along this road is an old burial ground with a Polynesian *marae* among the trees on a hillock behind. Many other similar *marae* are in the vicinity.

Continue along the Ara Metua and turn left up the road alongside Turangi Stream, on the far side of a small bridge. The **Turangi Valley** is larger and more impressive than Avana, and swamp taro is grown in irrigated paddies. Once again, you cycle halfway up and continue on foot.

Toward Ikurangi

At **Matavera** there's yet another lovely CICC church (1865) beside the road. Farther along, just a few km before Avarua, watch for a signboard on Maotangi Road pointing the way in to **Marae Arai-te-tonga,** on the Ara Metua. Marae Arai-te-tonga, the most sacred on the island, was a *koutu,* or place where the *ta'unga* (priest) invested and anointed the high chiefs *(ariki)* of the island. The route of the ancient Ara Metua is quite evident here, and there are other stone constructions 100 meters along it to the east.

Take the road inland between these ruins as far as Tupapa Stream, where two rather difficult climbs begin. Just a km up the trail is a fork in the path: the right fork leads to the top of **Ikurangi** (485 meters), while the one up the stream continues to **Te Manga** (653 meters). Neither climb is easy, so a local guide would be a good idea. From the top of Ikurangi (Tail of the Sky) you can see the whole wave-washed reef, tomato patches, and plantations of grapefruit, orange, tangerine, and lemon trees. This climb is best done in the cool hours of the early morning.

The Cross-Island Track

From Avarua walk three km up the Avatiu Valley. Just beyond the power station you get your first view of Te Rua Manga, **the Needle** (413 meters). In another 10 minutes the road ends at a concrete water intake; you continue up a footpath for 15 minutes until you reach a huge boulder. Pass it and head up the steep forested incline. This climb is the hardest part of the trip, but when you reach the top, the Needle towers majestically above you (the hike from the end of the road to the top takes less than an hour).

There's a fork at the top of the ridge: the Needle on your right, the trail down to the south coast on the left. After scrambling around the Needle, start down the trail to the south coast, past the giant ferns along the side of Papua Stream. On this part of the trek you really get to see Rarotonga's interior rainforest. The road out begins at **Papua Waterfall** at the bottom of the hill. The stream above Papua is a drinking water source, so save your swimming for the pool below the falls (often it will be dry unless there have been rains recently). The hapless Sheraton Resort is to your right just before you reach the main road.

Though sometimes slippery, the cross-island track can be covered in all weather and even if it has been raining, you can still do the trip the next day. Parts of the track are badly eroded, so it might not be a good idea to go alone. Allow 45 minutes to walk up Avatiu Road, then an hour and a quarter to climb to the Needle. Going down the Papua Valley takes two hours, and it's easier to do a roundtrip to the Needle from the end of the road on the Avatiu side, allowing a return to a parked vehicle. If you'll be hiking right across it's best done during the week as onward bus service on the other side will be limited or nonexistent on weekends. Several companies offer guided cross-island treks Mon.-Sat. at 0930 if the weather is okay, but lots of visitors do this hike on their own and you don't really need a guide.

Commercial Visitor Attractions

Monday, Wednesday, and Friday at 1000 the **Cultural Village** (Box 320, tel. 21-314, fax 25-557; admission NZ$39), on the back road in Arorangi, enthusiastically demonstrates Cook Islands history, medicine, cooking, arts, crafts, dances, and traditions during an informative three-hour program, which includes a lunch of local foods. Advance reservations through a hotel, travel agency, or directly by phone are required. Several readers have written in strongly endorsing the Cultural Village.

Another attraction accessible weekdays at 1000 is **Highland Paradise** (tel. 20-610; admission NZ$30 including lunch), a private botanical garden where old *marae* and other historic sites are scattered among the vegetation. The steep access road begins next to Rose Flats, a km south of the Cultural Village. The Arorangi people lived up here before being moved down to the coast by the missionaries.

SPORTS AND RECREATION

Dive Rarotonga (Barry and Shirley Hill, Box 38, Rarotonga; tel. 21-873, fax 21-878) offers scuba trips every afternoon at 1300 (including Sunday!). A one-tank dive is NZ$55 (NZ$45 if you have your own equipment), while two different dives at 0900 and 1300 on the same day are NZ$90 (or NZ$80 with your own equipment). Snorkelers can go along for NZ$20 pp (rental of snorkeling gear extra).

Scuba diving is also offered by Greg Wilson's **Cook Island Divers** (Box 1002, Rarotonga; tel. 22-483, fax 22-484), just up the road. Dive Raro-

Sharp spines on its back make the butterfly fish hard to swallow.

LOUISE FOOTE

tonga is a bit cheaper but if the weather looks at all bad they'll cancel that day's diving, whereas Cook Islands Divers tries to go out in almost any weather. Greg does two trips a day, at 0800 and 1300, and he runs a highly professional show. His four-day NAUI or PADI scuba certification course is NZ$425—what better place to learn?

Pacific Divers (Graham McDonald, Box 110, Rarotonga; tel./fax 22-450), also known as "Scuba Divers," opposite the Flame Tree Restaurant at Muri Beach, offers dives on the nearby Titikaveka Reef at 0800 and 1300 daily (at 1300 only on Sunday). It's NZ$60/100 for one/two tanks and two people together get a NZ$10 discount. A PADI open water certification course (four days) will run NZ$425. All three scuba operators offer discounts for three or more dives.

The **Aqua Sports Centre** (Junior Ioaba, Box 67, Rarotonga; tel. 27-350, fax 20-932) at the Rarotonga Sailing Club on Muri Beach rents kayaks (NZ$8 an hour), windsurfers (NZ$10 an hour), sailboats (NZ$20 an hour), and snorkeling gear (NZ$7 a half day). Lessons in windsurfing (NZ$20) and sailing (NZ$20) are given. A five-hour sailing course is NZ$130. Mornings from 0900-1300 they'll ferry you over to an uninhabited offshore island for NZ$5 return. Daily at 1100 Aqua Sports runs a glass-bottom coral reef boat tour costing NZ$15; combined with an afternoon lagoon cruise and barbecue lunch it's NZ$35 in total (on Sunday the glass-bottom boat trip is at 1330). Equipment rental is possible every day.

Captain Tama's Water Sportz World (Tamaiva Tuavera, tel. 20-810) at the Pacific Resort, Muri, rents out the same sort of gear and also does lagoon cruises in a boat with a

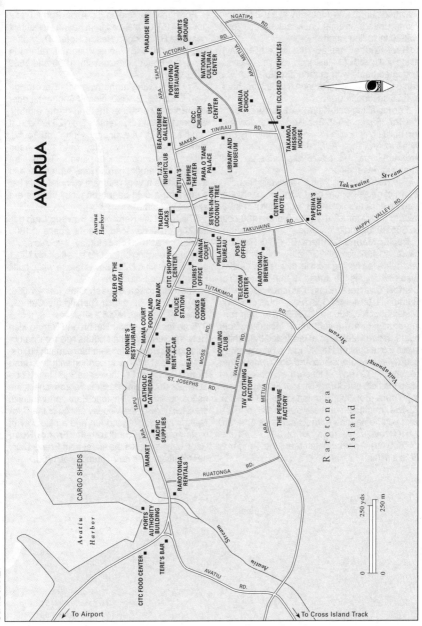

AVARUA

© DAVID STANLEY

thatched sunroof. Wednesday at 1100 Captain Tama does a special backpackers cruize at NZ$20 including lunch.

Reef Runner (tel. 26-780, closed Sunday), at the south end of Muri Beach, rents small glass-bottomed boats with outboard motors that you can use to explore the lagoon (NZ$35 first hour, NZ$25 second hour).

For kayaking call **Kayak Adventure Tours** (tel. 25-359, fax 29-223) based in a yellow and red building opposite Puaikura Community Services in Arorangi. A full day of paddling right around Rarotonga is NZ$90 pp plus tax. Call ahead for reservations.

The **Reef-Sub** (tel. 25-837) at Avatiu Harbor is a sort of glass-bottom boat with an underwater viewing deck (it's not a real submarine). The 90-minute trips Mon.-Sat. at 1000 and 1400 cost NZ$35/20 for adults/children.

Pacific Marine Charters (Box 770, Rarotonga; tel. 21-237, fax 27-237) at Avatiu Harbor offers deep-sea fishing from its fast yellow cruiser. Also at Avatiu is the larger 10-meter *Seafari* of **Seafari Charters** (Elgin Tetachuk, Box 148, Rarotonga; tel./fax 20-328). Four hours of fishing costs about NZ$100 pp (NZ$60 pp for non-fishing passengers), a light lunch included. Both boats depart weekdays at 0900 and the fishing takes place right off Rarotonga, so you get very good views of the island and don't waste time commuting. On both of these, the captain gets to keep the fish, but Brent Fisher of **Fisher's Fishing Tours** (Box 880, Rarotonga; tel. 23-356, fax 23-354) might let you keep your catch or even take you home for a barbecue. His catamaran, the *Corey-Anne,* goes out at 0800 or 1300 (NZ$60 pp). Another catamaran, the *Tangaroa III,* is similar.

For horseback riding it's **Aroa Pony Treks** (tel. 21-415), up the road from Kaena Restaurant near the Rarotongan Resort Hotel. They offer two-hour rides to Papua Waterfall, returning along the beach, weekdays at 1000 and 1500 (NZ$30 pp).

Try your swing at the nine-hole **Rarotonga Golf Club** (tel. 27-360; closed Sunday), under the radio towers near the end of the airstrip. Greens fees and club rentals are NZ$12 each. If you hit a mast, wire, or stay during your round, there's a compulsory replay; balls have been known to bounce back at players. There's an annual tournament here in late September and the club has a very pleasant colonial-style bar perfect for a cold beer (congenial visitors are always welcome).

The bar at the **Rarotonga Bowling Club** (tel. 26-277) on Moss Road, Avarua, opens at 1600 weekdays, at 1000 on Saturday. If you've never tried lawn bowling before, do so—it's only NZ$1 greens fees plus NZ$1 bowls hire (a white outfit is required on Saturday).

The **Rarotonga Squash Club** (tel. 21-056; daily 0900-2000), directly behind the Catholic cathedral, charges NZ$5 a session.

Both the Edgewater Resort and Rarotongan Resort Hotel have tennis courts open to the public, and the Edgewater also has squash courts.

Monday at 1730 you can jog with the **Hash House Harriers.** For the venue, call David Lobb at tel. 22-055 during business hours, check the notice outside the Westpac Bank, or scrutinize the back page of the Monday edition of the *Cook Islands News.* It's good fun and a nice way of meeting people. Similarly, the **Frangi Road Race** begins across the street from Frangi Dairy near Parliament every Thursday at 1700.

PRACTICALITIES

ACCOMMODATIONS

There's such a glut of accommodations on Rarotonga that you'd have to be very unlucky to arrive on a day when everything was full, and you can take advantage of competitive rates by not booking ahead from overseas. Bargaining for rooms isn't done but it's okay to ask if they have any specials on. If saving money is a concern, get a place with cooking facilities as restaurant meals can add up. All of the budget and medium-priced hotels are self-catering, but many of the upmarket resorts are not. When choosing, keep in mind that the west coast is drier and gets beautiful sunsets, while the finest snorkeling is at windy Titikaveka in the south and the top beach faces the gorgeous Muri Lagoon in the east. The places near Avarua are best for those more into shopping, sightseeing, and entertainment than beachlife.

Most places include the 12.5% VAT in the quoted rate but some charge it extra. Check out time at the motels is 1000. In past most of the budget hotels have provided free or inexpensive airport transfers to those who booked direct (there's pressure from the tour companies to change this). Even if you do get a free ride there, you'll probably be charged something for the ride back to the airport. The listings below are arranged counterclockwise around the island in each price category.

Shoestring

Aunty Noo's Beach Lodge (Box 196, Rarotonga; tel. 21-253, fax 22-275), halfway down to the beach behind Sunbird Laundry in Arorangi, offers the cheapest accommodations on Rarotonga and is thus the choice of backpackers on the barest of budgets. Beds in the four-bed dormitory and two double rooms are NZ$10-15 pp (depending on what the competition is charging), or you can camp in the back yard for NZ$7 pp. Rudimentary cooking facilities are provided and many guests sit and play cards at the picnic tables in the lounge all day. A party ensues whenever a duty-free bottle appears. Aunty Noo

is rather eccentric ("a lovely woman who treats her guests as real nephews and nieces" according to one reader) but it's unlikely you'll see much of her, and just forget the promised free breakfast. It's basic but a good place to meet other budget travelers (mostly male) and a nice beach is just half a minute away.

Maria's Backpackers Accommodations (Exham and Maria Wichman, Box 777, Rarotonga; tel. 21-180) is just off the Ara Metua in Arorangi, up near the trailhead of the Raemaru trek. From main road in Arorangi turn inland opposite Bunny's Restaurant. There are two self-catering rooms at NZ$15/25 single/double. This is a place for people who like peace and quiet; those interested in meeting other travelers should head elsewhere.

Piri's Coconut Beach Hostel (Box 624, Rarotonga; tel. 20-309), on the beach just west of the Sheraton site, offers 16 mattresses in an open dorm at NZ$12.50 or beds in a basic room at NZ$14 pp. There are communal cooking facilities but it's all really scruffy and to be avoided. The manager, Piri Puruto III, puts on a tacky coconut tree climbing show for tourists here Thursday at 1700 and Sunday at 1400. Watch out for him at the airport as he tends to pounce on fresh arrivals (we've received several complaints). On the plus side, the beach here is great but when snorkeling beware of dangerous currents in passes draining the lagoon.

Budget

The first budget place to the west of town is **Atupa Orchid Units** (Box 64, Rarotonga; tel. 28-543, fax 28-546), run by a German woman named Ingrid Caffery who has been in the Cooks since 1970. There are 10 rooms in four screened houses, each house with its own cooking facilities and hot water. Prices vary from NZ$25/48/68 single/double/triple in a budget room to NZ$45/65/80 in a more private flat. It's excellent value and discounts are available when things are slow. Rental bicycles are NZ$8. Quiet and comfortable, central Avarua is just a 10-minute walk away. The transfer from the airport is free but everybody pays NZ$4 pp to return to the airport.

Hugh Baker's **Matareka Hostel** (Box 587, Rarotonga; tel. 23-670, fax 23-672), on the hillside facing the far side of the airport, is Rarotonga's original budget hostel, founded in 1980. There are three breezy three-bed dormitories on the hilltop at NZ$15 pp, plus three rooms behind the owner's home below at NZ$25/40 single/double. The weekly rate is NZ$85 pp. A communal kitchen, laundry, and lounge area are available, and the washing machine is NZ$3 a load. In season, Hugh will give you all the fresh fruit you desire, and he rents some of the cheapest bicycles (NZ$5) and scooters (NZ$12) on Rarotonga. People who want a restful, do-your-own-thing type of holiday rather than 24-hour partying will like it here.

At the bottom of the hill below Hugh Baker's are the A-frame chalets and guesthouse of the popular **Tiare Village Dive Hostel** (Box 719, Rarotonga; tel. 23-466, fax 20-969). This friendly establishment has three fan-cooled, self-contained chalets, each with two singles and one double, at NZ$18/32/45 single/double/triple. In addition the main house has one double and three triples (NZ$15 pp to share). Tiare's 23 guests share the communal cooking facilities, lounge, and hot water showers in a family-style environment, and the tropical garden is bursting with fruit there for the picking. Free luggage storage is available. It's only a 30-minute walk from town (and provides a convenient base for hiking to the Needle). Ask for their free airport pickup.

The **Are Renga Motel** (Box 223, Rarotonga; tel. 20-050, fax 29-223) at Arorangi has 20 simple thin-walled units with well-equipped kitchens at NZ$25/40/55 single/double/triple. The quality varies, so ask to see another room if the first one you're shown isn't to your liking. Beware of rooms with open ventilation spaces near the ceiling, as these let in every sound from adjacent rooms. The Are Renga offers a reduced "backpacker's rate" of NZ$15 per bed in a couple of shared double rooms. The location is good with a store and other facilities nearby, and a lending library is available in the office. Use of their washing machine costs NZ$5, but there's no dryer. In season you may harvest fruit from the large orchard behind the property. Airport transfers are also free. When the motel is full, the Are Renga folk may offer you a room at **Airport Lodge** (tel.

20-050), near the Meteorological Station at the end of the airport runway. There are six self-catering duplex units, four of them facing the runway and two facing a coconut tree. It's rather isolated with no store nearby and only worth accepting as a last resort.

Backpackers International Hostel (Bill Bates, Box 878, Rarotonga; tel./fax 21-847) is in the southwest corner of the island, only 150 meters from a grocery store, the Island Bus, and the beach. They offer six rooms with double beds and another 12 rooms with twin beds at NZ$34 double. In addition, there are six singles at NZ$22 and 21 dorm beds in rooms of three to eight at NZ16 pp. A common TV lounge and cooking area are provided, and Bill will probably give you some free fruit. It's convivial, and on Saturday night the managers prepare a special buffet dinner at NZ$15 pp (NZ$18 for non-guests). Just ask Bill if you need to send an e-mail.

Under the same management as Backpackers International is **Rutaki Lodge** (Box 878, Rarotonga; tel./fax 21-847), a single-story building adjacent to Rutaki Store on the south side of the island. There are seven rooms: one single, three doubles (double beds), and three triples (three single beds). Communal cooking is available. It's mainly an overflow facility for Backpackers International, charging identical prices, and when things are slow on the island Rutaki remains closed.

The **Aremango Guesthouse** (Box 714, Rarotonga; tel. 24-362, fax 24-363) is just 50 meters from Muri Beach, south of the Muri Beachcomber. The 10 spacious fan-cooled rooms with shared bath are NZ$17 pp plus tax (airport transfers NZ$5 pp). Singles must be prepared to share or pay for both beds. Communal cooking facilities are available, and lockable cupboards for groceries are provided. Peace and quiet will be up to your fellow guests.

Vara's Beach House & Lodge (Vara Hunter, Box 434, Rarotonga; tel. 23-156, fax 22-619, www.varas.co.ck), on the south side of the Muri Beachcomber, consists of two distinct sections. The "beach house" right on Muri Beach has double rooms and a four-bed dorm, while the two large two-story "cottages" sleeping four or five are 400 meters up the hillside. The "lodge" is up above the cottages. At NZ$18 pp in a dorm, NZ$42 double with shared bath, or NZ$60 double with private bath, beds in both sections cost the same with discounts for stays of over a week. The accommodations on the hillside are of higher quality while those at the beach have the water only a few meters away. All guests have access to communal cooking facilities, fans, free laundry facilities, canoe rentals, and free airport pickups (NZ$6 to return to the airport). At Vara's you get to enjoy the same beach as guests at the adjacent Muri Beachcomber for a tenth the price.

The **Ariana Bungalows Motel** (Box 925, Rarotonga; tel./fax 20-521), also known as Ariana Backpackers Accommodation or the Ariana Hostel, a couple of km east of Avarua, offers quite a range of accommodations. The seven self-catering duplex bungalows are NZ$65 single, double, or triple with bath, whereas the six shared doubles are NZ$30/40 single/double with specials sometimes offered. The two segregated dormitories are NZ$18 pp (six beds for men, nine beds for women)—one of the only Rarotonga hostels with separate dorms for male and female. On a weekly basis it's 10% off. The pleasant grounds are peaceful and spacious, but it's 500 meters off the main road and quite a distance from town or the beach. On the plus side, this is one of the only budget properties with a swimming pool. Ariana is an excellent base from which to climb Ikurangi. Bicycles and scooters are for rent, and a few basic groceries are sold at the office for normal prices. Ariana is run by an American named Bob Healey who also heads the Cook Islands Budget Accommodation Council. Ask for Bob's free airport pickup.

Rarotonga's latest low-budget hostel is **Lovely Planet Backpackers** (Box 711, Rarotonga; tel./fax 25-100), opposite the Outpatients Medical Clinic at Tupapa, a km east of central Avarua. The five triple-bunk rooms start at NZ$20 pp. A shared kitchen, refrigerator, and laundry room are provided, and bicycles are for rent. Despite the name, this colonial-style home hostel with a spacious porch is run by Papa Ross Grant and has no connection with a certain mass-market Australian guidebook company.

Inexpensive

Wild Palms (Ronnie Siulepa, Box 489, Rarotonga; tel. 27-610, fax 27-611), directly behind the Tiare Village Hostel on the inland road, has six self-catering duplex bungalows at NZ$100

single or double, NZ$125 triple (children under 12 not accommodated). The units face a circular swimming pool and the design is attractive. It's a long way from the beach for these rates.

Ati's Beach Bungalows (Jim and Ati Robertson, Box 693, Rarotonga; tel. 21-546, fax 25-546), on the beach a little south of the church in Arorangi, offers nine self-contained units with cooking facilities and hot water showers. It's NZ$80/100 double/triple for one of the five garden bungalows or NZ$120/150 for one of the four deluxe beach bungalows. There's a communal TV lounge/bar, and you should try to get a room well away from both it and the office as the walls don't keep out the sound. The flagpole outside bears the flags of all the countries currently represented there. Ati's caters to an older clientele, and more youthful visitors may feel out of place. Airport transfers are NZ$10 pp return.

Etu Bungalows (Box 2136, Rarotonga; tel./fax 25-588), opposite Hugh Henry & Associates in Arorangi, has two self-catering bungalows at NZ$80 single or double (discounted weekly rates available).

Also try **Colin's Cottage** (Colin Brown, tel. 23-066 or 26-603, fax 25-546), on the road inland from the Kaena Restaurant near the Rarotongan Resort Hotel. The two self-catering apartments are NZ$70 single or double.

Daydreamer Accommodation (Bruce and Nga Young, Box 1048, Rarotonga; tel. 25-965, fax 25-964), also known as Moemoea Accommodation, offers five attractive self-catering units in one long block just west of the Sheraton site and across the street from Piri's Hostel. It's NZ$90 single or double.

Beach Lodge Apartments, also known as Turoa Villas, is the unmarked house adjacent to the west side of the residence of the Queen's Representative on the south side of the island. The three two-bedroom units with private cooking facilities are NZ$80 single, double, or triple a night or NZ$500 a week. The beach is just across the street and this is a nice, untouristed area. Information is available from Nan Noovao of Cook Islands Tours and Travel (Box 611, Rarotonga; tel. 20-270, fax 27-270) at the airport. Nan also has a variety of furnished houses for rent beginning at NZ$350 a week.

Daniel Roro's **Aroko Bungalows** (Box 850, Rarotonga; tel. 23-625, fax 24-625), at Ngatangiia facing Muri Beach, has five individual bungalows with basic cooking facilities at NZ$80 single or double roadside, NZ$90 beachside.

The **Sunrise Beach Motel** (Depot 8, Rarotonga; tel. 20-417, fax 22-991) at Ngatangiia has four beachfront bungalows at NZ$125 single or double, while the two garden units are NZ$95. Two rooms in a duplex block are cheaper and the rates are reduced when things are slow. All have cooking facilities and are excellent value. The beach here is poor but it's peaceful and a store is nearby. Some lovely nature hikes are available in the nearby valleys and it's an easy walk to Muri Beach.

The clean, pleasant **Kiikii Motel** (Box 68, Rarotonga; tel. 21-937, fax 22-937), a 30-minute walk west of Avarua, has an attractive swimming pool overlooking a rocky beach. Rooms in this solid two-story motel begin at NZ$54/67/113 single/double/triple, and even the four older "budget rooms" are quite adequate. The eight standard rooms in the west wing are 20% more expensive but they're large enough to accommodate a family of five. The six deluxe and six premier rooms (overlooking the sea) are 20% higher again. All 24 rooms have good cooking facilities, and the efficient staff is helpful in assisting with any special arrangements. Kiikii provides a good combination of proximity to town and beachside atmosphere, and several good bars and entertainment possibilities are nearby. Club Raro and its nightlife is only a stroll away (although you won't be bothered by the noise when you want to sleep). It's probably the closest you'll come to a U.S.-style motel, although much nicer. Airport transfers are NZ$7 each way.

A good bet very near Avarua's shopping, entertainment, and sightseeing possibilities is the **Paradise Inn** (Dianne Haworth, Box 674, Rarotonga; tel. 20-544, fax 22-544), just east of Portofino Restaurant. In a former existence "the Paradise" was the Maruaiai Dancehall, but it has been completely refurbished into a cozy little 16-room motel. The fan-cooled split-level rooms are NZ$72/80/93 single/double/triple, and there are two smaller budget singles that are a third cheaper. Cooking facilities are provided, and there's a large lounge and a nice terrace overlooking the ocean where you can sit and have a drink. Children under 12 are not accommodated.

The only hotel right in Avarua itself is the Cen-

tral Motel (Box 183, Rarotonga; tel. 25-735, fax 25-740), opposite the entrance to Rarotonga Breweries. The 14 units in this two-story concrete block edifice are NZ$95 single or double. No real cooking facilities are provided but a toaster, kettle, cups and plates have been added as an afterthought for making snacks. It's clean and convenient and might be okay if you were there on business.

Moderate

Puaikura Reef Lodges (Box 397, Rarotonga; tel. 23-537, fax 21-537) on the southwest side of the island offers 12 neat, orderly self-catering rooms in three single-story motel wings arranged around a swimming pool at NZ$126 single or double. A grocery store is adjacent, and the beach is just across the road with no houses blocking access to the sea. A paperback library is available for guests. The motel office is only open weekdays 0900-1600, Saturday 0900-1200, and the no-nonsense manager Paul Wilson would rather you booked from overseas through Air New Zealand instead of just showing up unannounced on his doorstep.

Lagoon Lodges (Box 45, Rarotonga; tel. 22-020, fax 22-021), on spacious grounds near the Rarotongan Resort Hotel, has 15 attractive self-catering units of varying descriptions beginning at NZ$140 single, double, or triple. There's a swimming pool, terrace café, and NZ$23 Sunday night barbecue for in-house guests only. It's a good choice for families with small children. Lagoon Lodges is run by Des Eggelton who arrived on Raro to help build the airport in 1973 just couldn't bring himself to leave.

Palm Grove Lodges (Box 23, Rarotonga; tel. 20-002, fax 21-998) on the south side of the island has 13 self-catering units beginning at NZ$140 single or double garden, NZ$185 beachfront. It's similar to Lagoon Lodges.

Raina Beach Apartments (Box 72, Rarotonga; tel. 22-327, fax 23-602) in Titikaveka has four self-catering units in a three-story main building at NZ$145 single or double. Its main advantages are proximity to a good snorkeling area and the view from the roof. If you're there on a Friday night you could be blasted by loud music from a local bar called Beach Kako across the street.

Travel writer Elliot Smith operates **Shangri-La Beach Cottages** (Box 146, Rarotonga; tel. 22-

779, fax 22-775) on the beach south of the Muri Beachcomber Motel. The six a/c cottages are NZ$145 single or double with jacuzzi, microwave, fridge, and lounge. After serving as a California judge for many years, Elliot dropped out of the legal profession and became a South Sea islander, sort of. His *Cook Islands Companion* is a best seller on Rarotonga and he'll be able to tell you on anything you want to know about Cook Islands.

Club Raro (Box 483, Rarotonga; tel. 22-415, fax 24-415) is a medium-sized resort just two km east of Avarua. The 39 fan-cooled rooms are NZ$120/165 double/triple standard, NZ$160/225 superior, including breakfast (no cooking facilities). Their all-inclusive meal and tour plan costs NZ$95 pp extra and twice a week the evening meal is off-site at a local restaurant. In 1995 an artificial beach was constructed and there's also a swimming pool. It's walking distance from town and might be a good choice for those interested in activities and having fun. Traditional dancing is staged Wednesdays and Fridays in their adjacent entertainment center.

Expensive

The **Oasis Village** (Box 2093, Rarotonga; tel. 28-213, fax 28-214), near the beach a bit south of Black Rock, has four a/c units at NZ$205 single or double. Children under 12 are not accepted. Cooking facilities are not provided but there's a convenience store adjacent to the property. It's overpriced.

The **Rarotongan Sunset Motel** (Box 377, Rarotonga; tel. 28-028, fax 28-026), in Arorangi next door to the Oasis Village, has 20 self-catering units in long blocks of four or five units at NZ$175 single, double, or triple in the garden or NZ$195 beachfront. These prices may be heavily discounted if you book direct on arrival and not through a travel agent. There's a swimming pool. It's popular and often full.

If your flight is delayed, Air New Zealand may accommodate you at the **Edgewater Resort** (Box 121, Rarotonga; tel. 25-435, fax 25-475), a crowded, impersonal cluster of two-story blocks, service buildings, and tennis courts facing a mediocre beach. This is Raro's largest hotel, with 182 a/c rooms beginning at NZ$200 single or double for those in the most unfavorable locations and rising to NZ$390 for an executive suite.

Third persons are NZ$50 extra. No cooking facilities are provided but there's traditional dancing twice a week. The original Edgewater was built in the early 1970s by controversial Czech "cancer specialist" Milan Brych to house his patients. Most ended up in a cemetery near the airport and Brych himself departed for greener pastures in the U.S. in 1978. Today those guests not sent here by an airline are on a package tour.

At Titikaveka is the **Moana Sands Resort** (Box 1007, Rarotonga; tel. 26-189, fax 22-189) with 12 units in a two-story building at NZ$179 single or double. These have only limited cooking facilities but the Moana Sands also has three beach villas with better cooking facilities at NZ$370. The beach is good and some water sports are offered.

The **Little Polynesian Motel** (Dorice Reid, Box 366, Rarotonga; tel. 24-280, fax 21-585), also at Titikaveka, has eight well-spaced self-catering duplex units at NZ$195 single or double, NZ$225 triple, plus a "honeymoon bungalow" that isn't as private as you might like. Children under 12 are not admitted. The motel faces one of the finest snorkeling beaches on the island (a swimming pool is also provided), and it has long been one of the most popular top-end places to stay on Rarotonga, too long in fact because the management has become rather complacent. Don't trust them to take telephoned messages, send your faxes, respond promptly to maintenance complaints, or provide advice. Inquiries outside of office hours (weekdays 0800-1600, Saturday 0900-1200) are unwelcome.

Near the south end of Muri Beach is the **Muri Beachcomber Motel** (Box 379, Rarotonga; tel. 21-022, fax 21-323) with 16 self-catering seaview units in eight duplex blocks at NZ$150/175/215 single/double/triple. Children under 12 are only accepted in two larger garden units facing the pool, which cost NZ$215 for up to four. There are also three "watergarden" units back near the road at NZ$200/225/285.

Premium

The **Rarotongan Resort Hotel** (Box 103, Rarotonga; tel. 25-800, fax 25-799), in the southwest corner of Rarotonga, has been the island's premier hotel since its opening in 1977. In 1997 the complex was fully renovated and made wheelchair accessible, one of the few South Pacific resorts where this is so. The 151 a/c rooms in nine one- and two-story blocks begin at NZ$240 single or double, NZ$300 triple, breakfast included (no cooking facilities). Children under 16 sleep free and some water sports are also included. The beach and swimming pool are fine, and island nights with traditional dancing are held twice a week. One Australian guidebook claims that nonguests can walk in here and use the pool, spa, and sporting equipment for free.

The **Pacific Resort** (Box 790, Rarotonga; tel. 20-427, fax 21-427) at Muri offers 54 self-catering rooms beginning at NZ$270 single or double, NZ$310 triple. The sandy beach is okay for swimming but not for snorkeling. A swimming pool, water-sports facility, and evening entertainment are part of this well-rounded resort. Their Barefoot Bar is fine for a hamburger and beer lunch but skip the stingy NZ$12 breakfast in their Sandals Restaurant.

Luxury

Crown Beach Resort and Villas (Stephen and Brenda Farnsworth, Box 47, Rarotonga; tel. 23-953, fax 23-951), south of the Edgewater Resort in Arorangi, opened in 1998. An a/c studio duplex is NZ$375 single or double, or NZ$525 for up to four persons in a two-bedroom duplex. A private villa will run NZ$495/645 for four/six persons. All 12 units have small kitchenettes, and a swimming pool and watersports are available. Airport transfers are NZ$24 pp return.

Packed together amid luxuriant vegetation next to the Flame Tree Restaurant is **Sokala Villas** (Box 82, Rarotonga; tel. 29-200, fax 21-222) with seven self-catering bungalows. The one garden villa without its own swimming pool is NZ$295 for up to three persons; the other six villas with pools or on the beach are NZ$410 and up. Most bookings are through travel agents abroad and there's a 25% "earlybird" discount if you pay 21 days in advance. Children under 12 are not admitted. Although billed as a honeymooner's hideaway such couples might find their neighbors too close for comfort, and in general it's overpriced.

The six two-story apartments at **Avana Marina Condominiums** (Box 869, Rarotonga; tel. 20-836, fax 22-991) are NZ$350 for up to five people (two or three bedrooms). Full cooking facilities are in each unit and they even throw in a rowboat. It's on a rocky shore facing the north side of Ngatangiia Bay but there is a swimming pool. The minimum stay is one week.

House Rentals

Renting a entire house by the week or month can be excellent value, and with hundreds of islanders moving to New Zealand each month, there are lots of places are available. Advertisements for furnished houses are often published in the classified section of the *Cook Islands News,* otherwise watch for signs around the island or ask at Cook Islands Tourism Corporation. Prices begin as low as NZ$100 a week plus utilities.

Kiikii Motel (Box 68, Rarotonga; tel. 21-937, fax 22-937) rents four fully equipped two-bedroom cottages near the Rarotongan Resort Hotel in Arorangi. These cost NZ$316 a week, plus about NZ$20 for electricity.

FOOD

Some upmarket restaurants don't include the value added tax in their menu prices, and if in doubt, ask when booking rather than get a 12.5% surprise on the bill. Most of the budget eateries popular among local residents are in Avarua but fancy tourist restaurants are found all around the island with a cluster near the Edgewater Hotel.

Budget Eateries

The cheapest meals are dispensed from food trailers at the market and there are covered picnic tables at which to eat.

Mama's Cafe (tel. 23-379; weekdays 0800-1630, Saturday 0800-1200), beside Foodland in Avarua, offers an interesting combination of healthy sandwiches and fattening desserts. The ice cream cones here are great! It's always crowded with locals.

The outdoor lunch counter at the **Cooks Corner Cafe** (tel. 22-345; open weekdays 0700-1500, Saturday 0700-1200) beside the Island Bus stop is also popular and specials are posted on blackboards.

Opposite Empire Theater is **Metua's Cafe** (tel. 20-850; open 0730-2200, closed Sunday) with lunch specials at NZ$6.50, dinner specials for NZ$11.90, all listed on a blackboard (large portions). It's good for a coffee or draft beer anytime.

In Arorangi **Flamboyant Takeaway** (tel. 23-958; open daily including Sunday 0800-0100), opposite Dive Rarotonga, serves inexpensive meals at their picnic tables. Friday at 1600 there's a special NZ$5 barbecue dish here. They also have good ice cream cones.

Avarua

Ronnie's Bar and Restaurant (Ronnie Siulepa, tel. 20-823; closed Sunday), on the Avarua waterfront, serves medium-priced lunches and dinners, and beside the restaurant bar is a pleasant, shady patio for cool drinks and conversation. Their *ika mata* (marinated raw fish) is excellent. It's okay to bring your own bottle of wine to dinner.

Much celebrated **Trader Jacks** (tel. 26-464) on the waterfront is a better venue for drinking or consuming *kati kati* (bar snacks) than ordering a full meal (although one reader recommended the seafood). It's one of the only places away from the resorts where you can get a beer on Sunday, and weekdays at happy hour you may meet some very senior, very drunk members of the local administration. It's lots of fun when the crew off one of the longliners working out of Avatiu Harbor rolls in.

The **Portofino Restaurant** (tel. 26-480), on the east side of town, specializes in Italian dishes such as pizza, pasta, and steaks. It opens for dinner at 1830 but is closed on Sunday. It gets good reviews from readers ("good food, lots of it, and well prepared") and could be crowded, so try to reserve. Just be aware that the menu in the window is the takeaway menu—the regular restaurant menu you'll be handed inside is much more expensive (tricky, tricky).

Arorangi

The **Oasis Steakhouse and Hopsings** (tel. 28-213; Mon.-Sat. from 1800), at the Oasis Village Motel, serves succulent steaks and is one of the only places on the island with a Chinese menu.

Alberto's Steakhouse (tel. 23-597; open Mon.-Sat. 1800-2100), near the Rarotongan Sunset Motel, offers steaks from NZ$17.50 to NZ$24.50 or pastas in the NZ$13-19 range. The cook is Swiss.

PJ's Sports Cafe (tel. 20-367; Mon.-Fri. 1200-1400/1800-2200, Saturday 1800-2200 only), 50 meters south of Alberto's and across the street, has less expensive burgers, chicken, fish and chips, and Chinese dishes you can carry out and consume at their roadside picnic tables. They also offer a more upmarket Chinese dinner

menu served in the main dining room with free transportation from most west coast hotels.

The much-advertised **Spaghetti House** (tel. 25-441; daily from 1700), at the entrance to the Edgewater Resort, offers pastas costing NZ$9.50-14, meats NZ$16.50-26.50, and pizzas NZ$10.50-12.50, plus tax.

Seafood, steaks, and chicken are available nightly 1800-2130 at the **Tumunu Tropical Garden Bar and Restaurant** (tel. 20-501), near the Edgewater Resort. This spacious bar opened in 1979 and the bartender, Eric, offers sightseers a popular guided tour of his picturesque establishment for a NZ$1 tip. Ask the waitress if you can see Eric's scrapbooks of life on Raro in the early 1970s.

Titikaveka to Muri

The **Vaima Cafe and Cocktails** (tel. 26-123), on the south coast just east of the Sheraton site, offers a reasonable lunch menu 1100-1500 and more upmarket dinner fare 1800-2200 every day. Friday to Monday nights there's live music.

Sails Restaurant (tel. 27-349; open daily), above the Rarotonga Sailing Club, serves good lunches, though dinner is more expensive. The downstairs Boardwalk Cafe section on the beach can be rather windy.

Under the same management as the Portofino in Avarua is the famous **Flame Tree Restaurant** (tel. 25-123), near Sokala Villas at Muri Beach, the island's top restaurant since it opened in 1988. Every day they offer a different set three-course menu for NZ$25, otherwise the seafood platter is NZ$30. À la carte starters are in the NZ$10-15 range and main plates run NZ$25-30. Owner Sue Carruthers was brought up in Kenya and some surprisingly exotic choices are on the menu (and in her two published cookbooks). This is one of the few restaurants on Rarotonga that doesn't allow smoking at the tables (only at the bar). It opens at 1830 daily and reservations are recommended.

Cafes

The **Blue Note Café** (tel. 23-236; daily 0800-1500, weekdays also 1800-2200), next to Banana Court, has the best coffee in town (NZ$3.50) and there's a stack of New Zealand newspapers on the counter for free reading. Check out the adjacent art gallery.

Fruits of Rarotonga (tel. 21-509; weekdays 0730-1700, Saturday 0900-1700), by the road in the southeast corner of the island, sells a variety of jams, chutneys, pickles, sauces, and dried fruits made on the premises. It's a great place to stop for coffee and muffins on your way around the island and you can snorkel right off their beach.

Sunday Barbecues

Several hotels prepare a Sunday barbecue dinner or "roast" open to everyone. The favorite of those in the know takes place at 1900 at Ati's Beach Bungalows (tel. 21-546), a bit south of the church in Arorangi (NZ$17.50 pp, reservations required). Return minibus transfers from anywhere on the island can be arranged at NZ$5 pp.

At the main hotels, there's one at the Rarotongan Sunset Motel (tel. 28-028) at 1730 (NZ$20 pp), at the Edgewater Resort (tel. 25-435) at 1830 (NZ$27.50), and at the Pacific Resort's Barefoot Bar (tel. 20-427) at 1900 (NZ$33). Call ahead to check times, prices, transportation arrangements, and bookings. Other possibilities may be advertised in the local paper.

Groceries

Every budget hotel provides kitchen facilities, so Rarotonga is perfect for those who enjoy preparing their own food. At the supermarkets newcomers to the South Pacific will be surprised to find the milk and juice in boxes on the shelves and long loaves of unwrapped bread in barrels near the check-out. Unfortunately it's almost impossible to buy fresh fish at Avarua market or elsewhere because the lagoons have been fished out and anything that's caught goes straight to the hotel kitchens.

CITC Food Center (tel. 27-000; Mon.-Thurs. 0800-1700, Friday 0800-1800, Saturday 0800-1300), next to Tere's Bar opposite Avatiu Harbor, is generally cheaper than Foodland Supermarket in town. **Meatco** (tel. 27-652), just down from Budget Rent-a-Car in town, usually has the least expensive vegetables and the best meat (except pork). The **Real Butcher** (tel. 27-418) opposite Metua's Cafe also sells quality meats.

Fresh milk and fruit juices are sold at **Frangi Dairy** (tel. 22-153), beside Parliament. You can also buy imported frozen meat and vegetables here, and super ice cream cones.

For beer or liquor, go to the **Liquor Center** (tel. 27-351; weekdays 1000-1630, Saturday 0900-1200) at Avatiu on the way to the airport.

On the south side of the island you can usually get everything you need at **Wigmore's Super Store** (tel. 20-206; Mon.-Sat. 0600-2100, Sunday 0600-0900/1400-2100) between the Sheraton site and Palm Grove Lodges.

The water on Rarotonga is safe to drink.

ENTERTAINMENT AND EVENTS

The **Empire Theater** (tel. 23-189) in Avarua projects feature films in two separate halls nightly except Sunday at 1930 and 2130 (NZ$4). On Saturday there's a matinee at 1000. It's almost worth going just to experience the enthusiasm of the local audience!

The most popular watering hole on the island used to be the historic **Banana Court** (tel. 27-797) in central Avarua in what was once a hostel for expatriate workers. Since 1994 the place has been in a state of limbo due to land disputes but it still opens on Friday nights with a live pop band for disco-style dancing. It's a genuine local scene.

The local teens spot is the **First Club,** behind Ronnie's Bar and Restaurant in Avarua, which opens from 1830 on Friday (NZ$2 admission).

T.J.'s Maruaiai Club (tel. 24-722), next to BECO Hardware Store just east of Metua's Cafe, opens Friday and Saturday around 1930. There's karaoke singing on Friday and a disco on Saturday. It's popular with the local teenagers, and dress regulations are in force to maintain standards.

The **Arorangi Clubhouse,** at the Raemaru Park Sports Ground, down the street opposite Southern Fried Chicken near the CICC church in Arorangi, has a good bar open on Friday and Saturday nights only. There's often live music. A predominately local crowd comes here and it can get rough, but it's a good place to mix.

A local spot near the accommodations at Muri is **Beach Kako,** also known as Beach Cargo, in a shed opposite Raina Beach Apartments. This occasionally rowdy drinking and dancing place opens intermittently on Friday and Saturday nights if the local rugby, cricket, or netball teams have scheduled a function. It's also used for fundraising barbecues by social groups, as is

Kent Hall, a bit west in Titikaveka. The *Cook Islands News* generally carries small ads for these events, sometimes printed in Maori.

Bars

Tere's Bar (tel. 20-352; closed Sunday), across the street from Avarua Harbor, is a breezy hangout with mugs of cold beer and occasional live music. It's the sort of place where you might expect to meet a former prime minister and other colorful local characters. Mention of "golden oldies" on the blackboard outside probably announces a dancing competition for senior citizens rather than Chubby Checkers or The Rondelles.

Another good drinking place is the **Cook Islands Game Fishing Club** (tel. 21-419; weekdays 1600-midnight, Saturday 1400-midnight) near Club Raro east of town. There's a terrace out back with picnic tables overlooking the beach and a large paperback library inside. This is a private club but a little tact and charm will see you through. Other agreeable bars include those at the **Rarotonga Bowling Club** (tel. 26-277; opens at 1600 weekdays) in Avarua and at the **Rarotonga Golf Club** (tel. 27-360) west of the airport. Both are closed on Sunday.

The **Returned Services Association Club** or "RSA" (tel. 20-590; weekdays 1200-2400, Saturday 1100-2400, public holidays 1300-2400, closed Sunday), directly across the street from the airport terminal, is a good place for a beer while you're waiting for a flight. They also have two pool tables, but food service is erratic. Tom Neale, who wrote a well-known book about his experiences living alone on Suwarrow atoll in the northern Cooks, is buried in the cemetery next to the club.

Cultural Shows for Visitors

Rarotonga is one place where the dance shows put on for tourists are worth seeing. Cook Islands dancers are renowned and "island night" performances are staged regularly at the hotels and restaurants. A buffet of traditional Cook Island food *(umukai)* is laid out and those ordering the meal can watch the show for free, otherwise there's usually a cover charge (around NZ$5-10). Things change, so call the hotels to check. Best of all, try to attend a show related to some special local event when the islanders themselves participate (look in the newspaper for listings).

Club Raro (tel. 22-415) does its island nights Wednesday at 2000 and Friday at 2100 (NZ$35 with dinner, otherwise NZ$5 cover). The Orama Dance Troupe, winner of many awards, often performs at Club Raro on Friday (Tuesday it's Awaiki Nui). The **Edgewater Resort** (tel. 25-435) has island nights Tuesday and Saturday at 2030, costing NZ$35 for the buffet or NZ$10 cover if you don't take dinner. The Taakoka Troupe often performs at the Edgewater on Tuesday with Orama on Saturday (ask). The **Rarotongan Resort Hotel** (tel. 25-800) usually has shows Wednesday and Saturday at 2030 (NZ$35 buffet or NZ$10 cover). The **Pacific Resort** (tel. 20-427) at Muri has an island night with children dancing Friday at 1900 (no cover change).

SHOPPING

Shopping hours in Avarua are weekdays 0800-1600, Saturday 0800-1200. Supermarkets in Avarua stay open about an hour longer, and small general stores around the island are open as late as 2000 weekdays and also on weekends. The **Dive Shop** (tel. 26-675) in Mana Court in Avarua sells quality snorkeling gear.

Raro Records (tel. 25-927), next to Empire Theater, sells Tahitian compact discs and cassettes a third cheaper than what you'd pay in Tahiti! **CITC Shopping Center** (tel. 22-000) nearby has more recordings of Cook Islands music.

The **Philatelic Bureau** (Box 13, Rarotonga; tel. 29-334, fax 22-428) next to the post office has colorful stamps, first-day covers, and mint sets of local coins, which make good souvenirs. In addition to the Cook Islands issues, they also sell stamps of Aitutaki and Penrhyn (only valid for postage on those islands). A crisp, new Cook Islands $3 bill costs NZ$7 here.

Crafts

Check out **Rosie's Are Crafts** (tel. 28-370), at the Avatiu Market, which carries grass skirts, baskets, dancing shakers, pandanus *rito* hats, and hat bands. *Tivaevae* quilts are available on request, NZ$200 and up for a medium-size one. This is the only shop where you can be sure that anything you buy is a genuine locally made handicraft. Also peruse the other handicraft stands in the market.

breadfruit leaf-shaped bowls carved from miro *wood on Mauke*

DAVID STANLEY

More commercial but also recommended is **Island Craft** (Box 28, Rarotonga; tel. 22-009), selling teak or *tamanu* (mahogany) carvings of Tangaroa, the fisherman's god (a fertility symbol), white woven hats from Penrhyn, mother-of-pearl jewelry, and good, strong bags. Other popular items include handbags, fans, tapa cloth from Atiu, replicas of staff gods, wooden bowls, food pounders, pearl jewelry, seats *(no'oanga),* headrests, slit gongs *(tokere),* and fishhooks. They've also got a branch at the airport that opens for international departures, but the selection in town is much better.

Pearls and Souvenirs
The black pearls of Manihiki may be inspected at the **Pearl Shop** (tel. 21-902, fax 21-903) at Cooks Corner. They provide certificates of authenticity, essential when you're spending hundreds of dollars for a single one! Cheaper, slightly imperfect gold-set pearls (with imperfections only obvious to an expert) are also available. Unfortunately, prices are not marked.

The **Beachcomber Gallery** (tel. 21-939; weekdays 1000-1630, Saturday 1000-1230), at the corner of the Ara Tapu and Makea Tinirau Road, is housed in a former London Missionary Society school building (1843). It's well worth entering this museum-like gallery to peruse the lovely pearl jewelry and other artworks on sale. Here all prices are clearly marked.

The **Perfume Factory** (tel. 22-690), on the Ara Metua behind town, sells a variety of coconut oil-based lotions and soaps produced on the premises. They also have the distinctive Tangaroa coconut coffee liqueur sold in souvenir ceramic Tangaroa bottles at NZ$40 for a large 500-ml bottle or NZ$20 for a 100-ml bottle. A regular 750-ml glass bottle of the same is NZ$30. Strangely, these items are not available at the airport.

Clothing
Visit the **Tav's Clothing Factory** (Ellena Tavioni, tel. 23-202) on Vakatini Road for the attractive lightweight tropical clothing and swimsuits screenprinted and sewn on the premises. Special-size items can be made to measure. Tav's designer garments are presently in fashion in Australia.

Get into style with some bright tropical apparel from **Joyce Peyroux Garments** (tel. 20-205) in the same mall as the ANZ Bank in Avarua and opposite the Are Renga Motel in Arorangi. Joyce Peyroux and other retailers carry beautiful selections of hand-printed dresses, pareus, tie-dyed T-shirts, bikinis, etc.—all locally made.

SERVICES AND INFORMATION

Money
Two banks serve Rarotonga, the Westpac Bank and the ANZ Bank, both open weekdays 0900-1500. Both change traveler's checks and give cash advances on Visa and MasterCard. The Westpac branch at the airport charges NZ$2.50

commission on traveler's checks, while the branch of the same bank in Avarua charges no commission. The ANZ Bank in Avarua charges NZ$2 commission on traveler's checks. If you're changing much, check both banks as their rates do vary slightly.

Post and Telecommunications
The post office in Avarua holds general delivery mail 28 days and there's no charge to pick up letters.

Telecom Cook Islands (Box 106, Rarotonga; tel. 29-680, fax 26-174) at the Earth Station Complex on Tutakimoa Road, Avarua, is open 24 hours a day for overseas telephone calls and telegrams. If you want to receive a fax here, the public fax number for Rarotonga is fax 682/26-174 and it costs NZ$2.20 to receive the first page, plus 50 cents per additional page.

Most public telephones around town are card phones but the Blue Note Café has a public telephone that accepts 20-cent coins.

Internet Access
If you'd like to catch up on your e-mail, Telecom Cook Islands (e-mail: info@oyster.net.ck) at the Earth Station Complex in Avarua has a "cyberbooth" available 24 hours a day at NZ$1.75 per five minutes. If you have a computer and are staying a while, you can get connected to the internet here for NZ$25 registration plus NZ$20 a month, which includes the first three hours (additional hours NZ$15 each). Of course, you'll need access to a phone line.

Visas and Officialdom
For an extension of stay go to the Immigration office (tel. 29-347) on the top floor of the Government Office Building behind the post office. Visa extensions cost NZ$70 to extend your initial 31 days to three months, then it's another NZ$70 to bring your total up to five months. Otherwise you can pay NZ$120 and get a five-month extension on the spot. The maximum stay is six months. If you lose your passport, report to the Ministry of Foreign Affairs in the same building.

The Honorary Consul of Germany is Dr. Wolfgang Losacker (tel. 23-304) near the tourist office in Avarua. The New Zealand High Commission (tel. 22-201; weekdays 1030-1430) is next to the Philatelic Bureau.

Other Services
Snowbird Laundromat (tel. 20-952), next to the Tumunu Restaurant in Arorangi, will do your wash for NZ$9 a load including washing, drying, and folding.

There are public toilets at Cooks Corner and at the Avatiu Market.

Yachting Facilities
Yachts pay a fee to anchor Mediterranean-style at Avatiu Harbor and are subject to the NZ$25 pp departure tax. The harbor is overcrowded and it's wise to do exactly what the harbormaster (tel. 28-814) asks as he's been around for a while. If you're trying to hitch a ride on a yacht to Aitutaki, Suwarrow, or points west, the harbormaster would be a good person to ask. There's a freshwater tap on the wharf, plus cold showers on the ground floor of the Ports Authority building. During occasional northerly winds Nov.-March, this harbor becomes dangerous and it would be a death trap for a small boat during a hurricane. Westbound from Rarotonga, consider stopping at unspoiled little Niue on the way to Vava'u.

Information
The government-run Cook Islands Tourism Corporation Visitor Center (Box 14, Rarotonga; tel. 29-435, fax 21-435; open weekdays 0800-1600), has brochures and information sheets giving current times and prices. Ask for a free copy of *What's On In The Cook Islands,* which contains a wealth of useful information.

The Statistics Office (Box 41, Rarotonga; tel. 29-390, fax 21-511), on the 2nd floor of the Government Office Building behind the post office, sells the informative *Annual Statistic Bulletin* (NZ$10).

The Bounty Bookshop (tel. 26-660), next to the ANZ Bank in Avarua, carries books on the Cook Islands, the latest regional newsmagazines, and the *Cook Islands News.* Pacific Supplies (tel. 27-770), next to South Seas International on the waterfront, also has the latest international newspapers and magazines. Good cultural books can be purchased at the Cook Islands Library and Museum and the University of the South Pacific Center.

The Postshop (tel. 29-992), in the mall opposite Dive Rarotonga, sells books on the Cook Islands, stationary, and postage stamps.

Panama Mini Mart (tel. 25-531), between the airport terminal and town, has a used paperback book exchange (NZ$1 to exchange, NZ$2 to buy).

Visitors can become temporary members of the Cook Islands Library (tel. 20-748; open Mon.-Sat. 0900-1300, Tuesday also 1600-2000) for an annual fee of NZ$25, of which NZ$10 is refunded upon departure.

Stars Travel (tel. 23-669) near the ANZ Bank is Rarotonga's most efficient and reliable travel agency. This agency and Island Hopper Vacations (tel. 22-026) next to the Banana Court arrange package tours to the outer islands with flights and accommodations included. Tipani Tours (tel. 25-266) is just west of the airport terminal.

Health

Rarotonga's main hospital (tel. 22-664), on a hill between the airport and Arorangi, is open for emergencies 24 hours a day. To call an ambulance dial 998.

The Outpatients Medical Clinic (tel. 20-066) at Tupapa, a km east of town, is open weekdays 0800-1600, Saturday 0800-1100. In the same building is the Central Dental Clinic (tel. 29-312), open weekdays 0800-1200 and 1300-1600.

With the Ministry of Health still reeling after massive budget cutbacks in 1996, you'll receive better service from a private practitioner, such as Dr. Robert Woonton (tel. 23-680; weekdays 0900-1400, Saturday 0900-1100), upstairs in Ingram House opposite Avatiu Harbor. He also has a clinic next to the Rarotongan Sunset Motel in Arorangi. Dr. Terepai Tairea has a Private Dental Surgery (tel. 25-210; weekdays 0800-1600) next to Dr. Woonton upstairs in Ingram House.

You could also turn to Dr. Teariki Noovao (tel. 20-835), between the Teachers College and the Golf Club opposite Avatea School on the Ara Metua. His medical clinic is open weekdays 1630-2030, Saturday 0900-1200. A private Dental Surgery (tel. 20-169; weekdays 0800-1600) is a few hundred meters east along the same road back toward town.

Dr. Wolfgang Losacker (tel. 23-304; weekdays 1000-1300), operates a medical clinic and photo gallery between the Banana Court and the tourist office in Avarua. He's a specialist in internal and tropical medicine, cardiology, and parasitology, and at his office he sells his own Cook Islands photo book (NZ$66) and quality postcards (NZ$1 each).

The CITC Pharmacy (tel. 29-292; weekdays 0800-1630, Saturday 0800-1200) is in central Avarua at CITC Shopping Center.

TRANSPORTATION

For information on air and sea service from Rarotonga to other Cook islands turn to the introduction to Cook Islands.

By Road

The **Cook's Island Bus Passenger Transport Ltd.** (Box 613, Rarotonga; tel./fax 25-512) operates a round-the-island bus service leaving Cooks Corner every half hour weekdays 0700-1600, Saturday 0800-1300. These yellow, 32-seat buses alternate in traveling clockwise (leaving on the hour) and counterclockwise (leaving on the half hour), stopping anywhere (no counterclockwise service on Saturday). The night bus leaves town Mon.-Sat. at 1800, 1900, 2100, and 2200, plus midnight and 0130 on Friday, and 2300 on Saturday. The current schedule is published in *What's On In The Cook Islands.* Fares are NZ$2 one-way, NZ$3 return, NZ$4 return at night, or NZ$5 for an all-day pass (NZ$12 for families). There's also a NZ$15 10-ride ticket that can be shared. Tourists are the main users of this excellent, privately run service and the drivers make a point of being helpful.

Taxi rates are negotiable, but the service is slightly erratic. Ask the fare before getting in and clarify whether it's per person or for the whole car. Some drivers will drive you the long way around the island to your destination. In Avarua the taxi stand is at the hut marked Are Tapaeanga across the street from the police station. Beware of prebooking taxis to the airport over the phone, as they often don't turn up, especially at odd hours. Service is generally 0600-2200 only. Hitchhiking is not understood here.

Rentals

A Cook Islands Driver's License (NZ$15 and one photo) is required to operate motorized rental vehicles. This can be obtained in a few minutes at the police station (tel. 22-499) in the center of Avarua any weekday 0800-1500, Saturday 0800-1200, upon presentation of your home driver's license (minimum age 21 years). This whole exercise is purely a moneymaking operation and the International Driver's License is not accepted.

If you wish to operate a scooter they'll require you to show something that states explicitly that you're licensed to drive a motorcycle, otherwise you may have to pass a test (NZ$5 extra) that involves riding one up and down the street without falling off. Bring your own scooter and keep in mind that if you fail the test you won't be allowed to ride any further and that day's scooter rental must still be paid. (In theory the person giving the driving tests takes lunch 1200-1300 and knocks off at 1500.) Without a license the insurance on the vehicle will not be valid and you'll be liable for a stiff fine if caught. No license is required to ride a bicycle.

Greg Sawyer of Lafayette, Indiana, sent us this:

I rented a scooter and went to get my required Cook Islands Drivers License and because my U.S. license had no motorcycle status, it was necessary to take a "practical driving test" first. The officer at the police station said, however, that the person doing the tests would return in 30 minutes. So off I scootered to run errands, returning half an hour later. No test person again, come back in one hour. Off I go, return in an hour, and still no tester. I returned in another hour: come back after lunch. Well, my patience gone and wishing to use my hard-won vacation time more vacation-like, I never went back. That's the hassle I got at the police station, but it's only half the story.

Late one night returning to my room, I was flagged down on my scooter by a man I thought was in distress. I was quickly surrounded on each side by one small and one very large man. The large one claimed to be a policeman, charged me with drunken driving, and demanded to see my license (which, remember, I had not). I responded by charging that he was no po-

liceman (which he obviously wasn't), that he was drunk (which he obviously was), and that my license was none of his business. To shorten the story, he became more nasty, more demanding of the license (claiming I had none), and seemed much larger. I asked what he wanted and he said NZ$20. So I gave it to him, preferring extortion to a doctor or dentist visit. Then he became very friendly and sent me on my way. As his expense to me was nearly the same as my untendered driver's license expense, I figure that I basically broke even. I feared to go to the police with my tale and let it slide. It's very possible these ruffians will keep this scam going.

You're supposed to wear a helmet while operating a motorbike. Although it's unlikely you'll ever see anybody with one on, and the local tourism brochures carry photos of girls on scooters with little more than flowers in their hair, an anti-tourist cop could always bring it up. Drive slowly, as local children tend to run onto the road unexpectedly, and beware of free-roaming dogs, which often cause accidents by suddenly giving chase at night. Take special care on Friday and Saturday nights, when there are more drunks on the road than sober drivers. The speed limit is 40 km per hour in Avarua, 50 km per hour on the open road, and driving is on the left.

The prices listed below are for the cheapest car. Rates include unlimited km, and the seventh consecutive day is usually free. Some places quote prices including the 12.5% government tax, others without the tax. Check all the agencies for special deals—most are also open on Sunday. Most cars and scooters rent for 24 hours, so you can use them for a sober evening on the town.

Two of the international chains are represented on Rarotonga. **Budget/Polynesian** (Box 607, Rarotonga; tel. 20-895, fax 20-888), in Avarua and at the Edgewater Resort and Rarotongan Resort Hotel, has the best quality cars and bicycles. Their cars are NZ$62 a day, jeeps NZ$75 a day, scooters NZ$25 a day, bicycles NZ$8 a day, tax and insurance included. You can also get a 12-passenger Mitsubishi van at

NZ$96 daily, great if you want to organize your own group tour.

Avis (Box 317, Rarotonga; tel. 22-833, fax 21-702), next to Cook Islands Tourism Corporation in Avarua, charges NZ$56 for cars, but tax and insurance are additional. Avis also has scooters at NZ$27/108 a day/week and bicycles at NZ$9/41, tax included.

Rarotonga Rentals (tel. 22-326), next to Odds 'n Ends opposite Avarua Market, has cars from NZ$55 a day (NZ$135 for three days) and scooters at NZ$20 a day (NZ$120 a week). Jeeps and a nifty MG sports car are also available.

Raymond Pirangi at **T.P.A. Rental Cars** (Box 327, Rarotonga; tel. 20-611, fax 23-611), opposite the Rarotongan Sunset Motel in Arorangi, has cars at NZ$38 daily, insurance and tax additional. Since Raymond offers the cheapest car rentals on the island, don't expect to receive a new car.

Tipani Rentals (Box 751, Rarotonga; tel. 22-328, fax 25-611), in Arorangi opposite the Edgewater Resort, charges NZ$60 a day for cars, tax and insurance included, scooters NZ$20 daily, bicycles NZ$8.

Many smaller companies rent motor scooters for NZ$15-20 a day, NZ$75-100 a week, and bicycles at NZ$8-10 daily—ask your hotel for the nearest. **Hogan Rentals** (Box 100, Rarotonga; tel./fax 22-632), 250 meters north of the Are Renga Motel in Arorangi, rents cars at NZ$55 a day, tax, insurance, and kms included. Hogan's 12-speed mountain bikes are NZ$8 daily or NZ$48 weekly (NZ$20 deposit). The bicycles have baskets on the front and are fairly sturdy, but there are no lamps for night riding. **BT Bike Hire** (tel. 23-586), right next to the Are Renga Motel, also has bicycles and scooters.

There aren't enough women's bicycles to go around, but men's cycles are easy to rent. The main advantage to renting a bicycle for the week is that you have it when you want it. Rarotonga is small enough to be easily seen by bicycle, which makes renting a car or scooter an unnecessary expense—you also avoid the compulsory local driver's license rip-off. Bicycles are also quiet, easy on the environment, healthy, safe, and great fun. One of the nicest things to do on a sleepy Rarotonga Sunday is to slowly circle the island by bicycle.

Tours

The **Takitumu Conservation Area** project (Box 817, Rarotonga; tel./fax 29-906) operates four-hour guided hikes into the bush up Avana Stream. You'll be shown the colorful *neinei* flower and the unique Rarotonga orchid, and hopefully catch a glimpse of the endangered *kakerori* or Rarotonga flycatcher that the group is working to save. A large colony of flying foxes may also be visited. At NZ$30 pp including light refreshments, it's good value and you'll be contributing to a worthy cause. Visit their office behind the post office in Avarua where distinctive T-shirts and posters are sold.

Pa's Nature Walk (tel. 21-079) is another good way to get acquainted with the natural history of the island. The four-hour hike through the bush behind Matavera includes a light lunch; both it and Pa's guided cross-island hike are NZ$35 pp with hotel transfers included. With his blond Rastafarian good looks, Pa is quite a character and it's worth signing up just to hear his spiel.

One reader wrote in recommending the 3.5-hour, NZ$25 circle-island tour offered weekdays by **Hugh Henry** (Box 440, Rarotonga; tel. 25-320, fax 25-420) in Arorangi. Call ahead and they'll pick you up at your hotel. The **Cultural Village** (tel. 21-314) offers a full-day combined circle-island tour and cultural show for NZ$60 including lunch.

BOB RACE

THE SOUTHERN GROUP

AITUTAKI

Aitutaki, 259 km north of Rarotonga, is the second-most-visited Cook Island and the scenery of this oversold "dream island" is actually quite lovely. The low rolling hills are flanked by banana plantations, taro fields, and coconut groves. Atiu-type coffee is grown here. A triangular barrier reef 45 km around catches Aitutaki's turquoise lagoon like a fishhook. The maximum depth of this lagoon is 10.5 meters but most of it is less than five meters deep. The 15 small islets or *motu* and many sandbars on the eastern barrier reef all have picture-postcard white sands and aquamarine water.

The main island is volcanic: its highest hill, Maungapu (124 meters), is said to be the top of Rarotonga's Raemaru, chopped off and brought back by victorious Aitutaki warriors. All of the *motu* are coraline except for Rapota and Moturakau, which contain some volcanic rock. Legend holds that just as the warriors were ar-

riving back with their stolen mountain they clashed with pursuing Rarotongans and pieces of Maungapu fell off creating Moturakau and Rapota. Moturakau served as a leper colony from the 1930s to 1967. Motikitiu at the south end of the lagoon is the nesting area of many of the Aitutaki's native birds as mynahs have taken over the main island. Be on the lookout for the blue lorikeet *(kuramo'o)* with its white bib and orange beak and legs.

The 2,300 people live in villages strung out along the roads on both sides of the main island and generally travel about on motor scooters. The roads are red-brown in the center of the island, coral white around the edge. The administration and most of the local businesses are clustered near the wharf at Arutanga. All of the villages have huge community halls built mostly with money sent from New Zealand. There's tremendous rivalry among the villages to have the

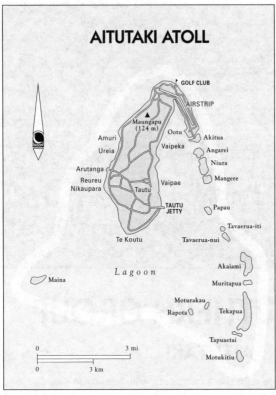

AITUTAKI ATOLL

GOLF CLUB

AIRSTRIP

Maungapu
(124 m)

Amuri   Ootu

Ureia   Akitua

Vaipeka   Angarei

Arutanga   Niura

Reureu   Vaipae   Mangere
Nikaupara

Tautu

TAUTU JETTY   Papau

Te Koutu   Tavaerua-iti

Tavaerua-nui

Lagoon   Akaiami

Maina   Muritapua

Moturakau

Rapota   Tekapua

Tapuaetai

0   3 mi   Motukitiu

0   3 km

© DAVID STANLEY

flies and mosquitoes are at their worst. They're more of a nuisance on the north side of the main island, far less so on the *motu.* Around Arutanga beware of theft from the beach and the back yards of the guesthouses by small children.

History

A Polynesian myth tells that Aitutaki is a giant fish tethered to the seabed by a vine. After a perilous journey from Tubuai in the canoe *Little Flowers,* the legendary hero Ru landed here with four wives, four younger brothers, and 20 virgins to colonize the island. Ru named the atoll Utataki-enua-o-Ru-ki-te-moana, meaning "a land sought and found in the sea by Ru," which the first Europeans corrupted to Aitutaki. Ru named various parts of the island for the head, stomach, and tail of a fish, but more places he named for himself. His brothers became angry when most of the land was divided among the 20 virgins, and they left for New Zealand where they won great honor. Ru himself suffered the consequences of his arrogance as higher chiefs eventually arrived and relegated him to the subordinate position held by his descendants today.

Captain William Bligh "discovered" Aitutaki in 1789, only 17 days before the notorious mutiny. In 1821, when the Tahitian pastors Papeiha and Vahapata were put ashore, it became the first of the Cook islands to receive Christian missionaries. Americans built the island's huge airfield during WW II. Tasman Empire Airways (now Air New Zealand) used Akaiami Island as a refueling stop for its four-engined Solent flying boats during the 1950s. The Coral Route, from Auckland to Tahiti via Suva and Apia, became obsolete when Faa'a Airport opened near Papeete in 1961. The Karaau Terminal Building at the airport was opened for the South Pacific Forum meeting in 1997.

biggest and best one, although they're unused most of the time. The *motu* are uninhabited, and there aren't any dogs at all on Aitutaki.

Aitutaki is the only Cook island other than Rarotonga where there's a good choice of places to stay, entertainment, and organized activities. One way to go is to catch a Thursday or Friday flight up from Rarotonga so as to be on hand for "island night" at the Rapae Hotel or Ralphie's that evening. Book a lagoon trip for Saturday and you'll still have Sunday to scooter around the island or laze on the beach. Fly back on Monday or Tuesday, having sidestepped Rarotonga's dull Sunday. This is probably too short a stay, however, and a week on the island would be much better.

Aitutaki is north of Rarotonga and therefore warmer. During the hot season Dec.-March, sand

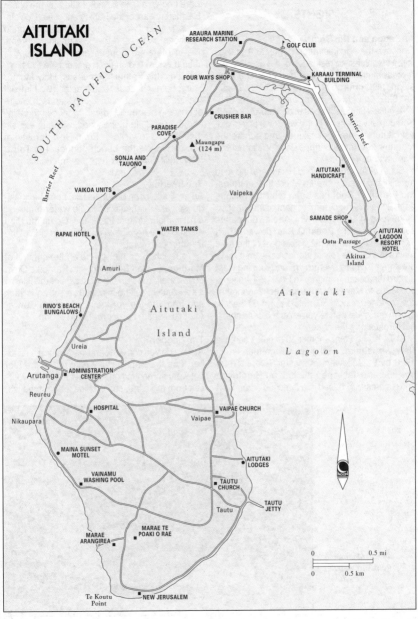

AITUTAKI ISLAND

SOUTH PACIFIC OCEAN

ARAURA MARINE RESEARCH STATION

GOLF CLUB

FOUR WAYS SHOP

KARAAU TERMINAL BUILDING

Barrier Reef

CRUSHER BAR

PARADISE COVE

▲ Maungapu (124 m)

SONJA AND TAUONO

AITUTAKI HANDICRAFT

VAIKOA UNITS

Vaipeka

Barrier Reef

SAMADE SHOP

RAPAE HOTEL

WATER TANKS

Ootu Passage

AITUTAKI LAGOON RESORT HOTEL

Akitua Island

Amuri

Aitutaki

RINO'S BEACH BUNGALOWS

Aitutaki Island

Lagoon

Ureia

Arutanga

ADMINISTRATION CENTER

Reureu

HOSPITAL

VAIPAE CHURCH

Nikaupara

Vaipae

MAINA SUNSET MOTEL

AITUTAKI LODGES

VAINAMU WASHING POOL

TAUTU CHURCH

TAUTU JETTY

Tautu

MARAE TE POAKI O RAE

MARAE ARANGIREA

N

MOON

0   0.5 mi
0   0.5 km

Te Koutu Point   NEW JERUSALEM

© DAVID STANLEY

SIGHTS

Arutanga and the South

Opposite the Administration Center at Arutanga is the colonial-style residence of the government representative set in lovely gardens. The limestone **CICC church** just to the south was begun in 1828, only a few years after Papeiha converted the islanders, but it's usually solidly locked. You can always peek in the windows of this oldest church in the Cook Islands and admire the monument to missionaries John Williams and Papeiha out front.

South of Arutanga beyond Nikaupara, the road turns inland at a dry stream where the old **Vainamu Washing Pool** has been rebuilt. Continue east along this road, turning right at the junction of the road to Te Koutu Point. About 700 meters south is **Marae Te Poaki O Rae,** down a short trail to the left. A signpost visible east of the road marks this double row of stones beneath a huge puka tree. A more overgrown road running west toward the beach from the Te Poaki O Rae junction leads to **Marae Arangirea.** Look for another line of stones about 150 meters down on the left, in high grass just before you enter the eerie chestnut forest along the coast.

At Te Koutu Point another 10 minutes south is **New Jerusalem,** a religious village founded in 1990 by the followers of Master Two. In 1986 this leader established the cult on Rarotonga and it's presently based in a thatched compound

there known as the "Land of Life," by the shore 100 meters east of the Parliament of the Cook Islands. Master Two's religion teaches a return to traditional ways, and the 33 Aitutaki adherents live in thatched houses arranged around a church where five chairs represent the five highest gods: the Father, Son Jesus, Holy Mother Mary, Father Joseph, and Master Two himself! Master Two's huge double bed stands in another building nearby. Members work communally, and they're quite friendly and willing to explain their beliefs to visitors. From New Jerusalem you can follow the beach northeast to **Tautu jetty,** built during WW II by the Americans.

The Interior

An easy afternoon or sunset hike from the guesthouses at Arutanga is up to the **water tanks** on a hill in the middle of the island. Go up the road marked Pirake/Vaipeka on the south side of the Paratrooper Motel.

To reach the radio towers on the summit of **Maungapu,** start from opposite Paradise Cove on the main road up the west side of the island. It's a leisurely half-hour jaunt up an obvious track and from the top you get a sweeping view of Aitutaki's entire barrier reef from on top.

The Lagoon

At low tide you can walk and wade along a sandbar from the Rapae Hotel right out to the reef but wear something on your feet to protect yourself from the coral, sea urchins, eels, stonefish,

view of Moturakau from Tapuaetai at Aitutaki

CLAIRE BRENN

algae, etc. Stonefish are not common, but they're almost impossible to spot until it's too late. At high tide snorkel out from the black rocks on the beach just north of the Rapae. Snorkelers and paddlers must keep at least 200 meters inside the main reef entrance at Arutanga, due to the strong outgoing current.

The finest snorkeling off the main island is at the far west end of the airstrip and to the south. Beware of dangerous currents in the passes near the edge of the reef here. Elsewhere on the main island the snorkeling is poor.

Wave-shelled giant clams (pahua) intended to restock the Aitutaki lagoon are reared at the **Araura Marine Research Station** established with Australian aid money just north of the west end of Aitutaki's airstrip. One tank contains an assortment of adult clams, baby sea turtles, sea slugs, sea urchins, and colorful fish. Weekdays you can take a tour and see a video for NZ$2.

The top beach on the main island is at the southeast end of the airstrip near the bridge to the Aitutaki Lagoon Resort Hotel. It's fine to swim here but there aren't many fish or corals to be seen by snorkelers.

SPORTS AND RECREATION

Neil Mitchell's **Aitutaki Scuba** (Box 40, Aitutaki; tel. 31-103, fax 31-310) offers diving at the drop-off once or twice a day (except Sunday). If you have your own equipment, diving is NZ$60 for one dive or NZ$55 each for two or more dives (NZ$10 extra if you need gear). Snorkelers are welcome to go along at NZ$20 pp when space is available. No reservations are required, but bring your own mask; wetsuits are handy June-December. The diving here is better March-November. Aitutaki is great place to learn to dive and Neil does four-day NAUI certification courses for NZ$490 (minimum of two persons). You'll find Neil about a hundred meters down the side road that branches off the main road at Sunny Beach Lodge. Aitutaki is not an easy dive destination. The lagoon may be great for snorkeling, but it's too shallow for serious diving and the dropoff outside the reef is very steep (not for beginners).

Aitutaki Sea Charters (Box 43, Aitutaki; tel. 31-281) offers deep sea fishing off the 10-meter cruiser Foxy Lady. A special "backpackers rate"

of NZ$50 pp applies when you book direct (2-8 persons). You'll often find Captain Jason or his father Don Watts at the Game Fishing Club around happy hour. Skipjack tuna, giant trevally, mahimahi, and barracuda are caught year-round off Aitutaki. The billfish (marlin) season is Nov.-March, while in August and September wahoo are frequently caught.

The **Aitutaki Golf Club** (Box 98, Aitutaki; no phone) beside the airport welcomes visitors. Greens fees are NZ$5 but there are no club rentals. If your ball falls on the airstrip, it's considered out of bounds. The Aitutaki Open Golf Tournament is in mid-October.

ACCOMMODATIONS

There are lots of places to stay on Aitutaki in every price category and the rooms are almost never fully booked. Air Rarotonga or Stars Travel can reserve any of the places mentioned below and discounts are possible if you stay a week or more. Most budget travelers stay at Tom's, Vaikoa Units, or Paradise Cove. Rino's and Maina Beach are the most popular of the medium-priced places. Packaged tourists are exiled to the Aitutaki Lagoon Resort Hotel, while Josie's, the Tiare Maori, Turia's, Paratrooper, and Sunny Beach are usually empty because the Rarotonga travel agencies don't book people into them. Most of the cheaper places offer rooms with shared bath only.

Budget

Arekoi Bungalows (tel./fax 31-327), also known as Bamboo Bungalows, is on a hill to the left of the road, 150 meters inland from the Administration Center in Arutanga. The two bungalows with kitchen, fridge, and private bath are good value at NZ$50/60/70 single/double/triple. There's no sign, so ask.

The pleasant **Tiare Maori Guest House** (Box 16, Aitutaki; tel. 31-119), formerly known as Mama Tunui's, in Ureia village, has seven rooms at NZ$32/42 single/double. Mama serves an all-you-can-eat dinner (NZ$15) including clams, chicken, and island vegetables. You can also use her stove, and watch the family television. She'll even give you a flower ai to wear to island night at the Rapae.

Josie's Lodge (Josie and David Sadaraka, tel. 31-111, fax 31-518), an older island house next door to the Tiare Maori, has four double and two single rooms with shared bath at NZ$26/36/45 single/double/triple. The rooms are screened to keep out insects, and communal cooking facilities are provided.

Tom's Beach Cottage (Box 51, Aitutaki; tel. 31-051, tel. 31-121 at home, fax 31-409) is a large island-style house (no sign) right on the beach just north of Rino's Bungalows. It's a favorite backpacker's hangout and also gets a lot of people who've booked budget packages through travel agents. The seven rooms with old fashioned brass beds and mosquito nets are NZ$32/48/58 single/double/triple but the two facing the street get considerable traffic noise. A nicer thatched "honeymoon" bungalow a bit closer to the beach is NZ$76/86 single/double. When things are slow these rates are reduced. A communal kitchen is available (beware of mice), plus a sitting room with photos of the family and a lounge with a pool table. Local calls on the house phone are 20 cents each. Tom will ferry you to Ootu Beach for kayak rentals.

Turia's Guesthouse (tel. 31-049) is a four-room concrete block house north of Tom's and almost opposite Tip Top Store. Dorm beds here are NZ$20 pp, but it's often closed.

The **Paratrooper Motel** (Box 73, Aitutaki; tel. 31-563 or 31-523), in Amuri almost opposite Swiss Rentals, consists of four wooden buildings in a crowded compound a block back from the beach. It's run by a laid-back ex-New Zealand paratrooper named Geoffrey Roi and his wife Maine who are shaking up the local tourist establishment by offering dis-count prices. Geoffrey's official rates are NZ$57 single or double for their two one-bedroom apartments with full cooking facilities, reduced to NZ$31 if you stay eight nights or more. The three two-bedroom family units come down to NZ$74 if you stay six nights. All rates are negotiable—this is one place where you can bargain when things are slow. It's more of a place for an extended stay than only one or two nights, and despite the name, there's no strict military discipline here.

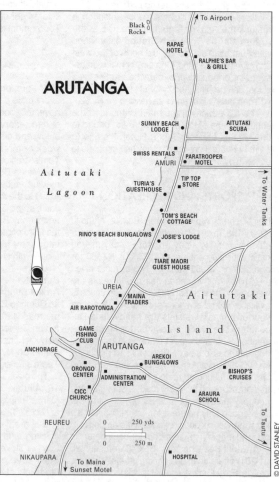

Vaikoa Units (Box 71, Aitutaki; tel. 31-145), a km north of the Rapae Hotel, offers six self-catering units in parallel wooden blocks at NZ$30/40 single/double. The nearest grocery store is a 15-minute walk away. It's right on one of the best snorkeling beaches on the main island and dugout canoes are loaned free. This attractive place is highly recommended.

Junior Maoate's **Paradise Cove Guesthouse** (Box 64, Aitutaki; tel. 31-218, fax 31-456) is at Anaunga, between the airstrip and the Rapae Hotel. Spacious grounds lead down to a white sand beach with excellent snorkeling just offshore. The five rooms in the main house are NZ$30/40 single/double, while the six thatched Polynesian beach huts with fridge and shared bath are NZ$40/60. Junior provides good communal cooking facilities and special reduced rates are sometimes offered.

Inexpensive

On the beach almost opposite Josie's Lodge is **Rino's Beach Bungalows** (Box 140, Aitutaki; tel. 31-197, fax 31-559) with four hotplate-equipped units in a two-story roadside block at NZ$55/85/95 single/double/triple. Four new beachfront duplex apartments are NZ$134 single or double complete with fridge, stove, washing machine, and terrace overlooking the lagoon. Rino's also has an older three-bedroom house across the street that is rented out at NZ$250 a week (up to six persons). This well-managed hotel also rents bicycles, scooters, and cars.

Sunny Beach Lodge (Box 94, Aitutaki; tel./fax 31-446), on the beach next to a grocery store toward the north end of the tourist strip, has a row of self-catering units in a new single-story block at NZ$72/80/95/110 single/double/triple/quad. If it's closed when you arrive, the owners live behind the Seventh-Day Adventist church across the street.

For years there's been talk of replacing the government-owned **Rapae Hotel** (Box 4, Aitutaki; tel. 31-320, fax 31-321), just north of Arutanga, with a flash resort on the same site, but as yet nothing has materialized. If it's still open, the 12 duplex rooms will cost about NZ$80 single or double, but the only one with cooking facilities is number 13 (about NZ$20 extra). Be aware that on Friday disco dancing continues half the night (other nights it's peaceful). Only minimal maintenance is being done on the bungalows at the moment and discounts are possible.

Moderate

In 1995 the **Maina Sunset Motel** (Box 34, Aitutaki; tel. 31-511, fax 31-611) opened in Nikaupara district, a 20-minute walk south of Arutanga. The 12 self-contained units are arranged in a U-shape around a freshwater swimming pool that faces the lagoon (poor beach). The eight rooms without cooking are NZ$145 double, while the four with cooking are NZ$175. It's peaceful as you don't get a lot of traffic noise down here but scooter hire is available. Their speedboat anchors at the landing directly in front of the motel and they'll shuttle you over to the fantastic snorkeling spots near Maina Island at NZ$30 pp with sandwiches and fresh fruit for lunch.

Expensive

Aitutaki Lodges (Box 70, Aitutaki; tel. 31-334, fax 31-333), near Tautu Jetty on the opposite side of the main island from Arutanga, offers six self-catering bungalows on stilts facing the lagoon at NZ$186 single or double, NZ$237 triple, with reductions for three or more nights. You'll need to hire a scooter if you stay here as it's far from everything. Although the lagoon view from your porch will be lovely, the beach below the units is too muddy for swimming and the water too murky for snorkeling. Most guests arrive on prepaid packages.

Premium

Aitutaki's top resort is the isolated **Aitutaki Lagoon Resort Hotel** (Box 99, Aitutaki; tel. 31-201, fax 31-202), on Akitua Island near Ootu Beach at the east end of the airstrip. It's connected to the main island by a small wooden bridge. The 16 a/c garden bungalows with private bath and fridge are overpriced at NZ$286 single or double, the nine lagoon bungalows NZ$427, and the five beachfront bungalows NZ$550. The plumbing fixtures are poorly maintained and cooking facilities are not provided. All rates include a buffet breakfast but no meal plan is available. Ordering à la carte in the restaurant is very expensive and you can't just walk across the street to a grocery store (the nearest is on the other side of Aitutaki). The Wednesday night seafood buffet is NZ$39, the Saturday island night NZ$30, both with traditional dancing. You get the feeling they're really out to fleece you: a Coke from the minibar in your room will be NZ$4.50 and it's NZ$8 to leave valuables in the office safe. No environmentally friendly bicycles are for hire, only motor scooters. Checkout time is 1030. There's a small swimming pool and the beach is lovely but the water offshore is murky and there's nothing much to see with a mask. Unfortunately the resort is also infested with tiny mosquitoes (bring a net to hang over your bed).

FOOD AND ENTERTAINMENT

Food
A small **vegetable market** operates 0800-1500 during the week at the Orongo Center near the wharf offering lots of bananas, cabbage, coconuts, green peppers, oranges, papaya, tomatoes, and watermelon. The **Seabreeze Cafe** (tel. 31-573; Mon.-Sat. 0800-1330/1730-2100) beyond the handicraft stalls serves fish and chips (NZ$7.50) to be consumed at picnic tables overlooking the lagoon.

Donald's CITC Branch (tel. 31-055; weekdays 0800-2000, Saturday 1700-2000) is one of several grocery stores near the wharf. **Maina Traders Ltd.** (tel. 31-219; Mon.-Sat. 0700-2000),

banana tree (Musa cavendishi)

between Tom's Cottage and the wharf, offers a good selection of groceries, fresh vegetables, and drinks.

Kuramoo Takeaways (Mon.-Sat. 1100-2100) serves a variety of seafood including parrot fish and octopus on their outdoor terrace near Maina Traders.

Tip Top Store, a few hundred meters north of Rino's, scoops out ice-cream cones as well as selling fresh vegetables.

Ralphie's Bar & Grill (tel. 31-418; daily 1000-1400/1800-2130), across the street from the Rapae Hotel, dispenses cheeseburger (NZ$4.50) or fish and chip (NZ$10.50) lunches that you can eat at the picnic tables outside. Dinner (F$16.50) is served in an a/c room and the food is good. They're open daily, but on Sunday only dinner is served. Free hotel pickups are available for diners.

The **Crusher Bar & Restaurant** (tel. 31-283; closed Friday), near Paradise Cove on the way to the airport, is a funky open air bar with picnic tables under a tin roof. Monday-Wed. from 1800 you can get a grilled steak or fish dinner with salad bar for NZ$15.50. Thursday night is island night with a Polynesian buffet (NZ$26 pp) followed by an excellent show by the dance group "Tiare Aitutaki." Saturday night is "backpackers nite" with main course and desert at NZ$10.50. The Sunday night roast or fish of the day is NZ$16.50 with desert. Nightly animation is provided by the infamous lady killer Ricky de Von (also an excellent cook). Call ahead for bookings and free hotel pickups.

Ask the people where you're staying if the water is safe to drink. It's always good to boil it and store it in your fridge, if you can.

Entertainment
Aside from the Thursday night show at the Crusher Bar, two Polynesian dance shows take place on Friday night. Most people start the evening with island night at the **Rapae Hotel** (tel. 31-320) where the buffet (NZ$30) begins at 1930, followed by the show at 2100. As soon as the one at Rapae finishes, almost everyone crosses the street to **Ralphie's Bar** (tel. 31-418) where the action starts at 2200 (be fast to get a reasonable seat). Neither place has a cover charge and a few drinks from the bar are all you need. The atmosphere at both places is excellent with as many locals present as tourists.

The **Aitutaki Game Fishing Club** (tel. 31-379, VHF channel 16; daily except Sunday from 1600), in a container behind the Ports Authority on the way to the harbor, has cheap beer and is a good place to meet people at happy hour.

PRACTICALITIES

Shopping
In 1995 the **Orongo Center** (closed Sunday) opened in the former banana packing house near the wharf. Aside from the farmers' market, there are several handicraft stalls with bright pareus and beachware.

Phillip and Jan Low run **Aitutaki Handicraft** (Box 77, Aitutaki; tel. 31-127) off the road along the side of the airstrip, 600 meters west of the Aitutaki Lagoon Resort. Jan works with tie dye fabrics, while Phillip carves beach hibiscus *(aue)* into tropical fish, ironwood *(toa)* into tangaroa figures, and mahogany *(tamano)* into slit drums.

Services
Traveler's checks can be cashed at the hotels but it's smarter to change your money on Rarotonga beforehand as the rates here are lousy. Trying to use one of the small banking agencies on Aitutaki can be a real pain.

The post office (weekdays 0800-1600) in the Administration Center opposite the wharf sells local telephone cards (NZ$10, NZ$20, and NZ$50), which can be used for international calls at the public telephone outside (dial 00 for international access). If you need to receive a fax here the number is fax 682/31-683.

Public toilets are behind the Seabreeze Cafe at the Orongo Center.

Outpatients are accepted at the hospital (tel. 31-002) Mon.-Fri. 0830-1200/1300-1600, Saturday 0830-1200, emergencies anytime. Some of the equipment here (such as the X-ray machine) seems to have been left behind by the U.S. military in 1945, so grab a flight back to Raro fast if anything serious goes wrong.

TRANSPORTATION

Because Aitutaki's small population doesn't justify a regular ferry service from Rarotonga, getting here is much more expensive than visiting similar outer islands in Tahiti-Polynesia, Tonga, and Fiji, almost always involving a stiff plane ticket. For flight and boat information see the Cook Islands introduction. **Air Rarotonga** (tel. 31-888, fax 31-414; weekdays 0800-1600, Saturday 0800-1200) has an office at Ureia.

The shipping companies have no local agent, but the people at the Ports Authority (tel. 31-050) near the wharf will know when a ship is due in. Dangerous coral heads and currents make passage through Aitutaki's barrier reef hazardous, so passengers and cargo on the interisland ships must be transferred to the wharf by lighters. The Americans built Arutanga Wharf during WW II. They had planned to dredge the anchorage and widen the pass, but the war ended before they got around to it. Blasting by the New Zealand military in 1986 improved Arutanga Passage somewhat, but it's still narrow, with a six-knot current draining water blown into the lagoon from the south. The depth in the pass is limited to two meters at high tide, but reader C. Webb reports that "the bottom of the pass is sand, so it's a good place to be somewhat aggressive." Once inside, the anchorage off Arutanga is safe and commodious for yachts. This is an official port of entry to the Cooks and the local customs officials readily approve visa extensions for yacht crews. "Having fun" is sufficient reason.

No taxis or buses operate on Aitutaki but there's considerable scooter and pickup traffic along the west coast. Mike Henry (tel. 31-379) does airport transfers at NZ$6 pp.

Rentals
Cook Islands driver's licenses can be obtained at the police office behind the Administration Center in Arutanga for NZ$2.50 and no photo is required (they're also valid on Rarotonga).

The T & M Ltd. gasoline station next to the Ports Authority at the wharf opens weekdays 0730-1630, Saturday 0730-1200.

Rino's Rentals (tel. 31-197, fax 31-559), near Tom's Cottage, and **Swiss Rentals** (tel. 31-600 or 31-223, fax 31-329) both have Suzuki jeeps (NZ$70 for 24 hours), Subaro cars (from NZ$40 daily), motor scooters (from NZ$20 the first day, NZ$15 subsequent days), and pushbikes (from NZ$8 daily). Rino's has a NZ$100 weekly rate for Honda 50s.

Aremati Bicycle Rentals, between Vaikoa Units and the Rapae Hotel, has mountain bikes at NZ$7 a day. Some of the guesthouses and hotels also rent bicycles—all you really need.

The **Samade Shop** (tel. 31-526) at Ootu Beach, not far from the Aitutaki Lagoon Resort Hotel, rents two-person canoe/kayaks at NZ$10 for four hours. They also serve drinks on their white sand terrace (when open). Call ahead if you want a kayak. From Ootu by kayaking you can reach Angarei in 15 minutes, Papua in an hour, and Akaiami in 2.5 hours.

Lagoon Tours

Several companies offer boat trips to uninhabited *motu* around the Aitutaki Lagoon, such as Akaiami or Tapuaetai (One Foot Island) where you can swim in the clear deep-green water, although the snorkeling there is mediocre. Unfortunately the very popularity of these trips has become their undoing as "desert islands" like Tapuaetai can get rather overcrowded when all of the tourist boats arrive!

Some trips also go to Maina, or "Bird Island," at the southwest corner of the lagoon. Only a few tropicbirds still nest on a sandbar called "Honeymoon Island" next to Maina as most have been scared off by marauding tourists and their guides. There's good snorkeling at Honeymoon Island as the fish are fed here. But when the wind whips up the sea it gets hard to snorkel and you miss out on half the fun.

Different tour operators concentrate on varying aspects and the smaller independent operators tend to serve you a bigger and better lunch for a lower price. If snorkeling is your main interest you should find out if they plan to spend all afternoon eating and drinking at Tapuaetai (also great fun). Bishop's Cruises is the most reliable company and they try to run on a schedule. This may be what you want if you have only one chance to get it right, but they're inevitably touristy and the amateur operators you learn about by word of mouth or from notices taped on the walls of the backpackers hostels are far more personal (and less dependable). It's also possible to arrange to be dropped off for the day on Akaiami or Maina for NZ$20-30 pp.

Bishop's Lagoon Cruises (Teina Bishop, Box 53, Aitutaki; tel. 31-009, fax 31-493), inland from Arutanga Wharf, offers lagoon trips daily except Sunday. One trip goes to Maina, another to Aka-

iami, and both continue to Moturakau and Tapuaetai. The Maina trip is the better and to get it you must specifically request a visit to Maina when booking, otherwise they'll only take you to Akaiami and Tapuaetai. Either way, the price is NZ$50 including lunch. **Paradise Islands Cruises** (Box 98, Aitutaki; tel. 31-248) operates the Aitutaki day tour cruises from Rarotonga, and both they and Bishop's are rather commercialized and jaded. Often the cooks can be rather miserly rationing out the fried fish in order to have an ample supply left over for themselves and the boat crews. You'll probably be whisked back to the main island earlier that you would have liked so the daytrippers from Rarotonga can catch their flight.

Tautu resident Mr. Tetonga Kepopua (tel. 31-264), better known as "Tu" and the leader of the local dance group "Tiare Aitutaki", takes visitors to Tapuaetai for a huge fish lunch Mon.-Sat. at 1000 (NZ$40 pp). He also does *motu* dropoffs at NZ$20 pp. **Vaipae Canoe Sailing** (tel. 31-207) offers *motu* trips at NZ$30 pp and exactly which island you'll visit depends on the wind. And if you're on a really low budget you can get comparable snorkeling right off the west end of the airstrip for free. Whatever you decide, take sunscreen and insect repellent.

Reef Tours

Sonja and Tauono (Box 1, Aitutaki; tel. 31-562), who live between Paradise Cove and Vaikoa Units, offer unique reef tours in a traditional outrigger sailing canoe. The NZ$25 pp fee (NZ$35 if you go out alone) includes a light lunch, and they'll prepare any of the fish you catch for an additional fee of NZ$10-25 depending on what you want. You may also take your fish back to your guesthouse and cook them yourself. If you'd like to do any reef walking or fishing with a bamboo rod you must go at low tide; the swimming and snorkeling are better at high tide. Tauono is a sensitive guide more than willing to explain Aitutaki's delicate reef ecology during the four hours the trips usually last. Call the night before to arrange a time. Tauono and Sonja keep the only organic garden on Aitutaki and it's always worth stopping by to pick up some vegetables, herbs, cakes, and fresh fish. Though their prices are higher than the local vegetable market, Sonja will happily spend time with you providing cooking suggestions and general information on their produce and the cuisine of the islands.

ATIU

The old name of Atiu, third largest of the Cook Islands, was originally Enuamanu, which means "land of birds." These days native birds are found mostly around the coast as the interior has been taken over by an influx of mynahs. Unlike neighboring Mauke and Mitiaro, which are flat, Atiu has a high central plateau (71 meters) surrounded by low swamps and an old raised coral reef known as a *makatea.* This is 20 meters high and covered with dense tropical jungle.

The red soil on Atiu's central plateau is formed from volcanic basalt rock and it's rather poor but it was once planted with pineapple to supply fresh fruit to New Zealand. This led to massive erosion and proved uneconomical due to erratic shipping schedules, and pineapples are now

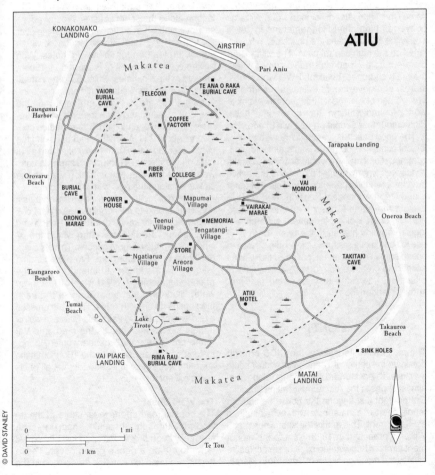

ATIU

© DAVID STANLEY

grown only on a small scale for local consumption (some patches are around the motel). Taro is presently the main cash crop and taro patches occupy the swamps along the inner edge of the *makatea*. The slopes up to the central plateau have been reforested to check erosion. Arabica coffee is grown, processed, roasted, packaged, and marketed as "Kaope Atiu."

Atiu is one of the only islands in Polynesia where the people prefer the center to the shore, and cooling ocean breezes blow across Atiu's plain. Once-fierce warriors who made cannibal raids on Mauke and Mitiaro, the islanders became Christians after missionary John Williams converted high chief Rongomatane in 1823. Today the 1,000 Atiuans live peacefully in five villages on the high central plain. The villages radiate out from an administrative center where the main churches, hospital, PWD workshops, stores, and government offices are all found. The women of Atiu meet throughout the week to work on handicrafts in their community halls. Pigs outnumber people on Atiu two to one.

The good beaches, varied scenery, and geological curiosities combine with satisfactory accommodations and enjoyable activities to make a visit well worthwhile. Atiu beckons the active traveler keen to experience a real slice of outer island life. It will appeal to hikers who want to explore the island's lonely roads, to adventurers who enjoy looking for caves and archaeological remains hidden in the bush, or to anyone in search of a restful holiday and a chance to spend some time on an unspoiled island without sacrificing creature comforts. Atiu has little to offer those interested in scuba diving, fancy resorts, or lagoon trips.

SIGHTS

The massive white walls of the **CICC church** dominate the center of Teenui village. Just south a road leads east toward Tengatangi village from almost opposite the Atiu Administration Building. On the right just beyond the house behind the tennis court is a stalagmite with twin inscribed stones in front. This marks the spot where John Williams preached in 1823. Next to the monument a row of huge stalagmites or stalactites indicates the rectangular site of **Teapiripiri Marae.**

Further south on the main road south into Areora village is the picturesque **Catholic mission.**

The East Coast
The 20-km road around Atiu is best covered in stages. From the motel it's a 15-minute walk down to **Matai Landing** and its white-sand beach. You can swim only if the sea is fairly calm but it's a nice picnic spot anytime. About 800 meters east of Matai Landing you'll come into a partly cleared area where pigs have been kept. Here search for a small trail out to the coast, where two **sinkholes** drain the reef. The lagoon along the south coast is a meter above sea level and when no waves are crashing over the reef sending water into the lagoon the whole lagoon drains through these sinkholes. With nowhere else to go, all of the lagoon fish congregate in the sinkholes, which become natural aquariums accessible to snorkelers. Due to the currents, it's safe to swim here only when the sea is very calm, and even then it's wise to remain on guard for changing or unexpected conditions. About 200 meters further east along the coast is a road down from the interior and a cut through the cliffs to **Takauroa Beach.** In calm weather at low tide you can also walk to the sinkholes along the reef from this beach.

A stretch of reefless shoreline on the northeast coast lets breakers roll right in to the cliffs. Look for the high white sands of **Oneroa Beach** and continue to **Tarapaku Landing** where the islanders keep their dugout canoes. There's a ladder down to the water here. From the landing take the Tengatangi road inland through the *makatea* watching for **Vai Momoiri,** a large water-filled cave that tunnels under the track then opens up on both sides. The route crosses a taro swamp passing **Vairakaia Marae,** a wall of upright stones right beside the road, and **Vai Inano** pool where the legendary chief Rongomatone's 12 wives used to bathe. (Rongomatane later adopted Christianity and forsook all of his wives except the youngest.)

The West Coast
The coastal road up the west shore of the island runs through a beautiful shady forest. A few really huge *puka* trees sport low bird's-nest ferns to create a dense green cover. These leaves are used to wrap fish for cooking in the

umu. **Taungaroro** is the nicest beach on Atiu, and one of the finest in the Cooks, with white sands descending far into the quiet blue-green lagoon, protected from ocean breakers by the surrounding reef. The cliffs of the *makatea* frame this scenic masterpiece.

Orovaru Beach, where Captain Cook arrived on 3 April 1777, is easily identified by a large coral rock that sits 15 meters out in the lagoon. On the island side of the road opposite Orovaru is a stone trail once used by Cook's crew to reach the main settlement of that time around **Orongo Marae,** the most important *marae* on Atiu. Once you're on the trail it's fairly easy to follow, bending right toward the end and terminating at a pig farm on an interior road. This interesting hike offers a chance to view the vegetation on the *makatea* up close. Beyond the pigs, turn right and go about 100 meters south on the road to a track on the right toward a huge Barringtonia or *utu* tree. Orongo Marae is just behind the tree—one of the best preserved archaeological sites in Cook Islands. Cut coral slabs and giant stalagmites form the walls of several rectangular structures here.

Farther north is **Taunganui Harbor** with a striking zigzag configuration, constructed in 1975. Barges can dock here in all weather but large ships must anchor offshore. The swimming and snorkeling in the deep, clear harbor water is good, and if you're here at 1500 you may be able to purchase fresh fish from returning fishermen. Stick to ocean fish, however, since in 1987 the ciguatera toxin appeared in reef fish. Below the cliffs just south of the harbor is the wreckage of the SV *Edna,* a two-masted Dutch sailing vessel built in 1916. One stormy night in 1990 this magnificent metal vessel was wrecked here while carrying cargo to the island from Rarotonga. Fortunately no lives were lost.

Lake Tiroto

According to legend, the eel Rauou dug Lake Tiroto and, when he was finished, traveled to Mitiaro to dig the lakes there. A tunnel runs under the *makatea* from the lake right through to the seashore and you can enter it with a lamp and guide if you're willing to wade through the muddy water. Wear old shoes and clothes, plus an old hat to protect your head from bumping against the cave's sharp roof. Retired schoolteacher

Vaine Moeroa Koronui (tel. 33-046) takes advantage of the visits to catch eels by organizing teams that herd the creatures up dead-end tunnels—a rare experience. Be sure to sign his Cave of Lake Tiroto visitors book.

Rima Rau Burial Cave

This cave near Lake Tiroto is said to contain the bones of those who died in a battle involving 1,000 Atiu warriors. Ask someone to tell you the legend of this cave's dead. Kiikii Tatuava (tel. 33-063) of Areora village can guide you to the cave, with side trips to the lake, taro fields, Katara Marae, and Vaitapoto Sinkhole.

Takitaki Cave

This cave is one of the few in the Cooks inhabited by birds: little *kopekas,* a type of swiftlet, nest in the roof. Their huge saucerlike eyes help them catch insects on the wing. They never land nor make a sound while outside the cave; inside, they make a cackling, clicking sound, the echoes of which help them find their way through the dank dark. Less than 200 pairs of this bird remain and their nesting success is poor. Visitors to the cave should keep at least two meters away from bird nests and discourage their guide from catching the tiny creatures.

Takitaki is in the middle of the *makatea,* east of the motel, a taxing 40-minute hike in from the road. A guide (NZ$15 plus NZ$5 pp) is required. The main part of the cave is large and dry, and you can walk in for quite a distance. Many stalactites, broken off by previous visitors, lie scattered about the floor. The story goes that Ake, wife of the hero Rangi, lived many years alone in this cave before being found by her husband, led to the spot by a *ngotare* (kingfisher) bird.

Keep an eye out for *unga* (coconut crabs) while exploring the *makatea,* and wear boots or sturdy shoes as the coral is razor-sharp. Go slowly and take care, as a fall could lead to a very nasty wound.

PRACTICALITIES

Accommodations

The **Atiu Motel** (Roger and Kura Malcolm, Box 7, Atiu; tel. 33-777, fax 33-775), eight km south of the airstrip, offers four comfortable self-catering chalets, each capable of accommodating four persons, at NZ$90/100/110 single/double/triple. There's also a six-bed family unit at NZ$110 single, plus NZ$10 per additional guest. The minimum stay is two nights. There's hot water but the electricity is off midnight-0500. These A-frame units are constructed of native materials with beams of coconut-palm trunks and cupboard fronts of hibiscus. In your room's pantry and fridge you'll find almost everything you might wish to consume—except vegetables and bread—and you pay for what you used upon departure. For vegetables make the rounds of the three main stores on the island and check the two bakeries for bread (a nuisance as they're far from the motel). You mark what you've used on a stock list and settle up when you leave (normal prices). Otherwise Kura will prepare your dinner at NZ$25 pp and up complete with her famous pavlova (order by 1500). An entertainment evening is staged some Saturday nights in the bar overlooking the grass tennis court. The motel doesn't have bicycles but Roger can arrange rentals from neighbor William Humphreys (tel. 33-041) at NZ$12 per day. Due to the ups and downs of Atiu's roads, motor scooters are more practical than bicycles as a means of getting around and Tauu Porio (tel. 33-050) rents Yamaha 50s at NZ$25. Inexpensive.

A less expensive place to stay is the **Are Manuiri Guest House** (Box 13, Atiu; tel. 33-031, fax 33-032) opposite the bakery in Areora village, 300 meters south of ADC/ANZ Store and on the left. This three-room family house with shared cooking and bathing facilities is NZ$25 pp in a shared room, NZ$50 single or double in a private room, or NZ$66 for a larger family room. There's a lounge and verandah. It's run by Andrea Eimke who arrived on Atiu in 1986 where she operates a small art studio and cafe. Her husband Juergen runs the local coffee factory and tours can be arranged (NZ$10 pp). They hire 18-speed mountain bikes at NZ$10, and return airport transfers are also NZ$10 pp. Budget.

Food

There are three main shops on Atiu and two bakers make bread weekdays and Sunday. **ADC/ANZ Shore** (weekdays 0700-1900, Saturday 0700-0900/1700-1900), in Areora village, may have a few fresh vegetables (cabbage, lettuce, tomatoes, green peppers).

Kura Malcolm runs the **Center Store** (tel. 33-773; Mon.-Thur. 0700-1830, Friday 0700-1930, Saturday 0700-1200/1700-1930), just beyond the CICC church, which dispenses liquor and cold drinks, as well as basic foodstuffs.

A third reasonable grocery store is next to the Air Rarotonga office, a block back from Center Store.

Areora Bakery Ltd. is between ADC/ANZ shop and the tennis court in Areora village. **Akai Bakery,** a bit beyond Atiu College, bakes bread at noon daily except Saturday.

Andrea Eimke's **Tivaevae Café** (tel. 33-027; weekdays 0800-1600, Saturday 0800-1300), at

pineapples galore on Atiu

DAVID STANLEY

the north end of Teenui village, serves excellent cups of Atiu coffee (NZ$2) with homemade cakes. It's pleasant to sit and chat with Andrea, and her **Atiu Fiber Arts Studio** here has women's jackets, dresses, and vests, plus wall hangings in the *tivaevae* quilt style.

Entertainment

Tennis is popular on Atiu and village rivalry has produced no fewer than nine tennis courts (for under 1,000 people). As each village constructed its tennis court it was made a little bigger than the last. The first village had a single netball court; the fourth built two tennis courts, two netball courts, and erected floodlights. The fifth village said it was "all too hard" and gave up.

Atiu won the Constitution Day dancing competitions on Rarotonga in 1982, 1983, 1984, 1985, 1988, 1992, 1993, and 1998 so ask where you can see them practicing. Special performances are held on Gospel Day and Christmas Day.

Bush Beer

Venerable institutions worthy of note are the bush beer schools, of which there are nine on Atiu. Bush beer is a local moonshine made from imported yeast, malt, hops, and sugar. The concoction is fermented in a *tumunu,* a hollowed-out coconut tree stump about a meter high. Orange-flavored "jungle juice" is also made. The mixing usually begins on Wednesday, and the resulting brew ferments for two days and is ready to drink on the weekend. A single batch will last three or four nights; the longer it's kept, the stronger it gets.

Gatherings at a school resemble the kava ceremonies of Fiji and the practice clearly dates back to the days before early missionaries banned kava drinking. Only the barman is permitted to ladle bush beer out of the *tumunu* in a half-coconut-shell cup and the potent contents of the cup must be swallowed in one hearty gulp. Those who've developed a taste for the stuff usually refer to regular beer as "lemonade." The village men come together at dusk, and after a few rounds, the barman calls them to order by tapping a cup on the side of the *tumunu.* A hymn is sung and a prayer said. Announcements are made by various members, and work details assigned to earn money to buy the ingredients for the next brew. After the announcements, guitars and ukuleles appear, and the group resumes drinking, dancing, and singing for as long as they can. The barman, responsible for maintaining order, controls how much brew each participant gets.

Nonmembers visiting a school are expected to bring along a kilo of sugar, or to put NZ$5 pp on the table, as their contribution (enough for the whole week). Guests may also be asked to work in the taro patches the next day.

Airport

A new airstrip (AIU) was built on Atiu's north side in 1983, after the old airstrip on the plateau, built only in 1977, was found to be too small. Roger Malcolm from the Atiu Motel is often there to meet flights (transfers NZ$8 pp each way). He'll give you a bit of an island tour on your way to the motel.

MITIARO

Mitiaro, formerly known as Nukuroa, is a low island with two lakes and vast areas of swampland. Of the lakes, Rotonui is much longer and broader than Rotoiti. This surprisingly large lake is surrounded by an unlikely combination of pine trees and coconut palms. The lake bed is covered by a thick layer of black and brown peat, and the eastern shore is firmer than the western. On one side of the lake is the small, coconut-studded island of Motu. Banana and taro plantations grow in the interior of Mitiaro and a stand of rare Mitiaro fan palms *(iniao)* remains in the south of the island. Like its neighboring islands, Mitiaro has a chronic water shortage.

The People
Before the arrival of Europeans, the people occupied the center of the island near their gardens. Today they all live in one long village on the west coast. The village is neat and clean, with white sandy roads between the Norfolk pines and houses. European-style dwellings predominate, though thatched cottages are still common on the back roads. Four different sections of the village maintain the names of the four original villages, and each has a garden area inland bearing the same name. Because the *makatea* cannot support crops, it's used for keeping pigs or growing coconuts. There are no mynah birds on Mitiaro, so you'll see abundant Pacific pigeons *(rupe)*, warblers, and reef herons.

The fine outrigger canoes of Mitiaro are made of hollowed-out *puka* logs, held together with coconut-husk rope. These are used for longline tuna and *paara* fishing outside the reef. Even from shore you'll see lots of fish on the reef at Mitiaro. From July to December flying fish swarm off Mitiaro for three days during the first quarter of the moon each month and local fishermen in outriggers scoop them up using handnets, returning to shore to unload again and again until every freezer on the island is full. Tradition dictates that it's not allowed to use outboard motors in this fishery or for the anglers to sell their catch but neither rule is followed these days.

Sights
The small church in the center of the village is quite exquisitely decorated. From the church a lane leads past a row of dugout canoes to a landing blasted out of the reef that serves as a saltwater swimming pool for the local kids. At low tide many people fish from the edge of the reef with long bamboo poles.

South of the village cut over to the beach when you reach the graveyard and football field. This long stretch of white sand is the best beach nearby and has many shallow pools in the reef where you can lounge while the tide is out. Walking along the reef at low tide all around Mitiaro is fascinating, and the restless rhythm and flow of the waves beating against the reef at low tide is almost hypnotic. If you're looking for secluded coves, you'll find many around the island.

Around the Island
It's 20 km around Mitiaro but the road across the center of the island offers more variety than the coastal road (no shade on either road, so be prepared). **Vai Marere,** to the left of the road from

MITIARO

AIRSTRIP

Okore

Makatea

Vai Ai

Lake Rotoiti

Atai
Auta

Omutu
Landing

Mangarei
■ Vai Marere

Vai
Nauri ■

Takaue

Lake
Rotonui

Parava

Makatea

Vai
Tamaroa

Te Pito o
■ Kare

TEPARE

Teunu

0   0.5 mi

0   0.5 km

© DAVID STANLEY

Takaue, is an easy 10-minute walk inland from the village. The locals enjoy swimming in the green, sulfur-laden waters of this cave *(vai).* Continue across the picturesque center of Mitiaro toward Teunu. Five minutes before you reach the coast you pass on your left **Te Pito o Kare,** a deep cave containing a pool that was once a source of drinking water for people living in the area.

Turn right at Teunu and follow the coastal road about 600 meters to an ironwood forest on your right. An obvious trail through this forest leads into the *makatea* to an old **Polynesian fort** *(tepare)* that the people of Mitiaro once used to defend themselves against raids from Atiu. Back at the Teunu junction you'll note the upright coral slabs of a small *marae* among the trees and 100 meters east on the coastal road to Parava is another larger *marae* just to the left of the road. Several more are on either side of the road to the east.

It's easy to find **Vai Tamaroa** on the east side of the island as there's a headstone commemorating the Boys Brigade Camp on Mitiaro in April 1985 at the trailhead. It's a rough 15-minute scramble over the *makatea* to this deep water-filled crevice but you probably won't be able to swim due to Vai Tamaroa's steep sides.

Less than a km north of the headstone is Parava with a small golden beach down by the seashore and a road in toward the east side of **Lake Rotonui.** Small, edible black tilapia are abundant, each with a red streak along its back fins. They grow to about 15 cm long and provide sustenance for lake's black eels *('itiki),* The much larger milk fish also found in the lakes are caught by humans for food. The lake water is fresh and clear, although the bottom is muddy. The low-lying surroundings are peaceful and serene, but the mud will make you forget about swimming.

About 600 meters north of the Lake Rotonui road is the access road to **Vai Nauri,** a cool, crystal-clear freshwater cave pool. A stairway leads down to the water's edge and on a hot afternoon a swim here is almost divine. From this pool it's about an hour's leisurely walk back to the village.

Practicalities

Mitiaro receives fewer than 50 tourists a year and there are no motels or tourist cottages. Several families take paying guests and in the past visitors have stayed with Joe and Mikara Herman (tel. 36-153) at the north end of the village, or with Nane Pokoati (tel. 36-107) next to the *ariki*'s house south of the church. Mii O'Bryan (tel. 36-106, fax 36-683) in the second house north of the church also takes guests (but no children).

The Rarotonga travel agencies and Air Rarotonga collect around NZ$65 pp a night including three meals for these arrangements, which makes Mitiaro a rather expensive island to visit, and two nights are quite enough here.

Two small stores on Mitiaro sell canned foods and bread is at the bakery opposite the CICC church.

MAUKE

Mauke, the easternmost of the Cooks, is a flat raised atoll. It and neighboring Mitiaro and Atiu are collectively known as Ngaputoru, "The Three Roots." As on its neighbors, the crops grow in the center of Mauke; the *makatea* ringing the island is infertile and rocky. Both the *makatea* and the central area are low, and you barely notice the transition as you walk along the road inland from the coast to the taro swamps and manioc plantations. Mauke exports bags of *maire* leaves to Hawaii, to be used in floral decorations, and taro is sent to Rarotonga. Pigs and chickens run wild across the island, and many goats can be seen. Thankfully dogs are banned from Mauke.

The men fish for tuna just offshore in small outrigger canoes and the women weave fine pandanus mats with brilliant borders of blue, red, yellow, and orange. There are also wide-rimmed pandanus hats and *kete* baskets of sturdy pandanus with colorful geometric designs. The men carve the attractive white-and-black *tou* or red-and-brown *miro* wood into large bowls shaped like breadfruit leaves. They also carve large spoons and forks, miniatures of chiefs' seats, and small replicas of the canoe of Uke, legendary founder of Mauke, who gave the island its name.

Mauke has the best beaches of the three neighboring islands, but it's too shallow for snorkeling. Coral overhangs provide shade at many of the beaches and in August and September whales are often seen off Mauke. It's a very friendly island to poke around for a few days and a good choice for a prolonged stay.

Sights

The harbor, market, Catholic mission, government residency, and administration building are all at **Taunganui Landing.** The area behind the administration building is known as **Te Marae O Rongo** with a stone circle and a large boulder once used as a seat by the chief. Inland at Makatea village, opposite a store with massive masonry walls, is the two-story concrete palace of the last queen of Mauke who died in 1982. Unfortunately the building is falling into ruins due to squabbles among her descendants. At one end of the taro swamp in the valley behind the palace is **Koenga Well,** a source of fresh drinking water in years gone by.

The **CICC church** (1882) at the hub of the island has an almost Islamic flavor, with its long

DAVID STANLEY

interior of Cook Islands Christian Church, Mauke

rectangular courtyard, tall gateways, perpendicular alignment, and interior decoration of crescents and interlocking arches. Due to an old dispute between Areora and Ngatiarua villages, the church was divided across the center and each side was decorated differently. The dividing partition has been removed, but dual gateways lead to dual doors, one for each village. The soft pastels (green, pink, yellow, and blue) harmonize the contrasting designs, and the pulpit in the middle unifies the two. Inset into the railing in front of the pulpit are nine old Chilean pesos. Look carefully at the different aspects of this building; it's one of the most fascinating in the Cook Islands.

Vai Tango Cave is fairly easy to find. From the Telecom office, go 500 meters northeast through Ngatiarua village and turn left after the last house. The cave is 500 meters northwest of the main road, at the end of a trail along a row of hibiscus trees. A large circular depression with Barringtonia trees growing inside, Vai Tango has a clear freshwater pool under the overhanging stalactites. The locals swim and bathe here. There are large rooms further back in the cave but you'd need scuba gear and lamps to reach them.

A *marae* called **Paepae A,** 50 meters beyond the Vai Tango turnoff, was reconstructed from scratch in 1997. The stalagmites standing on the *marae* platform are two pieces of a single pillar once carried by the legendary chief Kai Moko (Eater of Lizards). Siting on the ground behind Paepae A are four huge stones remaining from Marae Terongo. The origin of these volcanic rocks, unique on this coral island, is lost in the mists of time.

Back in Areora village, visit the woodcarvers who work in the house next to the Catholic church. One of their fine breadfruit leaf-shaped bowls would make a unique souvenir.

If you're still keen, you might wish to try to find **Moti Cave,** a large, open cave in the *makatea.* From the irrigation dam in the center of the island, follow the road south and take the left turn at a point where three roads separate. The cave is beyond the end of this road and you'll probably spend some time searching unless you have a guide. A guide is definitely required to find the freshwater pools of **Motuanga Cave,** the "Cave of 100 Rooms," which is deeper into the *makatea* from here. Limestone growth has made all but the first three rooms inaccessible.

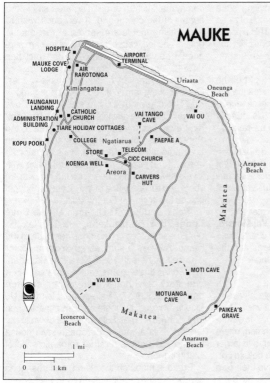

MAUKE

HOSPITAL
AIRPORT TERMINAL
MAUKE COVE LODGE
AIR RAROTONGA
Uriaata
Kimiangatau
Oneunga Beach
TAUNGANUI LANDING
CATHOLIC CHURCH
VAI TANGO CAVE
VAI OU
ADMINISTRATION BUILDING
TIARE HOLIDAY COTTAGES
KOPU POOKI
COLLEGE   Ngatiarua
PAEPAE A
STORE
TELECOM
KOENGA WELL
CICC CHURCH
Areora
CARVERS HUT
Arapaea Beach
Makatea
VAI MA'U
MOTI CAVE
MOTUANGA CAVE
Ieoneroa Beach
Makatea
PAIKEA'S GRAVE
Anaraura Beach

0   1 mi
0   1 km

© DAVID STANLEY

Around the Island

It's only 18 km around Mauke, and no one lives on the south or east sides of the island, so the secluded beaches there are ideal for those who want to be completely alone. There's good reef walking at low tide on the west side of Mauke, but ocean swimming is difficult everywhere. A coral trail just south of Tiare Cottages gives access to a small beach, and south around the point from this beach is a sea cave known as **Kopu Pooki** (Stomach Rock). It's about two meters deep and small fish congregate there.

About 450 meters southeast of Tukune junction, just past the second rock quarry, a trail leads 150 meters inland between the Barringtonia or *utu* trees to **Vai Ma'u**, a deep water-filled crack in the *makatea* with a tall coconut tree growing out. The water is very clear but the opening narrow and steep.

The finest beaches on Mauke are on the south side of the island and the white sands of **Ieoneroa** are just 500 meters

Cook Islands Christian Church, Mauke

DAVID STANLEY

southeast of Vai Ma'u. Also most inviting is the beach at **Anaraura,** where a long stretch of clean white sand borders a green lagoon. This piece of paradise is flanked by rugged limestone cliffs and backed by palm, pine, and pandanus. A short track leads down to the beach.

Two upright stone slabs to the right of the road about a km beyond Anaraura mark the site of **Paikea's grave.** A secluded white beach is just behind. Yet another good beach is found at **Arapaea,** three km north of Paikea's Grave.

At Oneunga, just under two km northwest of Arapaea, two huge stones thrown up between the shore and the road have trees growing out of them. Directly opposite these two rocks is a trail leading across the *makatea* to **Vai Ou,** a series of three caves. You can swim in the first cave's pool, about 800 meters in from the coastal road. A five-minute scramble beyond Vai Ou is **Vai Moraro,** and beyond that **Vai Tunamea.** The coastal road meets the road to the interior villages and the airstrip less than a km west of Oneunga.

Accommodations and Food

There are two excellent inexpensive places to stay on Mauke, both offering some privacy. **Tiare Holiday Cottages** (tel./fax 35-102), a few hundred meters south of Taunganui Landing, offers a duplex unit with two single rooms, two larger cottages with double beds, and one deluxe cottage with double beds. All units have their own fridge but only the deluxe unit has a private bathroom and shower. There's no hot water. Accommodations are NZ$25/35 single/double with the deluxe unit NZ$5 more expensive. If you stay a week the seventh night is free. A separate communal kitchen and dining area sits in the center of the compound. If you don't wish to cook, filling meals are served at reasonable prices, and tea, coffee, and tropical fruit are supplied free. Scooters (NZ$20) and bicycles (NZ$10) are for rent. Your hosts, Tautara and Kura Purea, are very helpful and make you feel like one of the family. If you try to book through Air Rarotonga they'll try to steer you to Cove Lodge (run by the airline's agent on Mauke) and may even claim that Tiare is full. In fact, the Pureas never turn away guests and will even accommodate unexpected arrivals in their own home, if necessary. This peaceful place with lovely sea views has been around for over 20 years and it's easily one of the nicest low-budget places to stay in the South Pacific.

Archie and Kura Guinea run **Mauke Cove Lodge** (Box 24, Mauke; tel. 35-888, fax 35-094), near the sea on the northwest side of the island. Archie's a semiretired Scottish doctor who settled here in 1983; Kura is a Maukean. They offer three rooms with private bath in a one-story coral house with a large covered porch at NZ$39/57/77 single/double/triple. No food is provided, but there's a communal kitchen and lounge. A coral pathway leads down to the lagoon. This attractive European-style house built in 1912 offers a rather romantic style of island living.

Bread is made on the island, and fresh tuna can be purchased directly from the fishermen at the landing. The brown insides of sea urchins, collected along the reef, are eaten raw (the egg cases are the most delicious part—the texture of raw liver and a strong taste of the sea).

MANGAIA

Mangaia is pronounced "mahng-ah-ee-ah," not "man-gaia," as there's no "g" sound in the Polynesian languages. It's 204 km southeast of Rarotonga and just north of the tropic of Capricorn, a position that makes it the southernmost and coolest of the Cook Islands. South of here you don't strike land again until Antarctica. At 52 square km it's also the country's second-largest island, just slightly smaller than Rarotonga. Without soaring peaks or an azure lagoon, Mangaia doesn't fit the tropical island stereotype and it remains an undiscovered tourist destination.

One of the major geological curiosities of the South Pacific, Mangaia is similar to Atiu and Mauke but much more dramatic. A *makatea* or raised coral reef forms a 60-meter-high ring around the island with sheer cliffs towering as high as 80 meters on the inland side. Lifted from the sea in stages over the past two million years, this outer limestone rim has eroded into quite remarkable rock formations with numerous caves hundreds of meters in length, some of them below sea level.

The volcanic earth inside the *makatea* is the only fertile soil on the island; this rises in rolling hills to slopes once planted with pineapples. At 169 meters elevation, Rangimotia is the island's highest point. Forested ridges radiate from this hill with the valleys between them used for farming. Near the inner edge of the *makatea,* where water is caught between the coral cliffs and the hills, low taro swamps are flanked by banana fields and miscellaneous crops. Nothing but bush and coconut palms grow on the *makatea* itself, and pigs are kept there in makeshift pens.

Legend tells how Rongo rose from the deep with his three sons to colonize the island. Captain Cook "discovered" Mangaia in 1777 and Polynesian missionaries followed in 1826. Mangaia was the last Cook Island to accept Christianity, and traditionally, the 1,100 Mangaians have a reputation for being a cautious lot, but you'll probably find them quite friendly when you get to know them. They live in three scattered coastal villages, Oneroa, Tamarua, and Ivirua. The population is static, with some continuing to migrate to New Zealand as others return. The Mangaians speak a language similar to that of Rarotonga, part of the great Austronesian family.

Crafts

Mangaia is represented in museum collections around the world by large ceremonial adzes, which were used to decapitate prisoners taken in battles. The head, right arm, and right leg were regarded as prized possessions because of the mana they possessed. Later the missionaries had the adzes changed to incorporate "steeple stands," reproducing church steeples. This was used to symbolize church authority over the *ariki.*

The yellow *pupu* shell necklaces *(ei)* of Mangaia are also unique. The tiny black *pupu* shells are found on the *makatea* only after rainfall. The yellow color comes from boiling them in caustic soda, though they can also be bleached white or dyed other colors. The shells are pierced one by one with a needle and threaded to make the *ei.*

Sights

A 30-km road along the coastal strip rings most of the island. It's 10 km from the airstrip to **Oneroa,** the main village, where a monument in front of the church recalls Mangaian church ministers and missionaries (such as the Rev. Wyatt Gill who served in the Cooks from 1852-83). If the church is open, enter to see the sennit rope bindings in the roof. On a large stone near Avarua landing are the footprints of the legendary giant, Mokea, and his son; both jumped across the island in a race to this spot. The huge stones on the reef to the north were thrown there by Mokea, to prevent a hostile canoe from landing. The queen of Mangaia still has a large flag given to her grandfather by Queen Victoria.

George Tuara (tel. 34-105) will guide you through **Teruarere Cave** for NZ$20 pp. Used as a burial ground in the distant past, the cave has old skeletons that add a skin-crawling touch of reality. The opening is small and you have to crawl in, but the cave goes on for a great distance. A lamp is necessary. Below Teruarere on the cliff is **Touri Cave.** Use indicators to find

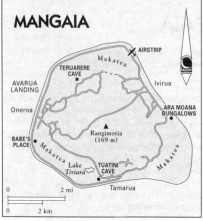

MANGAIA

AIRSTRIP

TERUARERE CAVE

AVARUA LANDING

Ivirua

Oneroa

ARA MOANA BUNGALOWS

BABE'S PLACE

Rangimotia (169 m)

Makatea

Lake Tiriara

TUATINI CAVE

Tamarua

0   2 mi

0   2 km

© DAVID STANLEY

your way back out—be careful not to get lost inside! There are two streams in this cave: one freshwater, the other salty.

An impressive cut leads up through the *makatea* from Oneroa. Follow a jeep track up to the flat summit of Rangimotia for varied views. From the plateau you can follow a footpath back down to Ivirua and return to Oneroa via **Tamarua,** a rather longish day-hike. The church at Tamarua has a sennit-bound roof.

A water-filled cave at **Lake Tiriara** is the legendary hiding place of the island hero Tangiia. Water from the lake runs through the cave under the *makatea* to the sea, and rises and falls with the tide. **Tuatini Cave** near Tamarua village has a huge gaping entrance, but gets narrower to-

ward the back. There's really nowhere safe to swim on the island.

Accommodations

Mangaia offers a choice of three places to stay. **Babe's Place** (Box 6, Mangaia; tel. 34-092, fax 34-078), just south of Oneroa, has six rooms with bath, fridge, fan, and TV at NZ$75/120/150 single/double/triple including all meals (cooking facilities not provided). Four of the rooms are in a long block, the other two in a family house. The bar here gets lively during the Friday and Saturday night dances. Island tours are NZ$40 pp, otherwise it's NZ$20 for an inflatable boat ride on Lake Tiriara. Bicycles can be arranged.

Mangaia Lodge, near the hospital above Oneroa, was closed for several years but reportedly it's reopened. Check with Air Rarotonga. If so, it has the advantage of providing cooking facilities for guests staying in the three rooms with shared bath in this large colonial-style house.

In 1997 **Ara Moana Bungalows** (tel. 34-278, fax 34-279) opened on the coast just southeast of Ivirua village, about five km from the airport. It's run by a Swede named Jan Kristensson and his local wife Tu. There are four tiny thatched cabins with shared bath at NZ$40/55 single/double, and two larger units with private bath at NZ$60/75. Airport transfers are included but add NZ$30-45 pp a day for meals (self-catering facilities are not available). Kawasaki 100 cc motor bikes are rented at NZ$30 a day, while an island tour by jeep or truck is NZ$35 pp with lunch. Bareback horses can also be hired. A nice beach is not far from Ara Moana.

OTHER SOUTHERN ISLANDS

Manuae

This small island consists of two islets, Manuae and Te Au O Tu, inside a barrier reef. The unspoiled wealth of marinelife in this lagoon has prompted the government to offer the atoll as an international marine park. It's said you can still catch large parrot fish in the lagoon by hand. There's no permanent habitation. Copra-cutting parties from Aitutaki once used an abandoned airstrip to come and go, though they haven't done so for years. In 1990 the 1,600 traditional Aitutaki-origin owners of Manuae rejected a gov-

ernment proposal to lease the island to an Australian company for tourism development. Captain Cook gave Manuae its other, fortunately rarely used, name, Hervey Island.

Takutea

Clearly visible 16 km off the northwest side of Atiu, to whose people it belongs, Takutea is in no place over six meters high. The island's other name, Enuaiti, means "Small Island." Until 1959 the people of Atiu called here to collect copra, but Takutea gets few visitors now. There are a few abandoned shelters and a freshwater collection tank. The waters along the reef abound with fish; many red-tailed tropic birds and red-footed boobies nest on the land. Permission of the Atiu Island Council is required for visits.

Palmerston

Palmerston, 367 km northwest of Aitutaki, is an atoll 11 km across at its widest point. Some 35 tiny islands dot its pear-shaped barrier reef, which encloses the lagoon completely at low tide. Although Polynesians had once lived on what they called Ava Rua ("two hundred channels"), Palmerston was uninhabited when Captain Cook arrived in 1774.

William Marsters, legendary prolific settler, arrived here to set up a coconut plantation in 1863. He brought with him from Penrhyn his Polynesian wife and her sister, who were soon joined by another sister. Marsters married all three, and by the time he died in 1899 at the ripe age of 78 he had begotten 21 children. Thousands of his descendants are now scattered around the Cook Islands, throughout New Zealand, and beyond, but the three Marsters branches on Palmerston are down to about 50. Marsters's grave may be seen near the remains of his original homestead.

Like lonely Pitcairn Island where the inhabitants are also of mixed British descent, on Palmerston the first language is English, the only island in the Cooks where this is so. The present population lives on tiny Home Island on the west side of the atoll, and as in any small, isolated community there's some tension between the three families. In 1995 officials from Rarotonga arrived on Palmerston and by playing one group off against another succeeded in undermining the authority of the island council and imposing centralized rule on the islanders.

Fish are caught at Palmerston using a circular net called a *rau* made of coconut fronds. People beat the water's surface with sticks to drive the fish into the net, which then closes upon them. Ships visit Palmerston three or four times a year to bring ordered supplies and to take away parrot fish and copra. Although unable to enter the lagoon, they can anchor offshore.

About a dozen yachts a year call at Palmerston, and since boats drawing over 1.5 meters cannot enter the lagoon, they must anchor outside the reef. Reader Sidsel Wold aboard *Northern Quest* send us this:

As soon as a sailboat is sighted there's a competition among the islanders to see who can get out first in a small boat to meet the yacht. That person's family then becomes the hosts of the visitors on Palmerston. The Marsters family told us that as long as we were on Palmerston we were regarded as Marsters too, and we certainly felt like part of the family. Every day we shared meals with them, joined them on fishing trips, etc. After crossing the Pacific, Palmerston became the highlight of our trip. We certainly didn't regret checking for their mail at the post office before leaving Rarotonga, or bringing cigarettes, magazines, books, coffee, tea, sugar, and fresh fruit. Such goods are always needed. We'd also been in touch with some Marsters people on Raro who gave us bananas and presents to take along. This atoll is certainly worth a stop, although the anchorage can be difficult.

BOB RACE

THE NORTHERN GROUP

The northern Cooks are far more traditional than the southern Cooks. All of the northern atolls except Penrhyn sit on the 3,000-meter-deep Manihiki Plateau; the sea around Penrhyn is 5,000 meters deep. These low-lying coral rings are the very image of the romantic South Seas, but life for the inhabitants can be hard and many have left for New Zealand. Reef fish and coconuts are abundant, but fresh water and everything else is limited. Now a commercial cultured pearl industry is bringing prosperity to several of the atolls.

All of the scattered atolls of the northern Cooks except Nassau have central lagoons. Only the Penrhyn lagoon is easily accessible to shipping, although yachts can anchor in the pass at Suwarrow. Until recently these isolated islands were served only by infrequent ships from Rarotonga, and tourist visits were limited to the ship's brief stop, as to disembark would have meant a stay of several weeks or even months. Now Air Rarotonga has flights to Manihiki and Penrhyn, taking four and a half hours each way.

Anyone desiring a fuller picture of life of the northern atolls should read Robert Dean Frisbie's *The Book of Pukapuka,* serialized in the *Atlantic Monthly* in 1928. Though interesting, Frisbie's book may seem distorted to some contemporary eyes, catering to European stereotypes.

Suwarrow

In 1814 the Russian explorer Mikhail Lazarev discovered an uninhabited atoll, which he named for his ship, the *Suvarov.* A mysterious box containing US$15,000 was dug up in 1855, probably left by the crew of a wrecked Spanish galleon in 1742. Later an additional US$2,400 was found. Early this century, Lever Brothers unsuccessfully attempted to introduce to the lagoon gold-lipped pearl oysters from Australia's Torres Straits. In the 1920s and 1930s A.B. Donald Ltd. ran Suwarrow as a copra estate, until the island became infested with termites and the export of copra was prohibited. During WW II New Zealand coastwatchers were stationed here—the few decrepit buildings on Anchorage Island date from that time.

At various times from 1952 onward, New Zealander Tom Neale lived alone on Suwarrow and wrote a book about his experiences titled, not surprisingly, *An Island to Oneself.* Tom never found the buried treasure he was searching for on Suwarrow, and in 1977 he died of cancer on Rarotonga. Today coconut-watchers serve on Suwarrow to ensure that none of the termite-infested nuts are removed. Officially Suwarrow is a Marine Park, and the caretakers live in Tom Neale's house. A government meteorologist may also be present, and pearl divers from Manihiki and Penrhyn visit occasionally.

Yachts often call on their way from Rarotonga or Bora Bora to Samoa. The wide, easy lagoon entrance is just east of Anchorage Island on the northeast side of the atoll and a 40-meter-long coral rock jetty points to the deep anchorage. There's good holding, but in stormy weather the lagoon waters can become very rough. Though Suwarrow is not an official port of entry, yachts often stop without clearing in at Rarotonga or Aitutaki. Passports must be taken to the caretakers in Tom's house, who also accept outgoing mail (yachties often volunteer to carry mail to/from Rarotonga). The table and chairs outside the caretaker family's home provide welcome neutral ground for whiling away the time.

Of the 25 *motu,* only five are sizable. The snorkeling in the lagoon is fantastic, with lots of shark action—they won't usually bother you unless you're spearfishing. Scuba diving is not allowed. In the past, hurricanes have washed four-meter waves across the island and during one storm in 1942 those present survived by tying themselves to a large tree (see *The Island of Desire,* by Robert Dean Frisbie). Thousands of seabirds, turtles, and coconut crabs nest on this historically strange and still mysterious island.

Nassau

Egg-shaped Nassau is the only northern island without an inner lagoon; instead, taro grows in

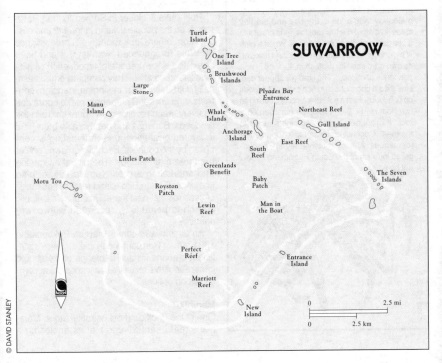

SUWARROW

Turtle Island
One Tree Island
Brushwood Islands
Large Stone
Manu Island
Plyades Bay Entrance
Whale Islands
Northeast Reef
Gull Island
Anchorage Island
East Reef
South Reef
Littles Patch
Greenlands Benefit
The Seven Islands
Motu Tou
Royston Patch
Baby Patch
Lewin Reef
Man in the Boat
Perfect Reef
Entrance Island
Marriott Reef
New Island

0   2.5 mi
0   2.5 km

© DAVID STANLEY

gardens at the center of the island. The American whaler *Nassau* called in 1835. Europeans ran a coconut plantation here until l945, when the government bought the island for £2,000 in order to get it back for the Pukapukans. In 1951, the chiefs of Pukapuka, 89 km to the northwest, purchased it from the government for the same amount and they've owned it ever since. Korean fishermen from Pago Pago stop illegally at Nassau to trade canned foods, fishing gear, and cheap jewelry for love. The children of these encounters add an exotic element to the local population. There's no safe anchorage here.

Pukapuka

An island sits at each corner of this unusual triangular atoll. Because of its treacherous reef, where no anchorage is possible, Pukapuka was

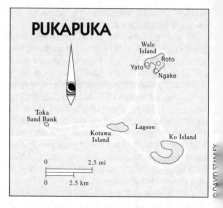

formerly known as "Danger Island." The only landing place for small boats or canoes is on the west side of Wale. Discovered by Mendaña in 1595 and rediscovered by Byron in 1765, Pukapuka was outrageously victimized during a Peruvian slave raid in 1863. Captain Gibson of HMS *Curacao* annexed the island in 1892.

Pukapuka is closer to Samoa than to Rarotonga, so the people differ in language and custom from other Cook Islanders. Three villages on Wale (pronounced "wah-lay") island have coexisted since precontact times, each with its own island council. They compete enthusiastically with each other in singing, dancing, contests, and cricket. The people make copra collectively, each receiving an equal share in the proceeds. Bananas and papaya also grow here in limited quantities; their harvesting is controlled by the councils. Each village owns one of the three main islands. The nicest swimming and snorkeling are off Kotawa Island, also known as Frigate Bird Island for the thousands of seabirds that nest there. Pukapuka's Catholic church is beautifully decorated with cowry shells.

An airstrip was constructed on Pukapuka in 1994 but Air Rarotonga only calls if there's sufficient demand. Their Rarotonga office should know about this as well as any possible accommodation options.

Manihiki

One of the Pacific's most beautiful atolls, Manihiki's reef bears 39 coral islets enclosing a

COCONUT CRABS

The coconut crab *Birgus latro* is a nocturnal creature that lives under logs, in holes, or at the base of pandanus or coconut trees. The females lay their eggs in the sea and the tiny crabs float around a few months, then crawl into a seashell and climb up the beach. When a crab is big enough, it abandons the shell and relies on its own hard shell for protection. Its food is ripe pandanus or coconut. The crab will appear dark blue if it's a coconut eater, rich orange if it feeds on pandanus. First it will husk a coconut using its two front claws, then break the nut open on a rock. It might take a crab two nights to get at the meat. Coconut crabs can grow up to three feet across. Althought tasty, they are endangered in much of the South Pacific and should not be eaten.

LOUISE FOOTE

FIELD MUSEUM OF NATURAL HISTORY, CHICAGO

This 19th-century model of a double-hulled Manihiki sailing canoe is inlaid with mother of pearl.

closed lagoon four km wide that's thick with sharks. The dark green *motu* are clearly visible across the blue waters. Until 1852, Manihiki was owned by the people of Rakahanga, who commuted the 44 km between the two islands in outrigger canoes, with great loss of life. In that year the missionaries convinced the islanders to divide themselves between the two islands and give up the hazardous voyages. In 1889 some disenchanted Manihiki islanders invited the

MANIHIKI

Tukao

✗ AIRSTRIP

Murihiti

Ngake

Lagoon

Tauhunu

Atimoono

Moto
Hakamaru

Motupae

0   2.5 mi
0   2.5 km

Porea

© DAVID STANLEY

French to annex their island. When a French warship arrived to consummate the act, anxious missionaries speedily hoisted the Union Jack, so the French sailed off. The same August Britain officially declared a protectorate over the island.

Mother-of-pearl shell was once taken from the lagoon by island divers who plunged effortlessly to depths of 25-30 meters. Today over a hundred farms on Manihiki produce cultured pearls from the 800,000 oysters hanging on racks below the surface of the lagoon. It's believed that with the growth in pearl farming over the past decade the Manihiki lagoon has already reached its maximum carrying capacity of oysters, and further development here would be disastrous. Unfortunately the money flowing in from this multi-million-dollar industry has eroded the authority of the *ariki* and led to drinking problems.

Manihiki is famous for its handsome people. The administrative center is Tauhunu, and there is a second village at Tukao. Permission of the chief of Tauhunu is required to dive in the lagoon. There's no safe anchorage for visiting ships but with the pearl boom in full swing, Air Rarotonga now flies here twice a week from Rarotonga (1,204 km) and two rooms are now available at **Danny's Bungalow** at NZ$45/75 single/double including meals.

Reader Robert Bisordi of New York sent us this:

We spent nine days on Manihiki and were told by the locals that we were the first tourists ever to stay overnight. Could that be true in this day and age? The difficulty in getting there was considerable. It cost about US$500 each from Rarotonga, and we had to provide Air Rarotonga with the name of the family we would be staying with, otherwise no plane reservations would be given.

Let me say that I have never seen such a happy group of people. We have been to all of the southern Cooks, Samoa, Fiji, and Tahiti, but here we encountered a warmth and happiness the source of which remains a mystery to us here in New York. In extremely tight clusters of homes they live, inescapably sharing each other's noises, emotions, and actions with a tolerance perhaps only possible in a homogeneous society in which so much is tacitly understood and accepted, to the point of resembling a genetic disposition. And the laughter, the giggling—it never ceased! It caused me anguish because it was the affirmation of an achievement that has always been beyond our reach: to be truly happy with so very, very little.

Our host was gracious and tender beyond justification. Of course, not only did we provide some monetary relief for putting us up, we took along pounds of meat, vegetables, and gifts for each member of the family. But I was convinced that none of this was the impetus for our most tender treatment.

Now for the downside. As soon as the aspiring snorkeler descends below the Manihiki lagoon, sharks come at you with the utmost curiosity. I saw at least three species, not to mention the black ones that attack you between the motu *(the* motu *themselves were absolutely gorgeous). Another prob-*

lem was the water situation. Clearly visible in a random glass of water from the cement tanks were little tadpolelike creatures swimming merrily about. This stuff shot through our systems like lightning, and to make matters worse, I contracted dengue fever. I was dehydrating and unable to drink the water, having to get up three or four times in the middle of the night and walk about 300 meters to the reef toilets with a flashlight, under a downpour.

Then, as if matters could not get any worse, there came the news that there may not be enough fuel on the island for our plane to make the return trip. It was all like a surreal nightmare—take the squatting, half-naked, 400-pound islander with torn shorts, bare feet, and a dried ring of taro around his lips telling me that the "contractual stipulations" of the ticket we bought meant the carrier was not obligated to make a special flight for us. I truly thought a squid would be more apt to speak those words than that guy—stereotypers beware!

The prospect of staying on Manihiki, dehydrating to a shrivel, was on the horizon as we waited for the next boat shipment of petrol. And, in typical island torture, I received so much misinformation about the flight that was or was not to be that I became numb until the day of our scheduled departure. Then that day, as if no one had ever said anything at all, it came and took us away, that bird of salvation, right on schedule.

In November 1997 Hurricane Martin passed near Manihiki leaving 19 people dead, Tauhunu village in a shambles, and pearl industry installations above water wiped out. Fortunately, most of the oysters survived. (During the hurricane, officials on Rarotonga tried to restrict media coverage of Martin out of fear that it might have an adverse impact on tourism! The same authorities were strongly criticized for the lack of warning they provided to the islanders and their inept rescue effort.)

Rakahanga

Two opposing horseshoe-shaped islands almost completely encircle the lagoon of this rectangular atoll. Still lacking the pearl wealth of Manihiki, this is a much quieter island. There are several small *motu* that can be reached on foot at low tide. Breadfruit and *puraka* (a tarolike vegetable) are the staples here, and copra is made for export. So that not too many coconuts are taken at one time, the island councils regulate visits to the *motu.* These usually take place only two or three times a year, so as to give nature a chance to regenerate. Coconut crabs, a delicacy on Rakahanga, are mostly caught on the small uninhabited *motu.* Nivano village is at the southwest corner of the atoll. Although unable to enter the lagoon, ships can anchor offshore. An airstrip in the middle of the west side of the atoll was destroyed by Hurricane Wasa in December 1991 and has not been repaired.

An old Polynesian legend explains the origin of Rakahanga and Manihiki. The mythological fisherman Huku caught an island he considered too small to take, so he tied it up to give it time to grow. After Huku left, the demigod Maui happened along and, with the help of a mermaid, finished Huku's work by fishing the island from the sea. When Huku returned, a great struggle ensued, and Maui leapt straight into the sky to escape, leaving his footprints embedded in the reef. His fishhook became the stars, and such was the force of his jump that the island was split in two, forming these neighboring atolls, which were later colonized by Huku's sister and her husband Toa, a warrior banished from Rarotonga.

Rakahanga has a place in the annals of Pacific exploration since it was on this island's reef that the raft *Tahiti Nui* met its end after sailing from Tahiti to Chile and back between 1956 and 1958. The expedition's leader, Éric de Bisschop, died in the mishap after having proved that the ancient Polynesians could have sailed to South America and returned.

Penrhyn

Penrhyn's turquoise 280-square-km lagoon is so wide that you can just see the roof of the church at Tautua from Omoka, the administrative center. The *motu* at the far end of the lagoon are too far away to be seen. The lagoon is thick with sharks, mostly innocuous black-tips; only the black shark is dangerous. The islanders ignore them as they dive for oysters. Now pearl farming is developing with 150,000 cultured oysters already hanging on racks in the lagoon and an oyster hatchery near Omoka is adding to their numbers every day.

Penrhyn was named for the British ship *Lady Penrhyn,* which arrived in 1788, although one of the Polynesian names is Tongareva. The legendary hero Vatea fished Penrhyn up from the sea using a hook baited with a piece of flesh from his own thigh. In 1863 four native missionaries on Penrhyn were tricked into recruiting their congregation for Peruvian slavers at $5 a head and sailed with them to Callao as overseers for $100 a month in the hope of obtaining enough money to build a new church! The blackbirders dubbed Penrhyn the "Island of the Four Evangelists" in gratitude. This tragedy wiped out the chiefly line and Penrhyn is today the only Cook Island without an *ariki.* Remnants of old graves and villages abandoned after the raid can still be seen on the *motu,* and the ruins of an unfinished church crumble away at Akasusu.

The island has a good natural harbor, one of the few in the Cook Islands, and vessels can enter the lagoon through Taruia Passage, just above Omoka, to tie up at Omoka wharf. In 1995 a fuel depot opened here for ships patrolling the fisheries zones of Cook Islands and Kiribati (Penrhyn is closer to Christmas Island than it is to Rarotonga). Development plans by the Rarotonga government have been resisted as various local factions vie for influence. Fine pandanus *rito* hats and mother-of-pearl shell jewelry are made on Penrhyn and visiting yachties can trade kitchen- and tableware, dry cell batteries, rope, and small anchors for crafts and pearls.

American forces occupied Penrhyn during 1942-46 and built a giant airfield at the south end of Omoka about five km from the present village. Aluminum from the wreck of a four-engined WW II Liberator bomber named *Go-Gettin' Gal* was used by the islanders to make combs and not much is left other than three engines near Warwick Latham's house and a fourth engine in the village. Concrete building foundations from the war and from a base camp that supported British and American atmospheric nuclear tests on Christmas Island in the early

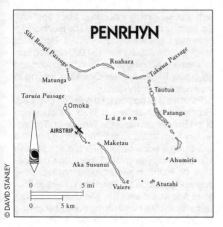

PENRHYN

Siki Rangi Passage

Ruahara

Takuua Passage

Matunga

Tautua

Taruia Passage

Omoka

Lagoon

Patanga

AIRSTRIP

Maketau

Aka Susunui

Ahumiria

0   5 mi

Vaiere   Atutahi

0   5 km

© DAVID STANLEY

1960s can be seen. The waters around the atoll are a rich fishing ground, and Penrhyn is used as a base for patrol boats and planes monitoring the activities of foreign fishing fleets.

Air Rarotonga flies once a week from Rarotonga (1,365 km) to this most northerly Cook island. The airfare (NZ$1,210 return from Rarotonga) is high due in part to an exorbitant landing fee levied by the island council. Soa Tini operates the **Tarakore Guest House** (tel. 42-018 or 42-087, fax 42-015) out of his own home at the center of Omoka village, charging NZ$55 pp including meals. As well, other families take guests and the local Air Rarotonga agent Warwick Latham (e-mail: penrhyn@airraro.co.ck) has a house for rent. Electricity is only available 0600-1200 and 1800-2400.

RESOURCES
INFORMATION OFFICES

REGIONAL

Tourism Council of the South Pacific, Box 13119, Suva, Fiji Islands (tel. 679/304-177, fax 679/301-995, www.tcsp.com; e-mail: spice@is.com.fj)

Tourism Council of the South Pacific, Box 7440, Tahoe City, CA 96145, U.S.A. (tel. 1-530/583-0152, fax 1-530/583-0154, e-mail: HPascal@compuserve.com)

Tourism Council of the South Pacific, 375 Upper Richmond Rd. West, East Sheen, London SW14 7NX, United Kingdom (tel. 44-181/392-1838, fax 44-181/392-1313)

Tourism Council of the South Pacific, Petersburger Strasse 94, D-10247 Berlin, Germany (tel. 49-304/225-6287, e-mail: tcsp.de@interfacetourism.com)

Tourism Council of the South Pacific, 13 rue d'Alembert, F-38000 Grenoble, France (tel. 33-4/7670-0617, fax 33-4/7670-0918)

Tourism Council of the South Pacific, Dirken-strasse 40, D-10178 Berlin, Germany (tel. 49-302/381-7628, fax 49-302/381-7641, e-mail: 100762.3614@compuserve.com)

Pacific Asia Travel Association, One Montgomery St., Telesis Tower, Ste. 1000, San Francisco, CA 94104-4539, U.S.A. (tel. 1-415/986-4646, fax 1-415/986-3458, www.pata.org, e-mail: patahq@pata.org)

Pata Pacific Division, Box 645, Kings Cross, NSW 2001, Australia (tel. 61-2/9332-3599, fax 61-2/9331-6592, e-mail: pata@world.net)

TAHITI-POLYNESIA

Tahiti Tourisme, B.P. 65, Papeete, 98713 Tahiti, Polynésie Française (tel. 689/50-57-00, fax 689/43-66-19, www.tahiti-tourisme.com, e-mail: tahiti-tourisme@mail.pf)

Tahiti Tourisme, 300 North Continental Blvd., Ste. 160, El Segundo, CA 90245, U.S.A. (tel. 1-310/414-8484, fax 1-310/414-8490, e-mail: tahitilax@earthlink.net)

Tahiti Tourisme, 36 Douglas St., Ponsonby, Auckland, New Zéaland (tel. 64-9/360-8880, fax 64-9/360-8891, e-mail: renae@tahiti-tourisme.co.nz)

Tahiti Tourisme, 620 St. Kilda Rd., Ste. 301, Melbourne 3004, Victoria, Australia (tel. 61-3/9521-3877, fax 61-3/9521-3867, www.ozemail.com.au/~tahiti, e-mail: tahiti@ozemail.com.au)

Pacific Leisure Group, 8th floor, Maneeya Center Building, 518/5 Ploenchit Rd., Bangkok 10330, Thailand (tel. 66-2/652-0507, fax 66-2/652-0509, e-mail: eckard@plgroup.com)

Tahiti Tourisme, Sankyo Building (No. 20) Room 802, 3-11-5 Ildabashi, Chiyoda-Ku, Tokyo 102, Japan (tel. 81-3/3265-0468, fax 81-3/3265-0581, e-mail: tahityo@mail.fa2.so-net.or.jp)

Oficina de Turismo de Tahiti, Casilla 16057, Santiago 9, Chile (tel. 56-2/251-2826, fax 56-2/251-2725, e-mail: tahiti@cmet.net)

Office du Tourisme de Tahiti, 28 Boulevard Saint-Germain, 75005 Paris, France (tel. 33-1/5542-6121, fax 33-1/5542-6120, e-mail: tahitipar@calva.net)

Fremdenverkehrsbüro von Tahiti, Bockenheimer Landstrasse 45, D-60325 Frankfurt/Main, Germany (tel. 49-69/971-484, fax 49-69/729-275)

Tahiti Tourisme, Piazza Castello 11, 20121 Milano, Italy (tel. 39-2/7202-2329, fax 39-2/7202-2306, e-mail: staff@aigo.com)

EASTER ISLAND

Servicio Nacional de Turismo, Ave. Providencia 1550, Santiago de Chile, Chile (tel. 56-2/236-1420, fax 56-2/236-1417, www.segegob.cl/sernatur/inicio2.html, e-mail: sernatur@ctc-mundo.net)

COOK ISLANDS

Cook Islands Tourism Corporation, Box 14, Rarotonga, Cook Islands (tel. 682/29-435, fax 682/21-435, www.cook-islands.com, e-mail: tourism@cookislands.gov.ck)

Cook Islands Tourism Corporation, 5757 West Century Blvd., Suite 660, Los Angeles, CA 90045-6407, U.S.A. (tel. 1-310/641-5621, fax 1-310/338-0708, e-mail: cooks@itr-aps.com)

Cook Islands Tourism Corporation, 1/127 Symonds St., Box 37391, Parnell, Auckland, New Zealand (tel. 64-9/366-1100, fax 64-9/309-1876)

Cook Islands Tourism Corporation, Box H95, Hurlstone Park, NSW 2193, Australia (tel. 61-2/9955-0446, fax 61-2/9955-0447, e-mail: cookislands@speednet.com.au)

Pacific Leisure, Tung Ming Building, 40 Des Voeux Rd., Central, Box 2382, Hong Kong (tel. 852/2525-1365, fax 852/2525-3290)

BIBLIOGRAPHY

GUIDEBOOKS

Davock, Marcia. *Cruising Guide to Tahiti and the French Society Islands.* Stamford, CT: Wescott Cove Publishing, 1985. Though researched nearly two decades ago, this large-format, spiral-bound guide is still a must for yachties. Available from Cruising Guide Publications, Box 1017, Dunedin, FL 34697-1017, U.S.A. (tel. 1-800/330-9542 or 1-813/733-5322, fax 1-813/734-8179, e-mail: cgp@earthlink.net).

Hammick, Anne. *Ocean Cruising on a Budget.* Camden, Maine: International Marine Publishing, 1991. Hammick shows how to sail your own yacht safely and enjoyably over the seas while cutting costs. Study it beforehand if you're thinking of working as crew on a yacht. Also from International Marine is Beth A. Leonard's *The Voyager's Handbook: The Essential Guide to Blue Water Cruising.*

Health Information For International Travel. "The Yellow Book" is an excellent reference published annually by the Centers for Disease Control, U.S. Public Health Service. Available from the Superintendent of Documents, Box 371954, Pittsburgh, PA 15250-7954, U.S.A. (tel. 1-202/512-1800, fax 1-202/512-2250, www.cdc.gov/travel/index.htm)

Kay, Rob. *Hidden Tahiti.* Berkeley, California: Ulysses Press. For the person who carries two guidebooks, Kay offers a reasoned second opinion on the top hotels and restaurants of the territory. For Cook Islands, Elliot Smith's *Cook Islands Companion* is recommended.

Laudon, Paule. *Randonnées en Montagne, Tahiti-Moorea.* Les Editions du Pacifique. The French-language guide describes 30 hikes ranging in difficulty from "easy" to "mountain-climbing experience required." For each hike, the author has provided a map, a brief description of the hike, the time required, the altitude gained, and an indication of the type of flora and fauna to be seen. The descriptions can be a little confusing (even if your French is good), yet it's a must for anyone serious about discovering the interior of these islands.

Pacific Travel Fact File. A reliable annual guide to upmarket accommodations all across the Pacific with exact prices listed. Travel agents will find it invaluable. Copies can be ordered from Box 622, Runaway Bay, Queensland 4216, Australia (fax 61-7/5537-9330, www.pacifictravel.com.au).

Parkinson, Susan, Peggy Stacy, and Adrian Mattinson. *Taste of the Pacific.* Honolulu: University of Hawaii Press, 1995. Over 200 recipes of South Pacific dishes.

Ryan, Paddy. *The Snorkeler's Guide to the Coral Reef.* Honolulu: University of Hawaii Press, 1994. An introduction to the wonders of the Indo-Pacific reefs. The author spent 10 years in the region and knows it well.

Schroeder, Dirk. *Staying Healthy in Asia, Africa, and Latin America.* Chico: Moon Publications. Order a copy of this book produced by Volunteers in Asia if you'd like to acquire a degree of expertise in tropical medicine.

Stanley, David. *South Pacific Handbook.* Chico, CA: Moon Publications. Covers the entire region in the same manner as the book you're reading. There's also a *Fiji Handbook.*

DESCRIPTION AND TRAVEL

Bell, Gavin. *In Search of Tusitala.* London: Picador, 1994. A young Scottish journalists' experiences in the Marquesas, Tahiti, Hawaii, Kiribati, and Samoa in the footsteps of Robert Louis Stevenson.

Danielsson, Bengt. *From Raft to Raft.* New York: Doubleday and Co., 1960. The story of one of the greatest sea adventures of modern times: Éric de Bisschop's raft voyage from Tahiti to South America and back, as told by one of the survivors.

Davis, Tom. *Island Boy: An Autobiography.* Suva: Institute of Pacific Studies, 1992. The story of a former Cook Islands prime minister who built an ocean-going canoe in which to sail across the Pacific.

Dodd, Edward. *Polynesia's Sacred Isle.* New York: Dodd, Mead and Co., 1976. An excellent account of Raiatea, its culture and history, based on the author's own researches, together with a vivid account of his many sojourns on the island.

Ellis, William. *Polynesian Researches.* Rutland, VT: Charles E. Tuttle Co., 1969. An early missionary's detailed observations of Tahiti during the years 1817-25.

Finney, Ben R. *Hokule'a: The Way to Tahiti.* New York: Dodd, Mead, 1979. The story of the *Hokule'a*'s 1976 voyage from Hawaii to Tahiti.

Finney, Ben. *Voyage of Discovery: A Cultural Odyssey through Polynesia.* University of California Press, 1994. A complete account of the 1985 journey of the traditional sailing canoe *Hokule'a* through Polynesia.

Frisbie, Robert Dean. *The Book of Pukapuka, A Lone Trader On A South Sea Atoll.* Honolulu: Mutual Publishing. A delightful depiction of daily life on one of the Northern Cook Islands in the interwar period. A 1944 sequel *The Island of Desire* deals with his time on Suwarrow.

Heyerdahl, Thor. *Fatu Hiva: Back to Nature.* New York: Doubleday, 1974. In 1936 Heyerdahl and his wife Liv went to live on Fatu Hiva. This book describes their year there.

Heyerdahl, Thor. *Kon Tiki.* Convinced that the mysterious origin of the Polynesians lies in the equally mysterious disappearance of the pre-Incan Indians of Peru, the author finds that only by sailing some 6,500 km across the Pacific in a balsa raft can he substantiate his theory.

Kyselka, Will. *An Ocean in Mind.* Honolulu: University of Hawaii Press, 1987. Analyzes the learning techniques of Nainoa Thompson, who successfully navigated without the use of modern navigational equipment the recreated traditional Polynesian sailing vessel, *Hokule'a,* during its second roundtrip journey between Hawaii and Tahiti in 1980.

Leimbach, Claire. *Tahiti: Celebration of Life.* Pacific Bridge Publishing, 56 Park Ave., Avalon, NSW 2107, Australia (tel. 61-7/5499-9440, e-mail: bob.e@bigpond.com). A coffee table look at Tahitian culture through reenactments on *marae,* tattooing, dance, and daily life, accompanied by Tahitian songs and poems.

Lewis, David. *We, the Navigators.* Honolulu: University of Hawaii Press, 1994. A 2nd edition of the 1972 classic on the ancient art of landfinding in the Pacific. Lewis' 1964 journey from Tahiti to New Zealand was the first in modern times on which only traditional navigational means were used.

McCall, Grant. *Rapanui: Tradition and Survival on Easter Island.* Honolulu: University of Hawaii Press, 1994. A comprehensive summary of what is known about the island and its current inhabitants.

Neale, Tom. *An Island to Myself.* New York: Holt, Rinehart, and Winston, 1966. Tom's tale of six years spent alone on Suwarrow atoll in the Cooks in the 1950s and early 1960s.

Stevenson, Robert Louis. *In the South Seas.* New York: Scribner's, 1901. The author's account of his travels through the Marquesas, Tuamotus, and Gilberts by yacht in the years 1888-90.

Sutton, Martin. *Strangers in Paradise.* Australia: Angus & Robertson Publishers, 1994. Illustrated stories of famous island visitors from

Captain Cook to Charles Darwin, Paul Gauguin, Marlon Brando, and Malcolm Forbes.

Syme, Ronald. *Isles of the Frigate Bird*. London: Michael Joseph Ltd., 1975. This and *The Lagoon is Lonely Now* (Wellington: Millwood Press, 1978) were autobiographical works by the founder of the former cannery on Mangaia.

Theroux, Paul. *The Happy Isles of Oceania*. London, Hamish Hamilton, 1992. The author of classic accounts of railway journeys sets out with kayak and tent to tour the Pacific.

GEOGRAPHY

Atlas of French Polynesia. Editions ORSTOM, 72 route d'Aulnay, 93143 Bondy Cedex, France. A major thematic atlas summarizing the geography, population, and history of the territory.

Crocombe, Ron, and Nancy Pollock, eds. *French Polynesia*. Suva: Institute of Pacific Studies, 1988. Overview of the history, customs, land, economy, development, migration, media, and politics.

Crocombe, Ron. *The South Pacific: An Introduction*. Suva: Institute of Pacific Studies, 1989. A collection of lecture notes covering a wide range of topics from one of the region's leading academics.

Oliver, Douglas L. *The Pacific Islands*. Honolulu: University of Hawaii Press, 1989. A 3rd edition of the classic 1961 study of the history and anthropology of the entire Pacific area.

Ridgell, Reilly. *Pacific Nations and Territories*. A high school geography text that provides an overview of the region and also focuses on the individual islands. *Pacific Neighbors* is an elementary school version of the same book, written in collaboration with Betty Dunford. Both are published by Bess Press, 3565 Harding Ave., Honolulu, HI 96816, U.S.A. (tel. 1-800/910-2377 or 1-808/734-7159, fax 1-808/732-3627, www.besspress.com).

NATURAL SCIENCE

Bahn, Paul, and John Flenley. *Easter Island, Easter Island*. London: Thames and Hudson, 1992. A well-illustrated study of man's impact on an isolated island environment, and how that led to his degradation. A message from our past for the future of our planet.

Bruner, Phillip L. *Field Guide to the Birds of French Polynesia*. Honolulu: Bishop Museum Press, 1972.

MacLeod, Roy M., and Philip F. Rehbock. *Darwin's Laboratory*. Honolulu: University of Hawaii Press, 1994. Evolutionary theory and natural history in the Pacific.

Mitchell, Andrew W. *A Fragile Paradise: Man and Nature in the Pacific*. London: Fontana, 1990. Published in the U.S. by the University of Texas Press under the title *The Fragile South Pacific: An Ecological Odyssey*.

Pratt, Douglas. *A Field Guide to the Birds of Hawaii and the Tropical Pacific*. Princeton, N.J.: Princeton University Press, 1986. The best in a poorly covered field.

Randall, John E., Gerald Robert Allen, and Roger C. Steene. *Fishes of the Great Barrier Reef and Coral Sea*. Honolulu: University of Hawaii Press, 1997. An identification guide for amateur diver and specialist alike.

Veron, J.E.N. *Corals of Australia and the Indo-Pacific*. Honolulu: University of Hawaii Press, 1993. An authoritative, illustrated work.

Whistler, W. Arthur. *Flowers of the Pacific Island Seashore*. Honolulu: University of Hawaii Press, 1993. A guide to the littoral plants of Hawaii, Tahiti, Samoa, Tonga, Cook Islands, Fiji, and Micronesia.

Whistler, W. Arthur. *Wayside Plants of the Islands*. Honolulu: University of Hawaii Press, 1995. A guide to the lowland flora of the Pacific islands.

HISTORY

Aldrich, Robert. *France and the South Pacific since 1940.* Honolulu: University of Hawaii Press, 1993. A lively view of the French presence in the islands.

Beaglehole, J.C. *The Life of Captain Cook.* Stanford, 1974. A well-written account of Cook's achievements in the context of the era in which Cook lived. Beaglehole also edited Cook's three volumes of journals.

Bellwood, Peter. *The Polynesians: Prehistory of an Island People.* London: Thames and Hudson, 1987. A succinct account of the archaeology of Polynesian expansion.

Buzacott, Aaron. *Mission Life in the Islands of the Pacific.* Suva: Institute of Pacific Studies. A reprint of the 1866 classic in which a long-standing LMS missionary on Rarotonga tells piously of the trials and triumphs of his mission.

Denoon, Donald, et al. *The Cambridge History of the Pacific Islanders.* Australia: Cambridge University Press, 1997. A team of scholars examines the history of the inhabitants of Oceania from first colonization to the nuclear era. While acknowledging the great diversity of Pacific peoples, cultures, and experiences, the book looks for common patterns and related themes, presenting them in an insightful and innovative way.

Gill, William Wyatt. *From Darkness to Light in Polynesia.* Suva: Institute of Pacific Studies. Originally published in 1884, it's a tale of treachery, war, cannibals, exiles, murder, forgiveness, and the calming effect of Christianity by an ethnographer and LMS missionary who worked on Mangaia for two decades. If the moralizing doesn't put you off, you'll find it fascinating.

Henningham, Stephen. *France and the South Pacific: A Contemporary History.* Honolulu: University of Hawaii Press, 1991. This lucid book brings French policy in the South Pacific into clear focus.

Hough, Richard. *Captain James Cook.* W.W. Norton, 1997. A readable new biography of Captain Cook that asserts that Cook's abrupt manner on his third journey may have been due to an intestinal infection that affected his judgment and indirectly led to his death at the hands of Hawaiian islanders.

Howarth, David. *Tahiti: A Paradise Lost.* New York: Penguin Books, 1985. A readable history of European exploration in the Society Islands until the French takeover in 1842.

Howe, K.R. *Where the Waves Fall.* Honolulu: University of Hawaii Press, 1988. A history of the South Seas from first settlement to the beginning of colonial rule.

Lamont, E.H. *Wild Life Among the Pacific Islanders.* Suva: Institute of Pacific Studies, 1994. The account first published in 1867 of the first foreigner to live on Penrhyn in the Northern Cooks.

Langdon, Robert. *Tahiti: Island of Love.* Australia: Pacific Publications, 1979. A popular history of Tahiti since the European discovery in 1767.

Maretu. *Cannibals and Converts: Radical Change in the Cook Islands.* Suva: Institute of Pacific Studies, 1983. Translated and edited by Marjorie Tuainekore Crocombe. The reminiscences of an elderly Cook Islander who personally witnessed the switch from paganism to Christianity, including the destruction of *marae,* breakup of polygamous families, epidemics, and struggles for power.

Moorehead, Alan. *The Fatal Impact.* Honolulu: Mutual Publishing. European impact on the South Pacific from 1767 to 1840, as illustrated in the cases of Tahiti, Australia, and Antarctica. Much information is provided on Captain Cook's three voyages.

Mulloy, William. *The Easter Island Bulletins of William Mulloy.* Los Osos, California: Easter Island Foundation, 1997. A reprint of all of Dr. Mulloy's reports and published papers on Easter Island archaeology.

Newbury, Colin. *Tahiti Nui: Change and Survival in French Polynesia, 1767-1945.* Honolulu: University of Hawaii Press, 1980. Describes major events, while providing many details of the social and economic processes (out of print).

Scott, Dick. *Years of the Pooh-Bah.* Auckland: Hodder & Stoughton, 1991. A history of the colonial era in the Cook Islands.

Stevenson, Christopher, ed. *Easter Island in Pacific Context.* Los Osos, California: Easter Island Foundation, 1988. A collection of 64 papers by 92 authors at the South Seas Symposium held at Albuquerque, New Mexico, in August 1997.

PACIFIC ISSUES

Cizeron, Marc, and Marianne Hienly. *Tahiti: Life on the Other Side.* Suva: Institute of Pacific Studies, 1983. Four lower-income urban Tahitians describe their experiences, and community leaders reflect on what must be done to help the Tahitian poor.

Danielsson, Bengt, and Marie-Thérèse Danielsson. *Poisoned Reign: French Nuclear Colonialism in the Pacific.* Penguin Books, 1986. An updated version of *Moruroa Mon Amour,* first published in 1977. A wealth of background on the former French nuclear testing program in Polynesia.

Dé Ishtar, Zohl, ed. *Daughters of the Pacific.* Melbourne: Spinifex Press, 1994. A stirring collection of stories of survival, strength, determination, and compassion told by indigenous women of the Pacific. The stories relate their experiences, and the impact on them by nuclear testing, uranium mining, neo-colonialism, and nuclear waste dumping.

Maclellan, Nic, and Jean Chesneaux. *After Moruroa: France in the South Pacific.* This timely examination of French colonialism from the French Revolution to the Matignon Accords speculates on France's future in the region in light of the end of nuclear testing and the political changes in Europe. Available from Ocean Press, GPO Box 3279, Melbourne 3001, Australia (tel. 61-3/9372-2683, fax 61-3/9372-1765, e-mail: ocean_press@msn.com.au).

Seur, Han, and Pieter De Vries. *Moruroa and Us.* Published in 1997 by the Centre de Documentation, B.P. 1027, 69201 Lyon Cedex, France. The testimony of 737 Polynesian workers at the former French nuclear test site in the Tuamotus, based on an independent sociological study carried out in 1996.

SOCIAL SCIENCE

Danielsson, Bengt. *Work and Life on Raroia.* Danielsson spent 18 months on this atoll observing Tuamotu life and this book published in 1956 is still the only detailed history of the Tuamotu Islands.

Levy, Robert. *Tahitians: Mind and Experience in the Society Islands.* Chicago: University of Chicago Press, 1973. Levy's study, based on several years of field work on Tahiti and Huahine, includes an intriguing examination of the *mahu* (transvestite) phenomenon.

Marshall, Don. *Raivavae.* New York: Doubleday and Co., 1961. The author, who is a professional anthropologist, did field work on this high island in the Austral group in 1957-58, to find out what was left of the old orgiastic pagan religion and sexual rites.

Oliver, Douglas L. *Native Cultures of the Pacific Islands.* Honolulu: University of Hawaii Press, 1989. Intended primarily for college-level courses on precontact anthropology, history, economy, and politics of the entire region; an abridged version of Oliver's *Oceania,* listed below.

Oliver, Douglas L. *Oceania: The Native Cultures of Australia and the Pacific Islands.* Honolulu: University of Hawaii Press, 1988. A massive, two-volume, 1,275-page anthropological survey.

Oliver, Douglas L. *Return to Tahiti: Bligh's Second Breadfruit Voyage.* Honolulu: University of Hawaii Press, 1988. Offers insights on the inhabitants of Tahiti and their customs at the time of European contact (out of print).

Pollock, Nancy J. *These Roots Remain.* Honolulu: University of Hawaii Press, 1992. Food habits of the central and western Pacific since European contact.

Tangatapoto, Vainerere, et al. *Atiu, An Island Community.* Suva: Institute of Pacific Studies, 1984. Eight residents of Atiu write about life on their island, with many invaluable insights on the traditional culture of the Cooks.

LITERATURE

Briand, Jr., Paul L. *In Search of Paradise.* Honolulu: Mutual Publishing. A joint biography of Charles Nordhoff and James Norman Hall.

Burdick, Eugene. *The Blue of Capricorn.* Honolulu: Mutual Publishing. Stories and sketches about the Pacific by the author of *The Ugly American.*

Davis, Tom. *Vaka: Saga of a Polynesian Canoe.* Suva: Institute of Pacific Studies, 1992. This historical novel's protagonist is a legendary voyaging canoe that sails between the diverse isles of Oceania for 12 generations. The lore of three centuries of Polynesian migration, including legends, customs, navigational and sailing techniques, genealogies, tribal hierarchies, and titles, is encapsulated in this simple chronicle. Prosaic elements such as female offspring, commoners, the passage of time, illness, and failure receive scant attention from Davis.

Day, A. Grove, and Carl Stroven, eds. *Best South Sea Stories.* Honolulu: Mutual Publishing. Fifteen extracts from the writings of famous European authors.

Day, A. Grove. *The Lure of Tahiti.* Honolulu: Mutual Publishing, 1986. Fifteen choice extracts from the rich literature of "the most romantic island in the world."

Hall, James Norman. *The Forgotten One and Other True Tales of the South Seas.* Honolulu: Mutual Publishing. A book about expatriate writers and intellectuals who sought refuge on the out-of-the-world islands of the Pacific.

Hall, James Norman, and Charles Bernard Nordhoff. *The Bounty Trilogy.* Retells in fictional form the famous mutiny, Bligh's escape to Timor, and the mutineers' fate on Pitcairn.

London, Jack. *South Sea Tales.* Honolulu: Mutual Publishing. Stories based on London's visit to Tahiti, Samoa, Fiji, and the Solomons in the early 20th century.

Loti, Pierre. *The Marriage of Loti.* This tale of Loti's visits to Tahiti in 1872 helped foster the romantic myth of Polynesia in Europe.

Maugham, W. Somerset. *The Moon and Sixpence.* Story of a London stockbroker who leaves his job for Tahiti and ends up leading an artist's primitive life that isn't as romantic as he hoped.

Maugham, W. Somerset. *The Trembling of a Leaf.* Honolulu: Mutual Publishing. The responses of a varied mix of white males—colonial administrator, trader, sea captain, bank manager, and missionary—to the peoples and environment of the South Pacific. Maugham is a masterful storyteller, and his journey to Samoa and Tahiti in 1916-1917 supplied him with poignant material.

Melville, Herman. *Typee, A Peep at Polynesian Life.* In 1842 Melville deserted from an American whaler at Nuku Hiva, Marquesas Islands. This semifictional account of Melville's four months among the Typee people was followed by *Omoo* in which Melville gives his impressions of Tahiti at the time of the French takeover.

THE ARTS

Charola, A. Elena. *Death of a Moai. Easter Island Statues: Their Nature, Deterioration, and Conservation.* Los Osos, California: Easter Island Foundation, 1997. Explores the problems involved in preserving the statues and rock art of Easter Island.

Danielsson, Bengt. *Gauguin in the South Seas.* New York: Doubleday, 1966. Danielsson's fascinating account of Gauguin's 10 years in Polynesia.

Gauguin, Paul. *Noa Noa.* A Tahitian journal kept by this famous artist during his first two years in the islands.

Guiart, Jean. *The Arts of the South Pacific.* New York: Golden Press, 1963. A well-illustrated coffee-table art book, with the emphasis on the French-dominated portion of Oceania. Consideration is given to the cultures that produced the works.

Holcombe, Bobby. *Bobby: Polynesian Visions.* Pacific Bridge Publishing, 56 Park Ave., Avalon, NSW 2107, Australia (tel. 61-7/5499-9440, e-mail: bob.e@bigpond.com). Color reproductions of the paintings of this Hawaiian artist who was so influential in the art and music of French Polynesia.

Kaeppler, Adrienne, C. Kaufmann, and Douglas Newton. *Oceanic Art.* New York: Abrams, 1997. The first major survey of the arts of Polynesia, Melanesia, and Micronesia in over three decades, this admirable volume brings the reader up to date on recent scholarship in the field. Of the 900 illustrations, over a third are new.

Lee, Georgia. *The Rock Art of Easter Island: Symbols of Power, Prayers to the Gods.* Monumenta Arqueologica 17. A readable 1992 examination of a fascinating subject. Also recommended are Alan Drake's *The Ceremonial Center of Orongo* and Dr. William Liller's *The Ancient Solar Observatories of Rapa Nui.* These and other excellent publications on Easter Island mentioned herein are available from the Easter Island Foundation, Box 6774, Los Osos, CA 93412-6774, U.S.A. (fax 1-805/534-9301, e-mail: rapanui@compuserve.com).

Seaver Kurze, Joan T. *Ingrained Images: Carvings in Wood from Easter Island.* Los Osos, California: Easter Island Foundation, 1997. A lavishly illustrated study of contemporary Rapanui wood carvings with comparisons to historic pieces.

Thomas, Nicholas. *Oceanic Art.* London: Thames and Hudson, 1995. Almost 200 illustrations grace the pages of this readable survey.

LANGUAGE

Anisson du Perron, Jacques, and Mai-Arii Cadousteau. *Dictionaire Moderne, Tahitien-Français et Français-Tahitien.* Papeete: Stepolde, 1973.

Buse, Jasper, et al. *Cook Islands Maori Dictionary.* Suva: Institute of Pacific Studies, 1995. Incorporates a wealth of knowledge on Cook islands language, culture, and society.

Carpentier, Tai, and Clive Beaumont. *Kai Korero.* Honolulu: University of Hawaii Press, 1996. This Cook Islands Maori coursebook comes with a cassette tape.

Haoa Rapahango, Ana Betty, and William Liller. *Speak Rapanui! Hable Rapanui!* Los Osos, Easter Island Foundation, 1996. A most useful trilingual language-phrase booklet.

Lynch, John. *Pacific Languages: An Introduction.* Honolulu: University of Hawaii Press, 1998. The grammatical features of the Oceanic, Papuan, and Australian languages.

Tryon, Darrell T. *Say It In Tahitian.* Sydney: Pacific Publications, 1977. For lovers of Polynesia, here is an instant introduction to spoken Tahitian.

REFERENCE BOOKS

Connell, John, et al. *Encyclopedia of the Pacific Islands.* Canberra: Australian National University, 1999. Published to mark the 50th anniversary of the Pacific Community, this important book combines the writings of 200 acknowledged experts on the physical environment, peoples, history, politics, economics, society, and culture of the South Pacific.

Craig, Robert D. *Dictionary of Polynesian Mythology.* Westport, CT: Greenwood Press, 1989. Aside from hundreds of alphabetical entries listing the legends, stories, gods, goddesses, and heroes of the Polynesians, this book charts the evolution of 30 Polynesian languages.

Craig, Robert D. *Historical Dictionary of Polynesia.* Metuchen, NJ: Scarecrow Press, 1994. This handy volume contains alphabetical listings of individuals (past and present), places, and organizations, plus historical chronologies and bibliographies by island group.

Douglas, Ngaire and Norman Douglas, eds. *Pacific Islands Yearbook.* Suva: Fiji Times Ltd. Despite the title, a new edition of this authoritative sourcebook has come out about every four years since 1932. Although a rather dry read, it's still the one indispensable reference work for students of the Pacific islands.

The Far East and Australasia. London: Europa Publications. An annual survey and directory of Asia and the Pacific. Provides abundant and factual political and economic data; an excellent reference source.

Fry, Gerald W., and Rufino Mauricio. *Pacific Basin and Oceania.* Oxford: Clio Press, 1987. A selective, indexed Pacific bibliography that actually describes the contents of the books, instead of merely listing them.

Jackson, Miles M., ed. *Pacific Island Studies: A Survey of the Literature.* Westport: Greenwood Press, 1986. In addition to comprehensive listings, there are extensive essays that put the most important works in perspective.

Motteler, Lee S. *Pacific Island Names.* Honolulu: Bishop Museum Press, 1986. A comprehensive gazetteer listing officially accepted island names, cross-referenced to all known variant names and spellings.

BOOKSELLERS AND PUBLISHERS

Many of the titles listed above are out of print and not available in regular bookstores or from www.amazon.com. Major research libraries should have a few, otherwise write to the specialized antiquarian booksellers or regional publishers listed below for their printed lists of hard-to-find books on the Pacific. Sources of detailed topographical maps or navigational charts are provided in the following section.

Antipodean Books, Box 189, Cold Spring, NY 10516, U.S.A. (tel. 1-914/424-3867, fax 1-914/424-3617, www.antipodean.com, e-mail: antipbooks@highlands.com). They have a complete catalog of out-of-print and rare items.

Bibliophile, 24A Glenmore Rd., Paddington, Sydney, NSW 2021, Australia (tel. 61-2/9331-1411, fax 61-2/9361-3371, www.ozemail. com.au/~susant, e-mail: susant@anzaab.com. au). An antiquarian bookstore specializing in books about Oceania. View their extensive catalog on line.

Bishop Museum Press, 1525 Bernice St., Honolulu, HI 96817-0916, U.S.A. (tel. 1-808/848-4135, fax 1-808/848-4132, www.bishop. hawaii.org/bishop/press). They have an indexed list of books on the Pacific; a separate list of "The Occasional Papers" lists specialized works.

Book Bin, 228 S.W. Third St., Corvallis, OR 97333, U.S.A. (tel. 1-541/752-0045, fax 1-541/754-4115, e-mail: pacific@bookbin.com). Their indexed mail-order catalog, *Hawaii and Pacific Islands,* lists hundreds of rare books and they also carry all the titles of the Institute of Pacific Studies in Suva. If there's a particular book about the Pacific you can't find anywhere, this is a place to try.

Books of Yesteryear, Box 257, Newport, NSW 2106, Australia (tel./fax 61-2/9918-0545, e-mail: patbooks@ozemail.com.au). Another source of old, fine, and rare books on the Pacific.

Books Pasifika, Box 68-446, Newtown, Auckland 1, New Zealand (tel. 64-9/303-2349, fax 64-9/377-9528, www.ak.planet.gen.nz/pasifika, e-mail: books@pasifika.co.nz). Besides being a major publisher, Pasifika Press is one of New Zealand's best sources of mail order books on Oceania, including those of the Institute of Pacific Studies.

Bushbooks, Box 1370, Gosford, NSW 2250, Australia (tel. 61-2/4323-3274, fax 61-2/9212-2468, e-mail: bushbook@ozemail.com.au). An Australian source of the publications of the Institute of Pacific Studies in Suva.

Cellar Book Shop, 18090 Wyoming Ave., Detroit, MI 48221, U.S.A. (tel./fax 1-313/861-1776, http://members.aol.com/cellarbook, e-mail: cellarbook@aol.com). Their catalog, *The 'Nesias' & Down Under: Some Recent Books,* includes a wide range of books on the Pacific.

Empire Books, Colin Hinchcliffe, 12 Queens Staith Mews, York, YO1 6HH, United Kingdom (tel. 44-1904/610679, fax 44-1904/641664, e-mail: colin@empires.demon.co.uk). An excellent source of antiquarian or out-of-print books, maps, and engravings.

Institute of Pacific Studies, University of the South Pacific, Box 1168, Suva, Fiji Islands (tel. 679/313-900, fax 679/301-594, e-mail: ips@usp.ac.fj). Their catalog, *Books from the Pacific Islands,* lists numerous books about the islands written by the Pacific islanders themselves. Some are rather dry academic publications of interest only to specialists, so order carefully. USP centers all across the region sell many of these books over the counter, including the one on Rarotonga. For internet access to the catalog, see the University Book Centre listing below.

International Marine Publishing Co., Box 548, Blacklick, OH 43004, U.S.A. (tel. 1-800/262-4729, fax 1-614/759-3641, www.pbg.mcgraw-hill.com/im). Their catalog, *Boating Books,* includes all the books you'll ever need to teach yourself how to sail. They also have books on sea kayaking.

Jean-Louis Boglio, Box 72, Currumbin, Queensland 4223, Australia (tel. 61-7/5534-9349, fax 61-7/5534-9949, www.ozemail.com.au/~boglio). An excellent source of new and used books on the French territories in the Pacific.

Michael Graves-Johnston, Bookseller, Box 532, London SW9 0DR, United Kingdom (tel. 44-171/274-2069, fax 44-171/738-3747). Sells antiquarian books only.

Mutual Publishing Company, 1215 Center St., Suite 210, Honolulu, HI 96816, U.S.A. (tel. 1-808/732-1709, fax 1-808/734-4094, www.pete.com/mutual, e-mail: mutual@lava.net). The classics of expatriate Pacific literature, available in cheap paperback editions.

Peter Moore, Box 66, Cambridge, CB1 3PD, United Kingdom (tel. 44-1223/411177, fax 44-1223/240559). The European distributor of books from the Institute of Pacific Studies of the University of the South Pacific, Fiji. Moore's catalog also lists antiquarian and secondhand books.

Serendipity Books, Box 340, Nedlands, WA 6009, Australia (tel. 61-8/9382-2246, fax 61-8/9388-2728, www.merriweb.com.au/serendip). Carries tand maintains the largest stocks of antiquarian, secondhand, and out-of-print books on the Pacific in Western Australia. Free catalogs are issued regularly.

South Pacific Regional Environment Program, Box 240, Apia, Samoa (tel. 685/21-929, fax 685/20-231, www.sprep.org.ws). They have a list of specialized technical publications on environmental concerns.

University Book Centre, University of the South Pacific, Box 1168, Suva, Fiji Islands (tel. 679/313-900, fax 679/303-265, www.usp.ac.fj/~bookcentre). An excellent source of books written and produced in the South Pacific itself. Check out their site.

University of Hawaii Press, 2840 Kolowalu St., Honolulu, HI 96822-1888, U.S.A. (tel. 1-888/847-7377 or 1-808/956-8255, fax 1-808/988-

6052, www2.hawaii.edu/uhpress). Their annual *Hawaii and the Pacific* catalog is well worth requesting if you're trying to build a Pacific library.

MAP PUBLISHERS

Defense Mapping Agency, Nautical Charts and Publications, Public Sale: Region 8, Oceania. NOAA Distribution Division N/ACC3, National Ocean Service, Riverdale, MD 20737-1199, U.S.A. (tel. 1-800/638-8972 or 1-301/436-8301, fax 1-301/436-6829, www.noaa.gov). A complete index and order form for nautical charts of the Pacific.

Liste des Cartes Disponibles. Service de l'Urbanisme, 11 rue du Commandant Destremeau, B.P. 866, 98713 Papeete, Tahiti. The main source of recent topographical maps of Tahiti-Polynesia.

Reference Map of Oceania. Honolulu: University of Hawaii Press, 1995. A most useful double-sided map of the Pacific by James A. Bier.

PERIODICALS

Ben Davison's In Depth. Box 1658, Sausalito, CA 94966, U.S.A. (www.undercurrent.org). A monthly consumer protection-oriented newsletter for serious scuba divers. Unlike virtually every other diving publication, *In Depth* accepts no advertising or free trips, which allows Ben to tell it as it is.

Center for South Pacific Studies Newsletter. Centre for South Pacific Studies, University of New South Wales, Kensington, NSW 2052, Australia (tel. 61-2/9385-3386, fax 61-2/9313-6337, www.arts.unsw.edu.au/Centres/South-Pacific/homepage.html, e-mail: J.Lodewijks@unsw.EDU.AU). A publication that catalogs scholarly conferences, events, activities, news, employment opportunities, courses, scholarships, and publications across the region.

Commodores' Bulletin. Seven Seas Cruising Assn., 1525 South Andrews Ave., Ste. 217, Fort Lauderdale, FL 33316, U.S.A. (tel. 1-954/463/2431, fax 1-954/463-7183, www.ssca.org, e-mail: SSCA1@ibm.net; US$53 a year worldwide by airmail). This monthly bulletin is chock-full of useful information for anyone wishing to tour the Pacific by sailing boat. All Pacific yachties and friends should be Seven Seas members!

The Contemporary Pacific. University of Hawaii Press, 2840 Kolowalu St., Honolulu, HI 96822, U.S.A. (tel. 1-808/956-8833, fax 1-808/988-6052, www2.hawaii.edu/uhpress, e-mail: uhpjourn@hawaii.edu, published twice a year, US$35 a year). Publishes a good mix of articles of interest to both scholars and general readers; the country-by-country "Political Review" in each number is a concise summary of events during the preceding year. The "Dialogue" section offers informed comment on the more controversial issues in the region, while recent publications on the islands are examined through book reviews. Those interested in current topics in Pacific island affairs should check recent volumes for background information.

Environment Newsletter. The quarterly newsletter of the South Pacific Regional Environment Program, Box 240, Apia, Samoa (tel. 685/21-929, fax 685/20-231, www.sprep.org.ws). Back issues are available for viewing on their website.

Europe-Pacific Solidarity Bulletin. Published monthly by the European Center for Studies Information and Education on Pacific Issues, Box 151, 3700 AD Zeist, The Netherlands (tel. 31-30/692-7827, fax 31-30/692-5614, www.antenna.nl/ecsiep, e-mail: ecsiep@antenna.nl).

German Pacific Society Bulletin. Dr. Freidrich Steinbauer, Feichtmayr Strasse 25, D-80992 München, Germany (tel. 49-89/151158, fax 49-89/151833). At DM 90 a year, Society membership is a good way for German speakers to keep in touch. News bulletins in English and German are published four to six times a year, and study tours to various Pacific destinations are organized annually.

Islands Business. Box 12718, Suva, Fiji Islands (tel. 679/303-108, fax 679/301-423, e-mail: subs@ibi.com.fj; annual airmailed subscription A$35 to Australia, NZ$55 to New Zealand, US$45 to North America, US$55 to Europe). A monthly newsmagazine with in-depth coverage of political and economic trends in the Pacific. It's more opinionated than *Pacific Islands Monthly* and even has a gossip section that is an essential weather vane for anyone doing business in the region. Travel and aviation news gets some prominence, and subscribers also receive the informative quarterly magazine *South Pacific Tourism.*

Journal of Pacific History. Division of Pacific and Asian History, RSPAS, Australian National University, Canberra, ACT 0200, Australia (tel. 61-2/6249-3140, fax 61-2/6249-5525, http://coombs.anu.edu.au/Depts/RSPAS/PAH/index.html). Since 1966 this publication has provided reliable scholarly information on the Pacific. Outstanding.

Journal of Pacific Studies. School of Social and Economic Development, University of the South Pacific, Box 1168, Suva, Fiji Islands (tel. 679/314-900, fax 679/301-487). Focuses on regional developments from a social sciences perspective.

Journal of the Polynesian Society. Department of Maori Studies, University of Auckland, Private Bag 92019, Auckland, New Zealand (tel. 64-9/373-7999, extension 7463, fax 64-9/3737409, www2.waikato.ac.nz/ling/PS/journal.html). Established in 1892, this quarterly journal contains a wealth of material on Pacific cultures past and present written by scholars of Pacific anthropology, archaeology, language, and history.

National Geographic. Dig out the June 1997 issue of this popular American magazine for an informative article on Tahiti-Polynesia.

Pacific Arts. Pacific Arts Association, c/o Dr. Michael Gunn, PAA Secretary/Treasurer, c/o A.A.O.A., The Metropolitan Museum of Art, 1000 Fifth Ave., New York, NY 10028-0198, U.S.A. (tel. 1-212/650-2209, fax 1-212/396-5039). For US$40 PAA membership, one will receive their annual magazine "devoted to the study of all the arts of Oceania" and intermittent newsletter.

Pacific Islands Monthly. Box 1167, Suva, Fiji Islands (tel. 679/304-111, fax 679/303-809, www.pim.com.fj, e-mail: fijitimes@is.com.fj; annual subscription A$40 to Australia, A$45 to New Zealand, US$40 to North America, and A$60 to Europe). Founded in Sydney by R.W. Robson in 1930, *PIM* is the granddaddy of regional magazines. In June 1989 the magazine's editorial office moved from Sydney to Suva and it's now part of the same operation that puts out *The Fiji Times.* Sadly, star columnists Roman Grynberg and David North recently left the magazine.

Pacific Magazine. Box 25488, Honolulu, HI 96825, U.S.A. (tel. 1-808/377-5335, fax 1-808/373-3953, www.pacificmagazine.com; every other month; US$15 a year surface mail, US$27 airmail to the U.S., US$39 airmail elsewhere). This business-oriented newsmagazine, published in Hawaii since 1976, will keep you up to date on what's happening in the South Pacific and Micronesia. The format is built around pithy little news bites on people and events rather than the longer background articles one finds in the other regional magazines.

Pacific News Bulletin. Pacific Concerns Resource Center, Box 803, Glebe, NSW 2037, Australia (tel./fax 61-2/9571-9039, e-mail: pacificnews@bigpond.com; A$15 a year in Australia, A$30 a year elsewhere). A 16-page monthly newsletter with up-to-date information on nuclear, independence, environmental, and political questions.

Pacific Studies. Box 1979, BYU-HC, Laie, HI 96762-1294, U.S.A. (tel. 1-808/293-3665, fax 1-808/293-3664, websider.byuh.edu/departments/ips, e-mail: robertsd@byuh.edu, quarterly, US$30 a year). Funded by the Polynesian Cultural Center and published by Hawaii's Brigham Young University.

Pacifica. Quarterly journal of the Pacific Islands Study Circle (John Ray, 24 Woodvale Ave., London SE25 4AE, United Kingdom, http://dspace.dial.pipex.com/jray/pisc.html, e-mail: jray@dial.pipex.com). This philatelic journal is exclusively concerned with stamps and the postal history of the islands.

Rapa Nui Journal. Box 6774, Los Osos, CA 93412-6774, U.S.A. (fax 1-805/534-9301, e-mail: rapanui@compuserve.com; quarterly, US$30 a year in North America, US$40 elsewhere). An interesting mix of scholarly reports and local news of interest to Rapanuiphiles. The June 1998 issue includes a fascinating study of Palmerston Island in the Cooks.

South Sea Digest. Box 4245, Sydney, NSW 2001, Australia (tel. 61-2/9288-1708, fax 61-2/9288-3322, A$150 a year in Australia, A$175 overseas). A private newsletter on political and economic matters, published every other week. It's a good way of keeping abreast of developments in commerce and industry.

Surf Report. Box 1028, Dana Point, CA 92629, U.S.A. (tel. 1-949/496-5922, fax 1-949/496-7849, www.surfermag.com; US$35 a year). Each month this newsletter provides a detailed analysis of surfing conditions at a different destination. Back issues on specific countries are available, including a 14-issue "South Pacific Collection" at US$50 (the last issue on Tahiti was 6#4 and on Tubuai 15#5). This is your best source of surfing information by far, and the same people also put out the glossy *Surfer Magazine* (US$25 a year).

Tahiti Pacifique. Alex Duprell, B.P. 368, 98728 Moorea (tel. 689/56-28-94, fax 689/56-30-07, www.tahitiweb.com/f/info, e-mail: tahitipm@mail.pf). For those who read French, this monthly magazine offers a style of informed and critical commentary quite unlike that seen in the daily press of the French territories.

Tahiti Today. Jan Prince, B.P. 887, 98713 Papeete, Tahiti (tel. 689/42-68-50, fax 689/42-33-56, subscriptions US$34 a year to North America). A newsy monthly magazine published by the same people who put out the *Tahiti Beach Press.*

Tok Blong Pasifik. South Pacific Peoples Foundation of Canada, 1921 Fernwood Rd., Victoria, BC V8T 2Y6, Canada (tel. 250/381-4131, fax 250/388-5258, www.sppf.org, e-mail: sppf@sppf.org; C$25 a year in Canada, US$25 elsewhere). This lively quarterly of news and views focuses on regional environmental, development, human rights, and disarmament issues.

Washington Pacific Report. Fred Radewagen, Box 26142, Alexandria, VA 22313, U.S.A. (tel. 1-703/519-7757, fax 1-703/548-0633, e-mail: piwowpr@erols.com; published twice a month, US$164 a year domestic, US$189 outside U.S. postal zones). An insider's newletter highlighting U.S. interests in the insular Pacific.

WorldViews. 1515 Webster St., No. 305, Oakland, CA 94612-3355, U.S.A. (tel. 1-510/451-1742, fax 1-510/835-9631, www.igc.org/worldviews, e-mail: worldviews@igc.org, subscription US$25 to the U.S. and Canada, US$45 overseas). A quarterly review of books, articles, audiovisual materials, and organizations involved with development issues in the third world.

OTHER RESOURCES

DISCOGRAPHY

Music lovers will be pleased to hear that authentic Pacific music is readily available on compact disc. In compiling this selection we've tried to list non-commercial recordings that are faithful to the traditional music of the islands as it exists today. Island music based on Western pop has been avoided. Most of the CDs below can be ordered through specialized music shops; otherwise write directly to the publishers.

Bagès, Gérard, ed. *Chants de L'Ile de Pâques* (92553-2). Buda Musique, 188 boulevard Voltaire, 75011 Paris, France (tel. 33-1/4024-0103). Sixteen traditional songs from Easter Island, in the collection "Musique du Monde" (recording date not provided).

Coco's Temaeva (S 65808). Manuiti Productions, B.P. 755, 98713 Papeete, Tahiti (fax 689/43-27-24). Founded by Coco Hotahota in 1962, Temaeva has won more prizes at the annual Heiva i Tahiti festivals than any other professional dance troupe.

Cook Islands National Arts Theater (CD MANU 1447). The drums, songs, and chants of the Cook Islands produced by Ode Record Company, Auckland (recording date not provided).

Fanshawe, David, ed. *Heiva i Tahiti: Festival of Life* (EUCD/MC 1238). Fanshawe has captured the excitement of Tahiti's biggest festival in these pieces recorded live in Papeete in 1982 and 1986. Famous groups led by Coco Hotahota, Yves Roche, Irma Prince, and others are represented. Order from ARC Music Inc., Box 2453, Clearwater, FL 33757-2453, U.S.A. (tel. 1-727/447-3755, fax 1-727/447-3820, www. arcmusic.co.uk, e-mail: arcamerica@ij. net), or Fanshawe One World Music (Box 574, Marlborough, Wilts, SN8 2SP, United Kingdom (tel. 44-1672/520211, fax 44-1672/ 521151, e-mail: fanshaweuk@mcmail. com).

Fanshawe, David, ed. *Spirit of Polynesia* (CD-SDL 403). Saydisc Records, Chipping Manor, The Chipping, Wotton-U-Edge, Glos. GL12 7AD, United Kingdom (tel. 44-1453/845-036, fax 44-1453/521-056, www.qualiton.com, e-mail: Saydisc@aol.com). An anthology of the music of 12 Pacific countries recorded between 1978 and 1988. Over half the pieces are from Tahiti-Polynesia and Cook Islands.

Holcomb, Bobby. *Bobby* (OCN CD 15). Océane Production, B.P. 3247, 98713 Papeete, Tahiti (tel. 689/42-69-00, fax 689/43-30-24). A collection of songs recorded on Tahiti by the late Hawaiian artist/musician Bobby Holcomb. A happy combination of traditional music and pop.

Linkels, Ad, and Lucia Linkels, eds. *Te Kuki 'Airani* (PAN 2099CD). The songs, rhythms, and dances of the Cook Islands recorded on Rarotonga and Atiu in 1992. The opening of the National Cultural Center at Avarua provided a unique opportunity to capture the diverse musical genre of the group. This and the other PAN Records compact disc listed below form part of the series "Anthology of Pacific Music" and extensive booklets explaining the music come with the records. Music stores can order PAN compact discs through Arhoolie, 10341 San Pablo Ave., El Cerrito, CA 94530, U.S.A. (tel. 1-510/525-7471, fax 1-510/525-1204).

Linkels, Ad, and Lucia Linkels, eds. *Te Pito O Te Henua* (PAN 2077CD). Thirty-two tracks of songs and dances of Easter Island recorded in 1995.

Music of Polynesia in the series "World Sounds" produced by Victor Entertainment, Inc., Tokyo, Japan, and distributed in the U.S. by JVC Music, Inc., 3800 Barham Blvd., Ste. 305, Los Angeles, CA 90068, U.S.A. (tel. 1-213/878-0101, fax 1-213/878-0202). This four-record services includes Vol. I (VICG 5271), with the music of Tahiti and the other Society Islands,

Vol. II (VICG 5272), music of the Tuamotu and Austral islands, Vol. III (VICG 5273), music of Easter Island and the Marquesas Islands, and Vol. IV (VICG 5274), music of Samoa and Tonga.

Nabet-Meyer, Pascal, ed. *The Tahitian Choir, Vol. I* (Triloka Records 7192-2). Triloka Records, 2415 Princeton Dr. NE, Suite L, Albuquerque, NM 87107, U.S.A. (tel. 1-800/578-44419, www.triloka.com). Recorded at Rapa Iti in 1991.

Nabet-Meyer, Pascal, ed. *The Tahitian Choir, Vol. II* (Shanachie 64055). Choral singing and chanting from Rapa Iti in the Austral Group (recording date not provided).

South Pacific Drums (PS 65066). Manuiti Productions, B.P. 755, 98713 Papeete, Tahiti (fax 689/43-27-24). A compilation of 39 of the best percussion recordings in Manuiti's archives—an excellent introduction to the traditional music of Polynesia.

Tumuenua Dance Group, *Cook Island Drums, Chants, and Songs* (CD VOY 1335). A 1991 release by Ode Record Company, Auckland, New Zealand. An outstanding selection of traditional Cook Island music. Distributed through the PAN network previously mentioned.

USEFUL INTERNET SITES

Aranui, Freighter to Paradise
www.aranui.com
When the awards are distributed for South Pacific websites, aranui.com will certainly be shortlisted. Viewers are taken taken to each of the ship's 17 ports of call, and clear schedule, price, and booking information is provided. It really makes you want to go.

Chris Davis' French Polynesia
www.cd-enterprises.com/french_polynesia
This commercial site is great for web surfing and it leads to a wide variety of sites, some just advertising but many full of specific information. The currency exchange rate is updated daily. Bookmark it right away!

Cook Islands News Online
www.cinews.co.ck
The best stories of the week from Rarotonga's daily paper, including local news, features, editorials, business, letters, and sports. It's an easy way of keeping up on political developments.

Cook Islands Business and Tourism
http://cookpages.com
Jim Bruce's Hawaii-based site is outstanding for its mix of useful tourist information and handy links. Check here for airfares, packages, resort prices, house rentals, events, etc.

Easter Island Home Page
www.netaxs.com/~trance/rapanui.html
Aside from the abundant links to everything associated with Easter Island, this site is entertaining to read.

France in Australia
www.france.net.au
An excellent source of links from the French perspective with many related to Tahiti.

La Dépêche de Tahiti
www.la-depeche-de-tahiti.com
Surprisingly, this French-language daily newspaper site provides mostly tourist information rather than news. It's better edited than some of the other tourist sites and occasionally discloses aspects not dealt with in official English-language publications.

Maui Pearls
www.mauipearls.co.ck
A buyers guide with good general information on the black pearls of Cook Islands.

Philatelic Center of Tahiti
www.tahiti-postoffice.com
The site of the Philatelic Bureau is appealing for the varied background information provided on local stamp issues and telephone cards. If you're curious about the arrival of the gospel in Polynesia, Tahitian music, seashells of Polynesia, the return of the Pacific Battalion, etc., look here. The site is bright and orderly—a pleasure to use.

Stars Travel Rarotonga
www.stars.co.ck
It's unlikely you'll find a more comprehensive price list of Cook Islands travel arrangements than this. Their New Zealand dollar rates are similar to what you'd pay locally and there's an online booking form.

Tahiti Black Pearl
www.tahiti-blackpearls.com
The site of GIE Perles de Tahiti contains excellent background on the black pearl industry and is certainly well worthy studying if you were thinking of buying a pearl. It's not just a sales pitch—plenty of technical information is there.

Tahiti.com
www.tahiti.com
Although heavy on advertising and weak on information, tahiti.com does provide a weekly news summary and a link to a local weather report from *USA Today*. Their Tahiti "yellow pages" may be the closest you'll come to an e-mail directory for the territory but check both the English and French versions as they're not consistent.

Tahiti Explorer
www.tahiti-explorer.com
Surprisingly, tahiti-explorer.com is a better source of tourist office-style information than the official Tahiti Tourisme site. You can learn about the black pearls, cruises, diving, flights, hotels, the weather, etc. There's a reader's forum, videos and music to download, and it's all regularly updated too.

Tahiti Invest
www.tahiti-invest.com
Anyone interested in doing business in Tahiti-Polynesia should look here. There's a wealth of investment information and background on local companies, plus an intriguing real estate section should you wish to own a piece of paradise.

Tahiti Nui Travel
www.tahiti-nui.com
Travel agents should check this very informative site for facts about the upmarket tourist facilities of the area. If you want to charter a yacht or book a cruise, look here. The current exchange rate of the Pacific franc is provided on the General Remarks page. Another nice feature is the section on Tahitian music with an opportunity to order compact discs.

Tahiti Pacifique
www.tahitiweb.com/f/info
The site of *Tahiti Pacifique,* a monthly magazine providing a lively commentary on economic, social, and political events in the territory. The monthly news summaries are a useful record and lead editorials are posted. It's available only in French.

Tahiti Vacations
www.tahitivacation.com
Air Tahiti's package tour wing provides good information on upmarket tours and tourist facilities with exact prices in U.S. dollars. It's well worth checking as a bottom line if you were planning to make advance bookings.

Tahiti Web
www.tahitiweb.com
This search engine calls itself the "Internet Guide to Tahiti and its Islands Web Sites." Indeed, tahitiweb.com gives access to many fascinating sites, including Joe Russell's excellent *Cruising Guide to the Marquesas Islands* under the "Cruises" heading. If you're concerned about the weather you'll find data here. It's also worth checking for upmarket travel information but be prepared for empty categories and links that don't work.

The Cook Islands
www.cook-islands.com
The official Cook Islands Tourism Corporation site can be rather annoying due to the small screen and constant switching back and forth. Their brochure-style information is uneven and the links irrelevant—hopefully improvements are on the way.

The Islands of Tahiti
www.tahiti-tourisme.com
This government-run tourist office's site contains mostly a posting of their standard brochures, unfortunately without specific prices. It's okay for basic information but you can't make bookings and much of it is out of date.

The Weather Underground
www.wunderground.com
Weather Underground's "Islands" section provides detailed two-day weather forecasts on nine islands in Tahiti-Polynesia and five in the Cooks, plus worldwide hurricane tracking. For Easter Island go to www.weatherlabs.com/city.htm and look under "South America." The same site has Tahiti-Polynesia under "New Zealand."

Welcome to Paradise
www.ck
An online Cook Islands travel guide with detailed descriptions of the 15 islands, accommodation prices in U.S. dollars, weekly news summaries, investment information, recommended reading lists, and a bulletin board. The two e-mail directories are excellent.

WEBSITE DIRECTORY

Tahiti-Polynesia
Aranui Cruises, California
www.aranui.com

Archipels Croisieres, Moorea
www.archipels.com

Bali Hai Hotels, Moorea
www.balihaihotels.com

Bora Bora Lagoon Resort
www.orient-expresshotels.com

Chris Davis
www.cd-enterprises.com/french_polynesia

Club Méditerranée
www.clubmed.com

Dolphin Quest, Moorea
www.dolphinquest.org

Government of France
www.outre-mer.gouv.fr/domtom

Hôtel Bora Bora
www.amanresorts.com

Iaora Tahiti Ecotours
www.iaora.com

Le Méridien Hotels, Tahiti
www.lemeridien-tahiti.com

Mana Internet Provider, Papeete
www.mana.pf

Office des Postes, Papeete
www.opt.pf

Outrigger Hotels of Hawaii
www.pacificinfoweb.com

Pacific Asia Travel Association
www.pata.org

Parkroyal Hotels
www.tahiti-resorts.com

Perles de Tahiti, Papeete
www.tahiti-blackpearls.com

Philatelic Bureau, Papeete
www.tahiti-postoffice.com

Radisson Seven Seas Cruises
www.rssc.com

Renaissance Cruises
www.renaissancecruises.com

Tahiti Communications Inc., Tahiti
www.tahiti.com

Tahiti Explorer, Los Angeles
www.tahiti-explorer.com

Tahiti Friendship Society, California
www.tahitinet.com

Tahiti Nui Travel, Papeete
www.tahiti-nui.com

Tahiti's Internet Guide
www.tahitiweb.com

Tahiti Tekura Travel, Papeete
www.tahiti-tekuratravel.com

Tahiti Tourisme, Papeete
www.tahiti-tourisme.com

Tahiti Vacations, California
www.tahitivacation.com

Tahiti Pacifique Magazine, Moorea
www.tahitiweb.com/f/info

The Moorings, Florida
www.moorings.com

Tourism Council of the South Pacific
www.tcsp.com

Vahine I. Resort, Taha'a
www.ila-chateau.com/vahine/index.htm

Easter Island

Easter Island Home Page
www.netaxs.com/~trance/rapanui.html

Kon Tiki Museum, Oslo
www.media.uio.no/Kon-Tiki

Mysterious Places
www.mysteriousplaces.com/
Easter_Isld_Pge.html

Secrets of Easter Island
www.pbs.org/wgbh/nova/easter

Cook Islands

Ara Moana Bungalows, Mangaia
www.ck/aramoana/aramoana.htm

Are Manuiri Guest House, Atiu
www.adc.co.ck

Cook Islands News, Rarotonga
www.cinews.co.ck

Crown Beach Resort, Rarotonga
www.crownbeach.com

Edgewater Resort, Rarotonga
www.edgewater.co.ck

Kiikii Motel, Rarotonga
www.kiikiimotel.co.ck

Pacific Divers, Rarotonga
www.pacificdivers.co.ck

Rarotongan Resort Hotel, Rarotonga
www.rarotongan.co.ck

Shangri-La Beach Cottages, Rarotonga
www.shangri-la.co.cx

Stars Travel, Rarotonga
www.stars.co.ck

Telecom Cook Islands, Rarotonga
www.oyster.net.ck

Cook Islands Tourism Corporation, Rarotonga
www.cook-islands.com

Vara's Beach House & Lodge, Rarotonga
www.varas.co.ck

E-MAIL DIRECTORY

Tahiti-Polynesia

Air Tahiti, Papeete
rtahitim@mail.pf

Air Tahiti Nui, Papeete
fly@airtahitinui.pf

Aranui Cruises
cptm@aranui.com

Archipels Croisieres
archimoo@mail.pf

Bathy's Club, Moorea
bathys@mail.pf

Bora Bora Beach Club
trhppt@mail.pf

Bora Bora Lagoon Resort
BBLR@mail.pf

Dolphin Quest, Moorea
dqfp@mail.pf

Dolphin Watch, Moorea
criobe@mail.pf

Institut Territorial de la Statistique
itstat@mail.pf

Kia Ora Village, Rangiroa
gecco@gte.net

Kuriri Village, Maupiti
Teiva@tahiti.com

Iaora Tahiti Ecotours
ecotours@mail.pf

Le Maitai Polynesia, Bora Bora
maitaibo@mail.pf

Le Méridien Hotels
sales@lemeridien-tahiti.com

Moana Beach Parkroyal, Bora Bora
borabora@parkroyal.pf

Moorea Beach Club
trhppt@mail.pf

Moorea Beachcomber Parkroyal
moorea@parkroyal.pf

Moorea Fun Dive
fundive@mail.pf

The Moorings Ltd., Raiatea
moorings@mail.pf

Nemo World Diving, Bora Bora
Divebora@mail.pf

Ono-Ono, Papeete
onoono@mail.pf

Outrigger Hotels of Hawaii
reservations@outrigger.com

Royal Tahitien Hôtel, Tahiti
royalres@mail.pf

Résidence Linareva, Moorea
linareva@mail.pf

Sofitel Hotels, Tahiti
coralia@mail.pf

Tahiti Beachcomber Parkroyal
tahiti@parkroyal.pf

Tahiti Country Club, Tahiti
trhppt@mail.pf

Tahiti Nui Travel, Papeete
info@tahitinuitravel.pf

Tahiti-Pacifique Magazine, Moorea
tahitipm@mail.pf

Tahiti Tourisme, Papeete
tahiti-tourisme@mail.pf

Tahiti Yacht Charter, Papeete
tyc@mail.pf

Tekura Tahiti Travel, Papeete
go@tahiti-tekuratravel.com

Te Tiare Beach Resort, Huahine
tetiarebeach@mail.pf

Tiki Village Theater, Moorea
tikivillage@mail.pf

Vahine Island Resort, Taha'a
vahine.island@usa.net

Cook Islands

Air Rarotonga, Penrhyn
penrhyn@airraro.co.ck

Air Rarotonga, Rarotonga
bookings@airraro.co.ck

Ara Moana Bungalows, Mangaia
jan@gatepoly.co.ck

Are Manuiri Guest House, Atiu
adc@adc.co.ck

Ariana Bungalows Motel, Rarotonga
bob@gatepoly.co.ck

Atiu Motel, Atiu
atiu@gatepoly.co.ck

Ati's Beach Bungalows, Rarotonga
atis@atisbeach.co.ck

Backpackers International, Rarotonga
annabill@oyster.net.ck

Budget/Polynesian Rentals, Rarotonga
rentals@budget.co.ck

Carolyn Short & Associates, Rarotonga
carolyn@gatepoly.co.ck

Central Motel, Rarotonga
stopover@central.co.ck

Club Raro, Rarotonga
holiday@clubraro.co.ck

Cook Island Divers, Rarotonga
divecook@oyster.net.ck

Cook Island Divers, Rarotonga
gwilson@ci-divers.co.ck

Cook Islands News, Rarotonga
editor@cinews.co.ck

Cook Islands Press, Rarotonga
cipress@gatepoly.co.ck

Cook Islands Tourism Corporation, Rarotonga
tourism@cookislands.gov.ck

Cook Islands Tours, Rarotonga
raroinfo@citours.co.ck

Crown Beach Resort, Rarotonga
crownltd@oyster.net.ck

Daydreamer Accommodation, Rarotonga
byoung@daydreamer.co.ck

Edgewater Resort, Rarotonga
stay@edgewater.co.ck

Hugh Henry & Associates, Rarotonga
hhenry@gatepoly.co.ck

Island Hopper Vacations, Rarotonga
travel@islandhopper.co.ck

Island Tours, Aitutaki
islands@gatepoly.co.ck

Kiikii Motel, Rarotonga
relax@kiikiimotel.co.ck

Lagoon Lodges, Rarotonga
des@lagoon.co.ck

Little Polynesian Motel, Rarotonga
lit-poly@gatepoly.co.ck

Matareka Hostel, Rarotonga
backpack@rarotonga.co.ck

Mauke Cove Lodge, Mauke
aguinea@gatepoly.co.ck

Moana Sands Resort, Rarotonga
beach@moanasands.co.ck

Muri Beachcomber Motel, Rarotonga
muri@beachcomber.co.ck

Oasis Village, Rarotonga
oasis@gatepoly.co.ck

Pacific Divers, Rarotonga
dive@pacificdivers.co.ck

Pacific Resort, Rarotonga
thomas@pacificresort.co.ck

Palm Grove Lodges, Rarotonga
beach@palmgrove.co.ck

Paradise Inn, Rarotonga
paradise@gatepoly.co.ck

Polyaccess, Rarotonga
republic@banana.co.ck

Puaikura Reef Lodges, Rarotonga
paul@puaikura.co.ck

Raina Beach Apartments, Rarotonga
raina@gatepoly.co.ck

Rarotongan Resort Hotel, Rarotonga
info@rarotongan.co.ck

Rarotongan Sunset Motel, Rarotonga
welcome@rarosunset.co.ck

Shangri-La Beach Cottages, Rarotonga
relax@shangri-la.co.ck

Sokala Villas, Rarotonga
stay@sokala.co.ck

Stars Travel, Rarotonga
holidays@starstravel.co.ck

Takitumu Conservation Area, Rarotonga
kakerori@tca.co.ck

Telecom Cook Islands, Rarotonga
info@oyster.net.ck

Tiare Village Dive Hostel, Rarotonga
tiarevil@gatepoly.co.ck

Tipani Tours, Rarotonga
tours@tipani.co.ck

Vara's Beach House, Rarotonga
backpack@varasbeach.co.ck

Wild Palms, Rarotonga
drink@ronnies.co.ck

GLOSSARY

aa lava—lava that is slow-moving, thick, and turbulent, creating a rough, chunky surface; *see also* pahoehoe

afa—a *demi* or person of mixed Polynesian/European blood

ahimaa—an underground, earthen oven. After A.D. 500, the Polynesians had lost the art of making pottery, so they were compelled to bake their food, rather than boil it.

ahu—a Polynesian stone temple platform

AIDS—Acquired Immune Deficiency Syndrome

aito—ironwood

anse—cove (French)

ANZUS Treaty—a mutual-defense pact signed in 1951 between Australia, New Zealand, and the U.S.

aparima—a Tahitian hand dance

archipelago—a group of islands

ariki—a Cook Islands high chief; the traditional head of a clan or tribe; in Tahitian, *ari'i*

Arioi—a pre-European religious society, which traveled among the Society Islands presenting ceremonies and entertainments

atoll—a low-lying, ring-shaped coral reef enclosing a lagoon

bareboat charter—chartering a yacht without crew or provisions

bark cloth—see *tapa*

barrier reef—a coral reef separated from the adjacent shore by a lagoon

bêche-de-mer—sea cucumber; an edible sea slug; in Tahitian, *rori;* in French, *trépang*

breadfruit—a large, round fruit with starchy flesh grown on an *uru* tree *(Artocarpus altilis)*

BYO—Bring Your Own (an Australian term used to refer to restaurants that allow you to bring your own alcoholic beverages)

caldera—a wide crater formed through the collapse or explosion of a volcano

cassava—manioc; the starchy edible root of the tapioca plant

CEP—Centre d'Expérimentation du Pacifique; the former French nuclear-testing establishment in Tahiti-Polynesia

CETAD—Centre d'études de Techniques Adaptés au Développement; a vocational training unit at the larger high schools

CFP—*Cour de Franc Pacifique;* the currency in Tahiti-Polynesia

chain—an archaic unit of length equivalent to 20 meters

ciguatera—a form of fish poisoning caused by microscopic algae

CMAS—Confédération Mondiale des Activités Subaquatiques; the French counterpart of PADI

coir—coconut husk sennit used to make rope, etc.

confirmation—A confirmed reservation exists when a supplier acknowledges, either orally or in writing, that a booking has been accepted.

copra—dried coconut meat used in the manufacture of coconut oil, cosmetics, soap, and margarine

coral—a hard, calcareous substance of various shapes, composed of the skeletons of tiny marine animals called polyps

coral bank—a coral formation over 150 meters long

coral head—a coral formation a few meters across

coral patch—a coral formation up to 150 meters long

cyclone—Also known as a hurricane (in the Caribbean) or typhoon (in Japan). A tropical storm that rotates around a center of low atmospheric pressure; it becomes a cyclone when its winds reach force 12 or 64 knots. At sea the air will be filled with foam and driving spray, the water surface completely white with 14-meter-high waves. In the Northern Hemisphere, cyclones spin counterclockwise, while south of the equator they move clockwise. The winds of cyclonic storms are deflected toward a low-pressure area at the center, although the "eye" of the cyclone may be calm.

deck—Australian English for a terrace or porch

desiccated coconut—the shredded meat of dehydrated fresh coconut

DGSE—Direction Générale de la Sécurité Extérieure; the French CIA

direct flight—a through flight with one or more stops but no change of aircraft, as opposed to a nonstop flight

DOM-TOM—Départements et Territoires d'Outre-Mer; the French colonial bureaucratic structure

dugong—a large plant-eating marine mammal; called a manatee in the Caribbean

EEZ—Exclusive Economic Zone; a 200-nautical-mile offshore belt of an island nation or seacoast state that controls the mineral exploitation and fishing rights

endemic—native to a particular area and existing only there

ESCAP—Economic and Social Commission for Asia and the Pacific

expatriate—a person residing in a country other than his/her own; in the South Pacific such persons are also called "Europeans" if their skin is white, or simply "expats."

FAD—fish aggregation device

fafa—a "spinach" of cooked taro leaves

farani—French; *français*

fare—Tahitian house

filaria—parasitic worms transmitted by biting insects to the blood or tissues of mammals. The obstruction of the lymphatic glands by the worms can cause an enlargement of the legs or other parts, a disease known as elephantiasis.

fissure—a narrow crack or chasm of some length and depth

FIT—foreign independent travel; a custom-designed, prepaid tour composed of many individualized arrangements

fringing reef—a reef along the shore of an island

gendarme—a French policeman on duty only in rural areas in France and French overseas territories

GPS—Global Positioning System, the space age successor of the sextant

guano—manure of seabirds, used as a fertilizer

guyot—a submerged atoll, the coral of which couldn't keep up with rising water levels

Havai'i—legendary homeland of the Polynesians

Hiro—the Polynesian god of thieves

HIV—Human Immunodeficiency Virus, the cause of AIDS

hurricane—*see* cyclone

jug—a cross between a ceramic kettle and a pitcher used to heat water for tea or coffee in Australian-style hotels

knot—about three kilometers per hour

lagoon—an expanse of water bounded by a reef

lapita pottery—pottery made by the ancient Polynesians from 1600 to 500 B.C.

lava tube—a conduit formed as molten rock continues to flow below a cooled surface during the growth of a lava field. When the eruption ends, a tunnel is left with a flat floor where the last lava hardened.

LDS—Latter-day Saints; the Mormons

leeward—downwind; the shore (or side) sheltered from the wind; as opposed to windward

lei—a garland, often of fresh flowers, but sometimes of paper, shells, etc., hung about the neck of a person being welcomed or feted

le truck—a truck with seats in back, used for public transportation on Tahiti

live-aboard—a tour boat with cabin accommodation for scuba divers

LMS—London Missionary Society; a Protestant group that spread Christianity from Tahiti (1797) across the Pacific

maa tahiti—Tahitian food

maa tinito—Chinese food

mahimahi—dorado, Pacific dolphinfish (no relation to the mammal)

mahu—a male Tahitian transvestite, sometimes also homosexual

mairie—town hall

makatea—an uplifted reef around the coast of an elevated atoll

mama ruau—actually "grandmother," but also used for the Mother Hubbard long dress introduced to Tahiti by missionaries

mana—authority, prestige, virtue, "face," psychic power, a positive force

manahune—a commoner or member of the lower class in pre-Christian Tahitian society

mangrove—a tropical shrub with branches that send down roots forming dense thickets along tidal shores

manioc—cassava, tapioca, a starchy root crop

maohi—a native of Tahiti-Polynesia

Maori—the Polynesians of New Zealand and the Cook Islands

mape—Tahitian chestnut tree

maraamu—southeast tradewinds or *alizés*

marae—a Tahitian temple or open-air cult place, called *me'ae* in the Marquesas

marara—flying fish

matrilineal—a system of tracing descent through the mother's familial line

Melanesia—the high island groups of the western Pacific (Fiji, New Caledonia, Vanuatu, Solomon Islands, Papua New Guinea); from *melas* (black)

Micronesia—chains of high and low islands mostly north of the Equator (Carolines, Gilberts, Marianas, Marshalls); from *micro* (small)

moai—an Easter Island statue

monoï—perfumed coconut oil

motu—a flat reef islet

NAUI—National Association of Underwater Instructors

NGO—Nongovernment organization

NFIP—Nuclear-Free and Independent Pacific movement

noanoa—perfume

no-nos—sand flies

Oro—the Polynesian god of war

ORSTOM—Office de la Recherche Scientifique et Technique d'Outre-Mer

ote'a—a Tahitian ceremonial dance performed by men and women in two lines

overbooking—the practice of confirming more seats, cabins, or rooms than are actually available to ensure against no-shows

pa—ancient Polynesian stone fortress

Pacific rim—the continental landmasses and large countries around the fringe of the Pacific

PADI—Professional Association of Dive Instructors

pahoehoe lava—A smooth lava formation with wavy, ropelike ripples created when very hot, fluid lava continues to flow beneath a cooling surface.

pandanus—screw pine with slender stem and prop roots. The sword-shaped leaves are used for plaiting mats and hats. In Tahitian, *fara*.

papa'a—a Tahitian word used to refer to Europeans

parasailing—a sport in which participants are carried aloft by a parachute pulled behind a speedboat

pareu—a Tahitian saronglike wraparound skirt or loincloth

pass—a channel through a barrier reef, usually with an outward flow of water

passage—an inside passage between an island and a barrier reef

patrilineal—a system of tracing descent through the fathers familial line

pawpaw—papaya

pelagic—relating to the open sea, away from land

peretane—Britain, British in Tahitian

pétanque—French lawn bowling in which small metal balls are thrown

pirogue—outrigger canoe (French), in Tahitian *vaa*

PK—*pointe kilométrique,* a system of marking kilometers along highways in Tahiti-Polynesia

poe—a sticky pudding made from bananas, papaya, pumpkin, or taro mixed with starch, baked in an oven, and served with coconut milk

poisson cru—(French) raw fish marinated in lime, in Tahitian *ia ota;* in Japanese *sashimi*

Polynesia—divided into Western Polynesia (Tonga and Samoa) and Eastern Polynesia (Tahiti-Polynesia, Cook Islands, Hawaii, Easter Island, and New Zealand); from *poly* (many)

punt—a flat-bottomed boat

pupu—traditional Tahitian dance group

raatira—Tahitian chief, dance leader

rain shadow—the dry side of a mountain, sheltered from the windward side

reef—a coral ridge near the ocean surface

roulotte—a mobile food van or truck

sailing—the fine art of getting wet and becoming ill while slowly going nowhere at great expense

scuba—self-contained underwater breathing apparatus

SDA—Seventh-Day Adventist

self-contained—a room with private facilities (a toilet and shower not shared with other guests); the brochure term "en-suite" means the same thing; as opposed to a "self-catering" unit with cooking facilities

sennit—braided coconut-fiber rope

shareboat charter—a yacht tour for individuals or couples who join a small group on a fixed itinerary

shifting cultivation—a method of farming involving the rotation of fields instead of crops

shoal—a shallow sandbar or mud bank

shoulder season—a travel period between high/peak and low/off-peak seasons

SPREP—South Pacific Regional Environment Program

subduction—the action of one tectonic plate wedging under another

subsidence—geological sinking or settling

symbiosis—a mutually advantageous relationship between unlike organisms

tahua—in the old days a skilled Tahitian artisan or priest; today a sorcerer or healer

tamaaraa—a Tahitian feast

tamure—a new name for Ori Tahiti, a very fast erotic dance

tapa—a cloth made from the pounded bark of the paper mulberry tree *(Broussonetia papyrifera)*. It's soaked and beaten with a mallet to flatten and intertwine the fibers, then painted with geometric designs.

tapu—taboo, sacred, set apart, forbidden, a negative force

taro—a starchy elephant-eared tuber *(Colocasia esculenta),* a staple food of the Pacific islanders

tatau—the Tahitian original of the adopted English word tattoo

tavana—the elected mayor of a Tahitian commune (from the English "governor") *tifaifai*—a Tahitian patchwork quilt based on either European or Polynesian motifs; in Cook Islands *tivaevae*

tiki—a humanlike sculpture used in the old days for religious rites and sorcery

timeshare—part ownership of a residential unit with the right to occupy the premises for a certain period each year in exchange for payment of an annual maintenance fee

tinito—Tahitian for Chinese

TNC—transnational corporation (also referred to as a multinational corporation)

to'ere—a hollow wooden drum hit with a stick

trade wind—a steady wind blowing toward the equator from either northeast or southeast

trench—the section at the bottom of the ocean where one tectonic plate wedges under another

tridacna clam—eaten everywhere in the Pacific, its size varies between 10 centimeters and one meter

tropical storm—a cyclonic storm with winds of 35 to 64 knots

tsunami—a fast-moving wave caused by an undersea earthquake; sometimes erroneously called a tidal wave

tu'i (Polynesian)—king, ruler

umara—sweet potato *(Ipomoea batatas)*

vigia—a mark on a nautical chart indicating a dangerous rock or shoal

volcanic bomb—lumps of lava blown out of a volcano, they take a bomblike shape as they cool in the air

VTT—vélo à tout terrain; mountain bike

windward—the point or side from which the wind blows, as opposed to leeward

zoreille—a recent arrival from France; from *les oreilles* (the ears); also called a *métro*

zories—rubber shower sandals, thongs, flip-flops

ALTERNATIVE PLACE NAMES

Bass Islands—Marotiri Islands
Bellingshausen—Motu One
Danger—Pukapuka
Easter Island—Isla de Pascua
Easter Island—Rapa Nui
French Polynesia—Tahiti-Polynesia
Hatutaa—Hatutu
Hatutu—Hatutaa
Hervey—Manuae
Hull—Maria
Isla de Pascua—Easter Island
Maiao—Tapuaemanu
Manuae—Hervey
Maria—Hull
Marotiri Islands—Bass Islands
Maupihaa—Mopelia
Maupiti—Maurau
Maurau—Maupiti
Mohotani—Motane
Mopelia—Maupihaa
Moruroa—Mururoa
Motane—Mohotani
Motu Iti—Tupai
Motu One—Bellingshausen
Mururoa—Moruroa
Penrhyn—Tongareva
Puamotu—Tuamotu
Pukapuka—Danger
Rapa Nui—Easter Island
Scilly—Manuae
Suvarov—Suwarrow
Suwarrow—Suvarov
Taha'a—Uporu
Tahiti-Polynesia—French Polynesia
Tapuaemanu—Maiao
Temoe—Timoe
Timoe—Temoe
Tongareva—Penrhyn
Tuamotu—Puamotu
Tupai—Motu Iti
Uporu—Taha'a

CAPSULE TAHITIAN VOCABULARY

ahiahi—evening
ahimaa—earth oven
aita—no
aita e peapea—no problem
aita maitai—no good
aito—ironwood
amu—eat
ananahi—tomorrow
arearea—fun, to have fun
atea—far away
atua—god
avae—moon, month
avatea—midday (1000-1500)

e—yes, also *oia*
eaha te huru?—how are you?
e haere oe ihea?—where are you going?
e hia?—how much?

faraoa—bread
fare—house
fare iti—toilet
fare moni—bank
fare niau—thatched house
fare punu—tin-roofed house
fare pure—church
fare rata—post office
fare toa—shop
fenua—land
fetii—parent, family
fiu—fed up, bored

haari—coconut
haere—goodbye (to a person leaving)
haere mai io nei—come here
haere maru—go easy, take it easy
hauti—play, make love
hei—flower garland, lei
here hoe—number-one sweetheart
himene—song, from the English "hymn"
hoa—friend

ia orana—good day, may you live, prosper
i nanahi—yesterday
ino—bad
inu—drink
ioa—name
ite—know

ma'a—food

maeva—welcome
mahana—sun, light, day
mahanahana—warm
maitai—good, I'm fine; also a cocktail
maitai roa—very good
manava—conscience
manu—bird
manuia—to your health!
manureva—airplane
mao—shark
mauruuru—thank you
mauruuru roa—thank you very much
miti—salt water
moana—deep ocean
moemoea—dream
moni—money

nana—goodbye
naonao—mosquito
nehenehe—beautiful
niau—coconut-palm frond

oa oa—happy
ohipa—work
ora—life, health
ori—dance
oromatua—the spirits of the dead
otaa—bundle, luggage
oti—finished

pahi—boat, ship
painapo—pineapple
pape—water, juice
parahi—goodbye (to a person staying)
pareu—sarong
pia—beer
pohe—death
poipoi—morning
popaa—foreigner, European
poti'i—teenage girl, young woman

raerae—effeminate
roto—lake

taapapu—understand
taata—human being, man
tabu—forbidden
tahatai—beach
tama'a—lunch
tama'a maitai—bon appetit
tamaaraa—Tahitian feast

tamarii—child
tane—man, husband
taofe—coffee
taote—doctor
taravana—crazy
tiare—flower

to'e to'e—cold
tupapau—ghost

ua—rain
uaina—wine
uteute—red

vahine—woman, wife
vai—fresh water
veavea—hot

NUMBERS

hoe—1
piti—2
toru—3
maha—4
pae—5
ono—6
hitu—7
vau—8
iva—9
ahuru—10
ahuru ma hoe—11
ahuru ma piti—12
ahuru ma toru—13
ahuru ma maha—14
ahuru ma pae—15
ahuru ma ono—16
ahuru ma hitu—17
ahuru ma vau—18
ahuru ma iva—19
piti ahuru—20
piti ahuru ma hoe—21
piti ahuru ma piti—22
piti ahuru ma toru—23
toru ahuru—30
maha ahuru—40
pae ahuru—50
ono ahuru—60
hitu ahuru—70
vau ahuru—80
iva ahuru—90
hanere—100
tauatini—1,000
ahuru tauatini—10,000
mirioni—1,000,000

CAPSULE FRENCH VOCABULARY

bonjour—hello

bonsoir—good evening

salut—hi

Je vais à . . .—I am going to . . .

Où allez-vous?—Where are you going?

Jusqu'où allez-vous?—How far are you going?

Où se trouve . . .?—Where is . . .?

C'est loin d'ici?—Is it far from here?

Je fais de l'autostop.—I am hitchhiking.

À quelle heure?—At what time?

un horaire—timetable

hier—yesterday

aujourd'hui—today

demain—tomorrow

Je désire, je voudrais . . .—I want . . .

J'aime . . .—I like . . .

Je ne comprends pas.—I don't understand.

une chambre—a room

Vous êtes très gentil.—You are very kind.

Où habitez-vous?—Where do you live?

Il fait mauvais temps.—It's bad weather.

le gendarmerie—police station

Quel travail faites-vous?—What work do you do?

la chômage, les chômeurs—unemployment, the unemployed

Je t'aime.—I love you.

une boutique, un magasin—a store

le pain—bread

le lait—milk

le vin—wine

le casse-croûte—snack

les conserves—canned foods

les fruits de mer—seafood

un café très chaud—hot coffee

l'eau—water

le plat du jour—set meal

Combien ça fait?—How much does it cost?

Combien ça coûte?

  Combien? Quel prix?

une auberge de jeunesse—youth hostel

la clef—the key

la route, la piste—the road

la plage—the beach

la falaise—the cliff

la cascade—waterfall

les grottes—caves

Est-ce que je peux camper ici?—May I camp here?

Je voudrais camper.—I would like to camp.

le terrain de camping—campsite

Devrais-je demander la permission?—Should I ask permission?

s'il vous plaît—please

oui—yes

merci—thank you

cher—expensive

bon marché—cheap

NUMBERS

un—1

deux—2

trois—3

quatre—4

cinq—5

six—6

sept—7

huit—8

neuf—9

dix—10

onze—11

douze—12

treize—13

quatorze—14

quinze—15

seize—16

dix-sept—17

dix-huit—18

dix-neuf—19

vingt—20

vingt-et-un—21

vingt-deux—22

vingt-trois—23

trente—30

quarante—40

cinquante—50

soixante—60

soixante-dix—70

quatre-vingts—80

quatre-vingt-dix—90

cent—100

mille—1,000

dix mille—10,000

million—1,000,000

THE ISLANDS AT A GLANCE*

ISLAND GROUP	LAND AREA (SQ KM)	HIGHEST POINT (M)	ISLAND POPULATION (1996)	LATITUDE	LONGITUDE
SOCIETY ISLANDS					
Bora Bora	29.3	727	5,767	16.45°S	151.87°W
Huahine	74.8	669	5,411	16.72°S	151.10°W
Maiao	8.3	180	283	17.67°S	150.63°W
Manuae	4.0	4	24	16.52°S	154.72°W
Maupihaa	3.6	4	30	16.87°S	154.00°W
Maupiti	11.4	380	1,127	16.45°S	152.25°W
Moorea	125.2	1,207	11,682	17.57°S	150.00°W
Motu One	2.8	4	12	15.80°S	154.55°W
Raiatea	171.4	1,017	10,063	16.82°S	151.43°W
Tahaa	90.2	590	4,470	16.62°S	151.49°W
Tahiti	1,045.1	2,241	150,721	17.63°S	149.50°W
Tetiaroa	4.9	3	14	17.00°S	149.57°W
AUSTRAL ISLANDS					
Raivavae	17.9	437	1,049	23.92°S	147.80°W
Rapa	40.5	650	521	26.60°S	144.37°W
Rimatara	8.6	84	929	22.67°S	153.42°W
Rurutu	32.3	389	2,015	22.48°S	151.33°W
Tubuai	45.0	422	2,049	23.35°S	149.58°W
TUAMOTU ISLANDS					
Ahe	12.2	4	377	14.50°S	146.33°W
Amanu	25.0	4	209	17.72°S	140.65°W
Anaa	37.7	4	411	17.50°S	145.50°W
Apataki	20.0	4	387	15.50°S	146.33°W
Aratika	8.3	4	260	15.55°S	146.65°W
Arutua	15.0	4	520	15.17°S	146.67°W
Faaite	8.8	4	246	16.75°S	145.17°W
Fakahina	8.3	4	104	16.00°S	140.08°W
Fakarava	13.8	4	467	16.17°S	145.58°W
Fangatau	5.9	4	150	15.75°S	140.83°W
Hao	18.5	4	1,412	18.25°S	140.92°W
Hereheretue	3.4	4	45	19.87°S	144.97°W
Hikueru	2.8	4	134	17.53°S	142.53°W
Katiu	10.0	4	208	16.52°S	144.20°W
Kauehi	15.0	4	699	15.98°S	145.15°W
Kaukura	11.0	4	379	15.72°S	146.83°W
Makatea	29.5	111	84	16.17°S	148.23°W
Makemo	13.1	4	588	16.43°S	143.93°W
Manihi	13.0	4	769	14.50°S	145.92°W
Marokau	4.5	4	65	18.00°S	142.25°W
Marutea South	4.0	4	214	21.09°S	135.06°W
Mataiva	15.0	4	227	14.88°S	148.72°W
Moruroa	10.5	6	1,062	21.82°S	138.80°W
Napuka	8.1	4	319	14.17°S	141.20°W
Nengonengo	0.7	4	56	18.70°S	141.77°W
Niau	21.6	5	160	16.18°S	146.37°W

* This chart covers only the permanently inhabited islands of Tahiti-Polynesia.

ISLAND GROUP	LAND AREA (SQ KM)	HIGHEST POINT (M)	ISLAND POPULATION (1996)	LATITUDE	LONGITUDE
TUAMOTU ISLANDS (CONTINUED)					
Nihiru	2.0	4	30	16.68°S	142.88°W
Nukutavake	3.6	4	190	19.18°S	138.70°W
Nukutipipi	0.8	4	1	20.67°S	142.50°W
Pukapuka	5.4	4	175	14.80°S	138.82°W
Pukarua	6.5	4	205	18.27°S	137.00°W
Rangiroa	79.2	4	1,913	15.80°S	147.97°W
Raraka	7.0	4	130	16.13°S	145.00°W
Raroia	7.5	2	184	15.93°S	142.37°W
Reao	9.4	4	313	18.47°S	136.47°W
Taenga	4.9	4	81	16.30°S	143.80°W
Taiaro	3.3	5	7	15.77°S	144.62°W
Takapoto	15.0	4	612	14.53°S	145.23°W
Takaroa	16.5	4	488	14.37°S	144.97°W
Takume	4.5	4	84	15.65°S	142.10°W
Tatakoto	7.3	4	247	17.28°S	138.33°W
Tematangi	5.5	4	54	21.64°S	140.62°W
Tepoto North	1.8	4	65	14.00°S	141.33°W
Tikehau	20.0	4	400	14.87°S	148.25°W
Toau	12.0	4	25	15.97°S	145.82°W
Tureia	8.3	4	205	20.78°S	138.50°W
Vahitahi	2.5	4	68	18.58°S	138.83°W
Vairaatea	3.0	4	70	19.23°S	139.32°W
GAMBIER ISLANDS					
Aukena	1.3	198	21	23.13°S	134.90°W
Mangareva	15.4	482	1,062	23.13°S	134.92°W
Taravai	5.7	255	4	23.13°S	135.03°W
MARQUESAS ISLANDS					
Fatu Hiva	83.8	960	631	10.40°S	138.67°W
Hiva Oa	315.5	1,276	1,837	9.78°S	138.78°W
Nuku Hiva	339.5	1,224	2,375	8.95°S	140.25°W
Tahuata	69.3	1,040	637	9.93°S	139.10°W
Ua Huka	83.4	884	571	8.92°S	139.56°W
Ua Pou	105.3	1,203	2,013	9.40°S	140.08°W
COOK ISLANDS					
Aitutaki	16.5	124	2,332	18.88°S	159.74°W
Atiu	29.1	71	960	19.99°S	158.10°W
Mangaia	34.5	169	1,104	21.94°S	157.90°W
Manihiki	5.2	4	662	10.40°S	161.20°W
Mauke	19.7	30	646	20.15°S	157.35°W
Mitiaro	22.8	15	319	19.86°S	157.70°W
Nassau	1.2	4	99	11.55°S	165.42°W
Palmerston	2.6	7	49	18.07°S	163.17°W
Penrhyn	9.8	4	600	9.00°S	158.00°W
Pukapuka	7.0	4	780	10.88°S	165.82°W
Rakahanga	4.0	4	249	10.50°S	161.10°W
Rarotonga	67.6	653	11,100	21.23°S	159.78°W
Suwarrow	1.7	3	4	13.25°S	163.08°W

ACCOMMODATIONS INDEX

INDEX

Bold *cross-references in the text refer to the general index.*

ARCHAEOLOGICAL SITES

DIVING

D

GARDENS

HIKING/CLIMBING

SURFING

ABOUT THE AUTHOR

Three decades ago, David Stanley's right thumb carried him out of Toronto, Canada, onto a journey that has so far wound through 171 countries, including a three-year trip from Tokyo to Kabul. His travel guidebooks to the South Pacific, Micronesia, Alaska, Eastern Europe, and Cuba opened those areas to budget travelers for the first time.

During the late 1960s, David got involved in Mexican culture by spending a year in several small towns near Guanajuato. Later he studied at the universities of Barcelona and Florence, before settling down to get an honors degree (with distinction) in Spanish literature from the University of Guelph, Canada.

In 1978 Stanley linked up with future publisher Bill Dalton, and together they wrote the first edition of *South Pacific Handbook.* Since then, Stanley has gone on to write additional definitive guides for Moon Publications, including *Fiji Handbook* and *Tonga-Samoa Handbook,* and early editions of *Alaska-Yukon Handbook* and *Micronesia Handbook.* He wrote the first three editions of Lonely Planet's *Eastern Europe on a Shoestring* as well as their guide to Cuba. His books have informed a generation of budget travelers.

Stanley makes frequent research trips to the areas covered in his guides, jammed between journeys to the 73 countries and territories worldwide he still hasn't visited. In travel writing David Stanley has found a perfect outlet for his restless wanderlust.

AVALON
TRAVEL
publishing

BECAUSE TRAVEL MATTERS.

AVALON TRAVEL PUBLISHING knows that travel is more than coming and going—travel is taking part in new experiences, new ideas, and a new outlook. Our goal is to bring you complete and up-to-date information to help you make informed travel decisions.

AVALON TRAVEL GUIDES feature a combination of practicality and spirit, offering a unique traveler-to-traveler perspective perfect for an afternoon hike, around-the-world journey, or anything in between.

WWW.TRAVELMATTERS.COM

Avalon Travel Publishing guides are available at your favorite book or travel store.

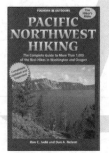

FOR TRAVELERS WITH
SPECIAL INTERESTS

GUIDES

The 100 Best Small Art Towns in America • Asia in New York City
The Big Book of Adventure Travel • Cities to Go
Cross-Country Ski Vacations • Gene Kilgore's Ranch Vacations
Great American Motorcycle Tours • Healing Centers and Retreats
Indian America • Into the Heart of Jerusalem
The People's Guide to Mexico • The Practical Nomad
Saddle Up! • Staying Healthy in Asia, Africa, and Latin America
Steppin' Out • Travel Unlimited • Understanding Europeans
Watch It Made in the U.S.A. • The Way of the Traveler
Work Worldwide • The World Awaits
The Top Retirement Havens • Yoga Vacations

SERIES

Adventures in Nature
The Dog Lover's Companion
Kidding Around
Live Well

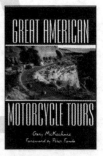

MOON HANDBOOKS

provide comprehensive coverage of a region's arts, history, land, people, and social issues in addition to detailed practical listings for accommodations, food, outdoor recreation, and entertainment. Moon Handbooks allow complete immersion in a region's culture—ideal for travelers who want to combine sightseeing with insight for an extraordinary travel experience.

USA

Alaska-Yukon • Arizona • Big Island of Hawaii • Boston
Coastal California • Colorado • Connecticut • Georgia
Grand Canyon • Hawaii • Honolulu-Waikiki • Idaho • Kauai
Los Angeles • Maine • Massachusetts • Maui • Michigan
Montana • Nevada • New Hampshire • New Mexico
New York City • New York State • North Carolina
Northern California • Ohio • Oregon • Pennsylvania
San Francisco • Santa Fe-Taos • Silicon Valley
South Carolina • Southern California • Tahoe • Tennessee
Texas • Utah • Virginia • Washington • Wisconsin
Wyoming • Yellowstone-Grand Teton

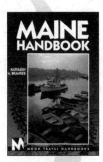

INTERNATIONAL

Alberta and the Northwest Territories • Archaeological Mexico
Atlantic Canada • Australia • Baja • Bangkok • Bali • Belize
British Columbia • Cabo • Canadian Rockies • Cancún
Caribbean Vacations • Colonial Mexico • Costa Rica • Cuba
Dominican Republic • Ecuador • Fiji • Havana • Honduras
Hong Kong • Indonesia • Jamaica • Mexico City • Mexico
Micronesia • The Moon • Nepal • New Zealand • Northern Mexico
Oaxaca • Pacific Mexico • Pakistan • Philippines • Puerto Vallarta
Singapore • South Korea • South Pacific • Southeast Asia • Tahiti
Thailand • Tonga-Samoa • Vancouver • Vietnam, Cambodia and Laos
Virgin Islands • Yucatán Peninsula

www.moon.com

Rick Steves shows you where to travel and how to travel—all while getting the most value for your dollar. His Back Door travel philosophy is about making friends, having fun, and avoiding tourist rip-offs.

Rick's been traveling to Europe for more than 25 years and is the author of 22 guidebooks, which have sold more than a million copies. He also hosts the award-winning public television series *Travels in Europe with Rick Steves*.

RICK STEVES' COUNTRY & CITY GUIDES

Best of Europe
France, Belgium & the Netherlands
Germany, Austria & Switzerland
Great Britain & Ireland
Italy • London • Paris • Rome • Scandinavia • Spain & Portugal

RICK STEVES' PHRASE BOOKS

French • German • Italian • French, Italian & German
Spanish & Portuguese

MORE EUROPE FROM RICK STEVES

Europe 101
Europe Through the Back Door
Mona Winks
Postcards from Europe

WWW.RICKSTEVES.COM

ROAD TRIP USA

Getting there is half the fun, and Road Trip USA guides are your ticket to driving adventure. Taking you off the interstates and onto less-traveled, two-lane highways, each guide is filled with fascinating trivia, historical information, photographs, facts about regional writers, and details on where to sleep and eat—all contributing to your exploration of the American road.

"Books so full of the pleasures of the American road,
you can smell the upholstery."
~ BBC radio

THE ORIGINAL CLASSIC GUIDE
Road Trip USA

ROAD TRIP USA REGIONAL GUIDE
Road Trip USA: California and the Southwest

ROAD TRIP USA GETAWAYS
Road Trip USA Getaways: Chicago
Road Trip USA Getaways: New Orleans
Road Trip USA Getaways: San Francisco
Road Trip USA Getaways: Seattle

www.roadtripusa.com

TRAVEL ✦ SMART ®

guidebooks are accessible, route-based driving guides. Special interest tours provide the most practical routes for family fun, outdoor activities, or regional history for a trip of anywhere from two to 22 days. Travel Smarts take the guesswork out of planning a trip by recommending only the most interesting places to eat, stay, and visit.

"One of the few travel series that rates sightseeing attractions. That's a handy feature. It helps to have some guidance so that every minute counts."

~ San Diego Union-Tribune

TRAVEL SMART REGIONS

Alaska
American Southwest
Arizona
Carolinas
Colorado
Deep South
Eastern Canada
Florida Gulf Coast
Florida
Georgia
Hawaii
Illinois/Indiana
Iowa/Nebraska
Kentucky/Tennessee
Maryland/Delaware
Michigan
Minnesota/Wisconsin
Montana/Wyoming/Idaho
Nevada
New England
New Mexico
New York State

Northern California
Ohio
Oregon
Pacific Northwest
Pennsylvania/New Jersey
South Florida and the Keys
Southern California
Texas
Utah
Virginias
Western Canada

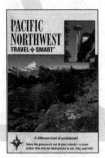

Foghorn Outdoors

guides are for campers, hikers, boaters, anglers, bikers, and golfers of all levels of daring and skill. Each guide contains site descriptions and ratings, driving directions, facilities and fees information, and easy-to-read maps that leave only the task of deciding where to go.

"Foghorn Outdoors has established an ecological conservation standard unmatched by any other publisher."
~ Sierra Club

CAMPING Arizona and New Mexico Camping

Baja Camping • California Camping
Camper's Companion • Colorado Camping
Easy Camping in Northern California
Easy Camping in Southern California
Florida Camping • New England Camping
Pacific Northwest Camping
Utah and Nevada Camping

HIKING 101 Great Hikes of the San Francisco Bay Area

California Hiking • Day-Hiking California's National Parks
Easy Hiking in Northern California
Easy Hiking in Southern California
New England Hiking
Pacific Northwest Hiking • Utah Hiking

FISHING Alaska Fishing • California Fishing

Washington Fishing

BOATING California Recreational Lakes and Rivers

Washington Boating and Water Sports

OTHER OUTDOOR RECREATION California Beaches

California Golf • California Waterfalls • California Wildlife
Easy Biking in Northern California • Florida Beaches
The Outdoor Getaway Guide For Southern California
Tom Stienstra's Outdoor Getaway Guide: Northern California

WWW.FOGHORN.COM

CiTY·SMaRT™

The best way to enjoy a city is to get advice from someone who lives there—and that's exactly what City Smart guidebooks offer. City Smarts are written by local authors with hometown perspectives who have personally selected the best places to eat, shop, sightsee, and simply hang out. The honest, lively, and opinionated advice is perfect for business travelers looking to relax with the locals or for longtime residents looking for something
new to do Saturday night.

*A portion of sales from each title
benefits a non-profit literacy organization in that city.*

CITY SMART CITIES

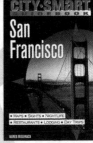

Albuquerque	Anchorage
Austin	Baltimore
Berkeley/Oakland	Boston
Calgary	Charlotte
Chicago	Cincinnati
Cleveland	Dallas/Ft. Worth
Denver	Indianapolis
Kansas City	Memphis
Milwaukee	Minneapolis/St. Paul
Nashville	Pittsburgh
Portland	Richmond
San Francisco	Sacramento
St. Louis	Salt Lake City
San Antonio	San Diego
Tampa/St. Petersburg	Toronto
Tucson	Vancouver

www.ricksteves.com

The Rick Steves web site is bursting with information to boost your travel I.Q. and liven up your European adventure. Including:

- The latest from Rick on what's hot in Europe
- Excerpts from Rick's books
- Rick's comprehensive Guide to European Railpasses

www.foghorn.com

Foghorn Outdoors guides are the premier source for United States outdoor recreation information. Visit the Foghorn Outdoors web site for more information on these activity-based travel guides, including the complete text of the handy *Foghorn Outdoors: Camper's Companion*.

www.moon.com

Moon Handbooks' goal is to give travelers all the background and practical information they'll need for an extraordinary travel experience. Visit the Moon Handbooks web site for interesting information and practical advice, including Q&A with the author of *The Practical Nomad*, Edward Hasbrouck.

U.S.~METRIC CONVERSION

1 inch = 2.54 centimeters (cm)
1 foot = .304 meters (m)
1 yard = 0.914 meters
1 mile = 1.6093 kilometers (km)
1 km = .6214 miles
1 fathom = 1.8288 m
1 chain = 20.1168 m
1 furlong = 201.168 m
1 acre = .4047 hectares
1 sq km = 100 hectares
1 sq mile = 2.59 square km
1 ounce = 28.35 grams
1 pound = .4536 kilograms
1 short ton = .90718 metric ton
1 short ton = 2000 pounds
1 long ton = 1.016 metric tons
1 long ton = 2240 pounds
1 metric ton = 1000 kilograms
1 quart = .94635 liters
1 US gallon = 3.7854 liters
1 Imperial gallon = 4.5459 liters
1 nautical mile = 1.852 km

To compute celsius temperatures, subtract 32 from Fahrenheit and divide by 1.8. To go the other way, multiply celsius by 1.8 and add 32.

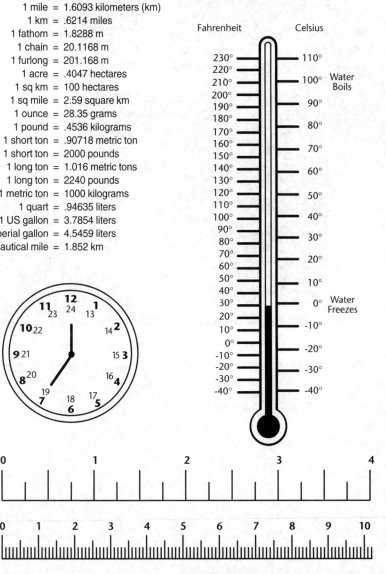

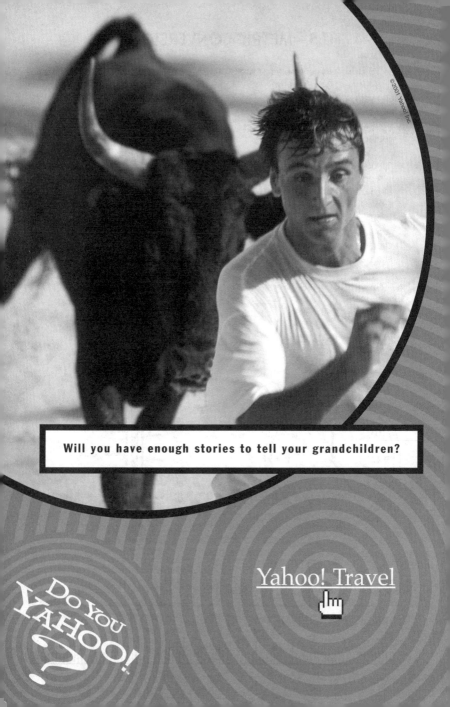

Will you have enough stories to tell your grandchildren?

Yahoo! Travel

DO YOU YAHOO!